The Gardener

David Whiting

COLORADO STATE UNIVERSITY

Kendall Hunt
publishing company

Cover image provided by the author.

Kendall Hunt
publishing company

www.kendallhunt.com
Send all inquiries to:
4050 Westmark Drive
Dubuque, IA 52004-1840

Printed in the United States of America
10 9 8 7 6 5 4 3

Contents

UNIT A

Benefits of Gardening

Jay Johnson

Chapter

1

Benefits of Gardening

Americans are constantly bombarded with stress-inducing information about environmental issues, economic concerns, health worries, and community strife. Gardening is a tool to abate life's stress, enhance the environment, develop individuals, and build communities.

LANDSCAPES CONTRIBUTE TO ENVIRONMENTAL QUALITY

Community forests can strongly influence the physical/biological environment and mitigate many impacts of urban development by moderating climate, conserving energy, sequestering carbon, improving air quality, controlling rainfall runoff and flooding, lowering noise levels, harboring wildlife, and enhancing the attractiveness of cities.[1]

Community forests play a key role in abating the energy crisis. On a community-wide basis, the value of the community forest in heating and cooling effects quickly adds up to millions of dollars in energy savings. Some figures to illustrate this point include:

- Trees contribute to energy conservation because they help reduce the cost of heating and cooling buildings. Summertime air temperatures in cities can be as much as 10° F warmer than in surrounding rural areas due to the replacement of soil and vegetation with concrete, asphalt, and metal.[2]

- Computer simulations suggest that a single 25-foot tree can reduce the heating and cooling costs of a typical residence by 8 to 10 percent.[3]

- In another study, windbreaks can reduce a typical home's heating demand by 5 to 15 percent.[4]

- In a Sacramento County case study, the value of the community forest in its annual cooling effects was calculated at approximately 157 GWh ($18.5 million) per year.[5]

Carbon sequestration is another measurable benefit of lawns and trees, which is important because increased greenhouse gases in the atmosphere have been linked with global climate change. Studies in Sacramento, California, showed that "in net, the urban forest removes approximately 3.3 tons per acre each year with an implied value of $3.3 million ($0.55 per tree). Carbon dioxide reduction by Sacramento's urban forest offsets the total amount emitted as a by-product of human consumption by 1.8 percent."[6]

A fast-growing forest tree absorbs up to 48 pounds of carbon dioxide a year; that adds up to 10 tons per acre of trees—enough to offset the carbon dioxide produced by driving a car 21,000 miles.[7]

GARDENING TECHNIQUES PROTECT AND ENHANCE THE ENVIRONMENT

Yard care and gardening activities have a direct impact on the neighborhood and community environment. Landscape design and maintenance sets a community standard of prosperity, tranquility, and serenity. This may be found in a small but charming inner city garden or tasteful rural home sites.

Many gardeners are unaware of how their yard care and gardening practices actually enhance or negatively influence the environment. As a point of illustration, let us consider the home lawn.[8]

- The lawn provides clean space for children (and adults) to enjoy the outdoors.

- An actively growing lawn provides significant cooling to the local surroundings.

- Grass traps and thereby helps control dust and pollen in the air that contribute to allergic reactions.

- Grass helps abate noise and reflected light, which are common irritants in the urban setting.

- Grass is a very effective element of the urban ecosystem to break down pollutants. Twenty-five square feet of actively growing grass converts enough carbon dioxide into oxygen for one person per day.

- Soil microorganisms associated with grass actively break down various pollutants, including air contaminants washed out of the air, pollen, and pesticides.

- A thick turfgrass allows fifteen times less runoff than a lower quality lawn. A healthy stand of turfgrass can reduce surface runoff to almost zero. In the landscape setting, grassy areas provide the primary process to abate pollution caused by surface runoff.

- Mowed lawns are a major fire control component in residential areas.

On the other hand, yard care and gardening practices can negatively influence the environment. For example:

- Lawn clipping and leaves mowed or blown onto the gutter and street account for sixty to eighty percent of the phosphate loading of surface water in the urban landscape.

- Excessive lawn fertilization promotes rapid growth, ultimately adding to the volume of yard waste.

- Excessive or careless fertilizer or pesticide applications contribute to water quality problems.

- According to data from the *Plant Health Care* (landscape maintenance) industry, over ninety percent of the pesticides typically applied in landscape maintenance are unwarranted and have little to no benefit.

- Irrigation water demand is becoming a critical factor in the arid west. Plant selection, and irrigation system design, maintenance, and management techniques determine water usage.

LANDSCAPING AND PROPERTY VALUES

Around twenty percent of the value of a house is tied up in the landscape. Landscape design and maintenance is a major factor in the marketability of a house. To illustrate the point, the county assessor's office lists the value of residential property in Larimer County, Colorado, at $16.9 billion.[9] This places the approximate value of residential landscapes in Larimer County at $3.4 billion!

Studies have shown that landscape plants, particularly trees, enhance property values and increase city assets. For example, in a study on a seven-acre tract of land, shade trees contributed 19 percent, or $57,000, to the total appraised value of $302,000.[10] In another study, real estate appraisers estimated that trees contributed as much as a twenty-seven percent increase in dollars for a lot that is two-thirds wooded compared to open land with no trees.[11]

A study on the contribution of landscaping to the price of single-family houses showed that a house that obtained an "excellent" rating for the landscape from a local landscape professional could expect a sale price four to five percent higher (depending on the size of the lot) than equivalent houses with a "good" landscape rating. Homes with landscapes rated "fair" or "poor" could expect a sale price eight to ten percent below equivalent homes with good landscape appeal.[12]

A survey of real estate agents revealed that eighty-four percent of the real estate agents feel a house on a lot with trees would be as much as twenty percent more salable than a house on a lot without trees. In addition, sixty-two percent of the respondents said the existence of healthy shade trees strongly influences a potential buyer's impression of a block or neighborhood; sixty percent thought healthy shade trees have a big influence on a potential buyer's first impression of a property; and fifty-six percent felt healthy shade trees are a strong factor in a home's salability.[13]

DOLLAR VALUE OF THE GREEN INDUSTRY

Home gardening activities are a significant part of agricultural economy in a region. For example, the wholesale value of Colorado Green Industry goods and services exceeds $1.67 billion annually, accounting for over one-fourth of the state's agriculture industry (2002 data). The green industry employs over 34,000 with an annual payroll in excess of $825 million dollars. In the United States, consumers spent $40.7 billion on garden products in 2002, after significant growth during the 1990s. The average household in Colorado spends over $1,000 annually on yard care and gardening supplies.[14]

GARDENING FOR NUTRITION AND HEALTH

Families with home vegetable gardens eat more fruit and vegetables for improved nutrition. For families on limited incomes, fresh fruits and vegetables may be a luxury they cannot afford. The home garden supplies fresh fruits and vegetables, and at the same time gives over a 20-fold increase in the value of produce grown compared to material costs.[15]

During a harvest day in a youth gardening project in Teller County, Colorado, a young boy came to the leaders and stated that his brother doesn't eat vegetables and that they had better cook something else. He was informed that his brother was on his second helping of the vegetable kabobs to which the naysayer replied, "*well this is different because we grew them*."

Gardening is also a key tool for improved health by providing exercise, stress reduction, and relaxation. From the medical perspective, researchers have documented that people who interact with plants recover more quickly from everyday stress and mental fatigue.[16]

It is amazing how fast weeds can disappear from the garden bed when the gardener is a little upset or angry, leaving the stress and anger in the compost pile with the weeds. I wish my neighbor would pull more weeds (weeds in their yard are taller than the wood fence) and yell less at the children.

For many, the garden is their escape from the pressures of the job and family responsibilities. This relaxation technique reduces stress levels and related issues like heart disease. Minnie Aumonier expressed it eloquently with, "*When the world wearies and society ceases to satisfy, there is always the Garden.*"

There has been an increased awareness in the restorative value of plants in hospitals, homes for the aged, and senior centers. In such places, "healing gardens" are constructed for clients, staff, and visitors.

GARDEN THERAPY: A TOOL TO DEVELOP INDIVIDUALS, STRENGTHEN FAMILIES, AND BUILD COMMUNITIES

Not only do plants contribute monetarily to the value of property, they also contribute to a higher quality of life and benefit society. Researchers found that accessibility to nature was the most important factor—after the marital role—in life satisfaction.[17] Yard care and gardening activities develop individuals, strengthen families, and build communities.

Gardening Therapy to Develop Individuals

For the individual, gardening provides exercise, stress reduction, and relaxation. For many Americans it provides a creative outlet, a sense of accomplishment, and the gardener's personal link to nature.

The garden is a great place to learn the "joy" that comes from work. In contrast to popular video games, gardening teaches that life does not always give instantaneous rewards. With gardening, as in real life, the rewards for one's efforts payoff sometime in the future.

For many individuals the garden is their piece of nature. Although most of us will never visit the tropical rain forests of Central America or the open plains of Africa, we can have our own piece of nature in the backyard. Although many of us will find some time to enjoy wildlife in the majestic Colorado Rockies, most of us will spend more time enjoying the beauties of nature in our own backyard. As evidenced in the following paragraphs, gardens are used in a variety of settings to develop individuals.

Discovering Self Worth

Master Gardeners were involved in a variety of community greening and gardening projects aimed at bringing the community together. The gardeners partnered with a youth service agency (whose mission was to teach job readiness skills) to do soil preparation on several of the project sites.

A crew of Master Gardener volunteers and four sixteen-year-old Hmong youth did the soil preparation work of adding compost and tilling the garden beds. On the first day with this crew of youth, one of the boys refused to take a turn on the tiller. He found our old tiller was rather scary. It was rather poor on the compacted soil, was noisy, and would jump out of the ground when it hit concrete chunks buried on the old gas station site that was to become a community welcome garden. However, peer pressure can be a strong influence on a sixteen-year-old, and his friends finally got him on the tiller. He tilled and tilled, and would be tilling there today had we not ran out of gas in the old tiller.

As the tiller stopped, he turned to me with a big smile covering his face and said, "*I'm not worthless, I can drive a tiller.*" For me, at sixteen, driving a tiller was no big treat. My dad was an avid gardener and I had been tilling since I was large enough to run it down a semi-straight row. However, for this young man, it changed his life. Driving a tiller, although work, was fun!

He told me a few days later, that his father (a Hmong refugee) had not stepped outside their tiny apartment in ten years. Social workers brought in food on Fridays, and his dad watched TV all day. His dad had taught him that work was evil and that if he played his cards right, he would never have a job.

This young, first-generation American found that he loved working in the garden. He was paid by the youth services agency for the first twenty hours that he worked with us. However, he put in over 300 hours of volunteer work in several of the community beautification projects that summer. He was always hoping that there would be a tiller to drive, but enjoyed planting, pulling weeds, or simply picking up trash. At the end of any work session, he always would stand back and comment on how good it looked and how fun it was to be involved. By tilling in compost, a young man found the joy of work and discovered the satisfaction of being involved.

Hug a Tree Therapy

One evening in a Master Gardener meeting in St. Paul, Minnesota, John (a Master Gardener volunteer) had the entire room in tears as he shared his personal story about gardening. Ramsey County Master Gardeners partnered with a community organization to beautify the Mississippi riverfront through downtown St. Paul with tree, shrub, and flower plantings. The Master Gardeners' roles were to work with various planting groups (such as Boy Scout and Girl Scout units, church groups, and community clubs) on "planting days" to mentor them in correct planting techniques on this extremely hard, rocky, compacted soil.

On planting days, John's role was to coordinate groups to various planting areas with plant materials. One Saturday, John was not feeling well. He had been in an accident and had a sprained ankle and broken fingers. He was planning to quickly return home as soon as he got the various groups working.

Just as he was ready to leave, an eight-year-old boy, Mark, and his mother showed up wanting to plant a tree. Mark was losing his sight, and a counselor had suggested that they do special events to mark his transition into a world without vision. Mark wanted to plant his tree to hug and help him remember what the world looked like. Because he lived in an apartment, the community tree planting provided him with the opportunity.

Well, John could not just have the boy and his mother join another group, Mark needed his own trees. So the three of them went to work. Designed as a flood control bank, the soil along the riverfront is very hard and rocky. Mark and is mother were rather inexperienced in working with a shovel in the hard ground, and John had his ankle wrapped due to the sprain. It took them six hours to dig the wide hole needed for the tree planting in the compacted soil. They laughed, sang, and cried during the planting event. They became good friends. It was the perfect day for Mark to remember!

It also changed John's life. John suffers from seasonal affective disorder (SAD); a type of depression common in the dark, gray winters of Minnesota). He had spent thousands of dollars and hundreds of hours in counseling and on medications. When John has a down day, he now has a little routine that really works for him. He hugs a large tree in his yard, reflecting on his rich life with a loving wife and family, a great job, beautiful home and garden, and on Mark and his mother who have so little, struggling to get by day by day. (And let's not forget that hugging a tree in Minnesota's 30 degrees below zero winter is no simple task.) I believe that all of us could use some tree hugging therapy some days.

St. Paul Children's Hospital

For many years, the Ramsey County Master Gardener Program has had a simple garden therapy program at the St. Paul Children's Hospital. Two days a week, Master Gardener volunteers work with children, cutting up large houseplants for propagation and planting rooted cuttings. The children love using bedpans for soil trays and syringes for watering cans. Each day, every child selects a rooted cutting to pot, water, and take back to their room. The success of the day is measured by the amount of laughter and giggles and the mess.

Leonard, one of the Master Gardener volunteers, tells that he knew something special happened by the reaction of the nurses assisting one day. One little boy said nothing, simply following what other children were doing. Like many, he over watered his plant with too many shots and it leaked on the table. The little boy started giggling that his plant went peepee on the table. "This little boy had shut down into a noncommunicating world of silence when he came to the hospital several days earlier. Even in rather painful treatments, he had not even responded to the pain stimulus. His plant going peepee on the table" brought him back into the world of communication.

Another day, Leonard was asked to take a small cart of plants and supplies to the room of a little girl who could not come to the activity room with the other children. As he got to the door, the nurse said, "I hope you are ready for this."

Inside, a small girl, who would not leave the oxygen and IV tubes alone, had her hand tied to the bed. With all the tubes, she had the mindset that she was dying, and no one could convince her otherwise. For days she had talked nonstop about death. *"Will it hurt?"* *"Will Grandma be there?"* *"Will my doggy be there?"* (Previously, her dog had been killed by a car.) Thinking of recently seeing Grandma in her coffin, *"...I'm afraid of the dark..."*

Leonard talked to her about the fun of caring for plants and she chose a pink and green leaf polkadot plant to be planted. Since her hands were tied, Leonard planted the plant and then convinced the nurse to untie her hands so she could give it shots (water the plant with a syringe).

The little girl gave the plant its shots and, with a big smile, turned toward her mother and asked if she could have chicken nuggets for lunch. She had to get better to take care of her plant, because it was pink, her favorite color. Welcome back to the world of the living!

Prison Gardens

Gardening is increasingly used as rehabilitation therapy in prison systems. When asked to document the influence of a gardening project in a Colorado prison system, a Colorado Master Gardener report included the following statements from prison inmates: *". . . it helped me to start caring about life. I'm more relaxed and see how living things are very fragile and need to be cared for and nurtured . . . We can be indifferent or even cruel and mean and destroy life or we can help life and take care of it and benefit everybody by just not hurting. I guess people are not much different than daisies. We need care, and nurturing, and balance in our growth. . . ."*Another inmate states, *"I have learned to deal with people as people instead of overpowering them or manipulating them as some sort of object to satisfy my wants."*

Garden Therapy to Strengthen Families

Family bonds are strengthened as families work together on yard care and gardening activities. Children learn work skills and team skills through gardening projects—as exemplified in the following paragraphs.

Neighborhood Beautification Project Strengthens a Family Unit

Ramsey County Master Gardeners were actively mentoring a variety of neighboring beautification projects in the "West Side" neighborhood of St. Paul, Minnesota. This is a neighborhood with high crime rates, and a lot of neighborhood tension caused by the extreme diversity in economic mobility, race, and ethnic groups. The objective was to bring the community together around gardening projects.

One of the projects was a park renovation on the bluff overlooking the Mississippi River. During the Great Depression, work crews had added beautiful stonewalls and benches. Currently, the park had minimal maintenance. A neighborhood group, led by Joan, coupled with Master Gardener volunteers to fixup the park.

During a planting night, Joan and her husband were working with her next door neighbor installing a flowerbed of iris and daylilies. For several years, they had never talked other than to exchange angry words over the fence about the neighbor's home remodeling mess and the children. During the planting event, it was discovered that both husbands were computer programmers working in specialized computer languages. This led to an invitation for hamburgers at Joan's home that evening.

Joan and her husband were surprised to learn more about the family next door. The young family had purchased the large old home next door when he had a great income from his computer business. With the computer industry's normal ups and downs, the young family was now struggling to make ends meet. In addition, their daughter had a brain tumor, leaving the family with staggering medical bills. That is why the home remodeling had stopped, leaving the house and yard in a mess.

Mom and dad were not disinterested parents, leaving the three latchkey children at home to cause mischief in the neighborhood (as Joan had assumed); rather, both parents were working to deal with the family's financial crisis. It is interesting that it took the "gardening activity" to open communication between the neighbors.

At Christmas time, Joan called thanking me for the effort of the Master Gardeners in mentoring the park renovation. With the interest and support of the neighborhood group, the park looked beautiful and had been reclassified by the city parks department to the routine maintenance level.

Joan added that her life was so full with her new grandchildren (the three latchkey kids next door that Joan previously disliked). The kids came to grandma's after school each day. They have cookies and milk, do their homework, have dinner and baths, and are ready for bed when their parents get home from work.

Grandpa took the boys ice fishing every week. The freezer was full of fish. Grandma was most proud of her new granddaughter. From the brain surgery for the cancer treatment, the young girl had learning disabilities, but was up to speed with her class in math and reading due to the tutoring from Grandma each day.

The neighborhood beautiful project was far more than just planting iris and daylilies. A new family unit emerged.

Building Communities

Gardening is a universal language that brings the community together. Gardening conversations and activities bring neighbors together, melting differences between racial and ethnic groups. Gardening is an effective tool to unite neighborhoods. Community gardens and community forestry projects contribute to lower levels of domestic violence.[18,19]

Building a Community Network

A study in Chicago used the number of trees on a property as a measurement of the quality of the landscape. As the number of trees in a neighborhood went up, the number of police calls went down. As the number of trees went up (quality of landscape improved), people spent more time outdoors, getting to know their neighbors. This developed a social network, reducing the crime rate.[20]

Experience Diversity

One of the inner city high schools called requesting a few Master Gardener volunteers to assist in a park cleanup as a Senior Slough Day activity. Early afternoon on the day of the event, Howie (one of the Master Gardener volunteers) called and asked if I had known that most of the teens there would be African American. I honestly answered that I had never thought of it in that way, but knew that the local community was primarily African American. "Why are you asking?" He replied that he had never been around African Americans before and would not have volunteered for the project if he had known (simply because it was outside his familiar zone). He however, added that they had a great time and he hoped for more opportunities like this.

Most of the teens at the event were not too excited about the park cleanup. However, one young man really stood out and they got talking as they planted a flowerbed together. The young man taught Howie rap songs and, in return, Howie taught the young man a Norwegian folk song. The young man, an honor student, indicated that he had dropped out of school (a couple of months before graduation) and was now in a street gang. Coming from extreme poverty, he felt that the future offered nothing for him.

Growing up in poverty himself, Howie could understand the young man's feelings about the future. At that point in Howie's young life, someone had given him a handup and Howie was a successful engineer with 3M. Howie could now pay it forward. They talked more and the young man returned to school and graduated. With a few phone calls, Howie found a full ride college scholarship for this young man to follow his dream of studying engineering.

Gardening can open up a world of diverse experiences, exploring different foods, cultures, and ways of life.

Celebrating Our Diversity

Master Gardener volunteers teamed with Community Action Programs (CAP) to mentor novice gardeners at a large community garden project. In the early fall, CAP called with praise for the efforts of the Master Gardeners. The many positive suggestions and education of the novice gardeners led to a very successful year. To celebrate, CAP wanted to have a garden fair and asked if I would judge the final products. I did not care for the idea of a fair, because there are always losers when you have winners, and cultivating the largest zucchini or head of lettuce was not what we were trying to teach the gardeners to harvest.

Knowing that there was a lot of interest in the assortment of vegetables grown, I suggested that they have a potluck and ask folks to bring a dish from the garden representing their cultural heritage.

The potluck was held at an adjacent community center. Early arrival to the potluck moved the central serving tables into four pods. One section for African Americans, another for Hispanics, a third group for Hmongs, with a fourth group for the European Americans. Participants just automatically segregated with their ethnic group.

During the meal, Master Gardeners were calling others to come over and taste this and that. "Hi Joe, you were asking what these bitter melons taste like. Come over and try them." "Hey, Kim, you like hot food. Come and try these hot peppers!" Before long, folks were tasting all kinds of different foods and having a great time.

The next summer, gardeners constantly asked if we were having the potluck again. They had planted extras just for the event. At the second year's potluck, there was no natural segregation. Just one large group having a great time sharing their heritage. It is amazing how gardening bridged the differences between race and ethnicity.

Gardening and Corporate America

Even corporate America is now including landscape considerations in its philosophy. When asked why they have emphasized landscaping, business owners cite the numerous positive aspects of trees and plants, including:[21]

- Increases employee productivity, morale, and pride in the workplace

- Helps recruit new employees

- Attracts customers or new business tenants

- Can be used as an employee benefit

- Creates a corporate image

- Has value as a marketing tool

MASTER GARDENERS FOSTER GARDENING SUCCESS

Since Extension Master Gardeners are not selling products, the gardening public looks to Master Gardener volunteers as an unbiased information source. Home gardeners verifying information received from green industry workers accounts for one-third of the inquiries processed by Colorado Master Gardeners (CMGs). Extension Master Gardeners also serve the community as a catalyst to encourage gardening activities.

Colorado green industry leaders readily recognize that CMGs directly influence the success of local gardeners. This in turn supports the success and growth of Colorado's green industry. The CMG training also provides a great learning opportunity for nursery and garden center employees. Past success encourages expanding links between the CMG Program and appropriate green industry training opportunities.

Gardening is a common topic of conservation at work, church, and between friends and relatives. The more involved a person is in garden-related activities, the more aggressive they will be in seeking out *reliable* garden information. These active gardeners also share their gardening wisdom *weekly* with other less active gardeners.[22]

This has direct implications on Master Gardener programs. Highly involved gardeners are more likely to seek the advice of Master Gardener volunteers, and in turn pass the information on to others. The level of expertise required to adequately respond to these advanced gardeners must continually rise and address emerging issues. To best serve the community, Master Gardeners need wisdom about water conservation and management techniques, alternative pest management options, as well as general gardening knowledge.

ENDNOTES

1. Dwyer, J.F., E.G. McPherson, H.W. Shroeder, and R.A. Rowntree. *Assessing the Benefits and Costs of the Urban Forest*. Journal of Arboriculture 18(5):227–234. 1992.

2. Akbari, H.S., S. Davis, J. Dorsan, J Haugn, and S. Wimmett. *Cooling Our Communities: A Guidebook on Tree Planting and Light-Colored Surfacing*.U.S. Environmental Protection Agency, Washington, DC. 1992.

3. McPherson, E.G., and R.A. Rowntree. *Energy Conservation Potential of Urban Tree Plantings*. Journal of Arboriculture 19(6):321–331. 1993.

4. Heisler, G.M. *Energy Savings With Trees*. Journal of Arboriculture 12(5):113–125. 1986.

5. Simpson, J.R. *Urban Forest Impacts on Regional Cooling and Heating Energy Use: Sacramento County Case Study*. Journal of Arboriculture 24(4):201–214. 1998.

6. McPherson, E.G. *Atmospheric Carbon Dioxide Reduction by Sacramento's Urban Forest*. Journal of Arboriculture 24(4) 147–190. 1998.

7. Simpson, J.R. *Urban Forest Impacts on Regional Cooling and Heating Energy Use: Sacramento County Case Study*. Journal of Arboriculture 24(4):201–214. 1998.

8. Mugaas, R.J., M.L., Agnew, and N.E.Christians. *Turfgrass Management for Protecting Surface Water Quality*. University of Minnesota Extension Service publication BU-5726.1995.

9. _____.Unpublished data from the from Larimer County Assessor's Office.2001.

10. Peters, L. *Shade and Ornamental Tree Evaluation*. Journal of Forestry 69:411–413. 1971.

11. Payne, H. *The Twenty-Nine Tree Home Improvement Plan*. Natural History 82:411–413. 1973.

12. Henry, M.S. *The contribution of landscaping to the price of single-family homes: A study of home sales in Greenville, South Carolina*. Journal of Environmental Horticulture2(2):65–70. 1994.

13. Arbor National Mortgage. *Survey of Realtors Opinions Concerning the Role of Trees in Determining the Value and marketability of Residential Property*. Arbor National Mortgage, Long Island, NY. 1993.

14. Thilmany, D., S. Davies, and P. Watson. *Green Industries of Colorado, Economic Contribution to the Colorado Economy* 2003. Colorado State University and GreenCo Foundation.2003.

15. *Gardens for All*. National Gardening Survey. 1979.

16. Relf, D. *The Pyscho-Social Benefits of Green Spaces*. Grounds Maintenance.March. 1996.

17. Relf, D. The Pyscho-Social Benefits of Green Spaces. Grounds Maintenance.March. 1996.

18. Sullivan, W.C., and F.E.Kuo, *Do Trees Strengthen Urban Communities, Reduce Domestic Violence?* Arborist News(4):33–34.1996.

19. Whiting, D.E. Unpublished data of the Ramsey County Master Gardener Program, University of Minnesota Extension Service. 1993.

20. Kuo, FE. *The Role of Arboriculture in a Healthy Social Ecology*, Journal of Arboriculture 19(3): May. 2003.

21. Relf, D. *The Pyscho-Social Benefits of Green Spaces*.Grounds Maintenance. March. 1996.

22. Keel, V.A., H.P. Zimmerman, R.A. Wearne, *Communicating Home Garden Information*. Phase 1 Report, Home Horticulture Project. ES-USDA.

UNIT B

How Plants Grow

Tip

Blade

Lateral vein

Margin

Midrib

Base

Petiole (leaf stalk)

Bud

Stipules

Learning Objectives

At the end of this unit, the student will be able to:

- Use correct terminology, enhancing communications and understanding about plants.

- Practice diagnostic skills of judiciously examining plants and plant parts for plant identification.

- Practice diagnostic skills of judiciously examining plants and plant parts and correlating observations with print information in the diagnostic process.

- Correlate plant structure and growth processes with common plant disorders.

Supplemental Reading

- Books

  —*Botany for Gardeners*. Brian Capon. Timber Press. 1990.

  —*Introduction to Botany*. James Schooley. Delmar Publishers. 1997.

  —*Manual of Woody Landscape Plants, Fifth Edition*. Michael A. Dirr. Stipes. 1998.

  —*Hartman's Plant Science, Third Edition*. Margaret J. McMahon, Anthon M. Kofranek, and Vincent E. Rubatzky. Prentice Hall. 2002.

  —*The Why and How of Home Horticulture*. D.R. Bienz. Freeman. 1993.

  —*Winter Guide to Central Rocky Mountain Shrubs*. Colorado Dept. of Natural Resources, Div. of Wildlife. 1976.

- References on Plant Taxonomy

  Books

  —*Gardener's Latin: A Lexicon*. Bill Neal.

  —*Manual of Woody Landscape Plants*. Michael Dirr.

  Web-based

  —*International Plant Name Index* at www.ipni.org

  —*Royal Botanic Gardens, Kew Resource Page* at www.kew.org./data/subjects.html

  —*U.S. Department of Agriculture Plant Database* at http://plants.usda.gov

  —Several web-based sites offer pronunciation guides for plant names. For example, http://www.finegardening.com/pguide/pronunciation-guide-to-botanical-latin.aspx

Chapter

2*

Communicating about Plants

Plant Classification and Taxonomy

Planet Earth is unique because of *plants*. They were the first complex organisms to evolve, and they are credited with making the atmosphere hospitable for animals and other life forms.

Plants make their own food using raw materials from the environment including carbon dioxide, water, soil nutrients, and sunlight in the process of photosynthesis.

HORTICULTURE AND RELATED FIELDS

Horticulture—The science and art of cultivating flowers, fruits, vegetables, turf, and ornamental plants in an orchard, garden, nursery, or greenhouse, on a large or small scale.

> **Horticultural**—An adjective used to describe something relating to horticulture, or produced under cultivation.

> **Horticulturist**—A noun referring to a specialist in horticulture.

The terms **ornamentals**, **landscape horticulture**, and **environmental horticulture** are used to identify the subgroupings of horticulture dealing with the landscape setting.

Botany—A branch of biology dealing with plant life (i.e., anatomy, taxonomy, genetics, physiology, ecology, etc.). The science of applied botany deals with plants grown in uncultivated settings.

Agronomy—A branch of agriculture dealing with field crop production and soil management.

Forestry—The science of developing, caring for, or cultivating forests; the management of growing timber.

Community forestry/urban forestry—A branch of forestry dealing specifically with the unique growth limitations and needs of trees in the landscape setting.

---

*Authors: David Whiting, Alison O'Connor, and Linda McMulkin, Colorado State University Extension. Artwork by Scott Johnson and David Whiting.

HORTICULTURAL CLASSIFICATIONS

With hundreds of thousands of plants used by mankind, it is impossible to talk about each one individually. Plants are grouped by various common characteristics to help us communicate similar ecological adaptations and cultural requirements. For example, the term "shade plants" indicates plants tolerant to various levels of shade. "Xeric" groups those plants requiring less supplemental irrigation. It is important to point out that any classification system will have plants that do not exactly fit the groupings.

The following are examples of some common classifications used in horticulture.

Classification by Use

I. Edibles
- A. Fruits
  - 1) Tree fruits
  - 2) Small fruits
- B. Vegetables
  - 1) Warm season vegetables
  - 2) Cool season vegetables
- C. Herbs
  - 1) Culinary
  - 2) Medicinal
- D. Nuts

II. Ornamentals/Landscape Plants
- A. Woody plants
  - 1) Trees
  - 2) Shrubs
  - 3) Vines and ground covers
- B. Herbaceous plants
  - 1) Flowers
  - 2) Vines and ground covers
- C. Grass/turf

III. Potted Plants, Houseplants, Gift Plants
- A. Flowering gift plants
- B. Foliage plants

> **Note**
>
> Do not confuse the multiple uses of the word "fruit."
>
> In reference to "fruits and vegetables," "fruit" refers to crops primarily used in Southern European cuisine as a dessert (peaches, apples, strawberries, and raspberries). "Vegetables" refers to crops served as part of the main entrée (potatoes, carrots, corn, and lettuce). In this frame of reference, tomatoes are vegetables.
>
> In reference to "fruit" as a part of plant anatomy (i.e., roots, stems, flowers, fruits, and seeds), tomatoes, squash, and watermelons are fruit.

Classification by Climatic Requirements

Temperature Requirements

Tropical plants originate in tropical climates with a year-round summer-like growing season, without freezing temperatures. Examples include cocao, cashew and macadamia nuts, banana, mango, papaya, and pineapple.

Subtropical plants cannot tolerate severe winter temperatures but need some winter chilling. Examples include citrus, dates, figs, and olives.

Temperate-zone plants require a cold winter season as well as a summer growing season and are adapted to survive temperatures considerably below freezing. Examples include apples, cherries, peaches, maples, cottonwoods, and aspen. In temperate-zones, tropical and subtropical plants are grown as annuals and houseplants.

Cool season plants thrive in cool temperatures (40°F to 70°F daytime temperatures) and are somewhat tolerant of light frosts. Examples include Kentucky bluegrass, peas, lettuce, and pansies.

Warm season plants thrive in warm temperatures (65°F to 90°F daytime temperatures) and are intolerant of frost. Examples include corn, tomatoes, and squash. Some warm season plants are subtropical and tropical plants grown as annuals in Colorado.

Tender plants are intolerant of cool temperatures, frost, and cold winds (e.g., most summer annuals, including impatiens, squash, and tomatoes).

Hardy plants are tolerant of cool temperatures, light frost, and cold winds (e.g., spring-flowering bulbs, spring-flowering perennials, peas, lettuce, and cole crops).

Heat zone refers to the accumulation of heat, a primary factor in how fast plants grow and what crops are suitable for any given area. This is only one factor that influences a plant's heat tolerance. On a heat zone map, the Colorado Front Range falls into zones 5 to 7.

Hardiness refers to a plant's tolerance to winter climatic conditions. Factors that influence hardiness include minimum temperature, recent temperature patterns, water supply, wind and sun exposure, genetic makeup, and carbohydrate reserves.

Cold Hardiness Zone refers to the *average annual minimum temperature* for a geographic area. Temperature is only one factor that influences a plant's winter hardiness. As of printing time, a new U.S. Department of Agriculture (USDA) Hardiness Zone Map is ready for release. With an extensive database, it will clear up some of the confusion created in previous versions and documents some zone creeping (zone moving north as temperatures warm).

Classification by Elevation and Plant Life Zones

Higher elevations have increasingly shorter growing seasons due to colder temperatures. High elevations have drier soils, stronger light, persistent winds, and greater temperature changes. Due to this harsh environment, alpine and tundra plants tend to be compact in form (Figure 2-1).

Classification by Ecological Adaptations

Many of our plant care problems arise as gardeners try to grow plants outside of their natural environment or "ecological adaptation."

For example, characteristics of the Colorado high plains and many areas of the west include low humidity, limited rainfall, and alkali soils low in organic matter. One of the most limiting factors is rapid temperature change. On the high plains, it can go from a beautiful warm spring day to a cold winter blizzard in just hours.

In higher mountain communities, the short frost-free season and low summer-growing temperatures significantly limit plant selection.

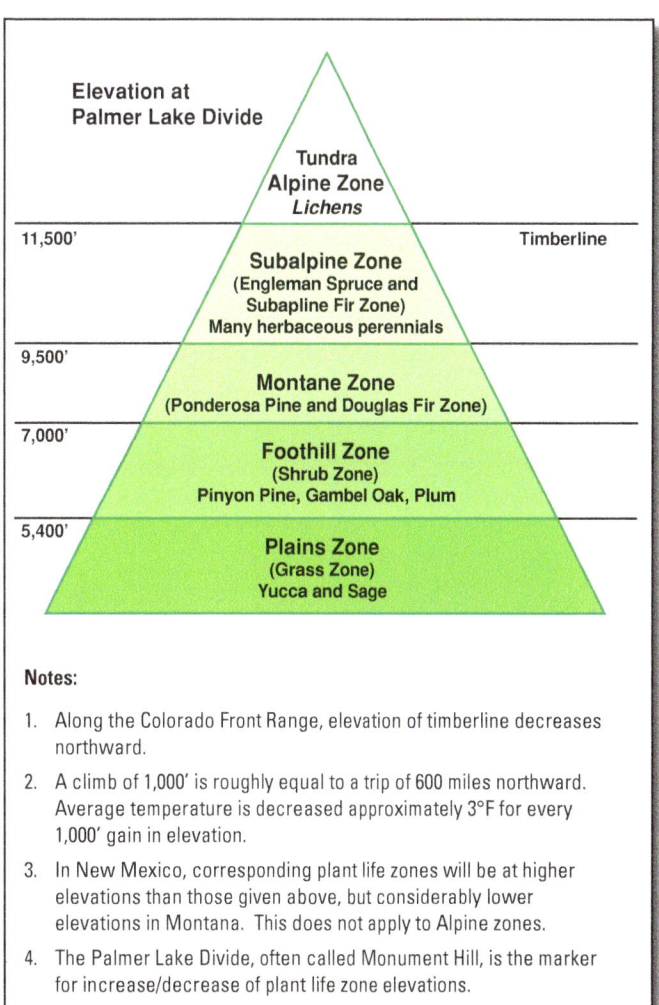

Figure 2-1 ▌ *Colorado Plant Life Zone.*

The following are a few examples of terms used to describe classifications based on ecological adaptation:

- **Alpine plants** tolerate the short growing season, cold, and wind of higher mountain elevations. They are typically low-growing, small-leaf perennials. Snow cover depth often dictates the plant's growing height.

- **Prairie plants** are adapted to the open sun and winds of the plains. These plants are further classified into dry, mesic, and wet prairie categories.

- **Woodland** plants are adapted to a low light conditions and soils rich in organic matter. They typically have large leaves and small flowers.

- **Wetland plants** tolerate continually moist soil conditions of a bog or a pond. Wetlands play a primary role in water quality as a filtering system for water-borne pollutants.

- **Xeric** plants tolerate conditions of low water, bright light, and warm temperatures due to a variety of adaptations such as thick, waxy, or fleshy leaves; hairy leaves; small narrow leaves; taproots; and succulent stems.

An excellent text on xeriscape gardening is *Xeriscape Plant Guide*, by Denver Water, published by Fulcrum Publishing.

Native and Adapted Plants for the Urban Landscape

Native (indigenous) plant refers to plants adapted to a given area during a defined time period. In America, the term often refers to plants growing in a region prior to the settlement by people of European descent.

The term is so overused that it has little meaning. With recent interest in water conservation, many gardeners mistakenly consider "native" plants as "xeric" plants, and "xeric" plants as "native" plants. The two terms are not interchangeable.

The concept of native should not refer to political boundaries, such as state or country, but rather to an ecological habitat during a defined chronological period. For example, Colorado blue spruce and quaking aspen are "native" to the ecological habitat referred to as the montane zone. They are not "native" to the Colorado high plains or elevations below 8,000 ft. From a chronological reference point, what is now the grassland of the Great Plains was once an inland sea. Therefore, aquatic plants such as kelp would have been "native" at one time. Over time, the ecological habitat changed, changing the "native" plants along with it. Environmental change is an ongoing process, based both on global climatic events and on the activity of all organisms, including mankind.

Adapted (or introduced) plants are those that reliably grow well in a given habitat without specific attention from humans in the form of winter protection, soil amendments, pest protection, water, etc. Adapted plants are considered to be "low maintenance" plants.

Urban environments—For gardening purposes, the urban setting needs to be recognized as a unique ecosystem. Characteristics of the urban environment include:

- Soil compaction
- Rooting areas covered with buildings, roads, and parking lots
- Increased surface runoff creating significant water quality problems
- Higher temperatures and lower humidity
- Air pollution

Characteristics of an urban environment cultivated by humans may include:

- Reduced wind
- Increased availability of water due to irrigation

- Increased organic matter and soil fertility

- Reduced pests

- Increased soil stability

- Slower temperature fluctuations

Classification by Stem and Leaf Texture

- **Herbaceous** plants have non-woody stems.

- **Woody** plants have woody stems that generally live for several years, adding new growth each year.

- **Deciduous** plants shed all leaves at approximately the same time annually.

- **Evergreen** plants retain some leaves longer than one growing season so that leaves are present throughout the year. Seasonal drop of some of the oldest interior leaves is a natural part of the life cycle.

- **Semi-evergreen** refers to plants that may retain their leaves, depending on the winter temperature and moisture.

- **Broadleaf** plants have a broad leaf blade (e.g., ash, maple, lilac, and beans) (Figure 2-2).

- **Narrowleaf** plants have needle-like leaves (e.g., pine, spruce) or awl-like leaves (e.g., junipers) (Figure 2-2).

- **Grass-like** plants have narrow leaves, usually arising from the base of the plant. The leaves may be soft (ornamental grasses) or stiff (yucca) (Figure 2-2).

Reminder:

- Some evergreens are broadleaf (e.g., Oregon grape, most true hollies, and evergreen euonymus).

- Some narrowleaf plants are deciduous (e.g., larch and bald cypress).

- **Conifer** refers to cone-bearing. Most conifers are narrowleaf evergreens. A few conifers are deciduous (larch, bald cypress).

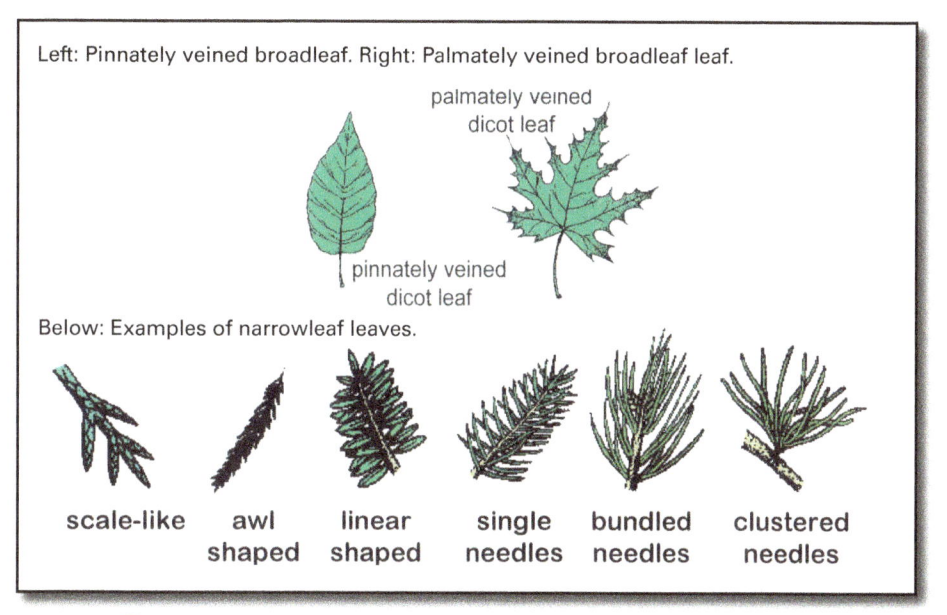

Left: Pinnately veined broadleaf. Right: Palmately veined broadleaf leaf.

palmately veined dicot leaf

pinnately veined dicot leaf

Below: Examples of narrowleaf leaves.

scale-like   awl shaped   linear shaped   single needles   bundled needles   clustered needles

Figure 2-2 ▮ *Leaf textures.*

Classification by Growth Habit

Growth habit refers to the genetic tendency of a plant to grow in a certain shape and to attain a certain mature height and spread (Figure 2-3).

- **Trees** typically have a single trunk and mature height over twelve feet (Figure 2-3).

- **Shrubs** typically have multiple branches from the ground and a mature height of less than twelve feet.

- **Vines** have a climbing, clasping, or self-clinging growth habit.

Note: Many landscape plants could be considered small trees or large shrubs. The terms "tree" or "shrub" would be applied based on the general appearance of the plant.

Plants have vastly different growth habits. It is important to understand growth habits in order to make knowledgeable decisions regarding plant placement, plant selection, pruning, and maintenance requirements.

The species, cultivar, and/or variety name sometimes indicates some characteristic of growth habit.

Columnar   Oval   Vase   Weeping   Pyramidal   Round

Figure 2-3 ▮ *Common forms of shade trees.*

Classification by Life Span

From a horticultural perspective, life span is a function of climate *and* usage. Many garden plants (including tomatoes and geraniums) grown as annuals in northern climates would be perennials in climates without freezing winter temperatures.

Annuals complete their life cycle (from seedling to setting seed) within a single growing season. However, the growing season may be from fall to summer, not just from spring to fall. These plants come back only from seeds.

  Summer annuals germinate from seed in the spring and complete flowering and seed production by fall, followed by plant death, usually due to cold temperatures. Their growing season is from spring to fall. Examples include marigolds, squash, and crabgrass.

  Winter annuals germinate from seed in the fall, with flowering and seed development the following spring, followed by plant death. Their growing season is from fall to summer. Examples include winter wheat and annual bluegrass. Many weeds in the lawn (such as chickweed and annual bluegrass) are winter annuals.

Biennials complete their life cycle within two growing seasons. Biennials germinate from seed during the growing season and often produce an overwintering storage root or bulb the first summer. Quite often, they maintain a rosette growth habit the first season, meaning that all the leaves are basal. They flower and develop seeds the second summer, followed by death. Many biennial flowers self-seed, giving the appearance of a perennial growth habit.

In the garden setting, we grow many biennials as annuals (e.g., carrots, onions, and beets) because we are more interested in the root than the bloom. Some biennial flowers may be grown as short-lived perennials (e.g., hollyhocks).

Perennials live through several growing seasons and can survive a period of dormancy between growing seasons. These plants regenerate from root systems or protected buds, in addition to seeds.

> **Herbaceous perennials** develop overwintering woody tissue only at the base of shoots (e.g., peony and hosta) or have underground storage structures from which new stems are produced. (Note: Golden Vicary Privet and Blue Mist Spirea (*Caryopteris* spp.) can be either herbaceous or woody perennials in northern climates.)

> **Spring ephemerals** have a relatively short growing season but return next season from underground storage organs (e.g., bleeding heart, daffodils).

> **Woody perennials** develop overwintering tissue along woody stems and in buds (e.g., most trees and shrubs grown in northern climates).

Combinations—Plants are usually classified as annual, biennial, or perennial on the basis of the plant part that lives the longest. For example, raspberries have biennial canes and perennial roots.

TAXONOMIC CLASSIFICATION

One of the most useful classification systems utilizes plant taxonomy. Taxonomy is the science of systematically naming and organizing organisms into similar groups. Plant taxonomy is an old science that uses the gross morphology (physical characteristics {i.e., flower form, leaf shape, fruit form, etc.}) of plants to separate them into similar groups. Quite often, the characteristics that distinguish the plants become a part of their name. For example, *Quercus alba* is a white oak, named because the underside of the leaf is white.

The science of plant taxonomy is being absorbed into the new science of systematics. The development of more sophisticated microscopes and laboratory chemical analyses has made this new science possible. Systematics is based on the evolutionary similarities of plants such as chemical make-up and reproductive features.

It should be noted that plant taxonomic classification changes with continuing research, so inconsistencies in nomenclature will be found among textbooks. Do not get caught up in which is correct, as it is a moving target. Rather focus on "are you communicating?"

An overview of plant taxonomy helps the gardener understand the basis of many cultural practices. For example, fire blight is a disease of the rose family; therefore, it is helpful to recognize members of the rose family to diagnose this disease.

Common Taxonomic Divisions

The scientific system of classification divides all living things into groups called **taxa** (singular, **taxon**). Plants are in the kingdom of ***Plantae***. Other kingdoms include ***Fungi***, ***Protista*** (one-celled organisms including yeasts, bacteria, and protozoans), and ***Animalia*** (animals).

The plant kingdom is divided into two taxa: **broyophytes** (including mosses and liverworts) and **vascular plants** (plants with a vascular system of xylem and phloem).

Vascular plants (sometimes called higher plants) are divided into two subgroups: seedless and seeded. The seeded plants divide into two taxa, ***Gymnospermae*** (Gymnosperms) and ***Angiospermae*** (Angiosperms). These make up most of the plants in the landscape.

These taxa divide into ***Divisions*** (or Phylum). Division names end in "phyta." Examples of phyla include *Ginkgophyta* (ginkgo), *Pinophyta* (conifers), and *Magnoliophyta* (flowering plants).

Gymnosperms (meaning naked seed) do not produce flowers, but rather produce seeds on the end of modified bracts, such as pinecones. Many have scale or needle-like leaves. Arborvitae, junipers, Douglas-fir, fir, pine, and spruce are examples of gymnosperms.

Angiosperms (*Magnoliophyta* or broadleaf flowering plants) produce seeds through flowering structures. Most have broadleaf leaves. Angiosperms are divided into two taxa: ***monocotyledon*** (monocots) and ***dicotyledon*** (dicots). Distinguishing between monocots and dicots is a common practice in landscape management. For example, some of our common herbicides work at the monocot/dicot level. Lawn weed sprays (such as 2,4-D and Dicamba) kill dicots (broadleaf plants like dandelions) but not monocots (the grass). Other herbicides will kill monocots but not dicots, allowing the gardener to kill grass (a monocot) in the shrub or flowerbed (dicots).

Additional taxa in descending order include **family**, **genus**, and **species**.

Families

Families of higher plants are separated from one another by characteristics inherent in their reproductive structures (flowers, fruit, and seed). Many family members share common characteristics in plant appearances, seed location and appearance, and growth habit. However, some families have a lot of diversity in appearance.

In gardening activities, the primary importance of families is that they share comparable cultural requirements and similar insect and disease problems. Pest management and cultural techniques are often discussed at the family level.

Family names end in "*aceae*." Examples of common families include the following:

- *Caprifoliaceae*—Honeysuckle family, including elders, honeysuckle, snowberry, and viburnum
- *Fabaceae*—Pea family, including Japanese pagoda, locust, and Siberian peashrubs
- *Oleaceae*—Olive family, including ash, forsythia, lilac, and privet
- *Rosaceae*—Rose family, including apples, cotoneaster, crabapples, potentilla, peach, plum, mountain ash, and 250 common landscape plants

Genus and Species

The taxonomic divisions beyond the family level are the genus and specific epithet names, together called the species. Plants are named using a binomial system. The genus name comes first and is analogous to a person's last name (like Smith). The specific epithet names follows as a more specific identifier. It would be analogous to a person's first name (like John).

Genus	*Specific epithet*
Smith	John
Catalpa	*speciosa*

Genera (plural of genus) are groupings whose members have more characteristics in common with each other than they do with other genera within the same family. Similarity of flowers and fruits is the most widely used feature, although roots, stems, buds, and leaves are also used.

Common names of plants typically apply to genera. For example, *Acer* is the genus of maples, *Fraxinus* of the ash, and *Juniperus* of the junipers.

Specific epithet generally refers to interbreeding subgroups of genus or groupings of individual plants that adhere to essential identification characteristics but display sufficient variation so as not to be categorized as replicas of one another. The specific epithet name is always used in conjunction with the genus.

When genus and specific epithet names are written, they should always be underlined or italicized to denote they are Latin words. The genus name is always capitalized, but the specific epithet name is not.

The singular and plural spelling of *species* is the same. In writing, the abbreviation "sp." following the genus indicates a single unidentified species and "spp." indicates multiple species. For example, "*Acer* sp." would indicate an unidentified species of maple, and "*Acer* spp." refers to multiple species in the maple genus. The "sp." or "spp." is not underlined or italicized.

In technical papers, the person who first identified the species, called the **Authority**, follows the specific epithet names. For example, Japanese Maple would be written *Acer palmatum* Thunberg or *Acer palmatum* T. The Irish potato would be written *Solanum tuberosum* Linnaeus or *Solanum tuberosum* L.

Some suggested sources of scientific names include the following:

- *USDA Plant Database* at http://plants.usda.gov/
- *Manual of Woody Landscape Plants.* Dr. Michael Dirr.
- *Hortus Third* or *Hortus Fourth*

Variety and Cultivar

The taxonomic divisions beyond the genus and species level are variety or cultivar. This is an even more specific identifier, similar to a person's middle name.

Genus	*Species*	*Cultivar*
Smith	John	'David'
Quercus	*rubra*	'Aurea'
Salvia	*greggii*	'Furman's Red'

Variety or **Subspecies** is a subgrouping of species assigned to individuals displaying unique differences in natural populations. The differences are inheritable and reproduce true-to-type in each generation. For example, cauliflower and cabbage are varieties of the same species *Brassica oleracea*.

In technical writing, variety and subspecies names must be denoted with "var." or "ssp." when following a species name. Names are italicized or underlined, while var. or ssp. is not italicized or underlined. For example, the thornless variety of honeylocust would be written *Gleditsia triacanthos* var. *inermis*. The use of trinomials *Gleditsia triacanthos inermis* is improper usage in scientific nomenclature. The big fruit evening primrose would be written *Oenothera macrocarpa* ssp. *incana*.

Cultivar is a subgrouping of species assigned to cultivated plants developed by a plant breeder ("cultivated variety") that display rather unique differences, and when reproduced by seeds or cuttings, retain its distinguishing characteristics. For example, 'Early Girl' and 'Big Boy' are cultivars of tomatoes.

In technical writing, the cultivar name follows the genus and specific epithet and is always capitalized and written inside single quotes but not italicized or underlined. For example, October Glory Red Maple is *Acer rubrum* 'October Glory.'

It is possible to have a cultivar of a variety. For example, *Cornus florida* var. *rubra* 'Cherokee Chief.'

Strain is a subgroup of cultivar with specific characteristics, like resistance to a disease or better color. For example, 'Early Girl VFN' tomato.

Clone is a subgroup of cultivar derived by asexual propagation (i.e., cuttings). The offspring have one parent and therefore are identical to the parent because no exchange of genetic materials has occurred.

Line is a subgroup of cultivar propagated by seed.

Form is based on selection by growth habit, not reproducible by seed (e.g., Columnar Norway Maple).

Scientific Names

Scientific names of plants are Latinized. When Linnaeus published the first books on classification, Latin was used in Western Europe as the language of science. Linnaeus continued this trend using Latin and Greek names.

Latin was the language of **Latium** (an area of ancient Italy) and Ancient Rome. French, Spanish, and Italian languages inherit a large part of their vocabulary and grammar from Latin.

Latin is still a part of science, medicine, law, and philosophy. For example, a prescription for a medication may use, "quater in die" (Q.I.D.) meaning "four times a day." "E Pluribus Unum," an early motto of the United States, means "out of many, one." Today, Latin has the advantage that it provides lingual neutrality between countries and languages.

Pronouncing Scientific Names

Genus and specific epithet names are universal in spelling (that is each plant has a single genus and specific epithet name, spelled the same, worldwide). By using Latin, plants can be positively identified from over 200,000 known plant species.

However, pronunciation of scientific names is not universal and will vary based on the local language. For example, the tomato may be pronounced "toe-may-toe" or "toe-mah-toe." Based on the native language and local dialect of the user, scientific names may actually sound rather different in various countries.

Many Latin names have become "generic" common names (e.g., anemone, rhododendron, crocus, and viburnum).

Here are a few basic guidelines for American English:

- Latin was meant to be entirely phonetic. There are no silent letters. What you see is what you say.
- Consonants are pronounced as you normally would. The letters "c" and "g" are normally in front of the vowels "a," "o," and "u." When in front of "i" and "e," the sound becomes soft ("Cecil" and "Gentle").
- The letters "ch" are pronounced like "k."
- Vowels are long in an accentuated syllable. For example, *Acer* becomes AY-ser and *Pinus* become PIE-nus.
- There are no silent syllables. For example, *Rudbeckia* becomes rood-BEK-ee-uh and *Miscanthus sinensis* becomes miss-can-thus seye-NEN-sis.
- Where the accent goes is a matter of local language styles. Here are some suggestions for American English.
  - In two syllable words, generally accentuate the first syllable. For example, *Cornus* become KOR-nus.
  - In most other words, accentuate the syllable before the last syllable. For example, *Rhododendron* becomes roo-doe-DEN-dron.
  - If the last syllable contains two vowels, accentuate on the third to last syllable. For example, *Buddleja* becomes BUD-lee-jah and *Campanula* becomes kam-PA-nu-la.
- When pronouncing a name based on a person's name, try not to change the sound; accentuate on the first part of the name.
- Examples
  - *Quercus macrocarpa* (bur oak)—KWER-kus ma-crow-CAR-pa
  - *Elaeagnus angustifolia* (Russian olive)—eel-a-EE-ag-nus an-gus-tih-FOL-ee-uh
  - *Ptelea trifoliata* (hoptree/wafer ash)—Tea-LEE-uh try-foal-lee-AH-tuh

Latin Names Add Meaning

Latin names often add meaning about the plant's description, for example:

- ***Americana*** = of America—*Fraxinus americana* (white ash)
- ***baccata*** = berry bearing—*Taxus baccata* (common yew)
- ***micro*** = little, small—*Antennaria microphylla* (littleleaf pussytoes)
- ***officinalis*** = medicinal—*Rosemarius officinalis* (rosemary)
- ***repens*** = creeping, crawling—*Mahonia repens* (creeping Oregon grape)
- ***undulata*** = wavy—*Quercus undulata* (wavyleaf oak)

- ***variegatus*** = variegated—*Miscanthus sinensis* 'Variegatus' (variegated Japanese silver grass)

- ***vulgaris*** = common—*Syringa vulgaris* (common purple lilac)

- ***alba*** = white—*Quercus alba* (white oak)

- ***niger*** = black—*Pinus nigra* (black pine)

- ***rubra*** = red—*Acer rubrum* (red maple), *Quercus rubra* (red oak)

- ***sanguineus*** = blood-red—*Geranium sanguineum*

Common Names

On the other hand, common names are often local in use and many times do not clearly identify the specific plant. For example, *Liriodendron tulipifera* is known as the tulip tree in the north and as yellow poplar in the south. *Carpinus caroliniana* goes by American hornbeam, blue beech, musclewood, water beech, and ironwood. The European white lily, *Nymphaea alba*, has fifteen English common names, forty-four French common names, 105 German common names, and eighty-one Dutch common names.

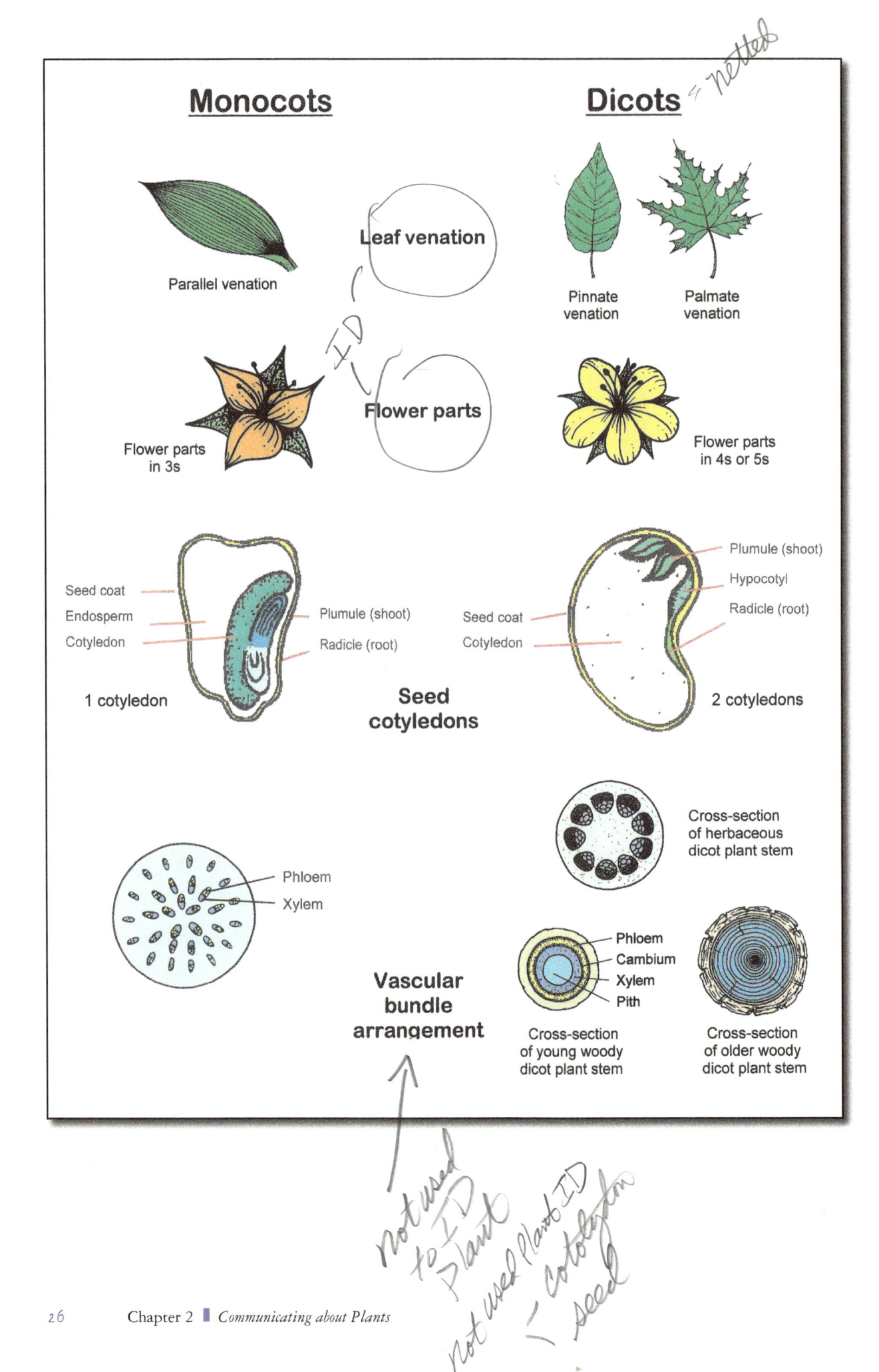

Monocots

Dicots ← netted

Leaf venation

Parallel venation

Pinnate venation

Palmate venation

Flower parts

Flower parts in 3s

Flower parts in 4s or 5s

Seed coat
Endosperm
Cotyledon
Plumule (shoot)
Radicle (root)

1 cotyledon

Seed cotyledons

Plumule (shoot)
Hypocotyl
Radicle (root)
Seed coat
Cotyledon

2 cotyledons

Phloem
Xylem

Vascular bundle arrangement

Cross-section of herbaceous dicot plant stem

Phloem
Cambium
Xylem
Pith

Cross-section of young woody dicot plant stem

Cross-section of older woody dicot plant stem

handwritten annotations: ID; not used to ID Plant; not used Plant ID; 1 cotyledon seed

Examples of Taxonomic Classification

Vascular plants

I. Seedless

    A. *Pteridophyta (Pterophyta)*—ferns

II. Seeded

    A. *Gymnospermae*—**Gymnosperms** (naked seed plants)

        1. *Cycadophyta*—Cycads

        2. *Pinophyta (Coniferophyta)*—**Conifers** (cone bearing plants)

            a) *Cupressaceae* (cypress family)
                1) *Juniperus* spp—**junipers**
                    a) *Juniperus horizontalis* (creeping Juniper)
                        1) *1Juniperus horizontalis* 'Blue Chip' (blue chip juniper)
                2) *Thuja spp.*—**arborvitae**

            b) *Pinaceae* (pine family)
                1) *Abies* spp.—**fir**
                2) *Larix* spp.—**larch**
                3) *Picea* spp.—**spruce**
                    a) *Picea pungens*—Colorado spruce
                      1) *Picea pungens* 'Bakeri'—Bakeri Colorado spruce
                4) *Pinus* spp.—pines
                    a) *Pinus ponderosa* —ponderosa pine
                5) *Pseudotsuga menziesii*—**Douglas-fir**

    B. *Angiospermae*—**Angiosperms** (flowering plants) / ***Magnoliophyta (Anthophyta)***

        1) *Aceraceae*—Maple family
            a) *Acer* spp.—**maples**
                1) *Acer platanoides*—Norway maple
                    a) *Acer platanoides* 'Crimson King'—Crimson King Norway maple

        2) *Salicaceae*—Willow family
            a) *Populus* spp.—**cottonwood, poplar,** and **aspen**
                1) *Populus deltoides*—eastern cottonwood
                    a) *Populus deltoides* 'Siouxland'—Siouxland eastern cottonwood
                2) *Populus tremuloides*—quaking aspen

        3) *Rosaceae*—rose family
            a) *Rosa* spp.—**roses**
                1) *Rosa rugosa*—Rugosa rose
                    a) *Rosa rugosa* 'Hansa'—Hansa rugosa rose
            b) *Cotoneaster* spp.—**cotoneasters**
                1) *Cotoneaster apiculatus*—cranberry cotoneaster

CHAPTER REVIEW
Questions

1. Define the following terms:
   a. Horticulture
   b. Botany
   c. Agronomy
   d. Community Forestry
2. Why do gardeners use plant classification?
3. Define the following terms:
   a. Warm season and cool season
   b. Tender and hardy
   c. Hardiness and hardiness zone
   d. Alpine, prairie, woodland, wetland, xeric, and native plants
   e. Herbaceous and woody
   f. Trees, shrubs, and vines
   g. Deciduous, evergreen, and semi-evergreen
   h. Broadleaf, narrowleaf, and needleleaf
   i. Annual, summer annual, and winter annual
   j. Biennial
   k. Perennial, herbaceous perennial, spring ephemerals, and woody perennials
4. Diagram the taxonomic breakdown of ferns, cycads, ginkgos, conifers, and angiosperms with monocots and dicots.
5. Why is it important to know the difference between monocots and dicots, especially when it comes to applying herbicides?
6. Why do horticulturists typically deal with plant *families*?
7. Give the protocol for writing scientific names. What is the difference between "sp." and "spp."?
8. Define the following terms:
   a. Variety
   b. Cultivar
   c. Clone
   d. Line
   e. Group
   f. Strain
   g. Form

Chapter

3*

Plant Structures

In reviewing plant physiology, plant cells are grouped into tissues based on similar characteristics, then into five distinct structures (organs).

Cells—Individual building blocks for life processes and growth. Common cells contain genetic matter (deoxyribonucleic acid, or DNA) and metabolic organelles, but they are mostly water. In green plants, they are the site of photosynthesis (Figure 3-1).

Tissues—Groups of cells that are similar in appearance and function, for example:

- **Epidermis** is the single exterior layer that protects the stems, leaves, flowers, and roots. The outside surface of the epidermis tissue is usually covered with a waxy substance called cutin, which reduces water loss.

- **Parenchyma** tissues are made of simple, thin-walled cells. In a carrot, for example, the parenchyma cells become a storage unit called the cortex. In leaves, a layer of parenchyma tissues under the epidermis is active in photosynthesis. When wounded, parenchyma cells can become meristematic and proliferate to grow over the wound.

- **Meristematic** tissues are comprised of actively dividing cells.

- **Sclerenchyma** tissues are thick-walled support cells found throughout the plant as fiber.

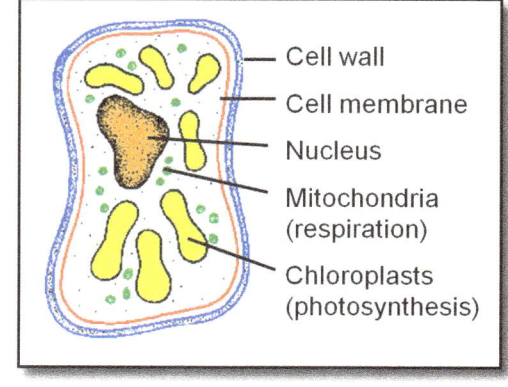

Figure 3-1 ■ *Plant cell.*

*Author: David Whiting, Colorado State University Extension. Artwork by Scott Johnson and David Whiting.

- **Xylem** is a structurally complex tissue that conducts water and nutrients from the roots to all parts of the plant. The xylem is comprised of a series of long tubes made up of shorter vessel members. In woody plants, the xylem tissue becomes the wood.

- **Phloem** tissue conducts *photosynthates* (metabolites from photosynthesis) throughout the plant, including down to the roots.

Structures (organs)—Groups of tissues working together with a common function (e.g., **roots, stems, leaves, flowers, fruits,** and **seeds**).

Plant—Made up of a number of coordinated structures to form a working unit.

ROOTS

The roots are the beginning of the vascular system pipeline that moves water and minerals from the soil up to the leaves and fruits. Roots make up around one-fourth to one-third of the total dry weight of a plant. The total length of root tissues in a single rye plant is around 380 miles!

To function, roots must have adequate levels of soil oxygen. Soil compaction or waterlogged soil situations, reducing soil oxygen levels, will kill roots and lead to a shallow root system.

The structure and growth habits of roots have a pronounced effect on:

- Size and vigor of the plants
- Adaptation to certain soils
- Response to cultural practices

Thought Questions

Explain the science behind the question.

- Last summer during a home remodeling project, we raised the soil level twelve inches in the yard. This summer my trees look stressed with small yellowish leaves. I don't see any insects. Could the problems be related to the soil change? My contractor assured us that trees are deep rooted.

- As you can't see the root system, what would be the symptoms of root and soil related problems?

Because they are out of sight, roots are often out of mind. They are widely overlooked as to their significance in plant health. Eighty percent of all plant problems start with soil/root problems.

Functions

- Anchor and support plants
- Absorb and conduct water and minerals
- Store products of photosynthesis (carbohydrates, sugars, proteins)
  - Winter survival of perennials
- Horticultural uses
  - Food and feed
  - Propagation
  - Soil erosion control

Structure

Epidermis—The outer layer of cells (see Figure 3-2).

>**Root hairs**—Absorptive unicellular extensions of epidermal cells of a root. These tiny, hair-like structures function as the major site of water and mineral uptake. Root hairs are extremely delicate and subject to desiccation. Root hairs are easily destroyed in transplanting (Figure 3-3).

Cortex—Primary tissues of a root bound on the outside by the epidermis and on the inside by the endodermis. In a carrot, the cortex becomes a storage organ (Figure 3-2).

Endodermis—A single layer of cells in a root that separates the cortex tissues from the pericycle (Figure 3-2).

Pericycle—A layer of cells immediately inside the endodermis. Branch roots arise from the pericycle (Figure 3-2).

Vascular system

>**Phloem** tissue conducts products of photosynthesis from leaves throughout the plant including down to the roots (Figure 3-2).

>**Xylem** tissue conducts water and minerals up from the roots up through the plant (Figure 3-2).

Zone of maturation—Pipeline section of the roots, conducting water and nutrients from the root hairs up to the stems (Figure 3-4).

Zone of elongation—Area where new cells are enlarging (Figure 3-4).

Meristematic zone

>**Root tip meristem**—Region of cell division that supports root elongation, found at the root tips just behind the root cap (Figure 3-4).

>**Root cap**—A thimble-shaped group of thick-walled cells at the root tip serves as a "hard hat" to push through soil. The root cap protects the tender meristem tissues (Figure 3-4).

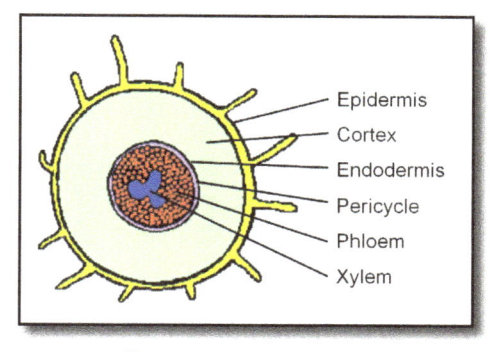

Figure 3-2 ■ *Root cross-section sectional view.*

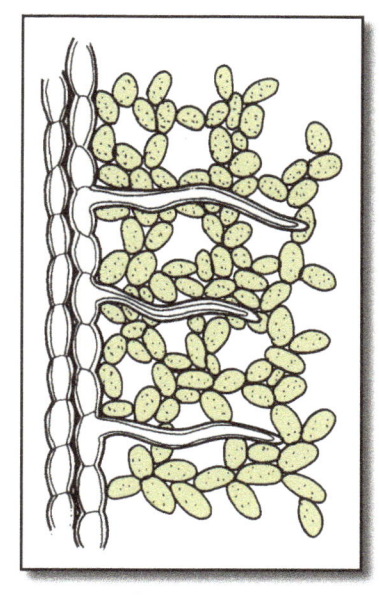

Figure 3-3 ■ *Root hairs are extensions of the epidermal cells.*

Types of Roots

Fibrous—Profusely branched roots that occupy a large volume of shallow soil around a plant's base (petunias, beans, peas) (Figure 3-5).

Taproot—Main, downward-growing root with limited branching, where soils permit (carrots, beets, radishes) (Figure 3-5).

Combination—In nursery production, the taproot of young plants (like oaks) is cut, forcing a fibrous growth pattern. This has a significant impact on the plant's ability to survive transplanting.

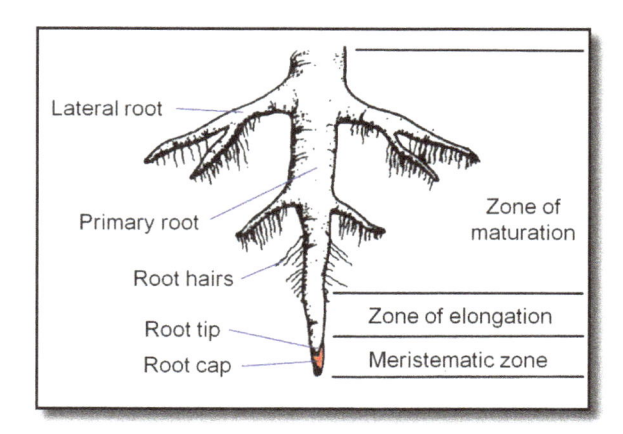

Figure 3-4 ■ *Lateral view of a root.*

Adventitious roots arise at an unexpected place. For example, the brace roots on corn and the short whitish bumps along a tomato stem are adventitious roots.

Aerial roots arise from above-ground stem tissues. On English ivy and poison ivy, the aerial roots support the vine. Aerial roots are common on philodendrons, pothos, and Christmas cactus.

Lateral root—Side root

Sinker roots make a sharp dive into deeper soils, following soil cracks where oxygen is available. Sinker roots are common on some tree species.

Storage or tuberous root—Enlarged roots that serve as storage organs (Canadian thistle, morning glory, sweet potato, dahlia).

Note: Tubers, bulbs, and corms are technically stem tissues.

Figure 3-5 ▍ *Root types. Left: Fibrous root system of corn. Right: Taproot system of carrot.*

Depth and Spread

The depth and spread of roots are dependent on the inherent growth characteristics of the plant *and* the soil's texture and structure. Roots require adequate levels of soil oxygen, so growth habit will be a factor of the soil's large pore space where oxygen is available (Figure 3-6).

- On compacted and clayey soils, roots will be shallow, remaining near the surface where oxygen is available.

- On droughty soils, the root system will spread farther, mining a larger soil area for moisture and minerals.

It is difficult to predict root spread of any plant. Under favorable growing conditions on loamy soils, the typical root spread of trees includes:

- Ninety to ninety-five percent in top thirty-six inches

- Fifty percent in top twelve inches

- Spreads two to three times tree's height or canopy (drip-line) spread

Figure 3-6 ▍ *Typical rooting pattern of trees, shallow and spreading.*

On compacted clayey soils, the typical root spread of trees includes:

- Ninety to ninety-five percent in top twelve inches or less

- Fifty percent in top four inches

- Potentially spreads five plus times the tree's height or canopy (drip-line) spread

Some plants are genetically programmed to have very deep, spreading root systems (i.e., they are more tolerant of low soil oxygen levels). This growth habit is an environmental adaptation. Examples include bindweed and prairie grasses.

Soil type is a key factor in water penetration and root uptake. Where soil allows, the primary water extraction depth extends to:

- Flowers   18 to 24 inches
- Turf   24 inches
- Vegetables   24 inches
- Shade trees   24 to 60 inches

Beneficial Microorganism Associations

Mycorrhizae are specific beneficial soil fungi forming symbiotic (mutually beneficial) associations with roots. While the role of mycorrhizae is not fully understood, they function to expand the root's contact with the soil profile, enhancing water and nutrient uptake. For additional information, refer to Chapter 7, Soil Tilth.

Rhizobium is a beneficial soil bacterium that forms a symbiotic relationship with plants, primarily those in the bean/pea family. These bacteria make atmospheric nitrogen available to plants. *Rhizobium* typically forms nodules on the roots of plants. These may be mistaken for insect injury or deformity. When alfalfa, a member of the bean/pea family, is left to mature then tilled into a field, it is considered "green manure" because the plant is rich in nitrogen due to the *rhizobium* in the roots.

STEMS

Stems are the part of a plant that bear leaves and flowers, and they are the continuation of the vascular system pipeline that starts in the roots.

Functions

- Framework for leaves, flowers, and seeds
- Continuation of vascular system carrying water and minerals from the soil, and photosynthates manufactured in leaves throughout the plant
- Green stems also manufacture food (photosynthesis)
- Food storage
- Horticultural uses
  - Aesthetic (winter interest in the landscape, appealing bark, etc.)
  - Feed and food
  - Fuel

Thought Questions

Explain the science behind the question.

- My trees have been under severe drought stress for the past few years. But why are they still showing stress when we had good moisture this year?

- Over the winter, rabbits girdled my tree all the way around down to the wood. My neighbor said it would die, but it leafed out nicely. Will it be OK? I planted several new trees over the past few years. How can I evaluate how they are growing? How can I tell if roots are established so I can begin structural pruning?

—Plant identification

—Propagation (cuttings and layering)

—Wildlife habitat

—Wood industry and construction

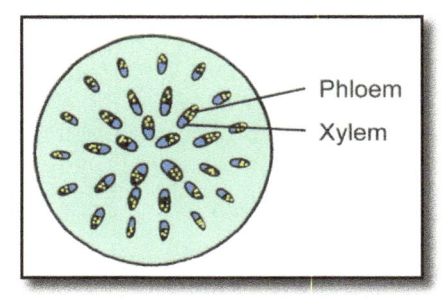

Structure

Internal Features

Apical meristem—Tissues at the tip of a stem capable of cell division, gives rise to stem elongation.

Epidermis—Outer layer of wax-coated cells that provides protection and covering (Figure 3-7).

Cortex—Primary tissues of a stem externally bound by the epidermis and internally by the phloem (Figure 3-7).

Vascular bundle

  Xylem tissues—Distribute water and minerals from the roots up through the plant. Xylem provides the structural support in plants, becoming the "woody " tissue (Figure 3-7).

  Cambium tissues are the single-celled layer of meristematic (dividing) tissues that continually divide to form phloem tissues toward the outside and xylem tissues toward the inside. Cell division of the cambium tissues adds width to the stem (Figure 3-7).

  Phloem tissues distribute **photosynthates** (sugars, carbohydrates, and proteins produced by photosynthesis) throughout the plant. It is important to understand what happens when the phloem is blocked, as when a tree is girdled with a tie or rope. The stem often enlarges just above the blockage due to the photosynthates moving down from the leaves for distribution throughout the plant. Tissues below the blockage slowly starve. Roots die back, eventually leading to death of the plant (Figure 3-7).

Pith—Center of dicot plant stems. In some plants, the pith breaks down forming a hollow stem. In older woody plants, the pith is filled with rigid xylem wood fiber (Figure 3-7).

Monocot or Dicot

Monocot and dicot stems differ in the arrangement of their vascular system.

In **monocot stems**, the xylem and phloem are paired in bundles, with bundles dispersed throughout the stem (Figure 3-8).

In **herbaceous dicot stems**, the vascular system makes a ring, with the phloem to the exterior and xylem to the interior (Figure 3-9).

In **woody dicot plants**, the rings grow to make a complete ring around the stem. Xylem growth makes the "annual rings" used to tell a tree's age. In woody dicot plants, water and mineral movement occurs in the more recent years of xylem rings. Drought reduces the size of the annual rings (size of xylem tubes) and thus the potential for water and nutrient movement. Multiyear droughts, with their corresponding reduction in xylem size, have long-term impacts on plant growth potential (Figure 3-10).

Pith—Woody dicot stems are used in tree and shrub identification. Features to look at include the cross-section shape of the pith (rounded, star, or triangular) and whether the pith is solid, hollow, or chambered (Figure 3-11).

Figure 3-7 ■ *Cross-section of stem.*

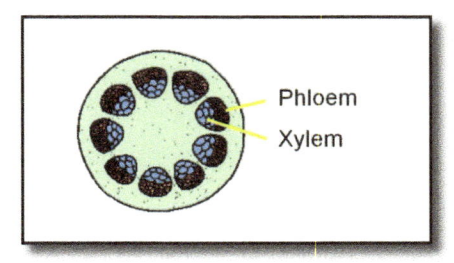

Figure 3-8 ■ *Monocot stem cross-section.*

Figure 3-9 ■ *Herbaceous dicot stem cross-section.*

External Features

Bud—A stem's primary growing point. Buds can be either leaf buds (vegetative) or flower buds (reproductive). These buds can be very similar in appearance, but flower buds tend to be plumper than leaf buds.

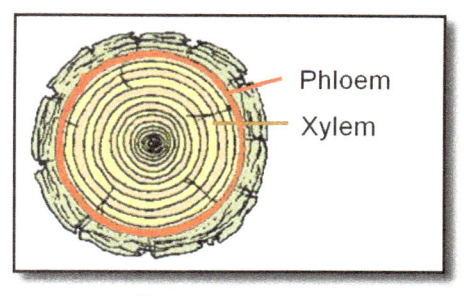

Figure 3-10 ■ *Woody dicot stem cross-section.*

> **Terminal bud**—Bud at the tip of a stem. In many plants, auxin (a plant hormone) released from the terminal bud suppresses development of lateral buds, thereby focusing the growth of the plant upward rather than outward. If the terminal bud is removed during pruning (or natural events) the lateral buds will develop and the stem becomes bushy (Figure 3-12).

> **Lateral buds** grow from the leaf axils on the side of a stem (Figure 3-12).

> **Bud scales**—A modified leaf protecting and covering a bud.

> **Naked bud**—Bud without a protective bud scale; characteristic of the Viburnum family.

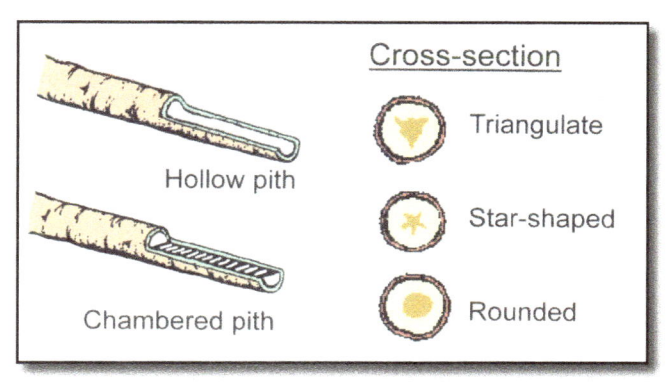

Figure 3-11 ■ *Stem pith is used in plant identification. It may be solid, hollow, or chambered. In a cross-section, the pith may be rounded, triangular, or star shaped.*

Leaf scar—Mark left on stem where leaf was attached. Often used in woody plant identification (Figure 3-13).

> **Bundle scar**—Marks left in the leaf scar from the vascular tissue attachment. Used in woody plant identification (Figure 3-13).

Lenticel—Pores that allow for gas exchange.

Terminal bud scale scars or **annual growth rings**—Marks left on stem from the terminal bud scales in previous years. Terminal bud scale scars are an external measure of annual growth. Therefore, they are important in assessing plant vigor (Figure 3-14).

Node—Segment of stem where leaves and lateral buds are attached (Figure 3-15).

Note: Roots do not have nodes.

Internode—Section of a stem between two nodes (Figure 3-15).

Bark—Protective outer tissue that develops with age. Used in woody plant identification.

All the features previously described can tell the knowledgeable horticulturist a great deal about a plant pertinent to its identification and health. These are common terms that frequently appear in literature.

Bud type—The type of bud is also used in plant identification. The following graphic illustrates bud types used in the *Manual of Woody Landscape Plants* (Figure 3-16).

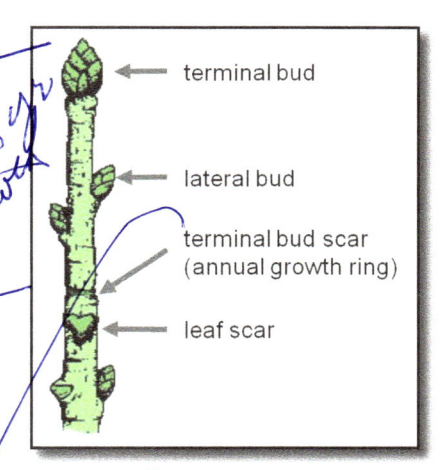

Figure 3-12 ■ *External features on a stem.*

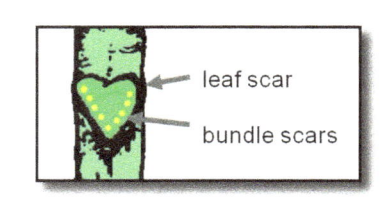

Figure 3-13 ■ *Leaf scar and bundle scar.*

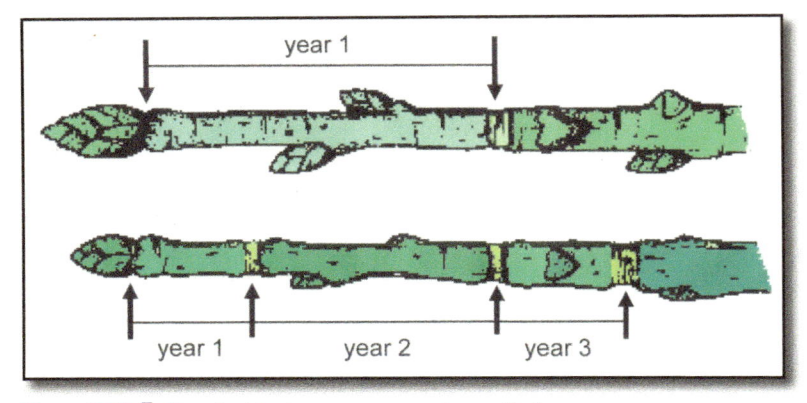

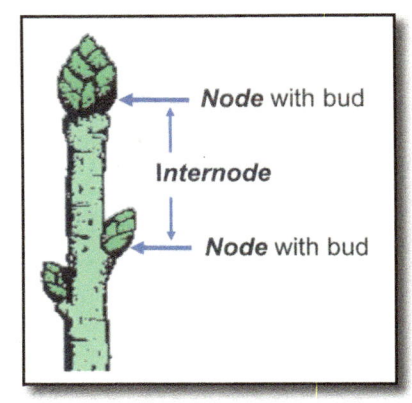

Figure 3-14 ▮ *Terminal bud scars or annual growth rings.*

Figure 3-15 ▮ *Stem with nodes and internodes.*

Common Types of Stems on Woody Plants

Shoot—First year growth on a woody or herbaceous plant

Twig—Woody stem less than one year old

Branch—Woody stem more than one year old

Trunk—Main support stem(s) of woody plants

Water sprouts—Juvenile adventitious shoots arising on a branch. Generally very rapid, upright growth, and poorly attached to the main limb.

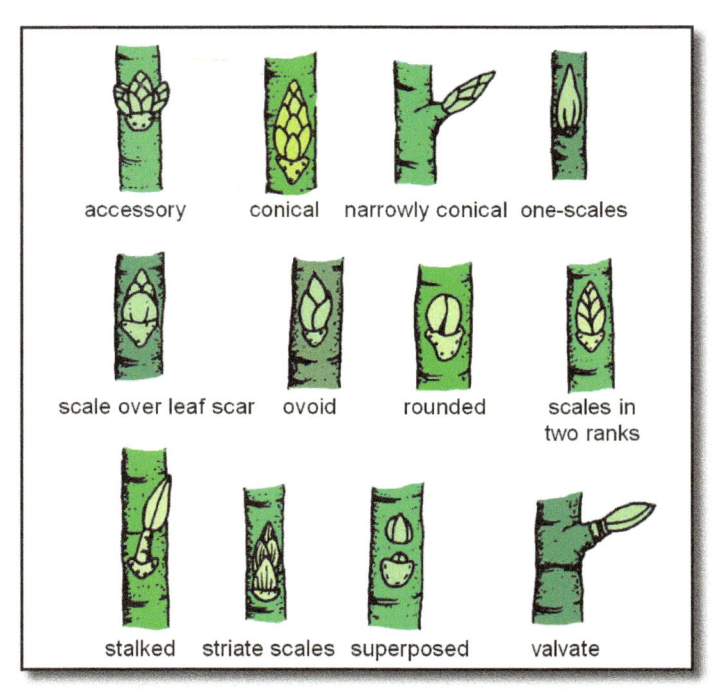

Figure 3-16 ▮ *Bud types.*

Suckers—Juvenile adventitious shoots arising from the roots, generally rapid, upright growth.

Canes—Stems with relatively large pith and usually living for only one to two years (roses, grapes, blackberries, raspberries).

Modified Stems

Bulb—Thickened, underground stem with fleshy storage leaves attached at base (tulips, lilies, onions) (Figure 3-17).

Corm—Short, thickened, underground stem with reduced

scaly leaves (gladiolus) (Figure 3-18).

Crown—Compressed stem having leaves and flowers growing above and roots beneath (strawberry plant, dandelion, African violet) (Figure 3-19).

Stolon (or runner)—Horizontal, above-ground stems often forming roots and/or plantlets at their tips or nodes (strawberry runners, spider plants) (Figure 3-20).

Rhizome—Horizontal, underground stems, typically forms roots and plantlets at tips or nodes (iris, bentgrass, cannas) (Figure 3-21).

Spur—Very compressed, fruiting twig found on some apples, pears, cherries, and ginkgo (Figure 3-22).

Figure 3-17 ▮ *Bulb.*

Figure 3-18 ▮ *Corm.*

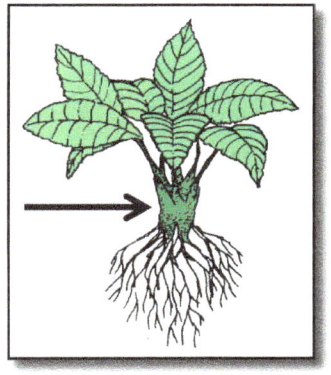

Figure 3-19 ▮ *Strawberry crown.*

Figure 3-20 ▮ *Strawberry plants with stolons.*

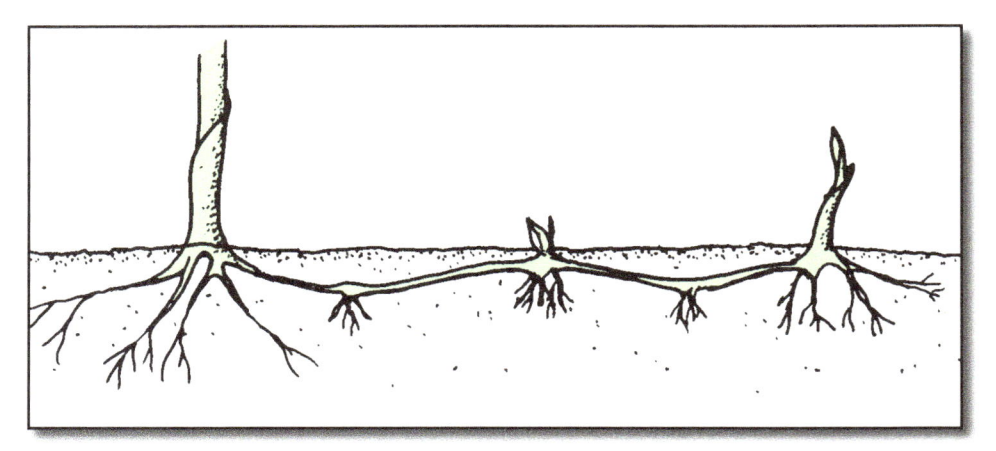

Figure 3-21 ▮ *Rhizome between plants.*

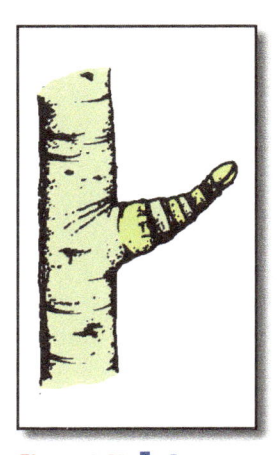

Figure 3-22 ▮ *Spur.*

Twining stems—Modified stems used for climbing. Some twist clockwise (hops, honeysuckle); others twist counter-clockwise (pole beans, Dutchman's pipe).

Tuber—Enlarged rhizome containing stored food (Irish potato, the eyes of the potato are modified buds) (Figure 3-23).

Tuberous stem—Short, flattened, modified storage stem (tuberous begonias, dahlias). Unlike tubers, which have buds scattered all over, tuberous stems only have leaf buds on the "up" end.

LEAVES

Leaves are the principle structure, produced on stems, where photosynthesis takes place. Cacti are an exception. The leaves are reduced to spines, and the thick green, fleshy stems are where photosynthesis takes place.

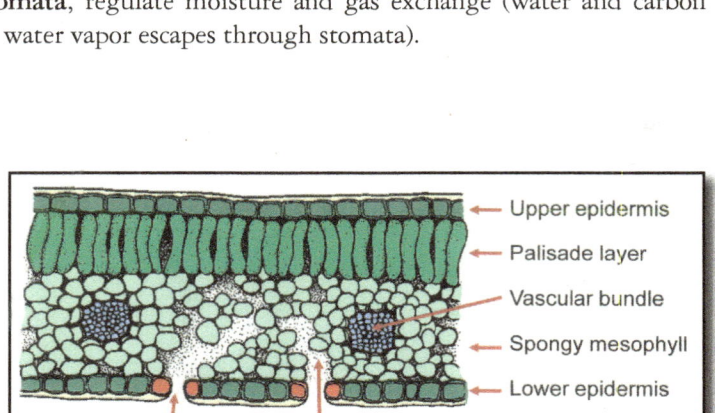

Figure 3-23 ▮ *Potato plant with tubers.*

Functions

- Photosynthesis

- Evapotranspiration from the leaves is what moves water and nutrients up from the roots.

- Small openings on the leaf, known as **stomata**, regulate moisture and gas exchange (water and carbon dioxide) and temperature (cooling effect as water vapor escapes through stomata).

- Horticultural uses

  —Aesthetic qualities

  —Feed and food

  —Mulch and compost

  —Plant identification

  —Propagation from cuttings

  —Summer cooling (evaporative cooling accounts for 70% to 80% of the shading impact of a tree)

  —Wildlife habitat

  —Wind, dust, and noise reduction

Figure 3-24 ▮ *Leaf cross-sectional view with stomata.*

Structure

Internal Features

The leaf blade is composed of several layers as follows.

Epidermis—Outer layer of tissues (Figure 3-24).

    Cuticle—Waxy protective outer layer of epidermis that prevents water loss on leaves, green stems, and fruits. The amount of cutin or wax increases with light intensity.

    Leaf hairs—Part of the epidermis.

Palisade layer—A tightly packed layer of parenchyma tissues filled with chloroplasts for photosynthesis (Figure 3-24).

> **Chloroplasts**—Subcellular, photosynthetic structures in leaves and other green tissues. Chloroplasts contain chlorophyll, a green plant pigment that captures the energy in light and begins the transformation of that energy into sugars.

Vascular bundle—Xylem and phloem tissues, commonly known as leaf veins (Figure 3-24).

Spongy mesophyll—Layer of parenchyma tissues loosely arranged to facilitate movement of oxygen, carbon dioxide, and water vapor. It also may contain some chloroplasts (Figure 3-24).

Stomata—Natural openings in leaves and herbaceous stems that allow for gas exchange (water vapor, carbon dioxide, and oxygen) (Figure 3-24).

Guard cells—Specialized kidney-shaped cells that open and close the stomata (Figure 3-24).

External Features

Leaf blade—Flattened part of the leaf (Figure 3-25).

Petiole—Leaf stalk (Figure 3-25).

Stipules—Leaf-like appendages at the base of the leaf (Figure 3-25).

For plant identification purposes, the shape of the leaf margin, leaf tip, and leaf base are key features to note. Remember, a leaf begins at the lateral or auxiliary bud.

Leaf Arrangement on Stems

Alternate—Arranged in staggered fashion along stem (willow) (Figure 3-26).

Opposite—Pair of leaves arranged across from each other on stem (maple) (Figure 3-26).

Whorled—Arranged in a ring (catalpa) (Figure 3-26).

Rosette—Spiral cluster of leaves arranged at the base (or crown) (dandelion).

Leaflet Arrangement on Petiole

Simple—Leaf blade is one continuous unit (cherry, maple, and elm) (Figure 3-27).

Compound—Several leaflets arise from the same petiole.

> **Pinnately compound**—Leaflets arranged on both sides of a common rachis (leaf stalk), like a feather (mountain ash) (Figure 3-27).

> **Palmately compound**—Leaflets radiate from one central point (Ohio buckeye and horse chestnut) (Figure 3-27).

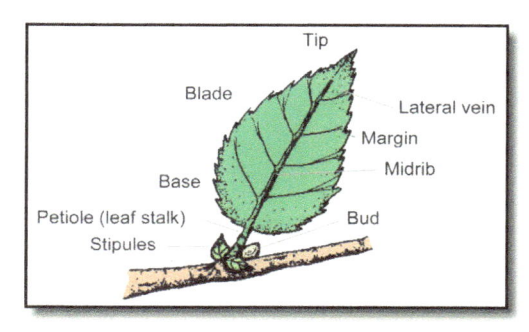

Figure 3-25 ▮ *External features of a leaf.*

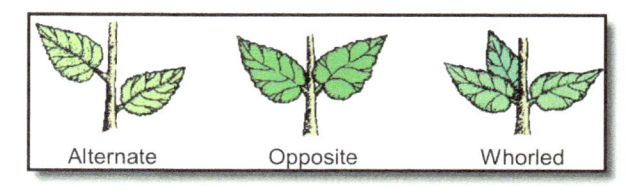

Figure 3-26 ▮ *Leaf arrangement on stem.*

Double pinnately compound—Double set of compound leaflets (Figure 3-27).

Note: Sometimes identifying a "leaf" or "leaflet" can be confusing. Look at the petiole attachment. A leaf petiole attaches to the stem at a bud node. There is no bud node where leaflets attach to the petiole.

Figure 3-27 ▪ *Leaf arrangement on petiole.*

Overall Leaf Shape

Leaf shape is a primary tool in plant identification. Descriptions often go into minute detail about general leaf shape and the shape of the leaf apex and base. Figure 3-28 shows common shapes as used in the *Manual of Woody Landscape Plants.*

Shape of Leaf Apex and Base

Shape of the leaf apex (tip) and base is another tool in plant identification. Figures 3-29 and 3-30 show the common tip and base styles as used in the *Manual of Woody Landscape Plants.*

Leaf Margin

The leaf margin is another tool in plant identification. Figure 3-31 shows common margin types as used in the *Manual of Woody Landscape Plants.*

Leaf Venation

Conifer types

- **Scale-like**—Mature leaves common on most junipers and arborvitae (Figure 3-32).

- **Awl-shaped**—Juvenile leaves common on some junipers (Figure 3-32).

- **Linear-shaped**—Narrow flat needles of spruce, fir, and yews (Figure 3-32).

- **Needle-like**—In pine, the single, bundle, or cluster of needles makes a rounded shape (Figure 3-32).

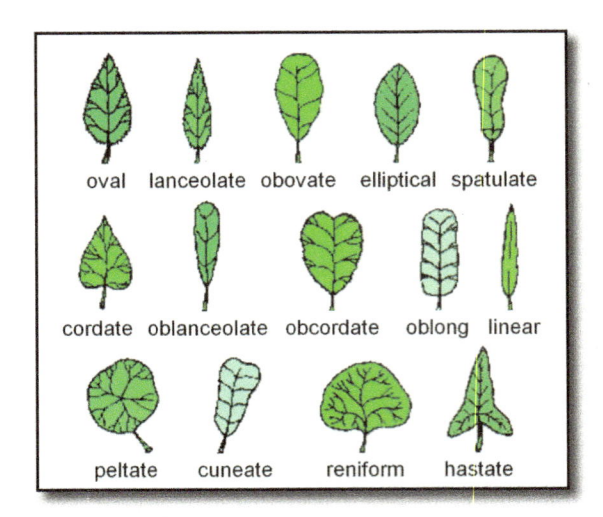

Figure 3-28 ▪ *Leaf shapes.*

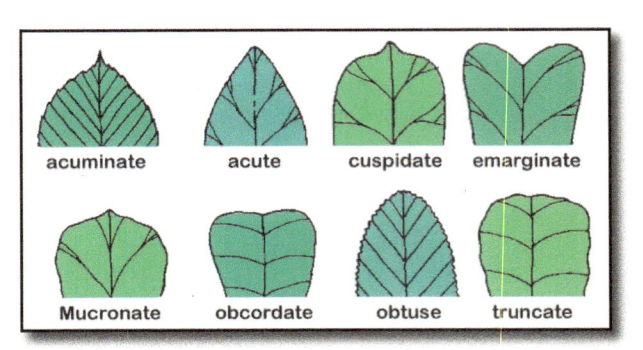

Figure 3-29 ▪ *Leaf tip shapes.*

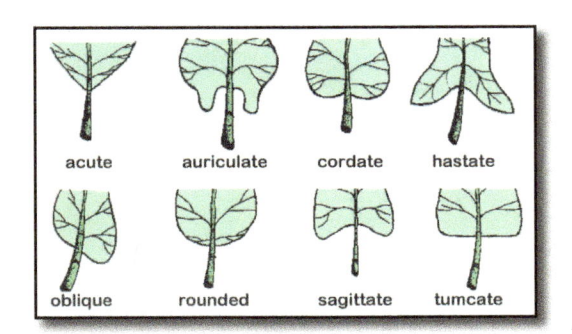

Figure 3-30 ▪ *Leaf base shapes.*

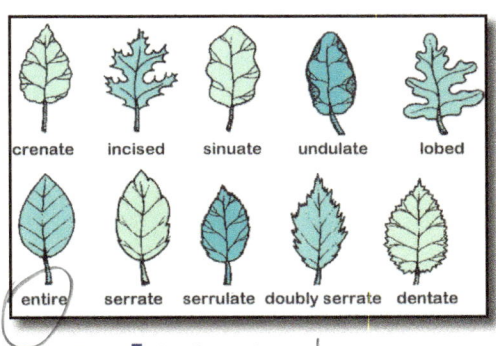

Figure 3-31 ▪ *Leaf margins.*

Ginkgo type

Dichotomous venation—Somewhat parallel vein sections, forming a "Y," found in ginkgo trees (Figure 3-33).

Monocot types

Parallel venation—Veins run in parallel lines (monocot plants [e.g., grasses, lilies, tulips]) (Figure 3-34).

Dicot types

Net-veined or reticulate-veined—Leaves with veins that branch from the main rib and then subdivide into finer veinlets (dicot plants).

Pinnate venation—Veins extend from a midrib to the edge (elm, peach, apple, cherry) (Figure 3-35).

Palmate venation—Veins radiate fan-shaped from the petiole (maple, grapes) (Figure 3-35).

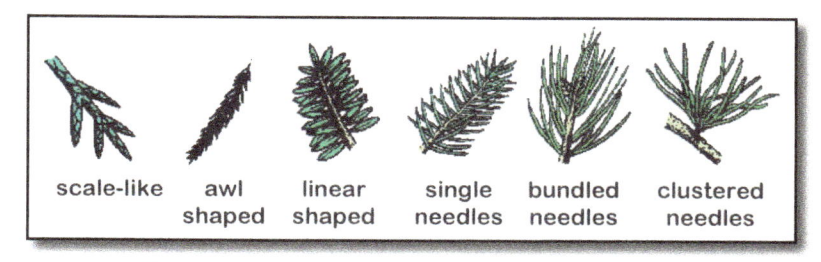

Figure 3-32 ▪ *Conifer leaf types.*

scale-like   awl shaped   linear shaped   single needles   bundled needles   clustered needles

Figure 3-33 ▪ *Dichotomous veined Ginkgo leaf.*

Figure 3-34 ▪ *Parallel veined monocot leaf.*

Modified Leaves

Adhesive disc—Modified leaf used for attachment mechanism. Sometimes referred to as a holdfast (Boston ivy).

Bract—Specialized, often highly colored leaf below flower that often serves to lure pollinators (Poinsettia, dogwood).

Spine or **thorn**—Modified leaf (barberry, pyracantha) (Figure 3-36).

Tendril—Modified sinuous leaf used for climbing or as an attachment mechanism (Virginia creeper, peas, grapes).

palmately veined dicot leaf

pinnately veined dicot leaf

Figure 3-35 ▪ *Venation of dicot leaves.*

Figure 3-36 ▪ *Thorns are modified leaves.*

FLOWERS

Flowers are the reproductive structures of a flowering plant. Flowers are the primary structures used in grouping plant families.

Function

- Reproduction, beginning with pollination and fertilization
- Advertisement and rewards to lure a pollinator
- Horticultural uses
  - Aesthetic qualities
  - Cut flowers and potted blooming plants
  - Edible flowers and herbs
  - Plant identification

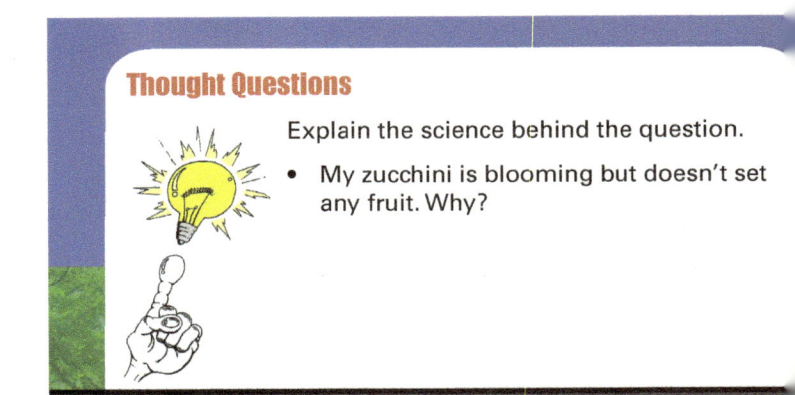

Thought Questions

Explain the science behind the question.

- My zucchini is blooming but doesn't set any fruit. Why?

Structure

Pistil—Central female organ of the flower. It is generally bowling-pin shaped and located in the center of the flower (Figure 3-37).

  Stigma—Receives pollen, typically flattened and sticky.

  Style—Connective tissues between stigma and ovary.

  Ovary—Contains ovules or embryo sacs.

  Ovules—Unfertilized, immature seeds.

Stamen—Male flower organ (Figure 3-37).

  Anthers—Pollen-producing organs.

  Filament—Stalk-supporting anthers.

Petals—Usually colorful petal-like structures making up the "flower," collectively called the **corolla**. They may contain perfume and nectar glands (Figure 3-37).

Sepals—Protective leaf-like enclosures for the flower buds, usually green, collectively called the **calyx**. Sometimes highly colored like the petal as in iris (Figure 3-37).

Receptacle—Base of the flower (Figure 3-37).

Pedicel—Flower stalk of an individual flower in an inflorescence (Figure 3-37).

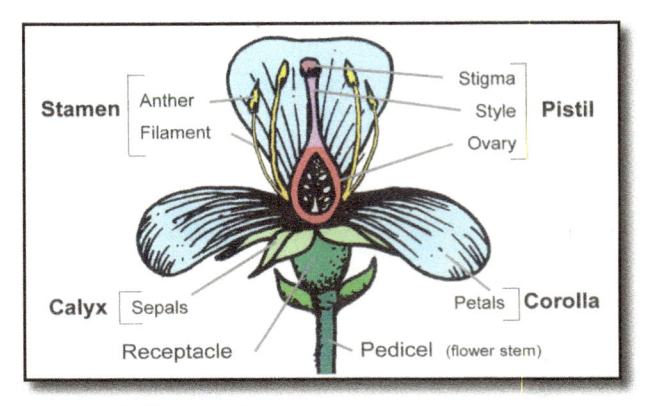

Figure 3-37 ■ *Parts of a flower.*

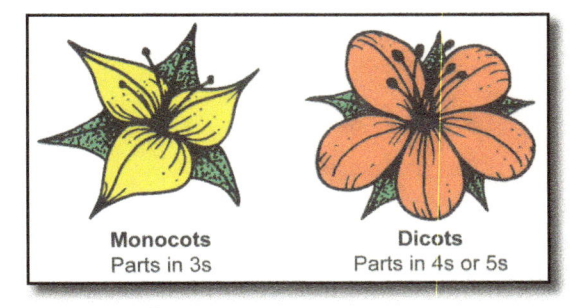

Figure 3-38 ■ *Monocot and dicot flowers.*

Monocot or Dicot Flower

The number of sepals and petals is used in plant identification. Dicots typically have sepals and petals in fours, fives, or multiples thereof. Monocots typically have flower parts in threes or multiples of three (Figure 3-38).

Terms Defining Flower Parts

Flowers

Complete—Flower containing sepals, petals, stamens, and pistil.

Incomplete—Flower lacking sepals, petals, stamens, and/or pistils.

Perfect—Flowers containing male *and* female parts.

Imperfect—Flowers with either male *or* female parts.

Pistillate—Flowers containing only female parts.

Staminate—Flowers containing only male parts.

Plants

Hermaphroditic—Plants with perfect flowers (apples, tulips).

Monoecious (mə-nē'shəs)—Plants with separate male flowers and female flowers on the same plant (corn, squash, and pine).

Dioecious (dīē'shəs)—Plants with male flowers and female flowers on separate plants (maple, holly, and salt brush).

Gynoecious—Plants with only female flowers.

Andromonoecious—Plants with only male flowers.

Inflorescence (Flower Arrangement on a Stem)

Catkin (ament)—A spike with only pistillate or staminate flowers (alder, poplar, walnut, and willows) (Figure 3-39).

Composite or Head—A daisy-type flower composed of ray flowers (usually sterile with attractive, colored petals) around the edge and disc flowers that develop into seed in center of the flat head (sunflower and aster). On some composites, the ray and disc flowers are similar (chrysanthemums and dahlias) (Figure 3-39).

Corymb—Stemlets (*pedicels*) arranged along main stem. Outer florets have longer pedicals than inner florets giving the display a flat top (yarrow, crabapple) (Figure 3-39).

Cyme—A determinate, flat or convex flower, with inner floret opening first (Figure 3-39).

Panicle—An indeterminate flower with repeated branching. It can be made up of racemes, spikes, corymbs, or umbels (begonia) (Figure 3-39).

Raceme—A modification of a spike with flowers attached to a main stem (*peduncle*) by stemlets (*pedicel*) (snapdragon, bleeding heart, Canterbury bells) (Figure 3-39).

Solitary (or single)—One flower per stem (tulip, crocus) (Figure 3-39).

Spadix—Showy part is a bract, or *spathe*, partially surrounding the male and female flowers inside (calla, caladium) (Figure 3-39).

Spike—Flowers attached to main stem, without stemlets, bottom florets open first (gladiolus, ajuga, and gayfeather) (Figure 3-39).

Umbel—Florets with stemlets attached to main stem at one central point, forming a flat or rounded top. Outer florets open first (dill and onion) (Figure 3-39).

Symmetrical—Symmetrical flowers (lily).

Asymmetrical—Asymmetrical flowers (snapdragon).

Figure 3-39 ▮ *Flower inflorescence.*

FRUIT

Fruit evolves from the maturing ovary following pollination and fertilization. Fruits can be either fleshy or dry. They contain one or more seeds.

Function

- Reproduction
- Horticulture uses
  —Feed, food, and oils
  —Aesthetic qualities
  —Plant identification

Structure

Fruit consists of carpels where the ovules (seeds) develop and the ovary wall or **pericarp**, which may be fleshy (as in apples) or dry and hard (as in an acorn). Some fruits have seeds (mature ovules) enclosed within the ovary (apples, peaches, oranges, squash, and cucumbers). The peel of an orange, the pea pod, the sunflower shell, and the skin flesh and pit of a peach are all derived from the pericarp (Figures 3-40–3-42).

Other fruit have seeds that are situated on the periphery of the pericarp (corncob, strawberry flesh).

Fruit Types

Conifers

Conifers are best known for their woody "pine cones." Junipers are an example of a conifer with a fleshy cone (Juniper berry). Upon close examination, the overlapping scales can be observed (Figure 3-43).

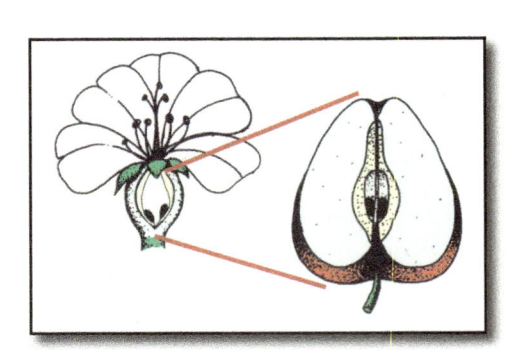

Figure 3-40 ▮ *In apples, the ovary wall becomes the fleshy part of the fruit. Notice the small fruit structure in the blossom.*

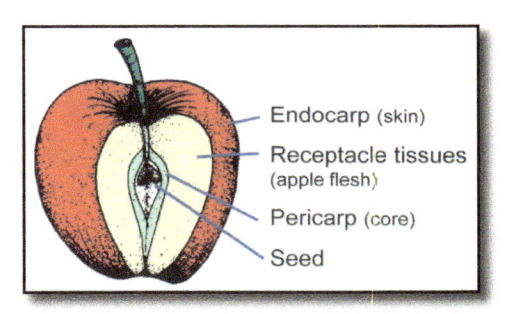

Figure 3-41 ▮ *Pome fruit (apple).*

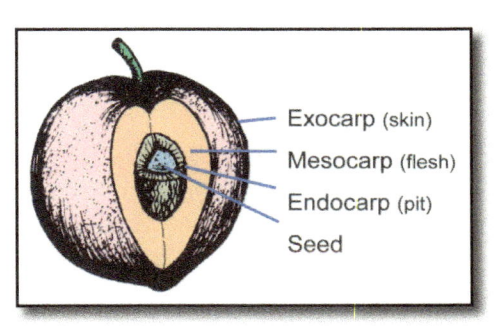

Figure 3-42 ▮ *Stone fruit (peach).*

Flowering Plants (Angiosperms)

Depending on flower structure and inflorescence type, fruits may be either simple, aggregate, or multiple.

Simple—Fruit formed from one ovary.

Aggregate—Fruit formed from a single flower with many ovaries. If not all of the ovaries are pollinated and fertilized, the fruit will be misshapen (raspberry, magnolia).

Multiple—Fruit developed from a fusion of separate, independent flowers born on a single structure (mulberry, pineapple, and beet seed).

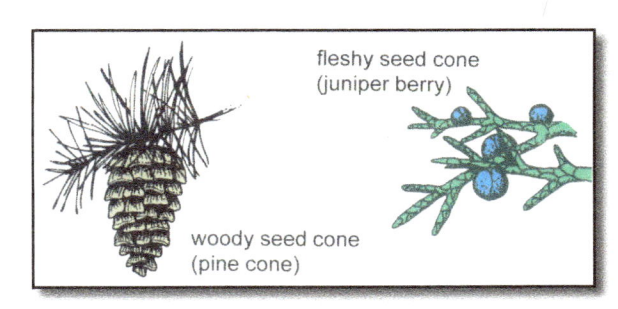

Figure 3-43 ■ *Conifer fruit. Left: Woody seed cone (pine cone). Right: Fleshy seed cone (juniper berry).*

Fruit Growth Terms

Bud development—On temperate-zone woody plants, buds typically develop mid-summer of the previous year. An exception is on summer flowering shrubs, where the buds develop on the current season's wood.

Pollination—Transfer of pollen from the male flower to the stigma of the female flower.

Fertilization—Union of the pollen grain from the male flower with the egg cell in the female flower.

Drop—Fruit drops when not pollinated or fertilized and when too much fruit sets on a tree.

Growth—What we see as growth is primarily cell enlargement as the cells fill with water.

Climacteric—Point when a fruit will continue to ripen if removed from a plant (e.g., pumpkins turning orange after being harvested).

SEEDS

A seed (mature ovule) is a miniature plant with a protective cover in a suspended state of development. Most seeds contain a built-in food supply called endosperm (orchid is an exception). The endosperm can be made up of proteins, carbohydrates, or fats.

Function

- Propagation
- Feed
- Horticultural uses
  —Feed, food, and oil

Structure and Emergence

Seeds of monocots and dicots differ in structure and method of emergence.

Monocot Seeds (Figures 3-57 and 3-58)

Seed coat—From the wall of the embryo sack (mother tissue).

Endosperm—Food supply containing three sets of chromosomes (two from the mother and one from the father).

Table 3-1. Key to Common Fruit Types

1a. Fruit fleshy.—go to 2

1b. Fruit dry at maturity.—go to 6

2a. Simple fruit: one that is derived from a flower with a single ovary.—go to 3

2b. Fruit derived from a single flower with many ovaries.—**Aggregate fruit** (raspberry and magnolia). Note: If not all of the ovaries are pollinated and fertilized, the fruit will be misshapen.

2c. Fruit develops from multiple separate flowers in an inflorescence, the fruits coalesce together to form a single "fruit" at maturity.—**Multiple fruit** (mulberry, pineapple, and beet seed).

3a. Fruit with a single seed enclosed in a hard pit. The *exocarp* (outer layer) becomes the thin skin, the *mesocarp* (middle layer) becomes thick and fleshy, and the *endocarp* (inner layer) becomes a hard stony pit.—**Drupe** (peaches, olives, cherries, and plums) (Figure 3-44).

3b. Fruit with more than one seed, the seed not enclosed in a hard pit.—go to 4

Figure 3-44 ▮ *Drupe (peach).*

4a. Fruit develops from the ovary only. Pulpy fruit from one or more carpels that develops few to many seeds, inner and outer walls fleshy.—**Berry** (tomatoes, eggplant, blueberries, and grapes) (Figure 3-45).

Berries with a leather rind containing oils, enclosing a pulpy juice sack (carpels).—**Hesperidium** (citrus: oranges, lemons, limes, grapefruit) (Figure 3-46).

4b. Fruits develop from the ovary plus other flower parts (accessory fruits).—go to 5

Figure 3-45 ▮ *Berry (tomato).*

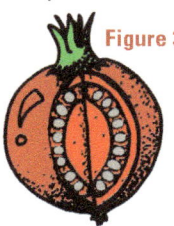

Figure 3-46 ▮ *Hesperidium (orange).*

5a. Simple fruits with relative hard rind at maturity, fleshy-watery interior with many seeds.—**Pepo** (cucumbers, melons, and squash) (Figure 3-47).

Figure 3-47 ▮ *Pepo (pumpkin).*

Table 3-1. Key to Common Fruit Types (continued)

5b.	Simple fruit with several carpels and papery inner wall (endocarp) and fleshy outer wall.—**Pome** (apple, pear, and quince) (Figure 3-48).	

Figure 3-48 ▪ *Pome (apple).*

6a.	Fruit not splitting at maturity.—go to 7
6b.	Fruit splitting open at maturity.—go to 10

Figure 3-49 ▪ *Samaras.*

7a.	One-seed achene fruit (elm and ash) or two-seed fruit (maple) with a wing-like structure formed from the ovary wall.—**Samaras** (Figure 3-49).
7b.	Fruit without wings.—go to 8

Elm   Ash   Double seeded = Maple

8a.	One-seeded fruit with hard stony shell (pericarp) surrounding the seed.—**Nut** (oak, filbert, and walnut) (Figure 3-50).
8b.	Fruit without hard shell.—go to 9

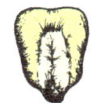

Figure 3-50 ▪ *Nut (acorn).*

9a.	Simple, one-seeded fruit with a thin seed coat (pericarp) surrounding and adhering tightly to the true seed.—**Caryopsis** (corn, rice, wheat, and barley) (Figure 3-51).
9b.	Simple, one-seeded, thin-wall fruit with seed loosely attached to ovary wall.—**Achene** (sunflower) (Figure 3-52).

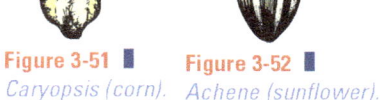

Figure 3-51 ▪ *Caryopsis (corn).*   **Figure 3-52** ▪ *Achene (sunflower).*

10a.	Fruit from two or more carpels, each with many seeds, splitting along or between carpel lines or forming a cap that comes off or a row of pores near the top.—**Capsule** (iris, poppy, jimson weed) (Figure 3-53).
10b.	Fruit splitting lengthwise along the edge.—go to 11

Figure 3-53 ▪ *Capsule (poppy).*

11a.	Fruits from two carpels with a central partition to which the seeds are attached. Splits to expose seeds along central membrane.—**Silique** or **Silicle** (mustards) (Figure 3-54).
11b.	Fruits not leaving a central partition.—go to 12

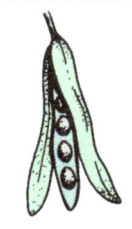

Figure 3-54 ▪ *Silique or Silicle (mustard).*

Table 3-1. Key to Common Fruit Types (continued)

12a. Fruit from a single carpel that splits along one suture only.—**Follicle** (Delphinium) (Figure 3-55).

12b. Fruit from a single carpel usually splits along two sutures. Found in members of the *Fabaceae* (pea) family.—**Legume** or **Pod** (peas and beans) (Figure 3-56).

12c. Fruit formed from two or more carpels that split at maturity to yield one-seeded halves.—**Schizocarp** (carrots, dill, parsley, hollyhock).

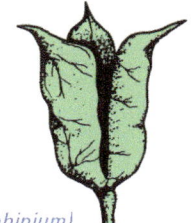 

Figure 3-55 ▮ *Follicle (delphinium).*   **Figure 3-56** ▮ *Legume or pod (pea).*

Embryo—Immature plant

Cotyledon—Seed leaf

Plumule—Shoot

Radicle—Root

Dicot Seeds (Figures 3-59–3-61)

Seed coat—From embryo sack wall and endosperm tissue. (During development, the endosperm stops dividing and is absorbed into the embryonic tissues.)

Embryo—Immature plant

Cotyledon—Food-storing seed leaf

Plumule—Shoot

Hypocotyl—Stem

Radicle—Root

Seed Growth and Development Terms

Dormancy—State of suspended growth to survive adverse conditions and aid in dispersion. Adapting plants to a variety of hostile environments, Mother Nature programs a variety of germination blocks. The following are common types.

Figure 3-57 ▮ *Cross-section of monocot seed (corn).*

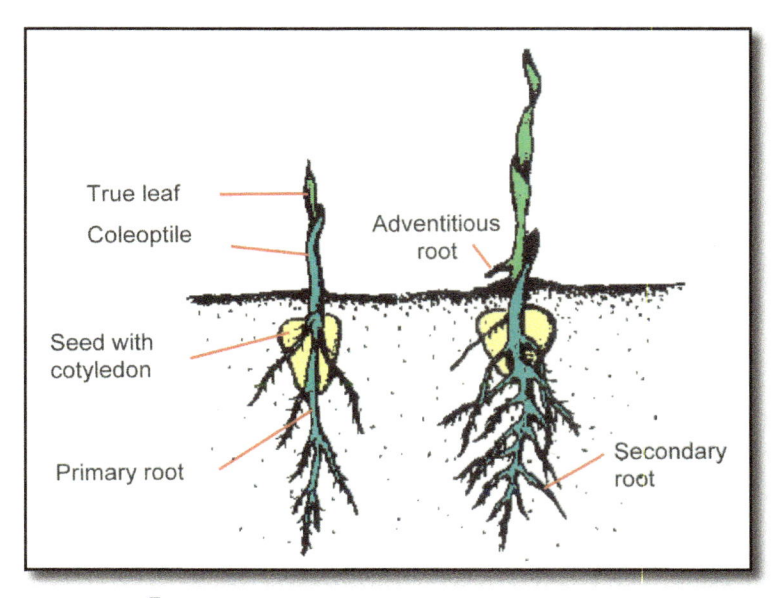

Figure 3-58 ▮ *Emergence of corn plant.*

Seed coat dormancy—When the seed coat is impermeable to water and gases (oxygen), it requires action by weathering, microorganisms, passage through an animal's digestive tract, or fire to soften the seed coat.

Embryo dormancy—Due to physiological conditions or germination blocks in the embryo itself, it requires a specific period of cold (or heat) with available moisture and oxygen. Embryo dormancy is common in woody plants.

Double dormancy—Condition of both seed coat and embryo dormancy.

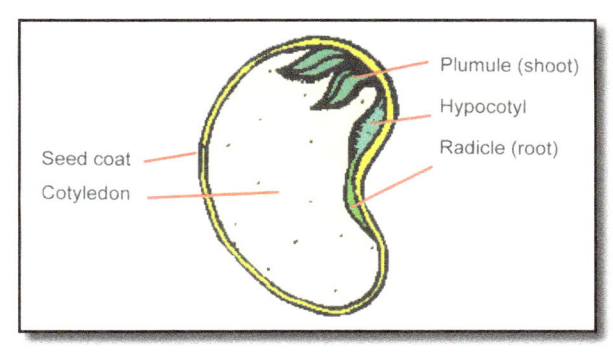

Figure 3-59 ▮ *Cross-section of dicot seed (bean).*

Rudimentary embryo dormancy—Situation where the embryo is immature and requires a growth period before it can germinate.

Chemical inhibitor dormancy—Seed contains some type of chemical that blocks germination. Many desert plants contain chemical germination inhibitors that are leached out in a soaking rain.

Stratification—Techniques used by a horticulturist to overcome dormancy.

For details on dormancy, stratification, and germination of any specific plant, refer to a book on plant propagation.

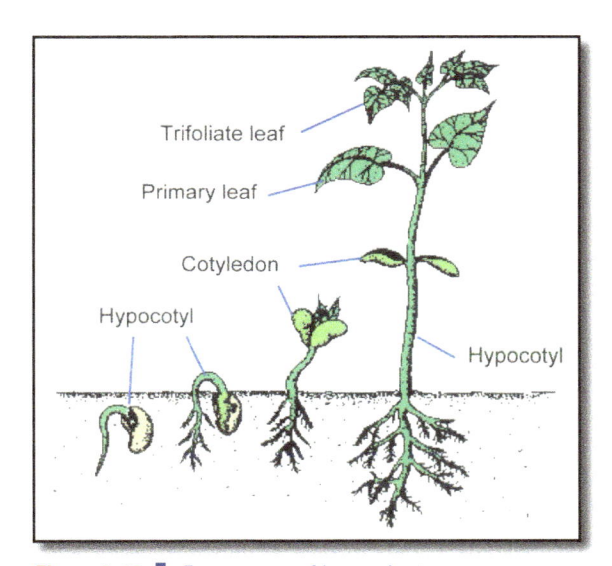

Figure 3-60 ▮ *Emergence of bean plant.*

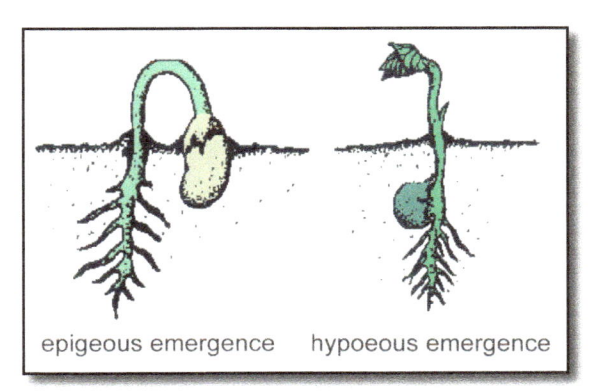

Figure 3-61 ▮ *Dicot seed emergence.*

1. Describe the relationships of *cells*, *tissues*, *structures*, and *plants*.

2. Describe the function of the xylem and phloem tissues.

3. List the three primary functions of roots. What percentage of plant problems begin as soil and root disorders?

4. Define and identify the following root terms:

   a. Primary roots

   b. Lateral roots

   c. Tap root system

   d. Fibrous roots system

5. Describe and identify the vascular bundle arrangement for monocot stems, non-woody dicot stems, and woody dicot stems and roots.

6. On a stem, identify the following parts: (Be able to label plant parts on a stem picture.)

   a. Nodes

   b. Internodes

   c. Terminal bud

   d. Lateral bud

   e. Terminal bud scar

   f. Leaf scar

   g. Bundle scar

7. Explain how to use the terminal bud scar (annual growth rings) to evaluate the vigor of a tree.

8. Describe the following internal characteristics of the stems used in plant identification:

   a. Solid

   b. Hollow

   c. Chambered pith

   d. Star-shaped pith

   e. Triangular pith

   f. Rounded pith

9. Define the following stem terms:

   a. Twig

   b. Branch

   c. Trunk

   d. Cane

   e. Sucker

   f. Water sprout

10. Define the following terms used in reference to modified stems:

    a. Bulb

    b. Stolon

    c. Rhizome

    d. Tuber

11. Describe and identify leaves from conifers, ginkgo, monocots, and dicots.

12. Define and identify the following leaf terms:

    a. Leaf blade

    b. Leaf tip

    j. Palmate venation

    k. Parallel venation

c. Leaf base

d. Mid-vein or midrib

e. Lateral veins

f. Petiole

g. Stipules

h. Bud

i. Pinnate venation

l. Simple leaf

m. Pinnately compound leaf

n. Palmately compound leaf

o. Double compound leaf

p. Alternate leaf arrangement

q. Opposite leaf arrangement

r. Whorled leaf arrangement

13. With compound leaves, how can you tell what is a leaf and what is a leaflet?

14. Describe how to identify monocot and dicot flowers.

15. On a flower, identify the following parts: (Be able to label plant parts on a flower picture.)

a. Sepals

b. Calyx

c. Petals

d. Corolla

e. Anthers

f. Filament

g. Stamen

h. Stigma

i. Style

j. Ovary

k. Ovules

l. Pistil

m. Receptacle

n. Pedicel

o. Floret

16. Define the following flower and plant terms.

a. Complete flower

b. Incomplete flower

c. Perfect flower

d. Imperfect staminate flower

e. Imperfect pistillate flower

f. Hermaphroditic plant

g. Monoecious plant

h. Dioecious plant

17. On a seed, identify the following parts:

a. Seed coat

b. Endosperm

c. Cotyledon

d. Plumule

e. Radicle

f. Hypocotyl

18. Describe the difference between monocot and dicot seeds.

19. Review *Thought Questions*.

Chapter

4*

Plant Growth

PHOTOSYNTHESIS, RESPIRATION, AND TRANSPIRATION

The three major functions that are basic to plant growth and development are as follows:

Thought Questions

Explain the science behind the question.

- What's the impact on air temperatures when restrictions in landscape irrigation create droughty urban landscapes?

- **Photosynthesis**—The process of capturing light energy and converting it to sugar energy, in the presence of chlorophyll using carbon dioxide and water.

- **Respiration**—The process of metabolizing (burning) sugars to yield energy for growth, reproduction, and other life processes.

- **Transpiration**—The loss of water vapor through the stomata of leaves.

Photosynthesis

A primary difference between plants and animals is the plant's ability to manufacture its own food. In **photosynthesis**, carbon dioxide from the air and water from the soil react with the sun's energy to form **photosynthates** (sugars, starches, carbohydrates, and proteins) and release oxygen as a byproduct (Figure 4-1).

Photosynthesis literally means *to put together with light*. It occurs only in the **chloroplasts**, tiny subcellular structures contained in the cells of leaves and green stems. A simple chemical equation for photosynthesis is given as follows:

―――――――――

*Author: David Whiting, Colorado State University Extension. Artwork by Scott Johnson and David Whiting.

$$\text{carbon dioxide} + \text{water} + \text{light energy} = \text{glucose} + \text{oxygen}$$
$$6CO_2 + 6H_2O + \text{light energy} = C_6H_{12}O_6 + 6O_2$$

This process is directly dependent on the supply of water, light, and carbon dioxide. Limiting any one of the factors on the left side of the equation (carbon dioxide, water, or light) can limit photosynthesis regardless of the availability of the other factors. An implication of drought or severe restrictions on landscape irrigation is a reduction in photosynthesis and thus a decrease in plant vigor and growth.

In a tightly closed greenhouse, there can be very little fresh air infiltration and carbon dioxide levels can become limiting, thus limiting plant growth. In the winter, many large commercial greenhouses provide supplemental carbon dioxide to stimulate plant growth.

The rate of photosynthesis is somewhat temperature dependent. For example, with tomatoes, when temperatures rise above 96°F, the rate of food used by respiration rises above the rate of which food is manufactured by photosynthesis. Plant growth comes to a stop and produce loses its sweetness. Most other plants are similar (Figure 4-2).

Figure 4-1 ■ *In photosynthesis, the plant uses water and nutrients from the soil, and carbon dioxide from the air with the sun's energy to create photosynthates. Oxygen is released as a byproduct.*

Respiration

In **respiration**, plants (and animals) convert the sugars (photosynthates) back into energy for growth and other life processes (metabolic processes). The chemical equation for respiration shows that the photosynthates are combined with oxygen releasing energy, carbon dioxide, and water. A simple chemical equation for respiration is given subsequently. Notice that the equation for respiration is the opposite of that for photosynthesis.

$$\text{glucose} + \text{oxygen} = \text{energy} + \text{carbon dioxide} + \text{water}$$
$$C_6H_{12}O_6 + 6O_2 = \text{energy} + 6CO_2 + 6H_2O$$

Chemically speaking, the process is similar to the **oxidation** that occurs as wood is burned, producing heat. When compounds combine with oxygen, the process is often referred to as "burning," for example, athlete's "burn" energy (sugars) as they exercise. The harder they exercise, the more sugars they burn so the more oxygen they need. That is why at full speed, they are breathing very fast. Athletes take up oxygen through their lungs. Plants take up oxygen through the stomata in their leaves and through their roots.

Again, respiration is the burning of photosynthates for energy to grow and to do the internal "work" of living. It is very important to understand that both plants and animals (including microorganisms) need oxygen for respiration. This is why overly wet or saturated soils are detrimental to root growth and function, as well as the decomposition processes carried out by microorganisms in the soil.

The same principles regarding limiting factors are valid for both photosynthesis and respiration.

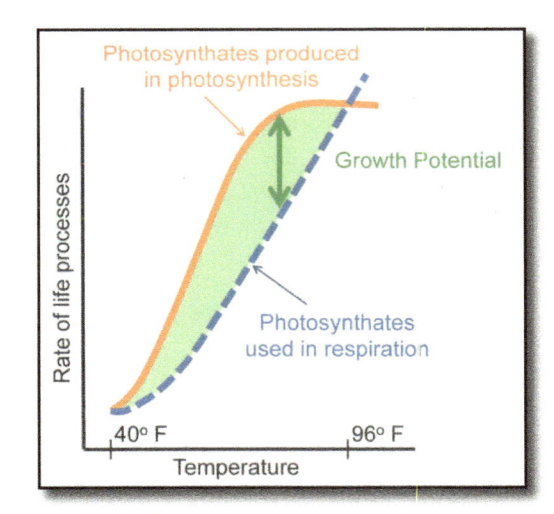

Figure 4-2 ■ *For the tomato plant, rates of photosynthesis and respiration both increase with increasing temperatures. As the temperature approaches 96°F, the rate of photosynthesis levels off, while the rate of respiration continues to rise.*

Transpiration

Water in the roots is pulled through the plant by **transpiration** (loss of water vapor through the stomata of the leaves). Transpiration uses about ninety percent of the water that enters the plant. The other ten percent is an ingredient in photosynthesis and cell growth.

Transpiration serves three essential roles:

- **Movement of minerals** up from the root (in the xylem) and sugars (products of photosynthesis) through out the plant (in the phloem). Water serves as both the solvent and the avenue of transport.

- **Cooling**—Eighty percent of the cooling effect of a shade tree is from the evaporative cooling effects of transpiration. This benefits both plants and humans.

- **Turgor pressure**—Water maintains the turgor pressure in cells much like air inflates a balloon, giving the non-woody plant parts form. Turgidity is important so the plant can remain stiff and upright and gain a competitive advantage when it comes to light. Turgidity is also important for the functioning of the guard cells, which surround the stomata and regulate water loss and carbon dioxide uptake. Turgidity also is the force that pushes roots through the soil.

Water movement in plants is also a factor of osmotic pressure and capillary action. **Osmotic pressure** is defined as water flowing through a permeable membrane in the direction of higher salt concentrations. Water will continue to flow in the direction of the highest salt concentration until the salts have been diluted to the point that the concentrations on both sides of the membrane are equal.

A classic example is pouring salt on a slug. Because the salt concentration outside the slug is highest, the water from inside the slug's body crosses the membrane that is his "skin." The poor slug becomes dehydrated and dies. Envision this same scenario the next time you gargle with salt water to kill the bacteria that are causing your sore throat.

Fertilizer burn and dog urine spots in a lawn are examples of salt problems. The salt level in the soil's water becomes higher than in the roots, and water flows from the roots into the soil's water in an effort to dilute the concentration. So what should you do if you accidentally apply too much fertilizer to your lawn?

Capillary action refers to the chemical forces that move water as a continuous film rather than as individual molecules. Water molecules in the soil and in the plant cling to one another and are reluctant to let go. You have observed this as water forms a meniscus on a coin or the lip of a glass. Thus when one molecule is drawn up the plant stem, it pulls another one along with it. These forces that link water molecules together can be overcome by gravity.

Comparison of Photosynthesis and Respiration

Photosynthesis	↔	Respiration
Produces sugars from energy		Burns sugars for energy
Energy is stored		Energy is released
Occurs only in cells with chloroplasts		Occurs in most cells
Oxygen is produced		Oxygen is used
Water is used		Water is produced
Carbon dioxide is used		Carbon dioxide is produced
Requires light		Occurs in dark and light

LIGHT

The quality, intensity, and duration of light directly influence plant growth.

Light Quality

Light quality refers to the color or wavelength reaching the plant's surface. A prism (or raindrops) can divide sunlight into respective colors of red, orange, yellow, green, blue, indigo, and violet.

Figure 4-3 ■ *Relative efficiency of various light colors in photosynthesis.*

Red and blue have the greatest impact on plant growth. Green light is least effective (the reflection of green light gives the green color to plants). Blue light is primarily responsible for vegetative leaf growth. Red light, when combined with blue light, encourages flowering (Figure 4-3).

Light quality is a major consideration for indoor growing.

Fluorescent cool white lamps are high in the blue range, and the best choice for starting seeds indoors.

For flowering plants that need more red light, use broad spectrum fluorescent bulbs.

Incandescent lights are high in red and red-orange, but generally produce too much heat for use in supplementing plant growth.

Light Intensity

The more sunlight a plant receives, to a degree, the higher the photosynthetic rate will be. However, leaves of plants growing in low light readily sun scorch when moved to a bright location. Over time, as the wax content on a leaf increases, it will become more sun tolerant.

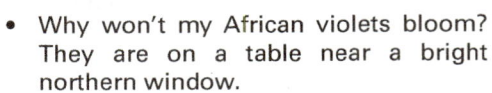

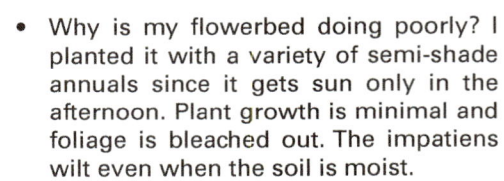

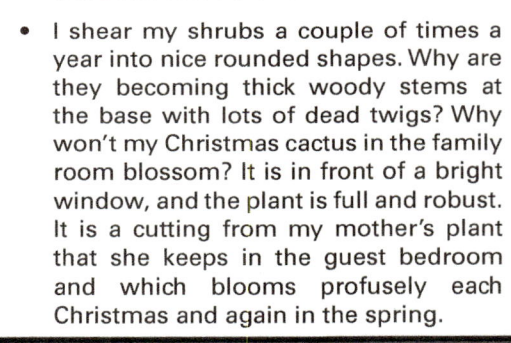

Thought Questions

Explain the science behind the question.

- Why won't my African violets bloom? They are on a table near a bright northern window.

- Why is my flowerbed doing poorly? I planted it with a variety of semi-shade annuals since it gets sun only in the afternoon. Plant growth is minimal and foliage is bleached out. The impatiens wilt even when the soil is moist.

- I shear my shrubs a couple of times a year into nice rounded shapes. Why are they becoming thick woody stems at the base with lots of dead twigs? Why won't my Christmas cactus in the family room blossom? It is in front of a bright window, and the plant is full and robust. It is a cutting from my mother's plant that she keeps in the guest bedroom and which blooms profusely each Christmas and again in the spring.

As illustrated in Box 4-1, light levels in most homes are below that required for all but low light house plants. Except for rather bright sunny rooms, most house plants can only be grown directly in front of bright windows. Inexpensive light meters are available in many garden supply stores to help the indoor gardener evaluate light levels.

Landscape plants vary in their adaptation to light intensity. Many gardening texts divide plants into sun, partial sun, and shade. However, the experienced gardener understands the differences between these seven degrees of sun/shade:

Full sun—Direct sun for at least 8 hours a day, including from 9 a.m. to 4 p.m.

Full sun with reflected heat—Where plants receive reflected heat from a building or other structure, temperatures can be extremely hot. This situation significantly limits the choice of plants for the site.

Morning shade with afternoon sun—This southwest- and west-reflected heat can be extremely hot and limiting to plant growth.

Morning sun with afternoon shade—This is an ideal site for many plants. The afternoon shade protects plants from extreme heat.

Filtered shade—Dappled shade filtered through trees can be bright shade to

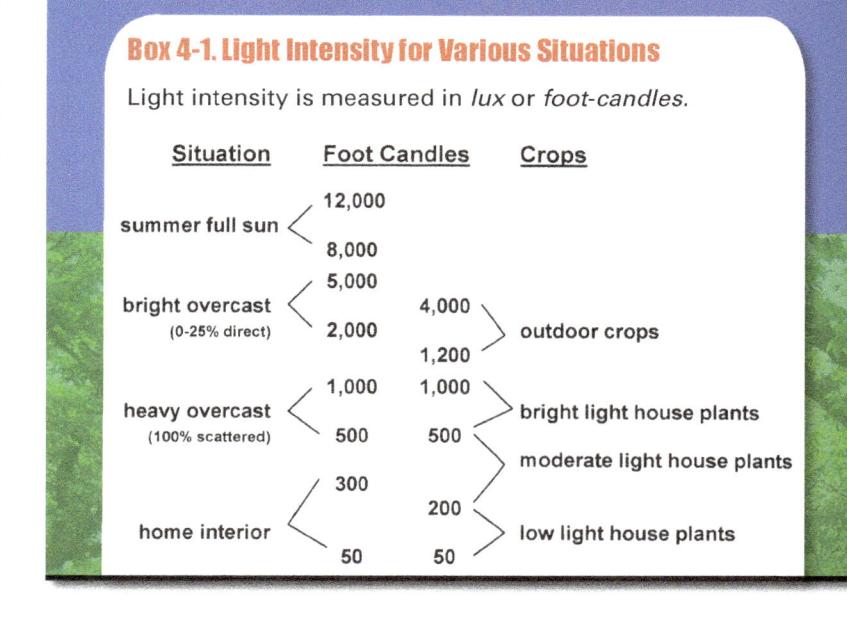

Box 4-1. Light Intensity for Various Situations

Light intensity is measured in *lux* or *foot-candles*.

Situation	Foot Candles	Crops
summer full sun	12,000 / 8,000	
bright overcast (0-25% direct)	5,000 / 2,000	4,000 / 1,200 outdoor crops
heavy overcast (100% scattered)	1,000 / 500	1,000 / 500 bright light house plants
home interior	300 / 50	200 / 50 moderate light house plants / low light house plants

dark shade depending on the tree's canopy. The constantly moving shade pattern protects under-story plants from heat. In darker dappled shade, only the more shade tolerant plants will thrive.

Open shade—Plants may be in the situation where they have open sky above, but direct sunlight is blocked during the day by buildings, fences, and other structures. Only more shade-tolerant plants will thrive here.

Closed shade—The situation where plants are under a canopy blocking sunlight is most limiting. Only the most shade-tolerant plants will survive this situation, like under a deck or covered patio.

In hot climates, temperature is often a limiting factor related to shade. Some plants, like impatiens and begonias, may require shade as an escape from heat. These plants will tolerate full sun in cooler summer climates.

Light penetration is a primary influence on correct pruning. For example, prune dwarf apple trees to a Christmas tree shape. This gives better light penetration for best quality fruit. Mature fruit trees are thinned each spring for better light penetration. A hedge should be pruned with a wider base and narrow top. Otherwise, the bottom thins out from the shading above. A common mistake in pruning flowering shrubs is to shear off the top. The resulting regrowth gives a thick upper canopy that shades out the bottom foliage (Figure 4-4).

Figure 4-4 ▮ *Light penetration is a primary influence in pruning. Left: Dwarf apple trees are pruned to a Christmas tree shape to allow better light penetration for best quality fruit. Right: Regrowth on flowering shrubs that are sheared on top is a very heavy upper canopy growth. This shades out the bottom giving a woody base.*

Light Duration

Light duration refers to the amount of time that a plant is exposed to sunlight. Travelers to Alaska often marvel at the giant vegetables and flowers that grow under the long days of the arctic sun even with cool temperatures.

When starting transplants indoors, generally give plants twelve to fourteen hours of light per day. Plants are generally intolerant of continuous light for twenty-four hours.

Figure 4-5 ▮ *Photoperiod and flowering. Left side: Short-day plants flower with uninterrupted long nights. Right side: Long-day plants flower with short nights or interrupted long nights.*

Photoperiod

The flowering response of many plants is controlled by the **photoperiod** (the length of uninterrupted darkness). Photoperiod response can be divided into three types (Figure 4-5).

Short-day plants flower in response to long periods of night darkness. Examples include poinsettias, Christmas cactus, chrysanthemums, and single-crop strawberries.

Long-day plants flower in response to short periods of night darkness. Examples include onions and spinach.

Day neutral plants flower without regard to the length of the night, but typically flower earlier and more profusely under long daylight regimes. Day neutral strawberries provide summer long harvesting (except during heat extremes).

TEMPERATURE

Temperature Considerations

Temperature factors that figure into plant growth potentials include the following:

- Maximum daily temperature
- Minimum daily temperature
- Difference between day and night temperatures
- Average daytime temperature
- Average nighttime temperature

Microclimates

The microclimate of a garden plays a primary role in actual garden temperatures. In mountain communities, changes in elevation, air drainage, exposure, and thermal heat mass (surrounding rocks) will make some gardens significantly warmer or cooler than the temperatures recorded for the area. In mountain communities, it is important to know where the local weather station is located so gardeners can factor in the difference in their specific location to forecast temperatures more accurately. Examples of factors to consider include the following.

Can alter
temp. 10-15

Thought Questions

Explain the science behind the question.

- Why did I have so much winter injury on my trees and shrubs? While it was dry and windy, temperatures were not extremely cold.

- My arborvitaes are bleached tan from the winter. Will they green-up with spring temperatures?

- With the rather hot summer, will the apple and peach crop be as sweet as normal?

Elevation—A 300-foot rise in elevation accounts for approximately 1°F drop in temperature.

Drainage—At night, cool air drains to low spots. Valley floors may be more than 10°F cooler than surrounding gardens on hillsides above the valley floor. That is why fruit orchards are typically located on the benches rather than on the valley floor (Figure 4-6).

Exposure—Southern exposures absorb more solar radiation than northern exposures. In mountain communities, northern exposures will have shorter growing seasons. In mountain communities, gardeners often place warm season plants, like tomatoes, on the south side of buildings to capture more heat.

Based on local topography, buildings, fences, plantings, and garden areas may be protected from or exposed to cold and drying winds. They may also be exposed to or protected from warm and drying winds (Figures 4-7 and 4-8).

Figure 4-6 ▮ *This magnificent garden on the hillside above Steamboat Springs, Colorado (a mountain community with a short frost-free season), has great drainage giving it a growing season that is several weeks longer than down in town.*

Thermal heat mass (surrounding rocks)—In many Colorado communities, the surrounding rock formations can form heat sinks creating wonderful gardening spots for local gardeners. Nestled in among the mountains, some gardeners have growing seasons several weeks longer than neighbors only a half mile away.

like a native plant finding a nurse rock

north facing exposure   south facing exposure

Figure 4-7 ▮ *Temperatures and growing season vary greatly based on exposure. A north-facing exposure will typically be cooler and moist. A south-facing exposure will typically be hot and dry.*

Figure 4-8 ▮ *The sidewalks and stone walls of this intercity plaza create a heat pocket with a frost-free periods 3 months longer than the surrounding neighborhood.*

In cooler locations, rock mulch may give some frost protection and increase temperatures for enhanced crop growth. In warmer locations, rock mulch can significantly increase summer temperatures and water requirements of landscape plants (Figure 4-8).

In Phoenix, Arizona, the urban heat island (with all their rock mulch instead of grass and trees) has significantly raised day and night temperatures. The upward convection of heat has become so strong that summer storms are going around the city and not raining on the urban heat island.

Impact of Heat on Plant Growth

Temperature affects the growth and productivity of plants, depending on whether the plant is a warm season or cool season crop.

Photosynthesis—Within limits, rates of photosynthesis and respiration both rise with increasing temperatures. As temperatures reach the upper growing limits for the crop, the rate of food used by respiration may exceed the rate at which food is manufactured by photosynthesis. For tomatoes, growth peaks at 96°F.

Temperature influence on growth—Seeds of cool season crops germinate at 40°F to 80°F. Warm season crop seeds germinate at 50°F to 90°F. In the spring, cool soil temperatures are a limiting factor for plant growth. In mid-summer, hot soil temperatures may prohibit seed germination.

Examples of temperature influence on flowering:

- Tomatoes
    - —Pollen does not develop if night temperatures are below 55°F.
    - —Blossoms drop if daytime temperatures rise above 95°F before 10 a.m.
    - —Tomatoes grown in cool climates will have softer fruit with bland flavors.
- Spinach (a cool season, short-day crop) flowers in warm weather with long days.
- Christmas cacti and poinsettias flower in response to cool temperatures and short days.

Examples of temperature influence on crop quality.

- High temperatures increase respiration rates, reducing sugar content of produce. Fruits and vegetables grown in heat will be less sweet.
- In heat, crop yields reduce while water demand goes up.
- In hot weather, flower colors fade and flowers have a shorter life.

The following table illustrates temperature differences in warm season tomatoes and cool season cole crops.

Comparison of Cool Season and Warm Season Temperature Needs

Temperature for	Cool Season: broccoli, cabbage, and cauliflower	Warm Season: tomatoes, peppers, squash, and melons
Germination	40°F –90°F, 80°F optimum	50°F–100°F, 80°F optimum
Growth	Daytime • 65°F–80°F preferred • 40°F minimum Nighttime • >32°F, tender transplants • > mid-20s°F, established plants	Daytime • 86°F optimum • 60°F minimum • A week below 55°F will stunt plant, reducing yields Nighttime • >32°F
Flowering	Temperature extremes lead to bolting and buttoning	• Nighttime <55°F, non-viable pollen (use blossom set hormones) • Daytime >95°F by 10 a.m., blossoms abort
Soil	Likes cool soils • Use organic mulch to cool soil • Because seeds germinate best in warm soils, use transplants for spring planting, and direct seeding for mid-summer plantings (fall harvest)	Likes warm soils • Use black plastic mulch to warm soil, increasing yields and earliness of crop

Heat Zone Map

A new concept in plant selection is **heat zone mapping**, a measurement of the typical summer heat accumulation. It will help identify geographic areas that have adequate heat accumulation to mature various crops.

The American Horticultural Society's Heat Zone Map can be viewed online at www.ahs.org/publications/heat_zone_map.htm.

Heat zones can be sorted by zip codes. To look up a heat zone by zip code, go online at www.ahs.org/publications/heat_zone_finder.htm.

It should be recognized that in mountain communities, minor changes in elevation and exposure (e.g., south slopes versus north slopes) make significant differences in heat accumulation. A heat zone for a community's zip code may not reflect the actual growing conditions in any specific garden.

Impact of Cold Temperatures

Plant Hardiness

Hardiness refers to a plant's tolerance to cold temperatures. Low temperature is only one of many factors influencing plant hardiness (ability to tolerate cold temperatures). Key hardiness factors include the following (Figure 4-9):

- Photoperiod
- Genetics (source of plant material)
- Low temperature
- Recent temperature pattern
- Rapid temperature changes
- Moisture
- Wind exposure   *right plant place*
- Sun exposure
- Carbohydrate reserve

• Photosynthate reserves

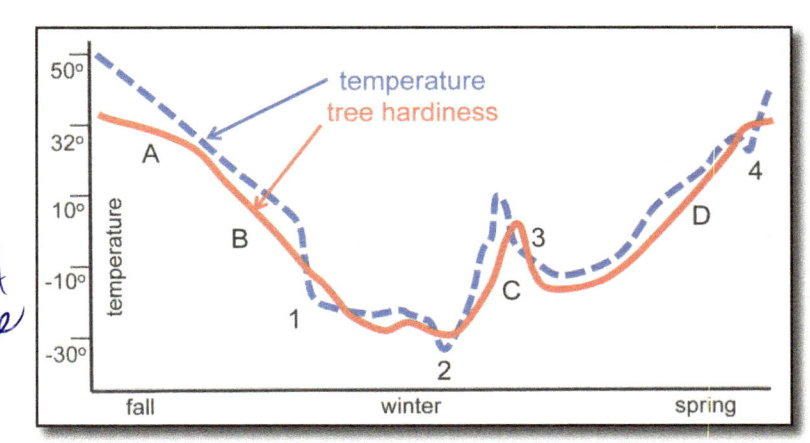

Figure 4-9 ▪ *Influence of temperature change on winter hardiness of trees. The solid line represents a tree's hardiness. Regions A to D represent various stages of hardiness through the winter season. The dotted line represents temperature. When the dotted (temperature) line drops below the solid (hardiness) line, damage occurs. Points 1 to 4 represent damage situations.*

A. Increased cold hardiness induced by shorter-day length of fall.
B. Increased cold hardiness induced by lowering temperatures.
C. Dehardening due to abnormally warm mid-winter temperatures.
D. Normal spring dehardening as temperatures warm.

1. Injury due to rapid drop in temperatures with inadequate fall hardening.
2. Injury at temperatures lower than hardening capability.
3. Injury due to rise and fall of mid-winter temperatures.
4. Injury due to spring frosts.

Hardiness Zone Map

Hardiness zone maps indicate the *average annual minimum temperature* expected for geographic areas. While this is a factor in plant selection, it is only one of many factors influencing plant hardiness.

In 2012, the U.S. Department of Agriculture released a new USDA Hardiness Zone Map at http://plant hardiness.ars.usda.gov/PHZMWeb/. The revised map has a large database correcting inherent problems with the 2003 version. It documents a climate zone creep, that is zone moving northwards in recent years. Zones are based on a 10°F difference in *average annual minimum temperature*.

Fall watering more critical before dormancy puts winter storage water in for

Average Annual Minimum Temperature

Zone 4	−20°F to −30°F
Zone 5	−10°F to −20°F
Zone 6	0°F to −10°F

Most of the Colorado Front Range area falls into Zone 5, with cool mountain areas in Zone 4. Warmer locations in the Denver Metro, Fort Collins, El Paso, and Pueblo Counties fall into Zone 6. Warmer areas of western, southwestern, and southeastern Colorado are in Zone 6.

Examples of Winter Injury

Bud kill and dieback—From spring and fall frosts.

Root temperature injury—Roots have limited tolerance to subfreezing temperatures. Roots receive limited protection from soil, mulch, and snow. Under extreme cold, roots may be killed by the lack of snow cover or mulch. Street trees are at high risk for root kill in extreme, long-term cold.

Soil heaving pushes out plants, breaking roots. Protect with snow cover or mulch.

Trunk injury—Drought predisposes trunks to winter injury.

Sunscald—Caused by heating of bark on sunny winter days followed by a rapid temperature drop, rupturing membranes as cells freeze. Winter drought predisposes tree trunks to sunscald (Figure 4-10).

Frost shake—Separation of wood along one or more growth rings, typically between phloem (inner bark) and xylem (wood), caused by sudden rise in bark temperature.

Frost crack—Vertical split on tree trunk caused by rapid drop in bark temperature (Figure 4-11).

Winter injury on evergreens (Figure 4-12)

Winter drought—Water transpires from needles and cannot be replaced from frozen soils. It is more severe on growing tips and on the windy side of trees.

Sunscald—Winter sun warms needles, followed by rapid temperature drop rupturing cell membranes. It occurs typically on southwest side, side of reflected heat, or with sudden shade.

Photo-oxidization of chlorophyll—Foliage bleaches during cold sunny days. Needles may green-up again in spring.

Tissue kill—Tissues killed when temperatures drop below hardiness levels.

Rest Period

An accumulation of cool units controls the flowering period of temperate-zone woody plants. The winter rest period (hours below 45°F) required to break bud dormancy includes:

Apricot	350–900 hours	Peach	800–1200 hours
Apple	250–1700 hours	Pear	200–1500 hours
Cherry, sour	600–1400 hours	Plum, European	900–1700 hours
Cherry, sweet	500–1300 hours	Plum, Japanese	300–1200 hours

Figure 4-10 ▮ *Southwest bark injury is common on trees under drought stress, such as this tree with a restricted root spread.*

Figure 4-11 ▮ *Vertical frost crack is common on trees when the temperature drops rapidly. Along the Colorado Front Range, it is common to go from a nice spring day back to cold storm with a 40° to 60° temperature drop in an hour!*

Figure 4-12 ▮ *Winter drought, sunscald, and photo-oxidization of chlorophyll are common on arborvitae. This is a poor plant choice for this windy site with little winter moisture.*

(handwritten margin note: tree wrap fall early Nov. remove April – disease insects)

WATER

In the arid west, water availability and quality can be a limiting factor in plant growth. Quality issues generally deal with excessive sodium or other soluble salts.

Available water limits potential for crops and gardens in many areas of the west. In cities, the cost of the infrastructure to supply water drives the need for water conservation.

Plants are 90% water [handwritten]

Role of Water

Plants are over ninety percent water. Roles of water are summarized in Table 4-1.

Thought Questions

Explain the science behind the question.

- Review how water stress impacts plant growth processes, then list common symptoms of drought stress.

turgid - leaves standing up [handwritten]

Table 4.1. Role of Water in Plant Growth

Role of water with plants	Impact of water shortage
Primary component of photosynthesis and transpiration	Reduced growth and vigor
Turgor pressure (pressure to inflate cells and hold plant erect)	Wilting
Solvent to move minerals from the soil up to the plant • NO_3^-, NH_4^+, $H_2PO_4^-$, HPO_4^{-2}, K^+, Ca^{+2}, Mg^{+2}, SO_4^{-2}, $H_2BO_3^-$, Cl^-, Co^{+2}, Cu^{+2}, Fe^{+2}, Fe^{+3}, Mn^{+2}, MoO_4^{-2}, and Zn^{+2}	Reduced growth and plant vigor Nutrient deficiencies
Solvent to move products of photosynthesis throughout the plant, including down to the root system	Reduced health of roots which leads (over time) to reduced health of plant
Regulation of stomatal opening and closure, thus regulating transpiration and photosynthesis	Reduced plant growth and vigor Reduced cooling effect = warmer microclimate temperatures
Source of pressure to move roots through the soil	Reduced root growth = reduced plant growth and vigor
Medium for biochemical reactions	Reduced plant growth and vigor

Common Symptoms of Water Stress

Drought

- Decreased growth
- Small, off-colored leaves
- Decline from top down

- Early fall color

- Reduced xylem growth = long-term growth reduction

- Stress may show up 5 or more years later

Waterlogged Soils

- Root activity slows or shuts down, and plants show symptoms of drought

- Decline in root growth slows plant growth processes

- Leaves may wilt from lack of water uptake

- Root rots are common in some species

- Lower interior leaves may yellow

Leaf scorch (short-term water deficiency in leaves)

- Marginal burning

- Often from the top down, on southwest side, or from the side with root injury or root restrictions

Factors contributing to leaf scorch

- Dry or overly wet soils

- Compacted soils

- Limited root spread

- Root injury

- Structural damage to xylem tissues

- Trunk and branch injury

- Excessive wind and heat

- Excessive canopy growth (from heavy fertilization)

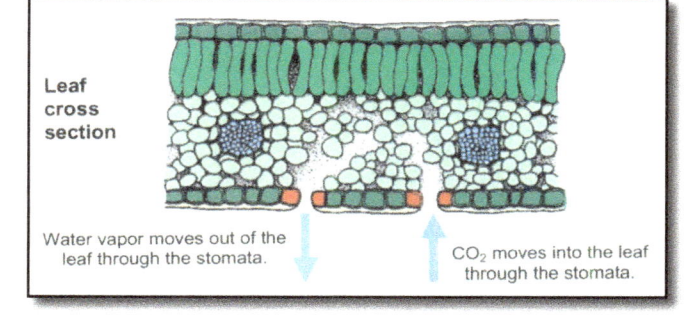

Figure 4-13 ▐ *Leaf cross-section.*

Relative Humidity

Water moves from areas of high relative humidity to areas of lower relative humidity. Inside a leaf, the relative humidity between cells approaches 100%. When the stomata open, water vapors inside the leaf rush out forming a bubble of higher humidity around the stomata on the outside of the leaf (Figure 4-13).

The difference in relative humidity around the stomata and adjacent air regulates transpiration rates and pulls water up through the xylem tissues. Transpiration peaks under hot dry and/or windy conditions. When the supply of water from the roots is inadequate, the stomata close, photosynthesis shuts down, and plants can wilt.

Outdoors—In the arid climate of the west, low summer humidity helps manage some insect and disease problems and can aggravate others. The relative humidity returns to normal levels within a few minutes of watering/irrigation.

Indoors—With forced air heating, many homes have very low relative humidity in the winter. Some homes can have excessively high relative humidity due to a large number of houseplants, cooking, and frequent long showers. Both extremely high and low indoor relative humidity are health concerns.

PLANT HORMONES

Plant Hormones and Plant Growth Regulators

Another factor in plant growth is the influence of plant hormones. **Hormones** are chemicals produced by plants that regulate the growth processes.

Plant growth regulators are chemicals applied by a horticulturist to regulate plant growth. In plant propagation, cuttings are dipped in a rooting hormone to stimulate root development. In greenhouse production, many potted flowering plants (like poinsettias and Easter lilies) may be treated with plant growth regulators to keep them short. Seedless grapes are treated with plant growth regulators to increase the size of the fruit. In special situations, turf may be treated to slow growth and mitigate the need for mowing. Because plant growth regulators are effective in parts per million or parts per billion, they have little application in home gardening.

Plant Hormones

Different hormones affect different plant processes. Understanding how hormones work allows horticulturists to manipulate plants for specific purposes.

→ Stem elongation

Auxins produced in the terminal buds suppress the growth of side buds and stimulate root growth. They also affect cell elongation (tropism), apical dominance, and fruit drop or retention (Figure 4-14). *in roots*

Gibberellins affect: *regulate stem elongation*

- The rate of cell division

- Flowering

- Increase in size of leaves and fruits

- Seed and bud dormancy

- Induction of growth at lower temperatures (used to green-up lawns 2 to 3 weeks earlier)

Figure 4-14 ■ *Auxins produced in the rapidly growing terminal buds suppress growth of side buds, giving a young tree a more upright form. As growth rates slow with age, reduction in apical dominance gives the maturing tree a more rounded crown.*

Cytokinins promote cell division and influence cell differentiation and aging of leaves.

Abscisic acid is considered the "stress" hormone. It inhibits the effects of other hormones to reduce growth during times of plant stress.

Hormone Influence on Pruning

Understanding hormones is key to proper pruning. **Auxin** produced in the terminal buds suppresses growth of side buds and stimulates root growth. **Gibberellins** produced in the root growing tips stimulate shoot growth. Pruning a newly planted tree removes the auxin, slowing root regeneration (Figure 4-15).

Heading cuts (removal of a branch tip) releases the apical dominance caused by auxins from the terminal bud. This allows side shoots to develop, and the branch becomes bushier. On the other hand, **thinning cuts**

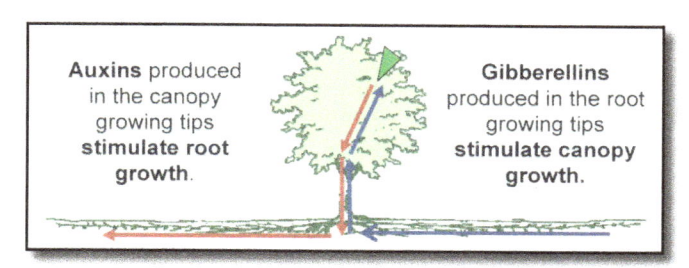

Figure 4-15 ▮ *Trees balance canopy growth with root growth by concentrations of auxins and gibberellins.*

remove a branch back to the branch union (crotch). This type of cut opens the plant to more light. Most pruning should be limited to thinning cuts. For details on pruning, refer to the chapter on pruning (Figure 4-16).

Tropisms

Auxins also play a key role in **tropism** (controlling the direction of plant growth) (Figures 4-17 and 4-18)

Figure 4-16 ▮ *Left: A **heading cut** releases apical dominance and the branch becomes denser as the lateral buds begin to grow. Right: A **thinning cut** removes a branch back at a branch union (crotch), opening the plant for better light penetration. Thinning cuts promote an open growth habit by redirecting sugars to the terminal shoots.*

Figure 4-17 ▮ **Geotropism**—*Under the influence of gravity, auxins accumulate in the lower side of a horizontal stem, causing cells to enlarge faster, turning the stem upright.*

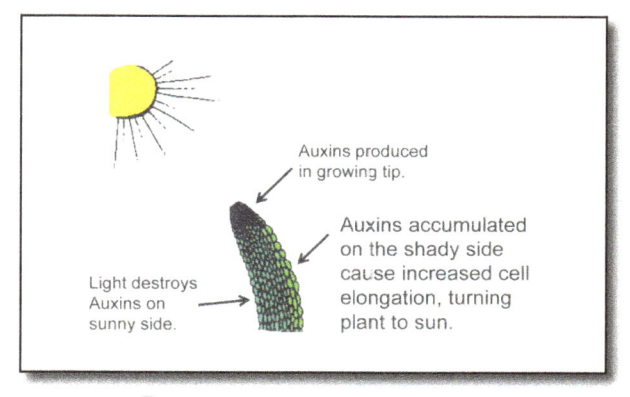

Figure 4-18 ▮ **Phototropism**—*The auxin concentration on the shaded side stimulates cell elongation, turning the stem to the sun.*

1. Give a simple equation for photosynthesis and respiration.

2. Define the terms:

    a. Photosynthesis

    b. Respiration

    c. Transpiration

3. What percentage of plant water is used for transpiration? Transpiration accounts for what percentage of the cooling effect of trees?

4. List the functions of transpiration.

5. List the seven degrees of sun and shade.

6. What is photoperiodism? For long- and short-day plants, give the response (i.e., vegetative or flowering) for long and short nights. What happens if the night is interrupted?

7. List factors that influence plant hardiness.

8. What does a hardiness zone map indicate?

9. How does a sudden dramatic drop in winter temperatures impact hardiness? How does a gradual yet significant drop in winter temperatures impact hardiness? How does early spring warming or late spring frost affect hardiness?

10. Define the following terms related to winter injury:

    a. Sunscald

    b. Frost crack

    c. Frost shake

    d. Winter drought

11. How do temperate-zone plants know when to start growing in the spring?

12. List the roles of water in plant growth.

13. Give common symptoms of drought stress and waterlogged soils.

14. What are the symptoms of leaf scorch? List factors that contribute to leaf scorch.

15. Define plant hormones and plant growth regulators.

16. Explain how a plant balances shoot growth with root growth.

17. Explain how a plant grows toward the sun. Explain how a plant knows up from down.

18. Review the thought questions.

Soils, Fertilizers, and Soil Amendments

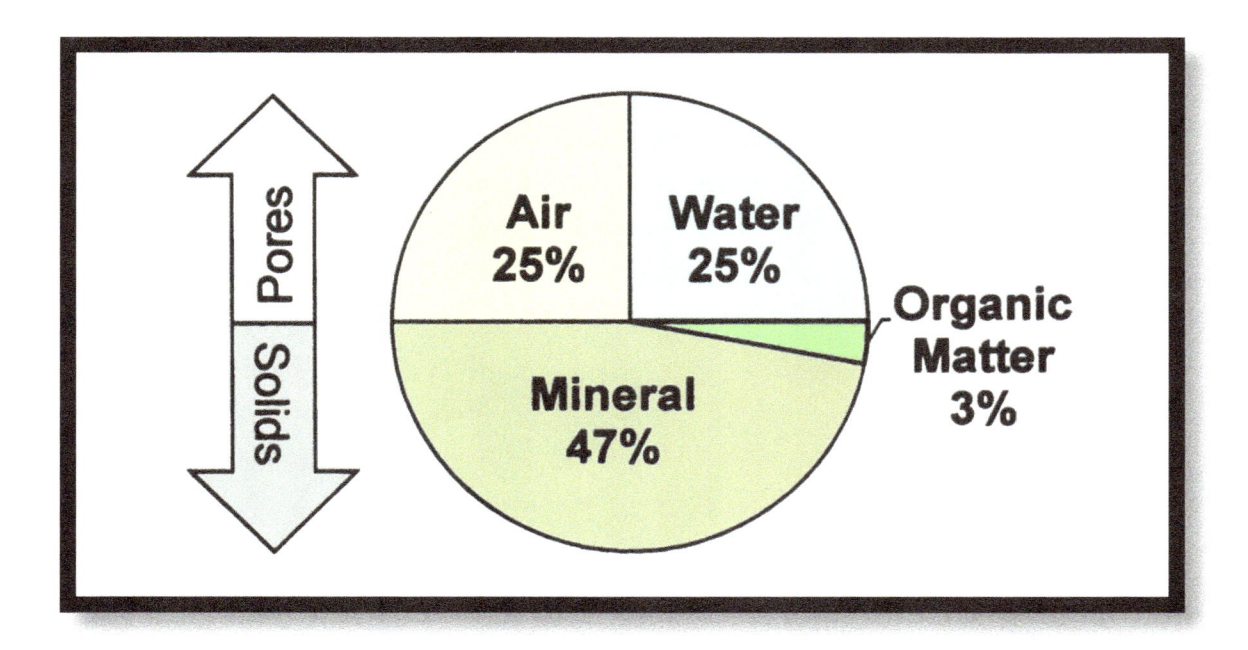

Learning Objectives

At the end of this unit, the student will be able to:

- Describe characteristics of a typical landscape soil and how it differs from native or agricultural soils.
- Describe how soil organisms directly and indirectly benefit the soil and plant growth.
- Describe management practices effective in nurturing soil organisms.
- Describe the relationship between soil *texture*, *structure*, *pore space*, and *tilth*.
- Describe effective management practices for sandy soils, clayey soils, and decomposed granite rocky soils.
- Describe effective management practices to prevent and reduce soil compaction.
- Describe considerations in selecting soil amendments.
- Describe considerations in selecting mulch.
- Describe considerations in selecting appropriate fertilizers.

Supplemental References

Books

- ***Urban Soil Primer.*** The Natural Resources Conservation Service, U.S. Department of Agriculture. 2005. Available online at http://www.nrcs.usda.gov/Internet/FSE_DOCUMENTS/nrcs142p2_052835.pdf
- ***Urban Soils: Applications and Practices.*** Phillip J Craul. John Wiley & Sons Publishing. 1999.

Colorado State University Extension fact sheets available at www.cmg.colostate.edu.

- *Choosing A Soil Amendment*, #7.235
- *Colorado Gardening: A Challenge to Newcomers*, #7.220
- *Composting Yard Waste*, #7.212
- *Diagnosing Saline and Sodic Soil Problems*, #0.521
- *Landscaping on Expansive Soils*, #7.236
- *Magnesium Chloride Toxicity in Trees*, #7.425
- *Managing Saline Soils*, #0.503
- *Managing Sodic Soils*, #0.504
- *Mulches for Home Grounds*, #7.214
- *Nitrogen Sources and Transformations*, #0.550
- *Organic Materials as Nitrogen Fertilizers*, #0.546
- *Preventing* E. coli *From Garden to Plate*, #9.369
- *Selecting an Analytical Laboratory*, #0.520

Chapter
5*

Introduction to Soils

SOIL ATTRIBUTES

What is soil? Gardeners know that soil is more than simply broken up rocks. Rather than being an inert unchanging material, soil is a dynamic living substance in which complex chemical and biological reactions are constantly occurring.

According to the Soil Science Society of America, soil is defined as, "the unconsolidated mineral or organic material on the immediate surface of the earth that serves as a natural medium for the growth of land plants." Unconsolidated materials are loose materials composed of multiple units (e.g., sand, gravel, etc.) unlike hard, massive materials like rock. Effective gardeners manage soils to produce healthy and resilient plants.

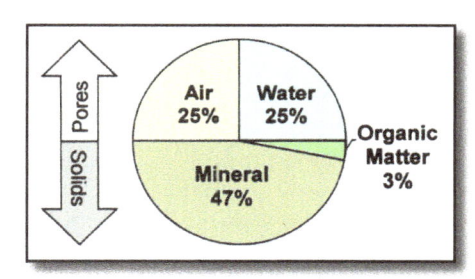

Figure 5-1 ▮ *A well-managed Western soil has 25% air, 25% water, 1 to 5% organic matter, and 45 to 49% mineral solids.*

Soil contains a variety of substances. In a well-managed western soil, usually around 50% of the soil's volume is composed of solid particles, while the other 50% is empty space. Soil scientists refer to these empty spaces as "pores" (Figure 5-1).

Most of the solid particles are derived from mineral sources such as decomposed rocks or sediments. Roughly one to five percent of the soil's volume is organic matter—plant, animal, and microbial residues in various stages of decomposition (Figure 5-1).

---

*Authors: Cathrine Moravec (Colorado Springs Utilities), David Whiting (Colorado State University Extension), and Jean Reeder, PhD (USDA-ARS, retired). Artwork by David Whiting.

The empty space between the solid particles can be occupied by water, air, or a combination of both. In a well-managed soil, about twenty-five percent of the soil's volume is air, while the remaining twenty-five percent is occupied by water. This combination of components provides a healthy environment for roots to grow.

SOIL-FORMING FACTORS

Soils vary across the landscape. A Western gardener may have noticed substantial differences between the soils in his or her yard compared to the neighbor's soil. Western soils are often dominated by clays, sands, or decomposed granite.

The factors that cause variation in soils in different locations are referred to as soil-forming factors. These factors differ in subtle and complex ways over the surface of the earth to create an infinite array of soils. Soil scientists recognize five soil-forming factors, including:

- Parent material
- Climate (precipitation, temperature, wind)
- Topography
- Biological organisms
- Time

The term **parent material** refers to the starting material for a soil. It consists of specific minerals (or organic materials) from which a soil is formed. The mineralogy of the parent material has a great effect on the mineralogy and properties of the soil.

Climatic factors influence soil formation in several ways. First, precipitation and temperature cause weathering of rocks. In dry climates (unlike warm, moist climates), wind is often more important than water in weathering rocks and transporting parent materials. Second, climatic factors often transport parent materials over long distances. Sometimes the parent material for a soil is **residual**, meaning it disintegrated in place to form the soil. In other cases, the parent material is **transported** by water (rivers and streams), wind, gravity, or glaciers. As with weathering, wind is the primary means of transport in dry climates of the West. Once the parent materials land on a stable surface, the process of soil formation can begin. The characteristics of the resulting soil will depend on the interaction of the remaining four soil-forming factors on the parent material. Together, these factors act over thousands of years to form the soil.

SOIL VARIATION

Soils are three-dimensional entities. Soil not only varies across the landscape, but also varies vertically with depth. Gardeners will notice changes in soil color, physical properties, and chemical properties as they dig deeper. Over time, the soil-forming factors change the undifferentiated parent material into a vertically differentiated soil. Soil scientists recognize **horizons**, or horizontal layers within a soil. Horizons are identified by letter codes. They may blend together gradually or have abrupt borders between layers (Figure 5-2).

The A Horizon (also referred to as "topsoil") is usually the surface horizon. This is an area of high biological activity with the greatest organic matter content. It is also a zone of leaching. As precipitation enters the A horizon, it dissolves soluble soil organic compounds and minerals. These dissolved compounds are then moved downward through the soil profile. Most plant roots are found in the A horizon. In dry climates like Colorado, the A horizon may be very thin to almost nonexistent (Figure 5-2).

The B Horizon (also referred to as "subsoil") lies underneath the A horizon. This layer usually contains less organic matter than the surface layer, but accumulates the dissolved materials leached from the A horizon (clays, iron oxides, aluminum, and dissolved organic compounds). For this reason, the B horizon typically contains more clay than the surface layer. The accumulated products in the B horizon increase over time as the soil forms (Figure 5-2).

The C Horizon contains unconsolidated material that has been minimally affected by the soil-forming factors. It lies beneath the B horizon and may or may not be the same as the parent material from which the soil formed.

Landscape Soils

Landscape soils differ significantly from agricultural or native soils. **Landscape soils** are soils that are found in a typical neighborhood community around homes, parks, schools, offices, parking lots, and buildings. Soil scientists often refer to landscape soils as "urban" soils.

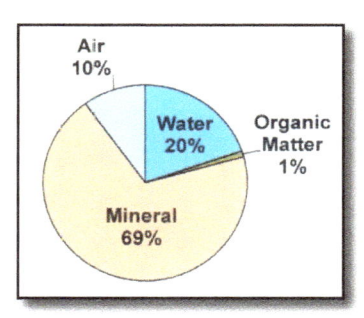

During the construction process, soils in communities are often graded by moving large volumes of soil. This process often removes the A horizon, taking with it the vast majority of organic matter. Furthermore, when construction workers drive large pieces of equipment over the soil it becomes compacted. Thousands of years of soil development can be destroyed in minutes with a bulldozer and other soil-moving equipment in a construction site.

Figure 5-3 ▍ *A typical compacted, unamended landscape soil has 10% air, 20% water, 1% organic matter, and 69% mineral solids.*

Sometimes construction debris, such as wood, trash, drywall, bricks, asphalt, or concrete, is buried in the soil during construction. Other possible landscape soil changes include increased variability, increased surface crusting, increased pH, decreased drainage, decreased soil microbial activity, and increased soil temperature. All of these factors can cause problems when managing soils around buildings.

Native, undisturbed soils typically have well-defined A, B, and C horizons. In compacted landscape soils, the horizons are scrambled and not defined, organic content is low, and air and water movement is reduced.

In comparison to native soils, the compacted unamended landscape soil typically has ten percent air, twenty percent water, one percent organic matter, and sixty-nine percent mineral solids. The most significant aspect of the compacted landscape soil is the reduction in air. Low soil oxygen is the most common limiting factor of plant (root) growth (Figure 5-3).

With soil conditions contributing to eighty percent of plant problems, what can the gardener do?

1. Understand soils as a living ecosystem. Nurture soil organisms by providing their food source (organic matter) and improving aeration and drainage (oxygen and water).

2. Understand the soil physical properties of *texture, structure,* and *pore space* as they relate to soil *tilth*. Compaction is a reduction in total pore space, but more importantly, compaction is a major reduction in large pore space where the air is located. Gardeners will be more successful in soil management by understanding what properties can be changed and what properties cannot be changed.

In summary, soils are important to gardeners because they strongly influence plant growth. Western soils vary substantially horizontally across the landscape and vertically with depth. In addition, landscape soils may vary considerably from agricultural or native soils. Landscapers and gardeners must take these changes into account when developing a soil management plan.

CHAPTER REVIEW
Questions

1. Explain how soils may vary horizontally and vertically. Describe characteristics of the A, B, and C soil horizons.

2. Describe how landscape soils differ from agricultural and native soils.

3. Describe the typical percentage of air, water, organic matter, and mineral solids for a native soil. How does this change for a compacted landscape soil?

The Living Soil

SOIL ORGANISMS IMPROVE GARDEN TILTH

Rather than being an inert material, soil houses a dynamic living ecosystem. The one to five percent of organic matter found in soils includes 0.2% of living organisms. Although most soil organisms are invisible to the naked eye, they help gardeners in multiple ways. One major benefit to gardeners is their ability to help improve soil tilth. Soil **tilth** is the suitability of a soil to support plant growth, especially as it relates to ease of tillage, fitness for a seedbed, impedance to seedling emergence, and root penetration. Soil organisms also play a central role in making nutrients available to plants. The community of soil organisms is varied, versatile, and adaptable to changing conditions and food supplies.

TYPES OF SOIL ORGANISMS

Soil contains an enormous number of living organisms. One cup of undisturbed native soil may contain:

Organism	Number
Bacteria	200 billion
Protozoa	20 million
Fungi	100,000 meters
Nematodes	100,000
Arthropods	50,000

Soil organisms are naturally active during certain times of the year. Most are active when the soil is warm and moist, like during late spring and early summer. If the soil dries out during the summer months, soil organism

*Authors: Cathrine Moravec (Colorado Springs Utilities), David Whiting and Adrian Card (Colorado State University Extension), and Jean Reeder, PhD (USDA-ARS, retired). Artwork by David Whiting and U.S. Department of Agriculture.

activity naturally declines. During fall, if there is rain or snow that moistens the soil while it is still warm, soil organisms may resume activity. As the soil cools in the fall, many soil organisms go dormant. Gardeners should note that fertilizers that require processing by soil organisms will be more available to plants when the soil is warm and moist and less available when the soil is cool or dry.

Despite their small size, soil organism activities have a large influence on plant growth. Soil organisms can be grouped into three categories: 1) organisms that are **beneficial** to plants—directly or indirectly, 2) **neutral** organisms—those whose activities have no effect on plants, and 3) organisms that are **harmful** to plants. Harmful organisms are often described as pathogens (such as the soil fungi that cause wilt diseases) or plant pests (such as white grubs that feed on plant roots).

DIRECTLY BENEFICIAL SOIL ORGANISMS

Some soil organisms have a close, mutually beneficial (**symbiotic**) relationship with plants. Two examples include rhizobia and mycorrhizae.

Rhizobia are bacteria that form symbiotic associations with legumes such as beans and peas. The bacteria form nodules on the roots of the host plant in which they fix nitrogen gas from the air. *Rhizobia* supply the plant with nitrogen and in turn, the plant supplies the bacteria with essential minerals and sugars. It may be helpful to add *Rhizobia* in the first planting of beans and peas in a soil area.

Mycorrhizae are specific fungi that form symbiotic associations with plant roots. Found in most soils, they are very host-specific (i.e., each plant species has specific species of mycorrhizae associated with it).

The Latin word *mycor* means fungus and *rhiza* means root. The terms "mycorrhiza" (singular) or "mycorrhizae" (plural) refer to the tissue that forms when fungi and roots develop a mutually beneficial relationship. Enlarging the surface-absorbing area of the roots by 100 to 1,000 times, mycorrhizae create filaments or threads that act like an extension of the root system. This makes the roots of the plant much more effective in the uptake of water and nutrients such as phosphorus and zinc. In exchange, the fungus receives essential sugars and compounds from the roots to fuel its own growth. Some species of mycorrhizae can be seen on roots, while most are invisible to the naked eye.

Mycorrhizae improve plant health. They enhance the plant's ability to tolerate environmental stress (like drought and dry winter weather). Plants with mycorrhizae may need less fertilizer and may have fewer soil-borne diseases.

A byproduct of mycorrhizal activity is the production of **glomalin**, a primary compound that improves soil tilth. In simple terms, glomalin glues the tiny clay particles together into larger aggregates, thereby increasing the amount of large pore space, which in turn creates an ideal environment for roots. For additional details, refer to the U.S. Department of Agriculture website at www.ars.usda.gov/is/AR/archive/sep02/soil0902.htm.

Mycorrhizal cocktails are sometimes incorporated in planting or post-planting care of trees and landscape plants. However, in research studies, results are variable. Over time, additional research will help clarify what procedures result in improved plant health and vigor.

INDIRECTLY BENEFICIAL SOIL ORGANISMS

In addition to directly beneficial organisms such as rhizobia and mycorrhizae, there are a large number of soil organisms whose activities indirectly help plants. Soil organisms collectively decompose organic matter, resulting in two principal benefits.

First, as soil organisms decompose organic matter, they transform nutrients into mineral forms that plants can use, a process called **mineralization**. Without soil microorganisms, insects, and worms feeding on organic matter, the nutrients in organic matter would remain bound in complex organic molecules that plants cannot utilize.

Second, as soil organisms break down organic matter, their activities help improve soil structure. Improved soil structure provides a better environment for roots, with less soil compaction and better water and air movement. Many gardeners know that organic matter improves soil, but it is important to note that its beneficial properties are only released after being processed by soil organisms.

Soils naturally contain these decomposers. Adding decomposers to the soil or compost pile is not necessary. Rather, nurture them with food (organic matter) and good aeration and drainage (air and water).

SOIL ORGANIC MATTER

Soil organic matter is composed of a wide variety of organic substances. Derived from plants, animals, and soil organisms, the soil organic matter "pool" can be divided into four categories. First are the living organisms and roots, making up less than five percent of the total pool. Second are the residues from dead plants, animals, and soil organisms that have not yet begun to decompose (less than ten percent). Third is the portion undergoing rapid decomposition (twenty to forty-five percent). Fourth is the stabilized organic matter (**humus**) remaining after rapid decomposition by soil microorganisms (fifty to eighty percent) (Figure 6-1).

The stabilized organic matter, or humus, is the pool of soil organic matter that has the longest lasting benefits for gardeners. After rapid decomposition occurs, a mix of stable, complex organic compounds remains, which decomposes slowly over time (about three percent per year). Humus is a mix of tiny solid particles

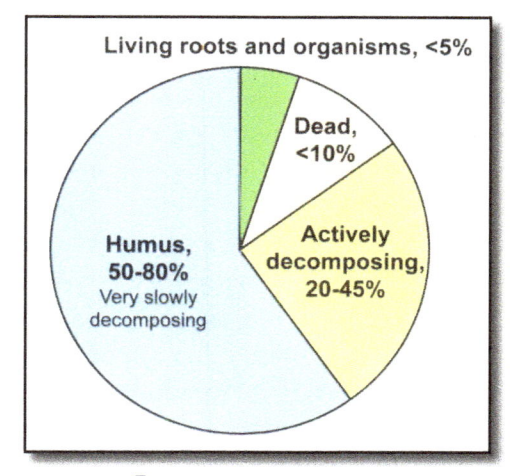

Figure 6-1 ▮ *Makeup of soil organic matter.*

and soluble compounds that are too chemically complex to be used by most organisms. Humus contains a potpourri of sugars, gums, resins, proteins, fats, waxes, and lignin. This mixture plays an important role in improving the physical and chemical properties of soil.

Humus improves the physical and chemical attributes of soil in several ways, including the following:

- Humus improves soil structure by binding or "gluing" small mineral particles together into larger aggregates, creating large soil pores for improved air and water infiltration and movement.

- Humus improves water retention and release to plants.

- Humus slowly releases nitrogen, phosphorus, and sulfur over time, which plants then use for growth and development.

- Because of its positive surface charge, humus improves soil fertility by retaining nutrients.

- Humus buffers the soil pH so it remains stable for plant roots.

- Humus can chelate or bind metals in soil, preventing metal toxicities.

As a point of clarification, garden stores sometime carry soil amendments labeled as humus. In reality these are generally "compost" and do not meet the soil scientist definition of humus as given here.

SOIL INOCULATION

Gardeners can purchase products at garden centers that are intended to introduce soil organisms to an existing soil. Adding decomposing bacteria from a purchased product is generally not necessary, because decomposing soil organisms are already present in the soil. Even if their populations are low due to unfavorable conditions, as soon as organic matter and water become available their populations rapidly increase. Thus, soil biologists encourage gardeners to nurture existing communities rather than introducing external organisms through purchased products.

In addition, inoculating with rhizobia is generally not needed, unless a vegetable gardener is planting a leguminous crop for the first time. In this case, the gardener should purchase the appropriate inoculant (bacteria) for the leguminous vegetable being planted. Inoculation in future years is not needed, because *Rhizobia* produce survival structures to overwinter.

Mycorrhizal products are considered highly experimental at this time, and are thus not currently recommended by Colorado State University Extension for general use.

SOIL FOOD WEB

Within the soil, organisms function within an ecological food web (the smaller becoming the food for the larger) cycling nutrients through the soil biomass. This soil food web is the basis of healthy, living soil. Significant soil organisms involved in the soil food web include: 1) bacteria, 2) fungi, 3) protozoa, 4) nematodes, 5) arthropods, and 6) earthworms.

Bacteria

Bacteria are simple, single-celled microorganisms. Bacteria inhabit a wide variety of habitats, including soil. In fact, a teaspoon of productive soil can contain from 100 million to 1 billion bacteria. Soil-inhabiting bacteria can be grouped as decomposers, mutualists, pathogens, or chemoautotrophs. Bacteria that improve soil quality feed on soil organisms, decompose organic matter, help keep nutrients in the root zone, enhance soil structure, compete with disease-causing organisms, and filter and degrade pollutants in soil.

Fungi

Fungi are a diverse group of multicellular organisms. The best known fungi are mushrooms, molds, and yeast, but there are many others that go unnoticed, particularly those living in soil. Fungi grow as long strands called hyphae (up to several yards long), pushing their way between soil particles, rocks, and roots. Fungi can be grouped as decomposers, mutualists, or pathogens. Fungi that improve soil quality decompose complex carbon compounds, improve accumulation of organic matter, retain nutrients in soil, bind soil particles into aggregates, compete with plant pathogens, and decompose certain types of pollution.

Protozoa

Protozoa are microscopic, single-celled microbes that primarily eat bacteria. The bacteria contain more nitrogen than the protozoa can utilize and some ammonium (NH_4) is released to plants. Protozoa also prevent some pathogens from establishing on plants and function as a food source for nematodes in the soil food web.

Nematodes

Nematodes are small, unsegmented round worms. Nematodes live in water films in the large pore spaces in soil. Most species are beneficial, feeding on bacteria, fungi, and other nematodes, but some cause harm by feeding on plant roots. Nematodes distribute bacteria and fungi through the soil as they move about. Predatory nematodes can consume root-feeding nematodes or prevent their access to roots.

Arthropods

Soil arthropods are small animals such as insects, spiders, and mites. They range in size from microscopic to several inches in length. Most live near the soil surface or in the upper 3 inches. Arthropods improve soil quality by creating structure through burrowing, depositing fecal pellets, controlling disease-causing organisms, stimulating microbial activity, enhancing decomposition via shredding organic matter and mixing soil, and regulating healthy soil food web populations.

Soil arthropods can be shredders (millipedes, sowbugs, etc.), predators (spiders, scorpions, pseudoscorpions, centipedes, and predatory mites, ants, and beetles), herbivores (symphylans, root-maggots, etc.), or fungal-feeders (springtails and turtle mites). Most soil-dwelling arthropods eat fungi, worms, or other arthropods.

Earthworms

Regarded by Aristotle as the "intestines of the earth," earthworms aid in soil fertility and structure, and contribute to overall plant health.

Earthworm Types

There are three types of earthworms:

Anecic (Greek for "up from the earth" or "out of the earth")

- Build permanent burrows into the deep mineral layers of the soil

- Drag organic matter from the soil surface into their burrows for food

- Include the familiar bait worm, the nightcrawler, or dew worm (*Lumbricus terrestris*)

Endogeic (Greek for "within the earth")

- Build extensive non-permanent burrows in the upper mineral layer of soil

- Feed on the organic matter in the soil

- Live exclusively in soil and usually are not noticed, except after a heavy rain when they come to the surface

Epigeic (Greek for "upon the earth")

- Live on the soil surface

- Form no permanent burrows

- Feed on decaying organic matter

- Common names: red worm, manure worm, brandling worm, red wiggler, and compost worm

The anecic (an-ess-ik) and endogeic (in-dough-gee-ik) are the types most often noticed in Colorado soils. Because the upper foot of soil freezes here during the winter, the epigeic worms are usually killed. In addition, the low organic matter content of Colorado soils will likely not support the food needs of epigeic earthworms. Anecic are larger than the endogeic.

Biology of Earthworms

Earthworms breathe through their skin and must be in an environment that has at least 40% moisture (at least as damp as a wrung out sponge). If their skin dries out, they cannot breathe and will die.

Earthworms prefer a near-neutral soil pH.

Instead of teeth, earthworms have a gizzard like a chicken that grinds the soil and organic matter that they consume. Their main intent is to eat the soil microorganisms that live in and on the soil and organic matter.

Worm excrement is commonly called worm casts or castings. These soil clusters are glued together when excreted by the earthworm and are quite resistant to erosive forces. Their castings contain many more microorganisms than food sources because their intestines inoculate the casts with microorganisms.

Earthworms become sexually mature when the familiar band (the clitellum) appears around their body, closer to their mouth. Each worm with a clitellum is capable of mating with other worms and producing cocoons that contain baby worms. Cocoons are lemon-shaped and slightly smaller than a pencil eraser.

Anecic worms are capable of burrowing to depths of 6 feet, often dragging surface litter (organic matter) into their burrows.

Benefits of Earthworms

Charles Darwin, known for his work with evolution of species, wrote a paper on earthworms during his final years. In it he surmised that most all of the fertile soil on earth must have passed through the gut of an earthworm. While not entirely accurate, earthworms do play an important role in soil and plant health.

Soil Fertility

Earthworms are part of a host of organisms that decompose organic matter in the soil. As earthworms digest the microorganisms and organic matter in soil, the form of nutrients is changed as materials pass through the earthworm's gut. Thus, worm casts are richer than the surrounding soil, containing nutrients changed into forms that are more available to plants. For example, one study found that in a sample of soil with four percent organic matter, worm casts contained 246 pounds of nitrogen per 1,000 square feet while the surrounding soil contained 161 pounds of nitrogen per 1,000 square feet (Source: ATTRA, Sustainable Soil Systems).

Soil Structure

The deep burrows of anecic earthworms create passages for air, water, and roots. Burrows provide easy avenues for the exchange of soil gases with the atmosphere. Clay soils with extensive earthworm burrows will allow water to infiltrate and percolate more readily than those without. Plants have the capacity to root deeper, and the lower layers of soil can recharge with air more quickly. Air is an essential component of root development.

Anecic worms mix the soil as they create their burrows and build soil organic matter and humus as they drag litter into their burrows and excrete castings in the soil.

Endogeic burrows contribute to soil tilth, tying together many of the large pore spaces in the soil and increasing soil porosity.

The mucus from the skin of earthworms aids in the formation of soil aggregates, which are integral components of the crumb of soil structure. Aggregates are also formed in castings.

Water-Holding Capacity

By increasing the organic matter content, soil porosity, and aggregation, earthworms can greatly increase the water-holding capacity of soils.

How to Encourage Earthworm Activity

Earthworms will not go where it is too hot/cold or too dry/wet. Soil temperatures above 70°F or below 40°F will discourage earthworm activity. While soil temperature is hard to alter, moisture can be managed. When soil becomes waterlogged, oxygen is driven out of the large pore spaces. Without this free oxygen, earthworms cannot breathe. Conversely, when soil dries beyond half of field capacity, earthworm skin dries in the soil. Maintaining moisture levels that are ideal for optimum plant growth in a landscape or garden will also be ideal for earthworm activity.

 Providing a food source in the form of organic matter is also important. Mulching grass clippings into the lawn, putting down a layer of organic mulch in beds, amending the soil with compost, and turning under a green manure are all excellent ways to feed earthworm populations.

Practices Detrimental to Earthworm Activity

- High rates of ammonium nitrate are harmful to earthworms.

- Tillage destroys permanent burrows and can cut and kill worms. Fall tillage can be especially destructive to earthworm populations. Deep and frequent tillage can reduce earthworm populations by as much as ninety percent.

- Earthworms are also hindered by salty conditions in the soil.

- Some chemicals have toxic effects on earthworm populations (Table 6-1).

Table 6-1. Earthworm Population Reduction by Pesticides*

Pesticide	Toxicity to Earthworms	Reduction
Sevin (carbaryl) insecticide	Severe	76–100%
Diazinon insecticide	Moderate	26–50%
2,4-D herbicide	Low	0–25%

* University of Kentucky Department of Entomology.

Transplanting Earthworms

To create worm populations in a soil without worms, simply dig a large spadeful of soil from an area with visible worm numbers and bury this soil in the area where worms are needed.

WAYS TO ENCOURAGE BENEFICIAL SOIL ORGANISMS

Creating a favorable environment for soil organisms improves plant growth and reduces garden maintenance. Encouraging their efforts is central to building a healthy fertile soil supportive to optimum plant growth.

- **Add organic matter to the soil.** Soil organisms require a food source from soil amendments (compost, crop residues) and/or mulch.

- **Use organic mulch.** It stabilizes soil moisture and temperature, and adds organic matter. Mulches may help prevent soil compaction and protect soil oxygen levels needed by soil organism and roots.

  Note: The term "mulch" refers to material placed on the soil surface. A mulch controls weeds, conserves water, moderates soil temperature, and has a direct impact on soil microorganism activity. The term "**soil amendment**" refers to materials mixed into the soil.

- **Water effectively.** Soil organisms require an environment that is damp (like a wrung out sponge) but not soggy, between 50°F and 90°F. Soil organism activity may be reduced due to dry soil conditions that are common in the fall and winter. Avoid over-irrigation because waterlogged soils will be harmful to beneficial soil organisms.

- **Avoid unnecessary rototilling**, as it will destroy the mycorrhizae and soil structure. Instead of tilling, mulch for weed control.

- **Avoid unwarranted pesticide applications.** Some fungicides, insecticides, and herbicides are harmful to various types of soil organisms.

- **Avoid plastic sheets under rock mulch.** This practice discourages microorganism activity by reducing water and air movement, and preventing the incorporation of organic matter.

1. Describe how organisms directly benefit the soil and plant growth.

2. Describe how organisms indirectly benefit the soil and plant growth.

3. Should gardeners inoculate their soil with rhizobia, mycorrhizae, and decomposers? Explain your answer.

4. What makes up the soil organic matter? Give a soil scientist's definition of *humus*. What are the benefits of humus?

5. How does a gardener enhance the living soil?

Chapter

7*

Soil Tilth

Texture, Structure, and Pore Space

SOIL TILTH

Gardening in Western soils can be a challenge due to poor soil tilth. Sandy soils hold little water and nutrients, while some Colorado soils are rocky and shallow.

Along Colorado's Front Range, many soils are clayey and compact readily. These soils may have poor drainage, which may lead to salt problems. Due to low soil oxygen levels, root systems are typically shallow, reducing the crop's tolerance to drought and hot windy weather.

Special attention to soil management is the primary key to gardening success. While gardeners often focus their attention on insect and disease problems, 80% of all plant problems begin with soil conditions reducing the plant's vigor.

The term **soil tilth** refers to the soil's general suitability to support plant growth, or more specifically to support root growth. Tilth is technically defined as the physical condition of soil as related to its ease of tillage, fitness of seedbed, and impedance to seedling emergence and root penetration.

A soil with good tilth has large pore spaces for adequate air infiltration and water movement. (Roots only grow where the soil tilth allows for adequate levels of soil oxygen.) It also holds a reasonable supply of water and nutrients.

Soil tilth is a function of soil texture, structure, fertility, and the interplay with organic content and the living soil organisms that help make up the soil ecosystem.

---

*Authors: David Whiting and Carl Wilson (Colorado State University Extension), Cathrine Moravec (Former CSU Extension employee), and Jean Reeder, PhD, (USDA-ARS, retired). Artwork by David Whiting unless otherwise noted.

These properties also influence how to manage the soil for successful gardening. Many gardeners give attention to the soil's nutrient content by applying fertilizers. However, fertilization is only one of the keys to a productive garden.

TEXTURE

Texture refers to the size of the particles that make up the soil. The terms **sand**, **silt**, and **clay** refer to relative sizes of the individual soil particles (Table 7-1 and Figure 7-1).

Based on the **Soil Textural Class Triangle** (Figure 7-2), the percentage of sand, silt and clay determine the textural class. (For example, a soil with 30% clay, 10% silt, and 60% sand is called a sandy clay loam. A soil with 20% clay, 40% silt, and 40% sand is a loam.)

A **fine-textured** or **clayey** soil is one dominated by tiny clay particles. A **coarse-textured** or **sandy** soil is one comprised primarily of medium to large size sand particles. The term "loamy soil" refers to a soil with a combination of sand, silt, and clay-sized particles.

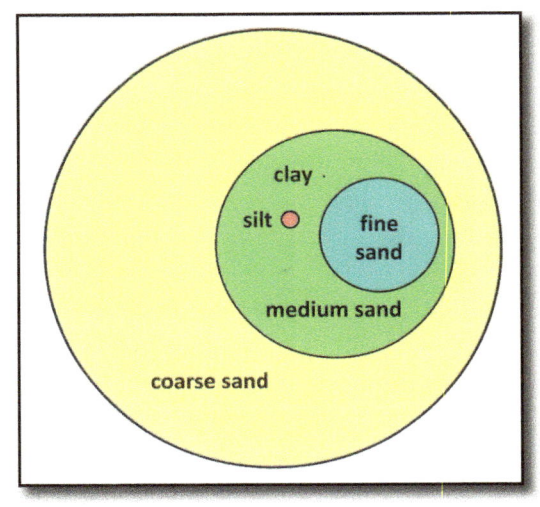

Figure 7-1 ▍ *Comparative size of clay to coarse sand. Clay is actually less than 0.002 mm (0.00008 inch) with coarse sand up to 1.0 m (0.04 inch).*

Table 7-1. The Size of Sand, Silt, and Clay

Name	Particle Diameter
Clay	below 0.002 mm
Silt	0.002 to 0.05 mm
Very fine sand	0.05 to 0.10 mm
Fine sand	0.10 to 0.25 mm
Medium sand	0.25 to 0.5 mm
Coarse sand	0.5 to 1.0 mm
Very coarse sand	1.0 to 2.0 mm
Gravel	2.0 to 75.0 mm
Rock	greater than 75.0 mm (~2 inches)

Clay—Clay particles are flat, plate-like, negatively charged particles. They are so tiny in size that it takes 12,000 clay particles in a line to make one inch. Clay feels sticky to the touch. Soils with as little as twenty percent clay size particles behave like a sticky clayey soil. Soils with high clay content have good water and nutrient holding capacity, but the lack of large pore space restricts water and air movement. Clayey soils are also rather prone to compaction issues.

Some types of clayey soils expand and contract with changes in soil moisture. These **expansive** soils create special issues around construction and landscaping. For homes on expansive clays, limit landscaping along the foundation to non-irrigated mulch areas and xeric plants that require little supplemental irrigation.

Avoid planting trees next to the foundation and direct drainage from the roof away from the foundation. For additional details, refer to Colorado State University Extension fact sheet #7.236, *Landscaping on Expansive Soils*, available at www. cmg.colostate.edu.

Silt—Silt has a smooth or floury texture. Silt settles out in slow-moving water and is common on the bottom of an irrigation ditch or lakeshore. Silt adds little to the characteristics of a soil. Water-holding capacity is similar to clay.

Sand—Sand, being the larger sized particles, feels gritty. There is a major difference in soil characteristics between fine sands and medium to coarse sands. Fine sands add little to the soil characteristics and do not significantly increase large pore space. An example of fine sand is the bagged sand sold for children's sandboxes.

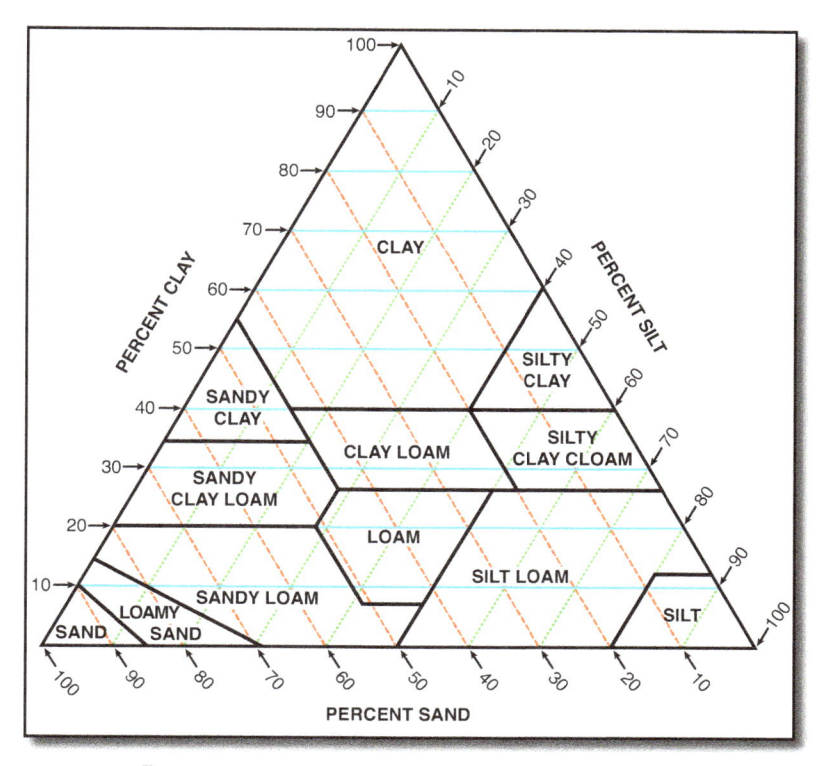

Figure 7-2. ▮ *Soil Textural Triangle (Source: U.S. Department of Agriculture).*

For a soil to take on the characteristics of a sandy soil, it needs greater than 50% to 60% medium to coarse size sand particles. Sandy soils have good drainage and aeration, but low water and nutrient holding capacity.

Gravel and rock—Some Western soils are dominated by gravel and rock, making them difficult for the gardener to work. Gravel and rock do not provide nutrients or water-holding capacity for the soil. Rather they often drain readily, being a droughty soil with low nutrient-holding capacity.

Texture directly affects plant growth and soil management as described in Table 7-2. A soil with as little as 20% clay may behave as a fine-textured, clayey soil, whereas a soil needs at least 50% to 60% medium to coarse size sand to behave as a sandy soil. Properties of the clay trumps property of the sand in a soil with 20% clay and 80% sand, behaving as a clayey soil (Table 7-2).

Table 7-2. Comparison of Fine-textured (Clayey) Soil and Coarse-textured (Sandy) Soil

	Clayey	Sandy
Water-holding capacity	High	Low
Nutrient-holding capacity	High	Low
Compaction potential	High	Lower
Crusts	Yes	No/sometimes
Drainage	Slow	Fast
Salinity buildup	Yes	Seldom
Warming in spring	Slow	Fast

Estimating Soil Texture by Measurement

1. Spread soil on a newspaper to dry. Remove all rocks, trash, roots, etc. Crush lumps and clods.

2. Finely pulverize the soil.

3. Fill a tall, slender jar (like a quart jar) one-quarter full of soil.

4. Add water until the jar is three-quarters full.

5. Add a teaspoon of powdered, non-foaming dishwasher detergent.

6. Put on a tight fitting lid and shake hard for ten to fifteen minutes. This shaking breaks apart the soil aggregates and separates the soil into individual mineral particles.

7. Set the jar where it will not be disturbed for two to three days.

8. Soil particles will settle out according to size. **After one minute,** mark on the jar the depth of the sand.

9. **After two hours,** mark on the jar the depth of the silt.

10. **When the water clears,** mark on the jar the clay level. This typically takes one to three days, but with some soils it may take weeks.

Figure 7-3 ▮ *Measuring soil texture.*

11. Measure the thickness of the sand, silt, and clay layers (Figure 7-3).

    a.   Thickness of sand deposit   _____

    b.   Thickness of silt deposit   _____

    c.   Thickness of clay deposit   _____

    d.   Thickness of total deposit   _____

12. Calculate the percentage of sand, silt, and clay.

    {clay thickness} / {total thickness} = _____ percent clay

    {silt thickness} / {total thickness}   = _____ percent silt

    {sand thickness} / {total thickness} = _____ percent sand

13. Turn to the soil texture triangle and look up the soil texture class.

Estimating Soil Texture by Feel

Feel test—Rub some moist soil between fingers (Figure 7-4).

- Sand feels gritty.
- Silt feels smooth.
- Clays feel sticky.

Ball squeeze test—Squeeze a moistened ball of soil in the hand (Figure 7-4).

- Coarse texture soils (sand or loamy sands) break with slight pressure.
- Medium texture soils (sandy loams and silt loams) stay together but change shape easily.
- Fine textured soils (clayey or clayey loam) resist breaking.

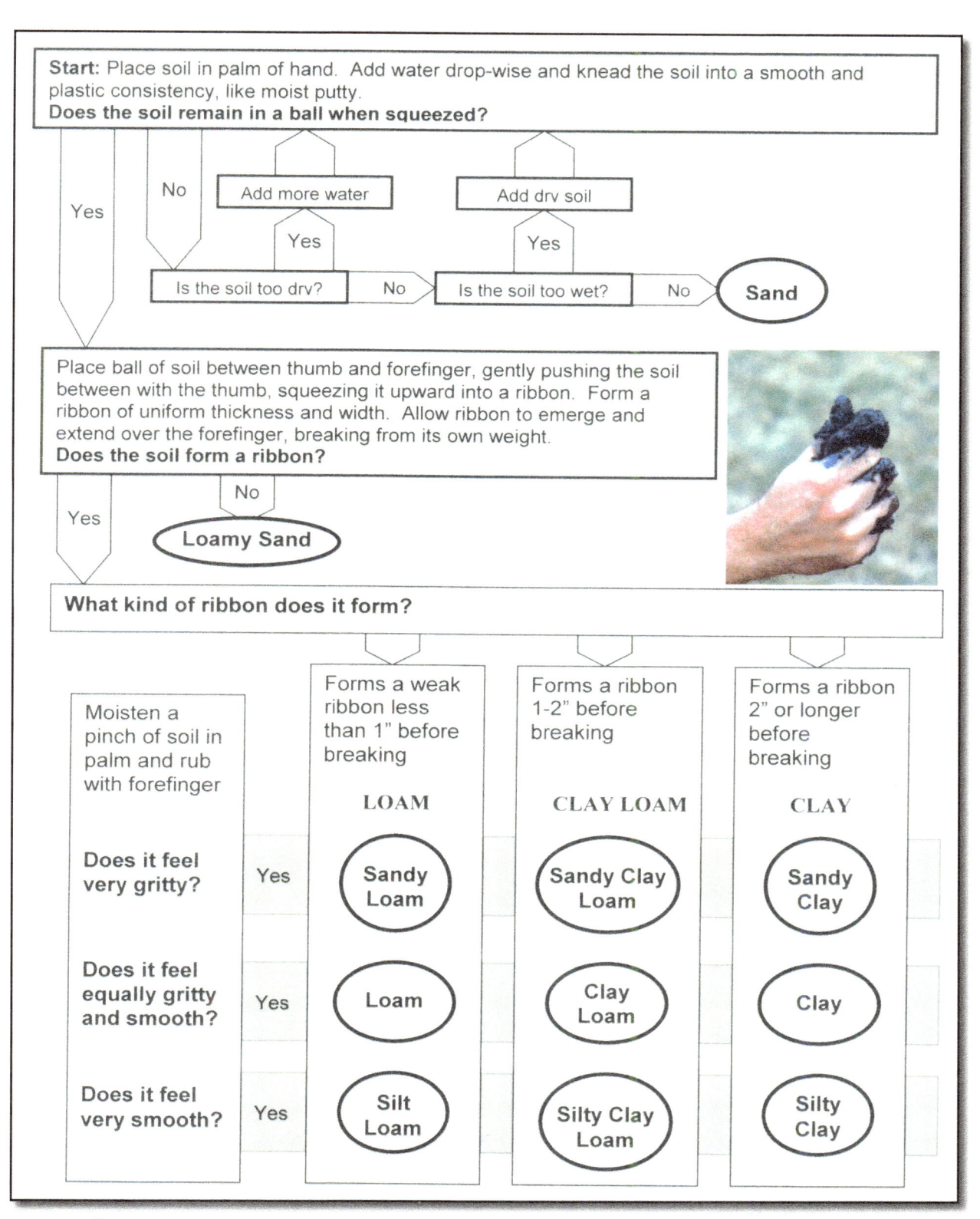

Start: Place soil in palm of hand. Add water drop-wise and knead the soil into a smooth and plastic consistency, like moist putty.
Does the soil remain in a ball when squeezed?

Yes

No

Add more water

Yes

Is the soil too drv? — No — Add drv soil

Yes

Is the soil too wet? — No — **Sand**

Place ball of soil between thumb and forefinger, gently pushing the soil between with the thumb, squeezing it upward into a ribbon. Form a ribbon of uniform thickness and width. Allow ribbon to emerge and extend over the forefinger, breaking from its own weight.
Does the soil form a ribbon?

Yes

No — **Loamy Sand**

What kind of ribbon does it form?

Moisten a pinch of soil in palm and rub with forefinger		Forms a weak ribbon less than 1" before breaking **LOAM**	Forms a ribbon 1-2" before breaking **CLAY LOAM**	Forms a ribbon 2" or longer before breaking **CLAY**
Does it feel very gritty?	Yes	Sandy Loam	Sandy Clay Loam	Sandy Clay
Does it feel equally gritty and smooth?	Yes	Loam	Clay Loam	Clay
Does it feel very smooth?	Yes	Silt Loam	Silty Clay Loam	Silty Clay

Figure 7-4 ▮ *Soil Texture by Feel.*

Ribbon test—Squeeze a moistened ball of soil out between thumb and fingers (Figure 7-4).

- Ribbons less than one inch
    - —Feels gritty = coarse texture (sandy) soil
    - —Not gritty feeling = medium texture soil high in silt
- Ribbons one to two inches
    - —Feels gritty = medium texture soil
    - —Not gritty feeling = fine texture soil
- Ribbons greater than two inches = fine texture (clayey) soil

Note: A soil with as little as 20% clay will behave as a clayey soil. A soil needs 45% to over 60% medium to coarse sand to behave as a sandy soil. In a soil with 20% clay and 80% sand, the soil will behave as a clayey soil.

STRUCTURE

Structure refers to how the various particles of sand, silt, and clay fit together, creating **pore spaces** of various sizes. Sand, silt, and clay particles are "glued" together by chemical and biological processes creating **aggregates** (clusters of particles). Mycorrhizae, earthworms, soil microorganisms, and plant roots are responsible for creating aggregates (Figures 7-5 and 7-6).

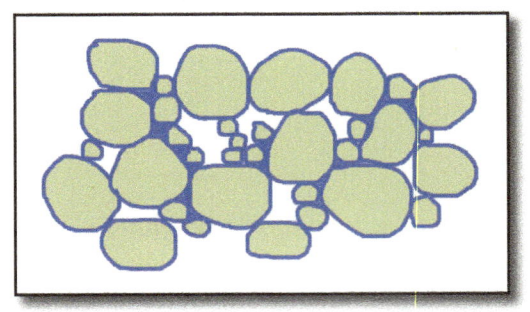

Figure 7-5 ▌ *The size of pore spaces between soil particles plays a key role in plant growth. Pore spaces are a function of soil texture and structure.*

Undisturbed native soils often have a granular structure in the A horizon (with rapid drainage) and block structure (with rapid to moderate drainage) in the B horizon. A platy structure (with slow to no drainage) is common in soils high in clay.

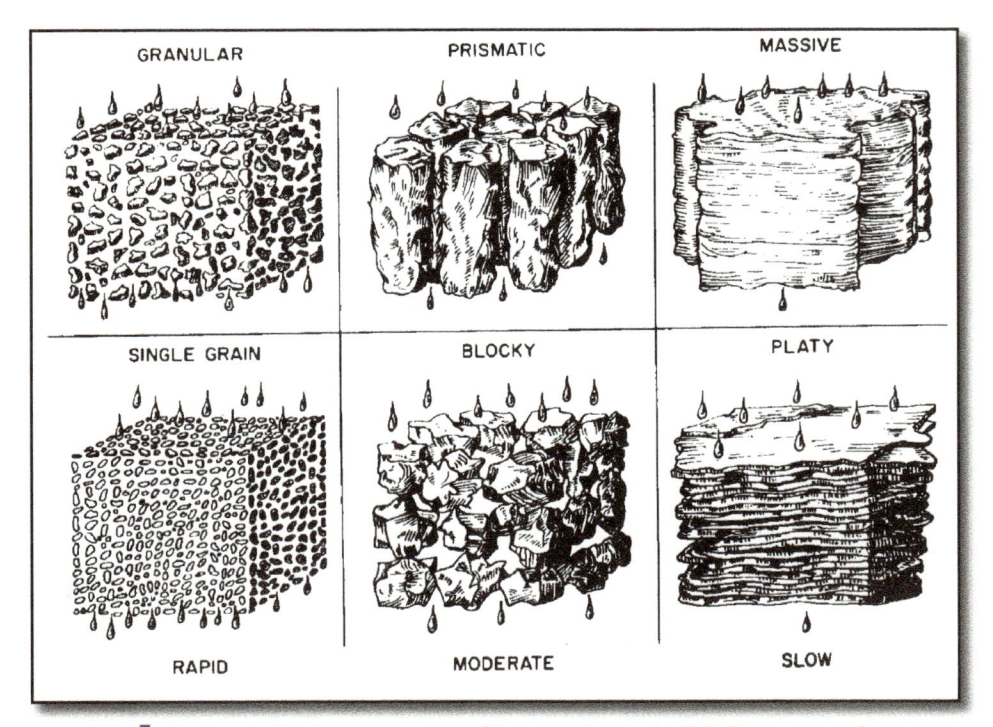

Figure 7-6 ▌ *Examples of soil structure types. (Line drawing by the U.S. Department of Agriculture.)*

Compacted, unamended landscape soils typically have a massive structure with no defined horizons, little organic matter, low total pore space, and most significantly low large pore space.

The term *"peds"* describes the soil's individual aggregates or dirt clods. Soils that create strong peds tolerate working and still maintain good structure. In some soils, the peds are extremely strong, making cultivation difficult except when the soil moisture is precisely right. Soils with soft peds may be easy to cultivate, but may readily pulverize destroying the soil's natural structure.

Primary factors influencing structure include the following:

- Texture

- Activity of soil mycorrhizae, earthworms, and other soil organisms

- Organic matter content

- Soil moisture (year round)

- The freezing/thawing cycle

- Cultivation—Tilling a soil has a direct impact on structure by breaking apart aggregates and collapsing pore spaces. Avoid tilling except to mix in organic matter, control weeds (limited use), or to prepare a seedbed.

- Soil compaction

To maintain good structure avoid overworking the soil. Acceptable ped size depends on the gardening activity. For planting vegetable or flower seeds, large peds interfere with seeding. In contrast, when planting trees peds up to the size of a fist are acceptable and pulverizing the soil would be undesirable.

PORE SPACE

Pore space is a function of soil texture, structure, and the activity of beneficial soil organisms. Water coats the solid particles and fills the smaller pore spaces. Air fills the larger pore spaces (Figure 7-7).

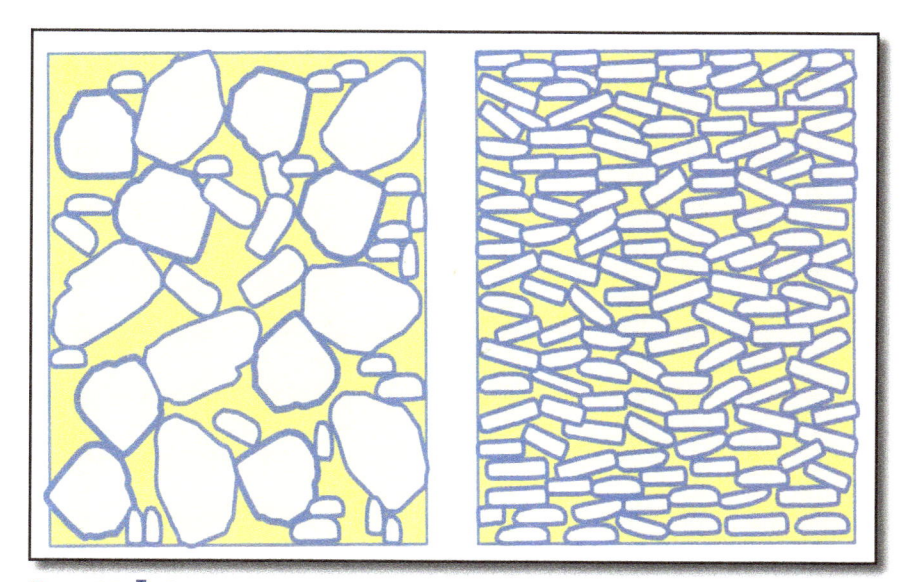

Figure 7-7 ▮ *Comparative pore space. Left: Soil with large pore space. Right: Soil lacking large pore space.*

To help understand pore space, visualize a bottle of golf balls and a bottle of table salt. The pore space between golf balls is large compared to the pore space between the salt grains.

The relative percent of clay size particles versus the percent of medium to coarse sand size particles influences the pore space of a soil. Silt and fine sand size particles contribute little to pore space attributes. Note in Figure 7-7 how large pore space is nonexistent to minimal until the sand strongly dominates the soil profile. Organic matter also plays a key role in creating large pore space (Figure 7-8).

Figure 7-8 ■ *Percent of small versus large pore space as a factor of soil texture.*

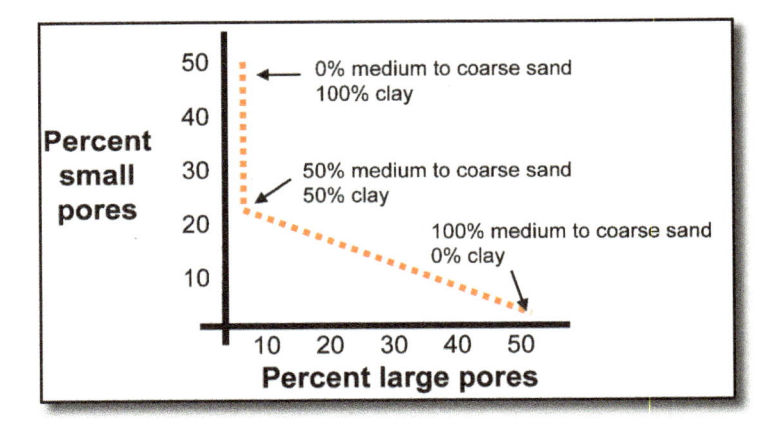

The quantities of large and small pore spaces directly affect plant growth. On fine-texture, clayey, and/or compacted soils, a lack of large pore spaces restricts water and air infiltration and movement, thus limiting root growth and the activity of beneficial soil organisms. On sandy soils, the lack of small pore space limits the soil's ability to hold water and nutrients.

Water Movement

Soil water coats the mineral and organic particles and is held by the property of **cohesion** (the chemical process by which water molecules stick together) in the small pore spaces. Air fills the large pore spaces.

Water movement is directly related to the size of pores in the soil. In the small pores of clayey soils, water slowly moves in all directions by **capillary action**. The lack of large pore space leads to drainage problems and low soil oxygen levels. On sandy soils with large pores, water readily drains downwards by **gravitational pull**. Excessive irrigation and/or precipitation can leach water-soluble nutrients, like nitrogen, out of the root zone and into ground water (Figure 7-9).

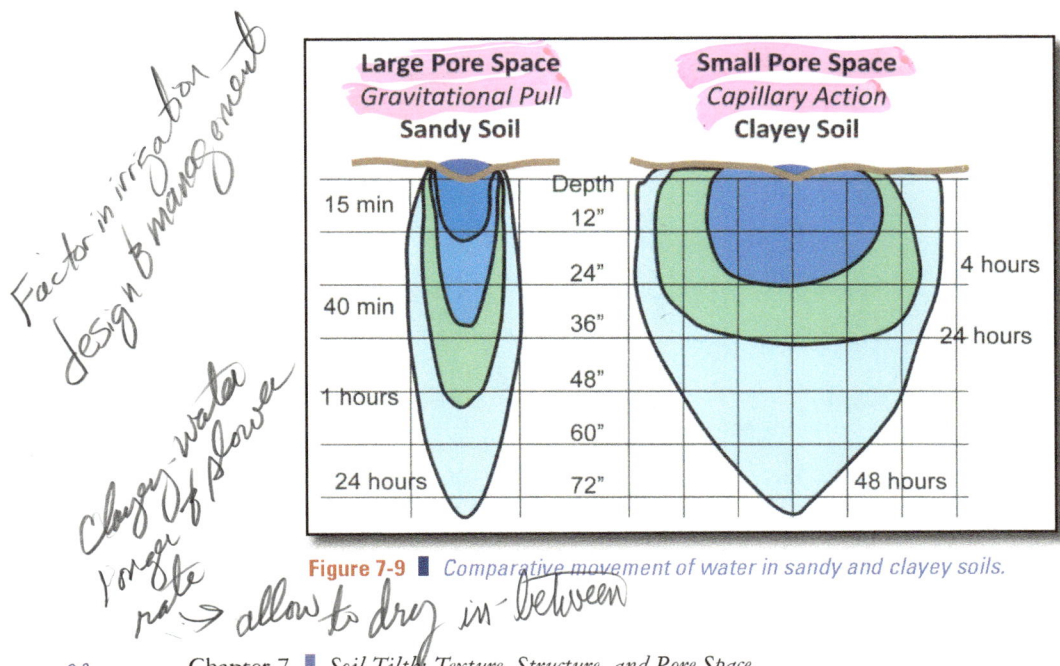

Figure 7-9 ■ *Comparative movement of water in sandy and clayey soils.*

Figure 7-10 ■ *Left: With clayey soil over sandy soil, water is slow to leave the small pore space of the clay. Right: With sandy soil over clayey soil, water is slow to move into the small pore space of the clay.*

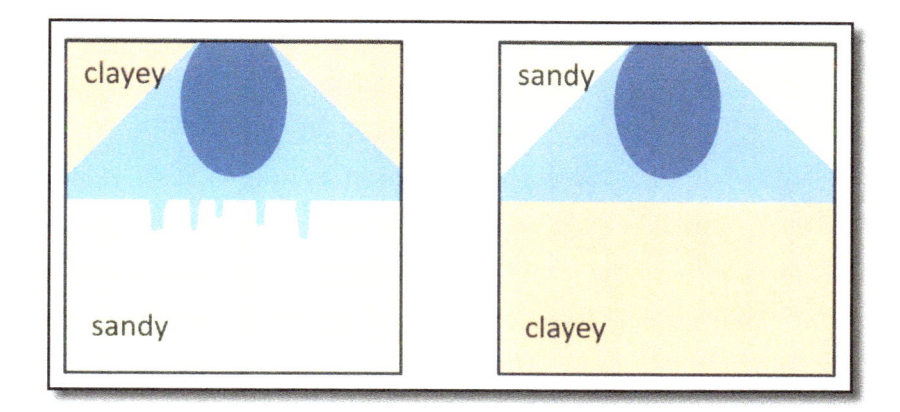

Texture Interface

Within the soil profile, a ***texture interface*** (abrupt change in actual pore space) creates a boundary line that affects the movement of water, air infiltration, and root growth. Water and air are very slow to cross a texture interface.

When a clayey and/or compacted soil layer (primarily small pore space) is on top of a sandy soil layer (primarily large pore space) water accumulates just above the change. Water is slow to leave the small pore space of the clayey soil due to the water properties of *cohesion* (water molecules binding to water molecules) (Figure 7-10).

Likewise, when water moving down through a sandy soil layer (primarily large pore space) hits a clayey and/or compacted soil layer (primarily small pore space), water accumulates in the soil just above the interface. This backup is due to the slow rate that water can move into the small pore space of the clayey soil. It is like a four-lane freeway suddenly changing into a country lane; traffic backs up on the freeway (Figure 7-10).

Perched water table—This change in water movement creates a **perched water table** (overly wet layer of soil) generally six inches thick or greater just above the change line. When creating raised bed boxes, mix the added soil with the soil below to avoid creating a texture interface. In tree planting, to deal with the texture interface between the root ball soil and the backfill soil, it is imperative that the root ball rises to the surface with no backfill soil over the root ball. In landscape soils that have a texture interface between soil layers, a perched water table may sit just above the interface line. In this situation, be cautious about frequent irrigation creating an oxygen deficiency in the roots below the perched water table (Figures 7-11 and 7-12).

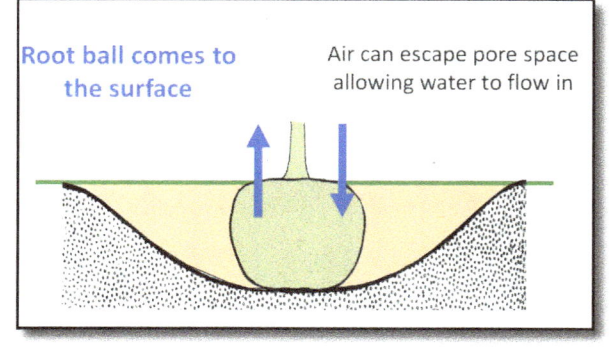

Figure 7-11 ■ *In tree planting, to deal with the texture interface between the root ball soil and the backfill soil, it is imperative that the root ball comes to the surface with no backfill soil over top of the root ball.*

Figure 7-12 ■ *On landscape soils with a texture interface in the soil profile, too frequent irrigation creates a perched water table above the interface line. Roots below the perched water table have low soil oxygen levels.*

MANAGING SOIL TILTH

Gardening on Coarse-Textured, Sandy Soils

The major limitation of sandy soil is its low capacity to hold water and nutrients. Plants growing on sandy soils do not use more water; they just need to be irrigated more frequently but with smaller quantities. Heavy irrigation wastes water because it readily leaches below the root zone. Water-soluble nutrients, such as nitrogen, also leach below the rooting zone with excessive irrigation or rain.

The best management practice for sandy soils is routine application of organic matter. Organic matter holds ten plus times more water and nutrients than sand. Sandy soils with high organic matter content (up to five percent) make an ideal gardening soil.

Gardening on Fine-Textured, Clayey Soils

The limitations of clayey soils arise from a lack of large pores, thus restricting both water and air movement. Soils easily waterlog when water cannot move down through the soil profile. During irrigation or rain events, the limited large pore space in fine-textured soils quickly fills with water, reducing the roots' oxygen supply.

The best management practice for clayey soils is routine applications of organic matter and attention to fostering the activity of soil microorganisms and earthworms. As soil microorganisms decompose the organic matter, the tiny soil particles bind together into larger clumps or aggregates, increasing large pore space. This improvement takes place over a period of years. A single large application of organic matter does not do the trick. A gardener may start seeing improvement in soil conditions in a couple of years.

As the organic content increases, earthworms and soil microorganisms become more active; this over time improves soil tilth.

On clayey soils, also take extra care to minimize soil compaction. Soil compaction reduces the large pore space, restricting air and water movement through the soil, thus limiting root growth. **Soil compaction is the primary factor limiting plant growth in landscape soils.** Soils generally become compacted during home construction. Methods of minimizing or reducing soil compaction are discussed in Chapter 8.

Gardening on Gravelly and Decomposed Granite Soils

Soils in Western foothills and mountains change greatly with topography and precipitation. Soils may be well developed with organic matter on north- and east-facing slopes and in valley floors, but on dryer south- and west-facing slopes soils are often shallow and extremely low in organic matter.

Gardening in the gravelly and decomposed granite soils, common to many foothills and mountain areas, may be extremely challenging. Large rocks, erratic depths for bedrock, very little organic matter, pockets of clayey soil, and rapid drainage with poor water-holding capacity characterize these coarse-textured soils. They erode readily once disturbed.

If the soil has been disturbed with the surface layer removed, decomposed granite soils will greatly benefit from organic matter. Add up to twenty-five percent by volume. For example, if tilling to a depth of eight inches, add two inches of compost or other organic materials. If only tillable to a depth of four inches, add one inch of compost. Use well-decomposed materials. In some situations, mixing in the organic matter may be very labor intensive or impossible.

When Soil Amendment Is Not Practical or Possible

In real-world settings, the ideal approach of improving soils by adding soil amendments may not be practical or possible. For example:

- In existing landscapes, it is easy to add amendments to annual flowerbeds and vegetable gardens, but amendments cannot be worked into the soil in the rooting zone of trees, shrubs, perennials, and lawn.

- In working with new landscapes, the new homeowner may not have the financial resources to purchase the amendments desired.

- The gardener may not have the physical ability for this intense labor.

- On slopes, removing the plant cover predisposes the soil to erosion.

- On rocky soils, it may be physically impractical or impossible to work in amendments.

Where amending is not practical or possible, gardeners need to consider alternatives. First and foremost, understand that without soil improvement the gardener may need to accept less than optimum plant growth and increased maintenance. When amending is not practical or possible, consider the following options:

- Focus on selecting plants more tolerant of the soil conditions. This includes tolerance to low soil oxygen and reduced root spread (compaction issues), poor drainage (tolerance to wet soils), drought (tolerance to dry soils), and low fertility (fertilizer need). These are characteristics of some rock garden or alpine garden plants. However, be careful about assuming that these characteristics apply to native plants as it may or may not be the case.

- Space plants farther apart to reduce competition for limited soil resources.

- Small transplants may adapt to poor soils better than either larger transplants or trying to grow plants from seed.

- Raised-bed gardening and container gardening may be a practical option when soils are poor.

- Pay attention to minimizing additional soil compaction with the use of organic mulches and management of foot traffic flow.

- Organic mulch (wood/bark chips) helps improve soil tilth over a period of time as the mulch decomposes and is worked into the soil by soil organisms. To allow this process to occur, do not put a weed fabric under the mulch and add material periodically.

- Established lawns, which have been in for more than some twenty years, come to equilibrium between root dieback and soil organic content.

Soil Practices to Avoid

The following is a summary of common practices that should be avoided in Western soils to maximize soil tilth and plant growth potential.

- **Avoid working the soil when wet**—Water lubricates soil particles, making the soil easier to compact.

- **Avoid excessive fertilization**—This has the potential for surface and ground water pollution and adds salts to the soil, which can become toxic to plants. Heavy fertilization will not compensate for poor soil preparation. Many gardeners have overapplied phosphate and potash.

- **Avoid adding too much organic matter**—This leads to salt buildup, large releases of nitrogen, the buildup of excessive phosphorus, and an imbalance in potassium, calcium, magnesium, and iron.

- **Avoid adding lime or wood ashes**—Being calcium sources, they are used to raise the soil pH. Most Colorado soils have a neutral to high pH. Lime or wood ashes would only be used on soils with a soil pH below 5.5.

- **Avoid adding gypsum (a calcium source)**—Gypsum is used to reclaim sodic soils by displacing the sodium with calcium.

- **Avoid creating texture interfaces**—For example, when making a raised bed, adding a different soil in the box creates an interface at the change line. Use similar soils and mix the soils.

- **Avoid trying to make dramatic changes in soil pH**—If the soil is high in *free lime* (calcium carbonate), lowering the pH is not effective.

1. Define the terms and explain how each are interrelated:

   a. Tilth

   b. Texture

   c. Structure

   d. Pore Space

2. Describe characteristics and management of the following soil types:

   a. Coarse-textured, sandy soil

   b. Fine-textured, clayey soil

   c. Gravelly and decomposed granite soils

3. Explain what is significant about large pore spaces and small pore spaces.

4. Describe how water moves through small pore spaces and large pore spaces.

5. In relation to root growth, air infiltration, and water movement, what happens when the soil has a texture interface?

6. List considerations when amending the soil is not practical or possible.

7. List common soil practices to avoid.

8*

Dealing with Soil Compaction

WHAT IS SOIL COMPACTION?

Soil compaction reduces total pore space of a soil. More importantly, it significantly reduces the amount of large pore space, restricting air and water movement into and through the soil. **Low soil oxygen levels caused by soil compaction are the primary factor limiting plant growth in landscape soils.** Soil conditions, primarily soil compaction, contribute to eighty percent of the plant disorders in the landscape setting. Figure 8-1 illustrates comparison in large pore space in a non-compacted and compacted soil. Soil compaction can change a block or aggregate structure (with good infiltration and drainage) into a massive structure (with poor infiltration and drainage) (Figures 8-1 and 8-2).

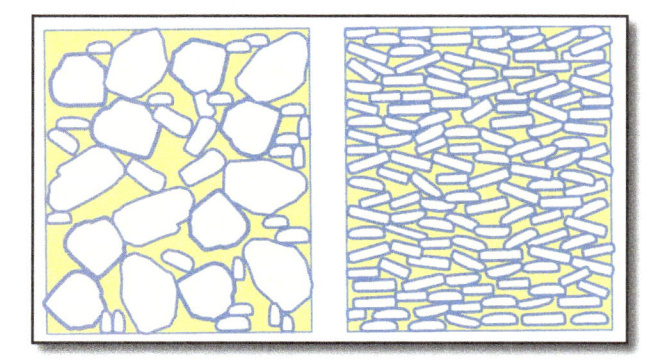

Figure 8-1 ▮ *Comparison of large pore space on non-compacted soil (Left) and compacted soil (Right).*

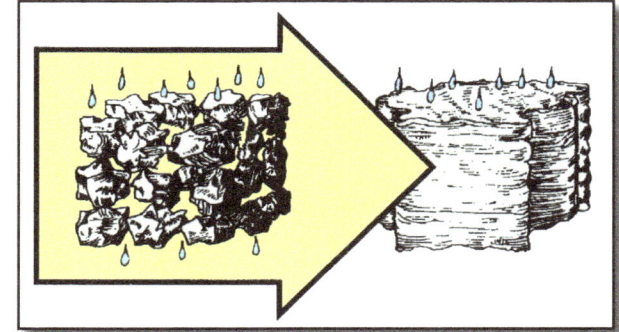

Figure 8-2 ▮ *Soil compaction can change a blocky or granular soil structure (with good air infiltration and drainage) into a massive structure with poor air infiltration and drainage. (Line drawing from the U.S. Department of Agriculture.)*

*Authors: David Whiting and Carl Wilson (Colorado State University Extension), and Jean Reeder, PhD (USDA-ARS, retired). Artwork by David Whiting unless otherwise noted.

Soil compaction is difficult to correct, thus efforts should be directed at preventing compaction. Soils generally become compacted during home construction. Foot traffic on moist soils is another primary compaction force in the home landscape. The impact of falling raindrops and sprinkler irrigation also compacts the surface of fine-textured clayey soils (Figure 8-3).

TECHNIQUES TO MINIMIZE SOIL COMPACTION
Adding Organic Matter

Ideally, cultivate organic soil amendments into the top six to eight inches of the soil. On compacted/clayey soils, anything less can lead to a shallow rooting system with reduced plant growth, lower vigor, and lower stress tolerance.

General application rate for organic soil amendments is based on the type of product and the salt content. Table 8-1 gives standard application rates for compost products. Compost made solely from plant residues (leaves and other yard wastes) is basically free of salt problems, so higher application rates are safe (Table 8-1).

Figure 8-3 ▮ *Foot traffic in the garden bed is a major source of compaction. The impact of raindrops and sprinkler irrigation also compacts fine-textured soils.*

Table 8-1. Routine Application Rate for Compost

Site	Incorporation Depth[b] (in inches)	Depth of Compost before Incorporation[a]	
		Plant-Based Compost and other compost known to be low in salts[c] (in inches)	Compost Made with Manure or Biosolids for which the salt content is unknown[d] (in inches)
One-time application such as lawn area	6–8	2–3	1
Annual application to vegetable and flower gardens—**first three years**	6–8	2–3	1
Annual application to vegetable and flower gardens—**fourth year and beyond**	6–8	1–2	1

[a]Three cubic yards (67 bushels) covers 1,000 square feet approximately 1 inch deep.

[b]Cultivate compost into the top 6 to 8 inches of the soil. On compacted/clayey soils, anything less may result in a shallow rooting depth predisposing plants to reduced growth, low vigor, and low stress tolerance. If actual incorporation depth is different than 6-8 inches, adjust the application rate accordingly.

[c]Plant-based composts are derived solely from plant materials (leaves, grass clippings, wood chips, and other yard wastes). Use this application rate also for other compost known, by soil test, to be low in salts.

[d]Use this application rate for any compost made with manure or biosolids unless the salt content is known, by soil test, to be low. Excessive salts are common in many commercially available products sold in Colorado. For a few products in the market with extremely high salt levels, even this low rate may be too high.

Compost that includes manure or biosolids as a component has a potential for high salts. Excessive salt levels are common in many commercially available products sold in Colorado. For compost made with manure or biosolids, the application rate is limited unless a soil test on that batch of product shows a low salt level. An amendment with up to 10 dS/m (10 mmhos/cm) total salt is acceptable if incorporated six to eight inches deep in a low-salt garden soil (less than 1 dS/m or 1 mmhos/cm). Any amendment with a salt level above 10 dS/m (10 mmhos/cm) is questionable.

> **Note:** dS/m or mmhos/cm is the unit used to measure salt content. It measures the electrical conductivity of the soil.

Do not leave compost in chunks, as this will interfere with root growth and soil water movement. As the soil organic content builds in a garden soil, the application rate should be reduced to prevent ground water contamination issues.

Manage Traffic Flow

Traffic over the soil is the major contributor to soil compaction. For example, a moist soil could reach seventy-five percent maximum compaction the first time it is stepped on and ninety percent by the fourth time it is stepped on.

Raised bed gardening techniques, with established walkways, eliminate compaction in the growing bed. On fine-textured clayey soils, limit routine traffic flow to selected paths.

Soils are more prone to compaction when wet. Soil water acts as a lubricant allowing the soil particles to readily slide together reducing large pore space.

Use Wood/Bark Chip Mulches

Some types of mulch effectively reduce the compaction forces of traffic. For example, three to four inches of wood or bark chips will minimize the effect of foot traffic.

Mulch minimizes the compaction forces of rainfall and sprinkler irrigation. On fine-textured clayey soil, keep garden beds mulched year round to minimize the compaction forces of summer and winter storms.

Organic mulches create an ideal home for beneficial earthworms and soil microorganisms, which play a key role in improving soil tilth.

Aerate Lawns and around Trees

In a lawn or tree's rooting area, where organic matter cannot be cultivated into the soil, reduce compaction with soil aeration. Make enough passes with the aerator to have plugs at two-inch intervals (Figure 8-4).

Avoid Excessive Cultivation

Avoid cultivating fine-textured clayey soils except to incorporate organic matter and fertilizer, and to prepare a seedbed. Use mulches to help manage weeds.

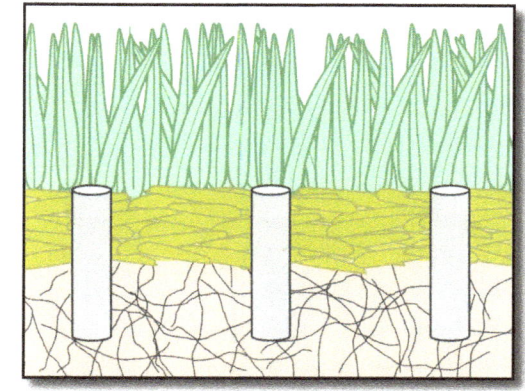

Figure 8-4 ▮ *Lawn aeration helps manage the impact of soil compaction if enough passes are made with the aerator to have plugs at two-inch intervals.*

Avoid Cultivating Overly Wet or Dry Soils

Never cultivate a clayey soil when wet as this will destroy soil structure; the dirt clods created by tilling wet clay may last for years. To check dryness, take a handful of soil and gently squeeze it into a ball. If the soil is dry enough to crumble, it may be cultivated. If the ball only reshapes with pressure, it is too wet for cultivation. On some

powdery

clayey soils, there may be only a few days (or even hours) between the time when the soil is too wet and too dry (too hard) to cultivate. In years when frequent spring rains prevent the soil from drying, planting will be significantly delayed.

Avoid Fill over Compacted Soil

Adding a thin layer of topsoil over compacted soil is a common practice that leads to future landscape management problems. It is often justified as "a way to get plants established." However, root growth into the compacted layer will be restricted or even minimal.

Do not create a layer with added topsoil that is of a different texture than the soil below. This change in texture (actually pore space) interferes with water movement and root spread. Where additional fill is desirable, lightly mix the fill with the soil beneath.

Long-term landscape management will be much easier by breaking up surface compaction with tilling and organic matter amendments. Before planting a yard, enhance soil organic content to the extent feasible. A minimum of three to four cubic yards of organic matter per 1,000 square feet is recommended.

What about Adding Sand?

Some gardeners try to improve fine-textured soils by adding sand. The practice may help the gardeners feel that they have done something, but it will have a limited or even negative impact on the soil. Adding sand to a clayey soil may actually reduce large pore space until enough medium to coarse size sand is added to reduce the clay content well below twenty percent. On clayey soils, this actually becomes a process of soil replacement rather than soil amendment. In some situations, adding sand to clayey soil can create concrete-like soil properties. To improve the soil, put efforts into adding organic matter, not sand.

What about Adding Gypsum?

Gypsum is a salt also known as calcium sulfate. When added to calcareous clayey soils (typical of Colorado), it simply increases the already high calcium content. Gypsum will not break up a compacted soil, but it can increase the soil's salt levels.

Gypsum is useful when a soil has a high sodium problem. Sodium has a unique physical characteristic that brings soil particles closer together, reducing large pore space and "sealing" soils to water penetration. The calcium in gypsum replaces the sodium on the soil cation exchange site, and the freed sodium is then leached out by heavy irrigation. Good quality (low salt) irrigation water must be available to successfully reclaim a high sodium soil.

The use of sulfur has also been incorrectly acclaimed to break up compacted soils. Over a period of time, sulfur may have an acidifying effect on a soil (if the soil is not high in lime). Adding sulfur to a calcareous soil only creates gypsum (calcium sulfate).

COMPACTION ISSUES AROUND TREES

The area where trees are especially intolerant of soil compaction is called the **Tree Protection Zone (TPZ)** or **Protected Root Zone**. This is typically about 40% larger than the dripline (reach of outer branches) area (Figure 8-5).

Figure 8-5 ■ *The* **Tree Protection Zone (TPZ)** *is a tree's rooting area particularly intolerant of any rooting issues, including soil compaction, adding soil, removal of soil, trenching, stockpiling of materials, and chemical spills.*

To approximate a tree's Tree Protection Zone:

1. Measure the tree's circumference (distance around the tree) in inches at 4.5 feet high.

2. Divide the number by 2.

3. This is the radius (distance out from the tree), in feet, of the Tree Protection Zone.

Example:

1. Circumference = 30 inches

2. $30 \div 2 = 15$

3. TPZ = 15 feet out from the tree

CHAPTER REVIEW Questions

1. In terms of pore space, water movement, and air infiltration, describe soil compaction.
2. Describe methods to help manage soil compaction.
   a. Adding organic matter
   b. Managing traffic flow
   c. Using mulch
   d. Aeration
   e. Avoid excessive cultivation
   f. Avoid cultivating overly wet or dry soil
   g. Avoid fill over compacted soil
3. What about adding sand and gypsum to deal with soil compaction?
4. Describe how to calculate the *Tree Protection Zone*.

Chapter

9*

Soil Amendments

TERMS

The term **soil amendment** refers to any material mixed into a soil. **Mulch** refers to a material placed on the soil surface. By legal definition, soil amendments make no legal claims about nutrient content or other helpful (or harmful) effects they will have on the soil and plant growth. In Colorado, the term **compost** is also unregulated, and could refer to any soil amendment regardless of microorganism activity.

By legal definition, the term **fertilizer** refers to soil amendments that guarantee the minimum percentages of nutrients (at least the minimum percentage of nitrogen, phosphate, and potash).

An **organic fertilizer** refers to soil amendments derived from natural sources that guarantee the minimum percentages of nitrogen, phosphate, and potash. These should not be confused with products approved for use by the U.S. Department of Agriculture (USDA) **National Organic Program**. The federal Certified Organic Label, *USDA Organic*, allows only certain regulated products as listed by the Organic Materials Review Institute (OMRI). For additional information on certified organic soil amendments and fertilizers, refer to the website at www.omri.org.

Many gardeners apply **organic soil amendments**, such as compost or manure, which most often do not meet the legal requirements as a "fertilizer" and generally add only small quantities of plant nutrients.

MANAGING SOIL TEXTURE AND STRUCTURE

Routine applications of organic matter should be considered an essential component of gardening and soil management. Organic matter improves the water- and nutrient-holding capacity of coarse-textured sandy soil.

---

*Authors: David Whiting, Carl Wilson, and Adrian Card (Colorado State University Extension), and Jean Reeder, PhD (USDA-ARS, retired).

On a fine-textured clayey soil, the organic matter over time glues the tiny clay particles into larger chunks or aggregates, creating large pore space. This improves water infiltration and drainage, air infiltration (often the most limiting aspect of plant growth), and allows for deeper rooting depths (allowing the plant to tap a larger supply of water and nutrients).

 Using **organic soil amendments** is a great way to turn otherwise useless products, like fall leaves and livestock manure, into compost for improving soil tilth.

 When using organic soil amendments, it is important to understand that only a portion of the nutrients in the product are available to plants in any one growing season. Soil microorganisms must process the organic compounds into chemical ions (NO_3^-, NH_4^+, HPO_4^{-2}, $H_2PO_4^-$, K^+) before plants can use them.

 Cultivate or hand-turn the organic matter thoroughly into the soil. Never leave it in chunks as this will interfere with root growth and water movement.

SELECTING SOIL AMENDMENT

Desired results—In selecting soil amendments, first consider the desired results. To improve the water and nutrient-holding capacity on sandy, gravelly, and decomposed granite soils, select well-decomposed materials like finished compost, aged manure, and peat. To improve aeration and infiltration (improve structure on clayey soils) select fibrous materials like composted wood chips, peat, and straw.

Potential for routine applications—Another important consideration is the potential for routine applications to improve the soil over time, as in a vegetable garden or annual flowerbed. In many landscape settings, the amendment is a one-time application added before planting lawns, perennials, trees, and shrubs (Table 9-1).

Longevity of the product merits consideration. Products that decompose rapidly (like grass clippings and manure) give quick results, while products that decompose slowly (like wood chips, bark chips, and peat) provide longer lasting results. For a quick improvement that lasts, use a combination of materials.

 Salts are a primary consideration. Products made with manure and/or biosolids are often very high in salts. Salt level may actually increase in the composting process, although water moving through the compost pile leaches out the salts. Use with caution! Plant-based products are naturally low in salts (Table 9-1).

Routine application rates depend on the salt potential of the material and the depth to which it will be cultivated into the soil. Table 9-1 gives standard rates.

In purchasing products, gardeners need to understand that there are no regulations about the quality of the product, salt content, or other beneficial or harmful qualities. Voluntary standards for bulk products may help in product evaluation. Use with caution! Many of the soil amendments sold in Colorado are high in salts!

Need for nitrogen fertilizer—Soil microorganisms release nitrogen tied up in organic matter over a period of time. Release rates from compost are very slow: over a period of years. The need for nitrogen fertilizer is based on the soil organic content. As the soil organic content increases, the need for fertilizer decreases (Table 9-2).

Over Amending

Over amending is a common problem. Some gardeners try to fix their soil limitations by adding large quantities of amendment in a single season. This can result in following problems:

- High salts
- High nitrogen
- Low nitrogen (from the tie up of nitrogen due to a carbon to nitrogen ratio imbalance)
- Holding too much water
- High ammonia (burns roots and leaves)

Table 9-1. Routine Application Rate for Compost

| Site | Incorporation Depth[b] (in inches) | Depth of Compost before Incorporation[a] | |
		Plant-Based Compost and other compost known to be low in salts[c] (in inches)	Compost Made with Manure or Biosolids for which the salt content is unknown[d] (in inches)
One-time application such as lawn area	6–8	2–3	1
	3–4	1–1.5	0.5
Annual application to vegetable and flower gardens—**first three years**	6–8	2–3	1
	3–4	1–1.5	0.5
Annual application to vegetable and flower gardens—**fourth year and beyond**	6–8	1–2	1
	3–4	1	0.5

[a]Three cubic yards (67 bushels) covers 1,000 square feet approximately 1 inch deep.

[b]Cultivate compost into the top 6 to 8 inches of the soil. On compacted/clayey soils, anything less may result in a shallow rooting depth predisposing plants to reduced growth, low vigor, and low stress tolerance. The 3- to 4-inch depth is shown as an illustration of how application rates need to adjust when the deep cultivation is not practiced.

[c]Plant-based composts are derived solely from plant materials (leaves, grass clippings, wood chips, and other yard wastes). Use this application rate also for other compost known, by soil test, to be low in salts.

[d]Use this application rate for any compost made with manure or biosolids unless the salt content is known, by soil test, to be low. Excessive salts are common in many commercially available products sold in Colorado. For a few products in the market with extremely high salt levels, even this low rate may be too high.

Table 9-2. Need for Nitrogen Fertilizer Based on Soil Organic Content

Soil Organic Content	Routine Application Rate for Gardens
1%	2 pounds actual N/1,000 square feet
2–3%	1 pound actual N/1,000 square feet
4–5%	0

Problems may also arise, over time, from the continual application of high rates. This can result in the following problems:

- High salts
- Excessive nitrogen, phosphate, and potash
- Ground water contamination
- Micronutrient imbalance

EVALUATING THE QUALITY OF ORGANIC AMENDMENTS

The quality of organic amendments can be determined by both visual evaluation and laboratory testing.

Visual Evaluation

Color—Dark brown to black.

Odor—Earthy, no ammonia smell.

Texture—Less than a half-inch particle size; lawn top dressing less than a quarter inch.

Foreign materials—Less than 1% and smaller than half-inch size.

Uniformity within the batch.

Consistency between different batches.

Raw materials—Concern of heavy metals (biosolids), human pathogens (manure), and salts (manure and biosolids).

Weed seeds—Test by germinating some material.

Laboratory Testing

C:N ratio—Less than 20 to 1 is acceptable; 10–12 to 1 is better.

Ash content—(This measurement of the mineral portion after the organic matter is burned off will determine if soil was a primary part of the mix.)

- Twenty to thirty percent is common
- Keep below 50%
- If greater than 50% to 60% it probably contains a lot of soil

Bulk density—Less than 1.0 gm/cc

pH—6.0 to 7.8

- May be higher in manure
- Near neutral (6.8 to 7.2) is best

Salts—Acceptable levels depend on use.

- Potting grade: <2.5 mmhos/cm
- Potting media amendment: <6 mmhos/cm
- Top dressing: <5 mmhos/cm
- Soil amendment in a low salt soil: <10 mmhos/cm

Sodium—Sodium adsorption ratio of less than 13%.

Ammonium—Less than one-third of total nitrogen. If higher, it may not be finished composting.

Heavy metals—A concern with biosolids but regulated by application permits.

Pesticide residues—Rarely a problem as they breakdown in composting.

Pathogens—*Escherichia coli* and other human pathogens are a potential in manure.

Nutrient content varies greatly from product to product.

Germination test—Seeds are started to check potential of toxic chemicals.

Stability (respiration rate) vs. maturity—Relative measurement of the completeness of microbial activity. If microorganisms are highly active, they may consume oxygen in the root zone causing root problems.

Bacterial and fungal diversity—Some compost has been found to suppress plant diseases. This is a high-tech field with commercial applications.

EXAMPLES OF SOIL AMENDMENTS

There are two broad categories of soil amendments: organic and inorganic. Organic amendments come from something that is or was alive. Inorganic amendments, on the other hand, are either mined or man-made. Organic amendments include sphagnum peat, wood chips, grass clippings, straw, compost, manure, biosolids, sawdust, and wood ash. Inorganic amendments include vermiculite, perlite, tire chunks, pea gravel, and sand.

Biosolids

Biosolids (sewage sludge) are a way to add slow release nutrients and organic matter to soil. They are available from some communities or sewer treatment districts in bulk and from garden stores in bags.

Some biosolids can be extremely high in salts. For example, tests on MetroGro report a salt content of 38.3 dS/m (38.3 mmhos/cm), which is considerably above acceptable tolerances for soil amendments. (A soil amendment above 10 dS/m is considered questionable.)

Biosolids typically have a five to six percent nitrogen content. Annual applications should be made only when the biosolids and garden soil are routinely tested for salt content.

Compost

Homemade or commercial compost is a great source of organic matter for the garden. Compost provides a food source for beneficial soil organisms, enhancing the soil food web and releasing nutrients over the long term. Composting is discussed in Chapter 10.

Green Manure and Cover Crops

A **cover crop** is simply a high number of plants (usually specific annual, biennial, or perennial grasses and/or legumes) growing and covering the soil surface. When the cover crop is tilled into the soil it is referred to as a **green manure** crop. Cover and green manure crops are discussed in Chapter 11.

Manure

For some gardeners, manure is readily available as a source of organic matter to build soils and add small amounts of nutrients. However, follow precautions with manure applications or they could become more detrimental than beneficial.

E. coli, *a Health Issue*

Due to the potential of transmitting human pathogens, such as *E. coli*, fresh manure should not be used on fruits and vegetables. On edible crops with soil contact (like carrots, beets, potatoes) fresh manure applications should be made at least four months prior to harvest. On other edible crops, fresh manure applications should be made at least three months prior to harvest. In other words, apply fresh manure only in the fall, but not in the spring or during the growing season. For additional details, refer to the Colorado State University Extension fact sheet #9.369, *Preventing* E. coli *From Garden to Plate*, available online at www.cmg.colostate.edu.

Nitrogen Release Rate Is Slow

Manure contains small amounts of plant nutrients and micronutrients. The nutrient composition of farm manure varies widely depending on bedding material, moisture content, exposure, and aging, even for the same species of animal. Where manure is routinely added, garden soils will likely have adequate phosphorus and potassium. Manure is a great source of micronutrients like zinc. Table 9-3 gives approximate amounts of nitrogen, phosphate, and potash.

The nitrogen in manure is not all available to growing plants the first year as much of it may be tied up in organic forms. Organic nitrogen becomes available to plants when soil microorganisms decompose organic compounds, such as proteins, and then convert the released N to NH_4. This process, known as **mineralization**, occurs over a period of years (Table 9-4).

The amount mineralized in the first year depends upon the manure source, soil temperature, moisture, and handling. In general, about thirty to fifty percent of the organic nitrogen becomes available the first year. Thereafter, the amount gradually decreases. A general estimate is fifty percent the first year, twenty-five percent the second year, twelve and one-half percent the third year, and so forth.

In gardens low in organic matter, it is common to find nitrogen deficiencies when the gardener relies solely on manure and/or compost due to the slow release rates. The gardener may need to supplement with a high nitrogen organic or manufactured fertilizer. As the soil builds in organic matter over the years, the problems with low nitrogen levels will improve.

Table 9-3. Approximate Nutrient Content of Manure*

Type		N	P_2O_5	K_2O
Beef	With bedding	1.1%	0.9%	1.3%
	Without bedding	1.1%	0.7%	1.2%
Dairy cattle	With bedding	0.5%	0.2%	0.5%
	Without bedding	0.5%	0.2%	0.5%
Horse	With bedding	0.7%	0.2%	0.7%
Poultry	With litter	2.8%	2.3%	1.7%
	Without litter	1.7%	2.4%	1.7%
Rabbit		2.0%	1.3%	1.2%
Sheep	With bedding	0.7%	0.5%	1.3%
	Without bedding	0.9%	0.6%	1.3%
Swine	With bedding	0.4%	0.4%	0.4%
	Without bedding	0.5%	0.5%	0.4%
Turkey	With litter	1.0%	0.8%	0.7%
	Without litter	1.4%	1.0%	0.9%

*At time of land application.

Sources: Colorado State University Extension Bulletin 552A, *Utilization of Animal Manure as Fertilizer*, except for rabbits from *Western Fertilizer Handbook* of the California Fertilizer Association.

Table 9-4. Approximate Percentage of Organic Nitrogen Mineralized in the First Year after Application

Manure Source	Percent of Organic Nitrogen Mineralized
Beef	35%
Dairy	35%
Horse	20%
Poultry	35%
Sheep	25%
Swine	50%

Source: Nebraska Cooperative Extension Bulletin EC89-117, *Fertilizing Crops with Animal Manures.*

Salts

Salt content may be high in fresh manure and decreases with exposure to rains and irrigation as salts are leached out. Continual and/or heavy applications of manure can lead to a salt buildup.

To avoid salt problems associated with the use of manure or compost made with manure, limit applications to 1 inch per year (when cultivated six to eight inches deep) and thoroughly cultivate the manure or compost into the soil. When cultivation is less than six to eight inches deep, adjust the application rate accordingly. Have a soil test for salt content before adding large amounts.

Manure or compost made with manure containing up to 10 dS/m (10 mmhos/cm) total salt is acceptable if cultivated six to eight inches deep into a low-salt garden soil (less than 1 dS/m or 1 mmhos/cm). Manure with a salt content greater than 10 dS/m (10 mmhos/cm) is questionable. Avoid use of manure on soils that are already high in salts (above 3 dS/m (3 mmhos/cm).

Note: dS/m or mmhos/cm is the unit used to measure salt content. It measures the electrical conductivity of the soil.

Other Disadvantages of Farm Manure

Other disadvantages of farm manure include the following:

- Potential burning of roots and foliage from high ammonia

- High potential for weed seeds

- Labor and transportation necessary to apply the manure to the garden

Horse manure is legendary for its potential to introduce a major weed seed problem into a garden. Composting the manure before application may kill the weed seeds if the pile heats to above 145°F and the pile is turned to heat process the entire product.

Feedlot manure is often high in salts if a salt additive is used in the livestock diet.

Poultry manure is particularly high in ammonia and readily burns if over applied. The ammonia content will be higher in fresh manure compared to aged manure. Laying hen manure can raise soil pH due to the calcium supplements in their diet.

Occasionally, gardeners may want to "fix" their soil by adding large quantities of organic matter at one time. Excessive applications of manure can lead to a reduction of plant growth due to excessive levels of nitrogen, ammonia burn, and salt damage to the roots.

Composted Manure

A growing trend in the use of manure is to compost it before application. Bagged composted manure is readily available in garden stores and nurseries. Composted manure has fewer odors. It is easier to haul and store than fresh manure because of the reduction in the weight of water and a decrease in overall volume by four to six fold. The composting process may kill weed seeds and pathogens if the pile heats above 145°F and the pile was turned to heat-process the entire product. Salts can be concentrated during composting as moisture is lost and volume is reduced. Many bagged manure products sold in Colorado are high in salts.

The nitrogen in composted manure will be primarily in stable organic forms, and first-year release rates will be significantly less than with fresh manure. For example, in composted dairy manure, only five to twenty percent of the nitrogen will be available the first year. In soils low in organic content, this can lead to a nitrogen deficiency unless an additional quick release nitrogen source is supplemented. This could be supplied with blood meal (approximately one to two pounds per 100 square feet) or with a manufactured fertilizer like ammonium nitrate (two-thirds cup per 100 square feet) or ammonium sulfate (one cup per 100 square feet). The ammonia content drops due to volatilization during composting, thereby reducing the burn potential.

Fresh manure without bedding materials is somewhat difficult to compost because of the high ammonia and moisture content. To speed decomposition and minimize foul odors from anaerobic decay, add some high carbon material, such as sawdust, straw, dried leaves, or wood chips. Depending on climatic conditions, on-farm manure composting takes six to more than ten weeks if turned weekly.

Peat

Sphagnum peat is a good soil amendment, especially for sandy soils, which will retain more water after sphagnum peat application. Sphagnum peat is generally acidic (i.e., low pH) and may help gardeners grow plants that require a more acidic soil. Sphagnum peat is harvested from bogs in Canada and the northern United States. The bogs can be revegetated after harvest and grow back relatively quickly in this moist environment. In recent years, however, harvest rates have become so high that it is raising questions on renewability.

Colorado mountain peat is *not* an acceptable soil amendment. It often is too fine in texture and generally has a higher pH. Mountain peat is mined from high-altitude wetlands that will take hundreds of years to rejuvenate, if ever. This mining is extremely disruptive to hydrologic cycles and mountain ecosystems.

Perlite and Vermiculite

Perlite and vermiculite are common inorganic amendments used in potting soils and planter mixes.

Vermiculite is made from heat-expanded silica (mica). It is used to increase pore space and has a high water-holding capacity. Perlite is made from heat-expanded volcanic rock. It is used to increase pore space and has a low water-holding capacity.

Worm Castings

Versatile worm castings can be used in potted plants, soil mixes, and in garden beds. Worm castings pose no threat of burning potted plants. Worms should have digested the batch of vermicompost for four months to ensure that microbial oxygen consumption has diminished sufficiently.

Red worm castings are the feces from compost worms. It has a slow release performance due to a mucus covering that is slowly degraded with microorganism activity. It contains highly available forms of plant nutrients that are water-soluble, has a neutral pH, and contains trace elements, enzymes, and beneficial microorganisms. The release time for nutrients is around 4 months. For continual release of nutrients, repeat application at four-month intervals.

Some batches made from livestock manure may have high salts depending if the animals producing the manure had access to a salt lick and if the compost maker leached them or not.

Castings can be applied as a top dressing, at a quarter inch deep, on potted plants, as twenty-five percent of a soil mix (1 to 4 mix) or tilled into a garden at one gallon per thirteen square feet or seven and one-half gallons (one cubic foot) per 100 square feet. Due to the high cost in Colorado, they are generally used in small gardens or potting mixes.

SUMMARY: CONSIDERATIONS IN SELECTING SOIL AMENDMENTS

Gardeners often inquire about the best amendments to use for their situation. There really is not a best. What is practical and available varies from gardener to gardener and within different communities. The important aspects are that: 1) soils are routine amended improving soil tilth and 2) the gardener follows the limitations for the specific product used. The following summarizes considerations in selecting soil amendments:

- Cost
  - —Local availability
  - —Cost of product
  - —Size of area to be treated (quantity needed)
  - —Depth of incorporation (application rate/quantity needed)
  - —Transportation costs
- Need for fertilizer after amending
  - —Soil organic content
- Precautions with specific products
  - —Salts (manure and biosolids)
  - —Weed seeds (manure and compost)
  - —Plant pathogens (compost)
  - —Human pathogens (manure)
- Alternatives to amending
  - —Potential to incorporate amendments
  - —Accepting a reduction in plant growth and vigor
  - —Accepting increased maintenance requirements
  - —Selecting plants more tolerant of poor soils
  - —Avoid crowding plants competing for limited soil resources
  - —Mulching with organic mulch to slowly improve soil over time
  - —Container and raised-bed gardening
  - —Preventing compaction forces

CHAPTER REVIEW
Questions

1. Define *soil amendment*, *mulch*, and *compost*.

2. Explain how organic soil amendments improve a clayey soil and a sandy soil.

3. Describe considerations in selecting a soil amendment as it relates to the following:

   a. Desired results

   b. Potential for routine application

   c. Longevity

   d. Salt

4. What is the routine application rate for soil amendments?

5. What is the precaution about over application at one time? What is the precaution about over amending over a period of years?

6. Explain the use and limitations on using manure as it relates to:

   a. *E. coli*

   b. Nitrogen release rates

   c. Salt

   d. Weed seeds

7. In summary, list considerations in selecting a soil amendment for a specific garden site.

Chapter

10*

~

Compost

COMPOST PRODUCTS

A home compost bin is an environmentally sound method to convert yard wastes into a valuable soil-building resource. Using compost has also been found to suppress some soil-borne plant disease pathogens in special situations.

Home compost has the advantage that the gardener controls what goes into the compost pile, and that weed seeds, diseased plants, and salt problems can be avoided.

There are many bagged compost-based products available in the retail trade. They could be any combination of plant residues, manure, and/or biosolids. Some products also have added rock minerals or animal byproducts. These bagged products will often be three times as expensive as manure and compost supplies available in bulk. They provide a long-term release of nutrients and add organic matter to soils, improving soil physical properties.

In Colorado (and most other states), compost is unregulated. Materials sold as "compost" could be anything (plant materials, manure, biosolids, animal byproducts, etc.) and could be at any stage of decomposition. Not all "composts" are good for the soil.

USING COMPOST

Application Rates and Salt Problems

General application rates for compost are based on the salt content of the compost and soil and on the depth to which it is cultivated into the soil. Ideally, cultivate the compost into the top 6 to 8 inches of the soil. On

---

*Authors: David Whiting and Carl Wilson (Colorado State University Extension), and Jean Reeder, PhD (USDA-ARS, retired).

compacted/clayey soils, anything less can lead to a shallow rooting system with reduced plant growth, lower vigor, and lower stress tolerance.

Table 10-1 gives standard application rates for compost. Compost made solely from plant residues (leaves and other yard wastes) is basically free of salt problems, and higher application rates are safe.

Compost that includes manure or biosolids as a component has a potential for high salts. Excessive salt levels are common in many commercially available products sold in Colorado. On compost made with manure or biosolids, application rate is limited unless a soil test on that batch of product shows a low salt level. An amendment with up to 10 dS/m (10 mmhos/cm) total salt is acceptable if incorporated six to eight inches deep in a low-salt garden soil (less than 1 dS/m or 1 mmhos/cm). Any amendment with a salt level above 10 dS/m (10 mmhos/cm) is questionable.

Note: dS/m or mmhos/cm is the unit used to measure salt content. It measures the electrical conductivity of the soil.

Compost needs to be thoroughly mixed into the upper six to eight inches of the soil profile. Do not leave compost in chunks, as this will interfere with root growth and soil water movement.

As the soil organic content builds in a garden soil, the application rate should be reduced to prevent ground water contamination issues. A soil test is suggested every four to six years to establish a baseline on soil organic matter content.

Table 10-1. Routine Application Rate for Compost

Site	Incorporation Depth[b] (in inches)	Depth of Compost before Incorporation[a]	
		Plant-Based Compost and other compost known to be low in salts[c] (in inches)	Compost Made with Manure or Biosolids for which the salt content is unknown[d] (in inches)
One-time application such as lawn area	6–8	2–3	1
Annual application to vegetable and flower gardens—first three years	6–8	2–3	1
Annual application to vegetable and flower gardens—fourth year and beyond	6–8	1–2	1

[a]Three cubic yards (67 bushels) covers 1,000 square feet approximately 1 inch deep.

[b]Cultivate compost into the top 6 to 8 inches of the soil. On compacted/clayey soils, anything less may result in a shallow rooting depth predisposing plants to reduced growth, low vigor, and low stress tolerance. If actual incorporation depth is different than 6-8 inches, adjust the application rate accordingly.

[c]Plant-based composts are derived solely from plant materials (leaves, grass clippings, wood chips, and other yard wastes). Use this application rate also for other compost known, by soil test, to be low in salts.

[d]Use this application rate for any compost made with manure or biosolids unless the salt content is known, by soil test, to be low. Excessive salts are common in many commercially available products sold in Colorado. For a few products in the market with extremely high salt levels, even this low rate may be too high.

Nitrogen Release

Typical nutrient content includes 1.5% to 3.5% nitrogen, 0.5% to 1% phosphate, and 1% to 2% potash, plus micronutrients. Thus, compost is more of a soil conditioner than a fertilizer. In gardens where compost is routinely added, phosphorus and potassium levels are likely to be adequate.

Like in other organic soil amendments, the nitrogen release rate from compost will be very slow (i.e., over a period of years). When the organic content is below five percent additional supplemental organic or manufactured nitrogen fertilizer may be needed.

- **5% organic matter**—Soils with five percent organic matter from compost will *mineralize* (release to plants) about 0.2 pound of nitrogen per 100 square feet per year. This should be sufficient for plant nitrogen needs.

- **3% organic matter**—Soils with three percent organic matter from compost will *mineralize* about 0.1 pound of nitrogen per 100 square feet per year. Additional nitrogen fertilizer will be needed for high nitrogen crops like broccoli, cauliflower, cabbage, potatoes, and corn.

- **1% organic matter**—In soils with one percent organic matter or less, the release rate for nitrogen will be too low to adequately provide the nitrogen needed for crop growth. A supplemental organic or manufactured nitrogen fertilizer may be needed.

Beware of Unfinished Compost

Finished compost is dark and crumbly, does not resemble the original contents, and has an earthy smell. Compost that has not thoroughly processed could be "hot" with high ammonia content. This could burn plant roots (when applied to the soil) or plant leaves (when applied as a mulch). If the compost smells like ammonia, it should be processed longer or be worked into the soil at least one month prior to seeding or transplanting in the area.

Compost maturity can be assessed in a laboratory by measuring the carbon dioxide (CO_2) production by the microorganisms living in the material. Lower levels of CO_2 indicate more mature compost (i.e., microbial activity is low because they have used the available nitrogen to decompose the carbon in the compost). Conversely, if microbes are producing CO_2, they are consuming oxygen (O_2). Unfinished compost can consume all of the O_2 from the root zone and greatly inhibit root growth. Finished compost should smell earthy, like healthy soil, not like ammonia.

When making compost at home, it is advisable to turn the pile when the compost heap temperatures drop below 120°F or when temperatures exceed 145°F. To encourage active microorganism processing, moisten the pile so that it feels like a wrung-out sponge. When temperatures do not rise above 120°F after turning to reheat, compost has entered its curing stage. It should cure for forty-five days before being considered finished. This curing period allows nitrogen and other chemical constituents to stabilize into forms suitable for placement around plants.

Weed Seeds and Diseased Plants

It is advisable not to compost diseased plants or weeds loaded with seeds. If the compost pile did not heat adequately or was not turned, the compost could be a source of weed seeds or plant disease pathogens. All parts of the compost should reach 145°F to kill weed seeds and plant disease pathogens. Because only the inner layers of the pile will reach this temperature, it is important that the outer layers are folded into the inner layers and the pile is allowed to reheat to 145°F. These temperatures must be maintained for at least three days. Temperatures of 130°F will somewhat minimize weed seeds and pathogens.

Livestock manure (horse, sheep, cow, swine, etc.) can also be a source of weed seeds in compost if the animals were fed hay with weed seeds or if seeds blew into a pile of manure.

Pet Manure

Do not add companion animal (cat, dog, etc.) feces to compost as this increases the incidence of nuisance animals rummaging through the compost pile and disease transmission to humans.

MAKING HOME COMPOST

Essential ingredients for the composting process include microorganisms, organic matter, water, and air (oxygen). The microbes that cause decomposition naturally occur on plant wastes. Compost starters or inoculums are not needed to start decomposition. The compost needs to be moist to the touch, but not soggy (excluding air). Air (oxygen) is essential for the microbes. Too fine of particle size, excessive water, large amount of soil, and packing of materials may decrease oxygen levels.

What Items Should and Should Not Be Composted?

Materials to Use

- Leaves
- Garden debris free of diseases and weed seeds (carrot tops, chopped corn stalks, pea vines, spent flowers, etc.)
- Weed, free of seeds
- Kitchen scraps—Free of meat, dairy, fats, and oils
- Shrub and tree pruning smaller than one-quarter inch in diameter
- Hay, straw, and other plant residues

Materials to Avoid

- Weeds with seeds—Seed may not be killed if compost piles does not heat to 145°F
- Diseased plants, including tomato and potato vines and potato peelings
- Tree branches greater than one-quarter inch in diameter—Large sizes should be run through a chipper first, as they will be very slow to decompose
- Meat and dairy products—Slow decomposition and attracts pests
- Fats, oils, and grease—Slow decomposition and attracts pests
- Kitchen scraps with meat, dairy, fats, oils, or grease
- Pet or human feces—May transmit diseases
- Synthetic or plastic fiber—Does not decompose
- Wood ash and lime—Drive up the pH of the soil

Materials to Use in Limitation

- Large amounts of grass clippings—Due to the small particle size and high nitrogen, they tend to smell unless mixed with brown materials. Rather, recycle the nutrients back to the grass by not bagging.
- Manure—Manures may contain strains of *Escherichia coli* and other bacteria that cause human illness. If manure is composted for food gardens, a 4-month curing process following composting is necessary to reduce pathogens.
- Large amounts of plants/weeds treated with pesticides (herbicides, insecticides, and fungicides)—Most pesticides readily break down in the composting process and present no threat as long the decomposition process had been completed.

- Large amounts of high tannin-containing leaves (oak and cottonwood) are also slow to decompose, but can be used in small quantities if chopped well and mixed with other materials.

- Large amounts of juniper, pine, spruce, and arborvitae pruning—Resins in these highly resinous wood and leaf prunings protect these materials from decomposition and extend the time needed for composting in comparison with other plant materials.

- Large amounts of paper products—Newsprint is best recycled through recycling collection operations rather than converted to compost. If paper is composted due to a shortage of dry materials, add no more than ten percent of the total weight of the material being composted. Higher amounts create imbalances in the carbon to nitrogen ratio. Do not use color printed glossy magazines as inks may not be safe as a soil additive.

- Large amounts of soil—Some gardeners like to sprinkle small amounts of soil into the compost bin as a source of microbes. However, this is not necessary as small amounts of soil are routinely added with the roots of weeds and other plants. Large amounts of soil increase weight, decrease oxygen infiltration, and can suffocate microorganisms. Soilless composting is often practiced.

What Is the Carbon to Nitrogen Ratio Talked about in Composting Literature?

For optimum processing, the ratio of carbon to nitrogen in the pile needs to be around 30 to 1. This is typically found with the combination of two parts green materials with one part brown materials. Compost piles too high in carbon will be slow to process or even not decompose. Piles too high in nitrogen develop strong ammonia odors.

Processing works best if the green and brown materials are mixed together before adding to the pile. An alternative is to layer the green and brown materials. Layers should not be more than two inches (fine materials) to six inches (coarse materials) deep.

When only brown materials are used, nitrogen fertilizer may be added to supply the needed nitrogen for decomposition. Standard rate is half a cup ammonium sulfate (or equivalent) per bushel of brown materials.

Table 10-2. Examples of Green and Brown Materials

Green Materials	Brown Materials
Vegetable wastes (12–20:1)	Dry leaves (30–80:1)
Coffee grounds (20:1)	Corn stalks (60:1)
Grass clippings (12-25:1)	Straw (40–100:1)
Cow manure (20:1)	Bark (100–130:1)
Horse manure (25:1)	Paper (150–200:1)
Poultry manure, fresh (10:1)	Wood chips and
Poultry manure, with litter (13–18:1)	sawdust (100–500:1)

What Is the Ideal Location of the Compost Bin?

Choose a composting site carefully. Considerations include the following:

- **Partial shade** avoids baking and drying in summer but provides some solar heating to start the composting action.

- **Wind protection** prevents too much moisture loss.

- **Water source** to keep the pile moist but not soggy.

- **City ordinances** often prohibit compost bins within ten to twenty feet of property lines.

- **Convenience** for loading and unloading of materials, but away from yard activities.

What Is the Ideal Size and Type of Compost Bin?

Structures are not necessary for composting but do help prevent wind and marauding animals from carrying away plant wastes. Open compost piles can be used in less-populated rural locales, but structures are a near-must in urban areas. Many composting structures can be purchased or built. They vary in how well they can be managed to meet the requirements for effective decomposition under Colorado environmental conditions.

Wire and wood structures are common for home composting. An inexpensive, easy-to-build type is made from hardware cloth (a stiff, lightweight wire mesh found in the fencing materials department at many hardware stores). A four foot high by thirteen foot length will make a small bin four feet across. Use wire to hold the length of hardware cloth into a round hoop. To unload the bin, unhook the wires holding the hoop in the circle.

Structures built of wire dry out faster, depending on exposure to drying winds. Plastic covers or tarps are often used to protect the outer lay from drying out. It is removed to add water and plant materials and to aerate the pile.

Wood structures do not dry as much but are generally more expensive to purchase or build. An inexpensive and easy-to-build bin is made with four wood pallets. Use wire and deck screws to fasten sides; add hinges to the front section to allow for easy access. (Figure 10-1).

An efficient wood structure is the three-chambered bin system that allows plant material to be aerated by turning it from one bin to the next as it decomposes. New materials are put in the first bin to begin decomposition. After a few weeks, it is turned to the second bin for active decomposition. As the process naturally slows, it is turned to the third bin for further curing (Figure 10-2).

Figure 10-1 ▮ *Simple compost bin made with wooden pallets for $5 to $25.*

Figure 10-2 ▮ *Three-chambered compost bin built for $200 to $300.*

Many brands of small home compost bins are available commercially typically running from $80 to over $100. Some are manufactured from recycled plastics. They work well for small yards that produce few plant wastes (Figure 10-3).

Size—A minimum volume of material is necessary to build up the heat necessary for efficient composting. When materials are heavy in green materials, keep the bin smaller to allow for better aeration. Three feet by three feet by three feet is considered minimum size to allow for heating. This small size may be adequate for small yards with limited materials to compost. If composting fall leaves and materials high in brown materials, a larger bin (five feet by five feet) may keep the processing going through the winter months.

In-ground pit composting presents problems with turning or aerating the plant material, and also can pool water, which leads to undesirable low oxygen conditions.

Figure 10-3 ▮ *Earth Machine™ compost bin.*

What Is the Routine Care of a Compost Pile?

The breakdown of organic yard wastes is a biological process dependent on microorganism activity. Like most living things, these microbes require favorable temperatures, moisture, oxygen, and nutrients.

Temperature—Plant-digesting microbes operate in a temperature range of 70°F to 140°F, but breakdown occurs slowly at the lower temperatures. Well-managed compost rapidly breaks down in summer when compost temperatures quickly reach 120°F to 130°F. If summer heat plus the heat produced by active microbes causes the temperature of the plant mass to exceed 160°F, the microbes will die. In Colorado winter temperatures, a well-constructed five foot by five foot pile will continue processing through the cold winter. Smaller piles will cool, stopping microbe activity and extending the time required to produce a finished product. In the spring, small piles may need to be turned and mixed with additional materials to enhance processing.

Moisture and oxygen—Moisture and oxygen are essential to microbial activity. In a region of limited rainfall such as Colorado, add moisture regularly to maintain composting. If parts of the composting material dry out, many microorganisms in the dry areas die. Even when moisture is added, the microbes that remain require time to multiply and resume plant digestion. The net result is slower composting. However, excess moisture displaces air and slows breakdown. Surplus water creates low oxygen conditions where certain microbes multiply and produce foul odors. The best description of the proper moisture level is moist or damp but not soggy. The entire mass of plant wastes should be moistened uniformly to the point where only a few drops of water can be squeezed from a fistful of plant material.

The size of plant particles that go into the compost also affects aeration. Large particles allow a lot of air to circulate around the plant chunks, but breakdown is slow because microbes can act only on the outside, not on the inside of the large chunks. Particles chopped into smaller chunks increase the surface area for microbes to operate. Particles chopped too small will compact and restrict air flow. Moderate-sized plant pieces of one-half to one and one-half inches are the best size to use and can be produced by hand or machine shredding. Chop woody materials into a smaller size. Leave soft plant parts in larger pieces for effective composting. Fluff or turn the material with a pitchfork or aerator tool at regular intervals to provide additional aeration and distribute microbes throughout the compost.

Nutrients—The microbes that break down plants use the plants for food. Nitrogen is the most important food nutrient, because a nitrogen shortage drastically slows the composting process. Woody and dried plant materials tend to contain little nitrogen in comparison to the total mass of the material. Green plant material, however, contains a high percentage of nitrogen. A mix of two parts green to one part brown material generally gives the best nitrogen balance. Add a plant fertilizer high in nitrogen when green materials are scarce.

Maintenance

- **How should materials be layered in the compost pile?**—Mixing of green and brown materials before placing it in the bin speeds decomposition. Otherwise, layer green and brown materials.

- **Does a compost pile require turning?**—No, but turning speeds decomposition and turns weed seeds and diseased plants into the center of the pile where temperatures are higher. Use an aeration tool to reach into the compost to lift and move plant materials. Turn the entire mass occasionally to provide uniform aeration.

- **What other routine care does a compost pile require?**—Keep it moist but not soggy. If overly wet, it will stink. Being dry stops the activity of microbes. The compost should feel moist to touch. But is too wet if more than a few drops of water can be squeezed out.

- **Will the compost process kill plant disease organisms and weed seeds?**—Only if the pile heats above 145°F and is turned regularly. Few home compost piles heat adequately, thus is it advisable not to compost weeds with seeds and diseased plants.

- **May fresh materials be added to the bin during processing?**—Yes, if small amounts are occasionally added. If a lot of materials are available, it would be better to start a new pile rather than combining a lot of fresh materials with nearly finished compost.

- **How can you tell when compost is finished?**—It will reduce in size by about half, will have lost the identity of the materials, and will smell "earthy." It typically takes 3 to 9 months, depending on type of materials, climatic conditions, and tending.

Compost Troubleshooting

Table 10-3. Compost Troubleshooting

Problem	Cause	Solution
Rotten odor	Anaerobic conditions (the lack of oxygen) • Excess moisture • Compaction • Small particle size	• Turn the pile • Make smaller pile • Add dry porous materials
Ammonia odor	Too much nitrogen (low C:N ratio)	Mix in brown materials Note: If compost high in ammonia is used as mulch, it may burn tender foliage. If mixed into soil as an amendment, it can burn roots.
Outside couple of inches is dry	Dry Colorado air	Water regularly and cover outer edge with tarp.
Low temperature	• Pile too small • Insufficient moisture • Poor aeration • Lack of nitrogen • Cold weather	• Make larger pile • Add water when turning pile • Turn pile to aerate • Mix in green materials or add N fertilizer • Increase pile size in winter
Pests (rats, bears, raccoons, insects)	Presence of meat, dairy, or fatty wastes	Do not compost kitchen scraps with meat, dairy, fats, oils, or grease.

CHAPTER REVIEW
Questions

1. Describe the use and limitation of compost at it relates to the following:

   a. Salts

   b. Nitrogen release

   c. Weeds and disease problems

2. What should and should not be put into a compost pile?

3. In composting, what is the carbon to nitrogen ratio? To achieve the ideal ratio, what is the routine combination of green materials to brown materials?

4. Explain basic procedures for making home compost.

Chapter

11*

Cover Crops and Green Manure Crops

A **cover crop** is simply a high numbers of plants, usually specific annual, biennial, or perennial grasses and/ or legumes, growing and covering the soil surface. When the cover crop is tilled into the soil it is referred to as a **green manure** crop.

BENEFITS
Cover Crops

Cover crops can protect the soil from wind and water erosion, suppress weeds, fix atmospheric nitrogen, build soil structure, and reduce insect pests.

Erosion protection—The primary erosive force for Colorado is wind. Winter winds are especially destructive, carrying away small particles of topsoil from the soil surface. A thick stand of a cover crop protects the soil surface from wind erosion, and the cover crop's roots can hold soil in place against water erosion during heavy downpours.

Weed suppression—Cover crops left in place for part or all of a growing season can suppress annual and some perennial weeds. Among the grasses, annual rye has alleopathic properties that prevent weed seeds from germinating and suppress weed seedlings around the root zone of the rye.

Nitrogen fixation—Legumes, inoculated with their specific *Rhizobium* bacteria, will take nitrogen out of the air (present in the soil) and store it in their plant tissues via nodules on the roots of the legume. Some of this nitrogen is available as roots die, but the majority becomes available when the legume is tilled under (green manure).

---

*Author: Adrian Card, Colorado State University Extension.

Soil structure creation—Plant roots exude a sticky substance then glue soil particles together, creating structure. Grasses are exceptional in their ability to do this.

Insect pest reduction—Cover crops encourage beneficial insect populations, often minimizing or eliminating the need for other insect control measures.

Green Manure Crops

Green manuring enhances soil fertility and soil structure by feeding soil organisms and gluing together soil particles into aggregates.

Soil fertility—When fresh plant material decomposes in the soil, its carbon-to-nitrogen ratio becomes low, allowing the nitrogen to be easily released into the soil chemistry by bacteria. Nitrogen accumulation is greater with legumes, which have nitrogen-fixing *Rhizobium* bacteria growing in nodules on the legume roots (Table 11-1). Notice the lower figure for rye.

Table 11-1. Nitrogen Accruement of Selected Cover Crops

Cover Crop	Nitrogen Accruement*
Hairy vetch	3.2 lbs/1,000 ft^2
Crimson clover	2.6 lbs/1,000 ft^2
Austrian winter pea	3.3 lbs/1,000 ft^2
Winter (annual) rye	2.0 lbs/1,000 ft^2

* Nitrogen accumulated in growing crop prior to tilling under.
Source: *ATTRA: Overview of Cover Crops and Green Manures.*

Soil structure—Microorganisms decomposing plant material and the plant material itself produce substances that glue soil particles together. These substances include slime, mucus, and fungal mycelia, which contain gums, waxes, and resins. These aggregate soil particles, thereby enhancing the tilth, porosity, and water-holding capabilities of soil.

BASIC RECIPES FOR COVER CROPS AND GREEN MANURE CROPS IN A GARDEN

Spring Planted

Most gardeners do not have enough space to forfeit to a cover crop for an entire growing season. However, if you do, a spring seeded clover would give your soil a great boost. Some seed companies will "rhizo-coat" seed with the specific *Rhizobium* for you. If not, apply *Rhizobium* as specified on the bag. It comes in a black powder specific to the species of clover. It also has a definite shelf life, so check the expiration date. Broadcast the seed/*Rhizobium* mix at a specified rate after the last frost with a handheld broadcaster (often used with pelleted fertilizer) into a loose seedbed and incorporate shallowly and water until germinated. Monitor water as you would in a lawn.

Till under at least two weeks prior to planting. Decomposing plant material consumes soil oxygen and can create plant health problems if not tilled in ahead of time. More than one tilling may be necessary to get an acceptable kill of the clover.

Fall Planted for Spring Till

Most will opt for a fall cover crop tilled under as a spring green manure. Seeding dates should be done by mid-October at the latest. Mid-September is ideal on the Front Range. In mountain elevations, plant in August or earlier. A rye/Austrian winter pea or rye/hairy vetch mixture will overwinter in Colorado. Hairy vetch is hardier than winter pea. Rye is extremely winter hardy. Prepare as above and broadcast at the rates in Table 11-2.

Table 11-2. Seeding Rates for Selected Winter Cover Crops

Cover Crop	Ounces per 100 Square Feet	Pounds per 1,000 Square Feet
Winter rye	4–6	2.5–3.75
Austrian Winter pea	4–6	2–4
Hairy vetch	2–3	1–2

Source: *Managing Cover Crops Profitability,* Sustainable Agriculture Network.

Overwintered cover crops become a veritable salad bar to geese and deer. A cover crop that is well established prior to winter temperature extremes should rebound from wildlife grazing in late winter/early spring.

Till the cover crop in mechanically or turn it under with a spade a month before you plan to plant/seed into that area. Decomposing plant material consumes soil oxygen and can create plant health problems if not tilled in ahead of time.

LANDSCAPE USES

Bare soil presents erosion and aesthetic issues for homeowners. During droughty periods, watering restrictions and the lack of natural precipitation may make turf establishment difficult or impossible. A temporary cover crop or long-term xeric grass may be the answer.

In this scenario, the homeowner has to understand that a cover crop will not look or feel like a healthy Kentucky bluegrass lawn, but should satisfy the need to cover the soil.

Annual Species Options

These are cool season grains that should be broadcast at two to three pounds per 1,000 square feet in February or March. Natural precipitation may be sufficient to get them established. They are suited for non-traffic areas, as they will grow to two feet tall and brownout in the heat of summer. The sterile triticale will not produce viable seeds so may be a good idea for areas that will eventually be put into turf or garden space. Winter rye seeds can be a weed problem in seeded turf grass and gardens (Table 11-3).

Table 11-3. Annual Species

Name	Bunch or Sod	Cool or Warm Season	Annual or Perennial	Turf?	Reseed?
Winter rye	Bunch	Cool	Annual	No	Yes
Pioneer sterile triticale	Bunch	Cool	Annual	No	No

Perennial Species Options

These are non-native grasses often used on roadsides for stabilization and cover. They are perennial and will be persistent (i.e., difficult to kill) once they are established. Water requirements for both are nine to ten inches of precipitation per year. Streambank wheatgrass has a slightly higher water requirement but is tolerant of very clayey soils, unlike crested wheatgrass. Broadcast in February or March at three to five pounds per 1,000 square feet (Table 11-4).

Table 11-4. Perennial Species

Name	Bunch or Sod	Cool or Warm Season	Annual or Perennial	Turf?	Reseed?
Streambank wheatgrass	Sod	Cool	Perennial	Yes	Some
Crested wheatgrass	Bunch	Cool	Perennial	Yes	Some

Native Species Options

These have the lowest water requirements at eight inches of precipitation per year and should be considered for areas of a landscape that are being converted to xeric management. This is a long-term management decision as the price of these seeds is more than the other options. These grasses will not feel like Kentucky bluegrass and will brownout like other cool season grasses. Seed as per perennial species options specifications. Seed for native species will be available from local seed sources, such as Pawnee Buttes Seeds (Table 11-5).

Table 11-5. Native Species

Name	Bunch or Sod	Cool or Warm Season	Annual or Perennial	Turf?	Reseed?
Indian ricegrass	Bunch	Cool	Perennial	No	Some
Squirreltail bottlebrush	Bunch	Cool	Perennial	No	Some

ESTABLISHMENT AND CARE

Before seeding—Prepare a seedbed for fine grass seed, ideally amending the soil with compost and tilling as deeply as possible. If possible, fence off the area from traffic.

Seeding—Water area prior to seeding if possible to establish ample soil moisture levels.

Broadcast the correct amount of seed per area onto a loosely tilled, fine (no soil pieces bigger than a quarter inch) seedbed. Shallowly incorporate seed with garden rake (not a leaf rake) to a depth of one-quarter to three-quarters inches deep.

For larger areas, consider hydromulching the seed. This will save time and increase germination of seeds.

After seeding—Consider laying a thin layer (less than one inch deep) of seed-free straw to hold in moisture and increase germination and survival of grass seedlings. Bird netting over the straw fastened to the ground with landscape fabric staples will keep the straw from blowing away.

Check moisture levels in the upper inch of soil at least every other day (soil should feel as moist as a wrung out sponge) and water if necessary (and if possible).

Mowing—If necessary, mow as high as possible.

Removing cover crops—For winter rye, either till under, mow and mulch heavily, or spray herbicide before it goes to seed. A seed bank can be sodded over or watered, germinated, and killed. Perennial grasses can be either mowed and mulched heavily prior to sodding, sprayed with herbicide and sodded, or sprayed with herbicide, tilled, and seeded.

1. What are cover crops and green manure crops?

2. List benefits of cover cropping and green manuring.

Chapter

12*

Mulching

TERMS

The term **mulch** refers to a material placed on the soil surface. By contrast, a **soil amendment** refers to a material mixed into a soil.

BENEFITS OF MULCHING

Depending on materials used, mulches have many benefits, including the following:

- Reduces evaporation from soil surface, cutting water use by twenty-five to fifty percent

- Organic mulches promote soil microorganism activity, which in turn improves soil tilth and helps lessen soil compaction

- Stabilizes soil moisture

- Prevents soil compaction

- Controls weeds, which rob soil moisture

- Moderates soil temperature extremes

- Controls erosion

- Gives a finished look, improving aesthetic quality

*Authors: David Whiting and Carl Wilson (Colorado State University Extension), and Jean Reeder, PhD (USDA-ARS, retired). Artwork by David Whiting.

EDGING AND SOIL GRADE

It is a common practice to add mulching materials above grade level. Without a defined edge, the mulch may readily spread off the bed onto lawns or sidewalks, creating a mowing or trip hazard (Figure 12-1).

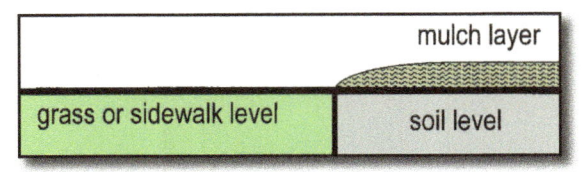

Figure 12-1 ■ *Mulch added above grade spills out onto the lawn or sidewalk.*

An effective alternative is to drop the soil level on the mulch bed three inches so the top of the mulch is at grade level. However, ensure that the mulched bed does not fill with water draining from higher areas (Figure 12-2).

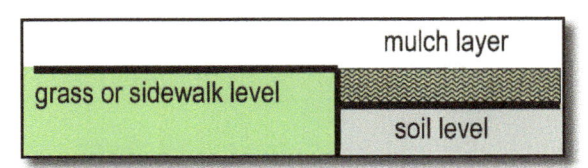

Figure 12-2 ■ *To keep mulch in place, drop the soil level in the mulch bed so the top of the mulch is at the grass or sidewalk level.*

An effective alternative is to round down the soil level along the edge of the bed. This gives a nice finished edge at grade level and creates a raised bed effect for the flowerbed (Figure 12-3).

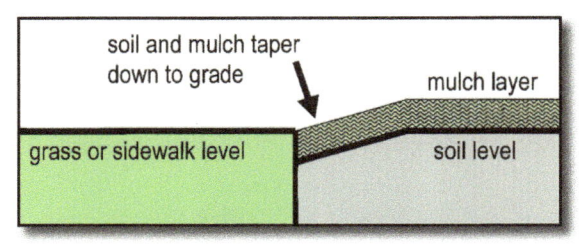

Figure 12-3 ■ *An alternative is to taper the soil level along the edge of the bed.*

WOOD/BARK CHIP MULCH
Benefits

Wood or bark chip mulch is great around trees, shrubs, perennials, and small fruits (Figure 12-4). A wood/bark chip mulch creates a favorable environment for earthworms and soil microorganisms. Over time, this helps reduce soil compaction.

In perennial and shrub beds, wood/bark chips can reduce the need for irrigation by as much as fifty percent. Mulching materials that mesh together are more effective at reducing water evaporation from the soil. Under acute water restrictions, gardeners with wood/bark chip mulch have been incorrectly accused of illegally irrigating because their plants are still faring well compared to the neighbors!

When placed on the soil surface as mulch, wood/bark chips do not tie up soil nitrogen. However, incorporating wood/bark chips into a soil can create a nitrogen deficiency due to a carbon-to-nitrogen imbalance and can interfere with seedbed preparation. It takes ten or more years for chips to decompose in a typical soil. The use of fine chips or sawdust as mulch can tie up soil nitrogen and can decrease soil oxygen levels.

Wood/bark chips are not recommended in vegetable or annual flowerbeds where the soil is routinely cultivated to prepare a seedbed.

Figure 12-4 ▮ *Wood/bark chip mulch in the perennial and shrub bed greatly enhances soil tilth over time.*

Product Selection

There is a wide variety of wood and bark chip products available for mulching. Wood chips have the advantage that they decompose faster, enriching the soil. Bark chips decompose slower, requiring less frequent replenishment. Primary selection is based on desired appearance and cost. Some can be colored to match the paint color of the home or landscape features.

Cedar mulch—A number of references discuss the phytotoxicity of cedar when used as mulch around young plants. Most of the information, however, refers to the use of cedar sawdust (smaller particles with more exposure to the surrounding plants and their roots) rather than chips that are typically used as mulch.

The other issue, and probably the more relevant question, is what plant is actually referred to as "cedar." In Colorado, we have very few true cedars (the genus of true cedar is *Cedrus*). What most people call "red cedar" is either a juniper (i.e., eastern red cedar, *Juniperus virginiana*) or arborvitae (i.e., Western red cedar, *Thuja* spp.). Neither of these have toxic qualities for young plants when used as a mulch.

Most "cedar" mulch in Colorado (unless they are bagged and shipped from another part of the country) will not be the true cedar. They will most likely be either the juniper or arborvitae, which are not toxic when used as mulch.

General Use

Depth

The desired depth of wood/bark chips depends on chip size. Smaller size chips should not exceed a one- to two-inch depth. Larger chips are typically applied at two to three inches deep. Thicker layers may reduce soil oxygen. Additional mulch needs to be added every few years to bring the mulch depth back to the desired amount.

With the larger chips from the tree pruning industry, three to four inches are needed for effective weed control and to eliminate the compaction forces of foot traffic. It is common to see where the mulch is too thin and does not provide for weed control and compaction management.

On compacted and/or clayey soil, three to four inches of wood/bark chips may reduce water evaporation from the soil surface so much that susceptible plants develop root rots in wet years or under frequent irrigation.

In wet soil situations, mulching may be undesirable as it may help hold excessive water leading to root rots.

Around Trees

Wood/bark chip mulch is great for trees and shrubs, protecting trees from lawnmower damage. However, do not make "mulch volcanoes" around tree trunks by applying chips up against a tree's trunk. Wet chips piled up against the trunk can cause bark problems and interfere with the natural trunk taper, making the tree more prone to wind throw. Keep the mulch back at least six inches from the trunk (Figure 12-5).

Windy Areas

Wood/bark chips move in strong winds. It is reported that the shredded-type chips are somewhat more wind resistant. Nevertheless, wood/bark chips often do not work in open windy areas. Wood/bark chips also float, and they are not suited to areas with standing water or heavy surface runoff during heavy rainfall.

Figure 12-5 ▍ *Never make a "mulch volcano." It leads to decay of the bark and interferes with trunk taper. Keep mulch back six inches from the trunk.*

Chips over Landscape Fabric or Newspapers

It is a common procedure to apply mulch over a landscape fabric to reduce weed growth. However, the chips will give a greater improvement on soil tilth where they can break down into the soil without the fabric layer in between.

Weed growth in a mulch bed is a problem when the mulch is not at an adequate depth! As an alternative to the weed fabric, maintain a proper mulch depth to manage weeds coming for seed. Weed seeds that germinate above the fabric layer will be difficult to pull.

Converting Lawn to a Mulch Area

In situations where a lawn is being converted to mulched beds, spray the lawn out first with Round-up (glyphosate). Apply the mulch after the lawn has died. Do not put mulch over a growing lawn.

Cultivating Chips into the Soil

Do not cultivate wood/bark chips into the soil. The high carbon content of the wood product ties up soil nitrogen. Chips create soil texture interfaces that interfere with air and water movement and root spread. Chips decompose only slowly, taking approximately ten years. Wood/bark chips on the surface do not tie up soil nitrogen. However, do not use sawdust for mulch as it may tie up soil nitrogen. Wood products need to be composted before use as a soil amendment.

GRASS CLIPPING MULCH

Grass clippings make good mulch when applied in thin layers and allowed to dry between applications. Add additional layers each week as the lawn is mowed. With a few layers, weed seed germination will be checked. Grass clippings decompose rapidly, requiring additional layers during the growing season. A grass clipping mulch recycles its nutrients into the garden bed.

Do not apply fresh grass in thick layers as it will mat, produce foul odors, reduce air and water infiltration, and even become hydrophobic.

Do not use clippings from lawns that have been treated with herbicides or other pesticides for at least four weeks after application.

Grass clippings are a good choice in vegetable and annual flowerbeds that receive annual cultivation to prepare a seedbed. Around leafy vegetables (such as lettuce, spinach, chard), carefully place the mulch at the base of the plant to avoid getting dry grass clippings stuck to the lettuce leaf (Figure 12-6).

Newspaper under Mulch

Newspapers make a good underlay for a wood/bark chips or grass mulch. The newspaper shuts out light, giving a quick stop to germinating weed seeds that were brought to the soil surface during cultivation for seedbed preparation. Newspaper shades out many, but not all, growing weeds.

Apply newspapers only one to two sheets thick and top with wood/bark chips or grass to hold it in place. As newspapers blow away with the slightest breeze, apply it just before covering with chips or grass. Do not use thick layers of newspaper; the high carbon content can tie up soil nitrogen (Figure 12-7).

In situations where the newspaper is wet from rains or sprinkler irrigation, it rapidly decomposes. Where it remains dry (like over a drip irrigation system), it may still be intact at the end of the growing season. Any remaining newspaper may be cultivated into the soil in the fall.

Newspapers are printed with soy-based inks and are safe for use. Do not use glossy magazines as their inks may contain heavy metals or other soil contaminants.

ROCK MULCH

Rock over landscape fabric is a common mulching material often considered as low maintenance. It is the preferred material for non-plant areas. Rock mulch has the advantage over wood/bark chips that it does not blow, float, or require additional amounts every few years as it decomposes (Figure 12-8).

Pea gravel over a weed mat helps reduce evaporation from the soil surface. The use of small size rock, such as pea gravel, has been reported to encourage plant growth due to warmer soil temperatures in the springtime. However, in Colorado's climate this may encourage early growth that is sensitive to late spring frosts.

Rock mulch may be desirable in some specialty gardens, like a cacti garden, rock garden, or alpine garden.

Rock mulch can become a heat sink, creating a significantly warmer afternoon, evening, and nighttime microclimate. Outdoor people space adjacent to rock mulch will be warmer and less comfortable for summertime afternoon and evening use. In planting beds, rock mulch increases temperatures and may increase water requirements.

Figure 12-6 ▮ *Grass clippings are great for the vegetable garden and around annual flowers. Directly from the bag, place them around the plants in thin layers, allowing each layer to dry before adding more.*

Figure 12-7 ▮ *Use newspaper under the grass or wood/bark chip mulch to shut out light and stop weed seed germination. Apply it only in thin layers to prevent a carbon-to-nitrogen imbalance.*

Figure 12-8 ▮ *Rock mulch is great for non-crop areas.*

Rock mulch may interfere with shrub rejuvenation. Because shrubs in rock mulch cannot be effectively renewed by rejuvenation pruning, they are replaced when the shrubs become overgrown and woody. In this situation, it would be better to consider the rock mulch as "deferred maintenance" rather than "low maintenance" (Figure 12-9).

Avoid using rock mulch beds adjacent to lawn areas. Rocks in the lawn are a safety issue with lawnmowers and ruin mower blades. For safety, avoid using rock mulch in children's play areas.

Rock over **black plastic** is very undesirable for planting areas. The plastic will reduce air infiltration into the soil and create soil moisture problems. The soil is often very dry or very wet under plastic.

Figure 12-9 ▮ *Rock mulch interferes with shrub rejuvenation pruning. Here a wood/bark chip mulch will help enhance soil tilth.*

SUMMARY: CONSIDERATIONS IN SELECTING MULCH

Gardeners often inquire about the best mulching material for their situation. There really is not a best. What is practical and available varies from gardener to gardener and within different communities. The following summarizes considerations in selecting mulches:

- Site
  - —Continual plant cover: trees, shrubs, perennials, and small fruit
  - —Annual soil preparation: annual flowers and vegetables
  - —Non-crop areas
  - —Specialty crops (rock garden, cacti garden, alpine garden)
- Function
  - —Soil improvement potential
  - —Frequency of reapplication
  - —Depth needed for weed management
  - —Depth needed to minimize soil compaction
  - —Appearance
  - —Heat sink
  - —Off-site movement by wind, water, and gravity
  - —Safety (children, lawnmowers)
- Cost
  - —Local availability
  - —Cost of product
  - —Appearance
  - —Size of area to be treated (quantity needed)
  - —Depth of application (quantity needed)
  - —Transportation costs

CHAPTER REVIEW
Questions

1. Describe the benefits of using mulch.

2. Describe the use and limitations of wood/bark chip mulch.

3. Describe the use and limitations of grass clipping mulch.

4. Describe the use and limitations of rock mulch.

Chapter

13*

Fertilization

PLANT NUTRITION

Fertility and Fertilization

Many people confuse plant nutrition with plant fertilization. Plant nutrition refers to the need for basic chemical elements for plant growth.

The term "fertilization" refers to the application of plant nutrients to supplement the nutrients naturally occurring in the soil. Nutrients may be applied as commercial manufactured fertilizers, organic fertilizers, and/or other soil amendments. Organic fertilizers and soil amendments are typically low in plant-available nutrient content.

Adequate soil fertility is only one of the many soil-related growth factors. Fertilizers will increase desirable plant growth only if the plant is deficient in the nutrient applied and other growth factors are not also significantly limiting plant growth. Fertilization will not compensate for poor soil preparation, the lack of water, weed competition, and other non-nutrient growth limiting factors! Fertilization will not enhance desired growth if the nutrients applied are not deficient.

From the nutritional perspective, a plant cannot tell if applied nutrients come from a manufactured fertilizer or a natural source. Plants use nutrients in ionic forms. Soil microorganisms must break down organic soil amendments, organic fertilizers, and many manufactured fertilizers before the nutrients become usable by plants.

*Authors: David Whiting and Carl Wilson (Colorado State University Extension), and Jean Reeder, PhD (USDA-ARS, retired). Artwork by David Whiting.

From a nutritional perspective, the primary difference between manufactured and organic soil amendments/organic fertilizers is the speed at which nutrients become available for plant use. For manufactured fertilizer, their release is typically, but not always, a few days to weeks. Some are specially formulated as "controlled release," "slow release," or "time release" products that release over a period of months. With natural-organic fertilizer, nutrients typically become available over a period of months or years. However, there are exceptions to this general rule. The high salt content of some manufactured fertilizers and some organic soil amendments could slow the activity of beneficial soil microorganisms.

Benefits of organic fertilizers and soil amendments include improvements in soil tilth (suitability of the soil to support plant growth). This should not be confused with fertilization, a distinctly different soil management objective. Organic soil amendments are typically low in nutrient content.

Remember that fertility is only part of the soil's role in supporting plant growth. The organic content of the soil also directly affects plant growth due to its influence on soil tilth and the activity of beneficial soil microorganisms. Relying solely on manufactured fertilizers is not recommended as this does not support good soil tilth.

Plant Nutrients

Plants need seventeen elements for normal growth. Carbon, hydrogen, and oxygen come from the air and water. Soil is the principle source of other nutrients. **Primary nutrients** (nitrogen, phosphorus, and potassium) are used in relatively large amounts by plants, and often are supplemented as fertilizers.

Secondary nutrients (calcium, magnesium, and sulfur) are also used in large amounts but are typically readily available and in adequate supply. **Micronutrients** or trace elements are needed only in small amounts. These include iron, zinc, molybdenum, manganese, boron, copper, cobalt, and chlorine (Table 13-1).

Table 13-1. Essential Plant Nutrients

Nutrient	Ions Absorbed by Plants
Structural elements	
Carbon, C	CO_2
Hydrogen, H	H_2O
Oxygen, O	O_2
Primary nutrients	
Nitrogen, N	NO_3^-, NH_4^+
Phosphorus, P	$H_2PO_4^-$, HPO_4^{-2}
Potassium, K	K^+
Secondary nutrients	
Calcium, Ca	Ca^{+2}
Magnesium, MG	Mg^{+2}
Sulfur, S	SO_4^{-2}
Micronutrients	
Boron, B	$H_2BO_3^-$
Chlorine, Cl	Cl^-
Cobalt, Co	Co^{+2}
Copper, Cu	Cu^{+2}
Iron, Fe	Fe^{+2}, Fe^{+3}
Manganese, Mn	Mn^{+2}
Molybdenum, MO	MoO_4^{-2}
Zinc, Zn	Zn^{+2}

Roots take up nutrients primarily as **ions** dissolved in the soil's water. The ions may be positively charged (**cations**) or negatively charged (**anions**). The nutrient ion soup in the soil's water is in a constant state of flux as the variety of ions dissolve in and precipitate out of solution.

Clay particles and organic matter in the soil are negatively charged, attracting the positively charged cations (like ammonium, NH_4^+, and potassium, K^+) and making the cations resistant to leaching. Negatively charged anions (like nitrate, NO_3^-) are prone to leaching and can become a water pollution problem. Both ammonium and nitrate are important plant nitrogen sources and are commonly found in salt forms in fertilizers.

The **cation exchange capacity (CEC)** is a measurement of the soil's capacity to hold cation nutrients. More precisely, it is a measurement of the capacity of the negatively charged clay and organic matter to attract and hold positively charged cations. CEC is useful in comparing the potential for different soils to hold and supply nutrients for plant growth.

WESTERN SOILS AND PLANT NUTRITIONAL NEEDS

Nitrogen

Nitrogen is the one nutrient most often limiting plant growth. The need for nitrogen varies from plant to plant. For example, tomatoes and vine crops (cucumbers, squash, and melons) will put on excessive vine growth at the expense of fruiting with excess nitrogen. Whereas potatoes, corn, and cole crops (cabbage, broccoli, and cauliflower) are heavy feeders and benefit from high soil nitrogen levels. Bluegrass turf and many annuals also benefit from routine nitrogen applications. Trees and shrubs have a low relative need for soil nitrogen. Colorado soils benefit from nitrogen fertilization of the right amount and frequency to meet plant needs. General symptoms of nitrogen deficiency are shown in Table 13-2 and Figure 13-1.

Table 13-2 and Figure 13-1. Symptoms of Nitrogen Deficiency

Leaves
- **Uniform yellowish-green**
- **More pronounced in older leaves**
- Small, thin leaves
- Fewer leaflets
- High fall color
- Early leaf drop

Shoots
- Short, small diameter
- May be reddish or reddish brown

Soil tests have limited value in indicating nitrogen needs for a home garden or lawn because the value is constantly changing due to organic content, microorganism activity, and changes in temperature and water.

Nitrogen is useable by plants in two forms, **ammonium** (NH_4^+), and **nitrate** (NO_3^-). Ammonium, being positively charged, is attracted to the negatively charged soil particles and thus is resistant to leaching (movement down through the soil profile). Soil microorganisms convert ammonium to nitrate. Nitrate, being negatively charged, readily leaches below the root zone with excess rain/irrigation on sandy soils. Prevent water pollution by avoiding over fertilization of nitrogen, particularly on sandy soils.

Soil microorganisms release nitrogen tied up in organic matter over a period of time. Release rates from compost are very slow (i.e., over a period of years). The need for nitrogen fertilizer is based on the organic content of the soils (Table 13-3).

Table 13-3. Need for Nitrogen Fertilizer Based o[...]

Soil Organic Content	Routine Appli[...] for Gar[...]
1%	2 pounds actual N/1,000 square feet
2–3%	1 pound actual N/1,000 square feet
4–5%	0

Iron

Iron chlorosis refers to a yellowing of leaves caused by an iron deficiency in the leaf tissues. Primary symptoms include interveinal chlorosis (i.e., a general yellowing of leaves with veins remaining green). Symptoms show first and more pronounced on younger leaves on the new growth. In severe cases, leaves may become pale yellow or whitish, but veins retain a greenish tint. Angular-shaped brown spits may develop between veins and leave margins may scorch (brown along the edge). Symptoms may show on a single branch or on the entire tree. General symptoms of iron chlorosis are shown in Table 13-4 and Figure 13-2.

Table 13-4 and Figure 13-2. Symptoms of Iron Chlorosis

Leaves
- General yellowing of leaf with veins remaining green
- More pronounced in younger leaves and new growth
- Angular brown spots and marginal scorch
- Smaller
- Curl, dry up, and fall early

Branches
- May show on a single branch or the entire plant

In Western, high pH soils, iron is not deficient but rather unavailable for plant uptake due to the soil's high lime (calcium carbonate) content. In Western soils, iron chlorosis is a general symptom of other problems, including the following:

- **Springtime overwatering** is the primary cause of iron chlorosis in Western soils! Attention to irrigation management, with season changes of the irrigation controller, will generally correct iron chlorosis.

- **Soil compaction** and low soil oxygen contributes to iron chlorosis.

- Iron chlorosis is an early symptom of **trunk girdling roots** (caused by planting tree too deep).

- Iron chlorosis expresses as a complication of **winter trunk/bark injury**.

Attention to these contributing factors is much more effective than adding iron products.

Phosphorus

Note: Phosphorus, P, is a primary nutrient in plant growth. The word **phosphate, P_2O_5,** refers to the ionic compound containing two atoms of phosphorus and five atoms of oxygen. The *phosphorus* content of fertilizer is measured in percent *phosphate*.

Phosphorus levels are naturally adequate in the majority of Western soils. Deficiencies are most likely to occur in new gardens where the organic matter content is low and the soil has a high pH (7.8 to 8.3). A soil test is the best method to determine the need for phosphorus fertilizers.

Phosphorus is also less available to plants when soil temperatures are cool. In the spring, the use of starter fertilizers with phosphorus may be beneficial on herbaceous flowers and vegetable transplants.

Phosphorus deficiency is difficult to diagnose because other growth factors will give similar symptoms. General symptoms include sparse, green to dark green leaves. Veins, petioles, and lower leaf surface may be reddish, dull bronze, or purple, especially when young. Phosphorus deficiency may be observed on roses in the early spring when soils are cold, but the condition corrects itself as soils warm.

Excessive phosphorus fertilizer can aggravate iron and zinc deficiencies and increase the soil salt content. Many home gardener soils are significantly over fertilized with phosphates, aggravating soil salts and iron chlorosis.

Potassium

Note: Potassium, K, is a primary nutrient in plant growth. The word **potash, K_2O,** refers to the ionic compound containing two atoms of potassium and one atom of oxygen. The potassium content of fertilizer is measured in percent potash.

Potassium levels are naturally adequate and even high in most Western soils. Deficiencies occasionally occur in new gardens low in organic matter and in sandy soils low in organic matter. A soil test is the best method to determine the need for potassium fertilizers.

Potassium deficiency is very difficult to diagnose because other growth factors will give similar symptoms. General symptoms include a marginal and interveinal chlorosis (yellowing), followed by scorching that moves inward. Older leaves are affected first. Leaves may crinkle and roll upward. Shoots may show short, bushy, zigzag growth, with dieback late in season.

Excessive potash fertilizer can aggravate soil salt levels. Many home garden soils are over fertilized with potash, leading to salt problems.

Zinc

Zinc deficiency occasionally occurs on sandy soils containing excessive lime and soils low in organic matter (typical of new yards where the topsoil has been removed). Excessive phosphate fertilization may aggravate a zinc problem. It will be seen more in years with cold wet springs.

Sweet corn, beans, and potatoes are the most likely vegetables to be affected. Symptoms include a general stunting of the plant due to shortening of internodes (stem length between leaves). Leaves on beans typically have a crinkled appearance and may become yellow or brown. On young corn, symptoms include a broad band of white-to-translucent tissue on both sides of the leaf midrib starting near the base of the leaf, but generally not extending to the tip.

Occasional manure applications will supply the zinc needs. If a soil test indicates zinc deficiency (less than 10 parts per million), apply a zinc-containing fertilizer according to label directions (typically two to four ounces per 1,000 square feet).

UNDERSTANDING FERTILIZERS

Fertility is only part of the soil management process. Colorado soils are naturally low in organic matter. To maximize productivity, our soils also need routine applications of organic matter to improve soil tilth. For flower and vegetable gardens, it is desirable to raise the soil organic content, over time, to four to five percent.

Manufactured fertilizers are popular with gardeners because they are readily available, inexpensive, easy to apply, and generally provide a quick release of nutrients for plant growth. Application rates depend on the nutrient need of the soil and the percent of nutrients in the specific fertilizer. In products containing multiple nutrients, the application rate is always based on the nitrogen content.

Fertilizer or Soil Amendment?

By legal definition, the term **fertilizer** refers to a soil amendment that guarantees the minimum percentages of nutrients (at least the minimum percentage of nitrogen, phosphate, and potash).

An **organic fertilizer** refers to a soil amendment derived from natural sources that guarantees the minimum percentages of nitrogen, phosphate, and potash. These should not be confused with products approved for use by the **U.S. Department of Agriculture (USDA) National Organic Program (NOP)**. The federal Certified Organic Label, USDA Organic, allows only certain regulated products as listed by the Organic Materials Review Institute (OMRI). For additional information on certified organic soil amendments and fertilizers, refer to the web site at: www.omri.org.

The term **soil amendment** refers to any material mixed into a soil. **Mulch** refers to a material placed on the soil surface. By legal definition, soil amendments make no legal claims about nutrient content or other helpful (or harmful) effects they will have on the soil and plant growth. In Colorado and most states, the term **compost** is also unregulated and could refer to any soil amendment regardless of active microorganism activity.

Many gardeners apply organic soil amendments, such as compost or manure, which most often do not meet the legal requirements as a "fertilizer" but add small amounts of nutrients.

What Is in a Fertilizer?

Analysis or Grade

By law, all products sold as fertilizer require uniform labeling guaranteeing the minimum percentage of nutrients. The three-number combination (fertilizer **grade** or **analysis**) on the product identifies percentages of nitrogen (N), phosphate (P_2O_5), and potash (K_2O), respectively. For example, a 20-10-5 fertilizer contains 20% nitrogen, 10% phosphate, and 5% potash.

The product may also identify other nutrients, such as sulfur, iron, and zinc, if the manufacturer wants to guarantee the amount. This may be done by placing a fourth number on the product label and identifying what nutrient was added in the ingredients.

Ratio

Fertilizer **ratio** indicates a comparative proportion of nitrogen to phosphate to potash. For example, a 15-10-5 fertilizer has a ratio of 3:2:1, and an 8-12-4 fertilizer has a ratio of 2:3:1. Fertilizer recommendations from a soil test are given in ratios.

When shopping for a fertilizer, select a product with a ratio somewhat similar to that desired. For example, if a soil test recommended a 2:1:0 ratio, the ideal fertilizer would be something like 8-4-0, 10-5-0, or 20-10-0. However, if you cannot find that exact fertilizer, an 8-4-2 would be similar. If a garden soil test calls for a 1:0:0 ratio, a 21-0-0 or 24-2-2 fertilizer would be similar.

Formulation

The **formulation** tells what specific kinds of fertilizer are in the product. Table 13-5 gives examples of manufactured fertilizers that could be mixed to derive any specific analysis, ratio, or brand name.

Table 13-5. Examples of Manufactured Fertilizers

Product	N%	P_2O_5%	K_2O%
Ammonium nitrate	34	0	0
Ammonium sulfate	21	0	0
Urea	48	0	0
Ammoniated super-phosphate	3–6	48–53	0
Di-ammonium phosphate	11	48	0
Mono-ammonium phosphate	11	48	0
Super-phosphate	0	18–50	0
Triple super phosphate	0	46	0
Potassium chloride	0	0	60
Potassium nitrate	13	0	44
Potassium sulfate	0	0	50
Potassium-magnesium sulfate	0	0	22

What else is in the fertilizer? In a manufactured fertilizer, the grade does not add up to 100% because the fertilizer also contains other elements like carbon, hydrogen, oxygen, sulfur, iron, zinc, etc. For example, ammonium nitrate ($NH_4^+\ NO_3^-$) has a grade of 34-0-0 with 34% of the content from nitrogen and 66% from hydrogen and oxygen. Ammonium sulfate ($NH_4^+\ SO_2^-$) has a grade of 21-0-0 with 21% from the nitrogen and 79% from the hydrogen, sulfur, and oxygen.

Time release or **slow release** fertilizers contain coating materials or are otherwise formulated to release the nutrients over a period of time as water, heat, and/or microorganisms break down the material (Table 13-6).

Table 13-6. Examples of Quickly and Slowly Available Nitrogen

Quickly available nitrogen • Lasts 4–6 weeks	Ammonium sulfate Ammonium nitrate Calcium nitrate Potassium nitrate Urea
Slowly available nitrogen • Available over weeks to months • Regulated by solubility or microorganism activity	Resin-coated urea Sulfur-coated urea Isobutylidene diurea Methylene urea Urea formaldehyde Manure Poultry wastes Blood meal

In an "organic" type fertilizer, the base is decomposed or processed plant and/or animal by-products. For example, fish emulsion is ground and processed non-edible fish or fish scraps. Its nutrient content would be around 8-4-2, with 8% from nitrogen, 4% from phosphate, and 2% from potash.

Some manufactured and "organic" fertilizers contain fillers, which are used to prevent caking, control dust, derive the desired grade, or to facilitate ease of application.

Complete fertilizer is a term used to identify fertilizers that contains nitrogen, phosphorus, *and* potassium. In the national home garden trade, most fertilizers are complete. However, in Colorado the majority of gardens do not need phosphorus or potassium. It is advisable to avoid heavy applications of phosphate and potash when unneeded as they contribute to soil salts.

Nitrogen Applications

Nitrogen is the nutrient needed in largest quantities as a fertilizer. Nitrogen is annually applied by manufactured fertilizer, organic fertilizers, and/or organic soil amendments. Application rates are critical, as too much or too little directly affects crop growth.

Application rate is based on the soil organic content. As the organic content increases, nitrogen will be slowly *mineralized* (released) by the activity of soil microorganisms. Standard application rates for gardens are given in Table 13-7.

Nitrogen fertilizer can be broadcast and watered in, or broadcast and tilled into the top few inches of soil. It can be banded 3 to 4 inches to the side of the seed row. Do not place the fertilizer in the seed row or root injury may occur.

Table 13-7. Nitrogen Fertilizer Application Rates for Home Gardens

	Soil Organic Content		
	Typical garden soil low in organic matter (1% organic matter)	Moderate level of organic matter (2–3% organic matter)	High level of organic matter (4–5% organic matter)
Nitrogen needed	0.2 lb actual N per 100 square feet	0.1 lb actual N per 100 square feet	0
Fertilizer to apply			
Ammonium sulfate 1-0-0	1 lb fertilizer per 100 square feet (approximately 2 cups)	0.5 lb fertilizer per 100 square feet (approximately 1 cup)	0
or Ammonium nitrate 34-0-0	0.6 lb fertilizer per 100 square feet (approximately 1.33 cups)	0.3 lb fertilizer per 100 square feet (approximately 0.66 cup)	0
or Urea, 45-0-0	0.4 lb fertilizer per 100 square feet (approximately 1 cup)	0.2 lb fertilizer per 100 square feet (approximately 0.5 cup)	0

Phosphate Applications

A soil test is the best method to determine the need for phosphate. When a fertilizer contains a combination of nitrogen with phosphate and/or potash, the application rate is always based on the nitrogen percentage, because nitrogen levels are most critical to plant growth. Phosphate fertilizers are best applied in the spring or fall when they can be tilled into the soil.

Phosphate levels are adequate in the majority of Western soil. With annual applications of compost or manure, phosphorus levels will likely be adequate. Deficiencies are most likely to occur in new gardens where the organic matter content is low and in soils with a high pH (7.8 to 8.3).

Excessive phosphorus fertilizer can aggravate iron and zinc deficiencies and increase soil salt content.

Where phosphate levels are believed to be low, the standard application rate without a soil test is one-quarter to one pound triple super phosphate (0-46-0) or ammonium phosphate (18-46-0) per 100 square feet.

When a phosphate fertilizer is applied to a soil, the phosphorus is quickly immobilized in the soil profile. It typically moves only about an inch. Therefore, it needs be tilled into the rooting zone to be most effective.

Phosphorus and Water Quality

In surface water, low phosphorus levels limit the growth of algae and water weeds. However, when the phosphorus content of surface water increases, algae and water weeds often grow unchecked, a process called *eutrophication*. This significant decrease in water quality is a major problem related to manure management in production agriculture and the handling of yard wastes from the landscape environment.

Popular press articles often incorrectly point to phosphorus-containing lawn and garden fertilizers as the major source of phosphate water pollution. Actually, phosphate fertilizers are rather immobile when applied at correct rates to lawn and garden soils. Phosphate is so immobile in the typical soil that it generally moves less than one inch after application and thus needs to be tilled into the rooting zone to be effective.

However, high rates of manure applied year after year will build soil phosphorus content where leaching becomes a water quality problem. On sandy soils coupled with high rainfall/irrigation, excessive application rates of organic or manufactured fertilizers may also lead to water quality concerns.

The primary source of water-polluting phosphorus in the landscape environment is the mowing, sweeping, or blowing of lawn clippings and leaves onto the gutter and street. When mowing, mow in a direction to blow the clippings onto the lawn rather than onto the sidewalk or street. Also, sweep any grass on the sidewalk/driveway onto the grass. When dealing with autumn leaves, avoid blowing them into the street (Figure 13-3).

It is also important to leave an unmowed buffer strip edging all lakes, streams, ponds, and wetlands rather than mowing plant residues into the water.

Second to yard waste management, overspreading fertilizers onto hard surface (sidewalks, driveways, and streets) adds to surface water pollution. When applying fertilizer, avoid spreading the fertilizer onto hard surfaces where it will wash into local surface water through the storm sewer system. Sweep any fertilizer that landed on the sidewalk/driveway onto the lawn area.

Another very important source of phosphorus pollution in the landscape setting is erosion of soil from new construction sites, unplanted slopes, and poorly maintained landscapes. When the soil moves, it takes the soil-bound phosphorus with it. For water quality, sloping ground needs to be planted with year-round plant cover to prevent soil erosion.

Figure 13-3 ▮ *Grass clippings and leaves mowed or blown into the street are the major source of phosphate pollution from the landscape environment. Mow in a direction to discharge clippings back onto the lawn and not into the street. Phosphate in fertilizer is immobilized upon contact with soil and is not a source of phosphate pollution when applied to a lawn (or garden) soil. However, fertilizer overspread onto the sidewalk, driveway, and street moves with surface runoff into local lakes, streams, and ponds. Exercise caution when fertilizing to keep the phosphate out of the street.*

Potash Applications

A soil test is the best method to determine the need for potash. When a fertilizer contains a combination of nitrogen with phosphate and/or potash, the application rate is always based on the nitrogen percentage because nitrogen levels are most critical to plant growth. Potash fertilizers are best applied in the spring or fall when they can be tilled into the soil.

Potassium levels are naturally adequate to high in most Colorado soils. With annual applications of compost or manure, potassium levels will likely be adequate. Deficiencies occasionally occur in new gardens low in organic matter and in sandy soils low in organic matter. A soil test is the best method to determine the need for potassium.

Excessive potash fertilizer can increase soil salt content.

Where potash levels are believed to be low, the standard application rate without a soil test is one-quarter to one-half pound potassium chloride (0-0-60) or potassium sulfate (0-0-50) per 100 square feet.

Movement of potassium in soils is dependent on soil texture. As the clay content increases, movement decreases. For most soils, it is important that applied potash be tilled into the root zone. In sandy soils, potassium could leach down past the root zone.

Specialty Fertilizers

For specific uses, specialty fertilizers may be preferred. For example, slow release fertilizers are recommended on lawns (see Lawn Care, Chapter 43, for details). **Slow release** or **time release** fertilizers give out small quantities of nutrients over a time period. The release may be controlled by water, temperature, or microbial activity. On trees and shrubs, use only slow release products.

In planters and hanging baskets, two popular specialty fertilizers include Osmocote and water solubles (MiracleGro, Peters, etc.).

Osmocote is a time release fertilizer designed for indoor and outdoor potted plants. Each time the soil is watered, a small amount of nutrients are released. Depending on the specific formulation, it should be applied to the soil once every three to nine months. In outdoor pots watered daily, it releases faster, having about half the life span of the product used on indoor plants. Gardeners sometimes see the Osmocote pellets in potted plants and mistake it for insect eggs.

Numerous brands of **water solubles** are popular in the home garden trade (e.g., MiracleGro, Peters, Schultz Plant Food, Fertilome Root Stimulator, etc.). Water-soluble fertilizers are mixed with the irrigation water, typically giving a blue or green color. This can be done in a bucket or hose-on fertilizer applicator. It is important to water the soil with the fertilizer water, not just wet the leaves. (**Note:** Hose-on fertilizer applicators and hose-on pesticide sprayers are not the same thing. Fertilizer applicators apply a heavier volume as the purpose is to water the soil. Pesticide applicators release a lower volume as wetting the leaf is the objective.) Water solubles are the standard in greenhouse production where the fertilizer is injected into the irrigation water.

For herbaceous transplants (flowers and vegetables), water-soluble fertilizers are recommended at planting and possibly two to four weeks after planting (depending on soil organic matter content). These are often marketed as *root stimulators*. It is the nitrogen content that promotes growth rather than any hormones or vitamins in the product. On cool springtime soils, the readily available phosphate may also be helpful. Woody plants (trees and shrubs) do not respond to water-soluble fertilizer at planting.

CALCULATING FERTILIZER APPLICATION RATE
Steps to Calculating Fertilizer Application Rate

Example is for a 40-foot by 100-foot lawn area, using a 20-10-0 fertilizer

1. **Calculating size of area to be fertilized**

    _____ ft. long   ×   _____ ft. wide   =   _____ square feet

    Example:

    40 feet   ×   100 feet   =   **4,000** square feet

2. **Calculating fertilizer application rate**

    $$\frac{\text{_____ lb nutrient per _____ square feet}}{\text{_____ \% nutrient in fertilizer}} = \text{_____ lb fertilizer / _____ square feet}$$

    Example:

    $$\frac{\text{1 lb nutrient per } \mathbf{1,000} \text{ square feet}}{\substack{\mathbf{20}\% \text{ nutrient in fertilizer} \\ (0.20)}} = \mathbf{5} \text{ lb fertilizer / } \mathbf{1000} \text{ square feet}$$

3. **Calculating pounds of fertilizer to apply**

lawn or garden area	×	application rate	=	pound of fertilizer per garden or lawn

    $$\frac{\text{_____ square feet}}{\text{garden or lawn}} \times \frac{\text{_____ lb fertilizer}}{\text{_____ square feet}} = \frac{\text{_____ lb fertilizer}}{\text{garden or lawn}}$$

    Example:

    $$\frac{\mathbf{4,000} \text{ square feet}}{\text{lawn}} \times \frac{\mathbf{5} \text{ lb fertilizer}}{\mathbf{1,000} \text{ square feet}} = \frac{\mathbf{20} \text{ lb fertilizer}}{\text{lawn}}$$

Fertilizer Application Rate Table

Because soil test recommendations for any given soil do not exactly match a fertilizer, select a fertilizer that gives comparative amounts of nitrogen, phosphorus, and potash as recommended by the soil test. In fertilizer application, it is most important to match the nitrogen requirement and compromise some for the phosphorus and potash. The amount of fertilizer to apply that will give the recommended amount of nitrogen can be obtained from Table 13-8.

Table 13-8. Amount of Fertilizer to Apply Based on Actual Nitrogen Recommendations

Nitrogen Rate		0.1 lb N/100 square feet	0.2 lb N/100 square feet	1 lb N/1,000 square feet
Fertilizer Grade		pounds fertilizer to apply per 100 square feet	pounds fertilizer to apply per 100 square feet	pounds fertilizer to apply per 1,000 square feet
45-0-0 (urea)		0.2	0.4	2.2
37-3-3		0.3	0.5	2.7
36-6-6		0.3	0.6	2.8
33-0-0		0.3	0.6	3.0
32-4-4	32-3-10	0.3	0.6	3.1
30-4-4	30-0-10	0.3	0.7	3.3
28-3-3	28-4-6	0.4	0.7	3.6
27-7-7	27-3-3	0.4	0.7	3.7
25-5-5	25-3-12	0.4	0.8	4.0
24-8-16	24-0-15	0.4	0.8	4.2
22-4-4	22-6-3	0.5	0.9	4.5
21-0-0	21-3-12	0.5	1.0	4.8
20-20-20	20-4-8	0.5	1.0	5.0
19-19-19	19-11-12	0.5	1.0	5.3
18-6-12	18-3-6	**0.6**	1.1	5.6
16-8-8	16-4-8	0.6	1.3	6.3
15-15-15	15-5-5	0.7	1.3	6.7
13-3-9	13-25-12	0.8	1.5	7.7
12-12-12	12-4-4	0.8	1.7	8.3
10-10-10	10-20-10	1.0	2.0	10.0
10-5-5	10-10-20	1.0	2.0	10.0
6-12-12	6-2-0	1.7	3.3	16.7
5-10-10	5-10-5	2.0	4.0	20.0

Example: If the nitrogen (N) recommendation is for 0.1 lb. N/100 square feet and the fertilizer grade selected has a ratio of 18-6-12 (column 1), apply 0.6 lb of this fertilizer per 100 square feet.

Note: Two cups (one pint) of dry fertilizer weighs about one pound.

ORGANIC FERTILIZERS

Terms

By legal definition, the term **fertilizer** refers to a soil amendment that guarantees the minimum percentages of nutrients (at least the minimum percentage of nitrogen, phosphate, and potash).

An **organic fertilizer** refers to a soil amendment derived from natural sources that guarantees, at least, the minimum percentages of nitrogen, phosphate, and potash. Examples include plant and animal by-products, rock powders, seaweed, inoculants, and conditioners. These are often available at garden centers and through horticultural supply companies.

These should not be confused with substances approved for use with the *USDA National Organic Program (NOP)*. The USDA NOP, with its "USDA Organic" label, allows for the use of only certain substances. The **Organic Materials Review Institute** (OMRI at www.omri.org) approves brand name products made with ingredients from the "National List" for use with the NOP. (For details refer to www.ams.usda.gov/nop and click "NOP Regulations" and then "National List Information"). Many of the organic fertilizers listed here will meet NOP standards (based on the national list). Growers participating in the NOP should consult with their certifier to ensure compliance for organic certification.

The term **soil amendment** refers to any material mixed into a soil. **Mulch** refers to a material placed on the soil surface. By legal definition, soil amendments make no legal claims about nutrient content or other helpful (or harmful) effects it will have on the soil and plant growth. In Colorado, the term **compost** is also unregulated and could refer to any soil amendment regardless of active microorganism activity.

Many gardeners apply *organic soil amendments*, such as compost or manure, which most often do not meet the legal requirements as a "fertilizer" but add small amounts of nutrients.

Release time—Organic products require the activity of soil microorganisms before nutrients are available for plant uptake. Microorganism activity is generally dependant on soil temperatures greater than 50°F in the presence of sufficient soil moisture. Dry and/or cold soil conditions will delay the release of nutrients from these organic sources. This period refers to how long these products are available if applied to the soil. Use this information to time the application of the product.

Application—Different products may be applied in various ways. Some may be tilled in (worked into the soil with a machine or hand tool), others may be applied as a foliar spray (mixed with a surfactant and sprayed in a fine mist on the leaf surface while temperatures are below 80°F), and some may be injected into a drip or overhead irrigation system (fertigation with a siphon mixer). Application rates in this fact sheet are generalized and based on some manufacturers' recommendations. Over- or under-fertilization may occur using these recommendations.

Plant By-Products

Alfalfa Meal or Pellets

Alfalfa meal or pellets are often used as animal feed. Primarily, they are used to increase organic matter in the soil but do offer nutrients and a high availability of trace minerals. They contain trianconatol, a natural fatty-acid growth stimulant (Table 13-9).

Table 13-9. Alfalfa Meal or Pellets

Typical NPK analysis	2-1-2
Release time	1–4 months
Pros	Available at feed stores
Cons	May contain seeds
Application	Till in 2–5 pounds per 100 square feet

Corn Gluten Meal

Corn gluten meal materials have a high percentage of nitrogen. It carries a warning to allow one to four months of decomposition in the soil prior to seeding. Allelopathic properties will inhibit the germination of seeds. However, there is no danger to established or transplanted plants. This product is also marketed as a pre-emergent weed control for annual grasses in bluegrass lawns (Table 13-10).

Table 13-10. Corn Gluten Meal

Typical NPK analysis	9-0-0
Release time	1–4 months
Pros	Very high nitrogen
Cons	Germination inhibitor, some are GMOs
Application	Till in 20–40 pounds per 1,000 square feet

Cottonseed Meal

Cottonseed meal is a rich source of nitrogen. Buyers should be aware that many pesticides are applied to cotton crops and residues tend to remain in the seeds. Pesticide-free cottonseed meal is available (Table 13-11).

Table 13-11. Cottonseed Meal

Typical NPK analysis	6-0.4-1.5
Release time	1–4 months
Pros	High nitrogen
Cons	Pesticide residues, most are GMOs
Application	Till in 10 pounds per 100 square feet

Soybean Meal

Used primarily as an animal feed product. Available bagged at many feed stores (Table 13-12).

Table 13-12. Soybean Meal

Typical NPK analysis	7-2-1
Release time	1–4 months
Pros	High nitrogen, available at feed stores
Cons	Almost half of the conventionally grown soy is GMO
Application	8 pounds per 100 square feet

Animal By-Products

Bat Guano—High N

Bat guano (feces) harvested from caves is powdered. It can be applied directly to the soil or made into a tea and applied as a foliar spray or injected into an irrigation system (Table 13-13).

Table 13-13. Bat Guano—High N

Typical NPK analysis	10-3-1
Release time	4+ months
Pros	Stimulates soil microbes
Cons	Cost
Application	Till in 5 pounds per 100 square feet or as a tea at 3 teaspoons per gallon of water

Bat Guano—High P

See the description for high N bat guano. The difference is that it is processed for high phosphorus content (Table 13-14).

Table 13-14. Bat Guano—High P

Typical NPK analysis	3-10-1
Release time	4+ months
Pros	Stimulates soil microbes
Cons	Cost
Application	Till in 5 pounds per 100 square feet or as tea at 3 teaspoons per gallon of water

Blood Meal

Blood meal, made from dried slaughterhouse waste, is one of the highest non-synthetic sources of nitrogen. If over applied, it can burn plants with excessive ammonia (Table 13-15).

Table 13-15. Blood Meal

Typical NPK analysis	12-0-0
Release time	1–4 months
Pros	Available at feed stores
Cons	Can burn. Expensive at garden centers
Application	Till in 5–10 pounds per 100 square feet

Bone Meal

A well-known source of phosphorus, bone meal is steam processed and widely available at feed stores and in garden centers. If purchased at feed stores, phosphorus is expressed on the label as elemental phosphorus and is

2.3 times higher than numbers shown on garden center labels for phosphate (i.e., 12% phosphate is the same as 27% phosphorus). However, recent Colorado State University research has shown that phosphorus from bone meal is only available to plants in soils that have a pH below 7.0 (Table 13-16).

Table 13-16. Bone Meal

Typical NPK analysis	3-15-0
Release time	1–4 months
Pros	Highly plant-available form of phosphorus
Cons	Cost
Application	Till in 10 pounds per 100 square feet

Feather Meal

Sourced from poultry slaughter, feather meal has fairly high nitrogen levels but is slow to release the nitrogen (Table 13-17).

Table 13-17. Feather Meal

Typical NPK analysis	N varies 7% to 12% on process
Release time	4+ months
Pros	Long-term fertilizer
Cons	Cost versus speed of nitrogen release
Application	Till in 2.5–5 pounds per 100 square feet

Fish Emulsion

Infamous for its foul smell, emulsions are soluble, liquid fertilizers that have been heat and acid processed from fish waste (Table 13-18).

Table 13-18. Fish Emulsion

Typical NPK analysis	5-2-2
Release time	1–4 months
Pros	Adds needed micronutrients
Cons	Some have foul smell
Application	Mix 6 tablespoons per gallon of water

Enzymatically Digested Hydrolyzed Liquid Fish

Enzymatically digested hydrolyzed liquid fish may have used enzymes to digest the nutrients from fish wastes instead of using heat and acids. This retains more of the proteins, enzymes, vitamins, and micronutrients than emulsions (Table 13-19).

Table 13-19. Enzymatically Digested Hydrolyzed Liquid Fish

Typical NPK analysis	4-2-2
Release time	1–4 months
Pros	More nutrients than emulsions
Cons	More expensive than emulsions
Application	Mix 5 tablespoons per gallon of water

Fish Meal

Fish meal is ground and heat-dried fish waste (Table 13-20).

Table 13-20. Fish Meal

Typical NPK analysis	10-6-2
Release time	1–4 months
Pros	Nitrogen and phosphorus source
Cons	Heat processed
Application	Till in 5–10 pounds per 100 square feet

Fish Powder

Fish power is dried with heat and turned into water-soluble powder. It is a high source of nitrogen. Many can be mixed into solution and injected into an irrigation system (Table 13-21).

Table 13-21. Fish Powder

Typical NPK analysis	12-0.25-1
Release time	Immediate to 1 month
Pros	Adds micronutrients
Cons	Heat processed
Application	Till in 1–2 ounces per 100 square feet *or* mix at 1 tablespoon per gallon of water

Compost, Manure, and Biosolid-Based Products

For information on compost made with compost, manure, biosolids, and worm casting, refer to Chapters 10, Compost.

Rock Powders

Rock powders relevant for use in Western soils are those that supply phosphorus. Those that serve as a potassium source (greensand, feldspar, potassium sulfate, biotite, etc.) are not necessary, as most Western soils are naturally high in potassium. Similarly, it is not necessary to add calcium (gypsum, lime, etc.) due to naturally high calcium levels in Western soils and arid conditions.

If you are making annual applications of manure and/or compost to your garden to add nitrogen, you should have sufficient levels of phosphorus in your soil. If you are applying manure or compost to your garden based on phosphorus needs, you might have an excess nitrogen supply. Excess nitrogen can lead to poor flower/fruit development and increases water pollution potential from nitrogen leaching from the soil.

Generally, plant or animal sources are the best value for phosphorus in the home garden. Colorado State University research results concluded that no rock phosphate (regardless of mesh size) is available for plant use unless the soil pH is below 7.0.

Colloidal Phosphate (Also Known as Soft Rock Phosphate)

This product is made by surrounding clay particles with natural phosphate. Total phosphate is about twenty percent while available phosphate is about two to three percent. This is why you can apply large amounts of colloidal phosphate, as it will release slowly over the years (usually more available the second year than the first). For home gardeners, the cost/return is adequate to apply colloidal phosphate at rates to supply phosphorus for this season's crops. This product also adds micronutrients to soil.

Micronized (passing through 1,000 mesh screen {1,000 wires per square inch}) sources may be more available than regular soft rock grinds in soils with a pH below 7.0.

Seaweed

Kelp is the most common form and is valued not for its macronutrient (nitrogen, phosphorus, and potash) contributions but for micronutrients, trace minerals, amino acids, and vitamins plus growth hormones that stimulate plant cell division.

Kelp is often mixed with fish products to enhance growth.

Three processes are available: extracts (as kelp meal or powder), cold-processed (usually liquid), and enzymatically digested (liquid). Ranked in quality of content and plant availability they are (highest to lowest): 1) enzymatically digested, 2) cold-processed, and 3) extracts.

Kelp Meal

Kelp meal, a product of the ocean, is used primarily as a trace mineral source. It is often combined with fish meal to add nitrogen, phosphorus, and potash value (Table 13-22).

Table 13-22. Kelp Meal

Typical NPK analysis	negligible
Release time	4+ months
Pros	Adds micronutrients
Cons	Insignificant NPK value
Application	Till in 1 pound per 100 square feet

Kelp Powder

Kelp powder is similar to kelp meal but ground fine enough to put into solution and applied as a foliar spray or injected into an irrigation system (Table 13-23).

Table 13-23. Kelp Powder

Typical NPK analysis	1-0-4
Release time	Immediate—1 month
Pros	Adds micronutrients
Cons	Insignificant NPK value
Application	Mix one-quarter to one-half teaspoon/gallon of water

Liquid Kelp

Usually cold-processed, liquid kelp will have higher levels of growth hormones than extracts. Some may also be enzymatically digested, making the growth hormones even more available to the plants (Table 13-24).

Table 13-24. Liquid Kelp

Typical NPK analysis	Negligible
Release time	Immediate—1 month
Pros	Adds micronutrients plus helps plant with stress
Cons	Insignificant NPK value
Application	Mix 1–2 tablespoons per gallon of water for foliar *or* mix at 0.25–1.25 teaspoon per gallon per 100 square feet and inject into an irrigation system

1. Define plant nutrition and fertilizer.

2. Will addition of fertilizer help plant growth when soil compaction is the limiting factor? Explain.

3. What are the typical symptoms of nitrogen deficiency? What are the problems associated with excessive nitrogen fertilization?

4. In Western soils, under what situations will phosphorus levels likely be adequate and deficient? How does one determine the need for phosphate fertilizer?

5. In Western soils, under what situations will potassium levels likely be adequate and deficient? How does one determine the need for potash fertilizers?

6. Define the following terms: *fertilizer*, *organic fertilizer*, *certified organic fertilizer*, and *soil amendment*.

7. What does grade or analysis indicate about a fertilizer? What is a fertilizer ratio?

8. What is a fertilizer formulation? What is a complete fertilizer? When applying a complete fertilizer, what is the application rate always based on?

9. What is the routine application rate for nitrogen fertilizer? How does it change based on soil organic matter?

10. In relation to phosphorus water pollution, what happens to phosphate fertilizers applied to: 1) a lawn or garden area and 2) overspread onto the street, sidewalk, or driveway? According to the research base, what is the major source of phosphate water pollution from the landscape setting?

Chapter
14*

Soil pH

Soil pH is a measurement of the acidity or alkalinity of a soil. On the pH scale, 7.0 is neutral. Below 7 is acid and above 7 is basic or alkaline. A pH range of 6.8 to 7.2 is termed **near neutral**. Areas of the world with limited rainfall typically have alkaline soils, while areas with higher rainfall typically have acid soils.

In Colorado, the majority of our soils are on the alkaline side, having a pH of 7.0 to 7.8 and above. Soils with a pH above 7.5 generally have a high calcium carbonate content, known as **free lime**. In some mountain soils and older gardens that have been highly irrigated and cultivated for many years, the pH may be in the neutral range or slightly acid.

Many gardening books list the preferred pH for common plants (generally 6.0 to 7.2). For most plants, however, what is preferred and what is tolerated are not related. Most garden and landscape plants tolerate a pH up to 7.5 to 7.8 with little problem. The exception is acid-loving plants, like blueberries, azaleas, and rhododendrons, which need acid soil. Blue hydrangeas also require a pH lower than 5.0 to induce the blue flower color (Table 14-1).

*Authors: David Whiting and Carl Wilson (Colorado State University Extension), and Jean Reeder, PhD (USDA-ARS, retired).

Table 14-1. Soil pH and Plant Growth

Soil Reaction	pH	Plant Growth
	>8.3	Too alkaline for most plants
	7.5	Iron availability becomes a problem on alkaline soils
Alkaline soil	7.2	6.8 to 7.2— "near neutral"
Neutral soil	7.0	6.0 to 7.5—acceptable for most plants
Acid soil	6.8	
	6.0	
	5.5	Reduced soil microbial activity
	<4.6	Too acid for most plants

pH AND NUTRIENT AVAILABILITY

Soil pH is an important chemical property because it affects the availability of nutrients to plants and the activity of soil microorganisms. The influence of pH on nutrient availability is illustrated in Figure 14-1. Iron chlorosis is common in Colorado due to alkaline soil pH. Phosphorus will become less available in highly alkaline soils. Zinc deficiencies are occasionally observed in sensitive field crops, like corn and beans (Figure 14-1).

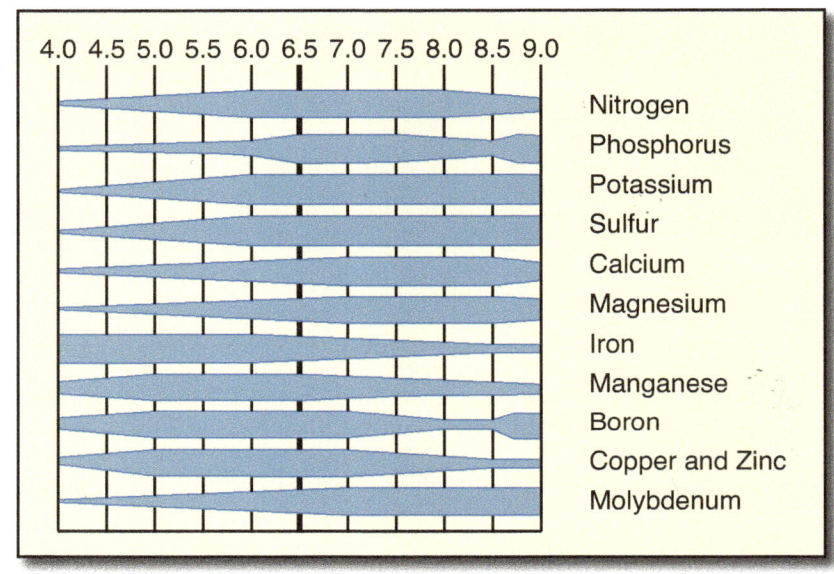

Figure 14-1 ▮ *Availability of nutrients based on soil pH.*

MANAGING ALKALINE SOILS

In Western soils with moderate to high alkalinity (pH above 7.5), manage the soil by giving extra attention to increasing the organic matter, using organic mulches, and light frequent irrigation. Plants are less tolerant of dry soil conditions when the pH is high. In Western soils, the major problem with high pH is iron chlorosis.

Soils with a pH above 7.3 and/or with free lime cannot be adequately amended for acid-loving plants like blueberries, azaleas, and rhododendrons.

In near-neutral pH soils rich with organic matter and without free lime, gardeners may find a slight decrease in soil pH over many decades. This occurs as irrigation leaches out some naturally occurring elements (calcium and magnesium) contributing to the higher pH. The growth of plants that secrete weak acids into the soil may also contribute to a gradual pH change.

Lowering the pH

Textbooks talk of sulfur applications to lower a soil's pH. This is effective in many parts of the country. However, it is not effective in many Western soils due to high levels of free lime (calcium carbonate) found in the soils.

To test for **free lime**, place a heaping tablespoon of crumbled dry soil in a cup. Moisten it with vinegar. If the soil-vinegar mix bubbles, the soil has free lime. **On soils with free lime, a gardener will not effectively lower the pH.**

On soils without free lime, the following products may help lower the pH.

- **Elemental sulfur** is one chemical that can be used to lower soil pH. The soil type, existing pH, and the desired pH are used to determine the amount of elemental sulfur needed (Table 14-2). Incorporate sulfur to a depth of 6 inches. It may take several months to over a year to react with the soil, lowering the pH. Test soil pH again three to four months after initial application. If the soil pH is not in the desired range, reapply.

Table 14-2. Pounds of Sulfur Needed to Lower Soil pH*

Material	pH Change	Pounds per 100 Square Feet†
Sulfur	7.5–6.5	1.5
	8.0–6.5	3.5
	8.5–6.5	4.0
Iron sulfate	7.5–6.5	12.5
	8.0–6.5	29.0
	8.5–6.5	33.2

*Effective only on soils without free lime; do the vinegar test.

†Higher rates will be required on fine-textured, clayey soils and soils with a pH 7.3 and above.

- **Iron sulfate** can also be used to acidify soils. This material reacts much faster than elemental sulfur, usually within three to four weeks following application. Do not apply more than nine pounds per 100 square feet in a single application. If higher rates are required, split applications to avoid excessive levels of soluble salts (see Table 14-2).

- **Aluminum sulfate** will also lower pH, but it is not recommended as a soil-acidifying amendment because of the potential for aluminum toxicity to plant roots.

- **Acid sphagnum peat** incorporated into the soil prior to planting will help provide a favorable rooting environment for the establishment of acid-loving plants in near-neutral soils. Incorporate peat at the rate of one to two cubic feet per plant. The positive effects of acid peat will last a few years, but unless other measures are used, the pH of the soil will eventually increase. The pH will be driven up with the high calcium in our irrigation water. Soil with a pH above 7.3 and/or with free lime cannot be adequately amended for acid-loving plants.

- **Fertilizers**—Use of **ammonium sulfate** or **urea** as nitrogen fertilizer sources will also have a small effect on lowering soil pH in soils without free lime. However, do not use these fertilizers at rates greater than those required to meet the nitrogen needs of the plants. For example, ammonium sulfate fertilizer, 21-0-0, at ten pounds per 1,000 square feet (maximum rate for crop application) may lower the pH from 7.3 to 7.2.

Fertilizers that contain nitrogen in the nitrate form will have a slight effect to increase the pH.

RAISING THE pH ON ACID SOIL

On acid soils, the pH can be raised by adding lime (calcium carbonate). The amount to add depends on the cation exchange capacity (nutrient-holding capacity) of the soil, which is based on the soil's clay content. Soil higher in clay will have a higher cation exchange capacity and will require more materials to raise the pH.

A laboratory test called **buffer index** measures the responsiveness of the soil to lime applications. The soil test will give recommendations on application rates based on the buffer index rather than just the pH. Table 14-3 gives an estimated amount of lime to apply to raise a soil's pH.

Table 14-3. Limestone Application Rates to Raise Soil pH to Approximately 7.0 for Turf

Existing Soil pH	Lime Application Rate (lb/1,000 square feet)		
	Sandy	Loamy	Clayey
5.5–6.0	20	25	35
5.0–5.5	30	40	50
3.4–5.0	40	55	80
3.5–4.5	50	70	80

Lime application rates shown in this table are for dolomite, ground, and pelletized limestone and assume a soil organic matter level of approximately 2% or less. On soils with 4% to 5% organic matter, increase limestone application rates by 20%.

Individual applications to turf should not exceed 50 pounds of limestone per 1,000 square feet.

Avoid the use of hydrated or burned lime because it is hazardous to both humans and turf (can seriously burn skin and leaves). If hydrated lime is used, crease application rates in the above table by 50% and apply no more than 10 pounds of hydrated or burned line per 1,000 square feet of turf.

Lime is commonly sold as ground agricultural limestone. It varies in how fine it has been ground. The finer the grind, the more rapidly it becomes effective in lowering pH. **Calcitic lime** mostly contains calcium carbonate ($CaCO_3$). **Dolomitic lime** contains both calcium carbonate and dolomite [$MgCa(CO_3)_2$]. On most soils, both are generally satisfactory. However, on sandy soils low in organic matter, dolomitic lime may supplement low magnesium levels.

HOME pH TEST KITS

In alkaline soils, home pH kits have questionable value. Inexpensive kits do not calibrate closely enough on alkaline soils to be meaningful, and small changes in techniques, such as how much water and the pH of the water used in the sample, can change results. Most home soil test kits are designed for acid soils.

CHAPTER REVIEW
Questions

1. What does soil pH measure? What is an acceptable range for most plants?

2. What is the typical pH for Western (Colorado) soils? What are the implications for gardening?

3. Can the pH of an alkaline soil be effectively lowered? Describe the function of the "free lime" vinegar test.

Chapter

15 *

Dealing with Iron Chlorosis

SYMPTOMS

The term **chlorosis** means a general yellowing of the leaves. Many factors contribute to chlorosis.

Iron chlorosis refers to a yellowing caused by an iron deficiency in the leaf tissues. The primary symptoms of iron deficiency include **interveinal chlorosis** (i.e., a general yellowing of leaves with veins remaining green). In severe cases, leaves may become pale yellow or whitish, but veins retain a greenish cast. Angular-shaped brown spots may develop between veins and leaf margins may scorch (brown along the edge) (Figure 15-1).

Iron chlorosis shows first and more severely on the newer growth at branch tips. Growing leaves may be smaller than normal. Leaves may eventually curl, dry up, and fall. Fruits may be small with a bitter flavor. Mildly affected plants become unsightly and grow poorly. In severe cases or if iron chlorosis persists over several years, individual limbs or the entire plant may die.

It is common for iron chlorosis to show on a single branch or on one side of a tree. This is particularly common for plant species with marginal winter hardiness and on the southwest side of the tree following winter injury. Plant species and varieties vary greatly in their susceptibility to iron deficiency.

Figure 15-1 ■ *Symptoms of iron chlorosis include yellowing of the leaf with veins remaining green.*

*Authors: David Whiting and Carl Wilson (Colorado State University Extension), and Jean Reeder, PhD (USDA-ARS, retired). Artwork by David Whiting.

On junipers, pines, and other evergreens, chlorosis usually develops as an overall yellowing of needles.

Iron is necessary for the formation of chlorophyll, which is responsible for the green color in plants and necessary for photosynthesis (sugar production in plants). Any reduction in chlorophyll during the growing season reduces plant growth, vigor, and tolerance to stress conditions. Plants with reduced vigor from iron chlorosis are more prone to winter injury, and winter injury may aggravate an iron chlorosis problem. Weakened plants also are more susceptible to other diseases and insect infestations.

Similar Symptoms

Iron chlorosis symptoms can be confused with other problems. In the high pH soils of the West, an iron chlorosis problem may actually be a combination of iron and manganese deficiencies. It is common for chlorotic trees to show a response to both iron and manganese treatments.

Zinc and manganese deficiencies result in similar leaf symptoms. Iron chlorosis appears first on the younger or terminal leaves. Under severe conditions, it may progress into older and lower leaves. By comparison, zinc and manganese deficiencies typically appear first on older, interior leaves.

Nitrogen deficiency shows as a uniform yellowing of the entire leaf (including the veins). Nitrogen deficiency shows first in the older leaves, while iron chlorosis shows first in the newer growth.

Damage from soil sterilants (i.e., Pramitol, Atrazine, Simazine, Ureabor, and Diuron) used to prevent weeds result in similar symptoms. With these weed killers, the area along the vein remains green. With iron chlorosis, just the vein itself remains green.

Natural aging of tissues may create similar symptoms in some plants. Root and trunk damage and some virus, phytoplasmas, and vascular wilt diseases may cause similar leaf symptoms.

CAUSES AND COMPLICATING FACTORS

The factors leading to iron chlorosis are complex and not fully understood. A number of chemical reactions govern iron availability and contribute to the complexity of iron chemistry in soils.

Many environmental factors also create or contribute to iron deficiency. These factors need to be evaluated and alleviated to the extent possible. In most situations, attention to watering and soil conditions will satisfactorily correct minor iron chlorosis problems.

Calcareous Soils

Many Colorado soils are naturally high in lime (calcium carbonate and other calcium compounds) driving the soil pH above 7.5. On these **calcareous** soils, iron chlorosis is common on susceptible plants.

Colorado soils are abundant in iron, as evidenced by the popular "red rock" formations. In alkaline soils (pH above 7.0), iron is rapidly fixed through a chemical reaction into insoluble, solid forms that cannot be absorbed by plant roots. Such iron will be tied up indefinitely unless soil pH changes. Soil applications of iron alone are ineffective, as the applied iron will quickly be converted to these unavailable solid forms.

Overwatering

Iron chlorosis is a common generic symptom of overwatering.

Overly wet or dry soils predispose plants to iron chlorosis. Iron chlorosis is more prevalent following wet springs, and where gardeners overwater in the spring. In Western calcareous soils, iron chlorosis can generally be avoided by eliminating springtime overwatering!

It is common for gardeners to allow sprinkler control settings to remain unchanged from the high summer water needs to the lower water needs of spring and fall. In this situation, the yard receives around 40% more water than is needed in the spring and fall. Changing the controller to meet seasonal needs will conserve water and correct iron chlorosis in most situations.

Soil Compaction

Soil compaction and other conditions that limit soil air infiltration (like surface crusting and use of plastic mulch) predispose plants to iron chlorosis by limiting effective rooting depth. These are key contributing factors in clayey soils. Using organic mulch (like wood or bark chips) helps prevent and reduce soil compaction. Avoid the use of plastic under rock mulch around landscape plants.

Trunk Girdling Roots

On trees, iron chlorosis is a common early symptom of trunk girdling roots. The primary cause of trunk girdling roots is planting trees too deep. Trunk girdling roots can lead to decline and death some twenty plus years after planting.

In tree planting standards, the top of the root ball should rise slightly above grade (one to two inches for newly planted trees). At least two structural roots should be located in the top one to three inches of the root ball.

On established trees, the trunk-to-root flare should be noticeable. If the trunk goes straight into the ground, suspect planting problems and possible development of trunk girdling roots over time. To check, perform a root collar excavation (carefully removing the soil around the base of tree) and examine the trunk/root flare.

Other Contributing Factors

- **Plant competition**—On susceptible plants, competition from adjacent lawns or flowers may aggravate iron chlorosis. Replace the grass under the tree canopy with wood/bark chip mulch. Thin perennials in the flowerbed.

- **Winter injury**—Trees with cankers and other winter injuries are prone to iron deficiency. Winter bark injury on tree trunks is caused by winter drought.

- **Soil organic matter**—Organic matter is a key to successfully gardening in Colorado's soils. Ideally, the soil's organic content is brought up to five percent. However, excessive amounts may aggravate iron problems.

- **Excessive salt levels**—High soil salt levels adversely affect uptake of water and nutrients, including iron.

- **Soil temperature and light intensity**—Extreme soil temperatures and high light intensity may increase iron chlorosis problems. Use an organic mulch to moderate soil temperature. Shading may help some crops.

- **Acid-loving plants**—Acid-loving plants are highly susceptible to iron chlorosis and not suited to Colorado's soil conditions. These include blueberries, azaleas, rhododendron, flowering dogwood, and heather.

- **Nutrients**—Excessive levels (from over application) of phosphate, manganese, copper, or zinc may aggravate iron chlorosis.

PLANT SELECTION—RIGHT PLANT, RIGHT PLACE

In Western high pH soils, a good method to prevent iron chlorosis is to select plant species tolerant of high soil pH and less affected by low iron availability. Avoid planting the more susceptible species (Table 15-1) on soils prone to iron chlorosis problems (pH above 7.5, compacted, clayish, or wet soils).

Table 15-1. Examples of Plants with High Susceptibility to Iron Chlorosis

Amur maple	Dawn redwood	Northern red oak
Apple	Douglas fir	Peach
Arborvitae	Elm	Pear
Aspen	Flowering dogwoods	Pin oak
Azalea	Grape	Pine
Beech	Honeylocust	Raspberry
Birch	Horse chestnut	Red maple
Boxelder	Juniper	Rhododendron
Bumald spiraea	Linden	Silver maple
Cherry	London plane tree (sycamore)	Spruce
Cotoneaster	Magnolia	Sweetgum
Crabapple	Mountain-ash	

some 250 other species

IRON ADDITIVES

Unfortunately, there is no easy, inexpensive, or long-term correction for iron chlorosis. Treatments may be rather expensive and give disappointing results. Because plant and soil conditions vary greatly, there is no single approach that is consistently best.

Focusing on reducing springtime overwatering, soil compaction, and other contributing factors is generally more effective than iron additives.

The first step in using iron additives is to know the soil pH and free lime (calcium carbonate) content. These soil factors directly affect the success of any approach. Determine soil pH by soil test. When the pH is above 7.5, effective approaches are limited.

To check for free lime, place a rounded tablespoon of dry crumbled soil in a small cup. Moisten the soil with vinegar. (The soil needs to be thoroughly moistened, but not swimming in vinegar.) If the soil-vinegar mix fizzes or bubbles, it has free lime. High lime content is typical of soils with a pH above 7.5. A standard approach in treating iron chlorosis is to lower the soil's pH. Lowering the pH is impractical to impossible if the soil contains free lime.

There are four general approaches to iron treatments: 1) lowering the soil's pH, 2) soil iron treatments, 3) foliar sprays, and 4) tree injections. Each has advantages and disadvantages. Each procedure gives variable results depending on plant species and soil conditions.

The two principal types of iron-containing products used for iron application include iron chelates and inorganic iron compounds (such as iron sulfate, ferrous sulfate). Several types of iron chelates are marketed under a variety of trade names. Soil pH dictates the type of chelate to use. Treatment of any iron product made mid-season may not produce satisfactory results.

Lowering Soil pH with Sulfur Products

A standard approach used in many products is to lower the soil pH. This approach merits consideration only if the soil does not have free lime (high calcium carbonate), and may show effectiveness over a period of years.

Due to the high pH and lime content of many Western soils, this approach seldom merits consideration. If irrigation water is hard, the calcium carbonate (lime) in the water will counter any acidifying effect. (As a side note, it is observed that in some older gardens the pH has dropped below natural levels as the lime content is slowly leached out with decades of irrigation.)

The pH is lowered by soil applications of sulfur products. See the product labels for specific application rate. (Use of aluminum sulfate to lower soil pH is not recommended due to a potential for aluminum toxicity.)

Soil Applications of Iron Sulfate Plus Sulfur

A simple approach is to apply a mixture of equal amounts of iron (ferrous) sulfate *and* sulfur to the soil. Examples of products include Copperas, Jirdon Super Iron Green, HiYield Soil Acidifier Plus Micros, and Fertilome Soil Acidifier Plus Iron. Over a period of months to years, an improvement may be noticed. When it is effective, treatments may last up to three or four years, depending on soil conditions.

This approach merits consideration only on soils without free lime.

For trees, apply the mixture in holes around the dripline of the tree, as described for chelates. Over time, the sulfur reacts to lower soil pH in a localized area. Broadcast applications, which dilute the material over a larger area, are less likely to give satisfactory results. Treat rows of berries or small shrubs by placing the mix in a furrow four inches deep and twelve to twenty-four inches away from the plant. See specific label directions for application rates. For best results, treat the soil in spring.

Soil Applications of Iron Chelates

Soil application of iron chelates may give a rapid response if the correct chelate is used and other contributing factors are minimal. Applications after May 1 are less likely to show results. Treatments may last less than a season to a couple of years.

Treat trees by placing the iron product in rings of holes in the ground beneath the dripline (outer reaches of the branches). Make holes one and one-half to two inches in diameter, six inches deep, and twelve inches apart in rings two feet apart. On smaller trees, make two to three rings of holes. For large trees, create four to more than five rings of holes, and rings may need to extend beyond the dripline. No holes should be made within two to four feet of the tree trunk on established trees (Figure 15-2).

Drill holes in the soil with a power or hand auger, bulb planter, or small trowel, removing the soil core. Using a punch bar that makes holes by compacting the surrounding soil may be less effective. To avoid damage to shallow utility lines, have the area staked before starting (Figure 15-2).

On soils with a pH above 7.5, only special chelates formulated for a high pH are effective. Examples include EDDHMA (Miller's Ferriplus) or EDDHA (Fe Sequestrene 138). Due to its higher cost, these products have limited availability. See product labels for specific application rates.

Figure 15-2 ▮ *Place soil additive in a ring of holes around the dripline of the tree.*

On acid to slightly alkaline soils, try other chelates like EDTA (Fe Sequestrene 330, Fertilome Liquid Iron) and DTPA (Miller's Iron Chelate DP). They lose effectiveness quickly as the pH rises above 7.2 to 7.5. See product labels for specific application rates.

Soil Applications of Iron Sucrate

Iron sucrate, a relatively new iron source, is manufactured from iron oxide and molasses to form an iron-containing organic complex with limited water solubility. It has an advantage that it is less prone to staining (due to its very low solubility).

Iron sucrate merits consideration in high pH soils, and additional scientific evaluation is warranted for Colorado soils. It is marketed as Lilly Miller Iron Safe.

Foliar Sprays

Foliar sprays of iron sulfate or iron chelates may provide quick response, often in a matter of days. However, the treatment is often spotty and only temporary. Multiple applications per season may be needed. Effects will not carry over into subsequent years.

Foliar applications are generally not recommended due to application limitations. Complete coverage of all leaves is essential. Individual leaves not treated may remain chlorotic. Coverage on large trees is impractical to impossible.

There is a small margin between an iron concentration that will green up the leaves and a concentration that will cause leaf burn. Leaf tissues are rather prone to turn black from an iron burn. Following an iron sulfate foliar treatment, it is common to see leaves that remain chlorotic, leaves that green up, and leaves with black burn spots on the same plant. Spray hitting the sidewalk, house, and other objects may leave a permanent rusty discoloration. Chelated iron sprays are inactivated by sunlight.

Foliar applications may be made with some iron chelates or with iron sulfate products. Both types of products are equally effective, but iron chelates are more expensive. See product labels for specific application rates and instructions. With foliar applications, spray in the evening or on cloudy days when drying time is slower. A few drops of liquid dishwashing soap or commercial wetting agent will enhance sticking properties.

Trunk Injections

Professional arborists have trunk implant or injection methods available for treating iron chlorosis on large trees. Trunk injections may last from one to five years. Refer to product information for application details.

CHAPTER REVIEW *Questions*

1. Describe the symptoms of iron chlorosis. What other situations can be confused with iron chlorosis? How can you tell them apart?

2. List primary factors that contribute to iron chlorosis.

3. What simple method identifies soils prone to iron chlorosis problems?

Chapter
16*

Dealing with Salty Soils

SOLUBLE SALTS

The term **soluble salts** refers to the salts (ions) dissolved in the soil's water. It is another soil factor limiting crop growth in some areas of the West.

Influence of High Salt on Plant Growth

High salt levels can reduce water uptake by plants, restrict root growth, cause marginal burning of the foliage, inhibit flowering, limit seed germination, and reduce fruit and vegetable yields. Irregular bare spots in gardens and uneven crop growth suggest salinity problems. Crop yields may be reduced as much as twenty-five percent without any damage being apparent. Salt injury generally is more severe during periods of hot dry weather, when water use is high (Figure 16-1).

Sensitivity to soluble salts differs among plant species/cultivars and also with their state of growth. Seed germination and seedling growth are more sensitive to salt stress than mature plants (Table 16-1).

Figure 16-1 ■ *Salt burn on bean leaf from high salts in compost.*

*Authors: David Whiting and Carl Wilson (Colorado State University Extension), and Jean Reeder, PhD (USDA-ARS, retired). Artwork by David Whiting.

Table 16-1. Relative Salt Tolerance of Cultivated Plants

Non-tolerant 0–2 dS/m	Slightly Tolerant 2–4 dS/m	Moderately Tolerant 4–8 dS/m	Tolerant 8–16 dS/m
Begonia	Apple	Beet	Arborvitae
Carrot	Cabbage	Black locust	Asparagus
Cotoneaster	Celery	Boxwood	Juniper
Green bean	Cucumber	Broccoli	Russian olive
Onion	Grape	Chrysanthemum	Swiss chard
Pea	Forsythia	Creeping bentgrass	
Radish	Kentucky bluegrass	Geranium	
Raspberry	Lettuce	Marigold	
Red pine	Linden	Muskmelon	
Rose	Norway maple	Perennial ryegrass	
Strawberry	Pepper	Red oak	
Sugar maple	Potato	Spinach	
Viburnum	Red fescue	Squash	
White pine	Red maple	Tomato	
	Snapdragon	White ash	
	Sweet corn	White oak	
		Zinnia	

Note: dS/m is the unit used to measure salt content. It measures the electrical conductivity of the soil. dS/m = mmhos/cm.

FACTORS CONTRIBUTING TO SALT PROBLEMS

Drainage

A common sign of salt problems is the accumulation of salts at the soil surface due to limited percolation in compacted and/or clayey soils. Soluble salts move with the soil water. Deep percolation of water down through the soil profile moves salt out of the rooting zone. Surface evaporation concentrates the salts at the soil surface. Salt deposits may or may not be seen as a white crust on the soil surface. As you drive around Colorado, it is common to see these soils with the white salt accumulation in low spots of fields and natural areas.

In some areas, salt naturally accumulates due to limited rainfall to leach the salt out. Salt levels drop when the soil undergoes irrigation. In other areas, salts may buildup when poor soil drainage prevents precipitation and irrigation water from leaching the salt down through the soil profile. Here, corrective measures are limited to improvements in soil drainage.

Soil Amendments

Manure, biosolids, and compost made with manure or biosolids may be high in salt. When using manure or compost made with manure, routinely monitor salt levels.

Excessive/Unnecessary Fertilizer Applications

Unwarranted application of fertilizers (such as phosphate or potash) increases the salt level. On soils marginally high in salts, potash fertilizers should be avoided unless a potassium deficiency is identified by soil tests.

Placing fertilizer and salty soil amendments too close to seeds or plant roots creates a salt burn of the tender roots. Germination failure or seedling injury can result.

De-Icing Salts

The use of **de-icing salts** on streets and sidewalks frequently results in high salt levels in adjacent soils. Along roads, salt injury has become a major concern. Highway salts may reach plants in two ways: movement to soil and uptake by plant roots, or movement onto plant stems and foliage through the air as vehicle "splash-back." Salts deposited on both soil and foliage have high potential to cause plant injury. Highway salts in road-melt runoff is another concern for plants and the wider environment.

Pet Urine

Damage by **pet urine** is also a salt problem. Water moves by osmotic pressure from the roots to the high salt concentration in the soil, dehydrating and killing roots.

MEASURING SOIL SALT LEVELS

Bean plants are rather salt sensitive and can be used to help assess salt problems. In a garden, if beans are doing well, soluble salts are not a problem. If the beans are doing poorly, consider salts as a possibility. Beans, tomatoes, and other easily germinated seeds can be used in a "pot test" on a windowsill to live assay the salt content of a soil. Assess plants' performance in light of the information in Table 16-1.

The amount of salt in a soil can be quantified only by a soil test. A soil test for soluble salts can be useful when investigating the cause of poor plant growth, determining the suitability of a new planting site, or monitoring the quality of fill soil or soil amendments for use on a landscape area.

Soil tests for soluble salts are based on electrical conductivity. Pure water is a very poor conductor of electric current, whereas water containing dissolved salts conducts current approximately in proportion to the amount of salt present. Thus, measurement of the electrical conductivity (ECe) of a soil extract gives an indication of the total soluble salt concentration in the soil. The ECe is measured in decisiemens per meter (dS/m) or millimhos per centimeter (mmhos/cm) (1 dS/m = 1 mmhos/cm) (Table 16-2).

Table 16-2. Soluble Salt Test Values and Relative Sensitivity Levels of Plants

Electrical Conductivity* (dS/m)	Salinity Level	Effect on Plant Growth
0–2	Non-saline	None
2.1–4	Very slight salinity	Sensitive plants are inhibited
4.1–8	Moderate salinity	Many plants are inhibited
8.1–16	Strong salinity	Most cultivated plants are inhibited
Over 16	Very strong salinity	Few plants are tolerant

*Saturated paste extract.

MANAGING SALTY SOILS
Leaching Salts

Leaching is the only practical way of removing excess salts. This is effective only to the extent that water moves down through the soil profile and beneath the root zone (drainage must be good). The amount of salts removed depends on the quantity and quality of water leached through the soil profile during a single irrigation period. Water should be low in salts (high quality) and must not run off the surface. It should be applied slowly so amounts do not exceed the ability of the soil to take in water (infiltration rate).

The following amounts of water applied in a single, continuous irrigation will dissolve and decrease soil salts by these fractional amounts:

- Six inches of water will leach about half the salt.

- Twelve inches of water will leach about four-fifths of the salt.

- Twenty-four inches of water will leach about nine-tenths of the salt.

Adding Soil Amendments

Because manure, biosolids, and compost made from manure or biosolids may be high in salts, do not add more than one inch per season without a soil test to evaluate salt levels. An amendment with up to 10 dS/m total salts is acceptable if mixed through the upper six to eight inches of a low-salt soil (less than 1 dS/m). Amendments with a salt content greater than 10 dS/m are questionable. Avoid these soil amendments in soils that are already high in salts (above 3 dS/m) when growing the salt sensitive plants.

Note: Because soil amendments are not regulated in Colorado, do not assume that products sold in bags or by bulk are necessarily low in salt content and good for the garden's soil. Many commercially available sources of manure, biosolids, and compost made with manure or biosolids have excessively high levels of salt.

On marginally salty soils, concentrate on gradually improving the soil organic content and activity of soil microorganisms and earthworms. Do not exceed recommended rates per application as large quantities of organic matter can hold salts next to plant roots and cause injury. Organic amendments applied over time improve soil tilth, which then will improve the potential for effective leaching as well as plant growth.

Other Management Techniques

Plants grown on salty soils are less tolerant of dry soil conditions. Plants will require more frequent irrigation, with reduced amounts of water.

Within pedestrian and vehicle safety limits, avoid the use of de-icing salts. Consider the use of sand or other abrasive materials for use on slick sidewalks and pavement. Where de-icing salts are routinely used, expect to find salt problems in adjacent soils and drainage swales where the snowmelt runs. Because soil salt levels from de-icing salts easily rise above the tolerance of even the most salt-tolerant plants, a rock mulch area without plants may be a better landscape design solution in salt use areas.

For additional details on soil salt issues, refer to the following Colorado State University Extension fact sheets #7.227, *Growing Turf on Salt-Affected Sites*, available at www.cmg.colostate.edu.

1. Describe plant problems associated with excess soil salt levels.

2. List sources/causes of high soil salts.

3. Describe the leaching process for salty soils. What about situations when excess salts cannot be leached out?

4. Describe other management strategies for salty soils.

Chapter

17*

Dealing with Soil Drainage

PORE SPACE CONTROLS SOIL DRAINAGE CHARACTERISTICS

Pore space controls soil drainage characteristics. In other words, drainage problems often arise from lack of large-sized pores.

In soils dominated by large pores (i.e., sandy soils), water moves rapidly. Soils that allow rapid *leaching* (water movement down through the soil profile) also pose environmental hazards because rain or irrigation water moving through the soil profile takes water-soluble pollutants with it. Ground water pollution is a sensitive issue on coarse-textured sandy soils.

In comparison, in soils dominated by small-sized pores (i.e., compacted soils and soils with greater than twenty percent clay content), water is slow to move or may not move at all. Soils easily waterlog.

Roots must have oxygen to survive, and root activity shuts down in waterlogged soils. Plants growing on wet soils are typically shallow rooted. Many plants are prone to root rot in wet soils. Prolonged periods of waterlogged soil conditions lead to the decline or even death of most plants.

When water does not leach through the soil profile, salts left behind by surface evaporation accumulate and create a white crust on the soil. This is frequently observed as a white deposit on low spots of pastures and fields. High soil salt content limits plant growth in some areas of Colorado.

Poor drainage is a common problem in many Colorado soils. In some areas, the surface soil allows water infiltration only to have the water stopped as it reaches a less permeable subsurface soil layer.

*Author: David Whiting, Colorado State University Extension. Artwork by David Whiting.

A simple test to evaluate soil drainage is to dig a hole twelve inches deep and fill it with water. If the water fails to drain in 30 minutes, the soil has a drainage problem. If the hole fails to drain in twenty-four hours, waterlogged soils may affect plant growth.

CORRECTING DRAINAGE PROBLEMS

Managing Soil Tilth

Attention to managing soil tilth plays a key role in soil drainage. On coarse-textured sandy soils, routine applications of organic matter increase the water-holding capacity. On compacted and fine-textured clayey soils, attention to organic matter and the "living soil" helps create large pores, improving drainage. For additional information, refer to Chapter 9.

French Drains

In some situations, a *French drain* facilitates water drainage. A French drain is a ditch-like trench that is filled with rock or gravel. The rock should round the top, preventing soil from covering the drain. The trench must slope at least one to three percent and flow to an outlet (Figure 17-1).

Surface Drainage and Runoff

To minimize surface runoff and soil erosion, sloping areas should be planted with perennial ground covers or turf. Mowed lawns or un-mowed naturalized grass areas make the best ground cover for slowing runoff. Some landscapes may also need terracing to control runoff.

Figure 17-1 ▮ *A French drain is a ditch-like trench filled with rock. Water must flow downhill to an outlet.*

To improve surface drainage problems, first identify and then correct the contributing factors:

- **Irrigation**—Many surface drainage problems arise from over irrigation (too much and/or too often).

- **Compaction**—Compaction is difficult to deal with, so prevention is the key. Soils around new homes are typically compacted from construction traffic. Break up the compacted layer by tilling, adding organic matter, and encouraging earthworms and soil organisms. For details, refer to Chapter 10.

- **Organic mulches**, like wood/bark chips, help manage compaction around trees and shrubs, perennials, small fruits, and garden paths. For details on mulching, refer to Chapter 12. On lawns and around shade trees, lawn aeration helps manage compaction.

- **Thatch in lawn**—A heavy thatch layer in a lawn slows water infiltration. Improve by aerating the lawn (making enough passes that plugs are at two-inch intervals) (Figure 17-2). (For details, refer to Chapter 43.)

- **Grading**—It is surprising how often the landscaper forgets that water only flows downhill. Sometimes, the grade may be deceiving.

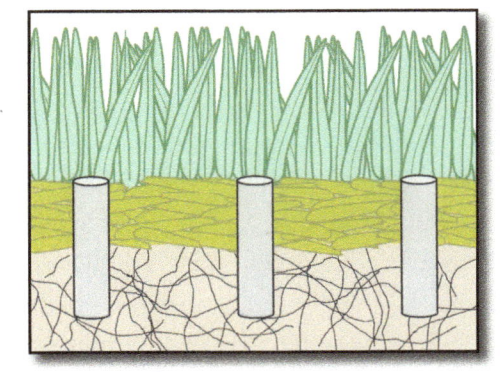

Figure 17-2 ▮ *A heavy thatch layer slows water infiltration. Routine aeration may be needed on compacted clayey soil to help reduce thatch and open the soil to air and water.*

- **Low spot without an outlet**—It is common to find standing water in low spots. Look at the irrigation schedule: is the area being overwatered or is irrigation running off instead of soaking in (aerate and use multiple shorter irrigation cycles)? Fill in the low spot, or install a French or underground drain with a gravity-flow outlet.

- **High water table**—High water tables may be difficult to deal with. Sometimes, the only solution is to raise the soil level (raised bed or berm gardening).

- **Impervious subsoil**—In Colorado, we find many soil profiles with an impervious soil layer under the surface. See the subsequent discussion on subsurface drainage.

Subsurface Drainage

Subsurface drainage problems are generally correctable only to the extent that large soil pore spaces can be increased to allow for better water movement. Use of soil drainage tiles are only effective to the extent that the soil will allow water to flow through it to the drain tile, and water in the drain tile can flow downhill to an outlet.

To improve subsurface drainage problems, first identify and then correct the contributing factors.

- **Impervious subsoil layer underlain with permeable soil**

  —If less than two feet thick, rip or double-dig when soil is dry. Irrigate to settle, and do final grade when soil re-dries.

  —If greater than two feet thick, bore holes through layer.

  —Holes are typically four to six inches in diameter at six-foot intervals. Fill with coarse sand or fine gravel.

- **Impermeable subsoil**

  —Increase soil depth.

  —Select shallow-rooted and water-tolerant plants.

  —These soils may have a salt problem.

- **Change in soil texture**—A change in soil texture creates water movement problems. This is a common problem when soils are added to a raised-bed box or applied as a top dressing.

  —Cultivate to mix layers.

1. Describe drainage problems as related to *pore space*, *surface runoff*, and *leaching*.

2. Why is it so important to identify the causes of a drainage problem before attempting corrections?

3. List common causes of surface drainage problems with possible corrective actions.

4. List common causes of subsurface drainage problems with possible corrective actions.

18*

Soil Tests

VALUE OF A SOIL TEST

On agronomic crops, greenhouse crops, and turf, an extensive research base for interpretation of soil test results makes soil testing a key tool in crop management for commercial producers.

In the home garden setting, soil testing is valuable to establish a baseline on soil limitations related to pH, salt levels, and the need for phosphate and potash fertilizers. A special lead test would be of concern to homeowners with lead-based paints on older homes.

However, in some gardening situations, soil testing has limited value. For example, soil testing for nitrogen has limited use for the home gardener because the nitrogen level constantly changes in response to soil organic matter additions, soil microorganism activity, and temperature and moisture levels.

The research base for interpreting results is also lacking for many landscape plants. For example, a test for a maple tree, native plants, or the gardener's favorite peony would simply be based on norms used for general agronomic crops. A research base to interpret needs for micronutrients is limited to specific agronomic and greenhouse crops.

Finally, a standard soil test will not identify the most common garden problems related to overwatering, underwatering, poor soil drainage, soil compaction, diseases, insects, weed competition, environmental disorders, too much shade, poor varieties, or basic neglect.

*Authors: David Whiting and Carl Wilson (Colorado State University Extension), and Jean Reeder, PhD (USDA-ARS, retired). Artwork by David Whiting.

Typical Test

A standard soil test typically includes the following:

- Texture (estimated by the hand-feel method)
- Organic matter (reported as a percent of the total soil)
  - About two-thirds of a pound of nitrogen per 1,000 square feet will be released (mineralized to nitrate) during the growing season for each one percent organic matter present
- pH
- Lime ($CaCO_3$ reported by percent)

  - On soils with free lime, sulfur will not effectively lower the pH
- Soluble salts (reported in mmhos/cm or dS/m)
- Nutrients (reported in parts per million)
  - Nitrate nitrogen
  - Phosphorus
  - Potassium
  - Micronutrients such as copper, iron, manganese, and zinc

Additional tests could be run for special needs like lead content or sodium problems. For additional details on soil testing, refer to Colorado State University Extension fact sheet #0.502, *Soil Test Explanation*, available at www.cmg.colostate.edu.

Frequency

For a gardener on a new site, a soil test gives a useful baseline on soil salts, phosphorus, potassium, and pH with free lime (or buffer index if acid).

In other parts of the country where lime is routinely added to raise the pH on acid soils, a soil test may be needed annually.

In the neutral and alkaline soils of Western soils, repeat the test when dramatic changes are made to the soil (such as addition of larger quantities of manure, biosolids, or compost that may be high in salts) or approximately every four to eight years to reestablish the baseline.

TAKING A SOIL SAMPLE

A soil sample may be taken at any time of year, although spring and fall sampling are usually the most convenient.

The results of a test are no better than the sample sent to the laboratory. The sample must be representative of the yard or garden being considered. Gardeners who try to shortcut the sampling procedure will not receive a reliable reading.

Submit a sample for each yard area that receives different fertilizer and soil management treatments. For example, if the front and back lawn are fertilized the same, the sample should include subsamples taken from each and mixed together. Because garden areas are managed differently from lawns, the garden should be sampled separately from the lawn. Sample various garden beds that receive differing amounts of fertilizers and soil amendments separately.

Samples are most easily collected using a soil tube or soil auger. A garden trowel, spade, bulb planter, or large knife also works. Discard any sod, surface vegetation, or litter. Sampling depth is critical and varies for the type of test taken and for various labs. Follow sampling depth directions given by the laboratory (Table 18-1).

Table 18-1. Example of Sampling Depth for Soil Test

Crop	Sampling Depth
Garden (vegetable and flower)	0–6 inches
Lawns, new (prior to planting)	0–6 inches
Lawns, established	0–3 inches
Lead test	0–0.75 inch

Each sample should be a composite of subsamples collected from randomly selected spots within the chosen area. Take five or more subsamples from a relatively small area in the home lawn, flower border, or vegetable garden. Take ten to fifteen subsamples for larger areas. Try to dig straight down rather than at an angle. Try to collect about the same amount of soil from each sampling area (Figure 18-1).

Collect the subsamples in a clean plastic pail, thoroughly mixing the subsamples together. Remove plant debris and break up clods. If possible, air-dry the soil by spreading it out on paper towel. (Do not oven-dry the sample.)

Place about two cups of the soil mix into the sample bag or box. Label the sample container (e.g., front lawn, vegetable garden, or flowerbed) and keep a record of the area represented by each sample taken. Send the samples to the soil-testing laboratory.

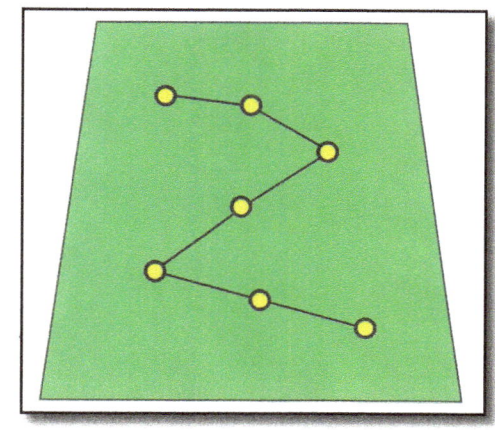

Figure 18-1 ■ *A proper soil sample is a composite of ten to fifteen subsamples.*

Many types of chemical solutions may be used to extract nutrients from soil in the laboratory. Processes used vary from laboratory to laboratory. Because climate and soil vary considerably in different parts of the country, select a local laboratory that processes for the alkaline calcareous soils of the Mountain West. Future testing should be done with the same laboratory in order to make comparisons.

Soil tests are available from many local providers. For a list of laboratories, refer to Colorado State University Extension fact sheet #0.520, *Selecting an Analytical Lab*, available online at www.cmg.colostate.edu.

SOIL TEST RECOMMENDATIONS

In production agriculture, it is not uncommon for a grower or fertilizer dealer to split a sample and send it to different laboratories. Because individual laboratories do not necessarily use the same soil test procedures, their **availability indexes** (the reported available nutrients) can, and frequently do, differ.

Laboratories can also differ in the objectives behind their recommendations. For example, are maximum yields the primary objective? In this scenario, fertilizer application will be highest, with increased costs, and higher potential for leaching of fertilizers into ground water. In another scenario, the crop's net return may be the primary objective, reducing production (fertilizer) costs, or minimizing potential for ground water pollution.

Fertilizer practices may also influence recommendations. For example, is the phosphate fertilizer recommendation based on an annual application or a single application to last several years? For a soil test for new turf, it is a standard practice to bring the phosphorus to a higher level when the fertilizer can be cultivated through the soil profile before the sod is laid.

The recommendations resulting from a soil test need to be made by the laboratory doing the work, based on cropping information provided by the grower/gardener. For additional details on soil testing, refer to Colorado State University Extension fact sheet #0.502, *Soil Test Explanation*, available at: www.cmg.colostate.edu.

HOME SOIL TEST KITS

Home soil test kits have questionable value. The actual process used on some procedures is based on soil pH. Most home test kits were designed for acid soils and have questionable accuracy on the alkaline soils of the West.

In addition, the accuracy in home soil test procedures may, at best, give a ballpark reading but not precise accuracy. For example, the calibration on a home soil pH kit will tell the gardener that the soil has a pH level between 7 and 8. How close to 7 or 8 makes a huge difference for the growth of some plants. More precise measurement requires more expensive equipment.

CHAPTER REVIEW
Questions

1. List situations when a soil test would be helpful. List examples of plant growth problems for which a soil test would *not* be helpful.

2. Describe the steps to a soil test.

3. Where does one find a list of soil testing laboratories?

UNIT D

Diagnostics and Pest Management

Learning Objectives

At the end of this unit, the student will be able to:

- Describe Plant Health Care (Integrated Pest Management) as it applies to the home landscape.
- Describe growth phases in the life cycle of trees.
- Describe steps in the diagnostic process.
- Describe steps to diagnose abiotic tree disorders.
- Identify the rooting area of trees.
- Identify common insects to taxonomic orders.
- Describe routine insect management techniques for the home landscape, selecting methods appropriate for various situations.
- Describe routine disease management techniques for the home landscape, selecting methods appropriate for various situations.
- Describe routine weed management techniques for the home landscape, selecting methods appropriate for various situations.

Supplemental Reading

Books

- *Abiotic Disorders of Landscape Plants: A Diagnostic Guide*. University of California Agriculture and Natural Resources Publication 3420. 2004.
- *Aspen: A Guide to Common Problems in Colorado*. Colorado State University Extension Publication 559A. 1996.
- *Garden Insects of North America.* Whitney Cranshaw. Princeton University Press. 2004.
- *Insects and Diseases of Woody Plants of the Central Rockies.* Colorado State University Cooperative Extension Bulletin 506A. 2004.
- *Pests of the West.* Dr. Whitney Cranshaw. Fulcrum Publishing. 1998.
- *Plant Health Care for Woody Ornamentals*. University of Illinois Cooperative Extension. 1997.

Web

- Colorado State University Extension fact sheets on home garden insect, disease, and weed management available online at www.cmg.colostate.edu.

19*

Integrated Pest Management

Plant Health Care

GARDENING AND THE ENVIRONMENT

Yard care and gardening practices may have positive or negative influences on health and the neighborhood environment. For example, turf enhances the environment by:

- Converting carbon dioxide to oxygen

- Increasing water infiltration into the soil

- Reducing surface runoff and erosion

- Reducing dust

- Providing a microecosystem that effectively breaks down pollutants

- Moderating summer temperatures

- Creating a pleasant "people" space

On the other hand, lawn care practices negatively affect the environment when grass clippings are mowed or blown onto the street (water quality problem), when fertilizers are overspread onto hard surfaces, and when unwarranted use of pesticides occurs.

Several terms (such as "Integrated Pest Management (IPM)," "Plant Health Care (PHC)," "sustainable farming/gardening," "best management practices," and "organic gardening") are used to describe farming/garden management systems designed to help farmers/gardeners maximize positive effects and minimize negative effects.

*Author: David Whiting, Colorado State University Extension.

INTEGRATED PEST MANAGEMENT

Integrated Pest Management, IPM, incorporates a variety of pest management strategies, including cultural methods, mechanical methods, use of bionaturals, and use of organic and manufactured pesticides. Objectives include minimizing pest damage, health-related hazards, and environmental hazards, while maintaining profitability.

Because insect and disease problems vary significantly from crop to crop, application of IPM principles is also crop-specific. IPM techniques used in an alfalfa field (perennial crop), a wheat field (annual crop), an apple orchard (perennial crop with minimal tolerance for pest damage), and the landscape (site with multiple plant species and higher tolerance to pests) will be vastly different.

PLANT HEALTH CARE

The term **Plant Health Care, PHC,** was coined by the International Society of Arboriculture to more clearly define IPM techniques as they apply to tree care and landscape maintenance.

PHC is a holistic approach to landscape management. The primary objective is to grow healthy plants and minimize the effects of pests in so doing. Concepts of PHC include the following:

- **Healthy plants have fewer pests.**—Many insect and disease problems only attack plants under stress. Minimizing stress prevents many common pests. For example, *Cytospora* fungus and most borers only attack trees under stress (primarily soil compaction and drought).

- **Healthy plants are more tolerant of pests.**—For example, aphids on shade trees generally do not warrant management efforts. An important exception is that trees under water stress (dry soils, non-established root system, limited root spread due to soil compaction or hardscape, root injury) are intolerant of aphid feeding.

- **Life cycle: Plant needs change with stages in their life cycle.**—A plant's needs for irrigation, fertilizer, pruning, tolerance to pests, etc., continually change through the growth cycles of the plant.

- **PIC cycle: Problems arise from a combination of stress factors.**—For example, overmaturity of forests coupled with drought leads to bark beetles in Western pine forests. Soil compaction leads to *Cytospora*.

The PIC Cycle

A basic principle of PHC is recognition that plant problems generally arise from a combination of stress factors. This concept is called the **PIC cycle.**

Predisposing factors reduce a plant's tolerance to stress. These factors should be considered in plant selection. Examples of predisposing factors include:

- Planting trees in a site where root spread will be restricted due to soil compaction or hardscape features

- Planting trees intolerant of wet soils (like crabapples) in heavily irrigated lawns (leads to root rots)

- Planting trees susceptible to iron chlorosis in soils with free lime

- Failure to structurally train young trees (predisposing trees to storm damage)

Inciting factors include primary insect, disease, and abiotic disorders that attack healthy plants, causing acute stress. Examples include:

- Soil compaction, the most common stress factor leading to many insect and disease problems

- Planting trees too deep (leads to trunk girdling roots)

- Drought

- Leaf chewing insects, such as caterpillars and sawfly larva

- Leaf sucking insects, such as aphids and leafhoppers

- Bark damage from lawn mowers

- Bark cankers and frost cracks from rapid winter temperature changes coupled with winter drought

Contributing factors include secondary insect, disease, and abiotic disorders that attack plants already under stress. They often lead to the plant's death and frequently cannot be controlled. Examples include:

- Bark beetles and borers (secondary to soil compaction, drought, and wind damage)

- *Cytospora* fungus (secondary to soil compaction, drought, and restricted rooting system)

- Trunk girdling roots caused by planting trees too deep

Management of contributing factors typically needs to be directed at the predisposing and inciting factors that stress the plant.

PLANT HEALTH CARE TECHNIQUES

Examples of techniques used in PHC include the following:

- Plant selection: right plant, right place—For the site, select plants to minimize future stress.

- Soils management—80% of all landscape plant problems relate to soil conditions.

  —Soil compaction (low soil oxygen and poor drainage)

  —Drainage

  —Improve soils tilth with routine applications of organic matter

  —Nutrient (fertilizer) management

- Water and irrigation management

  —Water requirements for plants to survive compared to the water needs for plants to grow may be vastly different

  —Plant tolerance to wet (wetland plants) or dry (xeric plants) conditions

  —Iron chlorosis is an issue of chronic, springtime overwatering

- Cultural care

  —Planting dates

  —Varieties with resistance to common pests

  —Plant diversity

  —Spacing and air flow

  —Exposure to sun and wind

  —Mulching

  —Pruning

- Weather influence on plant growth and pest potential

  —Temperatures

  —Wind and rain

  —Timing of insect activity

- Mechanical methods to manage pests

  —Covers and barriers

  —Traps

- Bionaturals for managing pests—Use of predators, parasites, disease organisms, and beneficial nematodes

  —**Preservation** is taking steps to encourage naturally occurring predators and parasites.

  —**Importation** is the purchase and release of predators and parasites.

- Pesticides, both "organic" and manufactured

Pest Management Questions

As part of PHC, ask the following questions to guide pest management:

1. **What is the plant?** Correctly identifying the plant will shorten the list of potential insects, diseases, and abiotic disorders.

2. **What is the disorder/pest?** Correctly identifying the disorder/pest will set the direction for effective management options. Gardeners often fail to control pests because they have misidentified the problems and are applying ineffective management techniques.

3. **What type of damage/stress does it cause?** In the landscape setting, most insect and disease problems are only cosmetic and may not warrant management efforts. To protect plant health, management may be needed on some pests. On fruits and vegetables, tolerance to insects and diseases is typically low.

4. **Under what situations will management efforts be warranted?**

   In production agriculture, **economic thresholds** determine how much damage can be tolerated before it becomes economically feasible to treat. For example, this may be determined by counting the number of insects per leaf, the number of insects in a square foot of soil, or the percent of leaves infected.

   In landscape horticulture, **aesthetic thresholds** characterize a relative level of cosmetic damage that can be tolerated before treatment is warranted. This threshold will vary considerably from individual to individual and from location to location.

   Spider mites are an example of a common pest generally kept in bounds by Mother Nature. However, management efforts may be warranted in situations where mite populations explode due to hot weather, drought, dust on the plants (interferes with activity of beneficials), or the use of some insecticides including imidacloprid (Merit) and carbaryl (Sevin).

5. **What management options are effective on the disorder/pest, and when are they applied?**

   Weather—While we do not control the weather, it directly influences the occurrence of many insects and diseases.

   Cultural—Such as watering more or less

   Mechanical—Such as washing down the plant with a forceful stream of water to wash of pests

   Bionaturals—Use of beneficial predators and parasites

   Pesticides—Including "organic" and manufactured

LIFE CYCLE OF A PLANT

Another key concept in PHC includes recognizing that the plant care changes with various stages of growth. Failure to relate cultural practices to the life cycle often leads to reduced growth and confusion about appropriate cultural practices. Tables 19-1 and 19-2 give an overview of the life cycle of trees.

Life cycle of a tree

1. Nursery production
2. Establishment phase
3. Growth phase
4. Maturity
5. Decline phase

Life cycle of a vegetable (annuals)

1. Seed germination and emergence
2. Seedling growth
3. Growth phase
4. Flowering and fruiting phase

Table 19-1. Life Cycle of a Tree

Growth Phase	Growth Objectives	Change to Next Growth Phase
Nursery production	Top growth = selling price	Planting
Establishment phase	Root establishment	When roots become established, length of annual twig growth significantly increases.
Growth phase	Period of canopy growth—Balance canopy growth with root growth	Growth slows as tree approaches mature size (for site limitations).
Maturity	Canopy growth slows as tree matures—Balance canopy growth with root growth.	Minimizing stress on aging trees prolongs tree life
Decline phase	Minimize stress levels	Death

Table 19-2. Influence of Life Cycle on Cultural Practices for Trees

Growth Phase	Irrigation Water Need	Fertilization	Pruning	Pest Tolerance
Nursery production	Water = Growth	Fertilizer pushes desirable top growth.	*Structural training* desirable.	Low: Could influence sales.
Establishment	Critical: Trees are under water stress due to the reduced rooting system.	None to very little as high nitrogen pushes canopy growth at the expense of root growth	Heavy pruning slows root establishment.	Low due to drought imposed by reduced root system.
Growth	Water = Growth Good tolerant to short-term drought. However, short-term drought will slow growth.	If other growth factors are not limiting, fertilization supports growth.	*Structural training* sets the tree's structural integrity for life.	High, except under stress situations.
Maturity	Good tolerance to short-term drought. Severe drought leads to decline.	Need for fertilizer reduces. Over fertilization could push out canopy growth that the roots cannot support in summer heat and wind.	Maturing trees that were structurally trained while young have minimal needs for pruning.	High, except under stress situations.
Decline	Intolerant of drought	Evaluate stress factors as fertilization can accelerate stress in some situations.	Pruning limited to *cleaning* (removal of dead wood). Do not remove healthy wood on trees under stress.	Low: Pests could accelerate decline.

CHAPTER REVIEW
Questions

1. Define IPM and PHC.

2. Describe concepts central to PHC.

3. What is the PIC cycle? What does it explain about plant care and pest problems?

4. In diagnosing *contributing* disorders, why is it important to also identify the *predisposing* and *inciting* factors to the extent possible?

5. Give examples of common PHC techniques used in home gardening.

6. In pest management, what are *bionaturals*? What is *preservation* and *importation* of bionaturals?

7. Explain the pest management questions.

8. Why is it important to talk about tree care issues as they relate to growth phases?

9. List the five growth phases of trees, giving growth objectives for each. Describe how to identify when trees have changed their phase.

10. Explain how water needs, fertilization, and pruning changes between growth phases.

Chapter

20*

The Diagnostic Process

SKILLS ESSENTIAL TO THE DIAGNOSTIC PROCESS

Judiciously examine the tree—Many homeowners have a difficult time describing their plants and plant problems. For example, the description "leaves are yellow" is so generic that nothing can be diagnosed without more details. When it comes to insects, a typical home gardener says they have "black bugs." What do they mean by "bug"? Are they saying they have a black insect? This is so generic that no diagnosis is possible without additional details.

Read—Part of the diagnostic process is to read, comparing the symptoms and signs of the problems with details in references. Do not simply work from memory.

Referring to multiple books on the same topic gives a better understanding of a pest's description and management situation. In diagnostic work, read for the details rather than general concepts.

Ask questions—Diagnosis requires extensive two-way conversations. Often, the horticulturist trying to diagnose the problem has not been onsite and has to totally rely on the descriptions of someone else. In this situation, diagnosis is difficult to impossible. Even with good samples or when visiting the site, questions about the care of the plant, history of the site, and progression of symptoms are needed in the diagnostic process.

Practice—Diagnostics is far more than applying knowledge that can be read in a book. The diagnostic process requires the integration of years of gardening wisdom and knowledge. It is learned by practice.

Patience—Diagnosing plant disorders is a process, not a simple answer to a question. It takes time and patience to work the process. Never jump at an answer just because it seems easy. Never guess. Rather, take the time to work the process, asking lots of questions.

---

*Authors: David Whiting and Carol O'Meara, Colorado State University Extension.

In pest management, first diagnose the problem and then discuss management options. Home gardeners often jump to management questions without diagnosing the problem. Because management options are very pest-specific, correct diagnosis of the problems must be completed before management can be discussed.

Asking Questions, Gathering Information

Ask questions that create dialogue. For example, "Tell me how you watered the plant." Avoid accusatory type questions (e.g., "Did you overwater the plant?").

Some disorders cannot be diagnosed.—We can only complete a diagnosis when detailed information is available. Generic descriptions, like "yellow leaves" or "poor growth" are inadequate descriptions for a diagnosis.

Diagnosis must be done in the context of the tree's environment.—For example, is the tree in a routinely irrigated lawn or in a site with limited irrigation? Does the site have an open area for root spread, or is the root system limited by poor soils or hardscape features?

For example, a client called with concerns that her tree looked wilted. Should she water more? After asking questions, it was discovered that the tree is located in a construction site and had most of the root system cut. Understanding the context of the root damage is essential to addressing the watering issue.

Questions asked may not reflect the real issues—Home gardeners frequently do not know what questions to ask. In the diagnostic process, Colorado Master Gardener volunteers must often help frame questions as well as provide answers. For example, in the previous situation with the tree in the construction site, an important question is the stability of the tree with respect to wind as most of the roots have been cut.

A useful tool in diagnosis is visualizing the plant, that is, painting a mental picture of the plant with its surroundings. As you paint the picture, ask questions about details. Every detail must be verified. For example, do not paint a nice green lawn in your mental picture until it is verified by asking questions. Painting creates a long list of questions to help discover details needed for diagnosis. Explaining to the client that you are trying to paint a mental picture of their tree encourages them to more patiently provide the needed information.

In working with clients, repeat back in your own words their descriptions. This helps clear up miscommunications about symptoms.

In working with clients, verbally explain how you rule out possible causes. This helps the client move on with you and may clarify miscommunication about symptoms.

As previously stated, diagnosis is not possible when generic symptoms are all we have to work with. Keep in mind that multiple problems will have similar symptoms.

Management should only be addressed after the diagnosis is complete.—Because disorders generally arise from a combination of factors, management must look at predisposing factors and inciting factors in the management discussion.

STEPS IN THE DIAGNOSTIC PROCESS

Diagnosis

1. Identify the plant.
2. Identify the problem(s).
   a. Look—Define the problem by describing the signs and symptoms.
   b. Read—Refer to reference materials describing similar signs and symptoms.
   c. Compare—Determine probable cause(s) through comparison and elimination.

Management

3. Evaluate if management efforts are warranted.
   a. What type of damage/stress does this disorder/pest cause?
   b. Under what situations would management efforts be warranted?
   c. Are management efforts warranted for this situation?

4. Evaluate management options effective for this disorder/pest and when they are applied.

STEP 1—IDENTIFY THE PLANT

There are hundreds of insects and diseases that attack landscape plants in any geographic region. Once the plant has been correctly identified, the list of potential insects and diseases that attack the specific plant drops to just a few. Additionally, insects and diseases account for only 20% of landscape plant problems. When working with abiotic disorders, plant identification will be helpful but will not shorten the list of potential possibilities as significantly.

Many gardeners are not familiar with plant materials and need help to correctly identify trees. Identification of a tree is not practical over the phone. The novice gardener cannot give adequate description over the phone for identification. Rather, a small branch sample with leaves should be brought to the Colorado State University Extension office.

STEP 2—IDENTIFY THE PROBLEM(S)

Step 2a—Look—Define the Problem by Describing the Signs and Symptoms

Take a close look at the plant and surroundings. A detailed description of the problem is essential for diagnosis. In situations where the description is limited or generic in symptoms, diagnosis will be impossible. Many landscape problems cannot be diagnosed! When diagnosing abiotic disorders, systematically evaluating the tree will help organize questions in a discovery process.

Symptoms are changes in the plant's growth or appearance in response to causal factors.

Signs are the presence of the actual organism or direct evidence of the casual factors.

Time development—Knowing the time frame for the development of signs and symptoms is a helpful tool. Did it occur suddenly or over a period of time? Keep in mind that the gardener may not actually know as he or she may not have observed the early development. Symptoms that occur suddenly and do not progress are typical of abiotic disorders. Symptoms that progressively develop are typical of living factors (insects and diseases).

Keep in mind that multiple problems have similar symptoms. Let the symptoms lead you to the diagnosis rather than trying to make a diagnosis fit a group of symptoms. Treatment without correct diagnosis is malpractice!

Terminology used to describe common symptoms includes:

- **Blight**—A rapid discoloration and death of twigs, foliage, or flowers.
- **Canker**—Dead area on bark or stem, often sunken or raised.
- **Chlorosis**—Yellowing—Chlorosis is so generic that without additional details diagnosis is impossible.
- **Decline**—Progressive decrease in plant vigor.
- **Dieback**—Progressive death of shoot, branch, or root starting at the tip.
- **Gall** or **gall-like**—Abnormal localized swelling or enlargement of plant part. It could be caused by insects, mites, diseases, or abiotic disorders.
- **Gummosis**—Exudation of gum or sap.

- **Leaf distortion**—The leaf could be twisted, cupped, rolled, or otherwise deformed.
- **Leaf scorch**—Burning along the leaf margin and into the leaf from the margin.
- **Leaf spot**—A spot or lesion on the leaf.
- **Necrosis**—Dead tissue—Necrotic areas are also so generic that without additional details diagnosis is impossible.
- **Wilt**—General wilting of the plant or plant part.
- **Witches broom**—Abnormal broom-like growth of many weak shoots.

Terminology used to describe signs includes:

- **Fruiting bodies**—Reproductive structures of fungi; could be in the form of mushrooms, puffballs, pycnidia, rusts, or conks.
- **Insects** and **mites** are common signs.
- **Mycelium**—Mass of fungal threads (hyphae) on the plant surface.
- **Rhizomorphs**—Shoestring-like fungal threads found under the bark of stressed and dying trees caused by the *Armillaria* fungi. They may glow!
- **Slime flux** or **ooze**—A bacterial discharge that oozes out of the plant tissues, may be gooey or a dried mass.

Examples of abiotic signs include:

- Girdling roots (caused by planting too deep)—sign of root starvation
- Lack of a root flare (sign that the tree was planted too deep with a high potential to develop girdling roots)
- Measuring soil compaction with a penetrometer
- Bark damage on a trunk from lawnmowers and weed eaters
- Standing water over rooting zone
- Plugged drip irrigation system emitters
- Record of springtime freezing temperatures or severe winter temperatures
- Hardscape over tree rooting area
- Soil tests show high salts

Define What is Normal versus Abnormal

It is common for the home gardener to suddenly observe normal characteristics of a tree and mistakenly attribute it to an insect or disease. For example, on evergreens:

- Needle problems and dieback of the new needles at the branch tip are abnormal.
- Yellowing and dropping of older needles from the inside of the tree are normal. The number of years that needles are retained is a factor of plant genetics and stress. Under stress, needles may drop sooner.

Other examples of "normal" occurrences often confused as problems include:

- Fuzz on underside of leaves.
- Male pollen cones on pine or spruce mistaken for insects or disease
- Less conspicuous fruit, such as juniper berries
- Mushrooms
- Bluegrass going to seed

- Spores on the underside of fern fronds

- Flowers and fruit on potatoes (potato fruit look like cherry tomatoes)

- Tomatoes dropping blossoms after a cool night

- Male squash blossoms

- June drop of apples and other fruit

- Aerial roots on tomatoes and corn

- Seed stalk on rhubarb and onions

Step 2b—Read—Refer to Reference Materials Describing Similar Signs and Symptoms

The reading will often send you back to the tree to look for more details.

A key in the back of the Colorado State University Extension publication *Insects and Diseases of Woody Plants* makes this step easy for diagnosing insects and diseases of landscape trees and shrubs in the Rocky Mountain and High Plains region. Similar publications are available from Cooperative Extension in other states and regions. The key is very good for most insects and fair for diseases (diseases are hard to describe in a few words). It does not include abiotic disorders.

Step 2c—Compare—Determine Probable Cause(s) through Comparison and Elimination

When the description of the disorder matches the details in the reference materials, diagnosis is complete. It requires careful reading of fine details. When things do not match, back up. Is the plant correctly identified? Work through the process again, paying attention to details missed.

Keep in mind that multiple problems have similar symptoms. Let the process guide you through the diagnosis rather than trying to match symptoms to fit a diagnosis.

Insects on trees are fairly easy to diagnose with the book *Insects and Diseases of Woody Plants*. Diseases are more difficult, and only a few tree diseases are common in Colorado. This book does not include abiotic disorders.

Abiotic disorders are generally difficult, if not impossible, to diagnose. A systematic evaluation of the tree will be helpful for diagnosing abiotic disorders. Abiotic disorders account for 80% of the samples diagnosed by Colorado State University Extension and often predispose the tree to insects and diseases.

STEP 3—EVALUATE IF MANAGEMENT EFFORTS ARE WARRANTED

Step 3a—What Type of Damage/Stress Does This Disorder/Pest Cause?

The primary question here is to determine if the disorder/pest is only cosmetic, if it adds stress to the tree, or if it is potentially life-threatening. This may depend, in part, on the general health of the tree before the disorder/pest started.

Step 3b—Under What Situations Would Management Efforts Be Warranted?

On healthy stress-free trees, most insect and disease problems are only cosmetic. However, trees under stress are much less tolerant of additional stress factors.

For example, aphids on shade trees are generally only cosmetic and normally do not warrant management efforts, unless they become a nuisance (like dripping honeydew on the car or patio table). However, under a water stress situation (due to drought, non-irrigated site, limited rooting spread, or non-established newly planted tree) aphid feeding adds to the water needs of the tree, creating a potentially serious stress issue. With water stress, mechanical (hosing off the tree with water), bionaturals (adding beneficials to feed on the aphids), or insecticidal management efforts would be warranted to protect the tree.

As a rule of thumb for leaf-chewing insects, healthy trees can tolerate the loss of one-third of the total leaving surface before stress becomes a management issue. Tolerance is much less for trees with growth-limiting factors such as poor soil tilth, limited rooting space, dry non-irrigated sites, previous defoliation, etc.

Predicting the potential population for caterpillars or sawfly larvae is difficult to impossible. Generally speaking, populations rarely remove more than one-third of the leafing area. However, outbreaks of some pests could leave the tree leafless.

Evergreens are much less tolerant because the needles last for multiple years. For example, a sawfly larva outbreak that takes off all the new needles would have an influence over multiple years; this would bring a healthy tree to a threshold where management would be warranted.

Step 3c—Are Management Efforts Warranted for This Situation?

The bottom line in Step 3 is to determine if management efforts are warranted for this situation. In other words, does the gardener need to do something about this situation? The answer needs to be focused on the specifics of this situation rather than generic considerations.

STEP 4—EVALUATE MANAGEMENT OPTIONS EFFECTIVE FOR THIS DISORDER/PEST

Management options may take many forms or directions. For example, on some insect pests, hosing off the tree with a strong force of water may be an effective mechanical option. In other situations, an insecticide may be needed.

Management efforts may take the approach of dealing with soil issues, such as lawn aeration to reduce soil compaction around a tree.

Other management efforts may go in the direction of irrigating a dry site during hot dry weather or reducing the overwatering with better irrigation system design and management.

Management options include far more than just spraying an organic insecticide. On landscape trees, only 4% of the insect problems warrant insecticides.

Timing of management efforts is another important consideration. Often, the effective spray window is past before the pest is observed.

Pesticide Use Questions

Note: The term "pesticide" is a generic term that includes *insecticides* (used for insect management), *fungicides* and *bactericides* (used for disease management), *herbicides* (used to control weeds), etc.

When pesticides are a management option, answer these important questions to guide pesticide application.

1. What pesticides are effective on this pest? (Refer to Colorado State University Extension fact sheets.)

2. Which have minimal health hazards? (Refer to the pesticide label.)

3. Which have minimal environmental hazards for the site? (Refer to the pesticide label.)

4. When are they applied to be effective? (Refer to Colorado State University Extension fact sheets.)

5. How are they applied to minimize health and environmental hazards? (Refer to the pesticide label.)

6. What are the re-entry period and the application-to-harvest interval following application? (Refer to the pesticide label.)

Answers to these questions often indicate that a pesticide is not warranted at the point in time. Only 4% of landscape pest problems warrant the use of pesticides.

STEPS TO SYSTEMATICALLY EVALUATE A TREE

In diagnostics, it is often important to systematically evaluate the entire tree as part of the diagnostic process (Step 2a). Professional arborists use a formal process in tree evaluation.

1. **Macro-look at tree**—Walk completely around the tree looking for things that stand out. These may be clues for other steps. For example, decline from the top down is typical of root problems and/or drought. Give extra attention to the soil and roots in Step 3.

2. **Macro-look at surroundings**—Insects and diseases are often host-specific. If symptoms are found on a variety of plants, it suggests abiotic disorders. Abiotic problems (like soil compaction) may also affect surrounding plants. How is the lawn under the tree doing? It shares the same soil problems.

3. **Soil and rooting area**—Soil problems contribute to 80% of the problems in the landscape. While we cannot see the root system, other clues will help evaluate the root system.

   - How is the lawn doing? It shares the same soil growth-limiting factors.

   - Push a screwdriver into the soil. How easy or hard it is to push into a moist soil provides an estimation of soil compaction.

   - With a soil probe, take some cores from the rooting area. It may indicate issues with soil texture changes and rooting.

   - Surface roots indicate soil compaction and/or wet soils, as the roots develop closer to the surface where oxygen is available.

   - The lack of a root flare suggests that the tree was planted too deeply or that soil was added over the rooting area (smothering the fine feeder roots). Planting too deep causes trunk girdling roots.

   - Trunk girdling (circling) is the most common cause of death in landscape trees. Trees often show a gradual decline from the trunk girdling roots 12 to 20 years after planting. The girdling root may be below the surface.

   - Decline of the tree from the top down or a uniform decline of the entire tree suggests root/soil problems.

4. **Trunk**—Things to look for include the following:

   - Cankers that go into the ground are always actively growing.

   - "Lawnmower decline" (bark damage at ground level from lawn mowers and weed trimmers) is common in many landscapes. If the bark is removed down to the wood on more than 50% around the tree, the tree is considered to have no value.

   - Look for evidence of decay in large size pruning cuts. A drum-like hollow sound when the trunk is tapped with a wood mallet is a symptom of extensive internal decay.

   - Ridges and valleys along the trunk are symptoms of internal problems and decay.

   - Borer exit holes indicate stress issues.

5. **Major branches** (scaffold branches or secondary trunks)—Things to look for include:

   - Cankers

   - Large pruning cuts and evidence of storm damage (suggest the possibility of internal decay)

   - Borer exit holes indicate stress issues

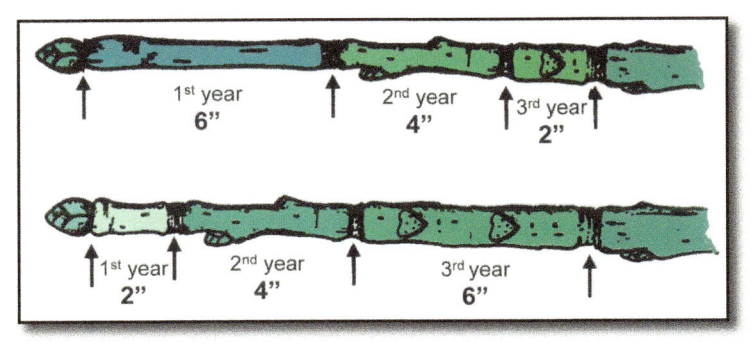

Figure 20-1 ▎ *Comparison of annual growth.*
- *Branch on top shows a decrease in stress levels as growth changes from 6 inches for the current season (1st year) to 4 inches for the 2nd year, and 2 inches in 3rd year.*
- *Branch on top shows an increase in stress levels as growth changes from 2 inches for the current season (1st year) to 4 inches for the 2nd year, and 6 inches in 3rd year.*

6. **Minor branches and limbs**

An important part of the evaluation is to get an assessment of the tree growth and vigor by comparing the annual growth increments of the twigs. Starting at the branch tip, look at the length back to the first **annual growth ring** (*terminal bud scar*). This is where the growth ended the previous year. The annual growth ring looks like a small ring or crown going completely around the twig. On some trees it is easy to identify, on other trees it is only a simple ring. To avoid confusing it with a side bud, the annual growth ring goes completely around the twig. On some trees, a slight change in bark color helps identify where the annual growth rings are located (Figure 20-1).

In evaluation, look at several branches around the tree. Going back 3 to 5 years, determine what is typical for each year, not what is longest or shortest. Is the annual growth what would be expected for that species of tree? For example, a young honeylocust tree in an open lawn could readily put on 18 to over 24 inches per year. The same tree where buildings and hardscape features limit root spread may put on only 6 to 12 inches per year. This reduced growth is in response to the restrictions in rooting.

Another important comparison is the change from year to year. For example, if the length of annual growth is shortening each year, it indicates that the stress levels are increasing. On newly planted trees, twig growth will be minimal until the root system establishes. A significant increase in annual twig growth indicates that the root system has established.

On mature trees, growth will naturally be reduced and must be evaluated by looking at the growth near the top rather than the bottom of the tree.

Evaluating annual growth helps interpret the effects of other problems (like soil/root issues) observed in previous steps.

Other things to look for include scale and other twig insects, borer exit holes (indicate stress issues), cankers, and galls.

7. **Foliage**—Things to look for include the following:

- Leaf color and size
- Leaf spots and other foliage diseases—Typically more serious on the lower inner foliage where humidity is higher
- Leaf chewing insects, sucking insects, mites, and galls
- Leaf scorch and dieback from the top down—Generic symptoms of root problems and/or drought
- Leaf scorch on a specific side—Suggests abiotic disorders coming from that side
- Early fall color—Generic symptom of stress

1. Describe essential skills used in the diagnostic process.

2. Explain how knowing the context of the situation helps in diagnosing the disorder.

3. Explain how painting a mental picture of a plant problem helps in diagnosing a disorder.

4. Explain how repeating back the details in your own words helps in diagnosing a disorder.

5. Explain how to tactfully change directions when the evidence leads down another road.

6. Why is it important to discuss management options only after the problems have been diagnosed?

7. List the steps, with substeps, in the diagnostic process.

8. Why is it important to correctly identify the plant?

9. Define *symptom* and *sign*. Give examples of each.

10. Define the following terms:

    a. Chlorosis

    b. Blight

    c. Dieback

    d. Decline

    e. Leaf spot

    f. Leaf scorch

    g. Canker

    h. Gall

    i. Fruiting bodies

    j. Mycelium

    k. Slime flux

11. Give examples of abiotic signs.

12. Explain why it is important to define what is normal versus abnormal about a plant problem.

13. Explain pesticide use questions.

14. List steps for systematically evaluating a tree.

15. If the average length of annual growth of twigs changes from four inches (current, year 1), two inches (year 2), one inch (year 3), and eight inches (year 4, older), what does it suggest about the tree's vigor? What if the growth changes from one inch (1 year, current season), two inches (year 2), three inches (year 3), and eight inches (year 4, older)?

Chapter

21*

Diagnosing Root and Soil Disorders on Landscape Trees

On landscape trees, symptoms of root and soil disorders are rather generic making diagnosis difficult. This chapter expands on **Step 3, Evaluate Roots and Soil**, in the **systematic evaluation of trees, Chapter 20.**

ROOT FUNCTION AND SYMPTOMS OF ROOT/SOIL DISORDERS

Roots account for approximately one-third of the tree's biomass. The functions of tree roots include the following:

- Water and nutrient uptake
- Anchoring the plant
- Production of gibberellins, a hormone that promotes canopy growth
- Storage of photosynthates (along with the woody tissues)

Symptoms of root/soil disorders are extremely generic in nature, including the following:

- Reduction in photosynthesis
- Reduction in root growth
- Reduction in canopy growth
- Reduction in winter survival
- Reduced tolerance to other stress factors (insects, diseases, drought, etc.)
- Poor anchoring of the plant, resulting in tree failure

---

*Author: David Whiting, Colorado State University Extension. Artwork by David Whiting.

Root, soil, and water issues contribute to 80% of landscape plant problems, for example:

- Soil compaction and/or drought are the inciting factors for many contributing insects (borers) and diseases (*Cytospora* and other cankers).

- Soil compaction and/or hardscape features often limit root spread, expressed as reduced growth and leaf scorch.

- Soil compaction reduces a tree's tolerance to common stress factors, including drought, heat and wind, aphids, mites, and other insects.

- Overwatering and drainage problems (soil compaction) are often expressed as iron chlorosis, root rots, leaf scorch, and limited growth.

- Trunk girdling roots, caused by planting too deep, is the most common cause of tree decline and death in the landscape.

DIAGNOSING ROOT AND SOIL DISORDERS

Uniform stress through canopy or stress from the top down suggests root-, soil-, and water-related problems. Diagnosis cannot be from the generic symptoms alone, but requires a more complete evaluation of the tree, its rooting system and growth. The following is a systematic approach to diagnosing root and soil disorders, based on common problems.

1. Define the Root System

Types of Roots

Root Plate—Zone of Rapid Taper

The **root plate** or **zone of rapid taper** comprises the primary structural roots extending out from the trunk. Roots branch readily, tapering in diameter. It is a continuation of the pipeline carrying water and nutrients from the absorbing and transport roots into the tree trunk (Figure 21-1).

The root plate is the tree's primary support in winds up to 40 mph. Thus, avoid routine digging or otherwise disturbing the soil and roots in the root plate area. Construction and hardscape features should not encroach into the root plate! When the tree fails by tipping over, often exposing the root plate, it is failure at the edge of the root plate.

As a rule of thumb, the radius of the root plate is three to six times the trunk DSH (diameter at standard height, 4.5 feet).

Transport Roots

Transport roots serve as a continuation of the pipeline carrying water and nutrients from the absorbing (feeder) roots to the root plate root and trunk. These are the major spreading roots of the tree and follow soil oxygen gradients across the rooting area. In compacted areas (with lower soil oxygen), they will come to the surface. In soils with good structure (higher oxygen), they will be deeper. They also provide additional support to the tree in winds above 40 mph (Figure 21-2).

Figure 21-1 ▮ *The rooting system of a tree is shallow and wide spreading. The Zone of Rapid Taper (Root Palate) area in highlighted in yellow.*

Figure 21-2 ▮ *Transport and absorbing roots are found through the entire rooting area beyond the zone of rapid taper.*

Transport roots are typically thumb-size in diameter, long, meandering, and with limited branching. Transport roots do not uniformly spread around the tree. Some areas may be void of roots, others heavily concentrated. In a hole dug in the rooting area, transport roots are readily observed sticking out the side (Figure 21-3).

Absorbing Roots

Absorbing (feeder) roots serve the function of water and nutrient uptake. These tiny roots are found near the soil surface throughout the entire transport rooting area. As a rule of thumb, they would be found in the top twelve inches on soils with good tilth, and in the top 4 inches or less in compacted, clayey soils (Figure 21-2).

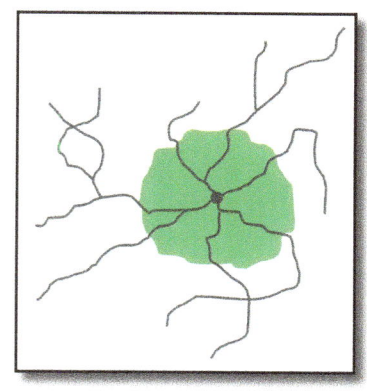

Figure 21-3 ▮ *Transport root are long and meandering. They are not uniformly disturbed out from the trunk.*

Absorbing roots have a short life, being replaced in four to five flushes of growth through the growing season. Short-term drought stress of ten days can turn off growth for one to five weeks. Long-term drought stress of twenty-two days can turn off growth for one to two years.

Sinker Roots

Sinker roots follow natural openings into deeper soil, as soil oxygen levels allow. It is unknown to what extent trees actually have sinker roots in the compacted soils of a landscape setting.

Sinker roots have the ability to extract water from deeper soil depths when the surface soil, with the absorbing roots, is dry. This helps explains how trees have good short-term drought resistance. It also helps explain the severe drought stress observed on trees when we have dry seasons with dry subsoil (Figure 21-4). Sinker roots also provide additional support in strong winds.

Tap Root

The tap root develops from the seed radical, being the primary root emerging from the germinating seed. Gardeners are very much aware of the tap root as they try to pull seeding maple or elm germinating as weeds in the garden.

However, beyond the seedling stage, the tap root is nonexistent on most trees. As the root system develops beyond the seedling stage, the roots grow into the root plate system due to low soil oxygen. Studies found less than 2% of landscape trees actually have a tap root. In nursery production, the tap root is cut while tiny, forcing a more branching root system that is tolerant of transplanting (Figure 21-5).

Figure 21-4 ▮ *Sinker roots follow cracks in the soil to deeper depths as oxygen levels allow. They extract water when the absorbing roots near the surface have dry soil.*

Figure 21-5 ▮ *The tap root develops from the seed radical. In the seedling stage, the tree develops the root plate system due to low soil oxygen. Tap roots are rare in landscape trees.*

Depth and Spread

The typical tree rooting system is shallow and wide spreading. Roots only grow with adequate levels of soil oxygen. Rooting depth and spread is a factor of: 1) the tree's genetic tolerance to soil oxygen levels, and 2) soil texture and structure (actual soil oxygen levels).

It is difficult to estimate the actual depth and spread of a tree's root system. Table 21-1 gives a rule of thumb on root spread. Roots will be more sparse and spreading on dryer soils, and more concentrated on moist soils (Table 21-1).

Table 21-1. Estimated Depth and Spread of a Tree's Root System

With good soil tilth:
- Ninety to ninety-five percent in top thirty-six inches
- Fifty percent in top twelve inches (absorbing roots)
- Spread two to three times tree height and/or canopy spread
- Modified to by actual soil conditions

With compacted/clayey soils:
- Ninety to ninety-five percent in top twelve inches or less
- Fifty percent in top four inches or less (absorbing roots)
- Spread more than five times tree height and/or canopy spread

Tree Protection Zone/Protected Root Zone

Obviously, not every root is essential for tree health. The **Tree Protection Zone**, TPZ (Protected Root Zone, PRZ) defines the rooting area with direct influence on tree health and vigor. The TPZ is the area of focus in tree care activities and evaluating root/soil-related disorders.

To protect trees in a construction area, there should be NO grading, trenching, parking, or stockpiling of materials in the TPZ. Several methods have been used to estimate the TPZ.

Dripline Method

The dripline (outer reach of branches) is often used in construction activities and by some city ordinances to define the TPZ. It may be suitable for a young tree with a broad canopy in an open lawn area. But it critically underestimates the critical rooting area for most landscape trees. It is not recommended (Figure 21-6).

Height Method

In this method, tree height equals the TPZ diameter or 40% of tree height equals the TPZ diameter. It comes from practices used in conifer forest management, but has little application to landscape trees. It is not recommended.

Trunk Diameter Method

The trunk diameter is probably the best method for general use on landscape trees. Size of the TPZ is based on the diameter of the trunk, increasing as the tree ages and becoming less tolerant of stress factors. It may be calculated by measuring the trunk circumference or DSH (diameter at standard height,

Figure 21-6 ■ *The dripline is the rooting area defined by the outer reach of the branches. It is a poor method for estimating a TPZ.*

4.5 feet). For trees with a broad canopy in an open lawn, it is approximately 40% larger in area than the dripline method (Figure 21-7).

Trunk Diameter Method by Circumference

TPZ radius = one foot per two inches of trunk circumference

1. Measure the tree's circumference at DSH (4.5 feet) in *inches*.

2. Divide the number of inches by two.

3. This is the radius, *in feet*, of the TPZ.

For example:

1. Circumference = 24 inches

2. $24 \div 2 = 12$

3. TPZ radius = 12 feet

Trunk Diameter Method by Diameter

TPZ radius = 1.5 feet per inch of trunk diameter at DSH

1. Measure the tree's diameter at DSH (4.5 feet) *in inches*.

2. Multiply the diameter (in inches) by 1.5

3. This is the radius, *in feet*, of the TPZ

For example:

1. Diameter = 8 inches

2. $8 \times 1.5 = 12$

3. TPZ radius = 12 feet

Area of the TPZ

The area of the TPZ can be calculated by the formula:

[TPZ radius]$^2 \times \pi$

For example—12 foot radius:

12 feet $\times$ 12 feet $\times$ 3.14 = 452 square feet

Stress Tolerance and Age Method

Sometimes in construction sites, the professional arborist must very tightly define the TPZ to accommodate the construction and still provide tree protection. In this situation, the **Stress Tolerance and Age Method** would be used. It takes into account the following items:

- Transplant response (tolerance) of the species

- Drought tolerance of the species

- Root pruning response (tolerance) of the species

- Compartmentalization (decay resistance) of the species

- Native range—Tolerance to stress outside the native ecosystem

Figure 21-7 ▮ *The Tree Protection Zone defined by the trunk formula method is a good estimate of the rooting area with direct influence on tree health and vigor. It is approximately 40% larger than the area defined by the drip line.*

2. Evaluate Root Spread Potential

The potential for the roots to spread is a primary consideration in evaluating a tree's root system. The mature size, growth rate, and longevity of a tree are directly related to the available rooting space. Many trees in the

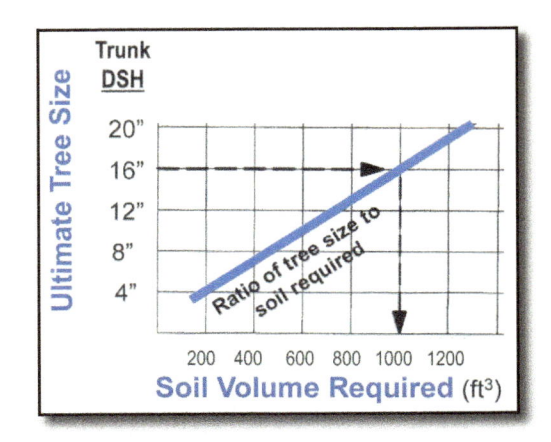

Figure 21-8 ■ *Tree size, growth rate, and longevity are directly related to the size of the available rooting area.*

For a tree in Colorado's clayey soils, effective rooting depth is probably less than one foot deep.

landscape are predisposed at planting to a short life and limited growth potential due to poor soil conditions and limited rooting space (Figure 21-8).

Figure 21-8 shows the relationship between root space and ultimate tree size. For example, a tree with a 16-inch diameter requires 1,000 cubic feet of soil. On a compacted clayey soil, rooting depth may be restricted to one foot or less, requiring an eighteen-foot or greater radius root spread. Anything less will reduce tree size, growth rates, vigor, and longevity.

Tree roots can generally cross under a sidewalk to open lawn areas beyond. The ability of roots to cross under a street depends on the road base properties. A good road base does not typically support root growth due to compaction and low soil oxygen levels.

The rooting area does not need to be rounded, but can be about any shape. Actual rooting areas are not necessarily round. Trees can share rooting space.

When roots fill the available "root vault" area and cannot spread beyond: 1) root growth slows, 2) canopy growth slows, and 3) trees reach an early maturity and go into decline. Routine replacement may be necessary.

3. Evaluating Soil Compaction

With trees, surface roots are an indication of low soil oxygen caused by soil compaction and/or overly wet soil. Soil compaction often expresses as low vigor and dieback. Soil compaction is the most common inciting factor leading to contributing factors in the decline process.

Soil compaction is a reduction in large pore space, reducing soil oxygen levels and decreasing soil drainage. As a result, rooting depth is reduced. Primary causes of soil compaction include construction activities, foot traffic. and the impact of rain on bare soil. Soils are extremely prone to compaction when wet as the water serves as a lubricant, allowing soil particles to slide closer together.

Evaluating Soil Compaction

Soil compaction is somewhat difficult to evaluate. Evaluation tools include the following:

- **How is the lawn?** It shares the same soil conditions as the tree and may be easier to evaluate. Is the lawn thick or thin?

- **Screwdriver test**—How easy can a screwdriver be pushed into the soil? For this penetration type test, the soil needs to have been watered the day before.

- **Soil probe**—With a soil probe, evaluate soil type, texture interfaces, and rooting. For this penetration test, it is better if the soil was watered the day before.

- **Penetrometer**—This instrument measures the amount of pressure it takes to push the probe into the soil. The colored dial sections indicate when root growth may be slowed or inhibited. For this penetration type test, the soil must be watered the day before (Figure 21-9).

- **Shovel**—Sometimes, the only way to evaluate the soil is with a shovel and some hard work.

Methods to Deal with Compaction around Trees

Standard methods of dealing with compaction in a garden setting (adding organic matter, cultivating the soil only when dry, and avoiding excessive tilling) do not apply to tree situations, as we do not cultivate the rooting zone.

Figure 21-9 ▮ *The soil penetrometer measures the pressure it takes to push the probe into the soil. It is a great tool to evaluate soil compaction.*

Practices Worth Considering

- **Aeration, with plugs at 2-inch intervals**—Lawn or soil aeration is helpful for tree root oxygen levels if enough passes are made over the area to have plugs at 2-inch intervals (Figure 21-10).

- **Managing traffic flow**—Established walks help minimize the compaction to other areas. The first time a cultivated soil is stepped on, it could return to 75% maximum compaction. The fourth time a newly cultivated soil is stepped on, it could return to 90% maximum compaction. As a point of clarification, the concern is foot traffic on a non-compacted soil. Foot traffic on a compacted soil causes little additional compaction. Soils are much more prone to compaction when wet, as the soil water acts as a lubricant allowing the soil particles to slide closer together.

Figure 21-10 ▮ *Aeration is a great tool to help reduce soil compaction around trees. To make a difference, plugs needs to be at two-inch intervals.*

- **Organic mulch**—A wood/bark chip mulch prevents soil compaction from foot traffic if maintained at adequate depths. For medium-sized chips, the ideal depth is 3 inches. Less does not give the protection from compaction; more reduces soil oxygen levels.

- **Soil renovation with an air spade**—This is a new method used by arborists on high-value trees (due to the expense). Steps include the following:

  1. Sod in the TPZ is removed with a sod cutter.

  2. Organic matter is spread and mixed into the soil with an air spade. The air spade is a high pressure stream of air that cultivates the soil without cutting the roots.

  3. The area is covered with organic wood/bark chip mulch. It does not work to replace the sod!

Practices of Questionable Value

- **Vertical mulching with an augur**—The TPZ is drilled with two-inch holes, typically at twelve to twenty-four inch intervals. Holes may be filled with coarse sand or organic matter. This method, formerly used by arborists, is currently out of favor. Long-term research finds that is does not aerate enough soil area for a significant increase in tree vigor (Figure 21-11).

Figure 21-11 ▮ *Vertical mulching with hole drilled throughout the tree protection zone.*

- **Trenching**—Trenches (dug between primary rooting paths) are backfilled with improved soil. This method, formerly used by arborists, is currently out of favor. Long-term research finds that while it improves root growth in the backfilled trenches, it does not support a long-term significant increase in overall tree vigor (Figure 21-12).

- **Punching holes with a pipe, pick, or bar**—This common practice by gardeners is not supported by research. It compacts the soil around the punch site, thus not increasing soil oxygen levels. To be effective, the soil cores must be removed. It does not aerate enough soil area for a significant increase in tree vigor.

- **Fracturing**—The soil is subjected to a high-pressure release of air or water, fracturing the soil profile. It has limited effectiveness in sandy soils. It may actually increase the compaction around the fracture lines on clayey soils.

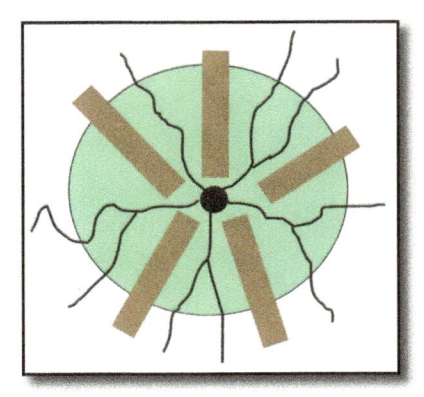

Figure 21-12 ▮ *Trenches dug between primary root paths does not result in significant improvements in tree vigor.*

In summary, there is NO quick, easy fix for compacted soils in tree rooting areas.

4. Evaluate Planting Depth

Trunk girdling roots are the most common cause of tree decline and death of landscape trees. Trunk girdling roots are caused by planting the tree too deep. It may show up some twelve to more than twenty years after planting, causing decline and death of trees as they have significant growth in the landscape. Thus in evaluating the rooting system of a tree, it makes sense to evaluate the tree planting depth (Figure 21-13).

Circling/girdling roots may also develop as trees are planted up from pot size to pot size in nursery production. They may be hidden inside the root ball.

Figure 21-13 ▮ *Trunk girdling roots are caused by planting too deep.*

Recently Planted Trees

Two considerations are important in evaluating the planting depth of trees: 1) the depth of tree in the root ball, and 2) the depth of root ball in the planting hole (Figure 21-14).

- **Depth of tree in the root ball**—Based on research, industry standards include the following:

  —Generally, as least two structural roots within the top one to three inches of the soil surface, measured three to four inches from the trunk.

  —For species prone to girdling roots (crabapples, green ash, hackberry, littleleaf linden, red maple, poplars, and possibly others), the top structural root should be within the top one inch of the soil surface.

- **Depth of root ball in planting hole**—To deal with the texture interface between the root ball soil and the backfill soil, the root ball must come to the surface with no backfill soil over the root ball. The top of the root ball on newly planted trees should rise one to two inches above grade (depending on root ball size). When the root ball mellows out, it will be at ground level.

Figure 21-14 ■ *Summary: Planting Hole Specifications.*

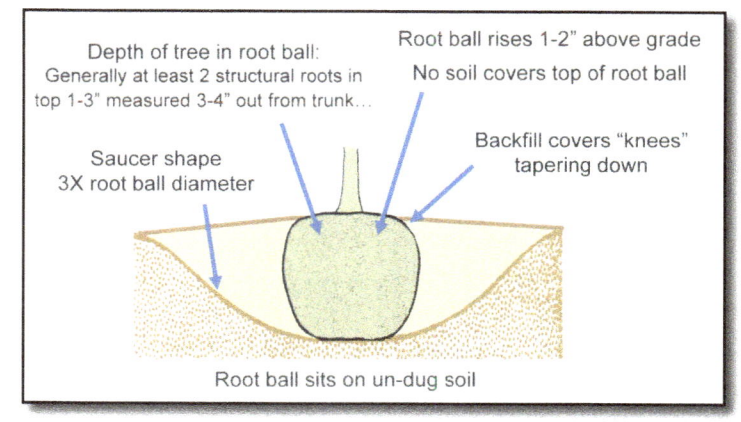

On recently planted trees, the height of the root ball should be slightly above grade or at grade level after the root ball mellows out. The root ball soil should be visible on the surface with the different site soil to the sides. With a small trowel, evaluate the planting depth of the root ball in the planting hole. With a small trowel or screwdriver, evaluate the planting depth of the tree in the root ball.

Recently Planted Tree, Planted Too Deep

- If the tree is stressed with poor vigor, replace the tree.

- If the tree is currently in good health:

  —Live with possible consequences of slower growth and trunk girdling roots. Check for circling/girdling roots.

  —Replant the tree—1) Dig around the tree exposing the root ball. 2) Wrap the root ball in burlap and twine to hold it together. 3) Lift the root ball from the hole. 4) Replant at correct depth. This would be difficult to do!

Established Trees Planted Too Deep

The lack of a visible root flare is an indication of planting too deep (or that soil has been added over the root system). If the root flare is not visible, check for trunk circling/girdling roots. Circling/girdling roots may be several inches below ground.

Circling roots not embedded into the trunk should be cut and removed. For girdling roots putting pressure on the trunk, cut and remove the root without causing injury to the trunk. The tree will likely recover without any long-term effects.

For girdling roots embedded into the trunk, cut the root without causing injury to the trunk, if possible. However, do not remove the girdling root section if it is embedded into the trunk, as this opens the trunk to decay and causes it to be structurally weak. The tree may or may not survive; only time will tell.

5. Evaluate Root/Shoot Hormone Balance

Auxins (plant hormones produced in the twig's terminal buds) stimulate root growth. Gibberellins (plant hormones produced in the root tips) stimulate canopy growth. The tree balances root growth versus canopy growth by these hormones (Figure 21-15).

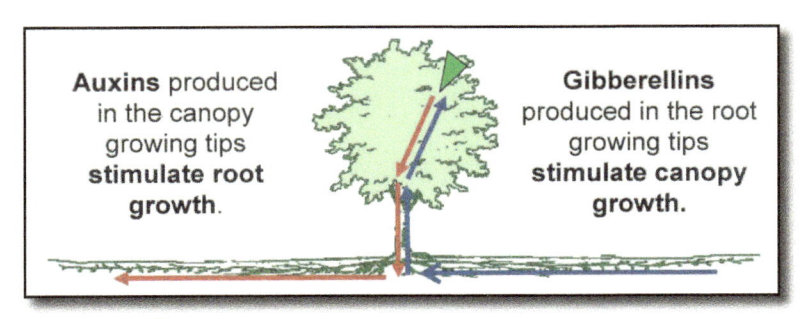

Figure 21-15 ▍ *Trees balance shoot and root growth based on the concentration of auxins and gibberellins.*

Soil factors that limit root growth will in turn influence canopy growth.

Storm damage or excessive pruning may reduce auxins, slowing root growth. Following storm damage, trees often put on heavy growth of water sprouts due to a low auxins/high gibberellins ratio (coupled with unobserved, limited root growth). This is followed by a decline in the canopy caused by the reduce root growth.

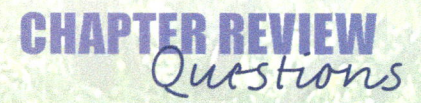
1. Describe the typical rooting system of a tree. Describe location and function of the following root types:

   a. Root plate or zone of rapid taper

   b. Transport roots

   c. Feeder roots

   d. Sinker roots

   e. Tap root

2. What two factors play into the rooting depth and spread?

3. What is the typical depth and spread of tree roots? How does this change for compacted/clayey soils?

4. Explain how to calculate the *critical rooting radius* and *tree protection zone (protected root zone)*.

5. Describe how potential rooting spread affects tree growth and vigor. What happens when a tree's root system cannot spread as needed?

6. Describe techniques to evaluate soil/root disorders and soil compaction.

7. Describe worthwhile techniques to reduce soil compaction around trees. Explain why questionable techniques to reduce soil compaction are out of favor.

8. What single factor accounts for the most deaths of landscape trees? What causes trunk girding roots? How long after planting can trunk girdling root develop? What can be done for a tree with trunk girdling roots?

9. Describe how a tree balances root growth with canopy growth.

22*

Identifying Insects

TAXONOMY OF ARTHROPODS (INSECTS AND INSECT RELATIVES)

Introduction

Insects and Mankind

Insects are the most abundant and diverse form of life found on earth. Over three-quarters of a million species are known to exist, more than the number of all kinds of animals and plants put together. Insects are a vital part of the world's ecosystem.

Insects are a major link in the world food chain. Insects like bees, wasps, flies, bugs, and beetles pollinate crops. Insects destroy various weeds in the same manner that they can injure crops. Insects improve the physical conditions of the soil and promote its fertility by decomposing plant residues and aerating the soil. Insects help control insect pests as predators and parasites. Only a few of the thousands of species are pests of mankind or his crops.

Most books list insect pests according to host plants, or by orders (beetles, bugs, flies, etc.) and families (aphids, scales, leaf beetles, etc.). When gardeners can identify insects by order, they will be able to identify the majority of pests by the process of elimination. Most routine garden pests are readily identifiable by order, some by families. However, there are always a few insects, with atypical appearances, that do not fit standard descriptions.

Insect Orders

Most common names for insects describe the insect orders. For example, "beetle" is the common name for members of the *Coleoptera* order, and "butterflies" and "moths" for the *Lepidoptera* order. A few common names

*Author: David Whiting, Colorado State University Extension. Drawings from the U.S. Department of Agriculture unless otherwise stated.

refer to families (or superfamilies). For example, aphids, leafhoppers, and psyllids refer to families in the *Homoptera* order.

"Order" is one of the levels of taxonomy. As illustrated in the following discussion, spiders, mites, and ticks are insect relatives.

Insect Identification

Identifying an insect is easy when:

- The insect is large enough to see.
- The insect is associated with plant damage.
- The insect has typical characteristics for the order and family.

Insect identification is more difficult when:

- The insect is too small to see characteristics.
- The insect is not associated with plant damage.
- The insect has atypical characteristics for the order or family.
- The insect has moved on, leaving only damage symptoms.

Taxonomy of *Arthropoda* (Insects and Insect Relatives)

The phylum *Arthropoda* includes insects, plus spiders, mites, tick, sowbugs, centipedes, millipedes, and more. They are characterized by chitinous exoskeletons, segmented bodies, and jointed appendages.

Class

- *Arachnida*—Spiders, mites, ticks, scorpions, daddy longlegs
- *Chipoda*—Centipedes
- *Crustacae*—Lobsters, crabs, shrimp, sowbugs, pillbugs
- *Diplopoda*—Millipedes
- *Symphyla*—Garden centipedes
- *Hexapoda* (or *Insecta*)—Insects
- etc.

Orders of Hexapoda

- *Coleoptera*—Beetles
- *Diptera*—Flies
- *Lepidoptera*—Butterflies, moths
- *Hemiptera*—True bugs
- *Homoptera*—Aphids, cicadas, leafhoppers, scales
- *Hymenoptera*—Ants, bees, hornets, sawflies, wasps
- etc.

Family

Some insects, such as beetles, are easy to indentify by family, while others, like flies, are more difficult.

Genus and Species

Actual identification of an insect to genus and species requires a very high level of expertise.

Insect Relatives

Class: *Arachnida—Spiders, Mites, Ticks, Scorpions, Daddy Longlegs*

Arachnids (spiders, mites, and ticks) have four pairs of legs and two body regions: the **cephalothorax** (a fusion of head and thorax) and the abdomen (Figure 22-1).

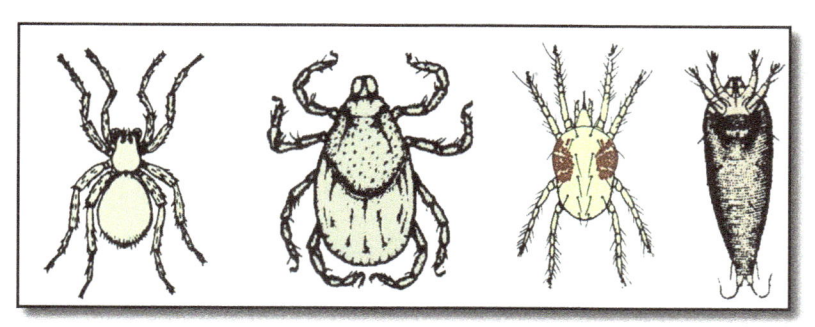

Figure 22-1 ▪ *Arachnids (left to right): spider, dog tick, two-spotted mite, eriophyid mite.*

Figure 22-2 ▪ *Sowbug.*

Class: Crustacea—*Sowbugs, Pillbugs, Shrimp, Lobster, Crayfish*

Pillbugs and sowbugs are land crustaceans that usually have five to seven pairs of legs. They have two pairs of antennae and two body regions. The pillbug will roll into a ball; the sowbug cannot (Figure 22-2).

Pillbugs and sowbugs are organic matter feeders, occasionally feeding on tender roots. Pillbugs and sowbugs can become a pest when numbers become very high or when they invade a home.

Class: Diplopoda—*Millipedes*

Millipedes have two pairs of legs per body segment (except the first three). The body is usually cylindrical, 1 to 1.5 inches long, with short antennae. They may have 15 to 150 body segments, with 30 being common (Figure 22-3).

Millipedes are usually found in damp and dark places, such as under leaves, under stones or boards, in rotting wood, and in soils high in organic materials. If touched or picked up when crawling, they will curl up. They frequently invade homes, especially after a heavy rainstorm. They are not known to bite people. However, some species will give off an ill-smelling fluid. Most are scavengers and feed on decaying plant materials and overripe fruit. A few species attack living plants.

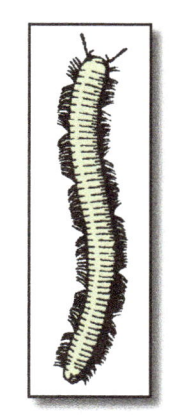

Figure 22-3 ▪ *Millipede.*

Class: Symphyla—*Garden Centipedes*

Centipedes have flattened bodies with typically 40 to 50 body segments and one pair of legs per body segment (Figure 22-4).

They are predatory, feeding on small spiders, carpet beetles, sowbugs, millipedes, and other small insects.

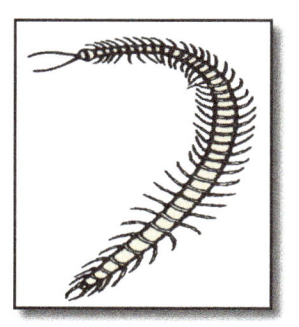

Figure 22-4 ▪ *Centipede.*

INSECT ANATOMY AND GROWTH

Identification and classification of insects is based on their structure and physiology. A basic understanding of insect physiology will enable the gardener to identify most insects by order and some by family.

External Structure

The exterior body wall, called an **exoskeleton**, provides the structural support for the insect. It is composed of five distinct layers made of waxy lipoproteins and *chitin* (a cellulose-like polymerized glucosamine). The acid-resistant exoskeleton protects the insect from excessive dryness, humidity, and disease organisms.

This external skeleton is somewhat cylindrical and typically made up of twenty-one hardened, ring-like segments. These segments are arranged in three groups or body regions: the **head**, **thorax**, and **abdomen**. The body may be covered by **setae** (hairs) and may have external protuberances, such as horns, spines, or spurs (Figure 22-5).

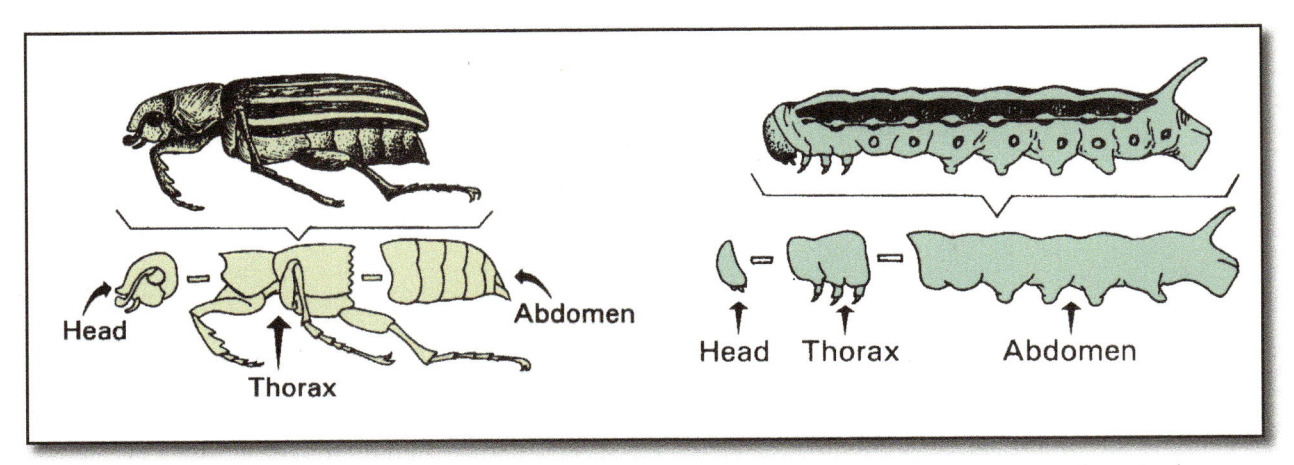

Figure 22-5 ▍ *Body regions of beetle (left) and caterpillar (right). (Line drawing by Colorado State University Extension.)*

Head

The head serves as a sensory center and for the intake of food. Main features of an insect's head include the eyes, antennae, and mouth parts.

Eyes

Insects have two types of eyes. To detect movement, most adult insects have a pair of lateral **compound eyes** comprised of multiple *ommatidium* (cornea). The number of ommatidia in the eye determines how well insects see. For example, dragonflies have approximately 50,000 per eye, house flies about 4,000, and ants about 50. These large compound eyes often occupy the greater portion of the insect head. Insects with large compound eyes are often predators, while insects with small compound eyes are often the prey.

The **ocelli** or simple eyes are used for light responsiveness. Two or three are typically located between the larger compound eyes on most insect adults. Some immatures may have one to eight lateral ocelli (Figure 22-6).

Antennae

All adult insects and many immature stages have a pair of segmented antennae, used for sensory function. Many modifications in form occur, and these variations are often used in identification.

Figure 22-6 ▍ *Grasshopper head. Note the large eyes, three ocelli between eyes, and large mandibles (chewing mouthparts). (Line drawing by David Whiting.)*

Figure 22-7 ▪ *Chewing mouth parts of a beetle. (Photograph by David Whiting.)*

Figure 22-8 ▪ *Piercing-sucking mouth parts of a cicada. Insects with piercing-sucking mouth parts feed on plant sap, blood, or in the case of predators, their victim's insides. They do not consume the plant or insect tissues. (Photograph by David Whiting.)*

Figure 22-9 ▪ *Lapping mouth parts. Flies are an example of an insect with lapping mouth parts. (Line drawing by Colorado State University Extension.)*

Mouth Parts

The most remarkably complicated structural feature of insects is the mouth. Mouth parts are modified for various types of feeding, chewing, or sucking.

The **mandibles** or **chewing mouth parts** move horizontally on insects. Insects with chewing mouth parts consume the plant or insect they are feeding upon (Figure 22-7).

Sucking-type mouth parts vary greatly for different feeding habits. **Piercing-sucking** mouth parts are typical of the *Hemiptera* (true bugs), *Homoptera* (aphids, scales) and blood-sucking lice, fleas, mosquitoes, and the so-called biting flies. These are designed to punch and suck on the plant's sap, victim's blood, or in the case of predatory insects to suck out the insides of the victims (Figures 22-8 and 22-9).

Figure 22-10 ▪ *Siphoning mouth parts. Butterflies and moths have a coiled siphoning tube. To reach the nectar in flowers, the uncoiled tube may be longer than the butterfly's body. (Line drawing by Colorado State University Extension.)*

The **siphoning** type found in butterflies and moths is a long coiled tube designed to suck up nectar. It looks like a cinnamon roll coiled up under the head (Figure 22-10).

Intermediate types of mouth parts include the **rasping-sucking** type found in thrips and the **chewing-lapping** types found in honey bees, wasps, and bumble bees.

Thorax

The **thorax** is made up of three segments (*prothorax*, *mesothorax*, and *metathorax*).

Legs—A pair of legs is attached on each thorax segment. The insect's leg consists of five independent movable parts. Legs may be specially adapted for leaping, walking, digging, grasping, swimming, etc.

Wings—Insects may have one or two pairs of wings or no wings. The wings are attached to the latter two thorax segments. The wing **venation** (arrangement of the veins) is different for each species of insect and is often a means of identification. Wing surfaces are covered with fine hairs, scales, or may be bare. On beetles, the thickened front wing, call **elytra**, serves for protection when not in flight (Figure 22-11).

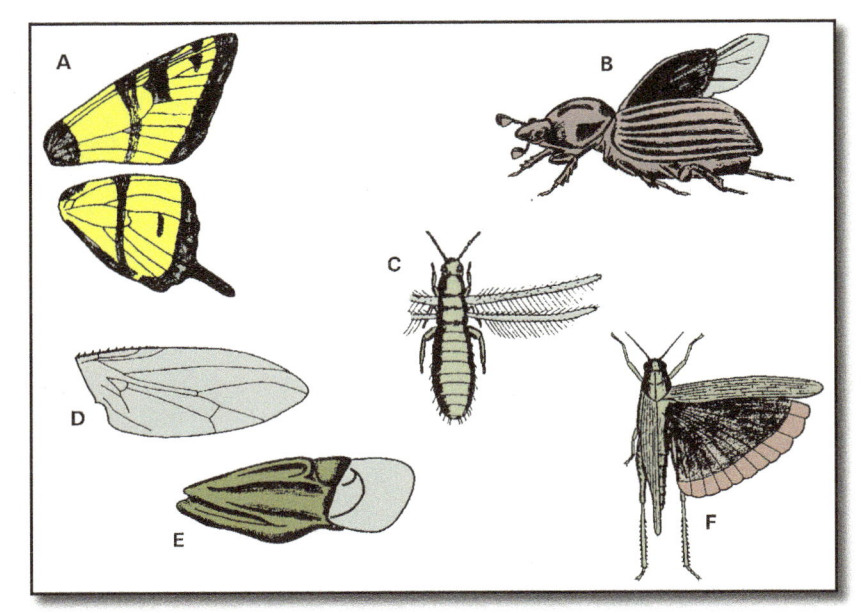

Figure 22-11 ▮ *Types of insect wings: (A) Scaly wing of moths and butterflies. (B) Armor-like (elytron) and membranous wings of beetles. (C) Feather wings of thrips. (D) Membranous wing of a fly. (E) Half-leathery/half-membranous wings (memelytron) of true bugs. (F) Wings of grasshoppers. (Line drawing by Colorado State University.)*

Abdomen

The **abdomen** may have eleven or twelve segments, but in most cases they are difficult to distinguish.

Prolegs (fleshy leg-like projections) occur on some larva such as caterpillars and sawfly larva. Prolegs, with tiny crochet-type hooks on the bottoms, help the insect cling to plants (Figure 22-12).

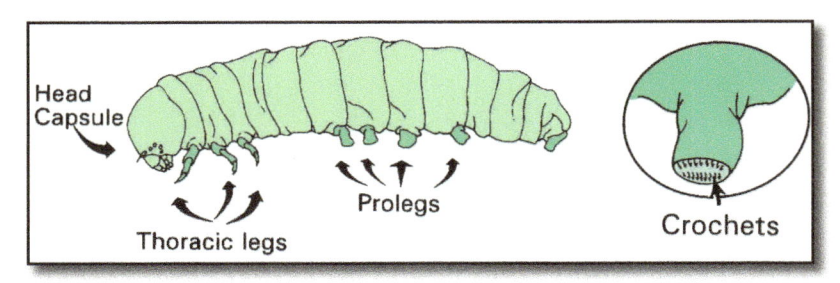

Figure 22-12 ▮ *Prolegs (leg-like appendages on the abdomen of caterpillars and sawfly larvae) have small crochet-like hooks that help the insect cling to plants. (Line drawing by Colorado State University Extension.)*

Some insects have a pair of appendages called **cerci** at the tip of the abdomen. The pinchers on earwigs are the best-known example of cerci. Cerci may be short, as in grasshoppers, termites and cockroaches, extremely long as in Mayflies or curved as in the earwigs. (Figure 22-13).

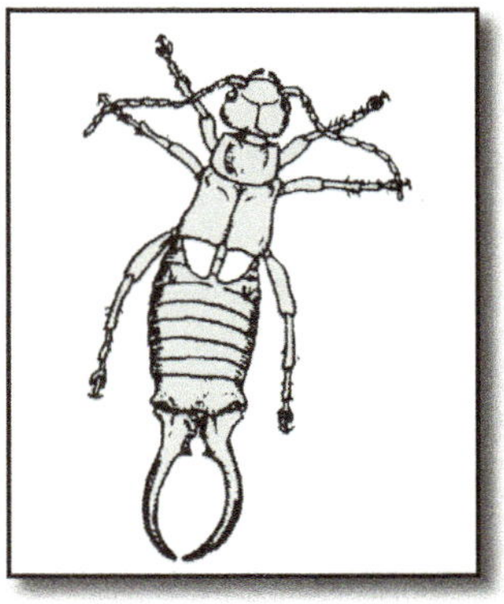

Figure 22-13 ▮ *Earwig with cerci (pinchers) on end of abdomen.*

Some groups have additional long segmented **filaments**, which appear like antennae (Figure 22-14).

The females of some insects have a prominent structure for depositing eggs, called an ovipositor. In bees, wasps, and ants, the ovipositor is modified into a stinger (Figure 22-15).

The **spiracles**, external openings used for respiration, are also present on the abdomen. Digestion, respiration, excretion, and reproduction are the main functions of the abdomen.

Internal Structure and Physiology

The muscular, digestive, circulatory, respiratory, nervous, and reproductive systems of insects are highly efficient. The insect's skeletal system has already been discussed, as part of the external structure.

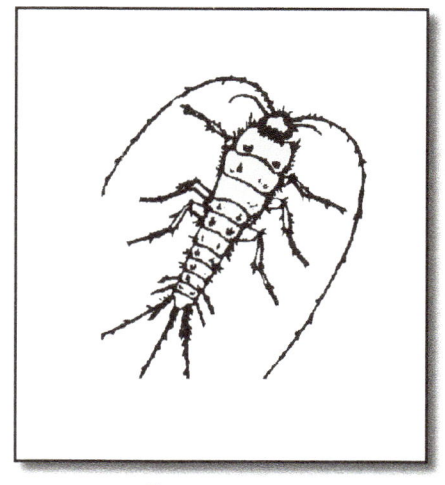

Figure 22-14 ▍ *Silverfish with three filaments on end of abdomen.*

While insect **muscles** are very small, they are very strong and often capable of extremely rapid contractions. Grasshoppers are said to have over 900 distinct muscles and some caterpillars over 4,000. In comparison to humans, insect muscle tissues are very strong.

The **circulatory system** of insects is an open type. The blood is pumped by the heart from the abdomen toward the head, bathing the organs in the body cavity. Blood functions to transport nutritive materials to the tissues and to carry away certain wastes. With a few exceptions, the blood of insects contains no red corpuscles and plays no part in respiration.

Figure 22-15 ▍ *Horntail with large ovipositor on end of abdomen.*

The **respiratory system** consists of a series of slender branching tubes or *tracheae*, which divide and subdivide throughout the body. Movement of oxygen and carbon dioxide is primarily by diffusion. Breathing-like movements help to ventilate the tracheae.

Insects have a two-part **nervous system**. The sympathetic nervous system controls functions of the heart, digestion, respiration, and possibly other systems. The peripheral nervous system controls sensory stimulations from the external environment.

Most insect **reproduction** is sexual (the union of an egg cell from the female with the sperm cell from the male). Some species are capable of producing young without fertilization (**parthenogenesis**). A few species carry the eggs internally, giving birth to live young (**ovoviviparous**). Glands of the insect reproductive systems are similar to that found in higher animals.

Growth and Metamorphosis

The series of events from egg to adulthood constitutes the insect's **life cycle**. The life cycle varies for each insect species. For example, mosquitoes under optimum environmental conditions may develop from egg to adult in ten days, whereas the periodical cicadas require thirteen to seventeen years to complete their life cycle.

An understanding of the insect's life cycle is a critical element in insect management practices.

Because the *exoskeleton* cannot expand sufficiently to accommodate an increase in size, it is cast off during the process called **molting**. The number of moltings varies considerably in the insect world. The form of an insect between successive molts is called an **instar**.

The *pupa* is a non-feeding stage during which the larval structures are transformed into adult structures. **Cocoon** refers to pupa cases made of silk from the modified salivary glands of the larva. **Chrysalis** is a term that denotes the pupa of a butterfly.

One of the most distinctive features of the insect world is **metamorphosis**, the marked or abrupt change in form, structure, and habit. Four basic types of metamorphosis are observed in the insect world.

No Metamorphosis

Upon hatching from the egg, the young insect with "no metamorphosis" development looks exactly like the adult except for size and minor differences in spines and setae (hairs). Size is the major change between each instar. Some species may molt after sexual maturity. The young and adults live in the same environment, and have the same types of mouthparts and feeding habits. These groups of very primitive, wingless insects include the *Thysanura* (silverfish) and *Collembola* (springtails) (Figure 22-16).

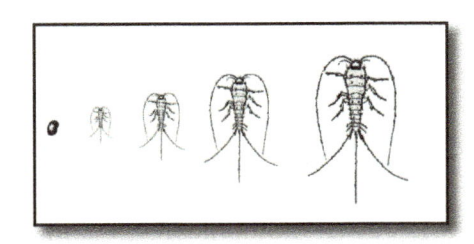

Figure 22-16 ■ *No metamorphosis of silverfish from left to right: egg, nymphs, and adult.*

Simple Metamorphosis

In simple metamorphosis, the insect goes through three basic changes: egg, nymph, and adult. The nymphs typically go through three to five instars. Some books further divide simple metamorphosis into gradual and incomplete types.

In **gradual metamorphosis**, the newly hatched insect resembles the adult in general body form, but lacks wings and external genital appendages. With each successive molt, the nymph resembles the adult more than it did in the previous instar. Both nymphs and adults have the same type of mouthparts and food habits. Grasshoppers, squash bugs, and aphids are examples of insects with gradual metamorphosis (Figure 22-17).

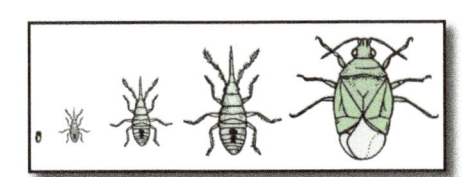

Figure 22-17 ■ *Simple-gradual metamorphosis of stink bug from left to right: egg, nymphs, and adult.*

Incomplete metamorphosis is characteristic of some orders with aquatic nymphs, such as *Emphemeroptera* (mayflies), *Odonata* (dragonflies), and *Plecoptera* (stoneflies). The changes that occur during the immature instar stages are more pronounced than in the case of insects with gradual metamorphosis, but not nearly so dramatic as in complete metamorphosis. The young, called *nymphs* or *naiads*, are aquatic insects found in rivers and streams, while the strikingly different fly-like adult is aerial (Figure 22-18).

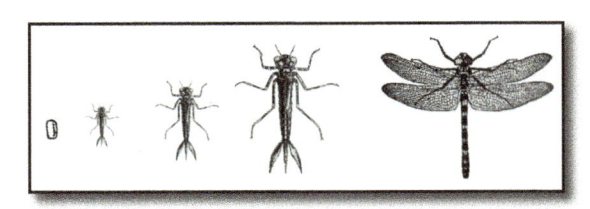

Figure 22-18 ■ *Simple-incomplete metamorphosis of dragonfly from left to right: egg, naiads, and adult.*

Complete Metamorphosis

Insects with complete metamorphosis have four developmental stages: eggs, larva, pupa, and adult. The insect may have several instars and molts as a larva, but it does not pick up the characteristics of the adult with each molting. The larval stage is primarily an eating and growing state. All larvae have chewing or modified chewing mouthparts (Figure 22-19).

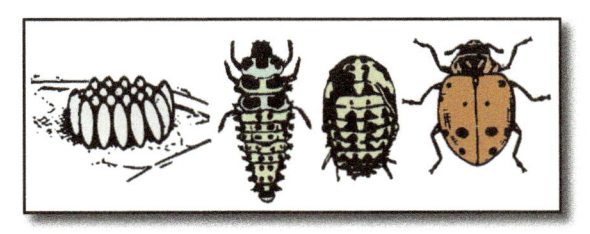

Figure 22-19 ■ *Complete metamorphosis of beetle from left to right: egg, larva (grub), pupa, and adult.*

Various names apply to the larvae of insects from different orders. Beetle larvae are known as **grubs**, butterfly and moth larvae are called **caterpillars**, and the larvae of flies are known as **maggots**. Grubs typically have three pairs of legs on the thorax segment and no prolegs on the abdomen. Caterpillars have three pairs of legs on the thorax segment and up to five pairs of prolegs (fleshy leg-like structures on the abdomen). By comparison, sawfly larvae have more than five pairs of prolegs. Maggots are typically legless.

When the larvae have attained maturity, it ceases to feed and following a period of inactivity transforms to the pupa stage. In the pupa stage, the insect usually remains inactive and does not feed, but undergoes marked physiological and morphological changes. The insect emerges from the pupa stage as a functional adult.

In the case of many insects, provisions are made by nature to protect the helpless pupa. Some seek protection in the ground, while others hide under the bark of trees. Some spin cocoons of silk (moths) or pupate in the last larval skin (flies).

The primary function of the adult insect is reproduction. In many insect groups, the adults die soon after mating and laying eggs. Some adults do little or no feeding.

Insects with complete metamorphosis may have entirely different types of mouthparts and food habits in the larval and adult stages. For example, caterpillars (larva of butterflies and moths) have chewing mouthparts and feed on a variety of materials, while the adults have siphoning mouthparts and normally feed on the nectar of plants. Flea larvae feed on inert organic materials with their chewing mouthparts, while the adults suck the blood of their hosts.

Diapause is defined as a state or period of suspended activity in any stage of the life cycle. This state is initiated or terminated by environmental stimuli, such as photoperiod (length of the daylight), temperature, moisture, nutrition, or a combination of these. Diapause should not be confused with the cycles in metamorphosis.

Because eggs and pupa are non-feeding stages, they are resistant to insecticides. This is an important point to remember when dealing with insect management.

Insect Names

All insects are classified into orders, families, genus, and species using scientific Latinized names. Scientific names are unique for that insect throughout the world. Genus names always begin with a capital letter, and species names are written entirely in lowercase. Scientific names are printed in italics or underlined. In technical papers, the first entry of an insect name is followed with the name of the author whom first described the species. For example, the honey bee, first described by Linnaeus, is written *Apis mellifera* Linnaeus.

Common names, generally used by the public, often refer the insect to its groups such as orders, suborders, families, or subfamilies, rather than individual species. For example, "beetles" applies to all species in the order *Coleoptera*; "leaf beetle" applies to species in the family *Chrysomelidae*.

Generally, only the insect species commonly known by the public have common names. Most insect species occurring in the world do not have a common name.

Most common names of insects that consist of a single word (i.e., beetles, earwigs, thrips, or termites) refer to an entire order. Most common names applying to families consist of two or more words, the last being the name of the larger groups. For example, carrion beetles, lady beetles, bark beetles, and blow flies.

Some common names are used for insects in more than one order, such as "fly" and "bug." The correct use and spelling of these words will help you identify orders. When a "bug" belongs to the *Hemiptera* order (often referred to as the "true bugs"), it is written as two words (bed bugs, stink bugs, water bugs). When it does not belong to this order, it is written as one word (sowbugs, pillbugs, ladybugs). The same principle applies to "flies" and the fly order *Diptera*. Insects in the *Diptera* (fly) order are written as two words (house fly, deer fly, flower fly). When the fly-like insect is of another order, it is written as one word (dragonfly, stonefly, Mayfly).

Changing Taxonomy

Like plants, the taxonomy of insects is constantly changing with new research.

New books combine *Hemiptera* and *Homoptera* into *Hemiptera* with the following subgroupings:

Hemiptera

- *Heteroptera*—True bugs
- *Sternohynncha*—Aphids, physllids, scales
- *Auchenorhynncha*—Leafhoppers, plant hoppers

In this book, we continue to teach the old taxonomy because most books gardeners will be using have the old taxonomy.

INSECT ORDERS

Anoplura—Sucking Lice

- Feeds by sucking blood from mammals
- Some species (head lice and crab lice) feed on humans

Metamorphosis: Simple/Gradual

Features: (Figure 22-20)

- Wingless
- Mouthparts: Piercing/sucking, designed to feed on blood
- Body: Small head with larger, pear-shaped thorax and nine-segmented abdomen.

Figure 22-20 ▮ *Sucking lice.*

Blattaria (Subclass of *Dictyoptera*)—Cockroaches and Woodroaches

- Most species are found in warmer subtropical to tropical climates.
- The German, Oriental, and American cockroaches are indoor pests.
- Woodroaches live outdoors feeding on decaying bark and other debris.

Metamorphosis: Simple/Gradual

Features: (Figure 22-21)

- Body: Flattened
- Antennae: Long, thread-like
- Mouthparts: Chewing
- Wings: If present, are thickened, are semitransparent with distinct veins, and lay flat.

Figure 22-21 ▮ *American cockroach.*

Coleoptera—Beetles and Weevils

- *Coleoptera* is the largest order of insects with 290,000 species worldwide and some 24,000 species in North America.
- Many species are plant feeders; some are predaceous (ground and lady beetles), scavengers (scarab and hide beetles), or aquatic.
- The term *weevil* refers to a snouted beetle.

Metamorphosis: Complete (Figure 22-22)

Adults: (Figure 22-23)

- Wings: Two pairs

  —Front pair, called **elytra**, are greatly thickened and shell-like (form fitting) and make a straight line down the back when at rest.

  —Hind wings are membranous and are protected by the front pair.

  —A few beetles are wingless or have only the front pair.

- Mouthparts: Chewing

- Antennae: Noticeable, generally quite stout

- Cerci (tail-like appendage): None

Larva:

- Legs:

  —Larva that feed externally on plants are the typical "grub" with head capsule, three pairs of legs on the thorax, and no prolegs on the abdomen (Figure 22-24).

  —Some larva that feed internally in plants (e.g., bark beetles and wood borers) may be maggot-like with no head capsule and no legs.

- Mouthparts: Chewing

Beneficial families include:

- Blister beetles, *Meloidae*
- Carrion beetles, *Silphidae*
- Checkered beetles, *Eleridae*
- Darkling beetles, *Tenebrionidae*
- Fireflies, *Lampyridae*
- Ground beetles, *Carabidae*
- Lady beetles, *Coccinellidae*
- Rove beetles, *Staphylinidae*
- Scarab beetles, *Scarabaeidae*
- Soldier beetles, *Cantharidae*
- Tiger beetles, *Cicindelidae*

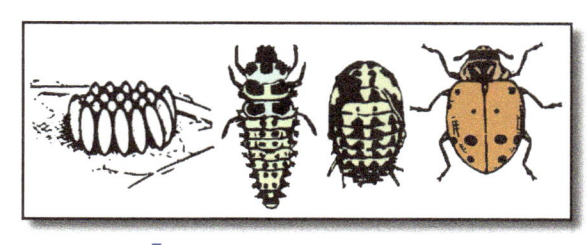

Figure 22-22 ▍ Coleoptera *metamorphosis (left to right): egg, grub, pupa, and adult.*

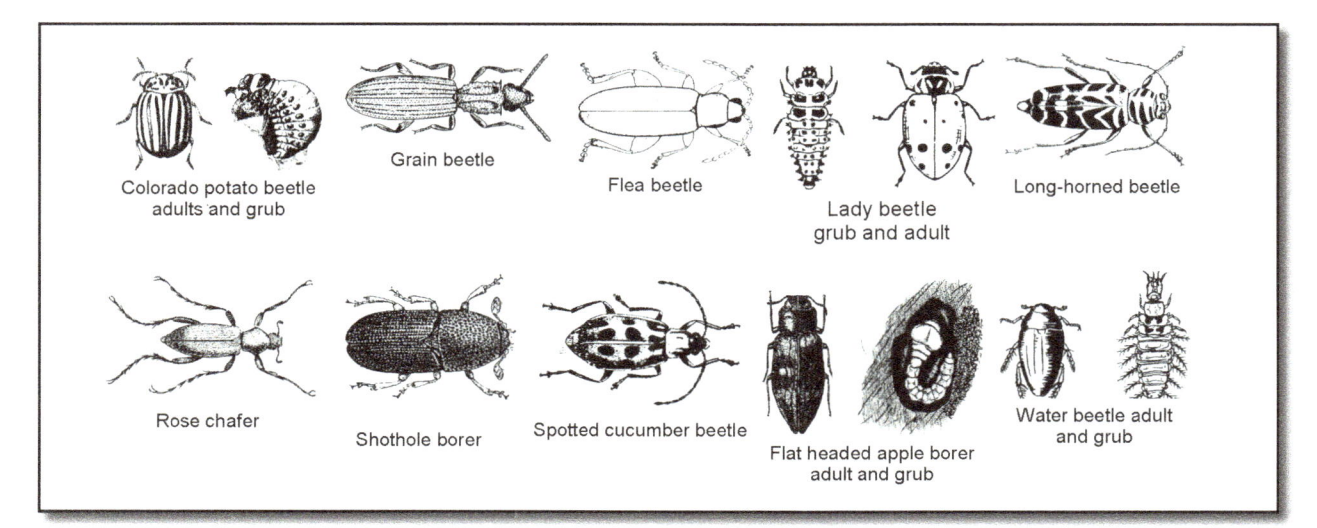

Figure 22- 23 ▍ *Examples of common beetles.*

Pest families include:

- Bark and ambrosia beetles, *Scolytidae*
- Blister beetles, *Meloidae*
- Carpet beetles, *Dermestidae*
- Click beetles or wireworms, *Elateridae*
- Ground beetles, *Carabidae*
- Leaf beetles, *Chrysomelidae*
- Longhorned beetles or roundheaded borers, *Cerambycidae*
- Metallic wood beetles or flatheaded borers, *Buprestidae*
- Sap beetles, *Nitidulidae*
- Scarab beetles including rose chafer, *Scarabaeidae*
- Seed beetles, *Bruchidae*
- Weevils, *Curculionidae*

Figure 22-24 ▮ *Grub with head capsule, three pairs of legs on the thorax, and no prolegs on abdomen.*

Collembola—Springtails

- Very tiny (1 to 2 mm) soft-bodied insect almost always associated with soil

- Very common but rarely observed due to tiny size

- Feeding: Most feed on algae, fungi, and other organic matter; some are predators of other insects and mites found in the soil

Metamorphosis: None

Features: (Figure 22-25)

- Wingless

- Mouth parts: Chewing

- "Springtail": (furcula) often present, used to jump

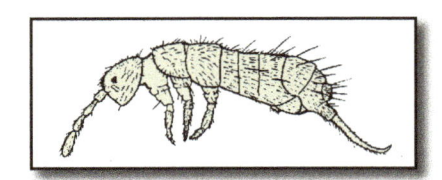

Figure 22-25 ▮ *Springtail.*

Dermaptera—Earwigs

- Introduced from Europe as a biological control.

Metamorphosis: Simple/Gradual

Features: (Figure 22-26)

- Mouthparts: Chewing; generally feed on decaying organic matter, occasionally feed on plants and insects

- Wings: Two pairs

  —Front wings are short, leathery, without venation, and meet in a straight line down the back when at rest.

  —Hind wings are membranous, broad, with veins radiating from a center, folded both lengthwise and crosswise when at rest

  —Note: Wings can be confused with those of beetles, but beetles do not have forceps-like cerci (tail-like appendage)

- Body: Elongated, flattened insects

- Cerci: Strong moveable forceps-like cerci on the abdomen end; cerci cannot produce a painful pinch, but the mouth parts can

- Habit: Overwinters as adults; during the day, earwigs like to hide in dark, moist areas

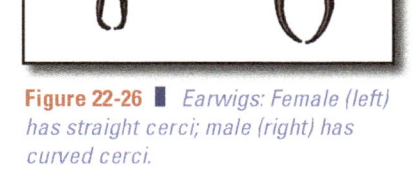

Figure 22-26 ▮ *Earwigs: Female (left) has straight cerci; male (right) has curved cerci.*

Diptera—Flies, Gnats, Midges, and Mosquitoes

- Around 99,000 species worldwide, with some 17,000 in North America

- Feeding habits vary widely, for example:

  —Scavenger (house fly, blow fly)

  —Blood sucking (mosquitoes)

  —Plant galls (gall midges)

  —Predators (flower flies, robber flies)

  —Aquatic

- Spelling hint: If the fly is a *Diptera*, the name is written as two words (house fly, deer fly, blow fly). If the fly is not a *Diptera*, the name is written as one word (sawfly, butterfly, whitefly).

Metamorphosis: Complete (Figure 22-27)

Adults: (Figures 22-27 and 22-28)

- Wings: One pair, membranous

  —One pair is a quick identifier for *Diptera*

  —Note: Count the wings! Some *Diptera* look like bees or wasps. Some *Hymenoptera* (bees and wasps) look like flies. *Diptera* has one pair. *Hymenoptera* have two pair; the hind pair is typically smaller and hidden under the front pair.

- Mouthparts: Highly variable

  —Sponging (house fly)

  —Cutting-lapping (horse fly)

  —Piercing-sucking (mosquito)

- Body: Typically soft bodied and often hairy

Larva: (Figures 22-27 and 22-28)

- Vary greatly in appearance

- Larva of advanced forms, like the house fly, are **maggot** type:

  —No head capsule

  —Mouth hooks

  —Legless

- Lower forms, such as mosquitoes, have a head capsule

Pupa: Typically pupate in last skin of larva.

Beneficial families include:

- Bee flies, *Bombyliidae*
- Crane flies, *Tipulidae*
- Gall gnats, *Cecidomylidae*
- Robber flies, *Asilidae*
- Syrphid or flower flies, *Syrphidae*
- Tachinid flies, *Tachinidae*

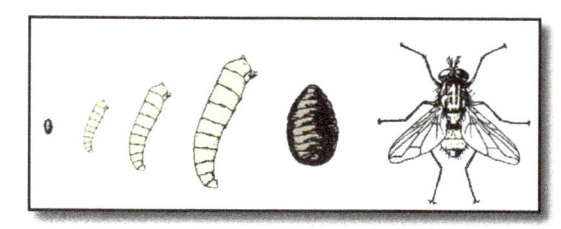

Figure 22-27 ▮ *Complete metamorphosis of flies.*

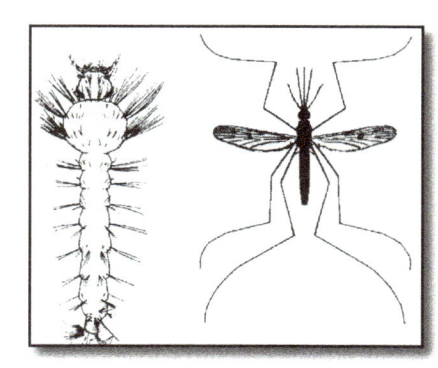

Figure 22-28 ▮ *Mosquito maggot and adult.*

Pest families include:

- Cabbage, onion, and seed corn maggots, beet leaf miner, *Anthomyiids*
- Biting midges, *Certopogonidae*
- Black flies, *Simuliidae*
- Blow flies, *Calliphoridae*
- Crane flies, *Tipulidae*
- Fruit flies, *Tephritidae*
- Gall gnats, *Cecidomylidae*
- Horse and deer flies, *Tabanidae*
- Horse bot flies, *Hippoboscidae*
- Leafminer flies, *Agromyzidae*
- Mosquitoes, *Culicidae*
- Muscids (house flies), *Muscidae*
- Sand flies (no-see-ums), *Psychodidae*
- Syrphid or flower flies, *Syrphidae*
- Vinegar flies, *Drosophilidae*

Ephemeroptera—Mayflies

- Small aquatic naiads found in the bottom of streams and lakes; serves as a source of food for fish

- No interaction with gardening activities

Metamorphosis: Simple/Incomplete

Adults: (Figure 22-29)

- Wings: Two pair

    —Front wings large and triangular shaped

    —Hind wings small and rounded

    —Wings held vertically over body

- Antennae: Small, bristle-like

- Filaments: Two very long tail-like filaments

- Mouthparts: Adults do not feed; live only a few days

Naiads: (Figure 22-30)

- Body: Aquatic naiads vary in shape; most are broad and have functional gills along the sides of the abdomen

- Mouthparts: Chewing

- Molting: Frequent; 20 to 60 times

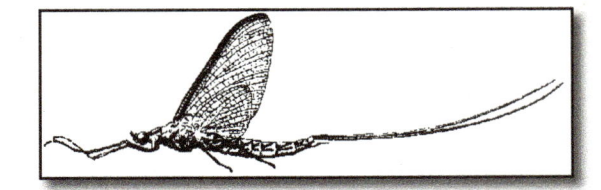

Figure 22-29 ▮ *Mayfly adult.*

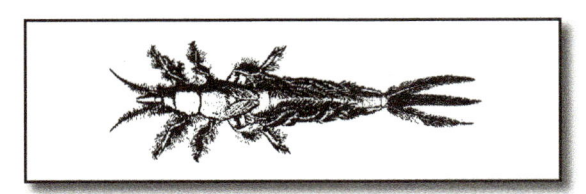

Figure 22-30 ▮ *Mayfly naiad.*

Hemiptera—True Bugs: Plant Bugs, Squash Bugs, and Stink Bugs

Note: New books combine *Homoptera* into the *Hemiptera* order. In this book, we continue to teach the old taxonomy because most books that gardeners will be using have the old taxonomic structure.

- This order includes many important insect predators.

- Spelling hint: If the bug is a *Hemiptera*, the name is written as two words (stink bug, water bug, squash bug). If the insect is not a *Hemiptera*, the name is written as one word (ladybug).

Metamorphosis: Simple/Gradual (Figure 22-31)

Features: (Figure 22-32)

- Mouthparts: Piercing-sucking

  —Jointed beak is typically visible and originates from top of head in front of eyes.

  —**Note:** By contrast, *Homoptera* mouthparts are not as visible and appear to arise from between the front legs.

- Wings: Two pairs

  —Front wings (called *hemielytra*) are thickened at base and membranous at end.

  —Hind wings are membranous.

  —When at rest, the wings overlap at the tips forming a large triangular plate (the *scutellum*) on the back.

- Body: Usually broad and somewhat flattened

Beneficial families include:

- Ambush bugs, *Phymatidae*
- Assassin bugs, *Reduvlidae*
- Coreids, *Coreidae*
- Damsel bugs, *Nabidae*
- Flower or minute pirate bugs, *Antocoridae*
- Leaf or plant bugs, *Miridae*
- Stink bugs, *Pentatomidae*

Figure 22-31 ▎ *Metamorphosis of stink bugs.*

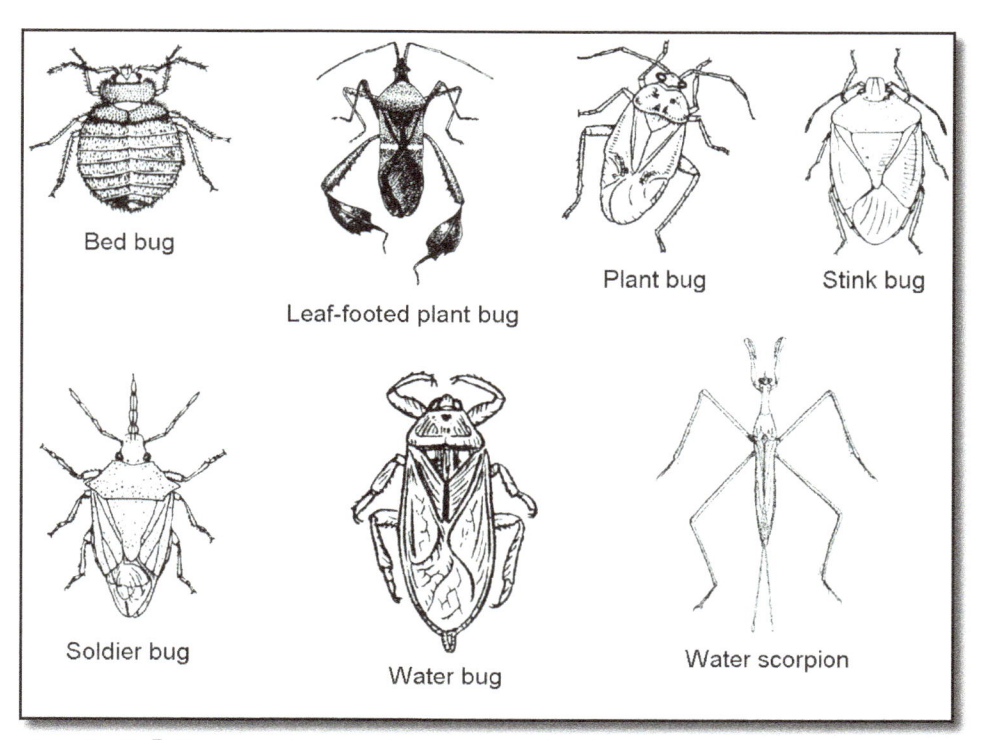

Figure 22-32 ▎ *Examples of common* Hemiptera *(true bugs).*

Pest families include:

- Chinch and lygus bugs, *Lygaeidae*
- Coreids, or squash bugs, *Coreidae*
- Lace bugs, *Tingidae*
- Stink bugs, *Pentatomidae*

Homoptera—Aphids, Cicadas, Leafhoppers, Mealybugs, Scale, and Whiteflies

Note: New books combine *Homoptera* into the *Hemiptera* order. In Colorado Master Gardener training, we continue to teach the old taxonomy because most books that gardeners will be using have the old taxonomic structure.

- All species are plant feeders, often feeding on phloem sap.

- Excretion of honeydew is common to many members of the order.

- Insects of this order are carriers of several plant pathogens.

Metamorphosis: Simple/Gradual

- Nymphs and adults similar in appearance (except male scales and whiteflies).

Features: (Figure 22-33)

- Mouthparts: Piercing-sucking

  —Jointed beak-like mouthparts not easily visible and originate from bottom of head so that it appears as if the beak is fastened between the front legs

  —**Note:** By contrast, in *Hemiptera*, mouthparts are more visible and originate from top of head, in front of eyes.

- Wings: Two pairs

  —Membranous

  —Typically held roof-like at rest

  —Many forms are wingless

  —Nymphs have no wings, but wing pads may be observed on some older nymphs

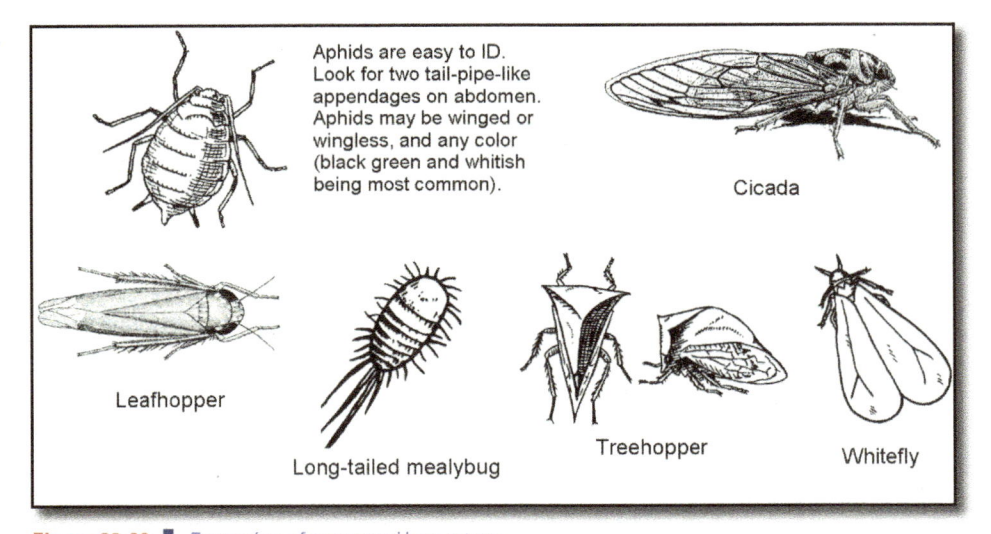

Figure 22-33 ▮ *Examples of common* Homoptera.

Pest families include:

- Adelgids, *Phylloxeridae*
- Aphids, *Aphididae*
- Armored scales, *Diaspididae*
- Cicadas, *Cicadidae*
- Leafhoppers, *Cicadellidae*
- Mealybugs, *Pseudococcidae*
- Planthoppers, superfamily *Fulgoroidea*
- Psyllids (many gall insects), *Psyllidae*
- Soft scale, *Coccidae*
- Spittlebugs, *Cercopidae*
- Treehoppers, *Membracidae*
- Whiteflies, *Aleyrodidae*

Hymenoptera—Ants, Bees, Horntails, Sawflies, and Wasps

- Large order with some 103,000 species worldwide and 18,000 in North America
- Order includes many important parasites and predators
- Has the most highly developed insect behaviors and social patterns
- Most species live in nests

Metamorphosis: Complete

Adults: (Figure 22-34)

- Wings: Two pairs, membranous

    —Hind wing is usually smaller and often hidden under front wing.

    —Front and hind wings may be attached.

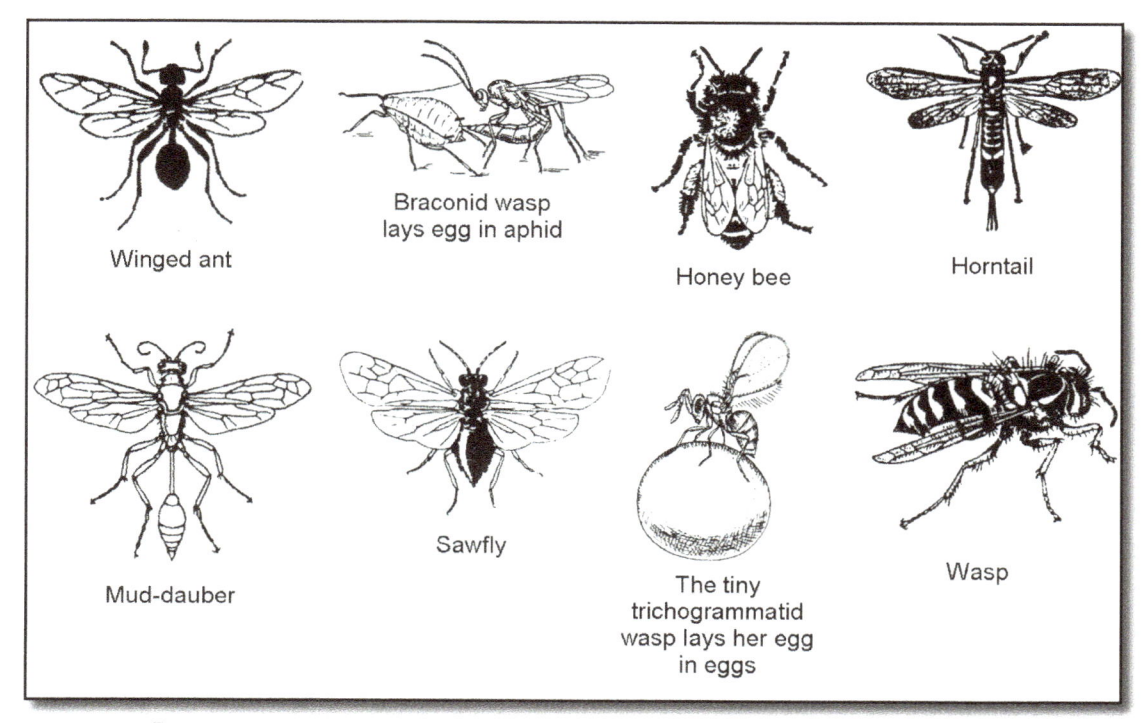

Figure 22-34 ▌ *Examples of common* Hymenoptera.

- Mouthparts: Typically chewing or chewing-sucking
- Body: Most species have a distinct constriction between the thorax and abdomen (wasp waist). The sawfly/horntail group does not have a "wasp waist."
- Antennae: Jointed, sometimes elbowed
- Stinger: Female abdomen usually provided with a saw, piercing organ, or stinger

Larva:

- Larvae of most species are rarely observed, often developing in a nest or as an internal parasite.
- Head: Distinct head capsule
- Legs: None (except sawfly larva)

  —Sawfly larva look like caterpillars but have six or more plus pairs of prolegs.

  —**Note:** Caterpillars (*Lepidoptera*) have five or fewer pairs of prolegs.

  —Some sawfly larva are legless and slug-like.

- Mouthparts: Chewing

Beneficial families include:

- Ants and parasitic wasps, superfamily *Scolioidea*
- Bees, superfamily *Apoidea*
- Chalcid wasps, *Chalcidoidea*
- Digger wasps, superfamily *Sphecoidea*
- Ichneumon and braconid wasps, superfamily *Ichneumonoidea*
- Social wasps, superfamily *Vespoidea*

Pest families include:

- Ants, superfamily *Scolioidea*
- Gall wasps, superfamily *Cynipoidea*
- Horntails, superfamily *Siricoidea*
- Sawflies, *Tenthredinoidae*
- Social wasps, superfamily *Vespoidea*

Isoptera—Termites

- Termites are social insects living in colonies. Colorado species live below ground.
- Workers avoid exposure and are rarely seen except when disturbed. Only the winged reproductive adults leave the colony.

Metamorphosis: Simple/Gradual

Features: (Figure 22-35)

- Color: Creamy white
- Wings: Two pairs that are the same size and longer than the body
- Body: Rectangular-shaped with no constriction (wasp waist) between thorax and abdomen
- Antennae: Straight and beaded
- Mouthparts: Chewing

Wasp or Bee?

Wasps have a slender and thin body; a narrow waist; slender, cylindrical legs; and a skin that generally lacks much hair. Yellow jackets, bald-faced hornets, and paper wasps are the most common wasps encountered by people.

Wasps are predators, feeding on insects and other arthropods. During late summer and autumn, when insect prey becomes more scarce, many wasps become scavengers and are especially attracted to sweets and other carbohydrates.

Bees are robust-bodied and very hairy compared with wasps. The hair on bees is branched, giving them a fuzzy or soft appearance. Their hind legs are flattened, with bristle-fringed areas for collecting and transporting pollen. Bees laden with pollen will appear to have yellow hind legs because of the pollen loads. Bees are vegetarians, feeding on nectar and pollen.

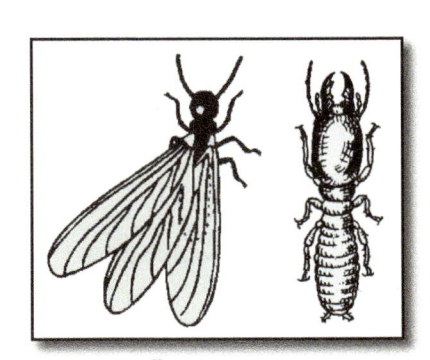

Figure 22-35 ▮ *Winged adult termite (left) and worker termite (right).*

Ant or Termite?

	Ant	Termite
Color	Black, red, yellowish, etc.	Creamy white
Waistline	"Wasp waist"	No constriction
Antennae	Jointed, sometimes elbowed	Straight and bead-like
Wings on adult	Front wing larger and hind wing smaller; wings may be attached	Front and hind wings same size, longer than body
Worker's body	Typical "ant" shape	Rectangular body with large chewing mouthparts
Observed	Commonly seen crawling around	Worker termite rarely seen except when disturbed

Lepidoptera—Butterflies and Moths

Metamorphosis: Complete

Adults: (Figure 22-36)

- Wings: Two pairs

  —Typically covered with small overlapping scales

  —Often but not always highly colored

- Mouthparts: Coiled sucking tube designed to siphon fluids like nectar

  —Some adults do not feed

Figure 22-36 ■ *The wings of butterflies and moths are generally covered with colorful scales.*

Larva—Caterpillars: (Figure 22-37)

- Legs: Three pairs on thorax

- Prolegs: Up to five pairs of prolegs (fleshy leg-like appendage with crochet-like hooks on the end which helps hold the insect to plants)

  —**Note:** Sawfly larva look like caterpillars but typically have six or more pairs of prolegs.

- Decorations: Often highly colored or decorated with spines or other appendages

- Mouthparts: Chewing, with voracious appetites

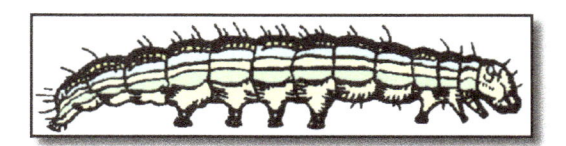

Figure 22-37 ■ *Caterpillars (larval stage of Lepidoptera) have three pairs of jointed legs on the thorax plus up to five pairs of prolegs on the abdomen.*

Pupa:

- Cocoon, made of silk spun from saliva glands

Families of interest include:

- Bagworm moths, *Psychidae*
- Carpenterworm moths, *Cossidae*
- Clearwing moths (squash vine borer, lilac borer), *Sesiidae*
- Giant silkworm moths, *Saturniidae*
- Leafrollers, *Tortricidae*
- Measuringworms, *Geometridae*
- Monarch, viceroy, red admiral, morningcloak, and angelwings butterflies, *Nymphalidae*
- Noctuids (cutworms, armyworms, fruitworms, corn earworm, cabbage loopers), *Noctuidae*
- Olethreutid moths, *Olethreutidae*
- Prominents (redhumped caterpillars), *Notodontidae*
- Pyralids (corn borer, sod webworm, meal moths), *Pyralidae*
- Royal moths, *Citheroniidae*
- Silkworm moths, *Bombycidae*
- Sphinx or hawk moth, hornworms, *Sphingidae*
- Swallowtail or parsleyworm, *Papilionidae*
- Tent caterpillars, *Lasiocampidae*
- Tineids (clothes moths), *Tineidae*
- Tussock moths, *Lymantriidae*
- White or yellow butterflies (imported cabbageworm), *Pieridae*

Mallophaga—Chewing or Biting Lice

- Tiny parasite of birds and some mammals

- Feeds on blood, feathers, hair, skin, or sebaceous fluids

Metamorphosis: Simple/Gradual

Features: (Figure 22-38)

- Flattened, oval

- Head larger than thorax

- Antenna short

- Eyes very small or absent

- No wings

- Legs short and modified to hold to feathers or fur

- Lives only on hosts

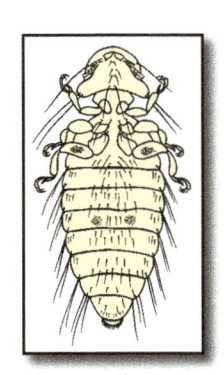

Figure 22-38 ▮
Chewing lice.

Mantodea—Mantids

- Predators of other insects, which they capture with front legs and eat

- Winter is spent in the egg mass covered with a tough polystyrene-like coat

Metamorphosis: Simple/Gradual

Features: (Figure 22-39)

- Legs: Foreleg designed for grasping and holding prey

- Body: Elongated

- Mouthparts: Chewing

- Antennae: Long, thread-like

- Wings: If present, are leathery and over abdomen; absent in nymphs

Figure 22-39 ▮ *Mantid.*

Neuroptera—Antlions, Lacewings, Snakeflies, and Dobsonflies

- Order includes many important predators

- No harmful species are known

- The antlion is the larva of the common lacewing; some forms are aquatic

Metamorphosis: Complete

Adults: (Figure 22-40)

- Wings: Two pairs

  —Membranous, similar in size and texture

  —Large membranous wing, usually with many veins and cross veins

  —Held roof-like over body when at rest

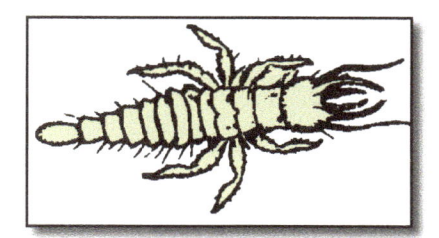

Figure 22-40 ▮ *Adult lacewing.*

- Mouthparts: Chewing; some are predators, while others feed on nectar or pollen

- Cerci: None

- Tarsus (foot): Five segments

Larva: (Figure 22-41)

- Mouthparts: Forward-projecting curved pointed jaws designed to grasp prey; they crush prey and suck out the insides

- Body: Often elongated

- Legs: Three pairs

Figure 22-41 ▮ *Antlion (lacewing larva).*

Odonata—Dragonflies and Damselflies

Metamorphosis: Simple/Incomplete

Adults: (Figure 22-42)

- Eyes: Very large eyes that may cover much of head

- Wings: Two pairs

  —Large, elongated, highly veined

  —Dragonflies hold wings horizontally when at rest; damselfly wings project back over body when at rest.

- Mouthparts: Chewing, prominent, used to capture and consume winged prey in flight

- Antennae: Small, bristle-like

Figure 22-42 ▮ *Dragonfly adult.*

Naiads: (Figure 22-43)

- Aquatic insect that feeds on mosquito larva and other aquatic life

- Eyes: Large

- Mouthparts: Uniquely hinged jaw that can project forward to capture prey

- Gills: Three leaf-like gills at end of abdomen (damselfly only)

Figure 22-43 ▮ *Dragonfly naiad.*

Orthoptera—Crickets, Grasshoppers, and Katydids

- **Note:** Older books place mantids (*Mantodea*), walking sticks (*Phasmida*), and roaches (*Blattaria*) in the order *Orthoptera*.

- Most are plant feeders. A few are predators or scavengers.

Metamorphosis: Simple/Gradual

Features: (Figure 22-44)

- Mouthparts: Chewing

- Wings: Two pairs

  —Front wings more or less parchment-like with distinct venations

  —Hind wings membranous and folded fan-like when at rest

  —Wings may be used to make sounds

- Legs: Hind legs enlarged for jumping

- Cerci (tail-like appendages): One pair on most adults

Pest families include:

- Crickets, *Gryliidae*

- Short-horned grasshoppers, *Acrididae*

- Long-horned grasshoppers (katydids, meadow grasshoppers, and Mormon crickets), *Tettigoniidae*

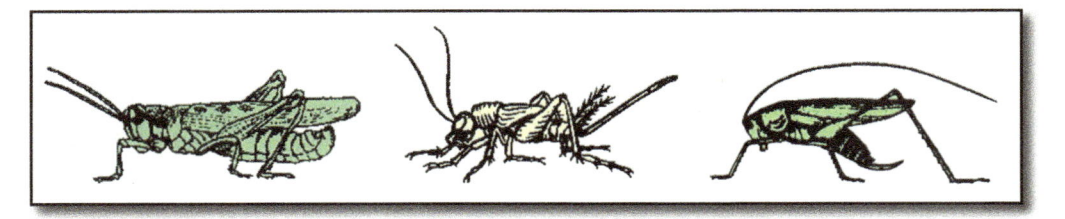

Figure 22-44 ▮ Orthoptera *(left to right): grasshopper, cricket, and katydid.*

Phasmida—Walking Stick

- Feeds on plant leaves

- Stick-like form provides great camouflage

Metamorphosis: Simple/Gradual

Features: (Figure 22-45)

- Body: Very elongated, stick-like
- Mouthparts: Chewing
- Wings: Typically none

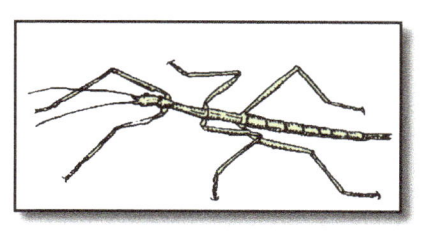

Figure 22-45 ▮ *Walking Stick.*

Plecoptera—Stoneflies

- Aquatic naiads cling to stones in streams and serve as food for other aquatic insects and fish.
- There is no direct interaction with gardening activities.

Metamorphosis: Simple/Incomplete

Adults: (Figure 22-46)

- Wings: Elongated wings fold flat over body when at rest
- Antennae: Long, filament-like
- Filament (tail-like): Two

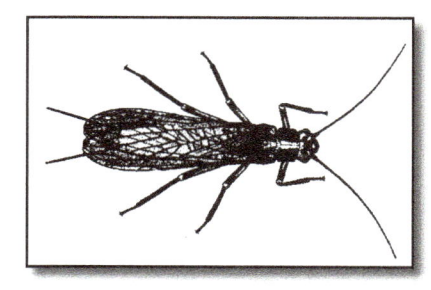

Figure 22-46 ▮ *Stonefly adult.*

Naiads: (Figure 22-47)

- Aquatic naiad typically found under stones in rivers and lake shores

Psocoptera—Psocids or Booklice

- Common but inconspicuous insect rarely observed due to tiny size
- Found in warm, damp places feeding on molds, fungi, cereals, pollen, etc.
- Occasionally invade the home

Metamorphosis: Simple/Gradual

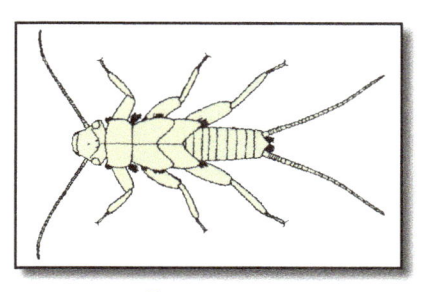

Figure 22-47 ▮ *Stonefly naiad.*

Features: (Figure 22-48)

- Size: Tiny, less than one-eighth inch
- Wings: Two pairs on some adults
  - —Held roof-like over body when at rest
  - —Front pair larger
  - —Veins prominent
  - —Unwinged specimens common
- Mouthparts: Chewing
- Antennae: Slender and as long or longer than body

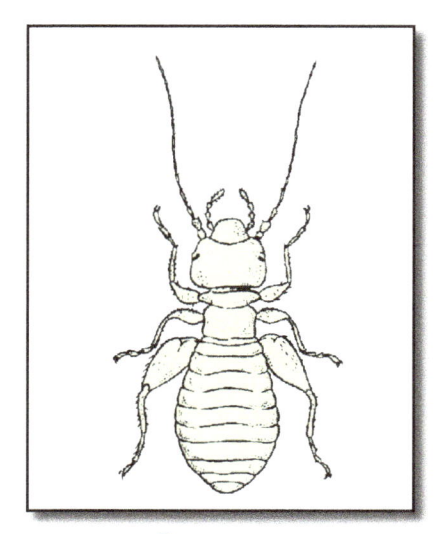

Figure 22-48 ▮ *Booklice.*

Siphonaptera—Fleas

- Household pest of pets and people

Metamorphosis: Complete

Adults: (Figure 22-49)

- Size: Less than one-eighth inch

- Wingless

- Body: Flattened sideways, dark colored, covered with bristles that project backwards

- Mouthparts: Piercing/sucking, designed to suck blood

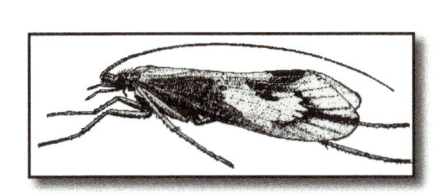

Figure 22-49 ▮ *Flea.*

Thysanoptera—Thrips

- It is a very common insect, but due to tiny size is rarely observed.

- Feeding leaves the plant looking scarred, as they rasp the leaf or flower surface and suck the fluids.

Metamorphosis: Simple/Gradual

Features: (Figure 22-50)

- Wings: Two pairs

  —Slender wings fringed with hairs

  —Often absent

- Mouthparts: Rasping-sucking; typically feed on flowers and leaves

- Tarsi (feet): One- or two-segmented, each with a balloon-like structure on the end

- Size: Minute, less than one-eighth inch long

Figure 22-50 ▮ *Thrips.*

Trichoptera—Caddisflies

- Aquatic naiad

- Not associated with gardening activities

Metamorphosis: Simple/Incomplete

Adults: (Figure 22-51)

- Wings: Two pairs

  —Covered with fine hairs

  —Held roof-like over body at rest

  —Resemble moths with hairy wings

- Antennae: Extended back over body

Figure 22-51 ▮ *Caddisfly.*

Naiads:

- Aquatic naiad

- Some live in cases constructed of silk, pebbles, sticks, and leaves; others construct silken nests

- Some are free-living and actively hunt other insects

Zygentomaa—Silverfish and Firebrats

- Found in cool, moist, dark places

- General feeder on starches and carbohydrates, including paper, wall paper, vegetables, and grain products

Metamorphosis: None

Features: (Figure 22-52)

- Size: Small, one-quater to one-half inch

- Wingless

- Mouthparts: Chewing

- Cerci: Pair, long tail-like

- Active, fast moving

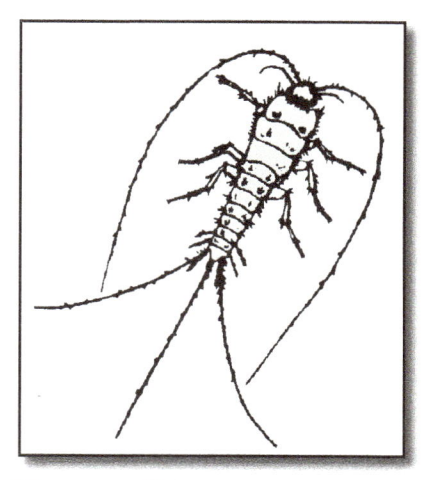

Figure 22-52 ▮ *Silverfish.*

KEY 1—KEY TO INSECTS ASSOCIATED WITH GARDENING

Notes:

- This key covers insect orders commonly associated with gardening and landscape maintenance. Key 2 includes additional orders.

- This simplified key covers insects showing common characteristics for the order. Species with atypical appearances will not work with this simplified key.

	1a.	Wings present.—go to 2
	1b.	Wings absent.—go to 8

(1a) | 2a. | One pair of membranous wings. The insect may look like a fly or bee. (Look carefully for a second pair of wings hidden beneath the front pair.)—***Diptera*** **(flies)**

(1a) | 2b. | Two pairs of wings present.—go to 3

(2b) | 3a. | Front and hind wings not similar in texture. Front wings parchment-like, shell-like, or leathery or thickened. Hind wings more delicate or membranous.—go to 4

(2b) | 3b. | Front and hind wings similar in texture. Either membranous, transparent or covered with powdery-like scales.—go to 6

(3a) | 4a. | Chewing mouthparts.—go to 5

(3a) | 4b. | Piercing-sucking mouthparts. Beak-like mouthparts usually easily visible and appear to arise from front of head, ahead of eyes. Front wings thickened at base but membranous and overlapping at tips, so that the wings form a triangle pattern on the back.—***Hemiptera*** **(true bugs)**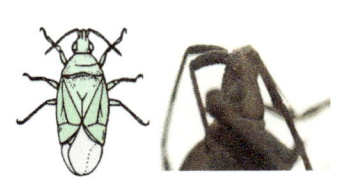

(4a) | 5a. | Leathery front wings, without veins, lay over body in a shell-like fashion, making a straight line between wings. Hind wings membranous. No cerci (tail-like appendages).—***Coleoptera*** **(beetles)**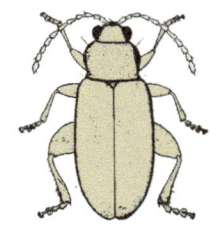

(4a) | 5b. | Front wings more or less parchment-like with a network of veins. Hind wings membranous and folded fan-like when at rest. Hind leg enlarged for jumping.—***Orthoptera*** **(grasshoppers, crickets, katydids)**

   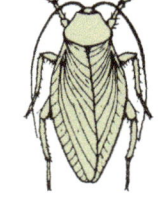

5c. | Front wings more or less parchment-like with a network of veins. Flattened bodies, thread-like antennae—***Blattaria*** **(cockroach)**

5d. | Front leg enlarged for capturing prey.—***Mantodea*** **(mantids)**

5e. Front wings short and leathery. Hind wings membranous. Elongated flattened body with distinct forceps-like pinchers (cerci).—***Dermaptera*** **(earwigs)**

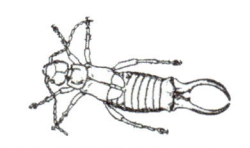

(3b) 6a. Wings membranous.—go to 7

6b. Wings usually covered with powdery-like scales. Mouthparts coiled sucking tube beneath the head.—***Lepidoptera*** **(butterflies, moths)**

6c. Wings very narrow and fringed with hair. Tiny insect (less than one-eighth inch). Foot ending in balloon-like swelling.—***Thysanoptera*** **(thrips)**

(6a) 7a. Piercing-sucking mouthparts. Jointed beak-like mouthparts not very visible and appear to arise from the area between the front legs. Wings generally held roof-like over body when at rest.—***Homoptera*** **(aphids, cicadas, leafhoppers, psyllids, treehoppers, and whiteflies)**

aphid   cicada   leafhopper   whitefly

7b. Front wing usually larger than hind wing. Wings may be connected. Chewing or chewing sucking mouthparts. Bee-, wasp-, or ant-like with narrow waist.—***Hymenoptera*** **(bees, wasps, ants)**

7c. Large membranous wings, usually with many veins and cross veins; similar in size and texture; held roof-like over body when at rest. Antennae longer, not extremely short or bristle-like. Tarsus (foot) with five segments. No cerci (tail-like appendage).—***Neuroptera*** **(lacewing)**

(1b) 8a. Piercing-sucking, jointed beak-like mouthparts.—go to 9

8b. Chewing mouthparts.—go to 10

8c. Rasping-sucking mouthparts. Tiny (less than one-eighth inch), slender insects. Balloon-like swelling on end of foot. Often noticed by scarring and deformation of leaves and flowers where it feeds.—***Thysanoptera*** **(thrips)**

(8a) 9a. Bug-like with jointed beak. Mouthparts usually easily visible and appear to arise from front of head, in front of eyes.—***Hemiptera*** **(true bugs)**

9b. Bug-like with jointed beak. Mouthparts not highly visible and appear to arise from the area between the front pair of legs.—*Homoptera* (aphids, cicadas, leafhoppers, mealybugs, psyllids, scale)

(8b) 10a. Larva-like (i.e., caterpillar-like, grub-like, maggot-like).—go to 11

10b. Bug-like with tail-like features (cerci, filaments).—go to 14

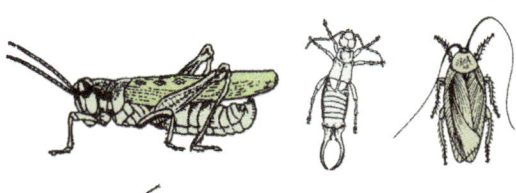

10c. Ant-like.—go to 15

10d. Dragon-like with lots of appendages and decorations.—go to 16

(10a) 11a. Caterpillar-like: soft bodied, three pairs of legs on thorax, fleshy leg-like prolegs on abdomen.—go to 12

11b. Grub-like: head capsule, three pairs of legs on thorax, and no legs on abdomen.—typical of *Coleoptera* (beetle grubs)

11c. Maggot-like, headless, legless.—go to 13

(11a) 12a. Up to five pairs of prolegs on abdomen.—*Lepidoptera* (butterfly and moth caterpillars)

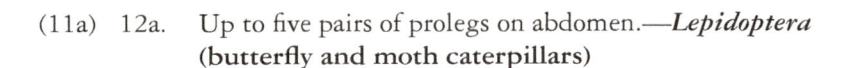

12b. Six or more pairs of prolegs on abdomen.—*Hymenoptera* (sawfly larva)

(11c) 13a. Maggot-like: no legs, no head capsule, mouth-hooks.—typical of *Diptera* (fly maggots)

13b. Legless, no head capsule, head area may be enlarged. Insect internal wood or bark borer.—some *Coleoptera* (borer larva)

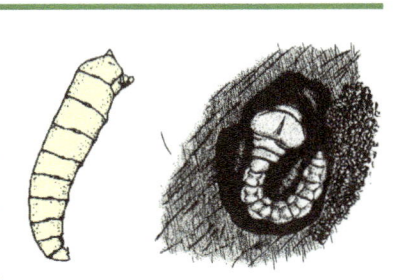

13c. Slug-like; foliage feeding.—*Hymenoptera* (typical of some sawfly larva)

13d. Maggot-like; larva found in nests.—*Hymenoptera* (larva of bees, wasps, and ants found in nest)

(10b) 14a. Elongated flattened body with distinct forceps-like pinchers (cerci) and short leathery front wings.—*Dermaptera* (**earwigs**)

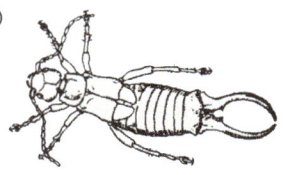

14b. Hind legs designed for jumping. Antennae tread-like.—*Orthoptera* (**grasshoppers, crickets, katydids**)

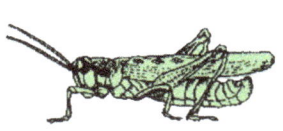  

14c. Flattened body, thread-like antennae, thick semitransparent wings with major venation. Household pest.—*Blattaria* (**cockroaches**)

14d. Front legs designed for grasping and holding prey. Body elongated. Long, thread-like antennae.—*Mantodea* (**mantids**)

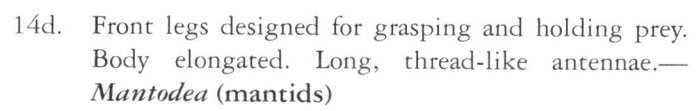

(10c) 15a. Three distinct body segments. Narrow waist. Elbowed antennae.—*Hymenoptera* (**ants**)

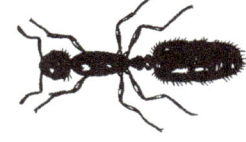

15b. Looks like a fat ant without a narrow waist. Creamy white. Straight beaded antennae.—*Isoptera* (**worker termites**)

(10d) 16a. Generally dark colored with bright markings and spines.—*Coleoptera* (**beetle grubs**)

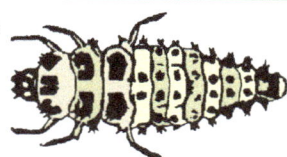

16b. Forward-projecting, curved pointed jaws designed to grasp prey; they crush and suck the insides of prey.—*Neuroptera* (**antlion**)

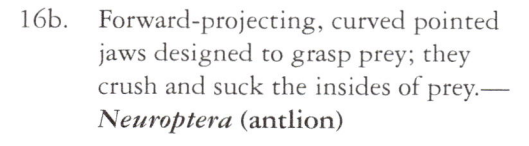 

KEY 2—KEY TO INSECT ORDERS

Notes:

- This key covers insect orders commonly and occasionally observed. However, it does not include all orders. Key 1 is similar, but easier, being limited to insect orders commonly associated with gardening and landscape maintenance.

- This simplified key covers insects showing common characteristics for the order. Species with atypical appearances will not work with this simplified key.

	1a.	Wings present.—go to 2	
	1b.	Wings absent.—go to 9	

| (1a) | 2a. | One pair of membranous wings. The insect may look like a fly or bee. (Look carefully for a second pair of wings hidden beneath the front pair.)—*Diptera* (**flies**) |  |
| | 2b. | Two pairs of wings present.—go to 3 | |

| (2b) | 3a. | Front and hind wings not similar in texture. Front wings parchment-like, shell-like or leathery or thickened. Hind wings more delicate or membranous.—go to 4 | |
| | 3b. | Front and hind wings similar in texture. Either membranous, transparent, or covered with powdery-like scales.—go to 7 | |

| (3a) | 4a. | Chewing mouthparts.—go to 5 | 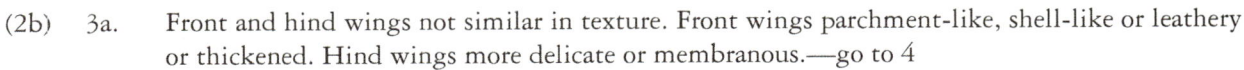 |
| | 4b. | Piercing-sucking mouthparts.—go to 6 | |

(4a)	5a.	Leathery front wings, without veins, lay over body in a shell-like fashion, making a straight line between wings. Hind wings membranous. No cerci (tail-like appendages).—*Coleoptera* (**beetle**)	
	5b.	Front wings more or less parchment-like with a network of veins. Hind wings membranous, usually broad with folds like a fan. Hind leg enlarged for jumping—*Orthoptera* (**grasshoppers, crickets, katydids**)	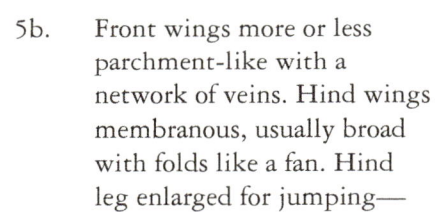
	5c.	Front wings more or less parchment-like with a network of veins. Flattened bodies, thread-like antennae — *Blattaria* (**cockroach**)	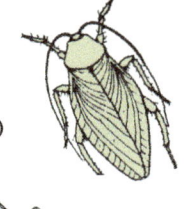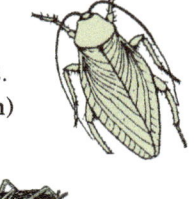
	5d.	Front wings more or less parchment-like with a network of veins. Front legs modified to catch and hold prey.—*Mantodea* (**mantids**)	
	5e.	Front wings short and leathery. Hind wings membranous. Elongated flattened body with distinct forceps-like pinchers (cerci).—*Dermaptera* (**earwigs**)	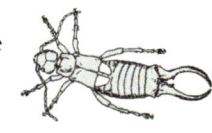

(4b)	6a.	Front wings thickened at base but membranous and overlapping at tips, so that the wings form a triangle pattern on the back. Beak-like mouthparts usually easily visible and appear to arise from front of head, ahead of eyes.—*Hemiptera* (**true bugs**)

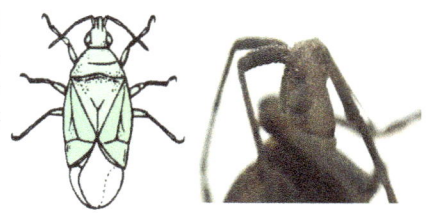

	6b.	Wings membranous folded tent-like at rest. Beak-like mouthparts not very visible and appear to arise from the area between the front pair of legs.—*Homoptera* (**leafhoppers, treehoppers**)

(3b)	7a.	Wings membranous—go to 8
	7b.	Wings usually covered with powdery-like scales. Mouthparts in the form of a coiled up tube beneath the head.—*Lepidoptera* (**butterflies, moths**)

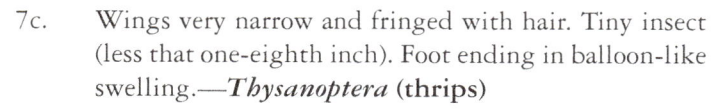

	7c.	Wings very narrow and fringed with hair. Tiny insect (less that one-eighth inch). Foot ending in balloon-like swelling.—*Thysanoptera* (**thrips**)

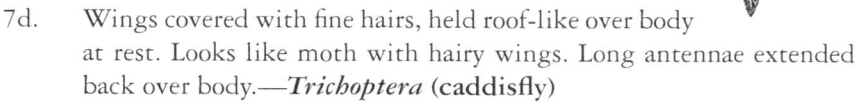

	7d.	Wings covered with fine hairs, held roof-like over body at rest. Looks like moth with hairy wings. Long antennae extended back over body.—*Trichoptera* (**caddisfly**)

(7a)	8a.	Piercing-sucking mouthparts. Beak-like mouthparts not very visible and appear to arise from the area between the front pair of legs. Wings generally held roof-like over body when at rest.—*Homoptera* (**aphids, cicadas, leafhoppers, psyllids, treehoppers, whiteflies**)

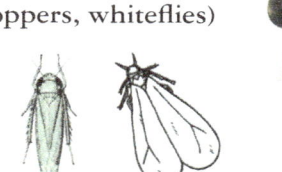

aphid   cicada   leafhopper   whitefly

	8b.	Front wing usually larger than hind wing. Wings may be connected. Chewing or chewing-sucking mouthparts. Bee-, wasp-, hornet-like.—*Hymenoptera* (**bees, wasps, hornets, winged ants**)

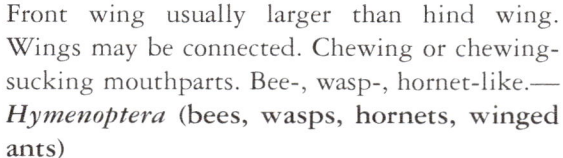

	8c.	Large wings in comparison to petite body. Wings usually with many veins and cross veins, held roof-like over body when at rest. Chewing mouth parts. No cerci (tail-like appendages).—*Neuroptera* (**lacewing**)

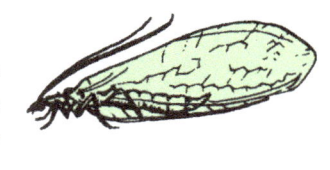

	8d.	Wings longer than body. Body whitish, looks like a fat ant without a slim waist. Straight and beaded antennae.—*Isoptera* (**winged termite**)

8e. Tiny (less than one-eighth inch). Wings held roof-like over body when at rest. Veins prominent. Hair-like antennae as long or longer than body. Whitish body.—*Psocoptera* (book lice)

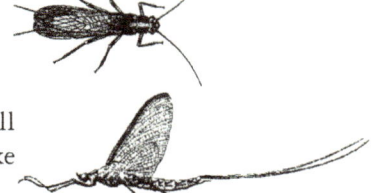

8f. Insect dominated by very large eyes. Wings elongated, highly veined. Slender, needle-like body. Chewing mouthparts used to capture and consume prey in flight.—*Odonata* (dragonflies and damselflies)

8g. Elongated wings fold flat over body when at rest. Long thread-like antennae. Two tail-like filaments.—*Plecoptera* (stonefly)

8h. Front wings large and triangular shaped. Hind wings small and rounded. Held vertical over body. Two very long tail-like filaments.—*Ephemeroptera* (Mayfly)

(1b) 9a. Piercing-sucking mouthparts.—go to 10

9b. Chewing mouthparts.—go to 11

9c. Rasping-sucking mouthparts. Tiny (less than one-eighth inch), slender insects. Balloon-like swelling on end of foot. Often noticed by scarring and deformation of leaves and flowers where it feeds.—*Thysanoptera* (thrips)

(9a) 10a. Bug-like with jointed beak. Mouthparts usually easily visible and appear to arise from front of head, in front of eyes.—*Hemiptera* (true bugs)

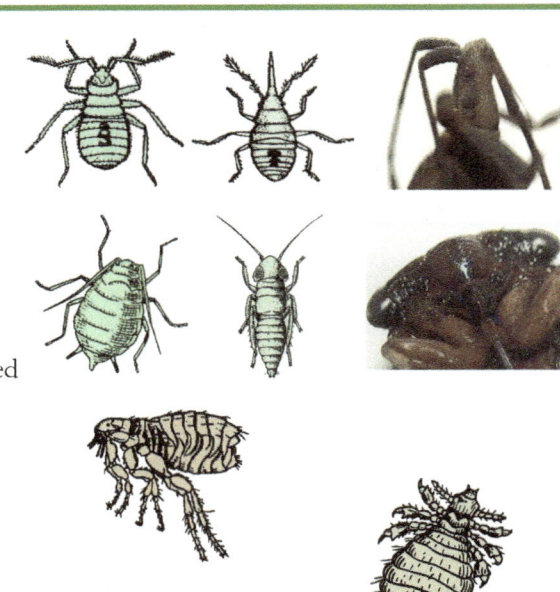

10b. Bug-like with jointed beak. Mouthparts not very visible and appear to arise from the area between the front pair of legs.—*Homoptera* (aphids, cicadas, leafhoppers, etc.)

10c. Tiny, hard-bodied, flattened sideways, covered with bristles that project backwards. Large hind legs designed for jumping, fast moving.—*Siphonaptera* (fleas)

10d. Small, flattened parasites of animals and people. Forelegs with claw designed to grasp hair or feathers. Head narrower than thorax.—*Anoplura* (sucking lice, including head lice and body lice)

(9b) 11a. Larva-like (caterpillar-like, grub-like, maggot-like).—go to 12

11b. Bug-like with tail-like features (cerci, filaments).— go to 15

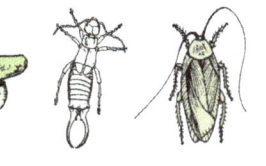

11c. Ant-like.—go to 16

11d. Dragon-like.—go to 17

11e. Tiny, bug-like.—go to 18

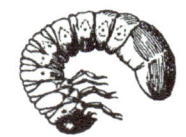

(11a) 12a. Caterpillar-like: soft bodied, three pairs of legs on thorax, fleshy leg-like prolegs on abdomen.—go to 13

12b. Grub-like: head capsule, three pairs of legs on thorax, no legs on abdomen.—typical of *Coleoptera* (**beetle grub**)

12c. Legless—go to 14

(12a) 13a. Up to five pairs of prolegs on abdomen.—*Lepidoptera* (**butterfly and moth caterpillar**)

13b. Six or more pairs of prolegs on abdomen.—*Hymenoptera* (**sawfly larva**)

(12c) 14a. Maggot-like: no legs, no head capsule, mouth-hooks.—**typical of** *Diptera* (**fly maggot**)

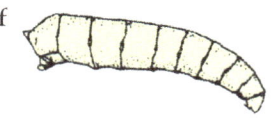

14b. Legless with enlarged head area.—typical of *Coleoptera* (**borer larva**) and some *Hymenoptera* larva

(11b) 15a. Elongated flattened body with distinct forceps-like pinchers (cerci).— *Dermaptera* (**earwigs**)

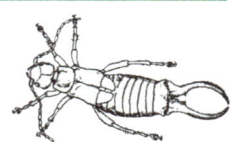

15b. Hind legs designed for jumping. Antennae tread-like. One pair of tail-like cerci on most adults.—*Orthoptera* (**grasshoppers, crickets, katydids**)

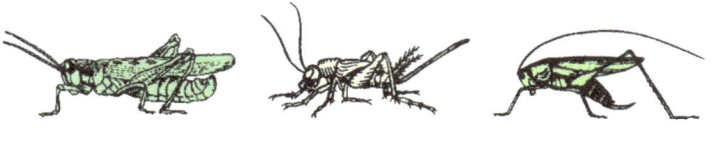

15c. Flattened body, long thread-like antennae.—*Blattaria* (**cockroaches**)

15d. Front legs designed for grasping and holding prey. Body elongated. Long, thread-like antennae.—*Mantodea* (**mantids**)

15e. Very elongated, stick-like insect.—*Phasmida* (**walking stick**)

15f. Two or three long, tail-like cerci. Fast moving. Small, one-quarter to one-half inch.—*Zygentomaa* (silverfish, firebrats)

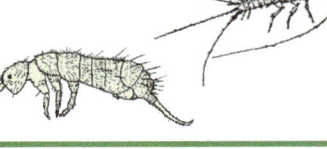

15g. Tiny (1 to 2 mm) soft-bodied insect. "Springtail" often present, used to jump.—*Collembola* (springtail)

(11c) 16a. Three distinct body segments. Ant-like with narrow ant waist. Elbowed antennae.—*Hymenoptera* (ant)

16b. Looks like a fat ant without a narrow waist. Creamy white. Straight beaded antennae.—*Isoptera* (termite)

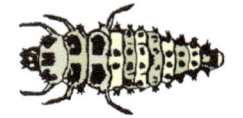

(11d) 17a. Generally dark colored with bright markings and spines. Lacking jaw as in 17b.—*Coleoptera* (lady beetle larva)

17b. Forward-projecting, curved pointed jaws designed to grasp prey, which they then crush and suck out the insides.—*Neuroptera* (antlion)

17c. Aquatic nymphs. ——

- *Coleoptera* (aquatic beetle larva)

- *Diptera* (mosquito larva)

- *Ephemeroptera* (Mayfly naiads)

- *Odonata* (dragonfly and damselfly naiads)

- *Plecoptera* (stonefly naiads)

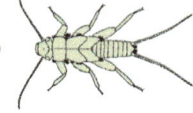

- *Trichoptera* (caddisfly naiads)

(11e) 18a. Tiny parasite of birds. Flattened body. Head as wide or wider than thorax. —*Mallophaga* (chewing or biting lice)

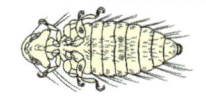

18b. Tiny, less than one-eighth inch. Hair-like antennae as long or longer than body. Whitish body.—*Psocoptera* (book lice)

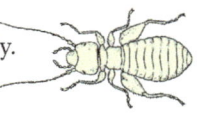

CHAPTER REVIEW
Questions

1. Describe the identifying characteristics of the following orders:

   a. *Coleoptera* (beetles)

      1) Adults

      2) Larva: Typical grub

   b. *Diptera* (flies)

      1) Adult

      2) Larva: Maggot

   c. *Hemiptera* (true bugs)

   d. *Hymenoptera* (bees, wasps, sawflies, etc.)

      1) Adult

      2) Sawfly larva

   f. *Lepidoptera*

      1) Adult butterfly

      2) Larva: Caterpillar

   g. *Orthoptera* (grasshoppers, katydids, and crickets)

2. How do you quickly tell the following orders of insects apart?

   a. Caterpillars (*Lepidoptera* larva) from sawfly larva (*Hymenoptera*)

   b. Flies (*Diptera* adults) from bees and wasps (*Hymenoptera* adults)

   c. *Homoptera* nymphs from *Hemiptera* nymphs

   d. *Homoptera* adults from *Hemiptera* adults

   e. Beetles adults (*Coleoptera*) from true bugs (*Hemiptera*)

Chapter
23*

Managing Insect Pests

Of the 750,000 species of insects, only a small portion are actually pests to humanity and crops. Most of the insects observed in the landscape are just part of the environment causing no harm. Some are actually beneficial, pollinating crops and feeding on pests.

Diagnosing insect pests on landscape plants is easy when following the basic steps in the diagnostic process.

1. **Identify the plant.** For any given host plant, this quickly cuts the list of possibilities from thousands down to just a handful.

2. **Identify the insect.** With good reference materials, insects on landscape plants are generally easy to identify when the insect is present, associated with plant damage, and large enough to see and describe. Identification will be difficult to impossible when the insect has done its damage and left, or is too small to be readily described.

   For various states and regions of the county, the Cooperative Extension System publishes local books and fact sheets to assist in insect pest identification and management. For the high plains and rocky mountain region, *Insects and Diseases of Woody Plants* (by Dr. Whitney Cranshaw, published by Colorado State University Extension) is the book of choice of insect and diseases of trees and shrubs. *Pests of the West* (by Dr. Whitney Cranshaw, published by Fulcrum Publishing) would be the reference for fruits and vegetables.

3. **Evaluate if management efforts are warranted.** Data from the landscape maintenance industry suggests that only four percent of landscape pests warrant the use of organic or manufactured pesticides (insecticides, fungicides, herbicides, etc.). Often, the insect damage is only cosmetic and management

*Author: David Whiting, Colorado State University Extension. Artwork by David Whiting.

efforts are not warranted for the health of the plant. Sometimes, the insect cannot be controlled with insecticides. For most insect pests, the time frame of effective insecticide application is limited to a few days or weeks.

4. **Evaluate management options effective for this insect.** Many landscape pests have a variety of management options. Some may have just a few effective methods. Each is different, so do not assume the effective approach for one insect will be similar to another pest.

    Examples of cultural methods include resistant varieties, planting times, irrigation management, and plant spacing. Examples of mechanical methods include row covers, traps, and hosing off the plants. Bionatural methods include the protection of beneficial insects, mites, and birds by avoiding unwarranted use of insecticides, by avoiding blanket spraying the entire yard, and by planting host plants for beneficials. The use of bionaturals could also include the importation and release of beneficial organisms (such as lady beetles).

    In limited situations, an organic or manufactured insecticide may be warranted to protect the health of the plant. By legal definition, insecticides include substances or organisms that prevent, destroy, repel, or mitigate insects, including extract from plants and animals, microbial products, microorganisms, or mineral-bearing rocks. Some are naturally occurring (called "organic"), and others are manufactured.

    In various states and regions of the county, Cooperative Extension (at the land grant university) publishes a variety of bulletins and fact sheets on insect management for that area of the county. For fact sheets from Colorado State University Extension, refer to the Colorado Master Gardener website at www.cmg. colostate.edu.

TYPES OF INSECT DAMAGE ON PLANTS

Books on landscape pests typically sort insects by the type of damage or by host plants. The following summarizes some of the common types of damage:

1. **Foliage feeders**

    a. **Defoliators**

        1) **Leaf-feeding caterpillars** (*Lepidoptera*)—There are hundreds of leaf-feeding caterpillars that feed on trees and other landscape plants. Most have a short list of host plants. They are identified by host plants, time of year, insect description, and location on the plant.

            As a rule of thumb, a healthy tree could lose one-third of the entire foliage before management efforts are warranted. Plants under stress are less tolerant. Most outbreaks cause rather minor damage. However, some could completely defoliate the plant in a few days.

            In the situation where chemical control is warranted, *Bacillus thuringiensis* is the bionatural (bacterium) insecticide of choice. It has minimal health and environmental risks. Most other home garden insecticides (including insecticidal soap) are effective. Complete coverage is required. For information on a specific insect, refer to Cooperative Extension bulletins in your state or region.

        2) **Leaf-feeding sawfly larva** (*Hymenoptera*)—A long list of leaf-feeding sawfly larva feed on trees and other landscape plants. Most species have a short list of host plants. They are identified by host plants, time of year, insect description, and location on the plant.

            Depending on the species, some sawfly outbreaks may be minor, but others can completely defoliate the plant in just a few days. In conifers, sawflies often attack a specific year of needles, like the new growth. Because conifers retain needles for multiple years, the loss of a single year's needles may become a major stress factor.

Many common home garden insecticides are effective on sawflies. However, *Bacillus thuringiensis, Bt,* (used for caterpillars) is not effective on sawflies. Thus, correct identification of the insect is critical. Complete coverage is essential. For information on a specific insect, refer to Cooperative Extension bulletins in your state or region.

Figure 23-1 ▮ *Flea beetle damage on beans.*

3) **Leaf-feeding beetles** (*Coleoptera*)— Leaf-feeding beetles are another common group of defoliants making tiny holes to consuming the entire leaves. Damage is done by both the larva (grub) and adult. Identification is primarily by host plant and insect description (Figure 23-1).

Management options when the beetle population is high vary with the specific pest. Refer to Cooperative Extension print information in your state or region for additional information.

b. **Leaf miners** feed on the inside of leaves or needles, leaving the upper and lower epidermis. Some make large patches, other make serpentine trails around the leaf. Identification is based on host plants (Figure 23-2).

Leaf miners on landscape plants rarely reach a population where management efforts are warranted. Most leaf miners have no effective control options. In leafy vegetables, like spinach, leaf miners often destroy crops. A floating row cover over the crop is effective. For information on a specific insect, refer to Cooperative Extension bulletins in your state or region.

Figure 23-2 ▮ *Spinach leaf miner on beet leaf.*

c. **Leaf-sucking insects** include aphids and other *Homoptera*, and true bugs (*Hemiptera*). Sap sucking *Homoptera* and *Hemiptera* are host-specific with a short list of host plants for each insect species. Feeding often causes twisting, cupping, curling, and other distortions of leaves; yellowing speckles or freckling of the leaves; and honeydew (sticky deposits that may drip from leaves and branches). Aphids are the most common insect in the landscape (Figure 23-3).

Without other stress factors, trees and other landscape plants are generally tolerant of low populations. Because these insects feed on the plant's sap, plants are rather intolerant of sucking insects when under water stress (including drought, limited irrigation, limited root spread due to hardscape features, lack of root spread due to poor soil conditions, newly planted, or root injury).

Figure 23-3 ▮ *Cupping of cherry caused by black cherry aphids.*

They are often kept in bounds by predators (such as lady beetles and predatory *Hemiptera*), insect diseases, birds, and driving rains. Hosing off the plant with a forceful stream of water often helps reduce populations.

When populations are high, organic or manufactured insecticides may be warranted. Many home garden insecticides are effective. With organic products like insecticidal soap and horticultural oils, complete coverage is essential. Being sap feeding, systemic insecticides are often most effective. For information on a specific insect, refer to Cooperative Extension bulletins in your state or region.

d. **Spider mites** are insect relatives with two body regions and four pairs of legs. They are tiny, barely visible to the naked eye, and are best viewed with a hand lens or microscope. Their feeding causes a bronzing of the leaves, and most species produce fine webbing. Various species of spider mites are host-specific. The most common, the two-spotted mite, however, has a long list of host plants (Figure 23-4).

Figure 23-4 ■ *Spider mite damage on beans with bronzing of foliage and fine webbing.*

Populations are driven by temperatures. A two-spotted mite can produce one million offspring in thirty days at temperatures of 90°F and above. Populations explode in hot dry summers. Some species, like the spruce spider mite, thrive in cool weather.

Plants are less tolerant of mites when under water stress. Driving rains are effective in reducing the spider mite population. Likewise, hosing off the plants with a forceful stream of water is helpful.

Spider mites are generally kept in bounds by a long list of predators, including predatory mites, some species of lady beetles, and other insects. However, dust on the leaves will interfere with predatory action. Hosing off the plants to reduce dust helps keep mite populations in bounds.

Spider mite populations may explode following use of carbaryl (Sevin) and imidacloprid (Merit) insecticides. Avoid use of these products on mite-sensitive plants.

A few insecticides in the home garden trade have limited effectiveness on mites. Insecticidal soap and horticultural oils require complete coverage. Commercial applicators have access to a few miticides that are more effective on landscape plants.

2. **Branch and twig feeders**—A variety of host-specific insects (aphids, hard scales, soft scales, twig borers, shoot moths, and galls) attack the branches and twigs of landscape plants. For information on a specific insect, refer to Cooperative Extension bulletins in your state or region.

Figure 23-5 ■ *Cooley spruce gall on spruce.*

3. **Galls** are abnormal localized swelling or enlargement of plant parts. They could be caused by insects, mites, diseases, or abiotic disorders. Common examples include Cooley spruce galls of blue spruce, poplar twig galls of aspen, assorted leaf and stem galls on oak, honeylocust seed pod galls, and nipple galls on hackberry leaves.

Galls rarely warrant management, and few have effective management options. For information on a specific insect, refer to Cooperative Extension bulletins in your state or region (Figure 23-5).

4. **Trunks and large branch insects**—Borers and bark beetles are common on many species of landscape trees. With few exceptions, borers and bark beetles only attack trees already under stress, most commonly soil compaction and drought.

   Management is centered on reducing the stress factors that predispose the tree to borer attack. Insecticide treatments may be effective in reducing reinfestations, and thus must be carefully timed to the flight of the egg-laying adults. Insecticides do not kill borers feeding inside the trunk. For information on a specific insect, refer to Cooperative Extension bulletins in your state or region.

5. **Root feeders**—A variety of host-specific insects feed on an assortment of plant roots. Most do not cause serious problems. The best known root feeders are in the vegetable garden where they can destroy a crop of radishes, carrots, or potatoes. For information on a specific insect, refer to Cooperative Extension bulletins in your state or region.

6. **Flower feeders**—A variety of host-specific insects feed on an assortment of plant flowers. For information on a specific insect, refer to Cooperative Extension bulletins in your state or region.

7. **Fruit feeders**—A variety of host-specific insects feed on the fruit of assorted plants. Common examples include codling moths of apples, corn earworm, tomato fruit worm, and peach twig borer. For information on a specific insect, refer to Cooperative Extension bulletins in your state or region.

1. Explain the four basic steps in managing insect pests.

2. List types feeding damage that occurs on plants.

3. List types of foliage defoliators.

Chapter 24*

Managing Plant Diseases

INTRODUCTION

Biotic versus Abiotic

A plant disease is usually defined as abnormal growth and/or dysfunction of a plant. Diseases are the result of some disturbance in the normal life process of the plant.

Diseases may be the result of living and/or non-living causes. **Biotic** diseases are caused by living organisms such as fungi, bacteria, and viruses. **Abiotic** diseases are caused by non-living environmental conditions.

Plant Disease Pyramid

Specific conditions must be present for biotic disease to develop. There must be a susceptible host plant, the pathogen (fungi, bacteria, viruses, etc.), and environmental conditions conducive to disease development; these must come together in a given point in time. These conditions make up what is called the "Plant Disease Pyramid." Biotic disease cannot occur if one of these pieces is missing (Figure 24-1).

Environmental conditions—Weather plays a large role in fungal disease development. Most fungi require free water or specific levels of humidity or moisture for prolonged periods of time to develop. Dry climates are not conducive

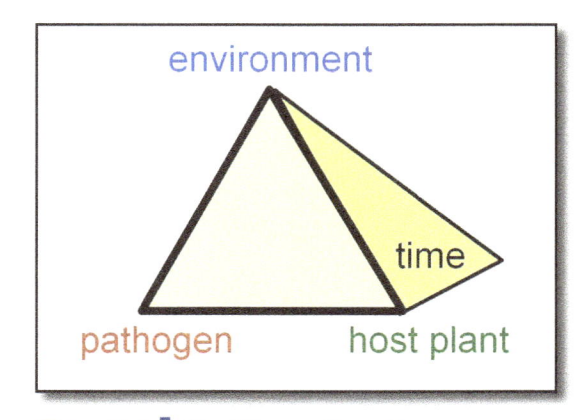

Figure 24-1 ▌ *Plant Disease Pyramid.*

*Authors: Mary Small and David Whiting, Colorado State University Extension. Artwork by David Whiting.

to their survival. The Rocky Mountain region has fewer fungal diseases than many other parts of the United States due to climatic differences. However, gardens and other microclimates may have conditions ideal for disease development due to poor air circulation, shade, high humidity, and high moisture.

Symptoms

Symptoms of disease are the plant's reaction to the causal agent. Plant symptoms include:

- **Blight**—A rapid discoloration and death of twigs, foliage, or flowers.
- **Canker**—Dead area on bark or stem, often sunken or raised.
- **Chlorosis**—Yellowing—Chlorosis is so generic that without additional details diagnosis is impossible.
- **Decline**—Progressive decrease in plant vigor.
- **Dieback**—Progressive death of shoot, branch, or root starting at the tip.
- **Distortion**—Malformed plant tissue.
- **Gall** or **gall-like**—Abnormal localized swelling or enlargement of plant part. It could be caused by insects, mites, diseases, or abiotic disorders.
- **Gummosis**—Exudation of gum or sap.
- **Leaf distortion**—The leaf could be twisted, cupped, rolled, or otherwise deformed.
- **Leaf scorch**—Burning along the leaf margin and into the leaf from the margin.
- **Leaf spot**—A spot or lesion on the leaf.
- **Mosaic**—Varying patterns of light and dark plant tissue.
- **Necrosis**—Dead tissue—Necrotic areas are also so generic that without additional details diagnosis is impossible.
- **Stunting**—Lack of growth.
- **Wilt**—General wilting of the plant or plant part.
- **Witches broom**—Abnormal broom-like growth of many weak shoots.
- **Insect feeding injury** is also a symptom used in diagnosis, but not a symptom of disease.

Even though a plant has symptoms on a specific part, it does not necessarily mean the damaged tissue contains the organism causing the symptoms. For example, a root rot can cause chlorosis and wilting of stems and leaves, but the disease causal organism is in the roots. It is imperative to examine as much of the plant as possible to determine exactly where the problem is originating.

Signs

Signs are the actual organisms causing the disease. Signs include:

- **Conks**—Woody reproductive structures of fungi.
- **Fruiting bodies**—Reproductive structures of fungi; could be in the form of mushrooms, puffballs, pycnidia, rusts, or conks.
- **Mildew**—Whitish growth produced by fungi composed of mycelium.
- **Mushrooms**—Fleshy reproductive structures of fungi.
- **Mycelium**—Thread-like vegetative growth of fungi.

- **Rhizomorphs**—Shoestring-like fungal threads found under the bark of stressed and dying trees caused by the *Armillaria* fungi. They may glow!

- **Slime flux** or **ooze**—A bacterial discharge that oozes out of the plant tissues, may be gooey or a dried mass.

- **Spore masses**—Masses of spores, the "seeds" of a fungus.

- **Insects** and/or their **frass** (excrement) are also signs, although not signs of disease.

BIOTIC DISEASE

Biotic causes of disease include fungi, bacteria, viruses, phytoplasmas, nematodes, and parasitic plants.

Fungi

Fungi are organisms that are classified in the kingdom *Fungi*. They lack chlorophyll and conductive tissue. Until a few years ago, fungi were considered lower forms of plants, but today are classified as a group by themselves. Because fungi cannot manufacture their own food (due to lack of chlorophyll), they must obtain it from another source as either a **saprophyte** or **parasite**. Most fungi encountered are saprophytic (feed on decaying organic matter). The parasitic fungi, those that derive their sustenance from living plants, are the group of interest in plant health. In dry climates like Colorado, fungi are the most frequent causes of plant diseases.

A fungus "body" is a branched filamentous structure known as **mycelium**. One single thread is called a hypha (hyphae, plural). Most fungi reproduce by spores, which are reproductive structures that contain little stored food, unlike seeds. Spores are the main dispersal mechanism of fungi and can remain dormant until germination conditions are appropriate. Many fungi overwinter as fruiting structures embedded in dead plant tissue.

When a spore comes in contact with a susceptible plant, it will germinate and enter the host if the proper environmental conditions are present. Hyphae develop from the germinated spore and begin to extract nutrients from host plant cells. The hyphae secrete enzymes to aid in the breakdown of organic materials that are ultimately absorbed through their cell walls. Fungi damage plants by killing cells and/or causing plant stress.

Fungi are spread by wind, water, soil, animals, equipment, and in plant material. They enter plants through natural openings such as stomata and lenticels and through wounds from pruning, hail, and other mechanical damage. Fungi can also produce enzymes that break down the cuticle (the outer protective covering of plants).

Fungi cause a variety of symptoms including leaf spots, leaf curling, galls, rots, wilts, cankers, and stem and root rots. Fungi are responsible for "damping off" symptoms associated with seedlings.

Damping Off

Damping off is the fungal infection of seeds or seedlings that leads to death. When infected with damping off, seeds may fail to germinate. In other situations, seedlings develop but eventually fall over and die. An examination of stems at the soil line reveals a discolored, "pinched in" appearance. Most plants are susceptible to damping off because of the soft immature nature of seedling tissue that is more susceptible to infection.

The best method to manage damping off is to avoid it in the first place. For starting seeds indoors, use pasteurized soil or planting mix and ensure that plants receive optimum light, water, and heat for rapid germination and growth. In home situations, damping off frequently develops due to poor lighting and overwatering. These conditions stress plants and make conditions optimal for the development of the soil-borne organisms that cause damping off.

In the garden, plant seeds at appropriate times (soil temperature for rapid germination) for the crop and avoid overwatering for optimal germination and growth. A strong healthy plant is better equipped to fight off infection.

Scientists continue to study the role of hyperparasites (parasites of parasites) in disease management. Several biological pesticides have been developed from naturally occurring hyperparasitic fungi and bacteria. The organisms protect plant roots against invasion by harmful soil pathogens. These biological pesticides must be applied prior to the development of damping off so the beneficial organisms have time to grow and colonize roots. They cannot be used as "rescue" treatments.

Figure 24-2 ■ *Cedar apple rust is a common leaf spot with a colorful border.*

Leaf Spots

One of the most common fungal plant symptoms is leaf spotting. Leaf spot symptoms are caused by many different fungi. Generally, fungal leaf spots possess a distinct dark brown or red margin between the interior (dead) and exterior (healthy green) tissue called a *border* (Figure 24-2).

Fungal fruiting structures (reproductive structures) are usually embedded in the dead interior. Frequently, a "halo" of yellow or red color develops around the border. A halo indicates recently killed tissue that will eventually die. Because of the cycle of killing tissue and creating a border, then killing more tissue and creating another border, many fungal leaf spots take on a target-like appearance.

To confuse matters, a series of drought events can cause damage that exhibits alternating light and dark bands. Additionally, fruiting structures may not be obvious in dry climates like Colorado. To positively identify a fungal leaf spot, it is best to either culture tissue from the sample or look for spores under a compound microscope.

For example, common leaf spot diseases in Colorado include *Marssonia* and *Septoria* leaf spots of cottonwoods and aspen, ink spot of aspen, and early blight of tomatoes and potatoes. For additional information, refer to the following Colorado State University Extension publications available online at www.cmg.colostate.edu.

- *Aspen and Poplar Leaf Spots*, Extension fact sheet #2.901
- *Aspen Leaf Spot*, Planttalk #1403
- *Marssonia Leaf Spot*—Planttalk #1476
- *Sycamore Anthracnose*, Extension fact sheet #2.930
- *Sycamore Anthracnose*, Planttalk #1406

Mildew

Powdery mildew is one of the most common diseases in dry climates like Colorado. General symptoms include a white or grayish powdery growth on leaves. It thrives in warm dry climates and often explodes in small yards with limited air movement and in the fall as nighttime humidity rises (Figure 24-3).

There are many species of mildew fungi, each being host-specific. In Colorado, for example, it is common on ash, lilac, grapes, roses, turfgrass, vine crops (cucumbers, melons, and squash), peas, euonymus, cherry, apple, crabapple, pear, Virginia creeper, and others.

Figure 24-3 ■ *Powdery mildew on lilac.*

Management is centered on a variety of cultural techniques. Avoid crowding plants as the lack of air circulation favors powdery mildew. Select resistant varieties where possible. Avoid late-summer application of nitrogen fertilizer as it may push growth of tender young leaves that are more prone to mildew. Avoid overhead irrigation as it raises relative humidity. Remove and destroy infected plant parts. A variety of fungicides found in the home garden trades are effective on powdery mildew.

For additional information, refer to Colorado State University Extension fact sheet #2.902, *Powdery Mildew*, available online at www.cmg.colostate.edu.

Figure 24-4 ▮ *Canker on honeylocust.*

Cankers

Cankers are discolored, sunken areas found on plant stems, branches, and trunks. They damage plants by killing the conductive tissue. Cankers may be caused by fungi, bacteria, virus, and abiotic disorders such as sunscald and hail (Figure 24-4).

Fungal cankers contain fruiting structures embedded in the discolored canker. Plants with cankers may exhibit branch dieback, leaf loss, and/or poor growth above the damaged area.

Common fungal cankers in Colorado *Cytospora* (*Cytospora* sp.) and *Thyronectria* (*Thyronectria* sp.). Common bacterial cankers in Colorado include fireblight (*Erwinia amylovora*). For additional information, refer to the following Colorado State University Extension publications available online at www.cmg.colostate.edu

- *Canker Diseases on Deciduous Trees*, Planttalk #1407
- *Cytospora Canker*, Extension fact sheet #2.937
- *Cytospora*—Planttalk #1451
- *Fire Blight*—Extension fact sheet #2.907
- *Fire Blight*—Planttalk #1411
- *Honeylocust Diseases—Extension* fact sheet #2.939

Root Rots

Root rots damage plants by stressing or killing root systems. Two common soil-inhabiting fungi that cause root rots include *Fusarium* sp. and *Rhizoctonia* sp.

Root symptoms of these (and other soil-borne) fungi include darkening, limpness, and mushiness. Rotted roots may break off easily. The cortex (the outer protective covering) of roots sloughs off, leaving behind the thread-like root core.

Leaves, stems, and entire plants may wilt, prompting one to think that the plant simply needs more water. (Unfortunately, additional water often makes the problem worse.)

Generally, the lower, interior leaves turn yellow, then brown and drop off. In addition, plants may be stunted. If enough roots are damaged, the plant eventually dies.

There are no root rot-resistant plants. Management strategies include avoiding overwatering and improving soil drainage. Roots stressed from overwatering or oxygen starvation easily succumb to root rots, because the organisms move through moist soil and water.

Sometimes, a plant with root rot may be salvaged by cutting off damaged roots and replanting in well-drained soil. Biological pesticides containing hyperparasites may help protect against root rot. These products are not designed to "rescue" plants from ongoing damage, but act as preventives.

In the green industry, root rots can be managed with a combination of the cultural management strategies and through use of fungicides. Because not all fungicides kill all root rot fungi, it is essential to determine which root rot organism is causing the problem through microscopic examination so the correct product can be recommended.

Bacteria

Bacteria are single-celled microorganisms. They contain no nucleus and reproduce by dividing into two equal parts (fission). As a result, they multiply and mutate rapidly. Bacteria function as either parasites or saprophytes.

Figure 24-5 ▍ *Fireblight on crabapple.*

Bacteria can infect all plant parts. Unlike fungi, bacteria must find a natural opening for entry. Bacterial cells can move from one plant to another in water, soil, and plant material, just as fungi do. However, bacterial pathogens are more dependent on water. Conditions must be very wet and/or humid for them to cause significant and widespread damage (Figure 24-5).

Bacteria move between plant cells and secrete substances that degrade plant cell walls so the contents can be utilized. Some produce enzymes that break down plant tissue, creating soft rots or water-soaking. Like the fungi, bacteria cause symptoms such as leaf blights and spots, galls, cankers, wilts, and stem rots.

Bacterial leaf spots appear different from fungal leaf spots due to their intercellular movement. Veins often limit the development of a lesion, so they appear angular or irregular, not round.

Bacterial diseases are not common in the Rocky Mountain region due to lack of natural moisture.

It is difficult for beginners to tell fungal and bacterial plant symptoms apart. Table 24-1 may be used to help distinguish symptoms caused by these pathogens.

Table 24-1. Comparison of Fungal and Bacterial Leaf Spots

Symptom Description	Fungal	Bacterial
Water-soaked appearance	No	Yes
Texture	Dry, papery	Slimy, sticky
Smell	No	Yes
Pattern	Circular, target-like	Irregular, angular
Disintegration	No	Yes
Color changes	Red, yellow, purple halos	No
Structures of pathogen	Mycelia, spores, fruiting structures	No

Common bacterial diseases in Colorado include bacterial wetwood (slime flux), fireblight (*Erwinia amylovora*), and bacterial leaf spot (*Erwinia* sp.). For additional information, refer to the following Colorado State University Extension publications available online at www.cmg.colostate.edu.

- *Bacterial Wetwood*—Extension fact sheet #2.910
- *Bacterial Wetwood*—Planttalk #1438

- *Fire Blight*—Extension fact sheet #2.907
- *Fire Blight*—Planttalk #1411

Viruses

Viruses are crystalline particles composed of nucleic acid (ribonucleic acid or deoxyribonucleic acid) and protein. They are obligate parasites, meaning they are unable to survive outside of their host. Small virus particles can be found in all plant parts and cannot be seen without an electron microscope.

To move from plant to plant, the particles must be transmitted by vectors and through a wound. The vector is typically an insect, nematode, or human. Insects and nematodes spread viruses between plants as they feed on them. The feeding injury creates the necessary wound. Usually, a plant virus is spread by only one kind of insect vector. Aphids, leafhoppers, and thrips are examples of virus vectors, but not all aphids, leafhoppers, or thrips spread virus.

Humans may spread plant viruses as they work in the garden. Mechanical abrasion from infected tools or touching and abrading plants with infected hands may be all that is needed.

Viruses overwinter in infected perennial plants or overwintering insects. A small portion of viruses can be transmitted through seeds. Some are transmitted through vegetative propagation.

Viruses cause mottling, spots, mosaic-like patterns, crinkling, and other malformations on leaves and fruits, and may stunt plants. Because viruses are systemic, infected plants must be rogued or discarded (Figure 24-6).

Viruses are named according to the first plant on which they were found and the type of symptom they cause (i.e., peony ringspot virus, rose mosaic virus).

Figure 24-6 ■ *Mosaic virus on cucumbers.*

For example, common virus diseases in Colorado include curly top virus of tomatoes, cucumber mosaic virus of vine crops and tomatoes, tomato spotted wilt virus of tomato, and a variety of greenhouse plant viruses. For additional information, refer to the following Colorado State University Extension publications available online at www.cgm.colostate.edu.

- *Greenhouse Plant Viruses*, Extension fact sheet #2.947
- *Recognizing Tomato Problems*, Extension fact sheet #2.949

Phytoplasmas

Phytoplasmas are classified as bacteria; however, they lack a cell wall and can take on a variety of shapes. They are obligate parasites, meaning they can only survive within their hosts. Phytoplasmas live in the phloem of host plants and are vectored by certain phloem-feeding insects, such as leafhoppers. This pathogen causes distortion, yellowing, wilting, and "**witches' brooms**" (a proliferation of growth). Immature leaf veins may appear clear (called "vein-clearing"). Flower parts may become vegetative and flowers that do develop produce sterile seeds.

Aster Yellows

Aster yellows damages over 300 species of broad-leafed herbaceous plants nationwide. Commonly affected flowering plants include *Echinacea* sp. (purple coneflower), cosmos, marigolds, asters, chrysanthemums, delphiniums, daisies, coreopsis, and zinnias. Vegetables affected include carrots, lettuce, and potatoes. Weeds such as dandelion, ragweed, plantain, wild lettuce, and thistles may also be infected (Figure 24-7).

Aster yellows is spread by the aster (or six-spotted) leafhopper. These insects are small (one-eighth inch long), gray-green, and wedge-shaped. They are called leafhoppers because they move or fly away quickly when plants are disturbed. They feed only on plant sap (phloem tissue) and generally on leaf undersides.

Aster leafhoppers do not overwinter in Colorado due to the cold climate, but are blown in from the Gulf of Mexico in late spring or early summer. Once a leafhopper feeds on an infected plant, about ten days to three weeks must elapse for the insect to become infective. Plant symptoms appear ten to forty days after infection. Dry weather can cause increased disease occurrence in the home garden as leafhoppers move from plants in prairies and pastures to irrigated yards. Generally, aster yellows symptoms appear in middle to late summer.

Figure 24-7 ▪ *Aster yellows on carrot.*

Although aster leafhoppers spread the disease, placing infected plants in the yard can also spread it. Management strategies for aster yellows include planting healthy plants, controlling weeds that may harbor the insects, and removing infected plants. Even though only one part of a plant appears infected, one must assume the phytoplasma is throughout the entire plant.

The pathogen can overwinter in plant crowns and roots. Leaves and stems that develop from this tissue will always be infected and provide a source of inoculum for other susceptible plants. Insecticidal control of aster leafhoppers is very difficult as they are constantly moving in and out of the garden, so it is not recommended.

For additional information, refer to Colorado State University Extension PlantTalk script #1452, *Aster Yellows*, available online at www.cmg.colostate.edu.

Parasitic Plants

More than 2,500 species of higher plants are known to live parasitically on other plants. Parasitic plants produce flowers and reproduce by seeds like other plants. The main difference is they cannot produce their own chlorophyll or produce only a small amount of chlorophyll. They must obtain sustenance from a chlorophyll-producing plant to survive. Parasitic plants are spread in various ways including animals, wind, and forcible ejection of their seeds.

Dwarf mistletoe and dodder are two examples of parasitic plants encountered in Colorado. Dwarf mistletoe has chlorophyll but no roots and depends on its host for water and minerals, although it can produce carbohydrates in its green stems and leaves. Dodder cannot produce its own chlorophyll and completely depends on its host for sustenance.

Plants damaged by parasitic plants appear wilted, stunted, distorted, and chlorotic. Some plants, particularly conifers, develop witches' broom symptoms.

For additional information, refer to the Colorado State University Extension fact sheet #2.925, *Mistletoe in Colorado Conifers*, available online at www.cmg.colostate.edu.

Nematodes

Nematodes are microscopic roundworms that live in soil, water, and plant material. They have a spear-like stylet mouthpart, require free water to move about, and reproduce by eggs. They spread in water, infected plant material, soil, and in some cases, insects.

Nematodes cause a variety of symptoms including stunting, yellowing, and wilting of plant tissue. Some infected plants simply appear unthrifty. Some develop strange, knot-like growths on their roots. Many saprophytic and parasitic species exist. Due to cold winters, nematodes as plant pathogens are uncommon problems in Colorado landscape plantings.

Pinewood nematode (*Bursaphelenchus xylophilus*) is a North American native nematode that invades exotic pines such as Austrian, black, and Scots pines.

Pinewood nematode causes pine wilt disease. The symptoms include needle necrosis, branch flagging, and eventual tree death. Trees may decline rapidly; whole tree death can occur in two weeks.

Pinewood nematodes are vectored two ways. The primary transmission is by maturation feeding of adult pine sawyer beetles (*Monochamus* sp.) on susceptible trees. Secondary transmission occurs when adult female pine sawyer beetles oviposit (or lay eggs) into phloem of susceptible trees. If this disease is suspected as the cause of pine tree death, samples must be sent to a diagnostic laboratory to accurately diagnose pine wilt disease.

Foliar nematodes are found occasionally in irrigated Colorado landscapes. They have a broad host range and can infect many plant species but especially anemone and chrysanthemum.

General Management of Biotic Plant Disease

Plant disease is best managed through an integrated approach, which includes a combination of cultural, mechanical, biological, and chemical practices.

Cultural management includes appropriate plant selection. Utilize plants that perform well in the local climate. Use disease-resistant varieties when possible. Plant certified seed or seed pieces.

Place plants in the appropriate environment for optimum growth. For example, grow shade-loving plants in the shade, not hot sun. Prepare soil before planting to improve root growth, reduce compaction in clay soils, and improve water holding of sandy soils. Apply fertilizer and water according to plant needs. Prune correctly, as needed, and at the correct time of year.

Mechanical management techniques include rototilling in the fall, which exposes pathogens, insect eggs, and weed seeds to cold winter temperatures. This action also speeds the decomposition of crop residues, improving soil organic matter. Clean up or prune out infested plant materials to reduce the source of inoculum on the property.

Rotate crops when possible to starve pathogens. For example, avoid planting solanaceous crops (tomatoes, peppers, eggplant, and potatoes) in the same area as pathogens specific to this group may build up in soil and infect new crops.

Apply mulch in gardens. Not only does this keep soil moister and cooler (helping roots thrive), it also creates a splash barrier against soil pathogens or pathogens on plant debris in the soil. Use soil solarization to reduce soil pathogens and weed seeds. Pull weeds and volunteer seedlings that hog precious water but also serve as a reservoir for pathogens and insects. Core-aerate turf once or twice yearly.

Biological controls include the use of compost, compost teas, and hyperparasite products, which may reduce pathogens by introducing beneficial microbes. Encourage beneficial insects by planting flowering plants attractive to all stages of development. Avoid blanket applications of pesticides, which may kill beneficials in addition to harmful insects. Spot treat pest problems instead.

Chemical control refers to the use of chemical fungicides, insecticides, and herbicides to manage a problem. Always identify the cause of a plant problem first, then select and use a product appropriate for the problem and follow label directions. Apply it at the correct time using the recommended method. Always spot treat.

ABIOTIC DISORDERS

Abiotic agents of disease are non-living factors such as soil compaction, spring frosts, hail, and lawnmower damage to tree trunks. Abiotic agents are noninfectious and non-transmissible. Plant diseases deriving from these agents have been referred to as physiological diseases or environmental diseases. For additional information, refer to Chapter 21, Diagnosing Abiotic Tree Disorders, and the following Colorado State University Extension publications, available online at www.cmg.colostate.edu.

- *Environmental Disorders of Woody Plants*, Extension fact sheet #2.932
- *Healthy Roots and Healthy Trees*, Extension fact sheet #2.926

Water Management

One of the major causes of abiotic plant disorders is improper water application. Too much water can be just as damaging as not enough water, as both kill roots. Examples of abiotic disorders related to water are leaf scorch, winter desiccation, and oxygen starvation (Figure 24-8).

Figure 24-8 ▮ *Water stress on trees often shows from the top down.*

Leaf Scorch

Symptoms of leaf scorch include necrosis (browning) of leaf edges and/or between the veins. These are naturally the least hydrated areas of a deciduous leaf, so when moisture is lost, symptoms appear there first. Scorch symptoms on needled evergreens appear as necrosis from the needle tips downward in a uniform pattern. The initial reaction to these symptoms is to provide more water, but that may only exacerbate the situation depending on what is causing scorch in the first place (Figure 24-9).

There are several causes of leaf scorch. There may not be enough water in the soil for root absorption. This occurs during drought periods as Colorado experienced in the early 2000s and during winters when soil water is frozen.

Figure 24-9 ▮ *Leaf scorch on linden caused by hardscapes over rooting zone.*

Water may be lost faster than it can be replaced. Warm, windy, and sunny weather during winter months causes rapid transpiration at a time when soil moisture may be frozen. During summer, sunny, hot, and windy weather causes such rapid transpiration that roots cannot physically keep up with the water loss.

Soil water may be available, but roots may not be functioning properly to absorb it. What causes roots to function poorly? Soil may be so compacted that roots cannot adequately explore soil for nutrients and moisture. Roots may be severed or otherwise damaged from construction activities or garden cultivation. Planting too deep limits oxygen availability for roots and stresses or kills them. A thick layer of mulch or black plastic covering root systems also injures them due to oxygen deprivation.

Mechanical damage on lower stems or trunks from mowing equipment, improper planting, improper staking, animal chewing, or boring insects may also prevent or slow water uptake. *The bottom line is that more water is lost than can easily be replaced.*

For additional information, refer to the following Colorado State University Extension publications, available online at www.cmg.colostate.edu.

- *Leaf Scorch*, Extension fact sheet #2.911
- *Tree Leaf Scorch*, PlantTalk #2112

Oxygen Starvation

Oxygen starvation occurs when excess water in the soil drives out oxygen, in effect "suffocating" roots. Plants respond by dropping the lower leaves that are usually yellowed or necrotic. Leaf loss is most noticeable from the inside of the plant out and the bottom up. In addition, leaves may be smaller than normal, growth increments may be small, and the plant may have an overall unthrifty appearance.

While oxygen starvation causes root damage, the first clue that something is wrong appears on the canopy, stems, and branches. These parts are the furthest from the water source, so the symptoms appear there first.

To control problems caused by water management issues, identify the likely causes and correct them if possible. This will require some detective work to determine which factor or (usually) combination of factors is causing the problem.

Management strategies are based on good horticultural practices. For example, add organic matter to vegetable and flower gardens before planting to improve drainage as well as water-holding capacity. Cut back on irrigation frequency or adjust the quantity of the water applied. Core aerate turf, which will also benefit tree roots growing in it. Apply and maintain mulch at levels appropriate for the material used. Remove any black plastic in the landscape.

Weather

Winter desiccation is caused by dry winter winds that result in leaf water loss. Water cannot be replaced in the plant because the soil is too cold and roots cannot absorb it. Symptoms of winter desiccation include necrotic leaf or needle tissue (typically from the tips inward), discoloration of needle or leaf tissue, and patchy damage distribution on individual plants in windy locations. Plants may not exhibit symptoms until the following summer when droughty summer conditions ensue (Figure 24-10).

To deter winter desiccation, water fall plants after they go dormant. Roots are still active and can absorb water until soil temperatures drop below 40°F. When the ground is not frozen, additional irrigation may be helpful monthly during the winter in the absence of snow cover or sufficient snowmelt or rainfall.

Figure 24-10 ▐ *Winter dehydration on pine shows at needle tips.*

For additional information, refer to the following Colorado State University Extension publications, available online at www.cmg.colostate.edu.

- *Environmental Disorders of Woody Plants*, Extension fact sheet #2.932
- *Fall and Winter Watering*, Extension fact sheet #7.211
- *Fall and Winter Watering*, PlantTalk #1706
- *Sunscald*, PlantTalk #2111

Temperature

Temperatures below optimal plant growth cause plant damage. The amount and type of damage depends on how quickly temperatures drop, the lowest temperature reached, and how long cold temperatures are sustained. Freeze injury may be caused by frost crystals that form in the freezing water outside of plant tissues or by freezing water inside plant cells. Damage from the latter is much more severe and resembles herbicide phytotoxicity, bacterial blight, and branch flagging due to insect borer activity (Figure 24-11).

Spring freezes damage exterior buds first, as these are the first to deharden. Fall freezes affect interior buds first as these are the last to harden. Damage of tissues is uniform. For example, newly developing conifer needles may be killed completely or from the tips inward.

Temperatures above optimal growth cause plant damage as well. The most severe injury occurs on leaves that are exposed to the sun and tissue that is furthest away from water such as outer branch tips, leaf margins, and between leaf veins.

Chemical Injury

Chemical injury is plant damage caused by pesticides, fertilizers, de-icing salts, and other products.

> Example 1. The client asks, "Why has my spruce tree has turned a different color after the certified arborist sprayed horticultural oil to control the Douglas Fir tussock moth?"

Herbicides

Herbicides (weed killers) damage plant tissues by causing symptoms such as chlorosis, necrosis, distortion, and elongated growth. Glyphosate, dicamba, and 2,4-D are examples of common herbicides that cause chemical injury to desirable plants when used incorrectly.

Herbicides that behave like plant growth regulators such as dicamba and 2,4-D translocate through both the xylem and phloem. They stimulate growth such as cell division, elongation, and fruit and flower production (Figure 24-12).

Figure 24-11 ▮ *Southwest bark injury on trees is a combination of rapid winter temperature change coupled with winter drought.*

Figure 24-12 ▮ *Damage on grapes from 2,4-D. Notice the distortion in leaf vein pattern.*

Excessive concentrations of these chemicals cause twisting and curling of stems, stem swelling, weakened cell walls, rapid cell growth, and cellular and vascular damage and death. Grasses are not affected by plant growth regulators apparently due to a different arrangement of vascular bundles (xylem and phloem).

Glyphosate is an amino acid inhibitor that interferes with synthesis of certain amino acids needed to build proteins. Glyphosate moves through the phloem to the new growth of shoots and roots. Injury symptoms include chlorosis, shortened internodes (compact growth or stunting), stem proliferation, and mimics damage caused by 2,4-D and other plant growth regulators, viruses, phytoplasmas, eriophyid mites, and environmental factors.

Fertilizers

An excess or shortage of the seventeen essential elements required for plant growth and development may cause plant damage. Excess amounts of fertilizers can "burn" plants due to the level of salts in fertilizers.

Symptoms of fertilizer damage include leaf margin necrosis (similar to drought stress in appearance), leaf discoloration, soft rapid growth, and vegetative growth at the expense of flower and fruit production.

Nutrient deficiencies include chlorosis, interveinal chlorosis, blossom-end rot, stunting, and purpling. Symptoms of nutrient excesses and deficiencies may be confused with disease, insect, mite, or other environmental problems. If a soil nutritional problem or salt injury is suspected, have the soil tested.

When excess fertilizer has been applied, apply water in an effort to leach salts from the root zone. Quick release fertilizers are more prone to "burn" plants. Follow label directions when applying fertilizers to avoid plant damage.

Salts

It is common practice in Colorado to use de-icing salts to remove snow and ice from roadways and sidewalks. Salts injure plants from: 1) salt burn on foliage, 2) root burn of salts, or 3) soil buildup that deteriorates soil structure, interfering with drainage and root growth.

Symptoms of salt spray on leaves include stem and leaf deformities, witches' brooms, and twig dieback of deciduous plants. Conifers exhibit needle browning at the tips of branches. Salt spray damage is only noticeable on the plant side adjacent to a road.

Symptoms of salt accumulation in soils are different from salt spray and include marginal leaf scorch, stunting, and twig dieback. Leaf scorch may not appear until later in the season or in following seasons.

To reduce salt burn, avoid de-icing salts or use alternatives such as calcium chloride, add organic matter and charcoal to the soil, leach with water, or protect plants using a barrier that will keep salt-laden snow away from plant material.

For additional information, refer to Colorado State University Extension fact sheet #7.425, *Magnesium Chloride Toxicity in Trees*, available online at www.cmg.colostate.edu.

Figure 24-13 ▪ *Salt damage on bean leaf burns the margin of the leaf. This was caused by using compost high in salts.*

Compost and other soil amendments can be high in salt when made with manure or biosolids. Symptoms of salt burn include marginal burning of leaves, stunting, root dieback, and death of plants. For additional information, refer to Chapter 9, Soil Amendments.

PLANT DISEASE DIAGNOSIS

Generic steps in the diagnostic process include the following:

1. Identify the plant.

2. Identify the problem(s).

    a. Look: Define the problem by describing the signs and symptoms.

        1) Identify "normal" characteristics of the plant.

        2) A systematic evaluation of the plant helps organize questions in a methodical process.

    b. Read: Distinguish between possible causes by comparing signs and symptoms with details in reference materials.

    c. Compare: Determine probable cause(s) through comparison and elimination.

3. Evaluate if management efforts are warranted.

    a. What type of damage/stress does this disorder/pest cause?

    b. Under what situations would management efforts be warranted?

    c. Are management efforts warranted for this situation?

4. Evaluate management options effective for this disorder/pest and when they are applied.

Determining the causal agent of plant damage can be a tumultuous endeavor, so let us expand on content around Step 2, Identify the problem(s). Taking a systematic approach when diagnosing plant damage and determination will become easier (see Chart 24-1). The probability of correctly diagnosing plant damage based on one or two symptoms is low. In contrast, probability of correctly diagnosing plant damage based on many symptoms and factors is high. Therefore, using investigative skills and asking many questions is imperative to arriving at a correct diagnosis.

For additional information on the diagnostic process, refer to Chapter 20, The Diagnostic Process.

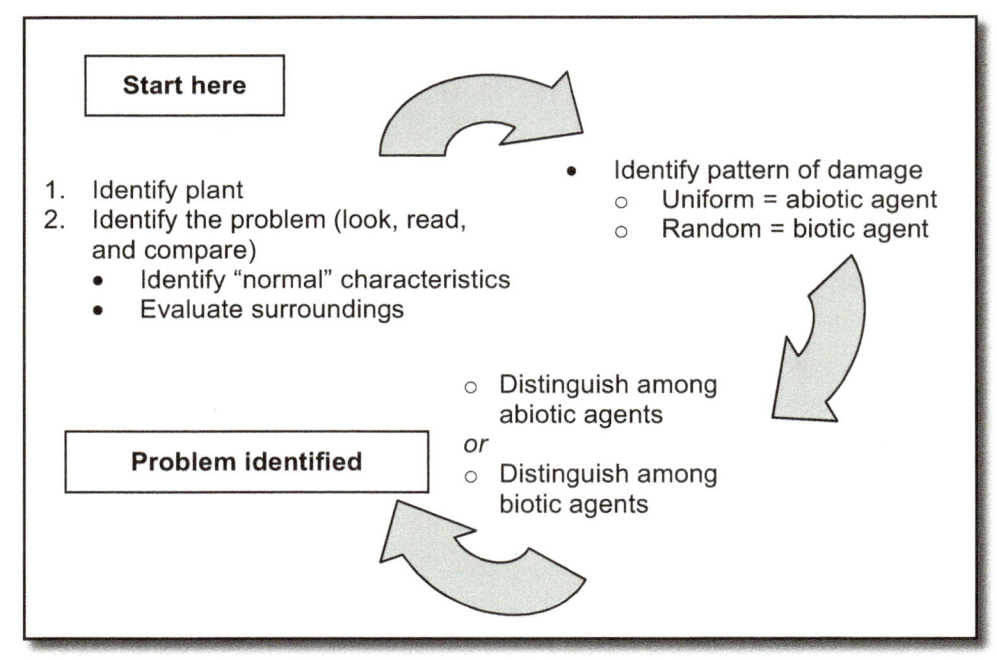

Chart 24-1 ▮ *A flow chart displaying the systematic approach to determining causal agents of plant damage.*

Sample Questions

Accurate diagnosis is absolutely dependent on accurate observation. When making observations, we must ask the following questions:

1. What symptoms are the plant expressing?

2. How many plants are affected?

3. Is there a pattern associated with the problem (i.e., is the problem located in one area, such as a low area, on the north side, south side, etc.)?

4. Are there any differences in susceptibility of varieties or species (i.e., is it just the tomatoes or are other plants also affected)?

5. Ask about obvious causes first, such as animals, frost, flooding, or mechanical damage.

6. Determine which part of the plant is actually damaged. Wilts, for instance, frequently are only a response to some damage to the roots. Dieback of branches is sometimes caused by cankers or mechanical damage further down the stem.

7. Are the roots healthy appearing (not black or mushy) and moist? Note: You may not be able to diagnose the problem without roots.

8. What about the texture and wetness of the soil? Is it clayey, sandy, or compacted? Is salt crusting evident?

9. What is the weed population? (Weeds may indicate a particular soil problem.)

10. Find out as much as possible about the previous history: fertilizer, pesticides, land leveling, cultivation methods, irrigation schedules, and climatic conditions.

11. There are many other questions that you may think to ask based on the specific sample in question.

Identify Plant and Its Normal Characteristics

Determine what the "normal" plant would look like during that time of year. Describe the damage using terms like "gall," "witches' broom," and "chlorotic." Establish the location on the plant where initial damage occurred. For example, there are leaf spots with fruiting structures on the underside of leaves, but these symptoms are not what caused tree death. Cankers along the branches and trunk are what killed the tree.

Example 1. The spruce sample is exhibiting interior needle loss in the fall. What is the diagnosis?

Distinguishing the factor that caused plant death from other symptoms and signs can be tricky. In turf grass, many times sclerotia, fruiting bodies, and conidia are spotted in necrotic and problematic areas. However, these disease-causing structures may not be related to turf grass death.

Identify Pattern of Plant Damage

Uniform damage patterns on individual plants and on many different plants in a specific area are typically characteristic of non-living or abiotic factors. Abiotic factors include mechanical, physical, or chemical factors.

Random damage patterns on individual plants or on a specific family or genus of plants typically indicates a living or biotic agent of disease. Biotic factors include fungi, bacteria, or nematodes.

Important note: You may come to a diagnosis based on the answers a client provided, but when double-checking the diagnosis, you may realize the diagnosis does not seem quite right. Keep an open mind, go back through your questions, and take a different diagnostic avenue.

Distinguish between Biotic and Abiotic Factors

Signs of biotic pathogen activity will always be present. It is a matter of whether the sign is observed. First, closely study plant damage. Mentally identify possible causal agents. Then look for signs that would accompany such damage. Signs of disease include fruiting structures, overwintering structures, mycelium, insect frass or carcasses, and ooze. Because some diseases are vectored by insects, signs that the vectors are present are equally as important as finding signs of the disease. Also, some types of disease symptoms mimic symptoms of insect or vertebrate damage. It is critical, therefore, to distinguish between insect and pathogen damage using observed or unobserved signs of both insects and pathogens.

If no signs are observed, abiotic activity should be considered. Ask questions regarding mechanical, physical, and chemical factors affecting the damaged plant. Mechanical factors include string trimmer damage to tree trunks, improper pruning cuts, injury during transportation of plant material, and guy wire damage. Physical factors include temperature extremes, light differentials, and extreme changes in oxygen and moisture levels. Chemical factors include pesticide damage, fertilizer damage, nutritional disorders, and pollutants.

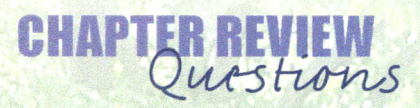
1. Define a plant disease.

2. What four components must be present for biotic disease development?

3. Another name for a living cause of disease is _____.

4. Another name for a non-living cause of disease is _____.

5. How are fungi dispersed? Bacteria? Phytoplasmas? Viruses?

6. Define the terms *chlorosis*, *canker*, *mycelium*, and *ooze*.

7. List four ways to manage foliar diseases.

8. A client brings you a foot-long branch of a chokecherry tree. The leaves on the branch tips are dark brown and wilted. The branch tip is bending over. Could this be fireblight? Why or why not?

9. What is the recommended pruning procedure for removal of fireblight-infected branches?

10. List two management techniques for tomato spotted wilt virus.

11. List two management techniques for canker diseases.

12. How are leaf scorch and winter desiccation similar?

13. Three characteristics of healthy roots are:

14. When diagnosing plant problems, why is it important to know what a "normal" plant looks like?

15. Random patterns of injury point to a/an _____ problem; uniform patterns of injury point to a/an _____ problem.

Chapter

25*

Managing Weeds

WHAT MAKES A PLANT A "LANDSCAPE WEED"?

A weed is any plant that becomes undesirable in the landscape because of the following:

- It is growing in a place where it is unwanted (lawn grass in a flowerbed, tree seedlings in a lawn, purslane growing between patio pavers, spearmint invading a raised vegetable bed).

- It is visually unattractive (color, texture, growth habit, growth rate makes it aesthetically unappealing to the eye).

- It poses a health or safety hazard (poisonous plants, thorny plants, fuel for fires).

- It outcompetes more desirable plants in the home landscape (competes for water, nutrients, light) or when it escapes into native landscapes (creating biodiversity problems).

- It acts as a host or shelter for other pests (alternate host for rust, attractive to injurious insects, food/shelter for damaging wildlife).

WHAT CHARACTERISTICS MAKE WEEDS SUCCESSFUL?

Characteristics that make weeds successful where they become a problem include the following:

- Rapid growth rate

- Prolific seed producer

*Authors: David Whiting, Tony Koski, Irene Shonle, and Kurt Jones, Colorado State University Extension.

- Long longevity of seed

- Deep roots, stolons, tubers, etc., making them tolerant of adverse growing conditions

- More "ecologically fit" than other plants in the landscape

- Adapted to readily spread (wind, animal manure, water, and human activities)

- Often adapted to disturbed soil/sites

- May not have insects and diseases to keep them in check

- May be better competitors for light, nutrients, or sun

Seed Bank

A seed bank builds up as a weed drops seed into the soil over many years—seed can remain viable for years. Persistence and vigilance to keep weeds from going to seed are keys to depleting the seed bank (Tables 25-1 and 25-2).

Weeds tend to be very competitive and are capable of taking advantage of disturbed areas. They often produce large amounts of seeds or are capable of quick reproduction. Weeds are generally a problem where the desired crop is doing poorly or the soil has been disturbed.

HOW DO WEEDS GET INTO OUR LANDSCAPES?

Major sources of landscape weeds include the following:

- Weeds going to seed (seed bank)

- Brought into garden in manure and soil amendments or with soils

- Disseminated from neighboring property's plants and weeds

- Deliberate introduction

Minor sources of landscape weeds include the following:

- Brought into garden with plant materials

- Brought into garden in irrigation water

- Brought into garden by humans or animals

- Using poor quality seed (weed content in seed)

Table 25.1. Seeds per Plant

Weed	Number of Seeds Produced per Plant
Dandelion	15,000
Canada thistle	680
Curly dock	29,500
Lamb's quarter	72,450
Mullein	223,200
Pigweed	117,400
Purslane	52,300

Table 25.2. Viability of Buried Seed

Weed	Viability of Buried Seed
Black mustard	50 years
Curly dock	80 years
Foxtail	30 years
Mallow	20 years
Plantain	40 years
Shepherd's purse	35 years

NOXIOUS WEEDS

Common weeds refer to weeds commonly found in various cropping situations, such as the lawn, vegetable garden, flowerbeds, or naturalized areas.

Noxious weeds refer to weed species declared by state or local statutes as a threat to agriculture and naturalized areas. Some designations require control under the law.

Examples of Legal Designations for Noxious Weeds

List A: All populations of List A species in Colorado are designated for eradication because they are not widespread (myrtle spurge, purple loosestrife).

List B: These weeds have discrete populations and will be managed to stop their continued spread or eradicated in certain areas (Chinese clematis, oxeye daisy).

List C: These weeds are already very widespread and not required to be controlled; however, education and research continue on these species (downy brome, field bindweed).

For additional information on Colorado's noxious weed laws, refer to the Colorado Department of Agriculture Noxious Weed Management Program at www.colorado.gov/ag/weeds.

WEED LIFE CYCLE

To control weeds, the gardener needs to know their life cycles.

Annuals

Summer annual—The seed germinates in the spring, the plant develops and produces seed during the summer, and the plant dies with killing frost in the fall. Examples include crabgrass and puncture vine.

Winter annual—The seed germinates in late summer or fall, and lives over winter as small tufts of leaves or rosettes, resumes growth in spring, matures seed early in the summer, and dies in summer heat. Examples include downy brome and shepherd's purse.

Keys to controlling annuals are preventing seed production, depleting the seed bank, and preventing germination.

- Timing is important.
- Winter annuals must be controlled before seed set in early summer.
- Summer annuals must be controlled before seed set in middle to late summer or early fall.
- The use of herbicides at the end of an annual's life cycle is often ineffective and does not make sense!
- Competition (from other plants and mulch) to prevent seed germination and seedling development.

Biennials

They require two seasons to complete growth cycle. Seeds germinate in spring; the following season, the plant flowers and matures seeds in summer and fall before dying. An example is the dame's rocket.

Keys to control are preventing seed production and depleting the seed bank, and preventing germination and seedling establishment.

Perennials

Simple perennials have a root crown that produces new shoots every year. They depend upon seed production to spread. Examples include foxtail barley and dandelion.

Creeping perennials propagate by seed, creeping above ground stems (stolons), and/or creeping underground stems (rhizomes). Examples include quackgrass and Canada thistle.

Keys to control are to prevent seed production and to kill the plant. Creeping perennials have a more extensive root system and are harder to control.

IPM: INTEGRATED WEED MANAGEMENT

"Integrated Pest Management, IPM, is a sustainable approach to managing pests by combining biological, cultural, physical, and chemical tools in a way that minimizes economic, health, and environmental risks."— National Integrated Pest Management Network

The best weed control is prevention!

- Plant weed-free seed, sod, nursery stock
- Avoid using plant species known to be invasive
- Use weed-free amendments, top dressing
- Use mulch where appropriate
- Maintain healthy, competitive plants
- Irrigate and fertilize appropriately

METHODS OF CONTROL
Cultural Methods

Irrigation

Irrigation methods and frequency have a direct influence on weeds. Infrequent, deep irrigation droughts out many shallow rooted weeds. Sprinkler irrigation (wetting the entire soil surface) encourages weeds. Drip irrigation (keeping most of the soil surface dry) discourages weeds. Keep non-irrigated areas dry to help suppress weeds.

Lawn Mowing

Many common garden weeds will not survive the frequent mowing of a lawn. However, mowing the lawn too short (less than two inches for Kentucky bluegrass) encourages weeds as it reduces vigor of the grass.

Mulching

If maintained at adequate depths, mulching has many benefits including preventing weed seed germination. For wood/bark chips, a depth of three inches is best for weed control. Less is ineffective. Mulching may not effectively control established perennials growing from root.

Landscape Fabrics

In landscape management, landscape fabric with wood/bark chips or rock mulch above is common. However, it prevents soil improvement by organic breakdown, decreasing plant vigor. Weed seeds that germinate above the fabric layer will be difficult to pull and must be removed with herbicides. Use of landscape fabric should be considered as a deferred-maintenance technique rather than a low-maintenance technique.

Crop Competition

Competition with the crops and weeds for light, water, nutrients, and growing space is an effective weed management tool. For example, mowing a cool season lawn (like Kentucky bluegrass) gives the lawn a growth advantage, shading out many weeds like crabgrass.

Block planting in the vegetable garden and close spacings in a flowerbed, with plants filling the bed space, helps suppress weeds.

Summary: Cultural Methods for Weed Management

Pros: This is the best long-term control as the gardener increases the conditions for desired plants to grow at the same time decrease the conditions for weeds.

Cons: Possibly more expensive and time-consuming; control may be slow.

Mechanical Methods

Tilling/Cultivating

Tilling or cultivating effectively controls 90% of annual and biennial weeds if done before seed set. It also brings a new set of weed seeds to the soil surface ready to germinate. When tilling for weed control, use only shallow cultivation. Deep tilling can damage crop roots. Cultivating/tilling may actually propagate most perennial weeds.

Hand Pulling

Hand pulling is quick when pulled while the weeds are small, and it is effective for small infestations. A few minutes on a weekly basis to keep the garden weed free will be more effective than a long weed pulling session as the weeds get large. For many gardeners, pulling weeds is a great way to vent stress. With hand pulling, most weed species require that they be pulled out by the roots. The weed will readily regrow if just the tops are removed. It is essential that weeds are removed before they go to seed, filling the seed bank. Some weed species, like purslane, must be removed from the garden bed. It can reroot if left in the garden.

Mowing Naturalized and Low-Maintenance Areas

Mowing is a common weed management tool in natural areas and lower-maintenance sections of a yard, reducing the unsightly appearance of the yard and fire hazard.

String Trimming ("Weed Whacking")

Use of a string trimmer is a form of weed management by mowing. It can be effective in preventing weeds from going to seed. However, it can sow seeds if done on weeds with seeds.

Flame (Propane Torch)

Flaming off weeds with a propane torch is a common practice in production agriculture and has limited application in landscape maintenance due to fire hazards. During the flaming process, heat from the flame is transferred to the plant tissues, increasing the thermal energy of the plant cells and resulting in coagulation of cell proteins if the temperature is above 50°F (122°F). Exposing plant tissue to a temperature of about 100°F (212°F) for a split second (0.1 second) can result in cell membrane rupture, resulting in loss of water and plant death. Thus, the weeds do not need to be burned up, but rather just scorched. Flaming works best on very young weeds.

It is rather expensive and many not be cost-effective in some production agriculture situations. It presents a fire and explosion hazard; use with caution. Fire prevention measures prohibit the use of flaming in many communities.

Burning

Burning of fields and ditch banks is a weed management tool in production agriculture. Generally, a permit is required. Most communities prohibit burning of weeds inside city limits.

Solarization

Solarization is a method of heating the soil to kill roots, weed seeds, and soil-borne insects and diseases near the soil surface. In regions with hot summer temperatures, it is effective in open areas with full sun. However, do not solarize the soil in the rooting area of trees, shrubs, and other desired plants. Steps include the following:

1. Remove vegetation and cultivate the soil to a six inch depth.

2. Sprinkle irrigate the area.

3. Cover the area with 4 mil clear plastic. Bury the edges of the plastic all the way around the plot.

4. Leave in place for three weeks during the summer heat of July and August.

5. After removing the plastic, avoid deep cultivation that would bring up weed seeds, insects, and disease pathogens from deeper soils.

Summary: Mechanical Method

Pros: Mechanical methods can be quick, inexpensive, environmentally friendly, and effective on small weed seedlings.

Cons: Mechanical methods have limited effectiveness on many established perennials and could be detrimental at the wrong time.

Biological Methods

Biological methods include the use of carefully screened insects to attack portions of the weed (i.e., stems, seeds, flowers, etc.). Development of biological methods with insects is rather complex and must be used with caution. The introduced insects must survive and become established in the new ecosystem. The insects need to reduce the weed population, but cannot entirely eliminate the weeds as that would eliminate the food supply. The insects must not attach to beneficial plants. The insects must not become insect pests. A great example of biological methods that failed is earwigs. They were intentionally introduced into the United States as a biological control agent and have since become a pest.

Biological methods also include the grazing of sheep, cows, horses, or goats. The purposeful use of grazing animals to control weed patches can be extremely expensive.

Pros: Biological methods can be an inexpensive, long-term control solution. They can be environmentally friendly and require little labor.

Cons: Biological methods are not always effective, may require a large population of weeds to maintain insect populations (will not work in backyard setting), and do not eradicate weeds. Insects can sometimes attack non-target plants.

Herbicides (Chemical Methods)

The use of herbicides is the use of chemicals that disrupt key physiological processes in plants, leading to plant death. Among the various herbicides, many different modes of action are found.

Pros: Use of herbicides is generally effective (if the correct herbicide is used), cost-effective, and provides quick control.

Cons: Use of herbicides can be environmentally problematic when incorrectly applied. Proper use includes proper selection of the specific herbicide for the weeds and for the growing crops in the area, timing of application, correct application rates, correct application procedures, and application safety measures to protect the application and non-target plants. Some require special licensing and may not be used in a home landscape or garden setting.

Be sure to follow the label; it is the law. Components of the herbicide label include the following:

- Trade name

- Common name

- Chemical name

- Signal words (e.g., danger, warning, caution)

- Use instructions

  —Weeds controlled

  —Plant tolerances

  —Application rate(s)

  —Application timing

  —Application technique

  —Application restrictions

- Safety

  —Applicator

  —Bystanders, pets

  —Wildlife

  —Non-target plants

How Herbicides Are Applied

- **Broadcast** application refers to a uniform application over a treatment area.

- **Spot treat** refers to application to a specific area, such as directly to individual weeds.

- **Foliar** application refers to application to the leaves.

- **Soil incorporation** refers to tilling or watering the herbicide into the soil after application.

Types of Herbicides

- **Systemic** or **Translocated** herbicides move internally in the plant. They must be applied during period of active growth with adequate water. Systemic herbicides are especially good for many perennials. Examples include glyphosate (Round-up), and 2,4-D.

- **Contact** herbicides only desiccate the portion of the plant that is contacted. Contact herbicides are most effective on annuals. Examples include vinegar and diquat.

- **Pre-emergent** herbicides are applied to soil prior to weed seed germination, killing germinating seeds. They will not kill growing weeds. Application timing is critical. For example, to control crabgrass in lawns, pre-emergent herbicides need to be applied late April to early May before the crabgrass germinates, about the time that common lilac blooms. Most require soil incorporation by irrigation.

  Some desired crops germinating from seeds may also be killed. For example, do not apply pre-emergent herbicides prior to seeding or laying sod. Uniform application and strict adherence to application rate are essential for attaining good weed control and for preventing injury to landscape plants.

- **Post-emergent** herbicides are applied to foliage of actively growing plants. Examples include 2,4-D and glyphosate (Round-up).

- **Selective** herbicides control a limited group of plants, like monocots versus dicots.

- **Non-selective** herbicides are effective on a broad range of plants.

Selective Herbicides for Broadleaf Weed Control in Lawns

Examples: 2,4-D, MCPP and MCPA, Banvel (dicamba), and Confront

Caution:

- Avoid drift and ground water movement to non-target crops. Tomatoes and grapes are extremely sensitive to 2,4-D products.

- Do not use with temperatures above 85°F.

- Do not broadcast apply under trees. Spot individual weeds.

- Banvel and Confront have higher toxicity on some shade trees including honeylocust, linden, and Japanese pagoda.

- Keep pets off treated area until lawn dries.

- Low human toxicity. Stay out of area until lawn dries.

Non-Selective Herbicides for Control of Herbaceous Plants

Example: Glyphosate (Round-up). Note: Many Round-up products in the home garden trade have a combination of other herbicides added for quicker kill or longer holding potential.

Caution:

- Requires application to leaf tissue. No soil action. Do not spray the ground.

- Neutralized upon contact with soil. Mix only with drinking quality water. The dirt in non-potable water may neutralize the product.

- Effective on most herbaceous plants. May or may not be toxic on woody plants.

- Low human toxicity, but avoid skin contact.

- Extremely toxic to dogs. Keep dogs out of treated area until spray dries.

Pre-Emergent Herbicides to Check Germinating Weeds in the Lawn

Examples: Balan, Betasan (bensulfide), Dacthal (DCPA, Ronstar (oxadiazon), Tipersan (siduron), etc.

Cautions:

- Requires soil incorporation by irrigation.

- Do not apply prior to seeding or sodding. (Refer to label direction.)

APPROACH TO CLIENTS HAVING WEED PROBLEMS

- The weed must be identified properly.

- What is the landscape setting (lawn, vegetable garden, flowerbed, shrub border, hardscape)?

- What is the health of the plants where the weeds are growing?

- What is the degree of weed infestation (by numbers, area, time, nearby sources of weeds)?

- What management has been done to date?

- Cultural issues: How is the area being managed (water, mowing, etc.)?

- Indicator species: Certain weeds "indicate" overwatering, too much/too little fertilizer, etc.

WEED ASSOCIATIONS WITH SPECIFIC ENVIRONMENTS AND CULTURAL CONDITIONS

Compacted Soils

- Annual bluegrass (*Poa annua*)
- Common chickweed (*Stellaria media*)
- Goosegrass (*Eleusine indica*)
- Knotweed (*Polygonum aviculare*)
- Mouse-ear chickweed (*Cerastium vulgatum*)
- Prostrate spurge (*Euphorbia supina*)

Dry Soil

- Black medic (*Medicago lupulina*)
- Dandelion (*Taraxacum officinale*)
- Bindweed (*Convolvulus* spp.)
- Kochia (*Kochia scoparia*)
- Stinkgrass (*Eragrostis cilianensis*)

Dry, Infertile Soils

- Black medic (*Medicago lupulina*)
- Yarrow (*Achillea millefolium*)

Moist or Poorly Drained Soils

- Annual bluegrass (*Poa annua*)
- Bentgrasses (*Agrostis* spp.)
- Common chickweed (*Stellaria media*)
- Crabgrasses (*Digitaria* spp.)
- Goosegrass (*Eleusine indica*)
- Ground ivy (*Glechoma hederacea*)
- Mouse-ear chickweed (*Cerastium vulgatum*)
- Violets (*Viola* spp.)
- Yellow nutsedge (*Cyperus esculentus*)

Moist, Fertile Soils

- Annual bluegrass (*Poa annua*)
- Curled dock (*Rumex crispus*)
- Henbit (*Lamium amplexicaule*)
- Yellow woodsorrel (*Oxalis stricta*)

Moist, Infertile (Low Nitrogen) Soils

- Black medic (*Medicago lupulina*)
- Plantains (*Plantago* spp.)
- White clover (*Trifolium repens*)

Low Mowing Height

- Annual bluegrass (*Poa annua*)
- Crabgrasses (*Digitaria* spp.)
- Yellow woodsorrel (*Oxalis stricta*)
- White clover (*Trifolium repens*)

New Seedings (Spring/Summer)

- Annual bluegrass (*Poa annua*)
- Barnyardgrass (*Echinochloa crusgalli*)
- Crabgrasses (*Digitaria* spp.)
- Purslane (*Portulaca oleracea*)
- Foxtail (*Setaria* spp.)

New Seedings (Fall)

- Henbit (*Lamium amplexicaule*)
- Storksbill (*Erodium cicutariuim*)
- Shepard's purse (*Capsella bursa-pastoris*)
- Annual mustards (many)

Old Lawns (25 to 30 or More Years)

- Bentgrasses, redtop (*Agrostis* spp.)
- Orchardgrass (*Dactylis glomerata*)

Shady Lawns

- Annual bluegrass (*Poa annua*)
- Common chickweed (*Stellaria media*)
- Ground ivy (*Glechoma hederacea*)
- Mouse-ear chickweed (*Cerastium vulgatum*)
- Nimblewill (*Muhlenbergia shreberi*)
- Violets (*Viola* spp.)

Formerly Agricultural/Farm Land

- Barnyardgrass (*Echinochloa crusgalli*)
- Bindweed (*Convolvulus* spp.)

- Canada thistle (*Cirsium arvense*)

- Foxtail (*Setaria* spp.)

- Quackgrass (*Elytrigia repens*)

- *Smooth bromegrass (Bromus inermis)*

WEED DESCRIPTIONS
Summer Annuals
Common Mallow, Malva neglecta

- Most frequent in cultivated ground, gardens, newly seeded lawns, or stressed lawns that lack density; found at 4,500 to 7,000 feet in elevation

- Prostrate, low-spreading annual, biennial, or perennial; deep taproot; foliage similar to geranium, pinkish-white flowers, fruits look like small round wheels of cheese

- Increase turf density

- Pull plants from moist soil

- Pre-emergent herbicides are effective

- Post-emergent herbicides can be effective

Common Purslane, Portulaca oleracea

- Summer annual, found in newly seeded or thinning, non-vigorous lawns and also in cultivated garden sites; up to 8,500 feet in elevation

- Smooth, thick, succulent, alternate (to sub-opposite) edible leaves; small yellow flowers in leaf axils; stems are smooth and reddish; plant is sprawling, prostrate, forming dense vegetative mats from shallow fibrous root system

- Increase turf density

- Pulls easily when soil is moist; easily re-roots after cultivation—remove and dispose of plant

- Pre-emergent herbicides may be helpful

- Post-emergent herbicide use is more effective when plants are young; difficult to kill with an herbicide when larger

Crabgrass, Digitaria sanguinalis

- Low-growing, prostrate, summer annual grass; leaf blades wider and lighter green color than Kentucky bluegrass with leaf sheaths with long stiff hairs

- Base of stems are often reddish-purple in color; plant spreads by rooting at the lower stem nodes as well as by seed; forms seedheads below mowing height; seedheads are composed of slender, finger-like spikes

- Crabgrass is less prevalent when turf has good density; mowing too low promotes crabgrass seed germination; maintain mowing height at 2.5 to 3 inches

- A pre-emergent herbicide applied correctly and at the proper time should provide control; do not use a pre-emergent herbicide on a newly-seeded or sodded lawn or when overseeding a lawn

- Post-emergent "crabgrass killer" sprays are not effective unless crabgrass plants are at the young seedling stage

Green Foxtail, Setaria viridis

- A summer annual grass with wider blades and a lighter green color than Kentucky bluegrass

- Faster growing than Kentucky bluegrass; seedheads (known as spikes) have bristles that give it a fuzzy appearance; may form a seedhead despite regular mowing

- Foxtail is much less prevalent when turf has good density; resod or reseed bare spots

- A pre-emergent herbicide applied correctly and at the proper time should provide control; do not use a pre-emergent herbicide on a newly-seeded or sodded lawn or when overseeding a lawn

- Post-emergent herbicides will kill foxtail seedlings (but not mature plants)

Kochia, Kochia scoparia

- Very prevalent in disturbed soils, cultivated fields, gardens

- In spring, seedlings have alternate leaves; lower leaves often wider than upper leaves; underside of leaves hairy, margins hairy

- Flowers are yellow, inconspicuous; seed production occurs from July to October

- Stems are 1 to 6 feet tall

- In fall, entire plant first becomes reddish-brown, then brown, becomes "tumbleweed"

- Germinates early; use pre-emergent herbicides before soil temps reach 38°F

- Post-emergent herbicides can be effective

- Mulch inhibits seedling development

Netseed Lambsquarters, Chenopodium berlandieri

- Summer annuals prevalent in disturbed soils, gardens, cultivated fields, waste areas

- Extremely variable in appearance; stems 1 to 6 feet tall, grooved, often reddish tinged; undersides of leaves whitish, mealy (mottled, granular appearance)

- Flowers inconspicuous, greenish, at tips of stems and leaf axils; seed production occurs from July to September

- Edible when plant is young and tender

- Competitive weed with rapid growth and high water use

- Can be hoed or pulled when young

- Pre-emergent herbicides applied at the right time in spring can provide good control

- Post-emergent herbicides can be effective

- Mulch inhibits seedling development

Prostrate Knotweed, Polygonum aviculare

- Prostrate summer annual from a thin taproot; tough, durable plant common along sidewalks, in turf that is stressed and less vigorous, and in gardens; found to 9,500 feet in elevation

- Thrives in dry, compacted soils or wherever there is excessive foot traffic

- Forms a tough, wiry mat of stems that are enlarged at each joint as well as a papery sheath at each leaf node; to differentiate from spurge, broken stem does not produce a milky sap; leaves and stems are not hairy, and leaves are alternate

- Flowers small, white, inconspicuous; found where leaf meets stem; produces many seeds
- Annual core aeration spring and/or fall will reduce knotweed infestation
- Apply pre-emergent herbicides in late fall/winter (knotweed can germinate in February or March)
- Post-emergent herbicides are mostly ineffective after plants become larger

Prostrate Spurge, Chamaesyce maculate

- Prostrate summer annual forming dense mats; found in thinning, less vigorous turf
- Leaves are opposite and each leaf has a reddish-purple spot in the center; small pinkish flowers in leaf axils; stems and leaves are both hairy; sap is milky latex; some people develop a rash after skin contact with sap
- Increase turf density
- Plants can be pulled and bagged if soil is moist; wear gloves because of the sap
- Post-emergent herbicides can be effective

Redroot Pigweed, Amaranthus retroflexus

- Coarse, summer annual; fast growing to 12 to 36 or more inches tall; dependent on moisture received
- Alternate leaves vary in appearance, but have prominent veins and midrib
- Lower stem reddish or red-striped; roots pink-red even down the taproot
- Flowers/seedheads at top of plant; prickly; produces many small black seeds
- Very toxic to cattle and swine
- Found in waste areas, gardens, disturbed soils, and in turf if thin and patchy in quality
- Hoe or pull from moist soil before seedheads mature; bag plants if pulled later
- Easy to kill with most herbicides, but apply according to label directions well before seedheads mature; herbicides suggested only where large numbers of plants exist or where large areas are infested

Scentless chamomile, Matricaria perforata

- Noxious weed in Colorado (List B)
- Annual forb that can persist as a biennial or short-lived perennial
- Stems of the plant are green, erect, often branched, glabrous, or slightly pubescent, and can range in height from 6 to 20 inches tall
- Leaves are alternate, 1 to 2 inches long, slightly pubescent or glabrous, and are finely divided into several short thread-like segments
- Terminal flowers are 0.75 to 1.25 inch in diameter, with a daisy-like appearance consisting of white petals surrounding a central yellow core
- Key to control is reducing seed production; hand pulling is effective, but may not be practical in larger patches; mowing conducted early in the growing season before plants flower and prior to seed production will reduce populations
- Maintaining healthy stands of desirable vegetation can also be an effective control measure because scentless chamomile seedlings cannot tolerate intense competition
- Post-emergent herbicides can be effective

Winter Annuals

Downy Brome/Cheat Grass, Bromus tectorum

- Noxious weed in Colorado (List C)
- Winter annual, extremely abundant in intermountain west; after maturity can become a fire hazard, especially when dry; found at 4,000 to 9,000 feet in elevation
- Leaf sheaths and blades are covered by dense soft hairs
- Droopy seedheads develop in spring; long awns; prolific seed producer; plants turn reddish-brown in early summer (mid to late June), and then fade to a blond color
- Competes vigorously with other perennial grasses for moisture because of its winter and early spring growth habit; root growth during winter can occur until soil temperature goes below 37°F
- Hand pulling effective for small infestations—repeat pulling over the season is necessary, as seeds will germinate irregularly; extract as much root as possible to prevent re-growth
- Infrequent in mowed turf; in the landscape, glyphosate (Round-up and others) works well in early spring prior to seedhead appearance; best when non-target species are dormant

Shepherd's Purse, Capsella bursa-pastoris

- Small winter annual with small white flowers early in spring; common in cultivated gardens and roadsides; common up to 9,000 feet in elevation
- Slender stems from basal rosettes; leaves are hairy below, smooth above, and often deeply lobed; seed pods are heart-shaped (or purse-shaped); seed production from April to September
- Hand pulling or hoeing before seed set is very effective—get on it early!
- Post-emergent herbicides should be labeled for use in turf grass

Biennials

Dame's Rocket, Hesperis matronalis

- Noxious weed in Colorado (List B)
- Can be a short-lived perennial
- Was introduced as an ornamental
- Flowers have four petals, are purple or white, clustered in loose stalks, and fragrant
- Mature plants range from 1 to 3 feet tall
- Can be aggressive in the landscape
- Pulling or cutting flower heads before seed set will control the plant, but this will need to be repeated for several years to exhaust seed bank
- For larger infestations, post-emergent herbicides can be effective
- Do not buy seed mixes that contain this plant

Diffuse Knapweed, Centaurea diffusa

- Noxious weed in Colorado (List B)
- A biennial, short-lived perennial, or occasionally an annual
- The plant develops a single shoot (stem), 1 to 2 feet tall that is branched toward the top; first-year rosette leaves and lower shoot leaves are finely divided; leaves become smaller toward the top of the shoot and have smooth margins

- Many solitary flowering heads occur on shoot tips; they are about one-eighth inch in diameter and 0.5 to 0.66 inch long; flowers usually are white but may be purplish; involucre bracts are divided like teeth on a comb and tipped with a slender spine that makes them sharp to the touch; sometimes the bracts are dark-tipped or spotted like spotted knapweed; the long terminal spine differentiates diffuse from spotted knapweed

- It reproduces and spreads from seed—keep from going to seed; hoeing or hand pulling before the plant goes to seed can accomplish this

- For larger areas, post-emergent herbicides can be effective

- Cultural controls include revegetating with desirable grasses

- Biological controls include the seedhead flies *Urophora affinis* and *U. quadrifasciata* and root-feeding insects such as the diffuse knapweed root beetle (*Sphenoptera jugoslavica*), the yellow-winged knapweed moth (*Agapeta zoegana*), and the knapweed root weevil (*Cyphocleonus achates*)

Musk Thistle, Carduus nutans

- Noxious weed in Colorado (List B)

- Musk thistle is a biennial or winter annual that can grow up to 8 feet tall

- Leaves are up to 10 inches long, dark green with a light green midrib, spiny, and deeply lobed; often have a white margin

- Solitary, lightly spiny, and nodding flower heads develop at the stem tips in midsummer and grow to a diameter of 1.5 to 3 inches and are deep rose to violet

- The key to control is not to let the plant go to seed; herbicides and hand pulling the rosette are both effective

- Applications should be made in late spring/early summer and again in the fall

Prickly Lettuce, Lactuca serriola

- Biennial or winter annual to 48 inches tall from a large taproot; invades disturbed garden soils

- Cut stems/leaves exude a "milky juice"; more common in areas from 4,500 to 6,000 feet

- Upper leaves lobed like oak leaves and are often twisted to lie in a vertical plane, also known as "compassplant" because leaves may "point" to north and south; lower leaves often not as lobed; leaves have prominent spines on back side of midrib

- Small yellow daisy-like flowers on elongated stems; seedheads are like those of dandelion

- Hoe or pull from moist soil before yellow flowers mature

- Easy to kill with most herbicides, especially when younger; apply according to label directions well before seedheads mature; herbicides suggested only where large numbers of plants exist or where large areas are infested

Yellow Sweet Clover, Melilotus officinalis

- Biennial herbaceous plants; second-year plants grow 3 to 5 feet high and are bush-like; sweet clovers are very fragrant

- Leaves are alternate, divided into three finely toothed leaflets; middle leaflet grows on a short stalk

- Flowers are crowded densely at the top 4 inches along a central stem; each flower is attached by a minute stalk

- There are one or two hard small seeds per flower; they stay viable in the soil for 30 years

- Strong taproot

- Can be good forage; however, moldy hay made from yellow sweet clover (or hay made from drought-stressed or frost-damaged plants) is toxic to livestock (contains coumarin which converts to dicoumarin, a blood thinner)

- The key to controlling sweet clovers is to keep them from flowering and then concentrate on depleting viable seeds in the soil

- Hoe, hand pull, or spray with post-emergent herbicide when young

Simple Perennials

Curly Dock, Rumex crispus

- Leaves emerge from stout taproot in spring

- Elongated leaves have wavy (curly) margins; leaves mostly basal, with long petioles

- Stems 2 to 4 feet tall, reddish, ridged; nodes sheathed with clear membrane

- Flowers greenish, May

- Winged fruits on flowering stems, reddish-brown

- Habitat—Fields, roadsides, railroads, waste ground, disturbed sites, turf/landscape

- Dig taproot, must remove at least 75% of the taproot to control

- Post-emergent herbicides can be effective

Myrtle Spurge, Euphorbia myrsinites

- Noxious weed in Colorado (List A)

- Mat-forming perennial to 9 inches tall

- Escaped ornamental; formerly sold as a drought-tolerant ground cover

- Blue-green succulent leaves form a "donkey tail"; has chartreuse bracts ("flowers")

- For small infestations, dig or pull out clumps with caution; white latex sap from stems and leaves can cause severe dermal reactions—always wear gloves if hand pulling

- For larger infestations, use a herbicide; the best time to treat myrtle spurge with herbicide is during late fall

- *Eradication of all plants is required throughout Colorado.* If you see it, contact your county weed supervisor or the state weed coordinator!

Spotted Knapweed, Centaurea maculosa

- Noxious weed in Colorado (List B)

- A short-lived, noncreeping perennial that reproduces from seed (primary means of spread)

- Produces one or more shoots that are branched and 1 to 3 feet tall; rosette leaves can be 6 inches long and deeply lobed

- Leaves are similar to diffuse knapweed

- Lavender to purple flowers are solitary on shoot tips and about the same size as diffuse knapweed flowers; involucre bracts are stiff and black-tipped; the tip and upper bract margin have a soft, spine-like fringe and the center spine is shorter than others

- For control measures, see diffuse knapweed

Creeping Perennials

Bouncingbet, Saponaria officinalis

- Noxious weed in Colorado (List B)
- An escaped ornamental, aggressive in landscapes and wild areas
- Spreads aggressively through rhizomes and seeds
- White to pink five-petaled flowers are clustered at the ends of branches
- Leaves are opposite, smooth, and have three veins from base
- Mature plants are up to 3 feet tall
- Saponins in plant are toxic to livestock
- Can be controlled by mowing or pulling several times a year—before seed production
- Post-emergent herbicides can be effective

Canada Thistle, Cirsium arvense

- Noxious weed in Colorado (List B)
- Colony-forming creeping perennial spreading primarily by horizontal roots (can grow as much as 18 feet in one season!) and to a lesser degree by seed; found from 4,000 to 9,500 feet in elevation
- Flowers are purple and are borne in clusters; spiny foliage with variable leaf shapes; when mowed in a lawn, will not develop full height and flower
- Highly invasive species; control is difficult because of its extensive root system; pulling generally is not effective due to the tremendous reserves in the root system; *regular, persistent* pulling may gradually starve root system; shoots should be pulled as they are noticed, as all shoots (leaves) are producing food reserves
- Increase density and competitiveness of turf
- Post-emergent herbicides can be effective
- Vinegar is a contact herbicide and will only brown leaves; these will be replaced by new shoots; frequent applications may be effective
- Biocontrol insects include a seed head weevil, a stem-mining weevil, and a gall-forming fly; these may not be significantly effective alone but can provide good results when combined with other control methods; biocontrol insect releases are best suited to large acreage infestations; backyard releases are generally impractical

Common Tansy, Tanacetum vulgare

- Noxious weed in Colorado (List B)
- Introduced from Europe as an ornamental and medicinal herb
- Found in yards, along roadsides, stream banks, and in waste places
- Spreads by rhizomes, can reach 3 to 4 feet tall
- Flowers are button-shaped and yellow in flat-topped clusters
- Leaves are deeply divided into narrow leaflets and rank smelling
- Is toxic to livestock, although unpalatable
- Mowing before seed production can limit spread, although it may have to be repeated several times in a season to prevent regrowth from rootstocks

- Hand pulling in damp soil can remove small infestations; wear gloves; will readily regrow from fragments in soils

- For larger infestations, post-emergent herbicides can be effective

Creeping Woodsorrel/Oxalis, Oxalis corniculata

- Prostrate, creeping perennial from slender taproot; stems root where they touch the ground

- Leaves have a shamrock appearance; plants often mistaken for a clover; leaves may "fold up" at night or on cloudy days; leaves turn purplish with the arrival of cooler weather in fall; some plants may have purplish leaves year-round

- Small yellow flowers

- Fruits "explode" when mature, scattering seed often more than 10 feet

- More common in thin, less vigorous turf given too frequent, light irrigation; increase turf density

- Pre-emergent herbicides may be helpful

- Post-emergent herbicides can be effective

Field Bindweed, Convolvulus arvensis

- Noxious weed in Colorado (List C)

- Creeping perennial; found as high as 10,000 feet in elevation; general range 4,000 to 8,000 feet

- Vining, sprawling, prostrate growth habit; may climb by twining around fence wire or around stems of other plants; not shade tolerant but drought tolerant due to large roots; leaves are arrowhead-shaped; attractive, white or pink bell-shaped flowers that resemble morning glory from late June until frost

- Increase density and competitiveness of turf

- Control is difficult because of its extensive root system, which can penetrate the soil profile to a depth of 20 feet; seeds also can remain viable for 20 to 50 years; pulling generally is not effective due to the tremendous reserves in the root system; *regular, persistent* pulling may gradually starve root system; shoots should be pulled as they are noticed, as all shoots (leaves) produce food reserves

- Post-emergent herbicides can be effective

- The bindweed mite has been used as a biological control with some success; initial impact is reduction of growth and limited flower and seed production; mowing moves mites around and stimulates plant growth for mites to feed on; survival is better in drier settings; excessive moisture may limit establishment; contact your local Colorado State University Extension office for information

Hoary Cress (White Top), Cardaria draba

- Noxious weed in Colorado (List B)

- A creeping perennial that reproduces by seed and creeping roots; one of the earliest perennial weeds to emerge in the spring

- It grows erect from 10 to 18 inches high and has a white color

- The alternate leaves clasp the stem and are oval or oblong with toothed or almost smooth margins; the leaves are often covered with very fine white hairs; each leaf is 0.5 to 2 inches long with blunt ends

- The flowers are white, one-eighth inch across, and numerous in compact flat-top clusters, which give the plant its name; each heart-shaped seed pod contains two oval, finely pitted, red-brown seeds each about one-twelfth inch long

- Due to the rhizomes of this perennial weed, mechanical control provides minimal control; diligent digging can provide control of very small infestations; hand pulling of above-ground plant parts is ineffective; successful digging requires complete plant removal within 10 days after weed emergence throughout the growing season for 2 to 4 years; cultivation 6 inches deep must be repeated within 10 days of weed emergence throughout the growing season for 2 to 4 years

- Revegetate with desirable vegetation

- Post-emergent herbicides can be effective

Leafy Spurge, Euphorbia esula

- Noxious weed in Colorado (List B)

- An erect plant that grows 1 to 3 feet tall

- Leaves are bluish-green with smooth margins, 0.25 to 0.5 inch wide, and 1 inch to 4 inches long

- Umbel flowers are surrounded by heart-shaped, showy, yellow-green bracts (an umbel looks like the stays of an umbrella if it is held upside down); flowers occur in many clusters toward the top of the plant; seeds are round to oblong, about one-twelfth inch long, gray or mottled brown with a dark line on one side

- Leafy spurge contains a white milky latex in all plant parts; latex distinguishes leafy spurge from some other weeds (e.g., yellow toadflax), particularly when plants are in a vegetative growth stage

- Leafy spurge has an extensive root system that is abundant in the top foot of soil, and it may grow 15 feet deep or more; roots contain substantial nutrient reserves that allow the weed to recover from stress, including control efforts; many vegetative buds along roots grow into new shoots

- Use a combination of methods to control leafy spurge; vigorous grass helps weaken leafy spurge through competition

- Post-emergent herbicides can be effective

Orange Hawkweed, Hieracium aurantiacum

- Noxious weed in Colorado (List A)

- Shallow, fibrous roots

- Leaves are hairy, spatula-shaped, up to 5 inches long, and basal

- Extensive stolons create a dense mat that practically eliminates other vegetation—makes mechanical control very difficult once established

- Stems and leaves exude a milky latex when cut or broken

- Up to 30 half-inch red to orange flowers appear in late May or June

- Post-emergent herbicides can be effective

- *Eradication of all plants is required throughout Colorado.* If you see it, contact your county weed supervisor or the state weed coordinator!

Oxeye Daisy, Chrysanthemum leucanthemum or Leucanthemum vulgare

- Noxious weed in Colorado (List B)

- A perennial from rhizomes with characteristic "daisy-like" flowers

- Plants initially develop as a basal rosette; lower rosette leaves occur on petioles and are from 1.5 to 6 inches long; leaves are lobed

- Flowers are white with a yellow center and range from 1.25 to 2 inches

- Oxeye daisy should be mowed as soon as flowers appear to reduce seed production; root systems are shallow and the plant can be dug up and removed; hand removal will have to be continued for several years because seeds may remain viable in the soil for a long time

- Post-emergent herbicides can be effective

- Native daisies are a good, non-invasive garden alternative

Purple Loosestrife, Lythrum salicaria

- Noxious weed in Colorado (List A)

- Escaped ornamental, aggressive in riparian areas

- Square stem, whorled leaves

- Purple-magenta flowers with five to seven petals in long racemes

- If left unchecked, a wetland may become a monoculture of loosestrife

- Control of small infestations can be managed through digging all the plants and roots—this will need to be monitored for a few years

- Large infestations should be controlled with an aquatic-labeled herbicide

- *Eradication of all plants is required throughout Colorado.* If you see it, contact your county weed supervisor or the state weed coordinator!

Quackgrass, Elytrigia repens

- Noxious weed in Colorado (List B)

- Very aggressive creeping perennial grass especially in moist soils; found from 4,500 to 9,000 feet in elevation; spreads by seeds and invasive rhizomes (underground stems)

- Rhizomes are yellow-white, with brown sections; rhizome ends are sharp-pointed and can penetrate hard soils; base of leaf blade with claw-like appendage that clasps the stem

- Believed to be allelopathic (release of a chemical that inhibits growth of nearby plants)

- Mechanical control is difficult as any rhizome segment produces new plants

- A few quackgrass plants can be spot-sprayed with glyphosate, or individual blades can be painted with glyphosate; note that glyphosate will kill any bluegrass it contacts; repeat applications will likely be needed

- Renovate severely infested lawn areas—spray area with glyphosate; repeat applications will likely be needed; ensure that quackgrass is killed before areas are resodded or reseeded

Russian Knapweed, Centaurea maculosa

- Noxious weed in Colorado (List B)

- Creeping perennial that reproduces from seed and vegetative root buds

- Emerges in early spring, bolts in May to June, and flowers through the summer into fall

- Shoots or stems are erect, 18 to 36 inches tall, with many branches; lower leaves are 2 to 4 inches long and deeply lobed; upper leaves are smaller, generally with smooth margins, but can be slightly lobed; shoots and leaves are covered with dense gray hairs

- The solitary, urn-shaped flower heads occur on shoot tips and generally are 0.25 to 0.5 inch in diameter with smooth papery bracts; flowers can be pink, lavender, or white

- Has vertical and horizontal roots that have a brown to black, scaly appearance, especially apparent near the crown

- Toxic to horses; allelopathic to other plants

- The key to Russian knapweed control is to stress the weed and cause it to expend nutrient stores in its root system

- An herbicide alone will usually not effectively manage Russian knapweed; combine treatment with perennial grasses sown in late fall; tillage is necessary to overcome the residual allelopathic effects of Russian knapweed

White Clover, Trifolium repens

- Creeping perennial that forms runners that root at nodes

- Many people like clover in lawns, while others find white flowers and the bees they attract objectionable

- A legume that fixes nitrogen, so it is often found in lawns having low fertility

- Increase turf density with proper watering, mowing, and fertilization

- Post-emergent herbicides can be effective

Wild Violet, Viola spp.

- Heart-shaped leaves on long petioles, purple flowers in spring; may also spread by rhizomes

- Difficult to control due to resistance to many herbicides

- Improve light penetration to shaded areas by pruning trees and shrubs

- Mow lawn higher to increase competition from grass

- Best control may be to pull plants when ground is moist

- Post-emergent herbicides can be effective

Yellow Toadflax, Linaria vulgaris

- Noxious weed in Colorado (List B)

- Yellow toadflax is a perennial that spreads sideways by underground rhizomes and by seeds

- Flowers are small, yellow, look like snapdragons, and bloom mid-late summer; leaves are linear

- Some people confuse a native plant, golden banner, with toadflax, but golden banner blooms very early and has three leaves, like a clover

- Yellow toadflax is difficult to control; its extensive root system lets it recover from control attempts

- Yellow toadflax is very variable, genetically; therefore the effectiveness of herbicides is also variable

- Hand pulling can be effective on small patches, especially in gravelly soils when you can pull a large part of the root; it will need to be pulled for several years; pull *before* it goes to seed

- Post-emergent herbicides can be effective

Woody Plants

Russian Olive, Elaeagnus angustifolia

- Noxious weed in Colorado (List B)

- Small tree 10 to 25 feet tall originally planted as an ornamental and for windbreaks

- Leaves are narrow and appear silvery

- Branches have long thorns 1 to 2 inches in length

- Small sweet smelling yellow flowers are followed by a berry-like fruit which is spread by birds

- Has become a serious weed in low-lying pastures, meadows, and waterways

- The most effective control is to cut the tree and immediately paint the stump with a herbicide

- Silver buffalo berry is an excellent native alternative plant

Tamarisk, Tamarix ramosissima

- Noxious weed in Colorado (List B)

- Tamarisk was sold as an ornamental plant for gardens during the 1800 and 1900s; tamarisk has now spread to most of the western United States, displacing the native cottonwoods and other plants

- Plants can grow to 6 inches tall during the first 2 months and can grow over 18 feet tall; the taproot can reach 100 feet down with a root spread of up to 150 feet; adventitious roots can produce new trees when buried!

- Mature tamarisk trees can produce millions of pollen-size seeds dispersed through wind and water; seeds can germinate while floating and establish themselves on wet banks within 2 weeks; newly formed sand banks are particularly susceptible; trees may reproduce in the first year, but typically they reproduce during the second year

- It is very "thirsty"—one tree can use up to 300 gallons of water per day, and it alters hydrologic conditions in riparian areas

- Salt glands on the leaves release salt, increasing salinity of soil

- Tamarisk is difficult to control; single treatment approaches to control tamarisk have not proven feasible because no method completely eliminates tamarisk or its regeneration; use revegetation in conjunction with other methods

- The saltcedar leaf beetle, *Diorhabda elongaa*, has been released on some stands, and has shown to be fairly effective

CHAPTER REVIEW
Questions

1. Define a weed.

2. List characteristics that make a plant "weedy."

3. List the three major sources of weed seeds.

4. Define *common weed* and *noxious weed*.

5. Describe methods and limitations of the following weed management techniques:

    a. Irrigation

    b. Lawn mowing

    c. Mulching

    d. Crop competition

    e. Tilling/cultivation

    f. Hand pulling

    g. Mowing naturalized areas

6. Define the following herbicide terms:

    a. Selective

    b. Non-selective

    c. Translocated

    d. Contact spray

    e. Pre-emergent herbicide

    f. Pre-plant herbicide

    g. Post-emergent herbicide

    h. Broadcast application

    i. Spot treatment application

    j. Foliar application

    k. Soil incorporated herbicide

UNIT E

Woody Plants

Identification, Selection, Placement, and Planting of Trees and Shrubs

Learning Objectives

At the end of this unit, the student will be able to:

- Using a plant key, identify common trees and shrubs.
- For a given home landscape situation, discuss right plant, right place considerations for tree placement.
- For a given home landscape situation, discuss right plant, right place considerations for tree selection.
- Describe tree planting steps for rapid root establishment.
- Describe post-planting tree care.

Supplemental Reading

Books

- *Colorado Flora, Eastern Slope.* William Weber and Ronald Wittman.
- *Colorado Flora, Western Slope.* William Weber and Ronald Wittman.
- *Gardener's Latin: A Lexicon.* Bill Neal.
- **Hortus Third** or **Hortus Fourth.**
- *Identification Key for Woody Plants of the Pikes Peak Region.* Colorado State University Extension, El Paso County.
- *Manual of Woody Landscape Plants.* Sixth edition. Michael A. Dirr. Stipes Publishing. 2009.
- *Principles and Practice of Planting Trees and Shrubs.* Gary W. Watson and E.B. Himelick. International Society of Arboriculture. 1997.
- *Trees and Shrubs of Colorado.* Jack L. Carter. 2006.
- *Winter Guide to Central Rocky Mountain Shrubs.* Colorado Department of Natural Resources, Division of Wildlife. 1976.
- *Woody Landscape Plants for the High Plains.* D.H. Fairchild and J.E. Klett. Colorado State University Cooperative Extension Bulletin LTLB93-1. 1993. To order call the CSU Cooperative Extension Resource Center toll-free at 877-692-9358.

Web

- **Dr. Ed Gilman's Tree Planting Site** at http://hort.ifas.ufl.edu/woody/planting.shtml
- **Front Range Tree Recommendation List** at http://www.ext.colostate.edu/pubs/garden/treereclist.pdf
- *International Plant Name Index* at www.ipni.org/
- *Royal Botanic Gardens, Kew Resource Page* at www.kew.org./data/subjects.html
- *U.S. Department of Agriculture Plant Database* at http://plants.usda.gov/
- Several web-based sites offer pronunciation guides for plant names. For example, http://www.finegardening.com/pguide/pronunciation-guide-to-botanical-latin.aspx

Chapter

26*

Identifying Trees and Shrubs

Plant identification is a skill that takes time and patience to develop. The reward for developing this skill is confidence when communicating with clients, improved access to plant diagnostics materials (most based on plant identification), and the personal satisfaction of knowing the names of plants in the community. The steps to plant identification involve observation, questioning, and research, similar to the process learned in diagnosing tree disorders.

Master Gardeners and green industry professionals are often asked to identify plants either over the phone or with a single leaf or plant part. Sometimes, asking questions about the plant may provide the details needed for successful identification, but more than likely it will be necessary to ask the client to bring in a sample, including the stem and leaves with flower or fruit when possible.

For details on the taxonomic system, including use of scientific names, refer to Chapter 2.

PLANT IDENTIFICATION TOOLS

The most important skill used in successful plant identification is the ability to observe and define the characteristics of an individual plant. Examine the plant and note the structure and texture of stems, leaves, flowers and fruit, as well as any available roots. Remember to use visual clues as well as the feel and scent of the plant. However, use caution, as some plants or plant parts are known to be irritating or toxic.

Simple tools such as a hand lens, ruler, and a sharp blade (knife, scalpel, or pruning shears) are helpful for examining plant parts. For more detailed work, a dissecting microscope is useful, especially for observing the details of flower parts.

---

*Authors: David Whiting and Linda McMulkin with Joanne Jones, Alison O'Connor, and Laurel Potts; Colorado State University Extension. Artwork by David Whiting and Scott Johnson

Plants collected from landscapes or native sites (with permission only) can be stored in resealable plastic bags in the refrigerator for up to a week or can be pressed between layers of newspaper for future reference.

There are many references available for plant identification, both print and electronic. While photo books are easy to use, they are often incomplete due to lack of space. Websites often require that the user already know the name of the plant, but they are useful to confirm identification or to obtain additional information regarding characteristics.

Plant Identification Keys

Keys are designed to systematically compare plant structures until the identification of a plant species is reached. Plant keys are generally the most complete and scientific references, consisting of a series of choices based on alternative plant characteristics.

Dichotomous Style Keys

A dichotomous key gives two choices at each step. Each couplet will compare variations in similar plant characteristics, such as:

> 1a. Leaves narrow, less than one-half inch (2)
> 1b. Leaves wider than one-half inch (7)

Read both statements in the couplet and choose the statement that best describes the plant being examined. Notice that each statement is followed by a number in parentheses, which indicates the next step. If leaf width is less than one-half inch, move down to the couplet labeled 2a and 2b. If leaf width is more than one-half inch, skip couplets 2 through 6 and resume the process at 7a and 7b.

Outline Style Keys

In outline style keys, compare options at each indentation level. These lines may not be adjacent in line order. For example, from the key below, the first choice would be A (needles single) or B (needles in clusters). If the needles were single, the next choice would be 1 (needles flat) or 2 (needles square).

> A. Needles single
>   1. Needles flat in cross-section and flexible
>   a. Leaf scar oval, bud tips pointed—*Pseudotsuga* (Douglas fir)
>   b. Leaf scar round, bud tips roundish—*Abies* (fir)
>   2. Needles square in cross-section and stiff—*Picea* (spruce)
> B. Needles in clusters of two or more—*Pinus* (pine)

Many key styles give you more than just two options to evaluate each level. Select the one that best describes the plant.

TERMINOLOGY

The terminology of plant identification can be intimidating to the beginning, as well as the experienced, plant taxonomist. For example, *Plant Identification Terminology: An Illustrated Glossary*, by James Harris, lists thirty-five terms that describe the hairs on the surfaces of stems and leaves.

Fortunately, keys and photo references often contain a glossary with definitions of most of the botanical terms used in that publication. With practice, commonly used words become familiar; however, many terms are used infrequently. A good taxonomist simply looks up the meaning of terms they are not familiar with. Do not try to memorize the terms and meanings; rather, look them up as needed. For future reference, it is often helpful to draw a picture of a structure or paraphrase a definition in the margin of your book.

THE PLANT IDENTIFICATION PROCESS

Plant identification is a process that begins with observing the plant as a whole, followed by evaluating the details of the plant parts. Gathering data and making notes of details before looking at references often saves time and frustration during the actual identification process. The details may seem trivial, but can play a major role in determining the species being identified.

Step 1—Collect Information Regarding the Plant

A. Determine If the Tree/Shrub Is a Conifer or a Broadleaf Flowering Plant

Conifers are woody trees and shrubs generally with needle-like or scale-like foliage, and usually evergreen. Seeds are produced in cones, which are generally woody (pine cone) but sometime fleshy and berry-like (juniper fruit). Examples include arborvitae, Douglas fir, fir, junipers, larch, pine, spruce, and yews (Figure 26-1).

Conifers (members of the *Gymnosperms* alone with ginkgos and cycads) do not flower but produce seed in a structure made up of modified leaves called "bracts." Gymnosperm means "naked seed" and refers to the exposure of the female reproductive structure during pollination rather than the actual seed being uncovered.

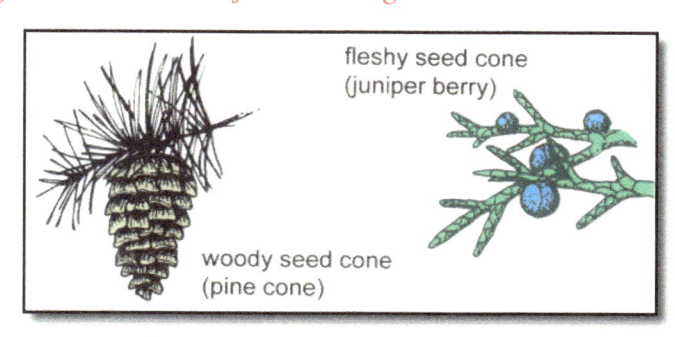

Figure 26-1 ▮ *Woody and fleshy cones of Conifers.*

Broadleaf flowering plants (members of the *Angiosperms*) are a highly diverse group of plants that produce seed via flowers. This group includes woody trees, shrubs, and vines and is often referred to as broadleaf plants due to the flattened leaf blade. Flowers range from tiny and inconspicuous to large and showy (Figure 26-2).

B. Determine If the Plant Is Deciduous or Evergreen

- **Deciduous** plants shed leaves in the fall. Most broadleaf flowering plants grown in northern climates are deciduous along with a few conifers such as some *Larix* (larch).

Figure 26-2 ▮ *Leaf of broadleaf type of Angiosperms.*

- **Semi-evergreen** plants may retain some leaves, depending on winter temperatures and moisture.

- **Evergreen** plants retain leaves for multiple seasons. Leaves (needles) will be present throughout the year. Most conifers are evergreen, along with some broadleaf plants such as *Mahonia* (Oregon Grape).

C. Determine the Growth Habit of the Plant

Growth habit refers to the genetic tendency of a plant to grow in a certain shape and to attain a certain mature height and spread.

- **Trees** typically have a single trunk and mature height over 12 feet.

- **Shrubs** typically have multiple branches from the ground and a mature height less than 12 feet.

- **Vines** have a climbing, clasping, or self-clinging growth habit.

Note: Many landscape plants could be considered small trees or large shrubs. The terms "tree" or "shrub" would be applied based on the general appearance of the plant. The species, cultivar, or variety name sometimes indicates plant characteristics, including form.

Step 2—Consult a Key to Lead You through the Identification Process

Each region of the county has a variety of keys written for trees in that region. Examples of keys for the Colorado region include the following:

- *Colorado Flora, Eastern Slope.* William Weber and Ronald Wittman.

- *Colorado Flora, Western Slope.* William Weber and Ronald Wittman.

- *Identification Key for Woody Plants of the Pikes Peak Region.* Colorado State University Extension, El Paso County.

- *Key to Common Landscape Trees and Shrubs of Colorado*, CMG GardenNotes #156 at www.cmg.colostate.edu/TreeID/156.html

- *Trees and Shrubs of Colorado.* Jack L. Carter.

- *What Tree Is This?* National Arbor Day Foundation, at www.arborday.org/trees/index-identification.cfm

IDENTIFYING CONIFERS: ARBORVITAE, DOUGLAS FIR, FIR, JUNIPER, PINE, SPRUCE, AND YEW

Characteristics of Conifers

Leaves

Most conifers (cone-bearing plants) are easy to identify to genus based on leaf type (Figure 26-3).

- *Pinaceae* family (pine, spruce, fir, and Douglas fir)—Needle-like leaves

- *Cupressaceae* family (juniper and arborvitae)—Scale-like or awl-like leaves

- *Taxaceae* family (yew)—Leaves flat and feather-like in arrangement

Seed Production

Conifers do not flower; they produce seed in a structure made up of modified leaves called bracts that become the "cone." Conifers are part of the *Gymnosperm* taxa (along with ginkgo and cycads). *Gymnosperm* means "naked

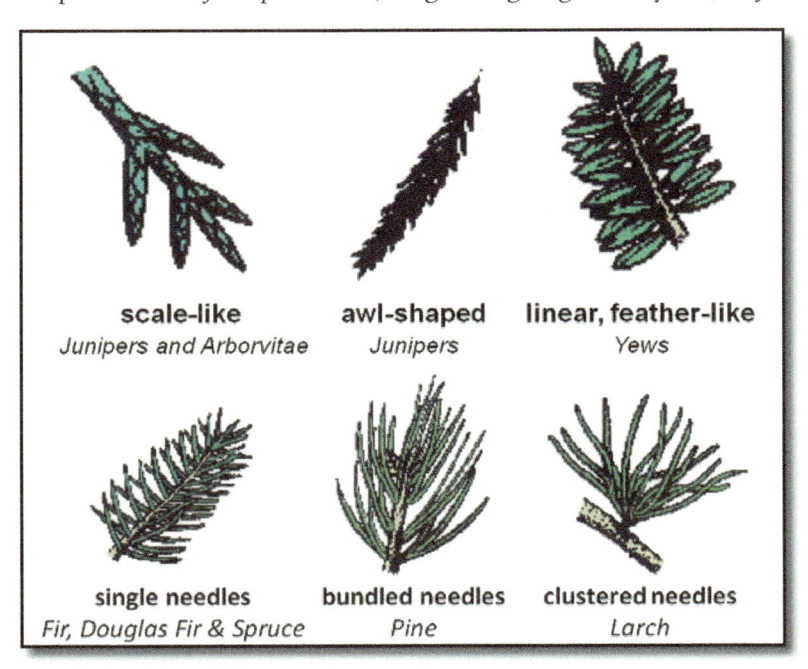

Figure 26-3 ▍ *Conifer leaf types.*

seed" and refers to the exposure of the female reproductive structure during pollination rather than the actual seed being naked.

The *Pinaceae* family (pine, spruce, fir, and Douglas fir) and arborvitae are monoecious plants (separate male and female flowers on the same plant). Male cones produce pollen and are normally short-lived. Female cones are generally larger and longer-lived, remaining on the tree until (or after) the seed matures. Junipers are dioecious plants (separate male and female plants). Yews are generally dioecious.

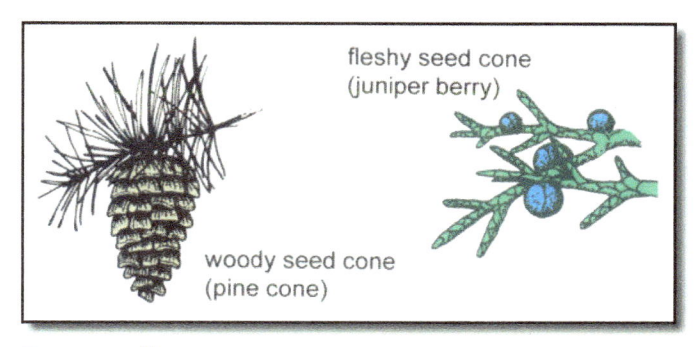

Figure 26-4 ▮ *Woody and fleshy cones of conifers.*

Cones of pines, spruce, and fir are made up of leathery or woody bracts, which open as the seed matures. The cones of junipers have fused scales, resulting in a more berry-like appearance (Figure 26-4).

Key to Conifers

Key to Conifers

A. **Leaves scale-like or awl-like.** Fruit berry-like cone with scales fused together—*Cupressaceae* family (junipers and arborvitae)
   1. Leaves scale-like or awl-shaped, often closely pressed to the branches. Foliage arranged around the branch, rather than flattened. Cones berry-like with scales pressed together—***Juniperus*** (junipers)
   2. Leaves small, scale-like hugging the stem. Foliage in flattened plate-like display. Cones berry-like with thick scales—***Thuja*** (arborvitae)

B. **Leaves needle-like**—*Pinaceae* family (pine, spruce, fir, and Douglas fir)
   1. Needles single
      a. Needles flat in cross-section and flexible
         1) Leaf scar oval, bud tips pointed. Cones have three-pronged lobed tongue-like "bract" that extend out beyond the scales—***Pseudotsuga menziesii*** (Douglas fir)
         2) Leaf scar round, bud tips roundish. Cones grow upright on the branch, usually disintegrating before falling to the ground—***Abies*** (fir)
      b. Needles square in cross-section and stiff. Older twigs studded with the persistent stumps of fallen needles—***Picea*** (spruce)
   2. Needles sheathed at the base in bundles of two to five. Cone scales thick and woody with swollen tips—***Pinus*** (pine)
   3. Short needles in tufts of ten or more. May be deciduous—***Larix*** (larch)

C. **Leaves flat, linear-shaped in a feather-like display.** Shrubs with dark green leathery leaves. Red, berry-like fruit—***Taxus*** (yew)

Key to *Abies* (Fir)

1. Young stems not hairy. Needles usually longer than 1 inch (but can be misleading). Cones grayish green, 7 to 12 cm long. Bracts of the cone scales with a short triangular tip—***Abies concolor*** (white fir)

2. Young stems hairy. Needles usually shorter than 1 inch. Cones dark brown/purple, 5 to 10 cm long. Bracts of the cone scale long with sublated tip. Native to higher elevations—***Abies lasiocarpa*** or ***Abies bifolia*** (subalpine fir)

Key to *Picea* (Spruce)

1. Needles very stiff, sharp, ¾ to 1½ inch long, often bluish, pointing outwards from stem. Stems not hairy. Cones 2½ inches to 4 inches long. Cone scales papery, furrowed, pointed/ragged. Bark black to dark grey furrowed. Native, generally below 9,000 feet elevation—***Picea pungens*** (Colorado spruce)

2. Needles somewhat blunt, not as stiff or sharp, pointed toward end of twig. Young stems somewhat hairy. Cones less than 2½ inches long. Cone scales rounded. Bark smooth, with purplish-brown to russet red scales on mature trees. Native—***Picea englemannii*** (Englemann spruce)

3. Needles ¼ to ½ inch long. Each branch very short (2 to 4 inches long). Landscape shrub—***Picea glauca*** 'Conica', (dwarf Alberta spruce)

Key to *Pinus* (Pine)

1. Two needles per bundle

   a. Needles ½ to 1¾ inches long, curved, medium green with white lines, some resin droplets. Cones small, rough, without prickles on scale. Seeds large (pine nuts). Shrubby tree. Native to the plateaus and mesas—***Pinus edulis*** (pinon pine)

   b. Needles 1 to 2 inches long, finely toothed, slightly twisted, curved, dark green, persisting 5 or more years. Branches out abruptly from trunk base, central leader not obvious, more shrub-like—***Pinus mugo*** (mugo pine)

   c. Needles 1 to 3 inches long, yellowish-green, slightly twisted. Cones small, less than 2 inches long, hard, one-sided with prickled tips on scales. Branches slender, slightly flexible. Bark scaly, not becoming platy. Native in dense forest stands in higher elevations—***Pinus contorta*** (lodgepole pine)

   d. Needles 1½ to 3 inches long, twisted, persistent 2 to 4 years. Cones 1½ inches long, scatter throughout the tree, without prickles on the scales. Older bark orange—**Pinus sylvestris (Scotch pine, Scots pine)**

   e. Needles 3 to 6 inches long, stiff, dark green, dense on the branch, persisting 4 or more years. Cones 2 to 3 inches long with small prickles on scales. Buds whitish. Older bark dark gray, furrowed—***Pinus nigra*** (Austrian pine)

2. Two and three needles per bundle, 3 to 10 inches long, medium green, crowded at end of branches on older trees, persisting 3 years. Cones 3 to 5 inches long, armed with sharp prickles on scales. Bark furrowed, eventually breaking into reddish plates. Native from outer foothills to subalpine regions—*Pinus ponderosa* (ponderosa pine)

3. Five needles per bundle—**White pines**

   a. White resin dots scattered on dark green needles, 1 to 1½ inches (25 to 38 mm) long. Cone scales long, sharp prickles. Native to higher elevations—***Pinus aristata*** (bristlecone pine)

   b. Needles 1 to 3 inches long, rigid, dark green, often clustered near branch ends, margins smooth, pointing forward, persist for 5 to 6 years. Cones 4 to 8 inches long on short stalk, with no prickles on scales. Branches very flexible. Bark silvery white to light gray. Small tree with irregular trunk and branching pattern. Native to higher elevation and high plains, often on open sites—***Pinus flexilis*** (limber pine)

   c. Needles 2 to 5 inches long, blue-green, very soft, thin, margin-toothed, persistent 2 years. Branches green-brown. Cones 3 to 8 inches long with 1-inch long stalk. Cone scales thin; do not bend back—***Pinus strobus*** (eastern white pine)

   d. Needles with a few small teeth near tip, not as soft as eastern white pine. Branchlets yellow-brown or red-brown. Cones are short-stalked. Cone scales bend back. Tall tree with straight, unbranched trunks. Native to San Juan Mountains. Sangre de Cristo and Rampart ranges—***Pinus strobiformis*** (southwestern white pine)

Key to *Thuja* (Arborvitae)

1. Foliage in vertical plate-like displays—***Thuja orientalis*** (oriental arborvitae)

2. Foliage in horizontal plate-like displays—***Thuja occidentalis,*** American (eastern arborvitae)

IDENTIFYING BROADLEAF FLOWERING TREES AND SHRUBS

Identification of broadleaf trees and shrubs is a skill mastered with practice and knowledge of the plant families. Most trees and shrubs can be readily identified to family and genus with a basic knowledge of the plant's characteristics and the use of a key. There are always a few exceptions with plants that do not look like their relatives. Identification to a specific epithet requires more skill and a closer look at plant characteristics. Identification to variety and cultivar is difficult to impossible, as the defining characteristics may not be clearly observable from plant samples. Most keys start with leaf arrangement and shape.

Leaf Characteristics

Arrangement on Stem (Figure 26-5)

- **Alternate**—Arranged in staggered fashion along stem (willow)

- **Opposite**—Pair of leaves arranged across from each other on stem (maple)

- **Whorled**—Arranged in a ring (catalpa)

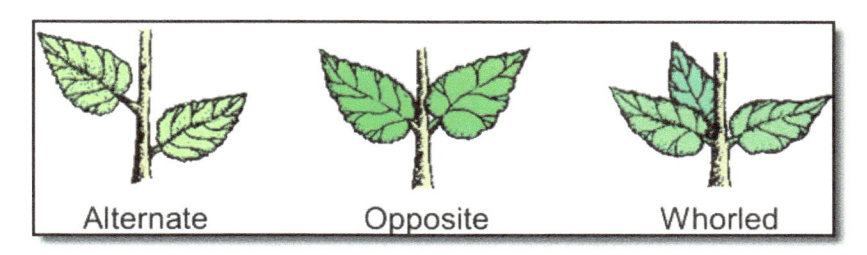

Figure 26-5 ▮ *Leaf arrangement on stem.*

Leaflet Arrangement on Petiole (Figure 26-6)

- **Simple**—Leaf blade is one continuous unit (cherry, maple, and elm)

- **Compound**—Several **leaflets** arise from the same petiole

  —**Pinnately compound**—Leaflets arranged on both sides of a common rachis (leaf stalk), like a feather (mountain ash)

  —**Palmately compound**—Leaflets radiate from one central point (Ohio buckeye and horse chestnut)

  —**Double pinnately compound**—Double set of compound leaflets

Note: Sometimes identifying a "leaf" or "leaflet" can be confusing. Look at the petiole attachment. A leaf petiole attaches to the stem at a bud node. There is no bud node where leaflets attach to the petiole.

Figure 26-6 ▮ *Leaflet arrangement on petiole.*

Venation (Figure 26-7)

- **Pinnately** veined leaves have a central vein down the center with veinlets branching off and extending to the edge (elm, peach, and linden).

- **Palmately** veined leaves radiate veinlets out in a fan-shaped pattern from a central point at the petiole (leaf stem) (maple, mulberry, and poplar).

Leaf Shape

Leaf shape is a primary tool in plant identification. Descriptions often go into minute detail about general leaf shape and the shape of the leaf apex and base. There

Figure 26-7 ▪ *Leaf venation.*

is no magic line where one type suddenly becomes another type; it is a judgment call. When using keys, look at several leaves and be flexible in your description. The following are common shapes as used in the *Manual of Woody Landscape Plants* by Michael A. Dirr (Figures 26-8 to 26-11).

Leaf Surface Texture

Look at all the surfaces, noting location, color, density, and length of scales and hairs. In addition to terms previously discussed, the following terms are commonly encountered when describing leaves:

- **Ciliate**—Orderly, widely spaced hairs along the edge (margin), also called fringed

- **Glandular**—Hairs bearing glands

- **Glutinous**—Sticky to the touch

- **Scabrous**—Hairs very short

- **Stellate**—Star-shaped hair (needs magnification)

- **Velutinous**—Dense hairs of equal height, like velvet

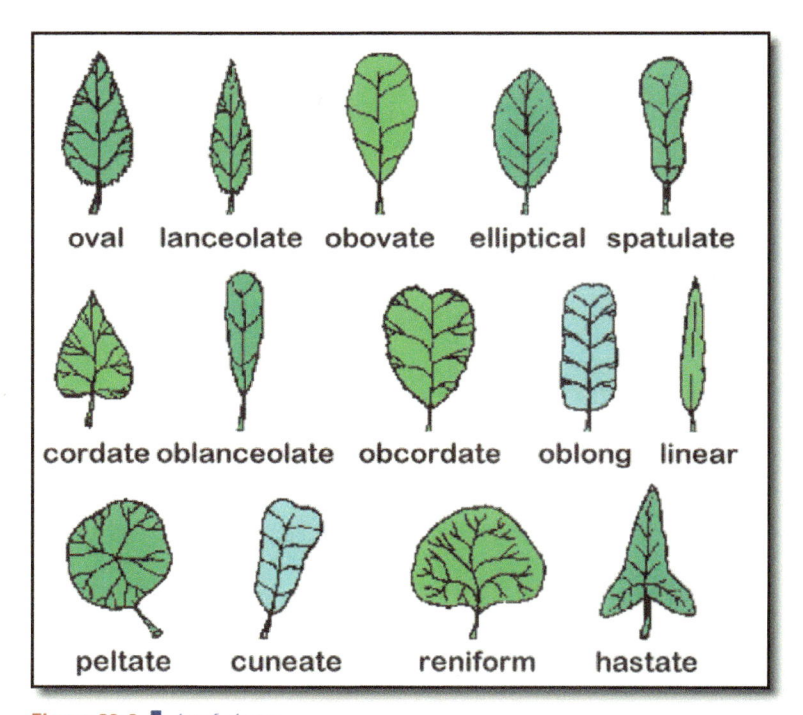

Figure 26-8 ▪ *Leaf shape.*

Stem Characteristics

Stems contain several features important to identifying plants. Cut into the stem to see the pith. Look at the epidermis, buds, arrangement of the nodes, and any surface coating or texture. For winter identification of woody plants, look at the pattern of the scales on the terminal and lateral buds and the shape of the leaf scars.

Bud Type

The type of bud is also used in plant identification. Figure 26-12 illustrates bud types used in the *Manual of Woody Landscape Plants*.

Leaf Scar and Bundle Scar Shape (Figure 26-13)

Leaf scar—Mark left on stem where leaf was attached. The shape of the leaf scar is often used in woody plant identification.

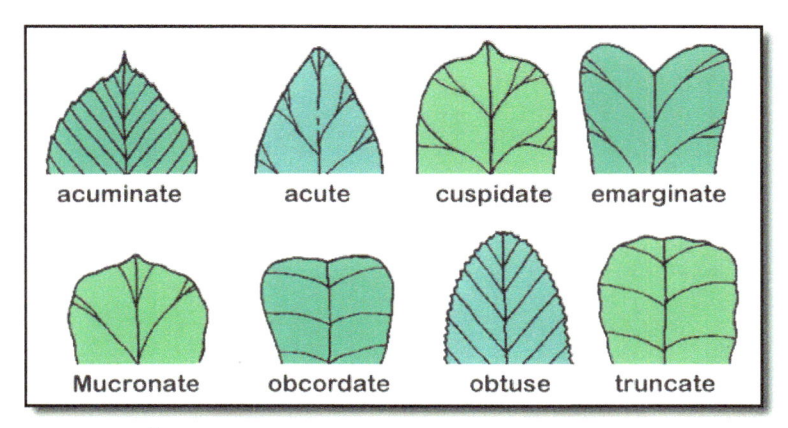

Figure 26-9 ▮ *Tip shape.*

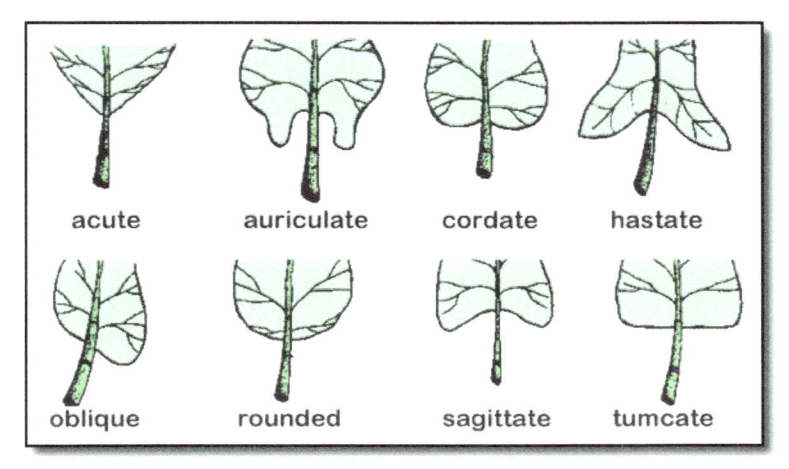

Figure 26-10 ▮ *Base shape.*

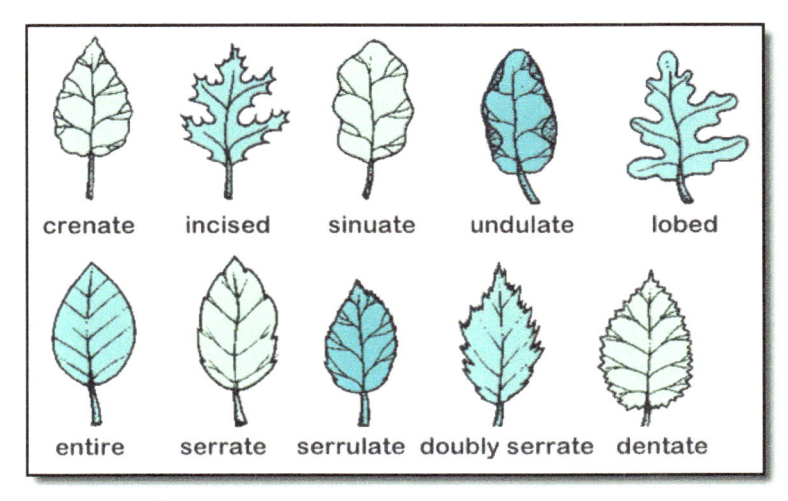

Figure 26-11 ▮ *Leaf margin.*

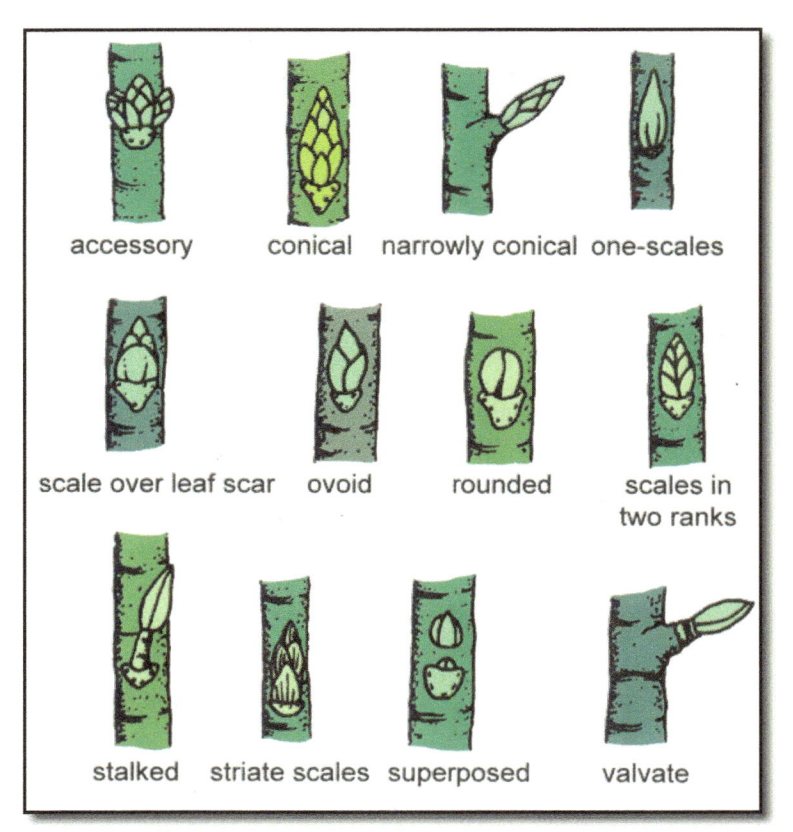

Figure 26-12 ▍ *Bud type.*

Bundle scar—Marks left in the leaf scar from the vascular tissue attachment. The shape of the bundle scar is often used in woody plant identification.

Stem Surface Texture

The surface of woody twigs may have a texture that can be used to distinguish one plant from another. Terms used to describe the surfaces of stems can also apply to leaves.

- **Farinose**—Covered with a mealy, powdery substance

- **Glabrous**—Smooth

- **Glaucous**—Having a bloom or whitish covering, often waxy

- **Hirsute**—Covered with coarse, stiff hairs, rough enough to break the skin

- **Pubescent**—Covered with hairs

- **Scurfy**—Covered with small scales

- **Tomentose**—Covered with short, matted or tangled, soft, wooly hairs

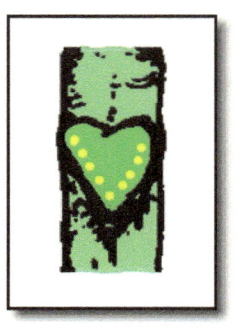

Figure 26-13 ▍
Heart-shaped leaf scar with v-shaped bundle scar inside.

Internal Stem Features

Pith is the tissue found at the center of stems and roots. Pith characteristics may provide identification clues. A diagonal cut across the stem reveals if the center of the stem is hollow or if the pith is solid or chambered. A straight cut across the stem reveals the shape of the pith (rounded, star or triangle) (Figure 26-14).

Fruit Characteristics

Generally, the identification of trees and shrubs is done without fruit, as the fruit is only around for a short season. However,

Figure 26-14 ■ *Internal stem features used in plant identification.*

when fruit is present, it can be a tool in plant identification. For example, double samaras indicate maples.

Examples of Fruit Found on Trees and Shrubs

1. **Simple fruit**—Fruit formed from one ovary

   A. Dry fruit

      1) Dehiscent fruits (splitting open when mature)

         a) **Capsule**—Many seeded fruits formed from more than one united carpels. Examples include *Deutzia* (deutzia), *Forsythia* (forsythia), *Philadelphus* (mockoranage), *Rhododendron* (rhododendron), and *Syringa* (lilac) (Figure 26-15).

         b) **Follicle**—Composed of one carpel but splits open at maturity along one suture exposing seeds. Examples include *Spiraea* (spiraea) and individual fruit of magnolia.

         c) **Legume** (pod)—Composed of one carpel that splits open along two sutures (like a pea pod). Characteristics of most members of the *Fabaceae* (*Leguminosae*) family. Examples include *Albizia* (silktree, mimosa), *Cercis* (redbud), *Gleditsia* (honeylocust), *Gymnocladus* (Kentucky coffeetree), Laburnum (goldenchain tree), and Robina (locust) (Figure 26-16).

      2) Indehiscent fruits (not splitting open at maturity)

         a) **Achene**—One-seeded fruit with seed attached at only one place to the pericarp. Pericarp is very close-fitted and does not split open, at least along regular established lines. Examples include *Calycanthus* (sweetshrub), *Chimonanthus* (wintersweet), and *Rosa* (rose and sunflower) (Figure 26-17).

         b) **Samara**—One- or two-seeded with a membranous wing. Examples include *Acer* (maples—double winged), *Fraxinus* (ash—single-winged), and *Ulmus* (elm—small, single-winged fruit) (Figure 26-18).

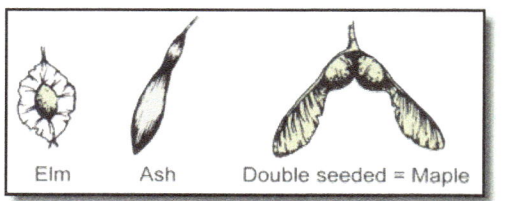

Figure 26-18 ■ *Samara of elm, ash, and maple.*

Figure 26-15 ■ *Capsule.*

Figure 26-16 ■ *Legume or pod.*

Figure 26-17 ■ *Achene of sunflower seed.*

c) **Nut**—A bony, hard, one-seeded fruit. Examples include *Castanea* (chestnut), *Corylus* (filbert), *Juglans* (walnut), and *Quercus* (oak) (Figure 26-19).

d) **Nutlet**—A tiny nut. Examples include *Betula* (birch), *Carpinus* (hornbean), and *Ostrya* (hophornbean).

B. Fleshy fruits

1) **Berry**—The entire pericarp is fleshy. Examples include tomato, *Lonicera* (honeysuckle), and *Vaccinium* (blueberry and cranberry).

2) **Drupe**—The pericarp is clearly differentiated into three layers; the exocarp is the epidermis; mesocarp (middle layer) is fleshy; and the endocarp (inner layer) is stony. Examples include ilex, *Prunus* (cherry, peach, and plum), *Sassafras* (sassafras), *Viburnum* (viburnum), and numerous other woody plants (Figure 26-20).

3) **Pome**—The pericarp is surrounded by the floral tube that become the fleshy edible fruit. Examples include *Malus* (apple), *Pyrus* (pear), and *Chaenomeles* (quince) (Figure 26-21).

2. **Aggregate fruits**—Develop from a single flower that contains many pistils. Several of the fruits are massed on one receptacle. Examples include the following:

- *Fragaria* (strawberry)—Aggregate of achenes

- *Liriodendron* (tuliptree) –Aggregate of samaras

- *Maclura* (osage-orange)—Aggregate of drupes

- *Magnolia* (magnolia)—Aggregate of follicles

- *Rubus* (raspberry)—Aggregate of drupes

3. **Multiple fruits**—Consists of several flowers that are more or less united into one mass. Examples include *Morus* (mulberry) and pineapples.

Online Identification Keys to Landscape Trees

- *Key to Common Landscape Trees and Shrubs of Colorado,* CMG GardenNotes #156 at www.cmg.colostate.edu/TreeID/156.html

- *What Tree Is This?* National Arbor Day Foundation, at www.arborday.org/trees/index-identification.cfm

Figure 26-19 ▮ *Nut: Oak acorn.*

Figure 26-20 ▮ *Drupe: Peach.*

Figure 26-21 ▮ *Pome: apple.*

Characteristics of Common Woody Plant Families with Opposite Leaf Arrangement on Stem

Family	Genera	Typical Leaf Shape	Noteworthy Flowers and Fruit
Aceraceae Maples family	• *Acer*—Maple and box elder	• Simple and palmately veined and lobed • Pinnately compound and pinnately veined • Simple and pinnately veined	• Fruit: Two-winged samaras
Caprifoliaceae Honeysuckle family	• *Lonicera*—Honeysuckle • *Sambucus*—Elders • *Symphoricarpos*—Snowberry, coralberry, and buckbrush • *Viburnum*—Viburnum	• Simple, pinnately veined • Simple and palmately veined and lobed • Pinnately compound • Leaves lacking stipules	• Fruit: Usually fleshy and berry-like
Oleaceae Olive family	• *Forsythia*—Forsythia • *Fraxinum*—Ash • *Ligustrum*—Privet • *Syringa*—Lilac	• Simple, pinnately veined • Pinnately compound (ash) • Without stipules	• Flowers: Often fused petals form a corolla tube • Fruit: Berry, drupe, or capsule • Ash has single-winged samara
Cornaceae Dogwood family	• *Cornus*—Dogwood	• Simple, pinnately veined	• Fruit: Drupe
Hippocastanaceae Horsechestnut family	• *Aesulus*—Horsechestnut and buckeye	• Palmately compound	• Flower: Often a showy cone of flowers • Fruit: Nut-like capsule

Characteristics of Common Woody Plant Families with Alternate Leaf Arrangement on Stem

Family	Genera	Typical Leaf Shape	Noteworthy Flowers and Fruit
Betulaceae Birch family	• *Alnus*—Alder • *Betula*—Birch	• Simple, pinnately veined	• Flowers: Male and female catkins • Fruit: Nutlet
Fabaceae Pea family	• *Cercis*—Redbud • *Caragana*—Peashrub • *Gleditsia*—Honeylocust • *Gymnocladus*—Kentucky coffee • *Sophora*—Pagodatree	• Simple, palmately veined • Pinnately compound • Bipinnately compound	• Fruit: Pea-like pod
Fagaceae Oak and beech family	• *Castanea*—Chestnut • *Fagus*—Beech • *Quercus*—Oak	• Simple, pinnately veined • Simple, pinnately veined and pinnately lobed	• Flowers: Catkin • Fruit: Nut (acorn)
Juglandaceae Walnut family	• *Juglans*—Walnut	• Pinnately compound	• Fruit: Nut

Moraceae Mulberry family	• *Morus*—Mulberry	• Simple and polymorphic (lobed and unlobed)	• Fruit: Multiple drupe
Platanaceae Sycamore family	• *Platanus*—Planetree and sycamore	• Simple, palmately veined and lobed	
Rosaceae Rose family	• *Amelancheir*—Serviceberry • *Aronia*—Chokecherry • *Cercocarpus*—Mountain mahogany • *Chaenomeles*—Quince • *Cotoneaster*—Cotoneaster • *Crataegus*—Hawthorne • *Fallugia*—Apache plume • *Fragaria*—Strawberry • *Kerria*—Kerria • *Malus*—Crabapple • *Physocarpus*—Ninebark • *Potentilla*—Potentilla • *Prunus*—Almond, apricot, cherry, peach, and plum • *Pyrus*—Pear • *Ribes*—Alpine currant • *Rosa*—Rose • *Rubus*—Blackberry and raspberry • *Sorbus*—Mountain ash • *Spiraea*—Spiraea	• Simple, pinnately veined • Simple, lobed • Pinnately compound • Palmately compound • Pair of stipules (leaf-like appendage) common where leaf stalk joins stem; stems often have thorns or spines	
Salicaceae Willow family	• *Populus*—Aspen, poplar, and cottonwood • *Salix*—Willow	• Simple • Simple and palmately lobed • Stipules at leaf base	• Fruit: Tiny, often catkin • Seeds wind dispersed with the aid of long hairs
Sapidaceae Soapberry family	• *Koelreuteria*—Raintree	• Pinnately or bipinnately compound	• Flowers: Large panicles of yellow flowers
Tiliaceae Linden family	• *Tilia*—Linden	• Simple	
Ulmaceae Elm family	• *Celtis*—Hackberry • *Ulmus*—Elm	• Simple, pinnately veined	• Elm fruit small samara with disc-shaped wing

CHAPTER REVIEW
Questions

1. What is the difference between a variety and a cultivar? Research for and name two plant varieties found in the plant trade; name two cultivars.

2. Why is Latin used for all scientific plant names?

3. Why is it important to try to use scientific names whenever possible? What challenges are there with using common names?

4. What important tools do you need in order to do plant identification?

5. Briefly explain how a plant identification key is used.

6. When using some plant keys, you must know if the plant is *evergreen* or *deciduous*. What do these terms mean?

7. What is the difference between *opposite* and *alternate* leaf arrangement? Name three trees/shrubs that have opposite and alternate leaf arrangements.

8. Define the terms *legume*, *samara*, and *pome*. Give examples of plants that bear these types of fruit.

9. If you are unsure if the sample you are identifying is a leaf or leaflet, what key feature should you look for on the branch?

Tree Selection and Placement

Right Plant, Right Place

The average life of a tree in the landscape is only eight years due to poor design and planting techniques. Homeowners and landscape designers often place trees in situations where trees have little chance to establish and thrive. Successful tree planting and establishment need attention in these five areas:

- Functional design

- Plant selection

- Pre-plant handling

- Planting techniques

- Post-planting care

TREE PLACEMENT IN LANDSCAPE DESIGN

In landscape design, placement of trees needs careful consideration to function and design elements. Trees are typically the major plant structure in a landscape. Trees give architectural form and organization to space.

In landscape design, trees should not be randomly placed around the property. Rather, place trees as specimens, group plantings, or mass plantings.

Specimen trees—The individual tree becomes the landscape feature. It is set off from other trees and plant materials by unique spacing, form, color, and/or texture. Specimen trees are often, but not always, a focal point in the design.

---

*Author: David Whiting, Colorado State University Extension. Artwork by David Whiting.

Group plantings—In group plantings, the trees *as a unit* become the landscape feature. Groupings are often, but not always, the same species. In group plantings, do not mix contrasting forms.

Mass plantings—In mass plantings, individual trees lose identity and appear as one larger unit in the design. A group planting may grow into a mass planting as trees mature.

Trees serve several key roles in landscape design. They often define space. Their spreading branches create a canopy that forms a ceiling for an outdoor room. Because we spend a lot of time indoors, people are more comfortable with this outdoor ceiling effect (Figure 27-1).

Trees are used to frame and mask views. Vertical views are effectively framed with trees on both sides. The yard should flow into the view. Avoid specimen plants that draw attention away from the view.

Figure 27-1 ▮ *Trees create a comfortable outdoor living space with their "ceiling effect."*

When framing a house, consider trees in front and to the sides as well as trees that can be viewed over the roofline. For framing, use the point of reference from which most people would view the house rather than straight on (Figure 27-2).

TREES AND ENERGY CONSERVATION

Tree placement can play a significant role in energy conservation. Winter sun entering south-facing windows can effectively heat many homes. Summer shade on south- and west-facing windows provides summer cooling.

In evaluating shading and heating patterns, be aware that shade patterns change with the season and with the latitude (Figure 27-3).

Figure 27-2 ▮ *When framing a house, consider how others would look at the home rather than straight on.*

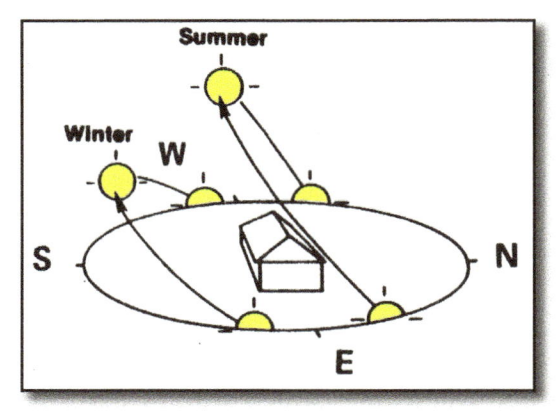

Figure 27-3 ▮ *The shade pattern changes with the season and with latitude.*

Maximizing Winter Solar Heating

Homes with south-facing windows have a great potential to capture winter solar heat.

In the winter, deciduous tree branches intercept twenty to fifty-five percent of the sun's radiation. For winter energy conservation, avoid placing trees where they would shade the windows in the winter, and open drapes to allow the sun's energy into the home. Winter shade patterns are large, approximately two and a half times the mature height of the tree at Colorado latitudes (Figure 27-4).

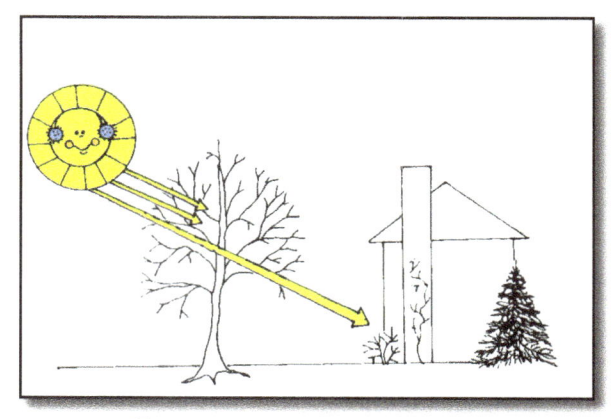

Figure 27-4 ▮ *For homes with south-facing windows, tree placement can compromise winter heating potential.*

Maximizing Summer Cooling

In the summer, trees block seventy to ninety percent of the sun's radiation on a clear summer day. When properly placed, trees can reduce air conditioning demands by ten to thirty percent. Along the Colorado high plains and mountain communities, where temperatures typically cool in the evening, shading a home may adequately moderate temperatures without the expense of air conditioning (Figure 27-5).

Evapotranspiration accounts for seventy to eighty percent of the cooling benefit. Under dry conditions (including water restrictions that prohibit landscape irrigation), evapotranspiration shuts down, photosynthesis stops (trees live off carbohydrate reserves), and the cooling effect is reduced. Community temperatures may rise significantly when landscape irrigation restrictions prohibit outdoor watering.

Figure 27-5 ▮ *Carefully placed trees can reduce home cooling costs by ten to thirty percent..*

Shading the House

In shading the house, there is a two- to three-hour lag time on sun heat hitting the house and the house becoming extremely hot. Shading priorities at Colorado latitudes include the following:

1. Shade windows on south and west
2. Shade south walls
3. Shade west walls
4. Shade air-conditioning units

Shading Pavement

As illustrated in Figure 27-6, a paved area stores approximately 50% of the sun's energy. In comparison, a grass area only stores 5% of the energy and uses 50% for evapotranspiration, resulting in a cooling effect. This cooling effect is only operational when the grass has water for active growth.

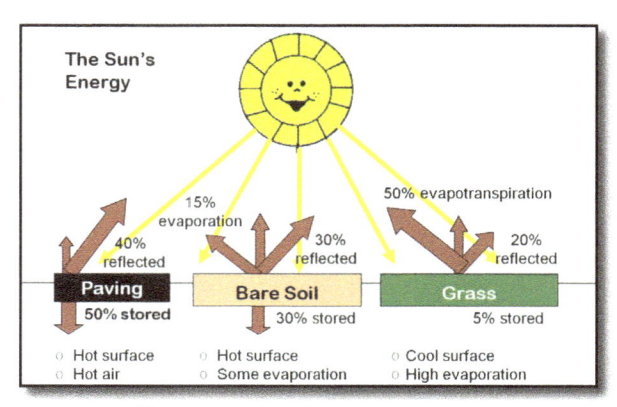

Figure 27-6 ▮ *The sun's energy.*

Another important cooling technique is to shade pavement and other heat-storing materials like the patio and driveway. Also, minimizing paved surfaces helps keep the living area cool (Figure 27-7).

Trees and other plant materials may also be used to shield the living space from stored and reflected heat (Figure 27-8).

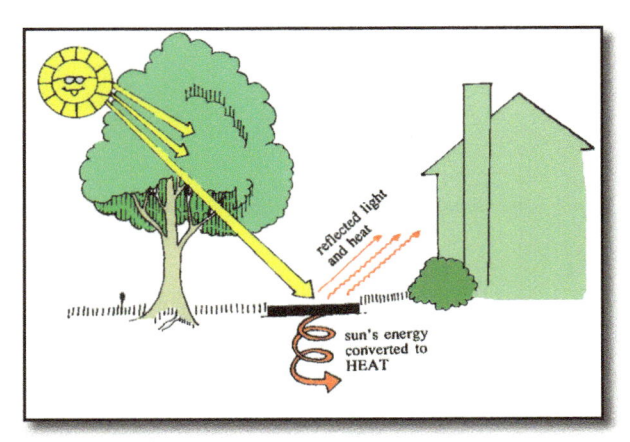

Figure 27-7 ▮ *For cooling, shade heat-storing areas and minimize heat-storing surfaces.*

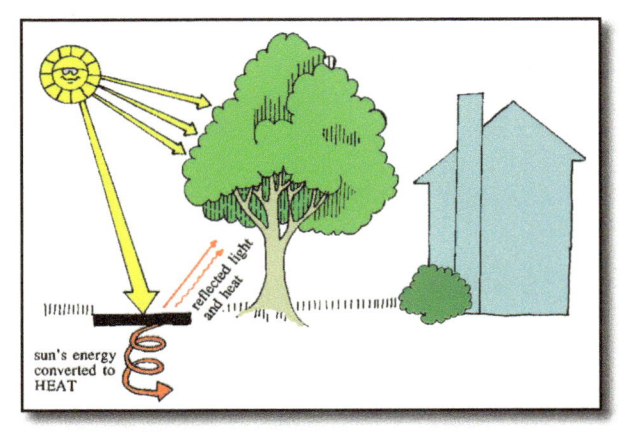

Figure 27-8 ▮ *Use trees to cool the air between the heat-storing surface and living space.*

Shading Streets

Older communities with tree-lined streets are noted for the pleasing, inviting surroundings that street trees create. Shaded streets are 10°F to 40°F cooler.

However, street trees are often predisposed to poor growth and limited life spans due to poor soil conditions. Tree roots can generally spread under a sidewalk into open lawn areas beyond. Root spread under a street is dependent on the soil properties created during road construction.

When the planting strip between the street and sidewalk is less than eight feet wide, tree health, vigor, and life span will be reduced. In most communities, planting strip width is set by the city ordinance in effect at the time of development.

An effective alternative for tree-lined streets is to plant trees in the lawn eight feet in from the street. This may give trees a better soil environment for root growth, resulting in improved tree vigor, growth, and longevity. In this situation, trees are also less likely to be hit by cars or damaged from road repairs. Eliminating the narrow planting area between the street and sidewalk is also an important water conservation technique as the "mow strip" is difficult to irrigate efficiently.

NOISE ABATEMENT WITH TREES AND SHRUBS

Tree and shrub hedgerows (planting belts) effectively abate noise pollution. To be most effective, place the hedgerow close to the noise source away from the living area. The hedgerow should be twice as long as the distance from the noise source to the living space. To be effective, the hedgerow needs to be dense. A few trees and shrubs here and there do little to abate noise (Figure 27-9).

Figure 27-9 ▮ *For effective noise abatement, place plant belt next to noise source rather than adjacent to the home.*

OTHER ENVIRONMENTAL BENEFITS OF TREES

In a study by the U.S. Department of Agriculture Forest Service, the 16,000 street trees in Fort Collins, Colorado, contribute $2.2 million in environmental benefits. The community forest has many important benefits, including:

- Energy saving from heating and cooling

- Noise abatement

- Carbon dioxide reduction—In a Sacramento, California, study, the carbon sequestration from the community forest more than offsets the inputs from human activity

- Air-pollution abatement

- Hydrology (stormwater runoff)

- Property values

The U.S. Department of Agriculture Forest Service evaluated the benefits of community forests. For each dollar that a city invests in a community tree program, large trees return $1.92 in environmental benefits. Medium-size trees return $1.36, while small trees return $1.00.

To maximize environmental benefits, the goal in community forestry is to have fifty percent of the land covered with tree canopy. That is, if we were to look down from an airplane, trees would cover fifty percent of the area. Here in the West, we have a great need to plant more trees in our communities. In wooded communities, the need may be to thin the forest.

To maximize the benefits of our community forests, homeowners and community leaders need to recognize that the primary benefits occur from large trees. We need to enhance efforts to protect and maintain large trees. We need to plan for large trees in landscape design. Small specimen trees may add to the landscape design, but large trees provide significantly more environmental benefits. We need to plant trees in situations where they have the potential to reach a mature size with longevity.

GROWING SPACE

Size is a primary consideration in tree selection. Trees should fit in the available growing space without pruning. This is of primary concern under utility lines as the utility has the right of way. Frequent pruning required to keep utility lines clear adds to our utility rates.

As discussed previously, environmental benefits are significantly greater for larger trees. Consider large tree species whenever the space allows. With proper structural training, large trees have minimal potential for storm and wind damage.

Homeowners often desire fast-growing trees. However, fast-growing species are typically more prone to insects, diseases, and internal decay. Fast-growing species typically have shorter life spans.

ROOTING SPACE

Rooting space should be a primary consideration in tree selection. The mature size, growth rate, and longevity of a tree are directly related to the available rooting space. Many trees in the landscape are predisposed at planting to a short life and limited growth potential due to poor soil conditions and limited rooting space.

Figure 27-10 shows the relationship between root space and ultimate tree size. For example, a tree with a sixteen-inch diameter

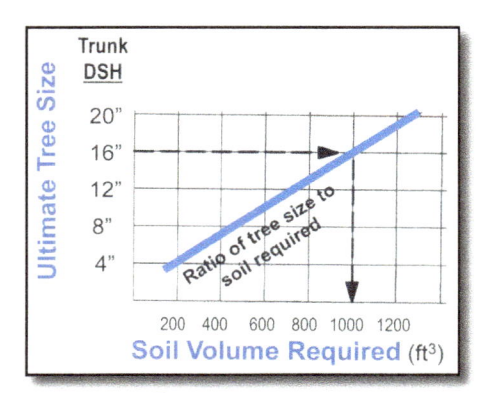

Figure 27-10 ■ *Ultimate tree size is set by the rooting space.*

requires 1,000 cubic feet of soil. On a compacted, clayey soil, rooting depth may be restricted to one foot or less, and spread would be an area thirty-six feet in diameter. Anything less will reduce tree size, growth rates, vigor, and longevity.

Tree roots can generally cross under a sidewalk to open lawn areas beyond. The ability of roots to cross under a street depends on the road base properties. A good road base does not typically support root growth due to compaction and low soil oxygen levels.

The rooting area does not need to be rounded; it can be about any shape. Trees can share rooting space.

Trees in Planters

Trees are often placed in planters and other sites with limited rooting potential. If the roots cannot escape the planting site (root vault) into other soils:

1. Root growth slows when the root vault area is filled

2. Tree growth slows

3. Tree declines

4. Routine replacement is required

The average life of trees in sidewalk planters and other restricted root vault sites is eight years. Home gardener and landscape designers need to understand that with restricted rooting space, growth potential and longevity are reduced accordingly.

SPECIES SELECTION

In any region, Cooperative Extensions and many cities have lists of suggested trees and shrubs for the region. Many species of trees and shrubs are well suited to Colorado landscapes. Colorado State University Extension publications listing trees and shrubs for Colorado, include the following (Extension publications available at www.cmg.colostate.edu):

- *Deciduous Shrubs*, #7.415
- *Evergreen Shrubs*, #7.414
- *Evergreen Trees*, #7.403
- *Front Range Tree Recommendation List*
- *Hedges*, #7.208
- *Large Deciduous Trees for Street and Shade*, #7.419
- *Native Shrubs for Colorado Landscapes*, #7.422
- *Native Trees for Colorado Landscapes*, #7.421
- *Shrubs for Mountain Communities*, #7.407
- *Small Deciduous Trees*, #7.418
- *Trees and Shrubs for Mountain Areas*, #7.423
- *Xeriscaping: Trees and Shrubs*, #7.229

In addition, many communities and nurseries have tree lists for local areas. Some communities have small arboretums in local parks where a variety of trees may be viewed.

In selecting trees for a home landscape, remember that there is no perfect tree. All trees have good and bad characteristics. Select trees based on site considerations as well as personal likes.

The best advice for selecting trees is to intentionally plant a diversity of species in the neighborhood and community. Avoid frequent use of only a few tree species as this increases the likelihood of insect and disease problems. Dutch elm disease spread through the United States due to the over-planting of elm trees. Ash trees became a common replacement for elms. Now the lilac/ash borer is commonplace. Currently, honeylocust is very popular, and pest problems on honeylocust are becoming common. Aspen is popular along the Colorado Front Range. While native to our mountains, it is not native to the high plains and has many problems in irrigated yards along Front Range communities.

Mature Size

Size is a primary consideration in tree selection. Trees should fit in the available growing space without pruning. This is of primary concern under utility lines as the utility has the right of way.

Because large trees give a higher return in environmental benefits, plant large tree species whenever the space allows. Large trees can be structurally strong if attention is given to structural training while young.

Growth Rates

Homeowners often desire fast-growing trees. However, fast-growing species are typically more prone to insects, diseases, and internal decay. Fast-growing species typically have shorter life spans.

Soil Considerations

Suitable rooting space is a major limiting factor in tree growth. Poor soil conditions contribute to eighty percent of tree health issues. Unfortunately, many homeowners and landscape designers fail to consider soil limitations in tree selection and planting. Impacts of poor soil conditions include:

- Many trees fail to establish or are slow to establish
- Growth rates will be reduced
- Tree vigor will be low, predisposing trees to insects, diseases, and other stress factors
- Mature size will be smaller
- Longevity will be shorter

Soil texture, structure, and tilth are considerations in tree selection. Some trees perform poorly in compacted or clayey soils (due to low soil oxygen levels). On compacted or clayey soils, drainage can be a limiting factor. Reference books often list trees that are "flooding or compaction tolerant" as an indication of trees more tolerant of low soil oxygen and more adaptable to compacted or clayey soils. Other trees do poorly in dry sandy soils (due to drought).

If the soil has free lime, iron chlorosis is a common problem for some species of trees in heavily irrigated lawns. Avoid planting species susceptible to iron chlorosis (like silver maple and aspen) in this situation (Figure 27-11).

Water Needs and Tolerances

Water needs and tolerances are primary considerations in light of Colorado's drought cycle. Gardeners need to understand that the water needed to maintain life is unrelated to the water needed for tree growth. Drought tolerance for any tree changes with the life cycle of the tree. Trees listed as drought-tolerant may not be suitable to extremely dry sites or prolonged water stress.

Figure 27-11 ▮ *Iron chlorosis (yellowing of younger leaves with veins remaining green) on aspen.*

Scientists cannot yet answer the common question, "How many gallons of water does this tree need?" At best, listing of trees more tolerant of dryer sites is only observational based on routine dry spells, not extreme drought situations.

Another common issue about tree selection is tolerance to wet soils. Due to poor irrigation system design, maintenance, and management, most home lawns are significantly over-watered. Some trees, such as crabapples and aspen, are rather intolerant of the excessive irrigation.

Management Concerns

Common management issues are a consideration in tree selection.

Pruning—Trees with a decurrent growth habit are more prone to storm and wind damage. Damage potential can be minimized if the trees are structurally trained while young.

Common insect and disease problems should be a consideration. What are the common pests of the tree? Which are only cosmetic, and which can affect tree health? How tolerant are you of cosmetic pests? Under what situations would management efforts become warranted? What is your interest and willingness to make pest management efforts?

For example, stressed ash trees are highly susceptible to the lilac/ash borer that may kill trees. For gardeners unwilling to routinely treat for borers, ash would be a poor choice, particularly on a site with limited rooting area. Aspen are highly susceptible to poplar twig gall when planted in a heavily irrigated lawn. If you do not like this cosmetic damage, do not plant aspen in routinely irrigated sites. Honeylocust are highly susceptible to the honeylocust spider mite (which can defoliate the tree midsummer) when planted on dry sites or with restricted rooting areas. If you are not willing to treat for spider mites, do not plant honeylocust on dry sites or those with restricted rooting areas.

Other maintenance factors include:

- Fruiting habit
- Leaf litter nuisance
- Seed germination
- Root and basal suckering

Climatic Adaptation

Exposure to sun, wind, heat, and cold are considerations in tree selection. Issues related to winter hardiness and winter burn can be reduced with winter watering on susceptible species.

Hardiness zones are an indication of the expected minimum low winter temperature. However, in Colorado, we occasionally have an extremely cold winter that challenges the hardiness zone data as we approach record lows.

Hardiness (the ability of a plant to withstand cold) comes from many interrelated factors:

Photoperiod and genetics—The length of night (photoperiod) is the first signal trees receive that winter is approaching. When parent materials are collected from the south and then moved north, they may not be adapted to the differences in photoperiod, and winter damage may be more pronounced. Growers are becoming aware of this important issue in selection of nursery stock.

Minimum temperatures that trees tolerate are set by the plants' genetics and influenced by recent temperatures.

Recent temperatures—A tree's tolerance to cold is heavily influenced by the temperature patterns of the previous few days. When temperatures gradually drop over a period of weeks, trees are generally tolerant of extreme cold. However, trees are less tolerant of extreme cold when it appears suddenly following moderate temperatures.

Rapid temperature change is a primary factor limiting our plant selection. In Colorado, it is common to have a spring thaw followed by an "arctic express" back to winter. Temperatures readily drop more than 50°F in an hour.

Water—Woody plants going into winter with dry soil conditions lose approximately 20°F in hardiness. Colorado's dry fall and winter weather reduces plant hardiness. Fall watering, after leaves drop but before soils freeze, helps minimize hardiness issues.

Wind exposure is another factor reducing hardiness in open areas of the high plains. Winter watering helps manage this issue.

Exposure to sun, including reflected sun from snow or structures, contributes to winter bark injury and frost cracks.

Carbohydrate reserves—Plants under stress, with lower carbohydrate reserves, are more susceptible to winter damage. For example, during the drought of 2002 to 2004, Colorado trees experienced extensive winter injury related to stress, even without extreme cold.

Microclimates—The typical yard has dryer and wetter sites, windy and less windy areas, and warmer and cooler areas. These microclimates may create a site that is more or less suitable for some specific plants.

Other Selection Criteria

- Potential damage to hardscapes (sidewalks, gutters, etc.) from root growth
- Utility right of ways for above-ground and below-ground utilities
- Vandalism in public access sites
- Car damage along streets
- Turf competition and herbicide use
- Pesticide drift from adjacent properties
- De-icing salts

The majority of landscape management problems are traceable back to the design flaws. Care in tree selection and placement will help minimize management problems.

SIZE CONSIDERATIONS
Size and Establishment

To give the "instant tree" appearance, larger-caliper trees are often the choice for homeowners and public access sites. However, the root systems of larger trees also take longer to redevelop in the establishment phase of the life cycle before the trees shift into the growth phase. During the establishment phase, canopy growth will be minimal. For this reason, smaller trees are recommended on sites where less than ideal growing conditions exist.

In hardiness zones 4 and 5, with good planting techniques and good soil conditions, it typically takes one growing season per inch of trunk caliper (measured at six inches above soil line) for roots to establish following transplanting. That is, a one-inch caliper tree will take one season for the roots to establish, while a three-inch caliper tree will take three seasons. In cooler regions with shorter growing seasons, it will take longer. With longer growing seasons, like the southern United States, the establishment phase will be measured in months.

On sites with poor soils and poor planting techniques, the establishment phase may be longer, and trees must live off carbohydrate reserves until roots become established. It is common to see trees planted with poor planting techniques and/or poor soil conditions that never establish, but rather decline over a period of time. In recent years, poor planting techniques have killed more trees than any insect or disease outbreak!

Moving Trees—A Weight Issue

Size (weight) is another factor in tree selection. It takes two people to move a two-inch caliper tree (measured six inches above the soil line). Larger trees require mechanical help. Trees up to four-inch caliper can be moved with front-end loaders used in landscape installation. For larger-caliper trees, special tree-moving equipment is required.

Minimum Root Ball Size

The minimum size of the root ball for trees and shrubs is set by the Colorado Department of Agriculture in the Rules and Regulations of the Colorado Nursery Act, as illustrated in the following.

Minimum Root Ball Diameter for Nursery-Grown, Balled and Burlapped Shade Trees

Tree Caliper*	Minimum Root Ball Diameter
½ to ¾ inch	12 inches
¾ to 1 inch	14 inches
1 to 1¼ inches	16 inches
1¼ to 1½ inches	18 inches
1½ to 1¾ inches	20 inches
1¾ to 2 inches	24 inches
2 to 2½ inches	26 inches
2½ to 3 inches	28 inches
3 to 3½ inches	32 inches
3½ to 4 inches	36 inches

*Measured 6 inches above soil line.

Maximum Size for Tree Spades

Spade Size	Deciduous Trees Caliper	Evergreen Trees Height
44-inch	2 to 3 inches	5 to 7 feet
60-inch	3 to 4 inches	7 to 9 feet
78-inch	4 to 6 inches	9 to 14 feet
85-inch	6 to 8 inches	14 to 18 feet

TYPES OF NURSERY STOCK

Bare-Root Stock

Bare-root plants are sold without an established soil ball. Bare-root stock is generally limited to smaller-caliper materials. Some evergreen materials will not transplant well as bare-root stock.

The cost of bare-root stock is significantly lower than the same plant as a container-grown or balled and bulapped (B&B) stock.

Roots dehydrate rapidly and must be protected. Bare-root stock is often marketed in individual units with roots bagged in moist sawdust or peat moss to prevent dehydration. Sometimes, bare-root stock is temporarily potted to protect roots. Some nurseries maintain bare-root stock in moist sawdust. As plants are removed at sale, roots are packed in moist sawdust for transport to the planting site. These need to be planted within twenty-four hours of purchase.

Survivability drops rapidly once the plant leafs out. Some nurseries keep bare-root stock in cold storage to delay leafing.

Field-Grown, Balled and Burlapped

Field-grown, B&B trees are dug from the growing field with the root ball and soil intact. In the harvest process, only five to twenty percent of the small roots are retained in the root ball, the other eighty to ninety-five percent is left behind in the field. This puts trees under water stress until roots can reestablish (Figure 27-12).

To prevent the root ball from breaking, the roots are balled and wrapped with burlap and twine (known as B&B). In nurseries today, there are many variations to B&B techniques. Some are also wrapped in plastic shrinkwrap, placed in a wire basket, or placed in a pot.

B&B stock is best transplanted in the spring or fall.

Figure 27-12 ▮ *Field-grown B&B nursery stock.*

The weight of the root ball readily becomes an issue with larger-caliper trees. A two-inch caliper tree is the largest size two people can expect to move. Equipment will be needed for larger trees.

In field production, the roots may be routinely cut to encourage a more compact root ball. While this process improves the transplantability of the tree, it slows growth, adding to production costs.

Container-Grown

Container-grown nursery stock is grown in the container. Because the root system is not seriously disturbed, container-grown nursery stock can be readily transplanted throughout the growing season: spring, summer, or fall (Figure 27-13).

Figure 27-13 ▮ *Container-grown nursery stock.*

Light-textured potting mixes are generally used in container production to reduce weight and waterlogging potential in the pot. However, this can make the newly planted tree more prone to drought during the first two years.

Because the roots cannot spread, the root system of container-grown stock will be only five to twenty percent of that found in field-grown plants. Thus, growth rates in the nursery may be slower.

There are many variations of container production. In many systems, like "pot-in-pot" and "grow-bags," the container is in the ground. This protects roots from extreme heat and cold and prevents trees from blowing over.

SELECTING PLANTS—DON'T BUY PROBLEMS

There are several considerations in plant selection at the nursery, including the following:

- Because **codominant trunks** (trunks of equal size) account for the majority of storm damage, avoid purchasing trees with codominant trunks. A single-trunk tree should have one trunk to the top, and all branches should be less than half the diameter of the adjacent trunk (Figure 27-14). (Refer to pruning fact sheets for details.)

- Consider what other **corrective pruning** will be needed to structurally train the tree. (Refer to pruning fact sheets for details.) Avoid trees with poor branching structure.

- Any **pruning wounds or bark injury** should be less than one inch or less than twenty-five percent of the trunk circumference.

- Trees should have good **growth** the past two to four years and good **leaf color**.

- Evaluate the potential long-term impacts of any **insect or disease problems**. While some insect and disease problems are not an issue, others could seriously affect the tree's health. Due to the water stress imposed by the harvest and planting process, young trees are less tolerant of most pests.

- **Planting depth of the tree in the root ball**— Generally, at least two structural roots should be within the top one to three inches of the soil surface, measured three to four inches out from the trunk. (For additional details, refer to Chapter 28.)

Figure 27-14 ■ *Codominant trunks account for the majority of storm damage. Avoid purchasing trees with codominant trunks or correct the situation with structural pruning.*

A visible trunk flare is another indication of proper planting depth in the root ball. However, on many small trees, the trunk flair is hardly noticeable. A small gap between the trunk and soil indicates that the tree is planted too deep.

- **Healthy roots** are whitish, while dead roots are dark. **Girdling roots** can become a serious problem and will need to be cut in the planting process.

SHIPMENT AND PRE-PLANT HANDLING

Pre-plant handling often predisposes new plantings to decline and death. Factors to pay attention to include the following:

- **Handle carefully.** The root ball is subject to cracking, killing the tree.

- **Lift by the root ball**, not the trunk. If lifted by the trunk, the roots may not be able to support the weight of the root ball soil, cracking the root ball.

- **Protect from mechanical injury** during shipment. The bark on young trees is tender and easily damaged by rubbing or bumping against the vehicle.

- **Protect from dehydration** during shipment. A shade cloth gives good wind protection. Many nurseries routinely wrap trees for shipment. Water upon delivery.

- **Protect from wind and heat** until planted.

- **Check water needs daily.**

- When possible, **plant immediately**.

- **Exposed roots** are readily killed by desiccation and should be cut off in the planting process.

1. What is the average life of a newly planted landscape tree? Why is it so short?

2. What five categories of plant care play in the success of tree plantings?

3. Describe functions of trees in landscape design.

4. Define a specimen tree, group planting, and mass planting.

5. For energy conservation, where should trees be placed to maximize summer shading and to maximize winter heating?

6. What percent of the sun's radiation will a tree block on a clear summer day?

7. What percent of the cooling effect of trees comes from evapotranspiration? How do drought and irrigation restrictions influence this cooling?

8. In order, list the four priorities for summer shading.

9. For energy conservation, what is the goal in urban forestry as to tree canopy cover?

10. For noise abatement, where should trees and shrubs be placed?

11. List benefits of shade trees.

12. What is the meaning behind "right plant, right place"? List examples of criteria to consider in selecting a tree species for a site.

13. Explain the criteria for above-ground space and below-ground rooting space in tree selection.

14. What happens when the root system cannot escape the root vault area?

15. Give examples of soil- and water-related considerations in tree selection.

16. Give examples of maintenance-related considerations in tree selection.

17. List factors that play into a tree's hardiness. What does a hardiness zone map tell about hardiness? Explain how hardiness changes through the winter in relation to weather.

18. Explain how the microclimate around a home influences plant selection.

19. Give examples of other criteria in tree selection.

20. Explain the rule of thumb for what it takes to move a tree with a 2-, 3-, and 4-foot wide root ball.

21. Where do you find standards (regulations) for plant-size to root-size relationships for various types of nursery stock?

22. What are the advantages of selecting a small-caliper tree? A larger-caliper tree? Which will be the largest size five years after planting?

23. Types of stock: Define the following terms and list advantages and limitations of each as indicated on the lecture slides.

    a. Container-grown

    b. In-ground, fabric grow bag

    c. Field-grown—B&B

    d. Field-grown—Balled and Potted

    e. Bare-root

24. To avoid purchasing problems, list key points in the selection and inspection of nursery plants.

25. List key points in pre-plant handling of nursery stock to minimize post-planting stress.

Chapter

28*

The Science of Planting Trees

This chapter outlines research-based tree planting steps. The procedures apply to deciduous trees, evergreen trees, and shrubs planted in a landscape setting.

The procedures apply to the home gardener planting trees (where rapid root establishment and tree growth is paramount and labor requirement is insignificant). In a commercial setting where someone is being paid to plant trees, some steps may be modified to reduce labor, and in doing so, may slow root establishment.

THE SCIENCE OF PLANTING TREES

Tree root systems are shallow and wide spreading (Figure 28-1). Based on nursery standards, a field-grown, balled and burlapped (B&B) tree or container-grown tree has less than five to twenty percent of the fine absorbing roots of the same size tree in a landscape setting. This creates stress when the tree moves from the daily care in the nursery setting to the landscape. The goal of the science of planting trees is promoting rapid root growth to reduce the water stress imposed by the

Figure 28-1 ▮ *A tree's rooting system is shallow and wide spreading. Based on nursery standards, the container-grown or field-grown, B&B tree has only five to twenty percent of the fine absorbing roots found on the same size tree in an open landscape. This places the new tree under stress.*

*Authors: David Whiting and Alison O'Connor, Colorado State University Extension. Line drawings and photographs by David Whiting.

limited root system. *Post-planting stress* (transplant shock) describes the stress factors induced by the limited root system.

STEPS TO PLANTING CONTAINER-GROWN OR FIELD-GROWN, BALLED AND BURLAPPED NURSERY STOCK

Note: Call before you dig. Whether you plan on planting the tree yourself or hiring the work done, the site needs to have underground utilities marked before digging to plant a tree. In Colorado this is easy to do by calling the **Utility Notification Center of Colorado** at 1-800-922-1987 or 8-1-1.) It can also be done online at www.colorado811.org. The utilities will be marked within 72 business hours, so plan ahead.

Step 1—Determine Depth of the Planting Hole

Planting trees too deep has become an epidemic leading to the decline and death of landscape trees. Trunk girdling roots, caused by planting too deep, leads to more deaths of landscape trees than all other factors combined!

Trunk girdling roots develop when a tree is planted too deep in the root ball and/or the root ball is planted too deep in the planting hole. Trunk girdling roots may lead to decline and death some twelve to twenty plus years after planting. Trunk girdling roots may be below ground.

To deal with this epidemic, an industry-wide working group developed the following standards for tree planting depth.

Note: These standards have been adopted industry wide, including endorsement by the American Nursery and Landscape Association, American Society of Consulting Arborists, American Society of Landscape Architects, Associated Landscape Contractors of America, International Society of Arboriculture, and Tree Care Industry Association.

Depth of Root Ball in Planting Hole

In tree planting, the root ball sits on undug soil. This prevents the tree from sinking and tilting as the soil settles. If the hole is dug too deep, backfill and firm the soil on the bottom to the correct depth. (Roots grow out from the root ball, not down.)

To deal with the *soil texture interface* (actually the differences in soil pore space) between the root ball soil and backfill soil, it is imperative that the root ball rise slightly above grade with no backfill soil over top of the root ball. For small (one-inch caliper) trees, the top of the root ball rises one inch above grade. For larger (two- to four-inch caliper) trees, the top of the root ball rises about two inches above grade. Backfill soil should cover the "knees" tapering down to grade (Figure 28-2).

If backfill covers the root ball, water and air will be slow to cross the texture interface. In this situation, water tends to move around the root ball and is slow to soak into the root ball. Root health will be compromised by lower soil oxygen levels (Figure 28-3).

Depth of Tree in the Root Ball

Generally, at least two structural roots should be within the top one to three inches of the root ball, measured three to four inches from the trunk.

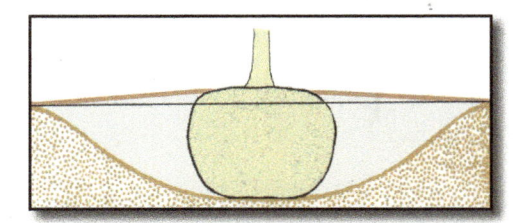

Figure 28-2 ▮ *Depth of root ball in planting hole. The top of root ball rises one to two inches above soil grade. No soil is placed over top of the root ball. Backfill soil covers the "knees" tapering downward to the original soil grade. Root ball sits on undug/firmed soil to prevent sinking.*

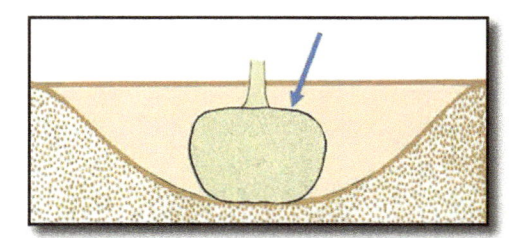

Figure 28-3 ▮ *It is imperative that the root ball comes to the surface, with no backfill on top of the root ball. When backfill soil is placed over top of the root ball, the soil texture interface impedes water and air movement into the root ball.*

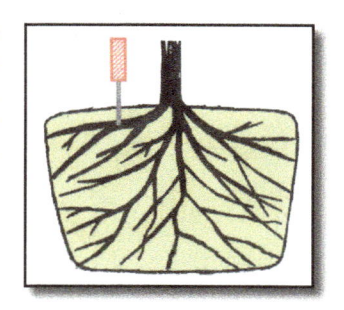

Figure 28-4 ▊ *Systematically probe the root ball with a slender screwdriver. Generally, at least two structural roots should be found in the top one to three inches of soil, three to four inches out from the trunk. On species prone to trunk circling roots (crabapples, green ash, hackberry, littleleaf linden, poplar, red maple, and other species with aggressive root systems), the top structural root should be within the top one inch of the root ball.*

On species prone to trunk-circling roots (crabapples, green ash, hackberry, littleleaf linden, poplar, red maple, and other species with aggressive root systems), the top structural root should be within the top one inch of the root ball.

Checking Depth of Tree in Root Ball

Check the depth of the tree in the root ball. Do not assume that it was planted correctly at the nursery.

- The presence of the root flare is an indication of good planting depth. However, small trees may have minimal root flare development, making it difficult to determine. Be careful not to mistake swelling of the trunk below the graft as the root flare.

- A good way to evaluate planting depth in the root ball is with a slender implement like a slender screwdriver, knitting needle, or barbeque skewer. Systematically probe the root ball three to four inches out from the trunk to locate structural roots and determine their depth (Figure 28-4).

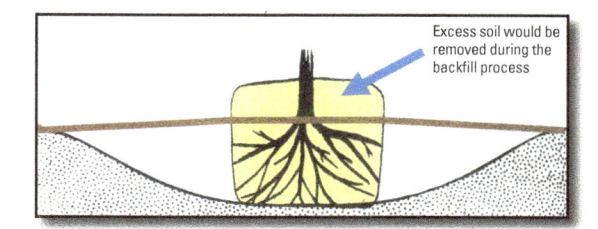

Excess soil would be removed during the backfill process

Figure 28-5 ▊ *Adjust the depth of the planting hole to bring the root flare to the correct depth.*

If the tree is planted too deep in the root ball, excess soil should be removed from the top in the backfill step of the planting process. Adjust the depth of the planting hole to compensate (Figure 28-5).

With trees planted too deep in the root ball, a better option is to not purchase the trees. In the root ball, the soil above the root flare generally does not contain roots, so the total volume of roots may be too small to maintain tree health. In container-grown stock, trees planted too deep readily develop trunk circling roots (Figure 28-6).

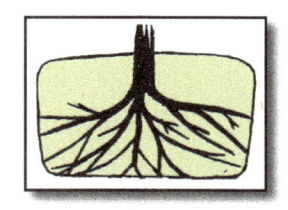

Figure 28-6 ▊ *Another issue with soil levels above the root flare is root ball size. With roots only in a portion of the root ball area, the root ball may be too small for the tree to thrive following planting.*

Summary: Depth of Planting Hole

Depth of the planting hole should be one to two inches less than the height of the root ball, adjusted (as needed) to correct the depth of the tree in the root ball.

For example, if a two-inch caliper tree has a root ball height of sixteen inches, depth of the planting hole would be fourteen inches. However, if the top structural roots are located five inches down in the root ball, between two to four inches of soil need to be removed from the root ball in the backfill process. Depth of the planting hole would be adjusted to ten to twelve inches.

Figure 28-7 ▪ *In digging, measure the depth of the planting hole with a straight board (like a rake handle) and a measuring tape.*

Figure 28-8 ▪ *Checking depth of root ball in planting hole with a straight board (like a rake handle).*

Step 2—Dig Saucer-Shaped Planting Hole Three Times Root Ball Diameter

Saucer-Shaped Planting Hole

To support rapid root regeneration, research suggests a wide, saucer-shaped planting hole. If the roots have difficulty penetrating compacted site soil (due to low soil oxygen levels), sloped sides direct roots upward and outward toward the higher oxygen soil near the surface rather than being trapped in the planting hole. Roots that do not penetrate the site soil may begin circling in the hole, leading to trunk girdling roots (Figure 28-9).

Waterlogging concerns—The saucer-shaped planting hole actually gives the tree a larger margin for error in overwatering. In the saucer-shaped planting hole three times the root ball diameter, the upper half contains eighty-five percent of the backfill soil and the upper quarter contains seventy-five percent of the backfill soil. Water could saturate the lower three-quarters of the backfill soil and only affect twenty-five percent of the root system!

When the planting hole is dug with an auger, cut down the sides with a shovel to help eliminate the glazing and create the preferred sloping sides. An alternative is to rototill a twelve- to twenty-four-inch ring of soil around the planting hole after planting (Figure 28-10).

Planting Hole Depth

Depth of the planting hole is determined in Step 1. To measure depth of the dug hole, place a straight board or shovel handle across the hole and measure from the board/handle height to the bottom of the hole.

For stability, it is imperative that the root ball sits on undug soil. If the hole is dug too deep, backfill and firmly pack the soil to the correct depth. Remember that the planting hole is shallow and wide. As a point of clarification, primary growth of roots is outward, not downward.

Figure 28-9 ▪ *When roots cannot penetrate the site soil (due to low oxygen levels), the saucer-shaped planting hole directs the roots upward and outward into soils with higher oxygen levels.*

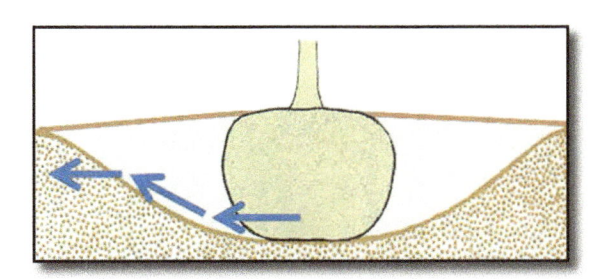

Figure 28-10 ▪ *When dug with an auger, cut down the sides into the saucer shape during backfill process.*

Planting Hole Width

Planting hole width is the key to promoting rapid root growth, reducing *post-planting stress.* In soils with great *tilth* (conditions supportive to ideal root growth), width is probably not a minor concern. However in a compacted clayey soil, typical of much of Colorado, root growth slows when roots reach the undisturbed site soil beyond the backfill area. This is due to lower soil oxygen levels in the undisturbed soil.

Twenty-five percent wider—A planting hole with vertical sides that is only twenty-five percent wider than the root ball hinders root growth. If the soil is compacted and difficult to penetrate, the roots circle inside the hole just as if the root system were in a container. Size of the root system (before growth is slowed by the lower oxygen levels of the site soil) is insufficient to reduce *post-planting stress.* Narrow planting holes are sometimes used as a labor-saving technique. However on less than idea soils, it will slow root establishment and may predispose the roots to circling.

Two times root ball—A saucer-shaped planting hole twice the diameter of the root ball will allow the root system to grow rapidly to 150% of the root ball size before growth is slowed by the lower oxygen levels of the site soil. This is not enough to avoid *post-planting stress* under normal conditions. A planting hole two times root ball diameter is common in commercial plantings as a labor-saving technique. However, on less than ideal soils, it may slow root establishment.

Three times root ball—A saucer-shaped planting hole three times the diameter of the root ball allows the root system to grow rapidly to 400% of the root ball size before being slowed by the lower oxygen levels of the site soil. This is enough to reduce *post-planting stress* under normal conditions. For example, a two-inch diameter tree with a twenty-four-inch (two-foot) wide root ball needs a seventy-two-inch (six-foot) wide saucer-shaped planting hole. To promote root growth, the planting hole is wide, shallow, and saucer-shaped!

The shallow but wide planting hole is the primary technique for encouraging rapid root growth, which is the objective in the *science of planting trees*. This is an important change in the mindset of many folks who have been planting into a narrow, deep hole.

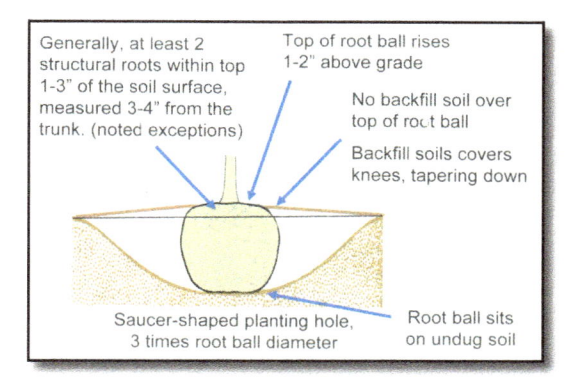

Figure 28-11 ▮ *Planting hole criteria to promote rapid root establishment, reducing post-planting stress.*

Summary: Planting Hole Specifications (Figure 28-11)

Modification for Wet Soils

On wet soils, raise planting depth so that one-third of the root ball is above grade. Cover root ball "knees" with soil, gradually tapering down to grade. Do not use mulch to cover knees, as roots will readily grow in moist mulch but will be killed when the mulch dries out (Figure 28-12).

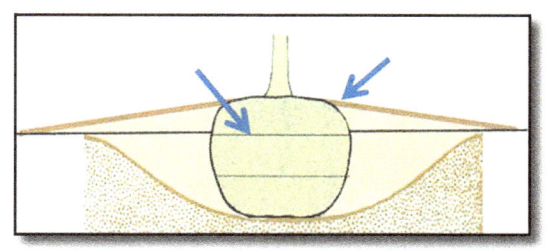

Figure 28-12 ▮ *On wet soils, place one-third of the root ball above grade, covering knees with soil tapering down to grade.*

Modification for Compacted Soils

On extremely compacted soils, rototilling a ring around the backfill area to a width of four, five, or more times the root ball diameter may be helpful. This should be done after planting is completed so the soil is not compacted by foot traffic during the planting process (Figure 28-13).

Planting on a Slope

When planting on a slope, plant "out-of-the-hill" by adjusting the grade around the planting hole, as illustrated in Figure 28-14.

Figure 28-13 ▮ *Rototilling a ring around the planting hole may help roots spread into compacted soil.*

Figure 28-14 ▮ *Planting on a slope: When planting on a slope, adjust the grade to plant "out-of-the-hill." Right: When planted "into-the-hill," roots on the uphill side will be too deep, slowing root establishment and growth.*

Labor-Saving Techniques

A labor-saving technique is to dig the hole twice the root ball width with more vertical sides. Place the tree in the hole, firm a ring of soil around the base of the root ball to stabilize it, remove wrappings, and check for circling roots. Then, with a shovel, cut the sides of the planting hole to form the saucer-shaped planting hole three times the root ball diameter. With this technique, part of the backfill soil does not have to be removed and shoveled back, but simply allowed to fall into the hole. Soil "peds" (dirt clods) up to the size of a small fist are acceptable. With this technique, it is not practical to mix in soil amendments, as amendments must be thoroughly mixed throughout the backfill soil (Figure 28-15).

A small tiller or "garden weeder" makes for quick digging. Simply place the tiller where the hole will be and walk around in a circle. Stop periodically to remove the loosened soil from the hole, and continue walking and tilling in a circle (Figure 28-16).

Figure 28-15 ▮ *Planting hole widened into saucer shape during the backfill process.*

Figure 28-16 ▮ *Digging the hole with a small tiller or "garden weeder."*

Step 3—Set Tree in Place, Removing Container/Wrappings

In setting the tree in the planting hole, if the tree has a "dogleg" (a slight curve in the trunk just above the graft), the inside curve must face north to reduce winter bark injury (Figure 28-17).

Vertically align the tree with the top centered above the root ball. Due to curves along the trunk, the trunk may not necessarily look straight. It will appear straighter with growth.

In this step, techniques vary for container-grown trees and B&B trees.

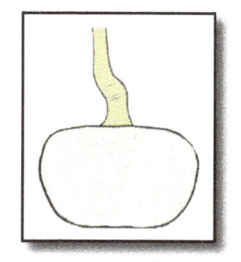

Figure 28-17 ▮ *The inside curve of the graft crook or "dogleg" must face north to reduce winter bark injury.*

Container-Grown Nursery Stock

Container-grown nursery stock refers to trees and shrubs grown in containers using a variety of production methods. Spread of the root system is limited to the container size. An advantage of container stock is that it can be planted in spring, summer, or fall. Smaller trees and shrubs are commonly grown in containers.

There are many variations of container production. In many systems, like "pot-in-pot" and "grow-bags," the container is in the ground. This protects roots from extreme heat and cold and prevents trees from blowing over.

In container-grown nursery stock, circling roots develop over time. These may be on the outside of the root ball (particularly at the bottom of the container) or just inside the root ball and not visible from the surface. Current research finds that the old standard of slitting the root ball on four sides does not adequately deal with circling roots. New standards call for the outer one to 1 and 1½ inches of the root ball to be shaved off with a knife, saw, or pruners in the planting process. This encourages roots to grow outward and does not affect tree growth potential (Figure 28-18).

Figure 28-18 ▮ *Container-grown nursery stock is prone to developing circling roots that will girdle the trunk several years after planting if not corrected.*

Techniques with Container-Grown Stock

Actual planting techniques in this step vary with the type of container and extent of root development. Generic steps include:

a. Lay the tree on its side in or near the planting hole.

b. Wiggle off or cut off the container.

c. Shave off the outer one to 1 and 1½ inches of the root ball with a knife, pruning saw, or pruners. This step is important to deal with circling roots.

d. Tilt the tree into place. Remember that the inside curve of any dogleg faces north.

e. Check depth of the root ball in the planting hole. If incorrect, remove the tree and correct the depth, firming any soil added back to the hole.

f. Align vertically.

g. Firm a shallow ring of soil around the bottom of the root ball to stabilize it (Figure 28-19).

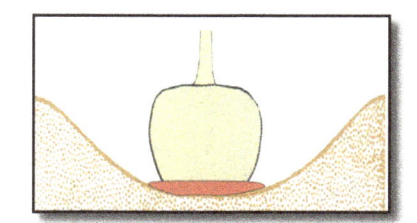

Figure 28-19 ▮ *Stabilize the tree by firming a small ring of backfill soil around the base of the root ball.*

- The ideal container-grown tree has a nice network of roots holding the root ball together. After the container is removed, the tree is gently tilted into place.

- If some of the soil falls off (often on the bottom), it may be necessary to adjust the depth of the planting hole. Backfill and pack the bottom of the planting hole to the correct depth.

- If most of the soil falls off the roots, the tree is planted as a bare-root tree (see subsequent discussion).

- Fabric grow bags must be removed from the sides. They are generally cut away after setting the tree in place.

- Generally, paper/pulp type containers should be removed. Most are slow to decompose and will complicate soil texture interface issues. Pulp containers often need to be cut off, as they may not slide off readily.

Figure 28-20 ▉ *If the container is easy to cut, many planters prefer to first cut off the bottom, then move the tree in place (helps hold root ball together), and then slit the container side to remove it.*

- In handling large trees (3-inch caliper and greater), it may be necessary to set the tree in place before removing the container.

- If the container is easy to cut, it may help to keep the root ball intact by first cutting off the bottom of the container, carefully setting the tree in place and tilting to align vertically, then cutting a slit down the side to remove the container (Figure 28-20).

Field-Grown, Balled and Burlapped Nursery Stock

Field-grown, balled and burlapped (B&B) trees and shrubs are dug from the growing field with the root ball soil intact. In the harvest process, only five two twenty percent of the feeder roots are retained in the root ball. B&B nursery stock is best transplanted in the cooler spring or fall season (Figure 28-21).

To prevent the root ball from breaking, the roots are balled and wrapped with burlap (or other fabrics) and twine (hence the name B&B). In nurseries today, there are many variations to B&B techniques. Some are also wrapped in plastic shrinkwrap, placed in a wire basket, or placed in a pot.

Larger plant materials are often sold as B&B stock. In field production, the roots may be routinely cut to encourage a more compact root ball. While this process improves the transplantability of the tree, it adds to production costs.

Figure 28-21 ▉ *Field-grown, B&B nursery stock needs to have the wrappings that hold the root ball together taken off after the tree is set in place.*

Depending on how long the tree has been held in the B&B condition, circling roots may begin to develop. If this has occurred, shave off the outer 1 to 1½ inches of the root ball as described previously for container-grown trees.

Techniques with Balled and Burlapped Nursery Stock

An advantage of the wider planting hole is that it gives room for the planter to remove root ball wrappings after the tree is situated in the hole.

Based on research, standard procedures are to remove root ball wrapping materials (burlap, fabric, grow bags, twine, ties, wire basket, etc.) from the upper twelve inches or two-thirds of the root ball, whichever is greater *after* the tree is set in place. Materials under the root ball are not a concern because roots grow outward, not downward.

Actual planting techniques in this step vary with the type of wrapping on the root ball. Generic steps include:

a. Remove extra root ball wrapping added for convenience in marketing (like shrinkwrap and a container). However, do not remove the burlap (or fabric), wire basket, and twine that hold the root ball together until the tree is set in place.

b. Set the tree in place. Remember that the inside curve of any dogleg faces north.

c. Check depth of the root ball in the planting hole. If incorrect, remove the tree and correct the depth, firming any soil added back to the hole.

d. Align vertically.

e. For stability, firm a shallow ring of soil around the bottom of the root ball (Figure 28-22).

f. Remove all the wrapping (burlap, fabric, twine, wire basket, etc.) on the upper twelve inches or upper two-thirds of the root ball, whichever is greater.

g. If circling roots are found in the root ball, shave off the outer one to 1½ inches of the root ball with a pruning saw and/or pruners.

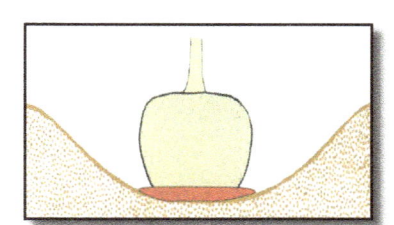

Figure 28-22 ▮ *Stabilize the tree by firming a small ring of backfill soil around the base of the root ball.*

Removal of the wire basket and burlap wrapping is a controversial issue. Some observational research reports that wire baskets do not cause problems (generally studies done in a year or two of planting). However, other observational studies report that the wire basket can cause root problems down the road as the roots grow around the wire, enclosing the wire in the root. So why take a chance that it may or may not cause problems? It is simple to remove the wire basket on the side. This also makes it easier to remove the burlap. Basket and burlap left on the bottom are not a problem, as the roots grow out, not down.

- Burlap may be slow to decompose and will complicate soil texture interface issues.

- Burlap that comes to the surface wicks moisture from the root ball, leading to dry soils.

- Jute twine left around the trunk will be slow to decompose, often girdling the tree.

- Nylon twine never decomposes in the soil, often girdling trees several years after planting.

- Wire baskets take 30 plus years to decompose and may interfere with long-term root growth.

- With tapered wire baskets, some planters find it easier to cut off the bottom of the basket before setting the tree in the hole. The basket can still be used to help move the tree and is then easy to remove by simply cutting the rings on the side.

Optional Step 4—Underground Stabilization

Several methods for underground stabilization are effective. They are applied prior to backfilling the planting hole (Figure 28-23).

- **Two or three wood dowels** driven into the ground at the edge of the root ball. The dowels will decompose over time.

- **A 2" × 2" wood triangle over the top of the root ball is screwed into 2" × 2" wood stakes** driven into the ground at the edge of the root ball. The wood will decompose over time.

- **Two metal root "staples"**—Several brands are on the market. The long leg of the staple goes into the ground at the edge of the root ball. The short leg of the staple goes into the root ball. The metal staple may pose a problem if the tree stump needs to be ground out in the future.

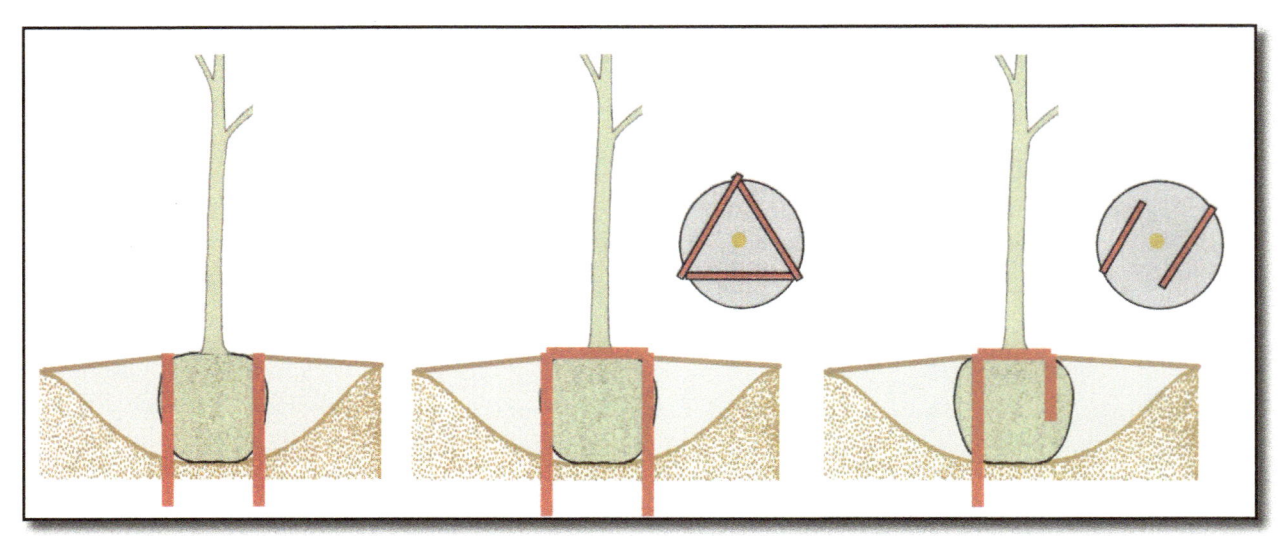

Figure 28-23 ▮ *Methods for underground stabilization Left: Two to three wood dowels are driven into the ground at the edge of the root ball. Center: Two by two lumber makes a triangle plate over the top of the root ball. It is screwed into wood stakes driven into the ground at the corners. Right: Metal root "staples" are driven into the ground at the edge of the root ball and hook into the root ball.*

Step 5—Backfill

In backfilling the planting hole, the best method is to simply return the soil and let water settle it. Avoid compacting the soil by walking or stamping on it. In the backfill process, the planting hole can be widened into the desired saucer shape.

No backfill soil goes on top of the root ball. Backfill soil covers the root ball "knees," tapering down to the original soil grade (Figure 28-24).

In preparing any garden for planting, it is standard gardening procedure to **modify** the soil structure (i.e., loosen the soil) by cultivating. It is also routine to **amend** the soil by adding organic matter to improve the water-holding capacity of sandy soils or to increase

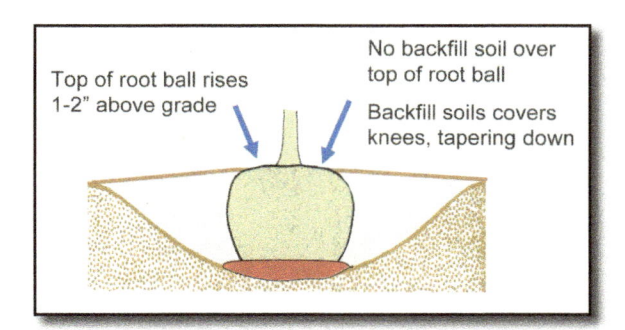

Figure 28-24 ▮ *Backfill soil covers the "knees," tapering down to the original soil grade. It is imperative that no soil cover the top of the root ball.*

large pore space in clayey soils. Modifying and amending, while related, are not the same process.

Ideally, soils in a tree's entire potential rooting area would be modified and amended to a 5% organic content.

Modifying the Backfill

When planting trees, soil in the planting hole is modified (loosened up) by digging the hole. The issue around "modifying the soil" is planting hole width, as discussed previously. Due to lower levels of soil oxygen in the site soil, root growth slows as roots reach the undisturbed site soil beyond the backfill. A saucer-shaped planting hole three times the diameter of the root ball supports rapid root growth, reducing post-planting stress. Amending backfill soil in a narrow planting hole will not substitute for modifying soil in the wider saucer-shaped planting hole.

For backfill, soil "peds" (dirt clods) up to the size of a small fist are acceptable. The soil does not need to be pulverized. In clayey soils, pulverizing the soil will destroy all structure and may lead to excessive re-compaction with minimal large pore space.

A labor-saving technique is to dig the planting hole two times the root ball diameter with rather vertical walls. Then in the backfill step, cut the hole to the three times root ball width, saucer-shaped hole. In this method, part of the soil does not have to be moved twice. Peds (dirt clods) up to fist size are acceptable in the backfill (Figure 28-25).

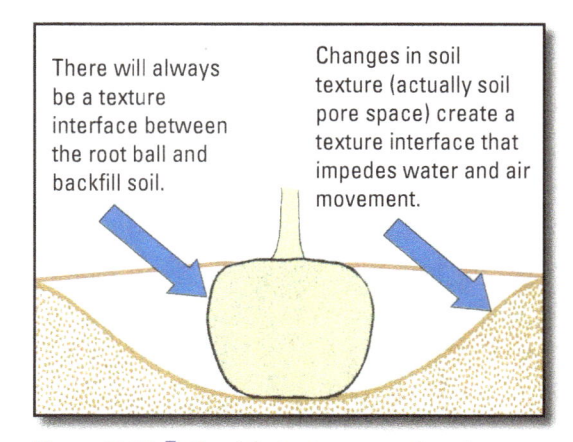

Figure 28-25 ▊ *A labor-saving method is to dig the planting hole two times the root ball diameter with more vertical walls and ease the tree in place. Then cut the planting hole into the three times root ball width and saucer shape during the backfill process. This way much of the soil does not have to be moved twice. Dirt clods up to fist size are acceptable in the planting hole.*

Amending the Backfill

Amending the soil just in the planting hole is a complex issue. Too many soil-related variables play into this amended planting pit for a simple directive. In tree planting, it is a common procedure to amend backfill soil with organic matter. It is a good marketing technique for the nursery to recommend soil amendments with the sale of a tree.

Amending the backfill soil to five percent organic matter is standard procedure in garden soil management and may be supportive to root growth in the planting hole during the first two years.

However, amending the backfill to twenty-five to fifty percent is a common mistake! It helps containerize the roots and may also hinder root spread beyond the planting hole. It may hold excessive amounts of water, reducing soil oxygen levels. As the organic matter decomposes, the total volume of soil in the planting hole diminishes, allowing the tree to topple over.

If amending the soil, the organic matter needs to be thoroughly mixed with the backfill soil. Never backfill with organic matter in layers or clumps as this creates additional texture interface lines. Amendments should be well aged. Never use unfinished compost or fresh manure as it may burn tender roots.

Texture Interface

Changes in soil texture (actually changes in soil pore space) create a *texture interface* that impedes water and air movement across the texture change. There will always be a texture interface between the root ball soil and backfill soil and between the backfill soil and undisturbed site soil. **Amending the backfill soil will not diminish the interface** (Figure 28-26).

There will always be a texture interface between the root ball and backfill soil.

Changes in soil texture (actually soil pore space) create a texture interface that impedes water and air movement.

Figure 28-26 ▊ *To minimize the texture interface, the root ball must come to the soil surface with no backfill over top of the root ball.*

To deal with the interface, it is imperative that the root ball comes to the soil surface with no backfill soil over top of the root ball. If backfill soil covers the root ball soil, the interface between the root ball and backfill soil will impede water and air movement into the root ball.

Summary: Modifying and Amending

For rapid root establishment, the focus needs to be on planting hole width and correct depth. In most situations, amending or not amending the backfill has little significance compared to other planting protocols.

Optional Step 6—Staking

Staking became a routine procedure when trees were planted in deep holes and the trees sank and tilted as the soil settled. In the science of planting trees, where trees are set on undisturbed soil and a ring of soil is firmed around the base before backfilling, staking is not needed in many landscape settings.

Consequences of Staking

The consequences of staking with traditional methods that wrap and hold the trunk include the following:

- The tree grows taller, faster.

- Staking (the lack of tree movement) slows root spread.

- The tree has less growth in trunk caliper near the ground but more near the top support ties. Staking often produces a reverse trunk taper that increases the potential for storm damage.

- Staked trees experience more wind damage than unstaked trees of equal height (the top of the tree is not free to bend in the wind).

- Bark is often damaged by the ties. In a survey of 10,000 street trees, ninety percent were damaged by the ties.

- If the stake is close to the trunk, it can develop uneven xylem growth where the stake shades the trunk, making the trunk tilt to the side. Keep stakes at least six inches away from the trunk.

Types of Staking

No staking—In most home landscape settings, no staking is necessary if the tree is set on undisturbed soil (where it cannot sink and tilt), with soil firmed around the base of the root ball before backfilling. Exceptions include the three types of staking below.

Protection staking is used where the tree needs protection from human activities, such as the football game on the front lawn or from passersby along a street planting.

Protection staking may include standard staking techniques with three or four posts and straps or a structure surrounding the tree but not actually touching the tree trunk (Figure 28-27).

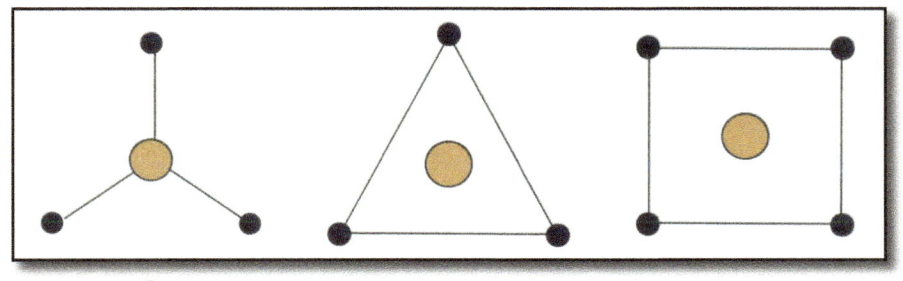

Figure 28-27 ▮ *Configurations for protection staking.*

Anchor staking—In areas of high winds, anchor staking may be needed. When anchor staking small trees, use two or three straps along the trunk about eighteen inches above the ground (Figure 28-28).

Support staking—If the tree has a floppy trunk that is not self-supporting, support staking will be needed. Straps would be located six inches above the point where the tree will stand upright, but at least three feet below the terminal leader.

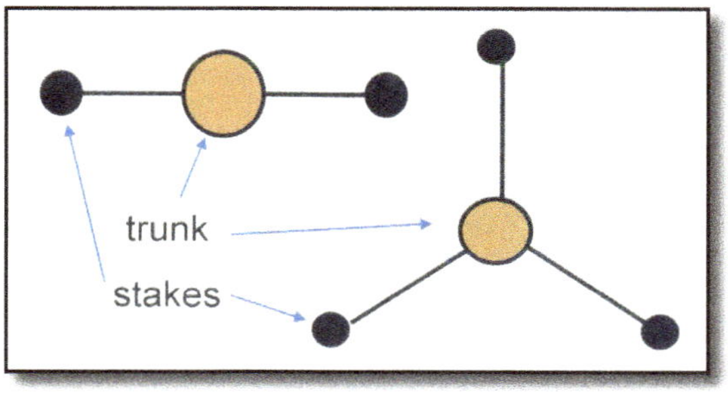

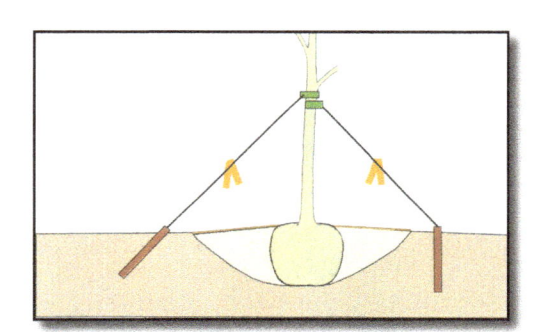

Figure 28-28 ▮ *Configurations for anchor staking. Anchor staking may be needed in areas of high winds.*

Above-Ground Staking Procedures

When staking, use flat, grommeted straps rather than ropes, wires, or hose segments against the trunk. The straps spread the pressure over a wider area, reducing the potential for bark damage. Straps should lie flat against the trunk and should not be bunched up or twisted. Two or three straps are routinely used in tree staking.

Straps may tie back to wood or metal posts or to anchors in the ground. Plastic caps are available as a safety measure for the tops of metal posts. Place posts at least fifteen to eighteen inches out from the trunk. Never tie a post to the trunk, as the shading will cause the trunk to curve (Figure 28-29).

With guy-lines and ground anchors, place the guy-lines at a 45-degree angle. Flag the guy-lines to help people see them and prevent injury. In the illustration, the anchor on the left may be more secure than the anchor on the right (Figure 28-30).

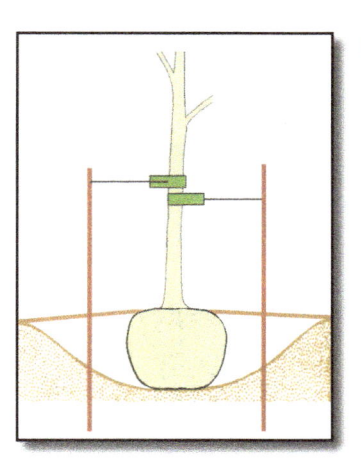

Figure 28-29 ▮ *Routine staking includes two or three posts, at least fifteen to eighteen inches out from the trunk. Use flat straps to spread pressure over a wider area, reducing bark damage.*

Figure 28-30 ▮ *TWhen staking with guy-lines, place guy-lines at a 45-degree angle. The ground anchor on the left is more secure than the anchor on the right.*

In any staking system, it is best if the tree trunk has a little flexibility. Some wind movement encourages root growth and trunk taper development. For example, Tree Stake Solutions (www.treestakessolution.com) offers metal staking systems that give underground stabilization with protection/anchor staking. The tree has limited movement inside the frame, reducing the limitation of traditional staking methods (Figure 28-31).

Figure 28-31 ▮ *Tree Stake Solutions offers underground stability with protection/anchor staking while allowing some movement of the tree. (Photographs courtesy of Tree Stake Solutions.)*

For one- to two-inch diameter trees, staking typically stays on for one or two seasons. On three- to four-inch diameter trees, staking may be needed for two or three years.

Step 7—Watering to Settle Soil

Watering is done after staking so the gardener does not compact the wet soil while installing the stakes. Watering is a tool to settle the soil without overly packing it (Figure 28-32).

Step 8—Final Grade

In the wide, shallow planting hole, the backfill soil may settle in watering. Final grading may be needed after watering (Figure 28-33).

Step 9—Mulching

A mulch ring of bark/wood chips is suggested around all trees to help protect the trunks from lawnmower damage. On newly planted trees, organic mulch can increase fine root development by 400% compared to grass competition. This results in twenty percent faster canopy growth. The increase in growth is due to the lack of competition between the tree and grass and weeds.

Site-specific water needs should be considered regarding the use of mulch. Mulch over the rooting area helps conserve moisture and moderate soil temperatures. However, on wet sites, the mulch may hold too much moisture, leading to root/crown rot, and may be undesirable. Wood/bark chips may blow in wind and therefore are not suitable for open, windy areas.

With newly planted trees, do not place mulch directly over the root ball. Rather mulch the backfill area and beyond. Never place mulch up against the trunk as this may lead to bark decay. Over the backfill area and beyond, three to four inches of wood chip mulch

Figure 28-32 ▮ *Water tree during planting; notice how soil has settled.*

Figure 28-33 ▮ *Final grade. Note how the root ball soil is visible on the surface, with no backfill covering the top of the root ball.*

gives better weed control and prevents additional soil compaction from foot traffic (Figure 28-34).

PLANTING BARE-ROOT TREES

Bare-root nursery stock is sold without an established soil ball and is generally limited to smaller-caliper materials. Some evergreen materials will not transplant well as bare-root stock.

Cost for bare-root stock is significantly lower than the same plant as container-grown or B&B stock. Survivability drops rapidly once the plant leafs out. Some nurseries keep bare-root nursery stock in cold storage to delay leafing.

Roots dehydrate rapidly and must be protected. Bare-root stock is often marketed in individual units with roots bagged in moist sawdust or peat moss to prevent

Figure 28-34 ▪ *Do not make mulch volcanoes. Mulch piled up against the tree trunk may lead to bark decay and reduced trunk taper. Excessive mulch can reduce soil oxygen.*

dehydration. Sometimes, bare-root stock is temporarily potted to protect roots. Some nurseries maintain bare-root stock in moist piles of sawdust. At the time of sale, plants are pulled from the sawdust, and the roots are wrapped with some moist sawdust for transport to the planting site. These need to be planted within twenty-four hours of purchase.

Techniques for Bare-Root Stock

Bare-root trees are planted with the same basic standards as container-grown or B&B stock, with the modification that the roots are spread out on a horizontal plane as the backfill soil is added. It is critical to minimize exposure of the roots as feeder roots dehydrate in minutes (Figure 28-35). Generic steps include the following:

1. Unpack roots to measure root spread. Cover or repack to protect roots while the hole is dug. Some gardeners like to soak the roots in a bucket of water for a couple of hours. However, do not leave them in the water for more than a half day.

2. Dig a shallow, saucer-shaped planting hole three times the diameter of the root spread. Depth of the planting hole should accommodate the planting depth standards mentioned above.
   - Top of backfill will be one inch above grade.
   - Generally, at least two structural roots should be within the top one to three inches of the soil surface.
   - On species prone to trunk circling roots (such as crabapples, green ash, hackberry, littleleaf linden, poplar, and red maple), the top structural root should be within the top one inch of the root ball soil surface.
   - The bottom root should rest on undug soil.

3. As backfill is added, spread roots out on a straight, horizontal plane.

4. Most bare-root trees will need staking.

5. Water the newly planted tree.

6. Complete the final grade.

7. Mulch as needed.

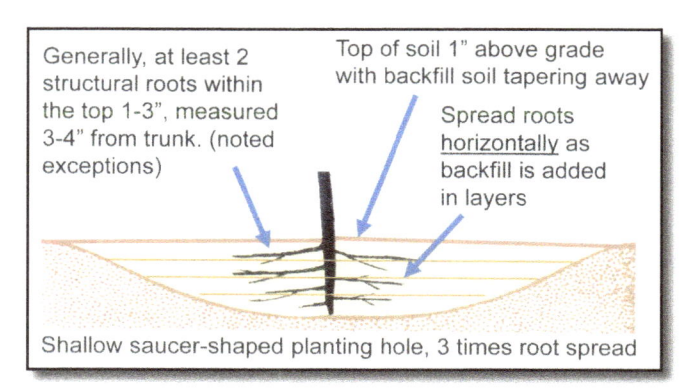

Generally, at least 2 structural roots within the top 1-3", measured 3-4" from trunk. (noted exceptions)

Top of soil 1" above grade with backfill soil tapering away

Spread roots horizontally as backfill is added in layers

Shallow saucer-shaped planting hole, 3 times root spread

Figure 28-35 ▪ *Planting bare-root trees.*

POST-PLANTING CARE
Root Establishment Phase

During the establishment phase in a tree's life cycle, primary growth occurs in the root system, with minimal growth in the canopy. The science of planting trees is aimed at encouraging this root growth, reducing *post-planting stress*.

With good planting techniques and soil conditions, the establishment phase takes one growing season per inch of trunk diameter (in hardiness zones 4 and 5). On small trees (up to four inches in diameter), trunk diameter is measured at six inches above the soil line. That is, a one-inch caliper tree typically takes one year for roots to establish. A two-inch diameter tree typically takes two years. In cooler regions with shorter growing seasons, it will take longer. In warmer regions, like the southern United States, the establishment phase is measured in months.

With poor planting techniques and/or poor soil conditions, the establishment phase may take many years. It is common to observe trees that never establish but rather simply hang on for a few years and gradually decline.

A significant increase in annual twig growth indicates that roots have become established and that the tree is shifting into the growth phase.

Watering

Regular irrigation after planting encourages rapid root development for tree establishment. Underirrigation often leads to slow establishment, canopy dieback, and bark splits (frost crack and sunscald) on the trunk. After the first couple of years, it is common to find underirrigated trees that have minimal root growth.

Recently planted trees and shrubs establish most quickly with light, frequent irrigation. For recently planted trees, primary water extraction is from the root ball and the root ball can become dry in just a day.

Larger volumes of water applied infrequently will not compensate for the need for frequent, light irrigation. On newly planted trees, soil amendments do not significantly reduce the need for frequent irrigation. Drought-tolerant species are not drought-tolerant until the root system becomes established. In sites without ideal irrigation management, smaller-sized nursery stock would be preferred because they establish faster.

When watering non-established trees, check the soil frequently, and water according to need. The soil could be dry in the root ball and wet in the backfill, or wet in the root ball and dry in the backfill. If the tree is planted in a newly sodded/seeded irrigated lawn, it is typically overwatered (Figure 28-36).

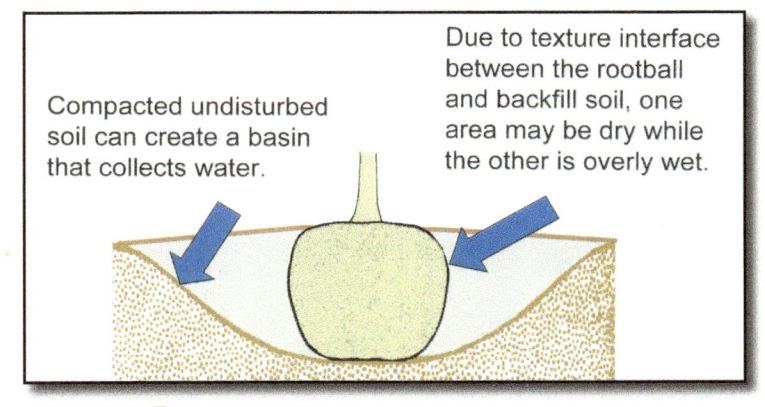

Compacted undisturbed soil can create a basin that collects water.

Due to texture interface between the rootball and backfill soil, one area may be dry while the other is overly wet.

Figure 28-36 ▪ *On non-established trees, check the water needs in the root ball and back fill soil frequently. Water according to observed needs.*

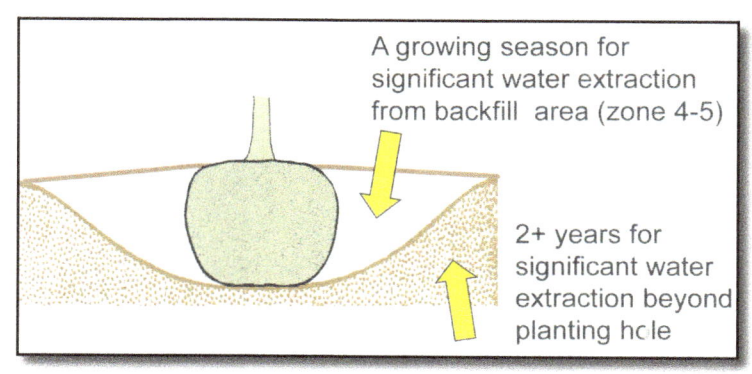

A growing season for significant water extraction from backfill area (zone 4-5)

2+ years for significant water extraction beyond planting hole

Figure 28-37 ■ *Check water needs in the root ball soil and the backfill soil.*

The only way to know the watering needs of non-established trees is to check soil moisture levels. A useful tool for the home gardener is a houseplant water meter. While somewhat inaccurate, it can indicate wet or dry. (**Note:** If the fertility is high, it will read on the wet side. If fertility is low, it will read on the dry side.)

Check both the root ball soil and the backfill soil. For a two-inch caliper tree in hardiness Zone 5, it takes one growing season for the roots to extract significant amounts of water from the backfill soil, and two or more years for significant water extraction from the soil beyond the planting hole (Figure 28-37).

Learn by carefully monitoring the amount and frequency of irrigation needed for each tree. Estimated irrigation needs are given in Table 28-1.

Table 28-1. Estimated Irrigation of Newly Planted Trees and Shrubs (during the growing season)—Check soil moisture and water as needed

Size of Nursery Stock	Irrigation Need for Vigor
<2-inch caliper	• **Check daily for 2 weeks and water as needed**—Depending on temperature and wind, apply 1 to 2 gallons per inch of trunk diameter. • **Check every other day for 2 months and water as needed**—Depending on temperature and wind, apply 2 to 4 gallons per inch of trunk diameter. • **Check weekly until established and water as needed** (two or more seasons).
2- to 4-inch caliper	• **Check daily for 4 weeks and water as needed**—Depending on temperature and wind, apply 1 to 2 gallons per inch of trunk diameter. • **Check every other day for 3 months and water as needed**—Depending on temperature and wind, apply 2 to 4 gallons per inch of trunk diameter. • **Check weekly until established and water as needed** (two to four seasons).
>4-inch caliper	• **Check daily for 6 weeks and water as needed**—Depending on temperature and wind, apply 1 to 2 gallons per inch of trunk diameter. • **Check every other day for 5 months and water as needed**—Depending on temperature and wind, apply 2 to 4 gallons per inch of trunk diameter. • **Check weekly until established and water as needed** (four or more seasons).

Check the actual water need before watering. A common mistake on compacted and clayey soils (with poor drainage) is to apply too much water per irrigation, waterlogging the planting hole. Never apply irrigation if soil is saturated.

Trunk diameter on small trees is measured at six inches above the soil line.

As a rule of thumb for hardiness zones 4 and 5, establishment takes one season per inch of trunk caliper.

In Colorado winters without routine moisture, water newly planted trees monthly. However, do not water if the ground is frozen.

In our dry, semiarid climate, there is benefit from applying additional irrigation outside the root ball area. This can be done with a ringed soil berm that allows water to percolate into the soil or a soaker-type hose running around the backfill area.

Mulch to Protect Tree from Lawnmowers, Weed Eaters, and Grass Competition

Wood/bark-chip mulch is highly recommended on newly planted trees. The mulch protects the trees from lawnmower and weed eater injury. Trees with a mulch ring typically have 20% more early growth compared to trees where grass grows up to the trunk. This is due to the lack of competition with the grass and/or weeds.

In a landscape setting, the mulch ring is typically two to four feet wide up to the width of the dripline (spread of branches). Wood chip mulch three to four inches deep gives better weed control and prevents additional soil compaction by foot traffic.

On newly planted trees, do not mulch over the root ball. On established trees, keep mulch back six inches from the trunk. Never pile wood/bark chips up against the trunk. Wet chips can lead to bark decay. Never make mulch volcanoes!

On wet sites, mulching may help hold excessive soil moisture and may be undesirable. On open windy sites, wood/bark-chip mulch blows away.

Fertilization

During the establishment phase, fertilization needs are none to minimal on woody plants. High-nitrogen fertilization rebalances the canopy-to-root growth ratio, encouraging canopy growth at the expense of root growth.

In situations where soil fertility is low—but water and other growth factors are not limiting—very light fertilization with a time-release product may be acceptable. Never use a quick-release fertilizer on trees.

Never fertilize trees in the establishment phase that are showing signs of stress. When a nonestablished tree is under stress, nitrogen fertilizer can push out canopy growth that the root system cannot support in hot windy weather. Woody plants do not respond to "starter fertilizers" like herbaceous plants.

Pruning

In the establishment phase of a tree's life cycle, pruning is undesirable. Pruning lowers the levels of auxin, a hormone produced in the canopy terminal buds that stimulates root growth.

Pruning should be limited to the removal of dead and broken branches and minimal pruning to maintain a single leader. In purchasing trees, select trees with good structure that will not require immediate pruning.

Structural training for the tree continues in the growth phase (after the roots have established and the canopy shows significant annual growth).

In situations where trees will not receive any structural training while young, it may be desirable to correct structural major defects as part of the planting process. This is primarily removal of codominant trunks and spacing of secondary trunks. However, major pruning at planting will slow root establishment.

1. What is the most limiting factor on a tree's root growth potential?

2. Compared to a field-grown, B&B tree or container-grown tree, what percent of the fine absorbing roots will be found in the nursery stock root ball?

3. What is meant by the "science of planting trees"?

4. What is the proper depth of a tree in the root ball? How can you tell if it is planted at the correct depth? What should be done by the planter if the tree is planted too deep in the root ball?

5. What is the proper depth of the root ball in the planting hole? Why should the tree sit on undisturbed soil? What should be done if the planting hole is accidentally dug too deep?

6. Explain the benefits of the saucer-shaped hole three times wider than the root ball. Explain the concerns about it filling with water.

7. If the planting hole is dug with an auger, how can it be readily modified so the tree has the benefits of a saucer-shaped hole?

8. Be able to diagram and label the routine planting specifications, including depth of tree in the root ball, depth of root ball in planting hole, and planting hole depth and width.

9. How are the recommended planting criteria modified for the following planting situations?

    a. Wet soil

    b. Compacted/clayish soil

    c. Planting on slopes

10. For container-grown nursery stock, discuss considerations in removing the container and setting tree in place.

11. For field-grown, B&B nursery stock, discuss considerations in setting tree in place and removing the wrappings.

    a. For B&B materials, why is the wrapping material removed after setting the tree in place and packing soil around the bottom?

    b. What about the packing materials on the bottom? Explain why it does not interfere with root growth.

    c. What packing materials should be removed from the sides? How far down?

    d. Do wire baskets interfere with root growth?

    e. Will burlap decay fast enough to not interfere with root growth?

    f. How fast do synthetic burlap, fabric grow bags, nylon twine, and wire baskets decay?

12. What should the planter do if the root ball has circling roots? What should the planter do if the root ball has roots sticking way out from the root ball?

13. Explain the statement that unamended backfill soil is not the same as unmodified backfill soil. Discuss the issue of amending the backfill. What criteria should be used to determine what criteria are appropriate for a given site?

14. List the four types of above-ground staking. Describe criteria for each.

15. Describe techniques used in below-ground stabilization.

16. Describe criteria for mulching around a newly planted tree.

    a.   How deep should the mulch be applied?

    b.   What about mulch up against the trunk?

    c.   What is the problem with "mulch volcanoes"?

17. Describe steps in planting bare-root nursery stock.

18. Describe the plan for watering newly planted trees based on size. How much should be applied? How often? For how long?

19. How should a tree in the establishment phase be fertilized?

20. What is the rule of thumb on how long the establishment phase lasts?

UNIT F
Pruning

Learning Objectives

At the end of this unit, the student will be able to:

- Explain how trees decay and the implications for pruning.
- Explain removal cuts, reduction cuts, and heading cuts.
- Structurally prune a young shade tree.
- Describe pruning of mature shade trees, including objectives (whys) and methods (hows).
- Prune flowering shrubs and evergreen shrubs.

Supplemental Reading

Books

- *An Illustrated Guide to Pruning, Third Edition.* Edward F. Gilman. Delmar. 2011.
- *Best Management Practices: Tree Pruning.* Edward F. Gilman and Sharin J. Lilly. International Society of Arboriculture. 2008.
- *American National Standards Institute A300 Pruning Standards, Part 1.* American National Standards Institute. 2008.

Web

- **Dr. Ed Gilman's Pruning website** at http://hort.ifas.ufl.edu/woody/pruning.shtml

Chapter

29*

Tree Growth and Decay

As forest scientists observed how trees respond to wounds, pruning techniques changed and pruning objectives were clarified.

This chapter provides background information on how trees grow and decay and therefore the implications of pruning cuts and structural training. Refer to Chapters 30 to 34 for additional details on pruning cuts, structural training, and basic pruning.

Note: in this publication, the term "trunk" refers to a trunk or parent branch and "side branch" refers to a side branch arising from the trunk (parent branch). The same relationship would exist between a side branch and a secondary side branch.

DEVELOPING A STRONG BRANCH UNION

In Colorado (and other snowy climates) the most common type of significant storm damage in landscape tree results from failures at the branch union (crotch), primarily with codominant trunks (adjacent trunks of similar size). Primary objectives in training young trees are to develop strong branch unions and eliminate structurally weak codominant trunks (Figure 29-1).

Structural strength of a branch union is based on the development of a branch collar. The branch collar is where the annual growth rings of the trunk overlap the annual growth rings of the side branch, like shuffling a deck of cards. In lumber, the branch collar is called the knot (Figure 29-2).

For the branch collar to develop, the side branch must be less than half the diameter of the adjacent trunk. Less than one-third is preferred. If the side branch is too large in diameter, prune back the side branch by 33% to

_____

*Author: David Whiting, Colorado State University Extension. Photographs and line drawings by David Whiting.

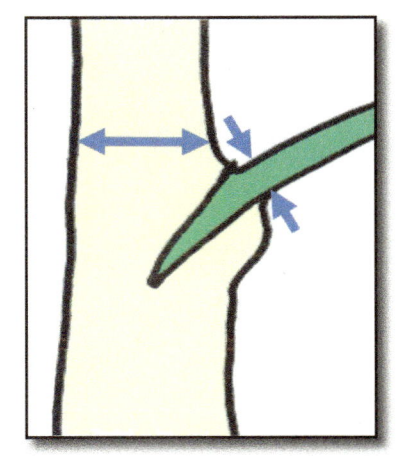

Branch Collar
Trunk tissues overlap with branch tissues

Branch Bark Ridge
Where trunk bark meets branch bark

Figure 29-2 ■ *Structural strength of the branch union (crotch) is based on development of a branch collar.*

67% to slow growth or remove the branch entirely. As the branch collar develops, side branch tissues connect into the trunk in a wedge shape, making a structurally strong unit (Figure 29-3).

The size relationship between the trunk and side branch is called Aspect Ratio. A branch union with high aspect ratio, like 1 to 1 (two trunks of the same diameter), is highly prone to failure in wind and snow loading. A branch union with a low aspect ratio, like 1 to 3 (side branch is 1/3 the diameter of the adjacent trunk), would not likely fail due to the development of the branch collar.

Figure 29-3 ■ *As the branch collar develops, side branch tissues connect into the trunk in a wedge shape making a structurally strong unit. For the branch collar to develop, the diameter of the side branch must be less than half the diameter of the adjacent trunk. Less than one-third is preferred.*

A branch collar will not develop on codominant trunks (adjoining trunks of similar size), making this branch union structurally weak (Figure 29-4).

Multiple branches arising at the same location also compromise the branch collar's structural strength. Some tree species (like elm, maple, and crabapple) naturally develop multiple branches at one location. This predisposes the tree to storm damage if the situation is not corrected by structural training when the tree is young (Figure 29-4).

Figure 29-4 ■ *(Left) A branch collar does not develop on codominant trunks, making the branch union structurally weak. (Right) Multiple branches arising at the same location are also structurally weak as the branch collars cannot knit together into a strong union.*

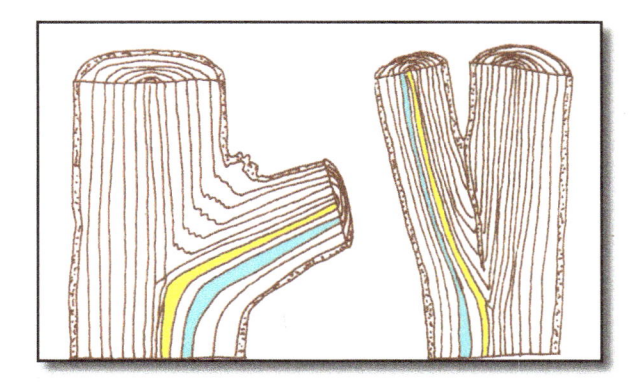

Figure 29-5 ▮ *Branch unions that form a right angle are more resistant to decay. A branch union with codominant trunks and a narrow angle of attachment is highly prone to the spread of decay.*

The development of a branch collar significantly reduces the potential spread of decay. In addition, branch unions with a right angle of attachment are more effective in preventing the spread of decay (Figure 29-5).

HOW TREES GROW

Xylem tissues—Each year, a tree puts on a new outer ring of wood (xylem tissue) under the bark, resulting in the increased diameter of a trunk or branch. The number of rings indicates the limb's age, and the width of individual rings indicates that year's growing conditions (Figures 29-6 and 29-7).

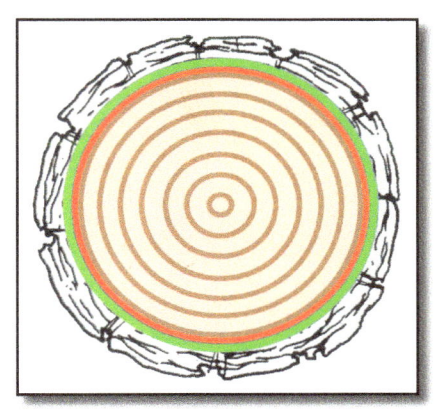

Figure 29-6 ▮ *Tree cross-section.*
Bark—*Outer protective covering*
Phloem *(green in drawing)—Inner bark tissue. Photosynthates (sugars and carbohydrates produced in the leaves by photosynthesis) move throughout the tree in the phloem tissues, including down to feed the roots.*
Cambial Zone *(red in drawing)—Layer of active cell division between bark and xylem.*
Xylem *(brown layers in drawing)—Each year, the cambium adds a new ring of xylem tissue just under the cambium layer, resulting in a growth in limb diameter. Xylem tissues are the technical name for the "wood."*

Figure 29-7 ▮ *The "wood" of a tree is the xylem tissue. Xylem tissues that grew in the spring and early summer enlarge and are the tubes in which water with minerals flows from the roots to the leaves. In a cross-section of the log, these are light-colored rings. Xylem tissues that grew mid-summer, at the end of the growth cycle, are higher in fiber content creating a wall to the outside. In a cross-section of a log, these are the darker-colored rings.*

Younger annual growth rings (annual rings of xylem tissue) with their living cells active in water transport and storage of photosynthates are called **sapwood**. Depending on the species and vigor, sapwood comprises approximately the five youngest (outer) annual growth rings. **Heartwood**, the older annual xylem rings no longer active in water transport, is very susceptible to decay organism. Due to chemical changes in these non-living cells, heartwood is often darker in color (Figure 29-8).

Ray cells grow through the annual growth rings, functioning like staples or nails to hold the growth rings together. Ray cells also function as the path to move photosynthates in and out of storage in the xylem tissues. On some species, ray cells are not readily visible. On other species, ray cells create interesting patterns in the wood (Figure 29-9).

The wood is a series of boxes or "compartments" framed by the annual growth rings and ray cells. Each compartment is filled with xylem tubes in which water with minerals moves from the roots to the leaves (Figures 29-10 and 29-11).

Figure 29-9 ▮ *The cracks on this willow stump show ray cells.*

Figure 29-8 ▮ *On this Douglas fir log, the* sapwood *is the light-colored annual growth rings active in water transport and storage of photosynthates. The darker-colored* heartwood *in the center has no resistance to decay.*

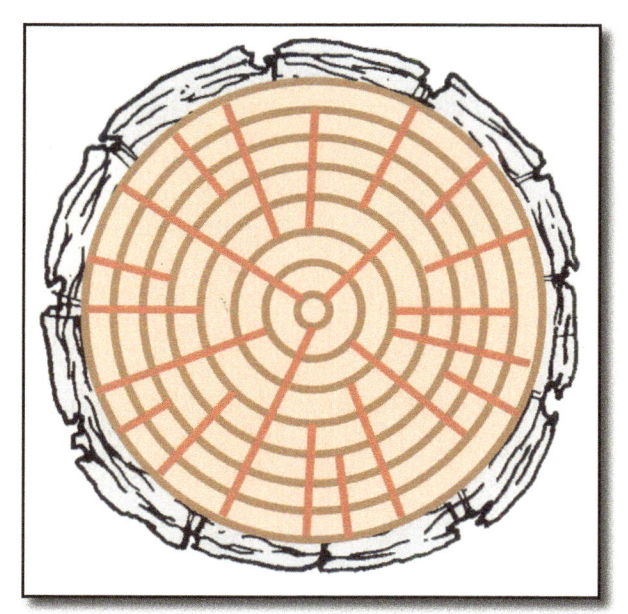

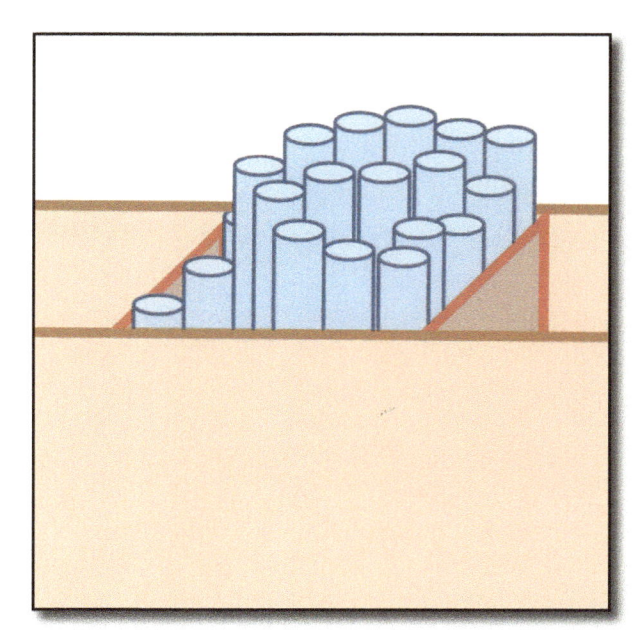

Figure 29-10 ▮ *The xylem tissue (wood) is a series of compartments or boxes created by the annual growth rings and ray cells.*

Figure 29-11 ▮ *Each compartment or box framed by the annual growth rings and ray cells is filled with xylem tubes. Water moves in the xylem tubes up from the roots.*

COMPARTMENTALIZATION OF DECAY IN TREES—HOW TREES DECAY

Unlike animals and people, trees do not replace damaged tissues. Rather, cells in the damaged area undergo a chemical change in a method to seal off or "compartmentalize" the damaged area from the spread of decay. This area of chemical change is called the reaction zone. In most species, a reaction zone appears as darker-colored wood.

The spread of decay is related to this compartmentalization of the xylem tubes in a box-like structure created by the annual growth rings and ray cells. In this box-like structure, the four walls differ in their resistance to the spread of decay (Figure 29-12).

Wall 1—Resistance to the spread of decay is very weak up and down inside the xylem tubes. Otherwise, the tubes would plug, stopping the flow of water, and kill the plant. From the point of injury, decay moves upwards to a small degree but readily moves downward. The downward movement may be twenty or more feet and can include the root system.

Wall 2—The walls into the older xylem tissues (toward the center of the tree) are also rather weak, allowing decay to readily move into older annual growth rings.

Wall 3—The walls created by the ray cells (being high in photosynthates) are somewhat resistant to decay organisms. This may help suppress the spread of decay around the tree.

Wall 4—New annual growth rings that grow in years after the injury are highly resistant to the spread of decay.

Resistance to the spread of decay by the new annual growth ring and ray cells creates a pipe-like structure with a decayed center. This concept of how decay spreads in a tree (as controlled by the annual growth rings and ray cells) is called CODIT, for *C*ompartmentalization *O*f *D*ecay *I*n *T*rees (Figures 29-12 and 29-13).

Evaluating Decay

Percent Shell

A trunk or branch with some internal decay is not necessarily at risk for failure. Structural strength is based on: 1) the minimum thickness of the healthy wood (xylem tissues), and 2) the structural strength of wood (tree species).

In evaluating potential hazards, arborists (tree care professionals) work with a technical term called **percent shell**. Percent shell is calculated by dividing the thickness of the healthy wood at the thinnest point (not including bark, reaction wood, or decaying tissue) by the radius of the trunk/branch (not including bark).

33% percent shell = high risk potential—Trees with a thirty-three percent shell or less are termed "high risk," with

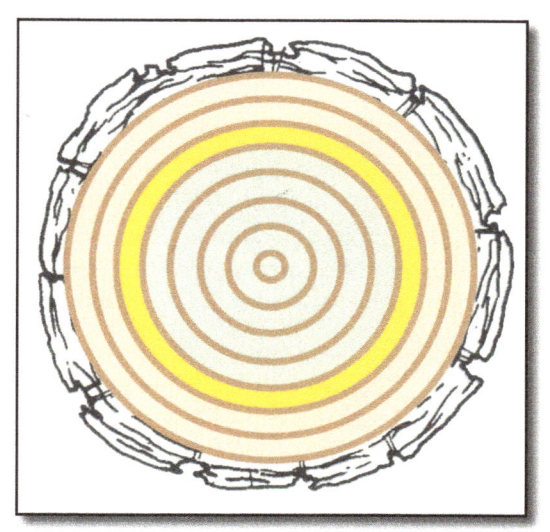

Figure 29-12. ▮ *Spread of decay in trees. The spread of decay in trees is suppressed by the four walls created by compartmentalization of the annual growth rings and ray cells. In the drawing, injury occurred three years ago when the yellow-colored annual growth ring was the youngest. That year and everything older (grayed annual growth rings) are subject to a reaction zone and decay. The two new annual growth rings (brown color) that grew in years after the injury are highly resistant to decay.*

Figure 29-13 ▮ *Decay in a tree creates a pipe-like structure with a hollow center. The light-colored wood represents new annual growth rings that grew after the year of injury. The darker-colored ring is a reaction zone created in the sapwood. The heartwood has completely decayed away.*

a statistically high probability of failure in a storm event. For example, a six-inch diameter (three-inch radius) trunk with only a one-inch thick ring of healthy wood would have a thirty-three percent shell with a hollow center. If injury or property damage would occur upon tree failure, corrective action (such as removal of the defective branch or removal of the tree) should be considered.

20 % shell = critical risk potential—Trees with a twenty percent shell or less are considered a "critical risk," with a very high probability of failure in storms. For example, a tree with a ten-inch diameter (five-inch radius) trunk with only a one-inch ring of healthy wood would be considered a "critical risk." If injury or property damage would occur upon tree failure, corrective action (such as removal of the defective branch or removal of the tree) should be taken (Figure 29-14).

The *Percent Shell Formula* is valid only when the decay column is centered in the trunk/branch. Researchers are developing other formulas to evaluate off-sided decay and open cavities, which are significantly weaker. On older mature trees, percent shell standards may overstate the thickness of healthy wood needed to be structurally acceptable. Additional research is needed to better clarify this standard for older/mature trees.

Figure 29-14 ▮ *This cottonwood branch has a twenty-five percent shell, putting it at "high risk" for potential failure. Percent shell is measured by dividing the thickness of the healthy wood at its narrowest point (not including the reaction wood [darker ring toward the center] and the bark) by the radius of the limb (not including bark).*

Measuring Decay

So, how thick is the healthy wood in a trunk or branch? Researchers are working to address this big question. At the present time, arborists are limited in their ability to measure and evaluate the internal structure of a trunk or limb. The following are procedures with limited potential to evaluate the internal structure of trees.

Visual Indicators of Decay

Large pruning wounds suggest the potential for internal decay. Often, decay may be observed within the pruning wound (Figure 29-15).

Cankers suggest the potential for internal decay. If the canker extends down into the soil, decay organisms will always be active.

Valleys, ridges, cracks, and splits along the trunk/branch suggest the potential for decay.

Wildlife living inside the tree is a sign of decay.

Abnormal swellings or shapes could be a sign that the tree is growing around a decayed area.

Figure 29-15 ▮ *The black material in the pruning cut is decay fungus. Notice the cracking; it also raises flags of structural integrity.*

Coring Devices

Note: All coring devices have a small potential to spread decay, as the coring tools break the strong exterior wall of a reaction zone and bring decaying tissues out through healthy wood in the removal. Thus, they are generally not used on living trees except when there is a special need to evaluate risk potential. Coring devices only indicate the decay potential at the point of drilling and do not represent the entire trunk or branch.

- An **increment borer** is a hand tool that removes a small core from a trunk or branch. The relative effort it takes to drill the borer through various layers of the tree and examination of the core removed gives the arborist some idea about the internal structure at this location. Increment borers are rarely used today in arboriculture.

- **Drill with small drill bit**—Drilling the trunk or branch with a one-eighth inch fully fluted drill bit is a tool used by some arborists. Pressure to push the drill through the annual growth rings and examination of the sawdust removed gives the arborist some idea about the internal structure at this location. An experienced arborist can be rather accurate in evaluation by drilling. Drilling has little value, however, for the inexperienced person (Figure 29-16).

- A **resistograph** is a specialized drill that graphs the pressure needed to push a small drill bit through various layers of annual growth rings. The graph gives a visual indication of internal structure at this location. Due to cost, few arborists have a resistograph (Figure 29-17).

- A **digital microprobe**, a specialized drill bit rotating at 7,000 rotations per minute, measures the pressure needed to drill/burn its way through tissues. Data are fed into a computer database for evaluation and printout. This equipment is new to the industry and cost-prohibitive for most arborists.

Figure 29-16 ■ *Examination of the sawdust and the pressure to push the drill through the annual growth rings give the experienced arborist a handle on internal decay. The yellow earplug on the drill bit helps the arborist know the depth as he works the drill bit in and out. With experience, the arborist could estimate percent shell for the spot drilled.*

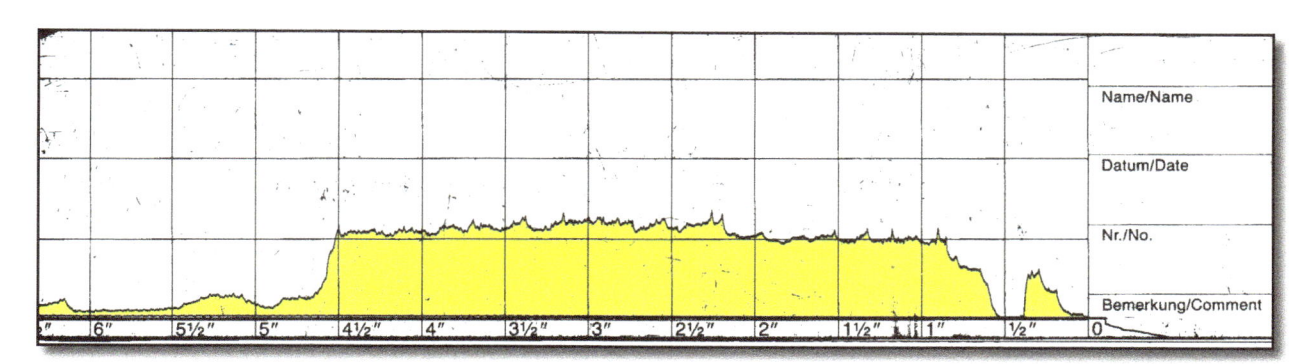

Figure 29-17 ■ *Sample printout of resistograph—This tree has a decayed center at 4½ inches from the outside bark.*

Listening and Radar Devices

- **Rubber mallet**—Tapping the trunk/branch with a rubber mallet and listening for a hollow sound may give some indication of critical internal decay. It will not give any percent shell to help evaluate risk potential and may not be effective on thick bark trees (like old cottonwoods). However, do not totally discount this technique, as it may give clues of where to use other tools.

- **PiCUS Sonic Tomography** is a new device that listens to how sound waves move through the trunk/branch using ultrasound technology. A series of listening devices are attached around the trunk/branch and connected to a computer. When the tree is tapped with a mallet, the computer measures how the sound moves through the wood and creates a graphic cross-section of the trunk/branch interior. Measurements taken at multiple heights up the trunk can generate a three-dimensional image. This type of equipment has the potential to totally change tree care when it becomes available to arborists. Currently, the cost is prohibitive for most arborists (Figure 29-18).

Figure 29-18 ■ *PiCUS Sonic Tomography equipment measures the speed of sound moving through the wood.*

Figure 29-19 ■ *Tree radar taking a look at the tree's wood structure.*

- **Electrical Impedance Tomography** is similar to sonic tomography and measures the distortion of the electrical field by wood conditions. Electrical impedance tomography is better at detecting "Y" crevices and cracks and thus is often used in conjunction with sonic tomography.

- **Tree Radar**—A handheld radar device is run around the trunk/branch. The computer database is sent to the company for evaluation. Currently, the cost is prohibitive for most arborists (Figure 29-19).

BREAKS IN THE PIPE-LIKE STRUCTURE

When a wound or pruning cut breaks the pipe-like structure of a trunk/branch, the tree is especially weak at this location, creating a higher potential for tree failure (Figure 29-20).

LACK OF TRUNK/BRANCH TAPER

Branch failure (often breaking a few feet to 1/3 of the branch length out from the branch union) is a common type of storm damage. Branch failures often cause minimal damage to the tree. However, failure of a major branch may create holes in the tree canopy, introduce decay and cracking, and make the tree look unacceptable. *Trunk failure* refers to breaking of the lower trunk, above ground level (not at a branch union).

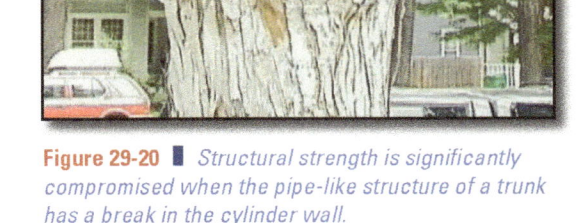

Figure 29-20 ■ *Structural strength is significantly compromised when the pipe-like structure of a trunk has a break in the cylinder wall.*

Branch and trunk failures are associated with lack of trunk/branch taper. That is the trunk/branch does not thicken adequately moving down the trunk/branch. This can be caused by pruning up the trunk too fast and by removing small branches and twigs on the lower trunk or lower interior canopy of the tree.

Very upright branches without a lot of side branches also typically fail to develop adequate taper. For structural integrity, shorten these branches with appropriate reduction cuts.

1. What is the branch collar?

    a. Explain how it develops.

    b. Explain the size relationship between the side branch and trunk/parent branch necessary for a branch collar to develop.

2. Explain how trees grow, adding xylem rings each year. Define the following terms:

    a. Phloem

    b. Xylem

    c. Sapwood

    d. Heartwood

    e. Ray cells

    f. Compartmentalization

3. Explain how trees respond to wounds (i.e., CODIT).

    a. What are the roles of annual growth rings and ray cells?

    b. In CODIT, explain why trees decay with a pipe-like structure. How does a break in the pipe-like structure impact structural strength?

4. What is percent shell? What are significant about 33% and 25% shells?

5. Describe methods to evaluate decay and cracking in trees.

Chapter

30 *

Pruning Basics
Pruning Cuts

A pruning cut may or may not predispose the tree to internal decay and cracking, depending on the type of cut used, technical precision of the cut, size of the branch removed, species, and general health of the tree.

In pruning, there are three primary types of pruning cuts: *removal (thinning)* **cuts**, **reduction cuts**, and **heading cuts**, each giving different results in growth and appearance.

Note: In this chapter, the term "trunk" refers to the trunk or parent branch, and "side branch" refers to the adjacent side branch arising from the trunk (parent branch). The same relationship exists between a side branch and secondary side branch.

MAXIMUM DIAMETER OF PRUNING CUTS

Sapwood, the living cells in the newer xylem rings active in water transport and storage of photosynthates, is resistant to decay. On branches two inches and less in diameter, sapwood dominates the branch structure making the branch resistant to decay. In a removal type cut, **woundwood** (the callus tissue that grows over pruning cuts or wounds) quickly grows over these small pruning cuts.

Heartwood, the older xylem rings no longer active in water transport, has no resistance to decay. Due to chemical changes in these non-living cells, heartwood is often darker in color. Depending on species and growth rates, heartwood becomes significant as branches reach two to four inches in diameter. At approximately four inches, heartwood dominates the branch structure, and the branch becomes highly susceptible to decay organisms and internal cracking (Figure 30-1).

*Authors: David Whiting, Eric Hammond, and Alison O'Connor, Colorado State University Extension. Photographs and line drawings by David Whiting.

In an ideal world, all pruning cuts would be two inches in diameter or smaller. This small size is especially important on tree prone to decay (a factor of species and tree vigor). On tree species resistant to decay, with good vigor and without growth limiting factors (such as severe soil compaction or drought stress), the two-inch or less standard may be pushed to 2-4 inches (Table 30-1).

Table 30-1. Tree Species Prone/Resistant to Decay

Weak Compartmentalizers Prone to Decay	Strong Compartmentalizers Resistant to Decay
• Beech (*Fagus* spp.) • Birch (*Betula* spp.) • Cherry, Peach, Plum and other *Prunus* spp.) • Crabapple (*Malus* spp.) • Hackberry (*Celtis* spp.) • Horsechestnut and Buckeye (*Aesculus* spp.) • Maples (some *Acer* spp.): Norway, Silver • Oak (some *Quercus* spp.): Pin, Shumard • Poplar, Cottonwood, & Aspen (*Populus* spp.) • Redbud (*Cercis* spp.) • Willow (*Salix* spp.)	• Black Locust (*Robinia pseudoacacia*) • Catalpa (*Catalpa* spp.) • Elm, American (*Ulmus Americana*) • Honeylocust (*Gleditsia* spp.) • Hornbean (*Carpinus* spp.) • Maples (some *Acer* spp.): Red, Sugar • Oak (some *Quercus* spp.): Bur, English, Live, Northern Red, White • Pine (some *Pinus* spp.) • Walnut (*Juglans* spp.) • Yew (*Taxus* spp.) Note: Will lose resistance with stress factors such as severe soil compaction, drought, hardscape over rooting area, etc.

However, we don't live in the ideal world. Sometime larger diameter cuts are needed. Any pruning cut four inches and larger needs to take into account the increased risk for failure and reduced health associated with internal decay and cracking. Cuts on large branches often create new problems with high potential for failure!

REMOVAL CUTS

Removal cuts (also known as thinning cuts or collar cuts) remove side branches back to the larger parent branch or trunk. If the branch union has a branch collar, removal cuts have the advantage of preserving the **branch defense zone,** providing a strong defense against internal decay (Figure 30-2).

Figure 30-1 ▍ *Cross-section of a Douglas fir. Dark wood in the center is the heartwood.*

Removal cuts reduce the canopy density but have little impact on height. Thinning with removal cuts allows better light penetration into the canopy, which encourages desired growth of interior branches. This improves trunk taper and increases the general vigor of primary branches and the trunk. Removal cuts reduce the weight on large branches, giving the tree resilience to snow loading. The primary use of removal cuts is in structural pruning of small middle-aged and older trees and on shrubs.

Two features on the branch, the *branch collar* and the *branch bark ridge*, help identify the proper cut angle. The **branch collar** is the area where the annual growth rings of the trunk fold in between the annual growth rings of the side branch, in a manner similar to shuffling a deck of cards. On some species, the branch collar is readily noticeable, while on other species the branch collar is less obvious (Figure 30-3).

The **branch bark ridge** is where the bark from the trunk joins the bark from the side branch. It looks like a dark line or small mountain range extending out from the crotch down both sides of the trunk/branch. It mirrors the angle of attachment of the side branch (Figure 30-3).

Within the branch collar is a narrow cone of cells called the **branch defense zone**. These cells activate the growth of **woundwood**, the callus tissue that grows over the pruning cut. With a proper cut, the woundwood grows out from all sides in a donut shape over the wound. If the branch collar is nicked, the woundwood does not grow from that point. It is common to see a pruning cut where the woundwood fills in only from two sides, indicating that the top and bottom of the branch collar were injured (Figures 30-4 and 30-5).

The branch defense zone also plays an important role in activating a strong reaction zone, inhibiting the spread of decay organisms into the trunk. If the branch collar is injured or removed during pruning, the branch defense zone will fail, limiting the growth of woundwood and predisposing the cut to decay. Thus, a primary objective in a correct removal cut is to preserve the branch collar intact.

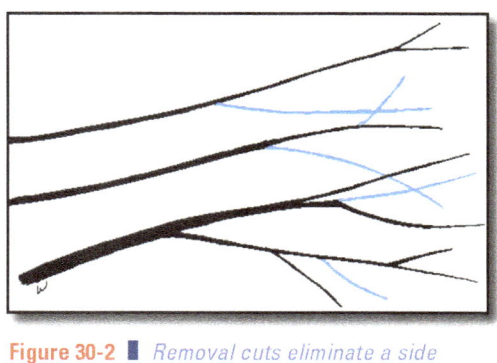

Figure 30-2 ▮ *Removal cuts eliminate a side branch back to the trunk or parent branch.*

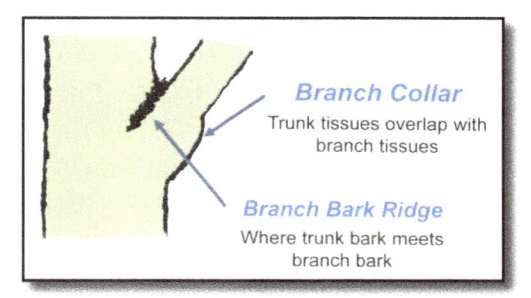

Figure 30-3 ▮ *Branch collar and branch bark ridge.*

Figure 30-4 ▮ *Branch Defense Zone—Within the branch collar is the branch defense zone, a narrow ring of cells that effectively initiates a strong reaction in which chemical changes protect the trunk from decay. If the branch collar is cut or nicked in pruning, the defense zone may fail, predisposing the wound to decay.*

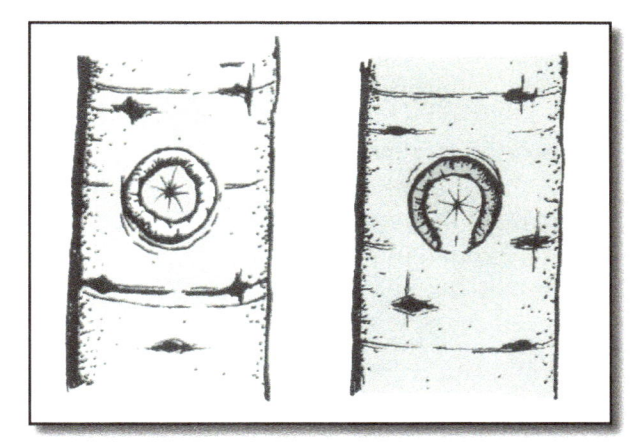

Figure 30-5 ▮ *Woundwood—On the left, a proper pruning cut was made. Woundwood grows over the cut in a donut-like fashion. On the right, the pruning cut nicked the branch collar on the bottom. See how the woundwood fails to grow where the collar was nicked.*

With a *removal cut*, the final cut should be just beyond the branch collar. Because the woundwood that grows over the pruning cut originates in the branch defense zone, it is imperative that the branch collar not be cut or otherwise injured in pruning. To eliminate error, cut a little beyond the collar region (i.e., one-eighth inch for small-diameter twigs and one-quarter inch for larger branches) (Figure 30-6).

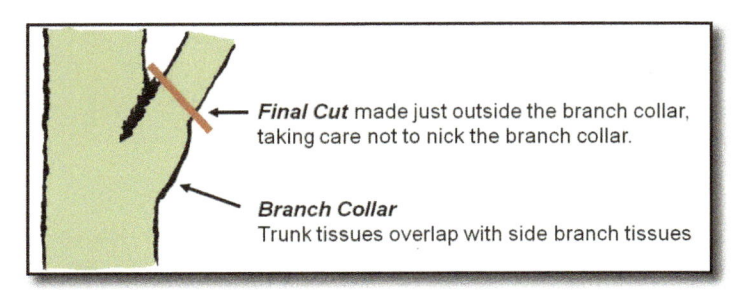

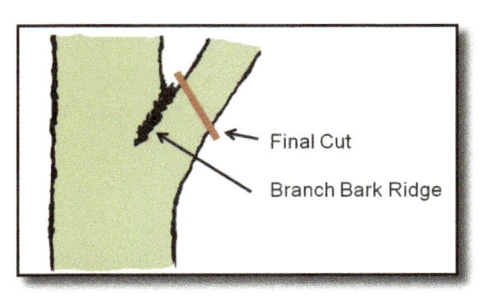

Figure 30-6 ▪ *Removal cut.*

Figure 30-7 ▪ *When the branch collar is not clearly identifiable, make the final thinning cut at the angle that mirrors the angle of the branch bark ridge.*

In species where the branch collar is not clearly identifiable, look for the branch bark ridge. Make the final cut at the angle that mirrors (lies opposite) the angle of the *branch bark ridge* (Figure 30-7).

When a branch union has no branch collar (the side branch is greater than half the diameter of the adjacent trunk), tilt the angle of the final cut out a little more to minimize the size of the wound. Be aware that in the absence of a branch collar, there is no branch defense zone to activate rapid woundwood growth and activate a strong reaction to suppress the potential for decay.

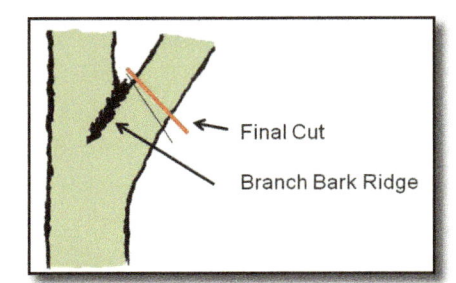

Figure 30-8 ▪ *When the branch union has no branch collar (the side branch is greater than half the trunk diameter), tilt the cut angle out a little more to reduce the diameter of the cut wound.*

When removing a dead branch, the final cut should be just outside the branch collar of live bark tissue. If a collar of live wood has begun to grow out along the dead branch, remove only the dead stub, leaving the collar intact. Do not cut into living tissues (Figure 30-9).

REDUCTION CUTS

Reduction cuts remove a larger branch or trunk back to a smaller-diameter side branch. Reduction cuts are commonly used in training young trees. They are also the only type of cut that will significantly lower a tree's height.

Figure 30-9 ▪ *When removing a dead branch, do not cut into or otherwise damage the branch collar or woundwood growing around the dead branch.*

However, reduction cuts do not have a branch defense zone, leaving the branch with a weak defense against decay. This is not a major concern on young, actively growing branches. However, reduction cuts are discouraged on mature trees and on limbs larger than two inches in diameter. On trees under stress or in decline, avoid reduction cuts as they can accelerate the decline.

In a reduction cut, make the final cut to bisect (split the difference) between the branch bark ridge angle and an imaginary line perpendicular to the stem being removed (Figure 30-10). Alternatively, the angle could be tilted up a little more to perpendicular to reduce the size of the wound. The exact angle is not critical as long as it is not flat on top (water needs to readily run off).

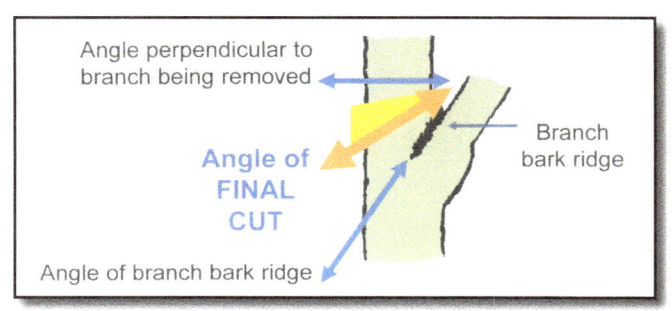

Angle perpendicular to branch being removed

Angle of FINAL CUT

Branch bark ridge

Angle of branch bark ridge

Figure 30-10 ■ *Reduction Cut—When pruning back a larger branch to a smaller branch, the angle of the final cut should split the difference between the angle of the branch bark ridge and the angle perpendicular to the branch being removed.*

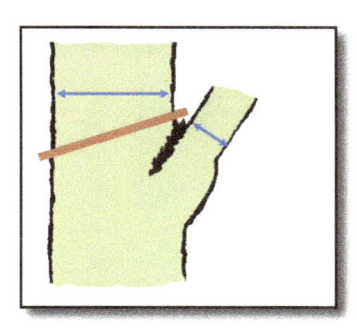

Figure 30-11 ■ *To prevent excessive suckering, the smaller branch should be at least one-third the diameter of the larger branch.*

Figure 30-12 ■ *This adventitious sucker growth from a reduction cut is structurally unsound and prone to storm damage as it grows.*

To prevent undesired suckering at this point, the diameter of the smaller side branch should be at least one-third (preferably one-half) the diameter of the larger branch being removed. If the diameter of the smaller branch is less than one-third the diameter of the larger branch being removed, the cut is considered a heading cut and is generally unacceptable in pruning standards (Figures 30-11 and 30-12).

HEADING CUTS

Heading cuts remove the growing tips of branches. This releases the side buds to grow, resulting in more dense growth at the point of pruning (Figure 30-13).

A type of undesirable heading cut is the removal of a large trunk/branch back to a smaller side branch when the side branch is less than one-third the size of the larger trunk being removed. Structurally unsound water sprouts often emerge along the branch, and the tree may become more unsound than before the pruning (Figure 30-14).

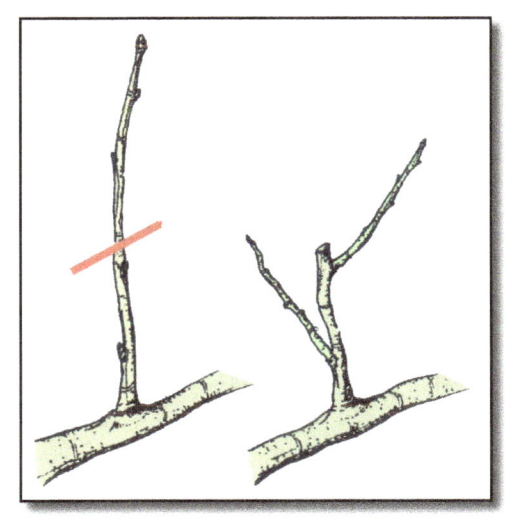

Figure 30-13 ■ *Heading cuts remove the growing tips of branches, releasing side buds to grow.*

Heading cuts are undesirable for most pruning objectives on shade trees. Topping a tree with heading cuts gives a surge of new branch growth at the tree's top. The new growth is often structurally unsound and prone to storm damage. Growth in the tree's interior thins out from increased shading, decreasing the tree's overall health and vigor.

On shrubs, heading cuts or "shearing" creates a very dense upper/outer canopy that shades out the lower/inner portion, creating a woody base.

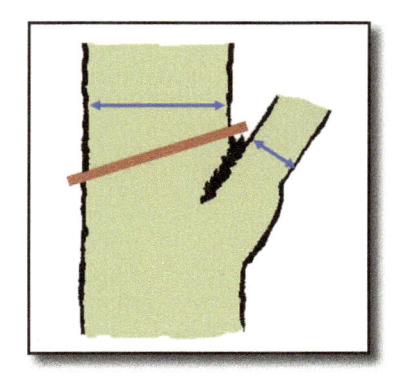

Figure 30-14 ■ *Removing a larger trunk or branch back to a small side branch when the side branch is less than one-third the diameter of the adjacent trunk is also considered a heading cut. This leads to structurally unsound growth of water sprouts and is not considered an acceptable pruning cut.*

THREE-CUT METHOD FOR LARGER BRANCHES

When removing any branch larger than one inch in diameter, use a three-cut method to protect the bark from tearing (Figure 30-15).

Cut 1. Coming out twelve to fifteen inches from the branch union (crotch), make an undercut approximately one-third to halfway through the branch.

Cut 2. Moving a couple of inches out past the first cut, make the second cut from above, removing the branch. This double-cut method prevents the weight of the branch from tearing the bark below the collar.

Cut 3. Make the third and final cut at the correct pruning point. For example, on a removal cut, just outside the branch collar. For woundwood growth, take extra caution not to cut into or otherwise injure the branch collar.

WOUND DRESSINGS

Wound dressings do not prevent decay organisms from moving in. In fact, the older, tar-type dressings actually interfere with the natural woundwood growth and may create conditions favorable for decay organisms. Generally, leave pruning cuts dry and untreated.

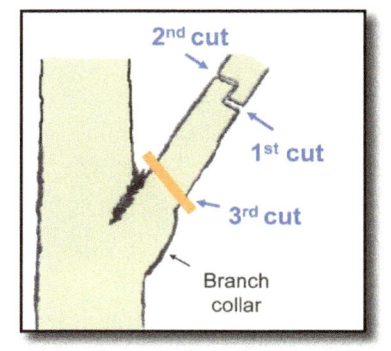

Figure 30-15 ■ *Three-cut method for any branch larger than one inch.*

Occasionally, a thin layer of water-based dressing or paint may be applied solely for aesthetic purposes. Never use an oil-based paint, tar, or other materials that contain petroleum solvents. A dark-colored material over a wound may predispose the wound site to winter injury. When managing diseases such as fire blight, a fungicide/bactericide may be used as a wound dressing.

The key to good wound closure is proper pruning, making a smooth cut just beyond the branch collar, and making all cuts on branches less than two inches in diameter. Trees under stress (soil compaction, drought, overly wet soils, insect or disease problems, lawnmower damage to the trunk, etc.) are less capable of fighting the invasion of decay organisms.

TIME OF YEAR TO PRUNE

Dead, diseased, and damaged wood can be removed any time of year as needed.

When it comes to removing live wood, there are better times of year for pruning. Light pruning—up to ten percent of the foliage—may generally be done any time of year on healthy trees without stress factors.

Late winter—Pruning in the late dormant season (before buds swell) is considered the routine pruning time on many tree species. However, some species are prone to bleeding if pruned in the spring. While this is more of a cosmetic issue than a health issue, most arborists avoid pruning bleeders in the late dormant season (Table 30-2).

Table 30-2. Examples of Trees Prone to Spring Bleeding

Birch	Kentucky coffeetree
Black locust	Maple
Elms	Mulberry
Goldenchain tree	Poplar
Hackberry	Walnut
Japanese pagodatree	Willow

Spring, during growth flush, is generally considered an undesirable time to prune trees. The bark and cambium tissues are easily damaged. Pruning may stimulate excessive water sprout growth or reduce overall vigor.

Midsummer, following growth flush (as leaves reach full size, harden, and turn dark summer green), is considered an excellent time to prune. It is the preferred time for spring bleeders. It may be the best time of year to suppress decay potential.

Late summer to fall is generally considered an undesirable time to prune. It may stimulate canopy growth and interfere with winter hardiness.

Late fall to early winter is generally considered an undesirable time to prune. Extreme cold (below zero) may cause cambium damage near the pruning cut.

Drought—Do not remove live wood from trees in drought stress. This removes stored photosynthates that the tree is living on during the stress.

Pest management consideration—In some insect management programs, pruning may need to be timed before insect flight periods or avoided during insect flight periods.

PRUNING EQUIPMENT

Hand pruners are used to cut small limbs up to one-quarter to one-half inch in diameter (depending on the wood hardness). The bypass or scissor-type pruner (cutting as the blade crosses past the hooked anvil in a scissor action) is considered the best type. The anvil type (cutting as the blade pushes against the anvil) is more prone to tearing and mashing the tissues. The best advice on pruners is to purchase the best pair you can afford. It will last for years. Inexpensive pruners are short-lived.

In using bypass-type hand pruners, place the blade toward the tree with the anvil toward the outside. This allows for a closer cut. For bypass pruners, sharpen only the beveled edge of the blade pointing toward the anvil, never the anvil side of the blade.

Loppers are used for larger branches, generally up to one-half inches in diameter. With long handles, they make quick work of cutting up prunings on the ground.

Pole pruners make poor-quality cuts. They are used to cut small branches out of reach from the ground.

Handsaws are used for branches larger than one-half inch. There are two general types of tree saws. Tree saws with curved blades cut as the saw is pulled and are considered safer to use. Tree saws with straight blades cut as the saw is pushed. To remove the moist sawdust, tree saws have a wider teeth spread than lumber saws. In a cut larger than 1 inch, a three-cut method should be used.

Chain saws are extremely dangerous. In the United States, 40,000 to 90,000 people have serious injuries, and forty to sixty are fatally injured each year from chain saw accidents. Most accidents occur to the left leg, the shoulders, and the face. Chain saws should only be used by someone specifically trained in chain saw safety. A common accident occurs when the limb kicks back as the cut is being completed. Personal protective clothing is needed. Safety glasses and boots are required by law. Helmet, hearing protection, gloves, and leg protection are also recommended.

1. Identify/define the following:

    a. Branch bark ridge

    b. Branch defense zone

    c. Reaction zone

    d. Woundwood

2. What is a removal cut?

    a. What are the advantages of a removal cut?

    b. When the branch bark ridge is visible, where is the removal cut made?

    c. If the branch collar is not easy to identify, where is the removal cut made?

    d. If the branch has no branch collar, where is the removal cut made?

    e. What happens when the branch collar is cut or injured?

    f. What happens when nubs or very short branches are left?

    g. With hindsight, how does one evaluate when the thinning cut was properly made?

3. What is a reduction cut?

    a. What are the uses and limitations of reduction cuts?

    b. What is the proper angle for a reduction cut?

    c. In a reduction cut, what is the proper size relationship of the branch being removed to the branch pruned back to? Why is it important?

4. What is a heading cut?

    a. How does it influence regrowth of the plant?

    b. What are the effects of using heading cuts on larger branches?

5. Explain the three-step method for pruning large branches. Why is it needed? When is it needed?

6. Describe the pros and cons of pruning live branches during the:

    a. Late winter (dormant)

    b. Spring (during growth flush)

    c. Midsummer (after leaves harden and turn dark green)

    d. Late summer and fall

    e. Late fall and early winter

    f. During drought

Chapter

31*

Structural Training of Young Shade Trees

PRUNING BASICS

Structural training is a multi-year investment requiring evaluation and corrective pruning on an annual basis. Young trees require little pruning. However, the training a tree receives while in the early "growth phase" of its life cycle determines its structural integrity for life. Many trees become prone to wind and snow damage as they mature due to the lack of structural training while young. Proper structural training of the young tree makes it especially resilient to storm damage when mature.

In this chapter, we look at the ideal structure for a young tree making it resilient to wind and snow loading. In selecting trees at the nursery, choose trees that will not require extensive pruning to reach the desired structure. In real world settings, not all trees will fit the ideal description. The objective is to set the direction of what is desirable, recognizing that some trees simply do not meet the preferred structure for storm resilience.

Time of Year

Structural pruning is typically done in late winter, before trees break dormancy. Pruning is generally avoided during the spring growth flush as bark is rather tender at this point in time. Mid-summer pruning is preferred for tree species prone to bleeding if spring pruned (including birch, black locust, elm, goldenchain tree, hackberry, Japanese pagoda tree, Kentucky coffeetree, maple, mulberry, poplar, walnut, and willow).

*Authors: David Whiting, Eric Hammond, and Alison O'Connor, Colorado State University Extension. Photographs and line drawings by David Whiting.

Size of Branches

Ideally, all pruning cuts are two inches in diameter and smaller. The structural training stage basically ends when pruning cuts would be greater than two inches. Any pruning cut four inches and larger must be justified by taking into account the potential for decay.

STRUCTURAL TRAINING STEPS

Structural training follows a series of steps. Considerations at each step determine the direction to take in following steps.

Step 1—Dosage: Maximum Amount of Live Wood/Foliage to Remove

The maximum amount of foliage/live wood that can be removed per season depends on the actual growth rate of the tree. Look at six to 12 branches around the tree to assess growth rates. Look for what is the typical growth rate for most branches, rather than fastest or slowest growing branches (Table 31-1).

Table 31-1. Dosage: Maximum Amount of Live Wood/Foliage to Remove per Season on Young, Actively Growing, Trees

Actual Annual Growth	Estimated Maximum Amount of Live Wood/ Foliage to Remove Per Season
3 to 4 plus feet.	25% to 50%.
1 to 2 feet	10% to 25%.
6 to 12 inches	Approximately 10%.
Little annual growth.	Limit pruning to a light dosage, correcting codominant trunks.
Tree under critical stress with minimal annual growth.	Limit pruning to cleaning (removal of dead and damaged branches).

In situations where trees are pruned annually (the ideal situation), the appropriate pruning dose would be light. However, in real world situations, trees are often pruned only once every several years. Here the appropriate pruning dose may be higher. In situations where heavy pruning is needed, complete the work over a period of years.

Excessive pruning can lead to watersprouts (upright, sucker-like shoots emerging on the trunk or branches). Waterspouts, a common response to over pruning and storm damage, are structurally unsound. Excessive pruning also creates a hormone imbalance between Auxins (produced in the terminal buds) which stimulates root growth, and Gibberellins (produced in the root tips) which stimulates canopy growth. Since roots have multiple regeneration periods each season, this imbalance puts the root system into a decline, resulting in a multi-year decline in canopy growth (Figure 31-1).

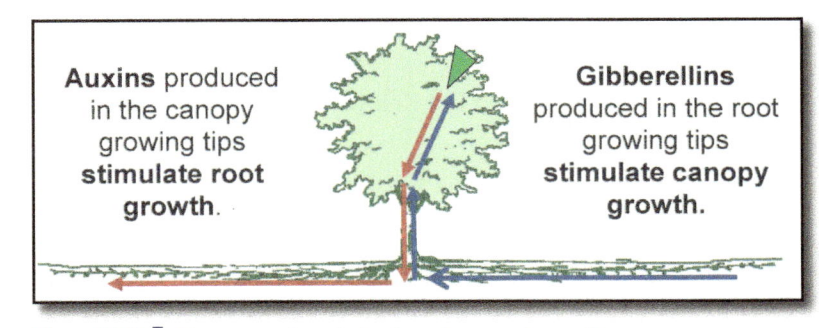

Auxins produced in the canopy growing tips **stimulate root growth**.

Gibberellins produced in the root growing tips **stimulate canopy growth**.

Figure 31-1 ▮ *Heavy pruning at planting slows root growth.*

Step 2—Growth Habit

The desired branching structure depends on the natural growth habit of the tree. Trees with an **excurrent** growth habit develop with a **central leader** (single trunk) to the top. Examples of excurrent trees include aspen, linden, and pine. Trees with a **decurrent** growth habit develop a more rounded form with multiple **scaffold branches** (secondary trunk-like branches) or secondary trunks originating from the trunk. Examples of decurrent trees include maple, ash, elm, and honeylocust.

Table 31-2 shows comparisons in pruning objective of excurrent and decurrent trees.

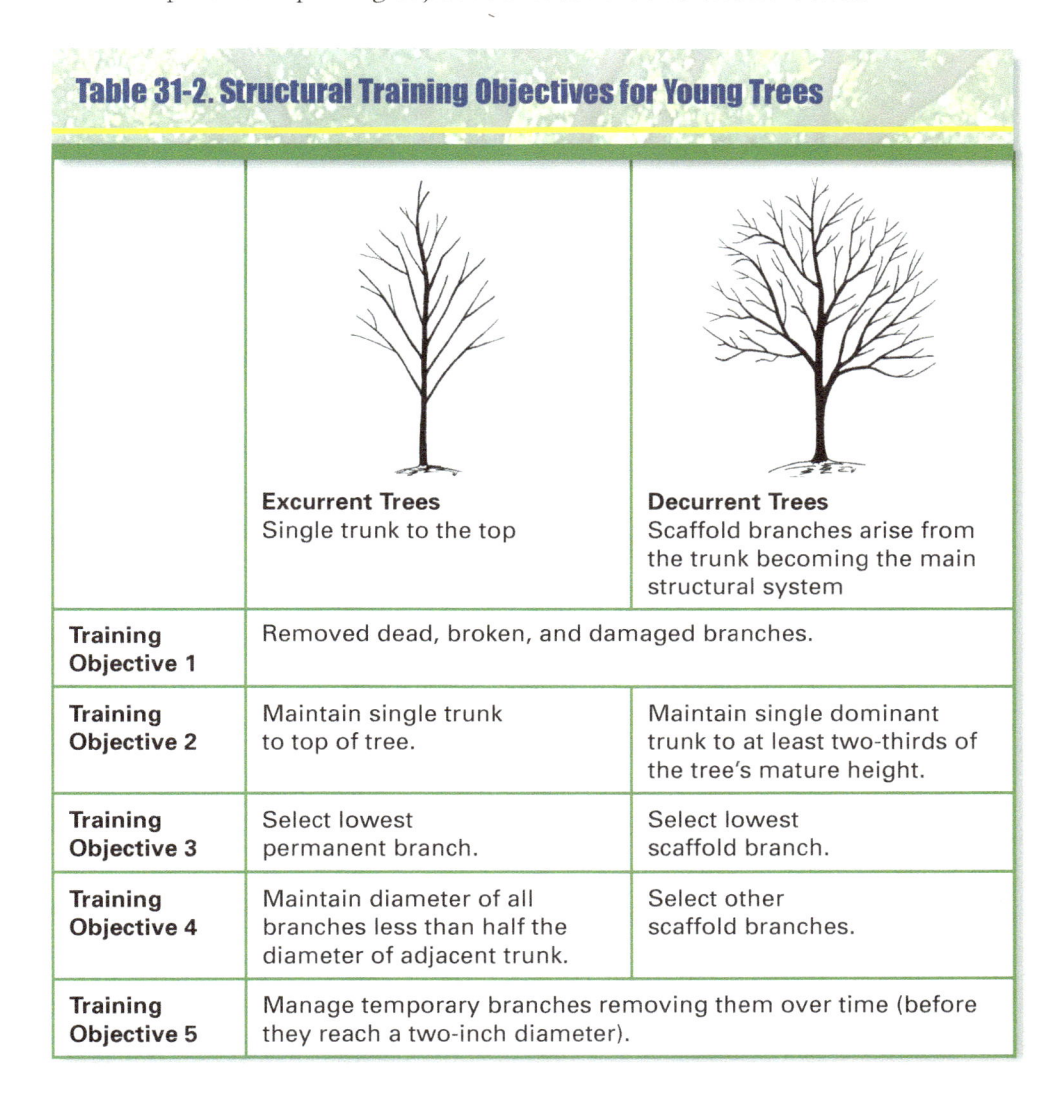

Table 31-2. Structural Training Objectives for Young Trees

	Excurrent Trees Single trunk to the top	**Decurrent Trees** Scaffold branches arise from the trunk becoming the main structural system
Training Objective 1	Removed dead, broken, and damaged branches.	
Training Objective 2	Maintain single trunk to top of tree.	Maintain single dominant trunk to at least two-thirds of the tree's mature height.
Training Objective 3	Select lowest permanent branch.	Select lowest scaffold branch.
Training Objective 4	Maintain diameter of all branches less than half the diameter of adjacent trunk.	Select other scaffold branches.
Training Objective 5	Manage temporary branches removing them over time (before they reach a two-inch diameter).	

Step 3—Pruning Objectives

Structural training of young shade trees is based on five pruning objectives. Evaluation of all five is generally done before actual pruning occurs, as considerations are interrelated.

Objective 1—Remove Broken and Damaged Branches

Actual pruning begins with the removal of broken, damaged, and rubbing branches (Figure 31-2).

Competing branches (branches growing in the same space) are also a consideration. However, which one to keep and which ones to remove generally sort out in the other steps.

Objective 2—Develop Trunk

The primary pruning objective is to eliminate multiple trunks. If multiple trunks start to develop, remove all but one. If the leader is killed, select a side branch to become the new leader, removing its competition (a multi-year process). It may be helpful to loosely tie the new leader to a stick to bend it to an upward orientation.

Codominant Trunks

In training trees, arborists have zero tolerance for **codominant trunks** (adjacent trunks of similar diameter). Codominant trunks account for the majority of wind- and snow-related tree failures in Colorado and other snowy climates.

Figure 31-2 ▮ *Rubbing branches.*

With codominant trunks, no branch collar develops to wrap the two trunks together. (The **branch collar** is the area where trunk wood wraps around the branch wood creating a structurally strong branch union.) The **branch union** (crotch) is structurally weak and prone to breakage as the trunks reach a size greater than three to four inches in diameter (Figure 31-3).

Note: In selecting a tree, it is advisable to avoid purchasing trees with codominant trunks.

Figure 31-3 ▮ *Codominant trunks—A branch union with two trunks of similar size is structurally weak and prone to storm damage. "Included bark" (hidden bark) between the trunks prevents the wood from growing together. Without a branch collar, wood of the two trunks does not knit together. In structural pruning, there is zero tolerance for codominant trunks.*

Excurrent Trees—Maintain Single Trunk to Top of Tree

On excurrent (central leader) trees, maintain a single trunk to the top of the tree. If a side branch begins growing upright in a trunk-like fashion, prune it back to redirect the growth to an outward direction or remove it entirely. Generally, do not prune or "head back" the central leader (trunk) (Figure 31-4).

Figure 31-4 ▮ *On excurrent trees, maintain a single trunk to the top.*

Decurrent Trees—Maintain Single Dominant Trunk to at Least Two-Thirds of the Tree's Mature Height

The overall objective with decurrent trees is to develop a structural system of *scaffold branches* rather than secondary trunks. **Scaffold branches** are the major structural, trunk-like branches that originate off of the trunk. By definition, a scaffold branch must be less than one-half the size of the adjacent trunk. Less than one-third is preferred. This allows for a branch collar to develop, creating a structurally strong branch union. In contrast, **secondary trunks** lack the size relationship for branch collar development, creating structurally weak branch unions.

In an open landscape setting, most decurrent trees naturally develop multiple secondary trunks often arising at the same location, predisposing the tree to storm damage.

On decurrent trees, maintain a single dominant trunk to at least two-thirds of the tree's mature height. For example, if the mature tree height is thirty feet, a single trunk should dominate to at least twenty feet. If the mature tree reaches sixty feet, a single trunk dominates to at least forty feet. Scaffold branches become the secondary framework of the tree. By training, secondary trunks are avoided (Figure 31-5).

Figure 31-5 ▮ *On decurrent trees, maintain a single dominant trunk to at least two-thirds of the tree's mature height.*

If vigorously upward-growing side branches begin to compete with the central leader, prune back the branch to a more outward growing side branch. Some tree species naturally put out many upward growing secondary trunks. Heavy pruning over a period of years is desirable to establish a dominant central leader with subordinate smaller side branches.

Generally, do not "head-back" (prune) the central leader.

Objective 3—Select Lowest Branch

It is often desirable to **raise** the canopy (remove lower branches) so they are out of the way of human activities like mowing the lawn and lawn games. For shade trees in lawns, patios, and along sidewalks, the lowest permanent branch generally starts seven to ten feet above ground level. On smaller specimen trees in a garden bed, lower branching may be preferred. Over streets, the lowest branches start at fourteen feet. In wooded settings, the canopy is raised to ten feet as a fire prevention technique.

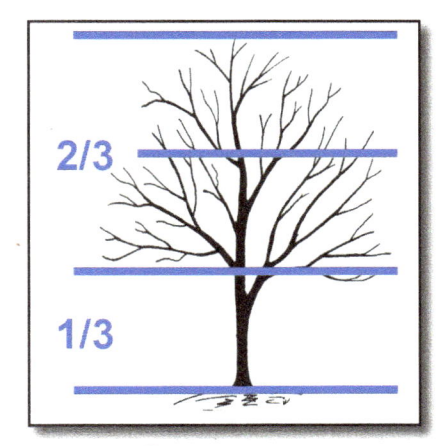

Figure 31-6 ▮ *To develop a strong trunk taper, at least one-half of the foliage must be in the lower two-thirds of the tree. Temporary branches below the lowest permanent branches will be removed over time. (Refer to Objective 5.)*

Many gardeners mistakenly plan to remove lower branches as the tree reaches a more mature size. Removing these larger branches as the tree matures opens the tree to internal decay. On decurrent trees, these lower branches typically make up a significant portion of the tree.

The objective is to identify what will be the lowest permanent branch at this early time in life, allowing the gardener to manage and remove lower branches over time. Branches below the lowest permanent branch are called **temporary branches**. Management and removal of the temporary branches will be discussed in Objective 5.

The lowest branch on any tree should originate in the bottom one-third of the tree. In establishing the lowest branch, do not "limb-up" a young tree too early in its growth. To develop a trunk taper resilient to wind, one-half of the leafing area should be found in the lower two-thirds of the tree. Lower **temporary branches** should be removed only as the tree grows in height, but before they reach two inches in diameter (Refer to Objective 5 for details.) (Figure 31-6).

On excurrent trees, select the lowest permanent branch. Branches below this point become temporary branches.

On decurrent trees, select the lowest permanent branch, which will become the first *scaffold branch*. Other scaffold branches will be selected based on the location of this branch. Branches below the lowest (first) scaffold branch become temporary branches.

Objective 4—Developing Branching Structure

In Objective 4, branches are managed differently for excurrent and decurrent trees.

Excurrent Trees: Maintain Diameter of All Branches Less Than Half the Trunk Diameter

For structural integrity, side branches must be less than one-half the diameter of the adjacent trunk. Less than one-third is preferred. Without this important size ratio, the branch collar fails to develop, creating a weak branch union (Figure 31-7).

If the diameter of a branch is growing too fast compared to the trunk, prune the branch back by one-thirds to two-thirds to slow its growth rate.

Spacing of branches along the trunk is not a critical structural issue on excurrent trees, as long as the trunk-to-side-branch ratio is within limits. Many species of excurrent trees develop branches in a whorl. This is structurally acceptable as long as the branch-to-trunk-size ratios are within limits. On some species of trees, thinning of competing branches (branches growing in the same space with the potential to rub and damage each other) may be desirable.

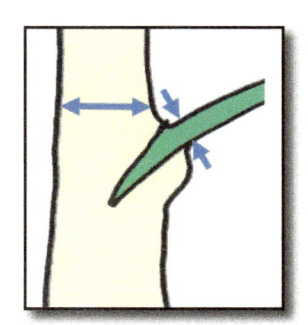

Figure 31-7 ▮ *For a branch collar to develop, the side branch must be less than one-half the diameter of the adjacent trunk.*

Decurrent Trees: Select Other Scaffold Branches

In the structural pruning of decurrent trees, an overall intent is to guide development of the branching structure, creating *scaffold branches* and eliminating secondary trunks. The intent is to create strong branch unions with a branch collar. For the branch collar to develop, the branch must be less than one-half (less than one-third preferable) the size of the adjacent trunk. Without the branch collar, secondary trunks are structurally weak and prone to breakage as the tree matures.

The selection of other scaffold branches takes place over a period of years as the tree grows in height. Branches along the trunk not destined to become scaffold branches are managed as **temporary branches** and are removed over time.

In selecting other scaffold branches, consider branch spacing and branch union (crotch) angles. In an open landscape setting, decurrent trees naturally develop more branches than is desirable, predisposing the tree to wind and snow damage as the tree matures. The objective of training is to correct this situation while the tree is young.

Branch spacing—Desired spacing for scaffold branches depends on the mature height of the tree. The rule of thumb is to allow at least 6 inches per 10 feet of mature tree height. Table 31-2 shows spacing for various mature heights (Table 31-2).

Table 31-2. Minimum Spacing for Scaffold Branches

Mature Tree Height	Minimum Scaffold Branch Spacing
20 feet	1 foot
30 feet	1.5 feet
40 feet	2 feet
50 feet	2.5 feet
60 feet	3 feet
70 feet	3.5 feet
80 feet	4 feet

Select scaffold branches with even distribution around the tree trunk. Where a scaffold branch is growing directly above another, vertical spacing should be at least sixty inches on trees with a mature height of thirty feet and taller, and eighteen to thirty-six inches on smaller trees (Figure 31-8).

Multiple branching at one location—When multiple scaffold branches arise from the same area, the branch collars cannot knit together into a strong branch union. These branches become vulnerable to wind and snow damage. In training a young decurrent tree, eliminate multiple branches arising at the same location. Many common shade trees, including maple, cottonwood, poplar, and elm, naturally develop multiple branchings at the same location (Figure 31-9).

Branch union angles—The problem with a narrow branch union (crotch) angle is the development of *included bark* (bark against bark inside the branch union) as the tree grows. With included bark, the branch collar cannot wrap the trunk wood around the side branch wood, creating a weak branch union. A branch union with a wide angle of attachment is also more resistant to the spread of decay.

In selecting scaffold branches, select outward-growing branches with a wide angle of attachment rather than upward-growing branches.

Objective 5—Manage Temporary Branches, Removing Them over Time

Temporary branches on the lower trunk are important to the tree's early growth. *Photosynthates* (carbohydrates and proteins produced by photosynthesis) produced in the lower canopy help develop the natural trunk taper, giving wind resilience. Shading by the lower foliage helps reduce sunscald of the tender bark.

Manage growth on temporary branches by keeping them short and removing them over time as the tree grows in height. Ideally, temporary branches are pruned back to a few buds. On temporary branches that have grown significantly before training begins, start by cutting them back by about 50%, removing more over time.

Temporary branches are removed before they reach a two-inch diameter. Pruning back a temporary branch slows the growth, giving more time before the branch must be removed due to size.

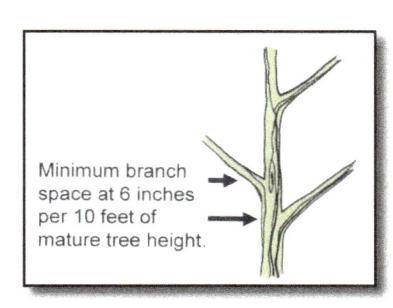

Minimum branch space at 6 inches per 10 feet of mature tree height.

Figure 31-8 ▮ *Minimum scaffold branch spacing is based on the mature height of the tree at six inches per ten feet of mature height. A tree that will grow to thirty feet should have scaffold branches spaced at least eighteen inches apart.*

Figure 31-9 ▮ *Multiple branches originating from the same location are structurally weak. An objective in structural training is to space scaffold branches.*

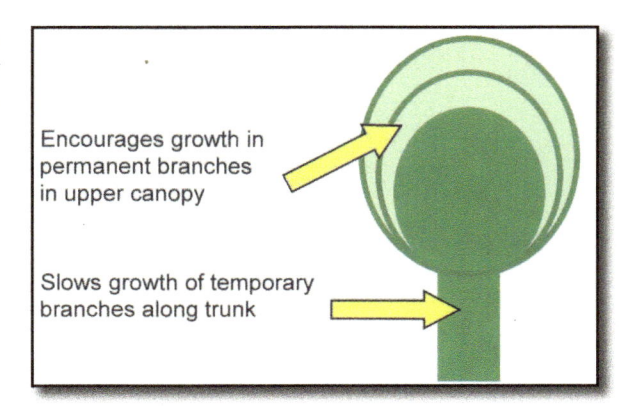

Keeping temporary branches short suppresses their rapid growth while encouraging the desired growth up in the scaffold branch structure. During the early training process, a young tree will have a cylinder of short temporary branches along the lower trunk (below the lowest permanent branch), with the tree's significant growth developing up in the permanent branch structure (Figure 31-10).

Preferred vertical spacing of temporary branches is four to six inches. Thus, some branches would be removed outright. On decurrent trees, no temporary branch should be within 6 inches of a scaffold branch. Branches between scaffold branches are also considered temporary branches. Maintain these temporary branches for one to five years, removing them before they reach a two-inch diameter.

On decurrent trees, it generally takes several years to manage and eventually remove temporary branches. Remember that the total amount of foliage that can be removed per season depends on the growth rate of the tree. In purchasing, select trees that require minimum corrective pruning to make them structurally sound.

1. In structural training of young shade trees, give the rule-of-thumb for dosage (i.e., the maximum amount of live wood/foliage removed per season)? How does the gardener determine the growth rates to set dosage? How is the dosage range adjusted for the specific tree?

2. Define *excurrent* and *decurrent* growth habits.

3. List the steps and pruning objectives for excurrent and decurrent trees.

4. Define codominant trunks. Why do arborists have zero tolerance for codominant trunks?

5. What are the options if multiple leaders develop? If the main leader is killed?

6. What is the standard height for the lowest permanent branch of sidewalk trees? Street tree? Trees in forest areas (fire management)?

7. What is the proper size relationship between the trunk and side branch? Why is it important? What are the options if a side branch is growing too large?

8. Define scaffold branch. What is the rule of thumb for minimum spacing of scaffold branches?

9. How do multiple branches arising at one site influence the branch collar and thus structural integrity?

10. What is the role of temporary branches on young trees?

11. Describe the management of temporary branches.

12. Given a young excurrent or decurrent tree (or a picture of a young excurrent tree), describe specific training for this tree.

13. When decurrent trees are not trained from early growth in the nursery and on the landscape site, it is often impossible to fully achieve the five training objectives. To minimize potential storm damage, what is the most important objective to pursue?

Chapter

32*

Pruning Maturing Trees

WHEN TO HIRE A PROFESSIONAL CERTIFIED ARBORIST

Pruning large trees is a safety issue beyond the training and experience of home gardeners. Hiring a bonded professional is the best approach for most tree pruning jobs. Look for arborists with certification from the International Society of Arboriculture (ISA). Many are listed in the phone book, and a list of ISA Certified Arborists working in the area can be found on the ISA website at www.isa-arbor.com. Be sure to ask about liability insurance coverage.

This chapter is written to help the home gardener understand issues around pruning mature trees and help with communication with certified arborists.

LIMITATIONS ON DIAMETER OF CUT

Ideally, all pruning cuts are two inches in diameter and smaller. On tree species resistant to decay, the standard could be pushed to two to four inches, maximum (depending on actual vigor and growth of the tree). These small wounds minimize the potential for internal decay. The two-inch diameter and smaller branch is primarily *sapwood* (newer xylem rings of living cells active in water transport and storage of photosynthates) that is not prone to decay.

Unless there is a strong justification, (taking into account the potential for a decay column and internal cracking) avoid removing branches larger than four inches in diameter. At approximately four inches, *heartwood* (older xylem rings of non-living cells no longer active in water transport) dominates the branch structure. The branch becomes prone to decay as heartwood has no resistance to the spread of decay and is prone to internal cracking.

---

*Author: David Whiting, Alison O'Connor and Eric Hammond, Colorado State University Extension. Photographs and line drawings by David Whiting.

(Note: Due to chemical changes in the cells, heartwood is often darker in color.) (Figure 1)

When a pruning cut or other injury opens a branch to decay, the decay column will take the current season of xylem ring and everything older. Decay creates a pipe-like structure in the branch. The healthy, undecayed wood will be the xylem rings that grow in future years. (Figure 2)

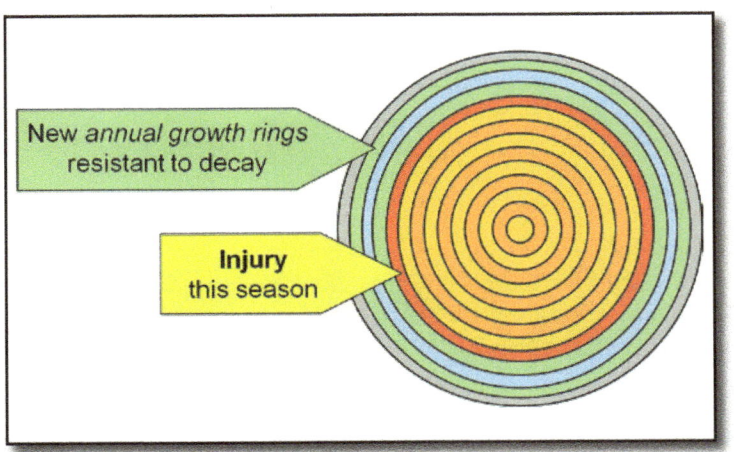

Figure 32-1 ▮ *Cross-section of Douglas fir. Light colored outer rings are sapwood. The dark wood in center is the heartwood.*

Figure 32-2 ▮ *When injury (such as improper pruning cuts) leads to decay, it takes the current season's xylem ring and everything older (inward). New growth (xylem rings that grow in future years) will be resistant to decay. Decay creates a pipe-like structure.*

For example, if a branch with eight-inch diameter xylem (wood) is pruned back to a trunk with 12-inch diameter xylem (wood) and decay results, the decay column in the trunk will be 12 inches wide (that is, the diameter of the trunk wood at the time the injury occurred). The tree would have to add six inches of healthy new growth to meet the minimum standards for structural strength (33% shell). If annual growth rings were ¼" wide, this would take 12 years! For additional information on tree decay and percent shell, refer to Chapter 29. (Figure 3)

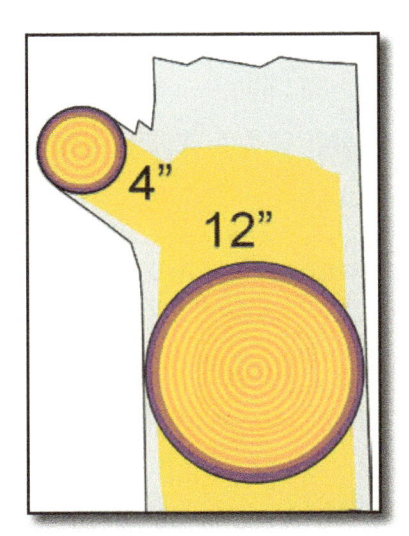

LIMITATIONS ON SIZE RELATIONSHIP WITH REDUCTION CUTS

Pruning often involves subordinating side branches or secondary trunks to a more dominant leader. This can only be achieved with ***reduction cuts*** (removing a larger trunk/branch back to a smaller side branch). In reduction cuts, the diameter of the side branch must be at least one-third the diameter of the trunk/parent branch removed. If the side branch is smaller, it becomes a ***heading cut***. (Figure 4)

A common mistake in lowering branch height is the use of heading cuts, which release waterspout (sucker) growth from the pruned branch. The regrowth will be structurally unsound, resulting in trees that may be more prone to storm damage than before pruning occurred. When pruning maturing trees, heading cuts are not acceptable in pruning standards! For additional details on reduction cuts refer to Chapter 30.

Figure 32-3 ▮ *The diameter of the decay column will be the diameter of the current season's xylem ring for the year that injury occurred and inwards. Structural weakness from the decay is offset by the growth of new wood (xylem rings) in future years.*

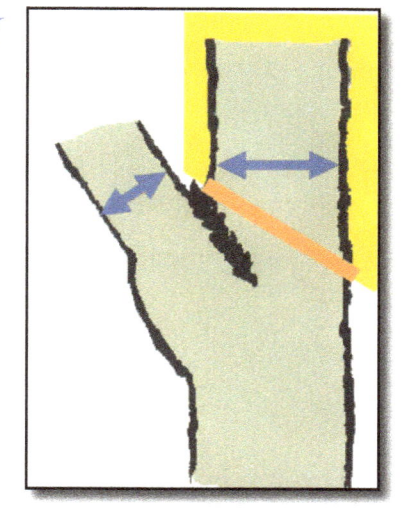

DOSAGE: MAXIMUM AMOUNT OF LIVE WOOD / FOLIAGE TO REMOVE

Do not indiscriminately remove branches with live foliage as this can add stress to the tree. **The amount of live wood and foliage to remove per season depends on the actual growth rate of the tree.** Young, actively growing, trees are rather tolerant of a heavy pruning dose. As trees become mature, they become intolerant of heavy pruning. Look at six to 12 branches around the tree to assess growth rates. Look for what is the typical growth rate for most branches, not the fastest or slowest growing branches.

- **Trees under severe stress putting on insignificant annual growth** – Limit pruning to *cleaning* (removal of dead and damaged branches). Live wood should not be removed on trees under severe stress (including drought stress). Heavy pruning simply removes the stored photosynthates that the tree is living on during the stress period!

- On **mature trees** (greater than 75% mature size for the site), pruning dose should be limited to 5% to 10%, based on actual growth and vigor of the tree.

- On **medium aged trees**, the dosage really depends on actual growth. Typical range would be 10% to 25% depending on actual growth and vigor of the tree.

In situations where trees are pruned annually (the ideal situation), the appropriate pruning dose would be on the lighter side. However, in real world situations, trees are often pruned only once every several years. Here the appropriate pruning dose may be heavier. In situations where heavy pruning is needed, complete the work over a period of years.

Excessive pruning can lead to watersprouts (upright, sucker-like shoots emerging on the trunk or branches). Waterspouts, a common response to over pruning and storm damage, are structurally unsound.

Excessive pruning also creates a hormone imbalance between Auxins (produced in the terminal buds of the canopy) which stimulates root growth and Gibberellins (produced in the root tips) which stimulates canopy growth. This puts the root system into a multi-year decline, resulting in a multi-year decline in canopy growth.

Storm damage may take of excessive amounts of live wood leading to heavy canopy growth and watersprouts the first year due to high Gibberellins. The natural root generation declines the first year due to low Auxins. This decline in root regeneration leads to a multi-year decline in root and canopy growth. The storm damage counts into the dosage of life wood removed. When storm damage takes off more than the appropriate dosage for the trees actual growth, limit pruning to cleaning (removal of dead and damaged) until the tree rebalances and resumes normal growth rates.

Removal of dead wood does not count into the dosage.

OTHER GENERAL GUIDELINES

- To maintain trunk taper resilient to winds, at least one-half of the foliage should be in the lower two-thirds of the tree. The lowest limb should originate in the bottom one-third of the tree's height.

- Pruning should maintain the tree's natural shape.

- Avoid "lion-tailing" where the small twiggy inner foliage is cleaned-out on the lower scaffold branches and secondary trunks. This shifts weight to the ends of branches and reduces the damping effect on the branch; increasing the potential for wind damage. It reduces the taper (widening of the branch/trunk as it moves downwards) increasing the potential for branch/trunk failure. It also reduces the stored photosynthate reserves in the lower branching structure decreasing resilience to stress factors.

- Avoid topping a tree. Topping opens the tree to internal decay and cracking. Regrowth of watersprouts (adventitious shoots) is structurally unsound.

- Written specification for any pruning job should include the following:

  —Clearly state which tree(s) will be pruned.

  —Clearly indicate the objectives for pruning (why prune), such as reduce risk of failure due to wind damage or snow loading, manage health, improve aesthetics, provide clearance, improve view.

  —Specify pruning methods (how to prune) to meet the objectives, such as structural pruning, cleaning, thinning, raising, reducing, restoration pruning.

  —State the size specification for the minimum and/or maximum branch size to be removed. For example, *"Cuts should be made on branches two inches and less in diameter"* and *"In a reduction cut, the side branch pruned back to should be at least one-third the diameter of the branch removed."*

  —Specify the dosage (maximum amount, by percentage, of live wood/foliage to be removed per season). For example, *"Pruning should not remove more than 15% of the live crown."*

  —In writing pruning specifications, the word "should" refers to a practice that is routine and recommended. The word "shall" refers to a practice that is mandatory.

  —Include these generic safety statements to reduce the homeowner's and pruning crew's liability. *"All work shall be performed in accordance with American National Standards Institute A300 Pruning Standards and Z133.3 Safety Standards." "All work shall be performed under the supervision of a licensed, International Society of Arboriculture certified arborist."*

PRUNING OBJECTIVES

Pruning should be based on pruning objectives (why to prune). Do not indiscriminately remove branches. Pruning objectives determine methods (how to prune) to be used, which in turn determine the type of pruning cuts made. Table 1 lists common objectives, methods and types of pruning cuts.

Table 32-1. Objectives and Methods for Pruning Maturing Trees

Objectives (Whys)	Methods (Hows)	Pruning Cuts
Reduce risk of failure (wind and snow)	Structural	Removal cut
Improve structure	Cleaning	Reduction cut
Maintain health	Thinning	Heading cut
Improve aesthetics	Raising	
Provide clearance	Reducing	
Improve view	Restoring	
Reduce shade	Pollarding	
Influence flowering and fruiting		

STRUCTURAL PRUNING

A common pruning objective with maturing trees is to reduce the potential risk of failure from wind and snow loading. Significant wind damage occurs on structurally weak trees with wind gusts of 60 to 75 mph. Even structurally sound trees may fail with wind gusts above 95 mph.

In Colorado (and other snowy climates), most significant storm damage is due to codominant trunks (trunks of similar size). Structural problems of this type should have been corrected while the tree was in the early growth stage. Arborists have a limited potential to correct structural defects on middle-aged and mature trees without predisposing the tree to internal decay, cracking, and creating an unsightly shaped tree. (Figure 5)

Structural pruning centers around developing a dominant trunk with subordinate side branches and secondary limbs. To be most effective, it requires annual pruning over a period of years, rather than an occasional one-time pruning.

Written pruning specifications for structural pruning of maturing trees should include the following:

Figure 32-5 ■ *Codominant trunks (adjacent trunks of similar size) account for the majority of storm damage in Colorado landscapes.*

- Identify branches where work will be done (for example, "*codominant trunk on south side of tree*").

- Identify the methods to be used in pruning (for example, "*the secondary trunk on the south side should be reduced by 10 feet*").

Subordinate Pruning Considerations

Structural pruning of maturing trees is often referred to as ***subordinate pruning***, where secondary trunks (and side branches) with weak branch unions are subordinated to a dominant trunk. To avoid removing too much foliage/live wood in one season, subordinate pruning generally requires work over a period of years.

In evaluating how to prune the maturing tree, take into account the following considerations:

What Is the Purpose for Pruning the Tree?

Structural pruning (subordinating weak side branches to a more dominant trunk) is more effective in reducing failure potential than general crown reduction or crown thinning. With general crown reduction or thinning, regrowth simply replaces what was pruned off in a few years.

Wind loading – To reduce potential of failure due to wind loading, the height of secondary trunks and side branches with weak branch unions must be lowered. This is done with reduction cuts, and proper reduction cuts may not be possible on many maturing trees without introducing decay and internal cracking, and structurally unsound waterspout growth.

For example, many cottonwood and popular trees will not have side branches of adequate size for proper reduction cuts (side branch prune back to must be at least 1/3 the diameter of the trunk removed).

A slight reduction in secondary trunk/branch height will not achieve the objective. To significantly reduce the risk of failure, reduction may need to be 1/3 or more of the branch length. On maturing trees, this may be into braches too larger for pruning by pruning standards. Not all branches can be effectively reduced.

Snow loading – To reduce potential of failure due to snow loading, the snow catching volume of the branch needs to be reduced. This is best achieved with structural pruning of weak branches.

What Is the Structural Integrity of the Branch Union?

To evaluate the structural integrity of the branch union (crotch) look at the **Aspect Ratio** (that is the diameter of the side branch to the diameter of the trunk). Any side branch with an aspect ratio larger than 1 to 2 (diameter of side branch greater than ½ the diameter of the trunk) will be structurally weak. For example, if the diameter of the trunk is four inches, all side branches should be less than two inches.

A structurally strong branch union has a **branch collar** (where the annual growth rings of the trunk wrap around the annual growth rings of the side branch). For a branch collar to develop, the side branch needs to be less than one-half the diameter of the adjacent trunk. Less than one-third is preferred. Branch unions with branch collars are also more resistant to the spread of decay. For more details on branch collars, refer to Chapter 29 (Figure 32-6).

Branch unions can also be compromised with narrow crotch angles, leading to **included bark** (bark against bark) and multiple branching originating in the same area.

Codominant trunks—In Colorado (and other snowy regions), most storm damage occurs due to **codominant trunks** (adjacent trunks of similar size). Structural problems of this type should have been corrected while the tree was in the early growth stage. Arborists have limited ability to correct structural defects on middle-aged and mature trees without predisposing the tree to internal decay and cracking.

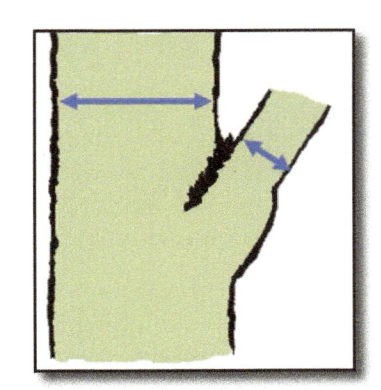

Figure 32-6 ■ *To evaluate the structural strength of a branch union, compare the diameters of the trunk and side branch. A branch union is structurally strong when it has a branch collar. For the branch collar to develop, the diameter of the side branch needs to be less than one-half the diameter of the adjacent trunk.*

What Is the Aesthetic Value of the Branch?

Is the branch in question important to the tree's balance and appearance? If the branch were removed, would its removal create a major gap in the canopy?

Where Should the Pruning Cut Be Made?

If the three previous questions lead to the conclusion that a secondary trunk or branch needs to be pruned, several considerations are needed to determine where to make the actual cut. Sometimes, none of the options meet pruning guidelines, and the better of the bad options is chosen.

For illustration, look at the tree in Figure 32-7. It has three trunks. If the branch unions do not have branch collars (that is, the secondary trunks are more than half the diameter of the primary trunk), the tree is prone to storm damage.

Figure 32-7 ■ *As drawn, the tree has three trunks. Evaluate the need for subordinate pruning by comparing the diameters of the secondary (left and right) trunks to the center trunk. To be structurally strong with branch collars, the left and right trunk need to be less than half the diameter of the center trunk.*

Considerations for the Secondary Trunk on the Left

As drawn in Figure 32-8, there are four sites where pruning could occur to lower the tree height (wind loading) and reduce the snow loading potential.

Considerations for locations A, B, and C with reduction cuts (removing a larger trunk back to a smaller side branch):

- If location A has a two-inch trunk with a one-inch side branch, it meets the pruning guidelines for both size (decay potential) and reduction cut (waterspout growth). However, as drawn, it may have little potential to minimize storm damage, as the height is not significantly lowered (wind loading), and the total potential for snow loading has not been significantly reduced.

- If location A has a two-inch trunk with a one-half-inch side branch, it does not meet the reduction cut guideline (waterspout growth), as the side branch is one-fourth the size of the trunk being removed. Due to the size relationship, this becomes a heading cut. Watersprouts regrowth on the trunk could make it more prone to storm damage than before pruning!

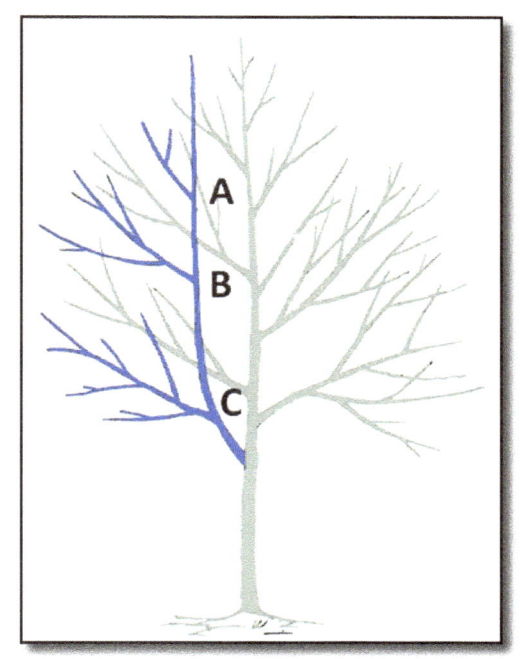

Figure 32-8 ▮ *As drawn, there are four locations where pruning could occur.*

- If location B has a four-inch trunk and a three-inch side branch, it violates the size (decay) guideline because the trunk is too large, predisposing the trunk to decay and internal cracking. This is typical when pruning maturing trees, as branches will be too large except in the outer canopy. The three-inch side branch is within the reduction cut (waterspout) guideline, making it a reduction cut.

- If location B has a four-inch trunk and a one-inch side branch, it violates both the size (decay) and the reduction cut (waterspout) guidelines.

- If location C has a six-inch trunk and a three-inch side branch, it violates the size (decay) standard. The three-inch side branch is within the reduction cut (waterspout) standard.

Considerations for location D with a removal cut (removing a smaller side branch back to a larger trunk/parent branch):

- Is the branch important to the aesthetics of the tree? As drawn, the removal of the entire branch would create a gap in the canopy.

- Removal of the left side secondary trunk plus additional pruning on the right side to aesthetically balance the tree would remove too much of the tree's foliage/live wood in a single season.

- If location D has an eight-inch trunk with a six-inch side branch (secondary trunk), it violates the size (decay) guideline. Being a removal cut (removing a smaller side branch back to a larger trunk/parent branch), it does not have a reduction cut standard. Without a branch collar, the branch union is prone to decay.

Better of the Bad Options

In reality, it is common that none of the potential cuts meets acceptable pruning guidelines, and the arborist looks for the better of the bad options. Due to the diameter of the limbs, large trees have few acceptable options based on the size guideline (potential for internal decay and cracking). It is common that secondary trunks may not have any side branches of an acceptable size relationship for a reduction cut.

- If the tree species is prone to decay, avoid compromising on the size (decay) guideline, opening the tree to decay and internal cracking.

- If the tree is in a stressed site (including limited water or root spread potential) avoid compromising on the size (decay) guideline, as the tree is more prone to decay.

- If the tree is vigorously growing or the total amount of foliage/live wood being removed is at the maximum allowed in pruning standards, avoid compromising on the reduction cut (waterspout) guideline, as the tree is more prone to waterspout growth. With growth, the tree may become more prone to storm damage than before pruning. If the tree will be pruned each year (dealing with the waterspout growth), this becomes less of an issue.

- If tree failure would not cause injury or significant property damage, no pruning may be the better option.

- If tree failure would cause injury or significant property damage, it may be better to accept limited decay and work with resulting structural issues from regrowth than to leave the tree at high risk for storm damage.

- Storm failures are more common on young and medium-sized trees as the codominant and secondary trunk reach three to four inches in diameter. Old, mature trees are actually less prone to storm damage, having had their weakness tested in previous megastorms.

ILLUSTRATIONS OF SUBORDINATE PRUNING SITUATIONS
Medium-Aged Tree with Codominant Trunks

With codominant trunks, one trunk is subordinated to a dominant trunk. Figure 32-9 illustrates this. It may require annual pruning over a period of years.

Figure 32-9 ▮ *Before and after pruning with codominant trunks. (A) Tree before pruning. (B) Codominant trunk on right subordinated to trunk on left. (C) Tree balanced with other, more upright-growing branches on left subordinated to the dominant trunk.*

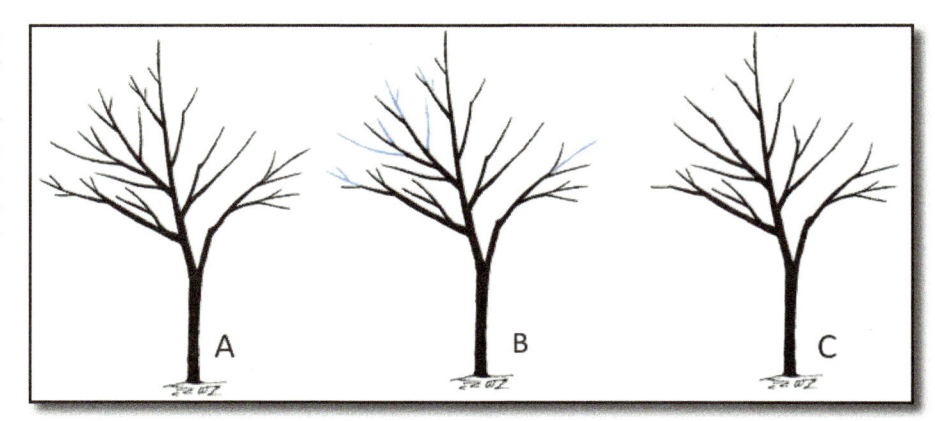

Vigorously Growing Branches Choke out the Central Leader

On species with opposite branching patterns, vigorously growing lower branches often choke out the central leader. Figure 32-10 illustrates the pruning approach. It may require annual pruning over a period of years.

Figure 32-10 ▮ *Before (A) and after (B) views of a tree whose vigorously growing branches choke out the central leader.*

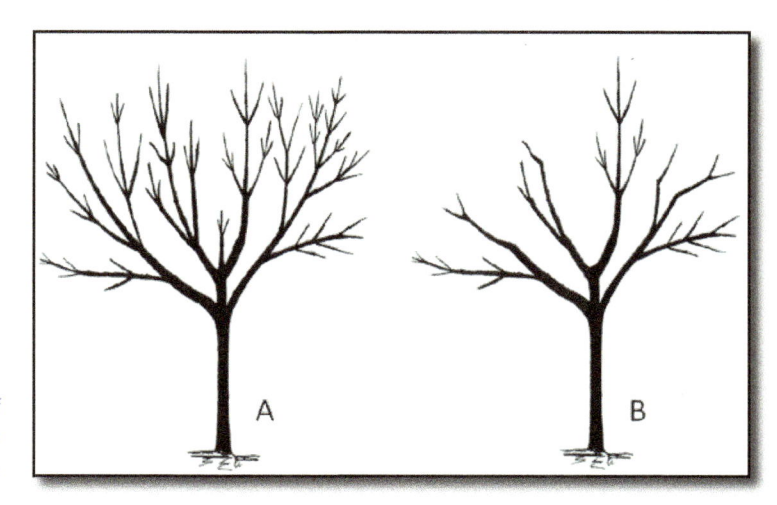

Young Tree Rounded with Heading Cuts

Trees should never be rounded with heading cuts. Figure 32-11 illustrates the pruning approach. It may require annual pruning over a period of years.

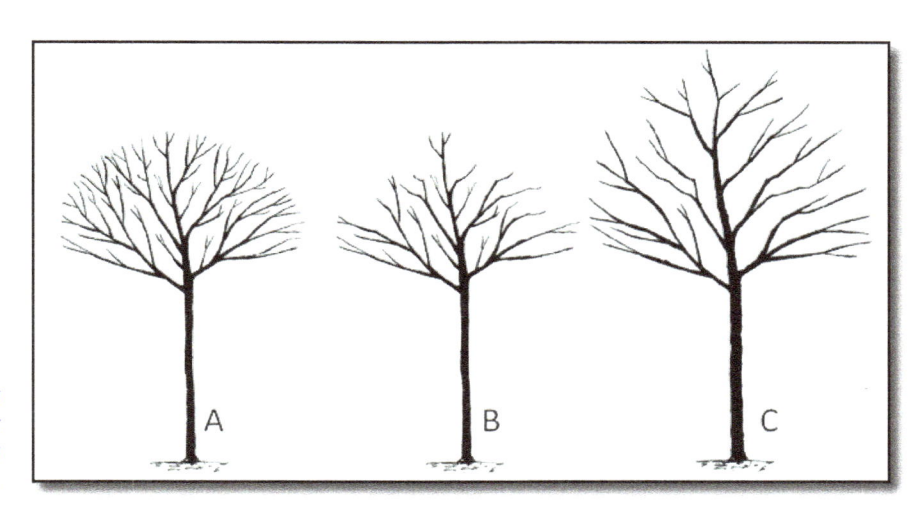

Figure 32-11 ▪ *Views of a young tree rounded with heading cuts; before pruning (A), after pruning (B), and with growth (C).*

Upright Growing Trees with Numerous Upright Growing Branches

Some species of trees (including Callery pear and some crabapple cultivars) have numerous upright growing branches. Figure 32-12 illustrates the pruning approach. It may require annual pruning over a period of years.

CLEANING

Cleaning is the removal of dead, diseased, cracked, and broken branches. This type of pruning is done to reduce the risk of branch failure, improve tree appearance, and to reduce the spread of insects and diseases. Most pruning of middle-aged and mature trees falls into this type. Trees under stress or declining trees may need cleaning every few months to every few years. All dead wood may be removed at one time. It does not count in the total of live wood/foliage removed. In cleaning, do not remove healthy branches and live foliage. Do not clean out healthy growth in the tree's interior (Figure 32-13).

Removing dead branches—To minimize risk if the branch were to fail, it is advisable to remove any dead branch larger than a two-inch diameter and higher than thirty feet. Dead branches may also become a source of insect and disease pressure in the tree.

Remove the dead branches using the three-step pruning technique. Do not cut into the branch collar, which would open a high potential for decay to spread into the trunk. If live wood has begun to grow out

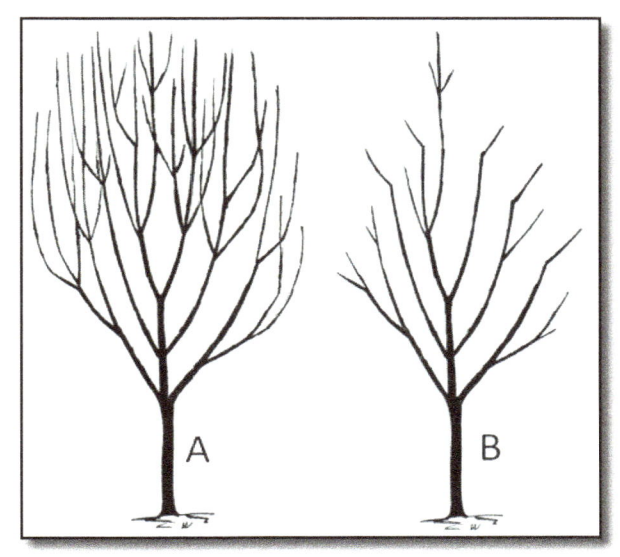

Figure 32-12 ▪ *Before and after views of an upright growing tree with numerous upright growing branches.*

Figure 32-13 ▪ *This old cottonwood needs cleaning to remove dead branches and reduce the risks associated with branch failure.*

along the dead limb, cut just beyond the live wood, being cautious not to nick the live tissue. Never "flush cut" the dead branch (Figure 32-14).

Figure 32-14 ▮ *When removing dead branches, do not cut into the living tissues.*

Written specifications for cleaning should specify the minimum size of dead branches to be removed. For example, "Clean branches one inch diameter and larger," or "Clean branches two inches in diameter and larger that are thirty feet and higher above the ground." The location of the branch to be removed should be specific if the entire crown is not going to be cleaned.

THINNING

Thinning is the selective removal of smaller branches (one-half inch to two and one-half inches in diameter) to reduce crown density. Because the majority of small branches are in the outer canopy, thinning focuses in this area. Thinning should retain crown shape and size, and provide an even distribution of foliage throughout the crown. Removal cuts are primarily used (Figure 32-15).

Figure 32-15 ▮ *Thinning is the selective removal of small branches, growing parallel to each other, in the leafy upper/outer tree canopy.*

Because thinning is in the upper/outer canopy, it requires a trained arborist with a high level of skill. Thinning is expensive, often running from $500 to over $1,000 per large tree when done correctly.

Thinning can include removal of suckers from the base of the tree and some waterspouts on the interior. Excessive removal of watersprouts at one time often promotes growth of additional watersprouts, and should be avoided.

Benefits of Thinning

- Thinning is the best way to minimize potential damage caused by snow loading, a primary situation leading to tree failures in Colorado. Thinning can reduce limb weight in order to compensate for structural defects.

- Thinning increases light penetration into the tree interior. This can invigorate the tree and help retain the tree's natural shape. Thinning may adequately reduce shade for shade-tolerant under-story plants below the tree. However, thinning middle-aged and mature trees will not adequately promote growth of sun-loving plants like Kentucky bluegrass.

- Thinning is a technique to partially open a view without removing or structurally affecting a tree. This is often referred to as *vista pruning*.

- On a tall tree, thinning may not be an effective technique to reduce wind sail and potential for breakage in strong winds. Reducing is the most effective way to deal with wind loading issues.

Effectiveness of Thinning

Researchers are questioning the effectiveness of overall tree thinning. Depending on growth rates, the tree may simply regrow the removed branches in a few years. Current thought in reducing storm loading is that structural pruning will be more effective than general thinning.

Clarification on Thinning

As a point of clarification, *thinning* is done on relatively small branches in the leafy upper/outer canopy. *Thinning* is not removing large lower branches, which could create gaps in the crown and encourage watersprouts. Thinning is not removal of the small twiggy branches in the inner canopy. Thinning will not significantly lower a tree's height (Figure 32-16).

Avoid **lion tailing**, which is the removal of the live small leafy twigs down in the tree's interior. These small interior branches are critical to the trunk's structural integrity and vigor. They also serve to dampen tree sway in the wind. Lion tailing shifts the wind loading to the outer canopy, increasing the tree's potential for wind damage (Figure 32-17).

Written specifications for a thinning job should specify the following:

- Clarify what percent of the tree's canopy may be removed. For example, "Pruning should not exceed fifteen percent of the total live canopy."

- Clarify where in the tree the pruning will occur. For example, "Pruning shall occur in the outer third of the crown."

- Clarify size of branches to be removed. For example, "Pruning should remove branches from one-half inch up to two and one-half inches in diameter."

Figure 32-16 ▮ *Left—Thinning focuses on small branches in the upper/outer tree canopy.*
Right—Thinning does not remove large branches, creating a gap in the tree canopy.

Figure 32-17 ▮ *Do not "lion tail" trees as in the photo. Removal of the smaller twiggy wood in the inner tree canopy decreases vigor on the major branches and trunk and shifts the weight to the top increasing the potential for wind damage.*

RAISING

Raising is the removal of lower branches to provide clearance for people, traffic, buildings, or a view. When removing lower branches, maintain at least one-half of the foliage in the lower two-thirds of the tree. The lowest branch should originate in the bottom one-third of the tree's height (live crown ratio) (Figure 32-18).

Raising should be part of the tree's structural training while young. Ideally, raising would be done before branches to be removed exceed a two-inch diameter. The potential for decay is high when the branch removed is larger than four inches or when a two-inch and larger branch is greater than half the diameter of the adjacent trunk (no branch collar to suppress decay).

On many trees, lower branches make up a significant portion of the tree's entire canopy and cannot be removed without significantly affecting tree health and appearance. When the branch to be removed is larger than two inches, consider other alternatives. Can the clearance required be achieved with removal and reduction cuts out along the branch rather than removing the entire branch? Leaving some small diameter branches on the lower trunk for a year helps close pruning wounds and lessens the potential for trunk cracking (Figure 32-19).

Excessive removal of lower branches increases the potential for tree failure by decreasing trunk taper, causing trunk cracks and decay, and transferring weight to the top.

Written specifications for raising should include the following:

- Clarify the clearance required. For example, *"The tree's crown will be raised to seven feet."*

- Clarify what branch(es) will be pruned and the type of pruning cuts (removal or reduction cut) to be used. For example, "The lowest branch on the south side shall be removed back to the trunk with a removal cut. The lowest branch on the north side will be reduced with a reduction cut at the branch five feet out from the trunk and a removal cut to the lowest side branch."

- Clarify what size of branches will be pruned. For example, "All cuts shall be two inches in diameter and smaller."

Figure 32-18 ▮ *When removing lower branches, maintain at least half of the foliage in the bottom two-thirds of the tree. The lowest branch should originate in the lower one-third of the tree.*

Figure 32-19 ▮ *In raising branches on maturing trees, consider if required clearance can be achieved with removal and reduction cuts out along the branch rather than removing large branches entirely.*

REDUCTION

Reduction is the selective removal of branches to decrease the height and/or spread of a tree. It requires the use of *reduction cuts*, which remove larger branches back to smaller side branches (Figure 32-20).

Reduction is a method to reduce potential wind loading on large trees with structural defects. Reducing and thinning both decrease potential failure from snow loading. However, researchers are questioning the effectiveness of overall tree reduction. Depending on growth rates, the tree may simply regrow the removed branches in a few years. Current thought in reducing storm loading is that selective structural pruning on weak secondary trunks will be more effective than general tree reduction.

Not all trees can be reduced without predisposing the tree to decline and death. Crown reducing requires the extensive use of *reduction cuts*, which can predispose the branch/trunk to internal decay. On older trees showing stress or decline, reduction cuts can accelerate decline and death (Figure 32-21).

In a proper *reduction cut*, the side branch pruned back to will be at least one-third the diameter of the trunk/parent branch removed. Under American National Standards Institute pruning standards, if the side branch is less than one-third, it is considered a *heading cut*, which is generally unacceptable.

It is very difficult to use crown reducing to permanently maintain a tree at a small size without causing tree decline. Ideally, trees were selected with adequate space for their mature size. Where size control is necessary, it is best to begin reduction pruning as the tree reaches acceptable size, rather than when the tree becomes overgrown.

In crown reducing, first visualize the new outer edge of the smaller canopy. Then prune the tree back to appropriate branch unions for a proper reduction cut or removal cut. Some branches will be left taller than the visualized outer edge, while others will be cut back below the visualized canopy edge. Do not make heading cuts and avoid rounding off the tree canopy (Figure 32-22).

In shortening primary upward-growing trunks/primary branches to a lateral branch, a side branch that is somewhat upward growing with a narrow branch union angle may be stronger than a branch union with a wide angle (Figure 32-23).

Figure 32-20 ▮ *Reducing is the selective removal of branches to decrease a tree's height and/or spread. Just being tall does not indicate that a tree is structurally weak and prone to storm damage.*

Figure 32-21 ▮ *Not every tree should be reduced. Notice the dieback associated with the previous reduction on this old cottonwood. On old trees and trees showing stress or decline, reduction cuts and heading cuts may accelerate the decline cycle.*

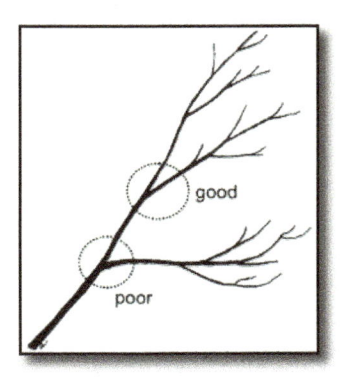

Figure 32-22 ▮ *Left—In reduction, visualize the new outer edge of the smaller canopy. Prune back to branch unions that make proper reduction and thinning cuts. Some branches will be taller than the new outer edge, some shorter. Right—This tree is incorrectly rounded off with heading cuts.*

Figure 32-23 ▮ *In shortening a main upward-growing branch, pruning back to a narrow branch union may be stronger than a wide branch union.*

Just because a tree is tall does not indicate that it is structurally unsound. Potential risk of failure should be evaluated by an experienced arborist based on branching structure, branch union integrity, signs of internal decay, and previous damage.

Written specifications for reduction pruning should include the following:

- Clarify the desired reduction in height/spread.

- Specify criteria for reduction cuts. For example, "All cuts should be made on branches less than two inches in diameter. Diameter of the side branches pruned back to should be at least one-third the diameter of the branch removed."

- Percentage of foliage to be removed. For example, "Pruning should not exceed ten percent of the total foliage."

RESTORATION

Restoration is the selective removal of branches, sprouts, and stubs from trees that have been damaged by improper pruning, vandalism, and storms. The objective is to restore the tree's structure, form, and appearance to the extent possible. Restoration generally requires annual pruning over a period of years.

Actual pruning procedures vary with the situation. When dealing with situations of excessive watersprouts, a rule of thumb is to remove one-third and reduce one-third with each annual pruning. Removing all of the watersprouts at one time often stimulates the growth of more watersprouts.

POLLARDING

Pollarding is a training system that involves creating "heads" on secondary branches where small tertiary branches arise. The small tertiary branches are all removed back to the head every one to three years (depending on growth rates).

Pollarding started as a method to produce shoots for fuel, shelter, and products made from the young shoots. Today, it is used as an art form. Pollarding is common in some parts of Europe to keep tree small and shaped as living screens. Pollarding is not topping and should not be considered a routine method to keep large trees small. Due to annual labor involved, it is uncommon in the United States.

FREQUENTLY ASKED QUESTIONS ABOUT PRUNING MATURE SHADE TREES

What about Topping a Tree?

Shade trees should **never** be topped. The regrowth of a topped tree is structurally unsound. Topping required by utility right-of-way pruning is starkly obvious and sets an unfortunate community standard followed by others. Instead of topping, use *cleaning*, and/or proper *structural pruning* methods (Figure 32-24).

What about Utility Right-of-Way Pruning?

Pruning for utility line clearance does not always follow desirable pruning techniques regarding appearance and health of the tree. In this situation, the needs of the utility right of way take priority over the tree.

Figure 32-24 ▮ *Never top a tree; the regrowth is structurally unsound, making it very prone to wind and storm damage.*

When a tree under a power line requires frequent reduction, consider having the tree removed. Utility companies are generally eager to accommodate. In planting trees, selection criteria (i.e., size and placement) should be followed so that a tree's health and appearance will never be compromised by the need for utility pruning.

I Am Concerned about My Tree Breaking in Storms, but I Really Do Not Want to Lose the Shade. Do I Really Need to Have the Tree Pruned or Removed?

This is a two-part question. First, does the tree show signs of being highly susceptible to storm damage (i.e., previous storm damage, dieback or dead branches, structural problems such as codominant trunks, weak branch unions, or internal decay)? This should be evaluated by an experienced ISA Certified Arborist.

Second, if yes, what would the tree or branch hit should it fail? If it would cause significant property damage or threaten life, the tree should be pruned or removed as a preventive measure.

Cleaning and **structural pruning** may reduce the potential storm hazard without compromising the shade. In some situations, the risk of failure cannot be reduced without removal. Remember that healthy structurally sound trees are generally windfast even when mature.

Storm damage is usually, but not always, related to structural problems that could have been addressed with proper structural training when the tree was young. Codominant trunks account for the majority of tree failures in Colorado. The hazard of wind damage is higher on the regrowth of trees that have been "topped." Consult an ISA Certified Arborist for additional details.

How Should Storm-Damaged Trees Be Pruned?

First, focus on *cleaning* (removing broken and damaged limbs), keeping in mind the structural integrity of the tree. Realize that you may have to accept less than ideal pruning techniques by Mother Nature.

Second, focus on *structural pruning* to restore the tree's structural integrity and shape to the extent possible. This may take place over a period of years.

The maximum amount of tree canopy that can be removed without putting the tree and its root system under stress includes the live wood/foliage removed by the storm. When Mother Nature removes too much live wood/foliage, limit pruning to cleaning.

On storm-damaged trees where excessive live wood and foliage were removed by storm damage, wait until the roots and crown stabilize (as measured in canopy growth) before doing thinning, reducing, or other structural pruning. This may be a multi-year period.

Keep the tree if it can be pruned back to structurally sound wood and will be esthetically pleasing. Often when one side of the tree is gone, the best option is to remove the entire tree (Figure 32-25).

How Should Trees with Root Damage Be Pruned?

Focus on *cleaning*. Avoid removing live wood and foliage, as this could speed the decline. Removing live wood lowers the *auxin* content, which is the hormone that promotes root growth. Removing foliage reduces photosynthesis and levels of stored carbohydrates that the tree is living on during the recovery period. Trees in a construction site with damaged roots may require cleaning every three to twelve months for five or more years.

How Should Declining Trees Be Pruned?

Focus on *cleaning*. Avoid removing live wood and foliage as this could speed the decline. Removing live wood lowers the *auxin* content, which is the hormone that promotes root growth. Removing foliage reduces photosynthesis and levels of stored carbohydrates that the tree is living on. Old declining cottonwoods and poplars may warrant cleaning every one to five years.

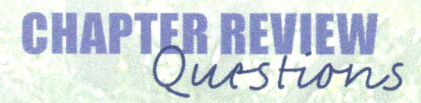

1. List the objectives (whys) for pruning a mature tree.

2. List the methods (hows) of pruning to achieve purposes.

3. Describe key elements in writing specifications for general pruning of maturing trees.

4. What is the overall objective in structural pruning of medium-aged and mature trees? Why will it generally require work over a period of years? How does larger branch size influence the potential for structural pruning?

5. Describe *subordinate pruning*. What factors should be considered when deciding where to make a subordinate pruning cut?

6. Describe how to subordinate prune a medium-aged tree with the following situations:

   a. Codominant trunks

   b. Rounded off

   c. Choked out central leader

   d. Too many upright-growing branches

7. Describe key elements in writing specifications for structural pruning of medium-aged trees.

8. Define *cleaning*. In cleaning, how much of the live wood should be removed? Why?

9. When is it important to remove dead branches? At what size and height does dead branch removal become an important management issue?

10. When woundwood is growing out along a dead branch, where is the final cut made?

11. Describe key elements in writing specifications for cleaning.

12. Describe thinning:

    a. What are the purposes of thinning the crown?

    b. Will thinning lower a tree's height?

    c. In thinning the crown, what types of cuts are made?

    d. What is the general maximum size of branches to be removed?

    e. What is the long-term effectiveness of overall crown thinning in reducing storm damage potential? What pruning method would be more effective?

13. What is *lion tailing*? How does it differ from thinning the crown? What are the problems associated with lion tailing?

14. Describe the key elements in writing specifications for thinning.

15. In raising, what is live crown ratio? What is the rule of thumb on how fast a tree can be pruned up?

16. In raising, what options may be workable other than removal of lower branches? Why may removal of lower branches cause problems?

17. Describe the key elements in writing specifications for crown raising.

18. Describe the reasons for reduction. Describe the limitations of reduction.

19. List points on reduction, as given in this chapter.

20. What is the long-term effectiveness in overall crown reduction in reducing storm damage potential? What pruning method would be more effective?

21. How does topping a tree affect its structural integrity and internal decay potential?

22. Describe the key elements in writing specifications for reduction.

23. In restoration, what is the rule of thumb on dealing with excessive sucker growth?

24. Explain the pruning objectives for the following situations:

    a. Storm-damaged trees

    b. Old and declining trees

    c. Root-damaged trees

    d. Hazard trees

Chapter

33*

Pruning Evergreens

Most types of evergreen trees and shrubs need little to no pruning. Pruning may make the new growth bushier, but will not effectively control size. Select plants based on mature size to minimize pruning needs. If frequent pruning is necessary to keep plant growth in bounds and prevent interference with a walk, driveway or view, consider replacing the plant. Evergreen trees and shrubs are pruned according to species growth characteristics.

PRUNING EVERGREEN TREES

On evergreen trees, avoid pruning the central leader (trunk). This results in the development of multiple leaders that are prone to wind and snow damage. If the central leader is killed back, select one branch to become the new leader and remove potentially competing leaders.

Never allow codominant trunks (trunks of similar size) to develop. If multiple trunks begin to develop, select one and remove others.

For structural integrity on evergreen trees, all side branches should be less than half the diameter of the adjacent trunk (less than one-third is preferred). If the diameter of a side branch is too large, prune back part of the needled area to slow growth or remove the branch entirely back to the trunk.

Removing Large Branches on Evergreen Trees

New needles will not grow from branches without needles. When a side branch is removed on an evergreen, cut back to the trunk just outside the **branch collar** (the enlarged connecting area on the trunk around the limb).

*Authors: David Whiting with Robert Cox, Carol O'Meara, and Carl Wilson, Colorado State University Extension. Artwork by David Whiting and Colorado State University Extension.

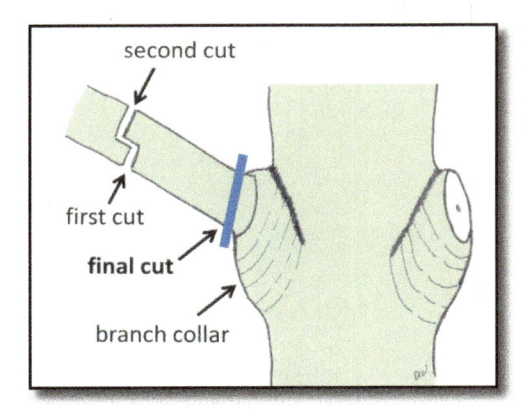

Do not cut into or otherwise injure the branch collar. Do not make flush cuts. Remove the branch using a three-cut method (Figure 33-1).

Cut 1. Coming out twelve to fifteen inches from the trunk, make an undercut a third to halfway through the branch.

Cut 2. Moving a couple of inches out past the first cut, make the second cut from the top, removing the branch. This double-cut method prevents the weight of the branch from tearing the branch below the branch collar.

Cut 3. Make the third and final cut just outside the branch bark collar. Take extra caution to not cut into or otherwise injure the branch bark collar.

PRUNING SPRUCE, FIR, AND DOUGLAS FIR

Spruce (*Picea* spp.), fir (*Abies* spp.), and Douglas fir (*Pseudotsuga menziesii*) generally need little to no pruning.

On young trees, pruning is useful in situations where bushier new growth is desired. Because these species produce some side buds, branch tips can be removed encouraging side bud growth. Prune late winter or early spring (Figure 33-2).

Figure 33-2 ■ *Pruning spruce and fir back to a side bud or side branch will encourage growth of side branches.*

Spruce, fir, and Douglas fir that are overgrowing their space are somewhat tolerant of being pruned back as long as they are not pruned back past the needles. However, with constant pruning, the branches may begin to show needle browning and dieback. In situations where the branch must be pruned back past the needles, remove it back to the trunk.

In landscape design, small to mid-size evergreen trees, with their pyramidal form, generally look best with their lowest branches allowed to drape to ground level.

On large trees, primary growth occurs at the top with minimal growth at the lower levels. Due to slow growth, pruning of the lower branches may give a "pruned look" for a long time. On large trees, limb up lower branches only if they are in the way.

Very slow-growing species, like the dwarf Alberta spruce (*Picea glauca* var. *albertiana* "Conica"), blue nest spruce (also known as dwarf black spruce [*Picea mariana* "Nana"]), and bird's nest spruce (*Picea abies* "Nidiformis") are rather intolerant of pruning.

PRUNING PINE

Pines generally need little to no pruning.

On young plants, if a more compact new growth is desired, "pinching" may be helpful. Using the fingers, snap off one-third of the new growing tips while in the "candle" stage (in the spring, when young needles are in a tight cluster). Avoid using pruners or a knife, as they will cut the remaining needles, giving a brown tip appearance (Figure 33-3).

Because pines produce few side buds, they are intolerant of more extensive pruning. If the terminal bud on a branch is removed, growth on that shoot is stopped, with additional growth occurring only from existing side branches. Do not shear pines.

Like other evergreen trees, small to mid-size pine trees look best (from the landscape design perspective) with their lowest branches allowed to drape down near ground level. When a lower branch has to be pruned back for space issues, remove it back to the trunk.

Figure 33-3 ▪ *On pines, for bushier new growth "pinch" growing tips by snapping off one-third of the "candle" tips with the fingers. Because pines produce few side buds, they are intolerant of more extensive pruning.*

PRUNING JUNIPER AND ARBORVITAE

Juniper and arborvitae generally need little to no pruning.

They may be pruned at any time except during subzero weather. The best time is early spring, prior to new growth.

The best pruning method is to cut individual branches back to an upward-growing side branch. This method of pruning is time-consuming, but keeps the plant looking young and natural (Figure 33-4).

While shearing is quick and easy, it is not recommended, especially after midsummer. Shearing creates a dense growth of foliage on the plant's exterior. This in turn shades out the interior growth, and the plant becomes a thin shell of foliage. Frequently sheared plants are more prone to show needle browning and dieback from winter cold and drying winds.

Figure 33-4 ▪ *Pruning junipers and arborvitae back to a side shoot hides the pruning cut.*

Any pruning that tapers in toward the bottom of the plant will lead to thinning of the lower branches due to shading. To keep the bottom full, the base of the shrub needs to be wider than the top portion.

It is common to see junipers and arborvitae that have overgrown their space. Because new growth comes only from the growing tips, branches cannot be pruned back into wood without needles. If the shrub is pruned back to bare wood, it will have a permanent bare spot.

For shrubs that are getting too large, it is better to prune them back as they begin to overgrow the site. Pruning back severely overgrown shrubs generally gets into wood without needles. Consider replacing severely overgrown plants with smaller cultivars or other species.

Junipers and arborvitae growing in the shade are rather intolerant of pruning due to slow growth rates.

1. How can a gardener make a young spruce, fir, or Douglas fir bushier? What about a pine?

2. A large evergreen tree is overgrowing the space. Explain options to prune back the bottom branches for spruce, fir, and Douglas fir. Explain options for pruning back bottom branches for pine. Why is pine different from spruce, fir, and Douglas fir?

3. Explain what happens when a gardener shears a mugo pine shrub.

4. On junipers and arborvitae, explain the pros and cons of:

   a. Shearing

   b. Thinning

5. Explain the problems associated with trying to prune back a severely overgrown juniper or arborvitae.

Chapter
34*

Pruning Flowering Shrubs

WHY PRUNE?

Pruning has a major influence on a shrub's flowering habit, shape, size, and pest problems.

Prune to Encourage Flowering

Pruning has a major influence on shrub flowering. Over time, an unpruned flowering shrub becomes woody, with little new growth to support flower bud development.

Spring-flowering shrubs bloom on one-year-old wood (twigs that grew new the previous summer). Buds develop in midsummer through fall for the following spring. Pruning in the fall and winter removes flowering wood with buds. Spring-flowering shrubs can be rejuvenated or thinned (as described in the following) in early spring before flowering or growth starts Thinning can also be done right after bloom to maximize the next season's flowers. (Figures 34-1 and 34-2).

Spring-flowering shrubs include forsythia (*Forsythia* spp.), Nanking cherry (*Prunus tomentosa*), quince (*Chaenomelea* spp.), bridalwreath and Vanhoutte spireas (*Spiraea prunifolia*, *S. plenaflora* 'Plena' and *S.* x *vanhouttei*), viburnum (*Viburnum* spp.), beautybush (*Kolkwitzia amabilis*), lilac (*Syringa* spp.), honeysuckle (*Lonicera* spp.), peashrub (*Caragana* spp.), deutzia (*Deutzia* spp.), and weigela (*Weigela* spp.).

On spring-flowering shrubs, it is recommended to "deadhead" spent blooms (remove flowers after they fade). While time-consuming, deadheading conserves the plant's energy, which would otherwise be spent on seedpod and seed development. On many shrubs, the spent flowers and seedpods are not attractive (lilacs).

---

*Authors: David Whiting, Carl Wilson, and Robert Cox, Colorado State University Extension. Photographs and line drawing by David Whiting, unless otherwise noted.

Figure 34-1 ▮ *Spring-flowering shrubs bloom from buds that developed on new wood the previous summer.*

Figure 34-2 ▮ *Fall shearing of this spring-flowering lilac removed flower buds on the lower section of the shrubs.*

Summer-flowering shrubs bloom on new wood that grew earlier in the growing season. Summer-flowering shrubs are also pruned by thinning or rejuvenation in the early spring before growth starts (Figure 34-3).

Summer-flowering shrubs include most butterfly bush (*Buddleia* spp. and *Cassia* spp.), blue mist spirea (*Caryopteris* x *clandonensis*), Hancock coralberry (*Symphoricarpos* x *chenaultii* 'Hancock'), mockorange (*Philadelphus* spp.), potentilla (*Potentilla* spp.), bumald and Japanese spirea (*Spiraea* x *bumalda* and *S. japonica*), Annabelle and peegee hydrangea (*Hydrangea arborescens* 'Annabelle' and *H. paniculata*), shrub althea or rose of Sharon (*Hibiscus syriacus*), snowberry (*Symphoricarpos albus*), and St. John's wort (*Hypericum* spp.).

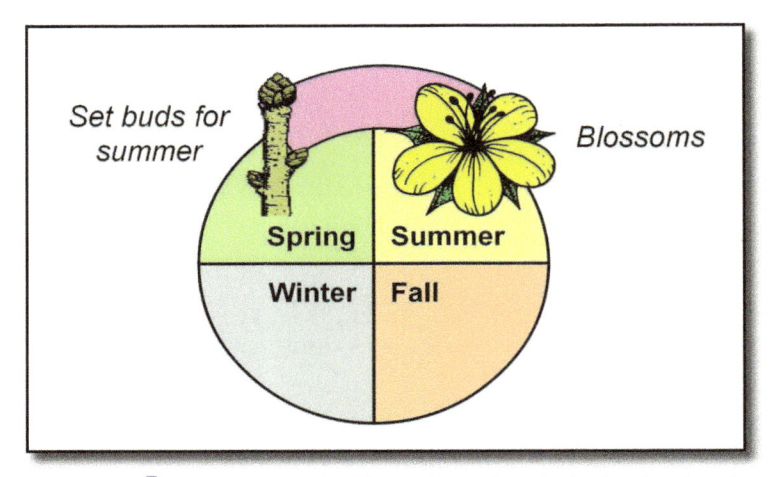

Figure 34-3 ▮ *Summer-flowering shrubs bloom from buds that developed on new wood that grew earlier this growing season.*

Removing older canes of flowering shrubs also allows better sunlight penetration into the shrub. This results in better flowering throughout the shrub, instead of flowers just at the top where sunlight is sufficient.

On shrubs noted for their bark color, like red-twig dogwood (*Cornus sericea*), the new shoot growth has more brilliant color. Routine pruning at the base encourages new shoots, which have the desired red color.

Prune to Direct Shape

Shaping is another reason for pruning shrubs. Shape can be managed to some degree by pruning to side buds or branches growing in the desired direction. While pruning can provide some control over size, it is not an effective method to keep a large shrub in a small space. Where shrubs have overgrown their space, consider replacing the plants with smaller cultivars or other species (Figures 34-4 and 34-5).

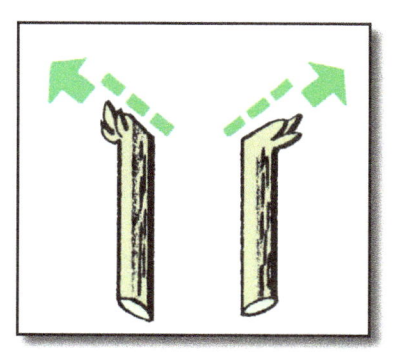

Figure 34-4 ▪ *Shape can be managed to some extent by pruning to buds and branches growing in the desired direction of growth.*

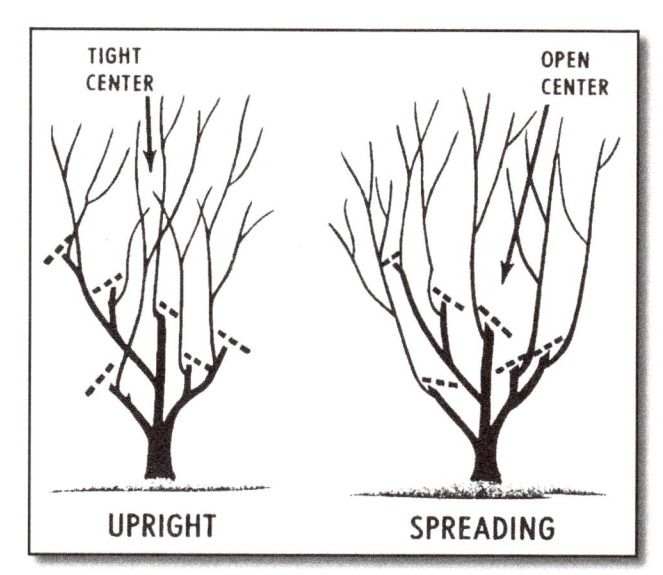

Figure 34-5 ▪ *Pruning to inward-growing buds or branches results in narrower shrubs. Pruning to outward-growing buds or branches results in wider shrubs. (Line drawing by the U.S. Department of Agriculture.)*

Prune to Manage Pests

Pruning is a management technique for some insect or disease problems. For example, removing the older wood in lilac reduces oystershell scale and borer problems. Thinning a shrub to increase air circulation reduces the incidence of powdery mildew and leaf spot diseases.

PRUNING METHODS FOR FLOWERING SHRUBS

The primary objective in pruning flowering shrubs is to encourage new (flowering) growth from the base. This is best accomplished by thinning at the base, or rejuvenation.

Branch-by-Branch Shaping

Branch-by-branch shaping involves shortening the length of excessively long branches by cutting them back one-by-one. Cuts are made back in the shrub, leaving branches at varying lengths. Avoid making cuts at a uniform "edge," creating a rounded ball. Make cuts at appropriate branch unions (crotches) or buds (Figure 34-6).

This method maintains a more naturally shaped shrub but does not significantly encourage new growth of flowering wood for maximum bloom. Branch-by-branch shaping is a slow process.

Shearing to Shape

Shearing shrubs to round balls or other desired shapes is a common pruning technique because it is quick and easy. However, sheared shrubs lose their natural shape, and the rounded "balls" may detract from a more natural, informal landscape design. Shaping spring-flowering shrubs after midsummer removes the new wood with next year's blossoms. Frequent shearing does not encourage new growth from the base, which is needed to promote flowering.

Figure 34-6 ▪ *With branch-by-branch shaping, long branches are cut back into the shrub, giving a more natural shape. Avoid making cuts at a uniform "edge," creating a rounded ball.*

With frequent shearing, the plant becomes bushier on the exterior. The thick outer foliage may shade out the interior and lower foliage, and the plant becomes a thin shell of foliage with a woody interior and base. The thin shell of foliage is prone to browning and burning from wind and cold weather. Over time, shrubs become woody, with lots of dead branches and few flowers. When shrubs become overly woody from routine shearing, replacement is the best option to refresh the landscape design (Figures 34-7–34-11).

Figure 34-7 ▪ *Flowering shrubs pruned by topping or shearing become woody at the base. (Line drawing by the U.S. Department of Agriculture.)*

Figure 34-8 ▪ *Over time, sheared shrubs become woody with dead sections. The only treatment at this point is to replace the shrub.*

Figure 34-9 ▪ *Sheared forsythia in full bloom. Shearing does not encourage new wood with blossoms.*

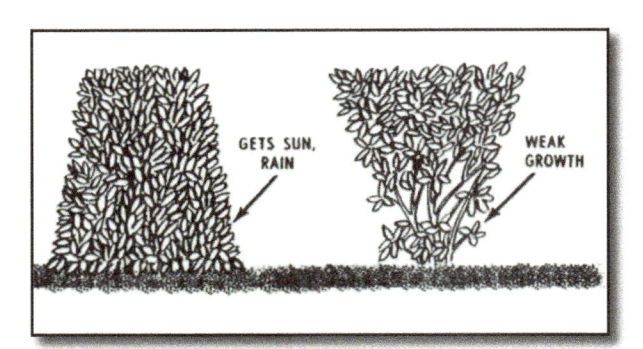

Figure 34-10 ▪ *In shearing hedges, maintain the natural shape of the plant. A common mistake is to shape shrubs with a wide top and narrow base. Lack of sunlight shades out lower interior growth, resulting in a woody base. (Line drawing by the U.S. Department of Agriculture.)*

Figure 34-11 ▪ *Properly pruned hedge, wider at the base.*

Thinning

One method to encourage shrub flowering is annual thinning. The objective is to remove one-third of the oldest wood to the ground each year, which in turn stimulates new, better-flowering growth from the base of the shrub. Thinning is more easily done with leafless branches in early spring before growth starts but can also be done in summer. This method is time-consuming and does not work well on twiggy, multistem shrubs, like spirea (Figure 34-12).

Cutting back and thinning an overgrown shrub will not restore its natural, informal form. It will look like an overgrown shrub that has been pruned. Rejuvenation pruning followed by thinning is better for overgrown shrubs.

Figure 34-12 ▮ *Annual thinning removes one-third of the oldest wood to the base each spring. This encourages new growth from the base, keeping the shrub youthful looking. (Line drawing by the U.S. Department of Agriculture.)*

Rejuvenation Pruning

Many shrubs can be easily renewed with rejuvenation pruning. The shrub is cut entirely to the ground in the early spring before growth starts. The shrub regrows from roots, giving a compact, youthful plant with maximum bloom. Rejuvenation can have a major effect on size. This method is preferred for many flowering shrubs because it is quick and easy with great results. Initial rejuvenation should be followed by thinning new canes to several strong ones over the next several years. Remove weak cane growth at the base (ground level).

Rejuvenation is typically done no more than every three to five years when a shrub begins to look gangly and woody. It works very well on multistemmed, twiggy-type shrubs such as spirea, *Caryopteris* (blue mist spirea), *Potentilla*, red-twig dogwood, sumac (*Rhus* spp.), and hydrangea. (**Note:** *Caryopteris* flowers best if renewed each spring.) Also use this method to rejuvenate lilac, privets (*Ligustrum* spp.), barberry (*Berberis* spp.), forsythia, flowering quince, honeysuckle, mockorange, flowering weigela, beautybush, many viburnums, elderberry (*Sambucus* spp.), and others.

Limitations:

- Spring-flowering shrubs will not bloom the year of rejuvenation.

- On shrubs with a rock and weed fabric mulch, rejuvenation may not be successful due to decreased root vigor and interference of the mulch with growth from the base.

- Extremely overgrown shrubs with large woody bases may not respond well to rejuvenation pruning.

- Shrubs with a lot of dead branches will not respond well to rejuvenation pruning. As a rule of thumb, if more than one-third of the branches are woody, without healthy foliage, the shrub will probably not respond.

- Some shrubs are structurally more like small trees, with only one or a few primary trunks. They include several *Viburnum* and *Euonymus* species, and shrubby forms of *Rhamnus* (buckthorn). Do not cut these shrubs to the ground. Prune by thinning branches back to side branches.

- Lilac cultivars budded onto common lilac rootstocks should not be cut to the ground. Regrowth will be common lilac rather than the selected cultivar.

Replacement

Shrubs that have been repeatedly sheared often become woody and filled with dead twigs. The best option may be to replace them. On many commercial sites, labor issues prohibit routine pruning. When shrubs become overgrown, they are simply replaced as a low-maintenance alternative. Shrubs can also be overwhelmed by weedy invaders seeded by birds, squirrels, or wind (common buckthorn, *Rhamnus cathartica*; walnut, *Juglans* spp.; elm, *Ulmus* spp.). If routine clearing of these invading woody species is not done, the original shrubs may be compromised or lost. Replacement may again be needed.

CHAPTER REVIEW
Questions

1. What is the difference in flowering habit and pruning of spring-flowering shrubs and summer-flowering shrubs?

2. Many gardeners prune flowering shrubs by topping them. Describe the impact on growth and flowering.

3. Explain the pros of, and limitations for, shrub pruning by:

   a. Shearing to shape

   b. Thinning old wood

   c. Pruning to the ground

   d. Replacement

4. What types of shrubs are successfully renewed by pruning to the ground? List situations where this approach may not work.

UNIT G

Herbaceous Plants

Flowers

Learning Objectives

At the end of this unit, the student will be able to:

- Select plants for different garden situations.
- Describe factors that influence microclimates.
- Describe methods to create and exploit microclimates.
- Interpret catalog and plant label descriptions, as they relate to:
  —Life cycles
  —Exposure
  —Irrigation requirements
  —Drought tolerance
  —Soil requirements
- List other selection considerations related to right plant, right place.
- Describe clues to overly well-adapted plants in relation to noxious weeds.

Supplemental Reading

Books

- *Annuals for Connoisseurs.* Wayne Winterrowd. Prentice Hall. 1992.
- *Best Perennials for the Rocky Mountains & High Plains.* Celia Tannehill and James E. Klett. Word Press. 2002.
- *Encyclopedia of Perennials: A Gardener's Guide.* Christopher Woods. Facts on File. 1992.
- *Gardening in the Mountain West.* Barbara Hyde. Johnson Printing. 1999.
- *Hardy Herbaceous Perennials.* Leo Jelitto and William Schacht. Timber Press. 1990.
- *Illustrated Encyclopedia of Perennials.* Ellen Phillips and C. Colston Burrell. Rodale Press. 2004.
- *Rodale's Flower Garden Problem Solver.* Jeff Ball. Rodale Press. 1995.
- *Sunset Western Garden Book.* Seventh edition. Sunset Publishing. 2001.
- *The Perennial Garden: Color Harmonies Through the Seasons* Jeff and Marilyn Cox. Rodale Press. 1985.
- *Tough Plants for Tough Places.* Peter Loewer. Rodale Press. 1992.
- *Waterwise Landscaping.* Jim Knopf. Chamisa Books. 1999.
- *Well-Tended Perennial Garden: Planting and Pruning Techniques.* Tracy Disabato-Aust and Steven M. Still. Timber Press Inc. 1998.
- *Xeriscape Colorado.* Connie Ellefson and David Winger. Westcliffe Publishers. 2004.
- *Xeriscape Plant Guide.* Denver Water. Fulcrum Publishing. 1996.

Web

- Assorted Colorado State University Extension fact sheets, Colorado Master Gardener GardenNotes, and PlantTalk Colorado Scripts (available at www.cmg.colostate.edu).

Chapter

35*

Herbaceous Plants (Flowers)

Right Plant, Right Place

CLIMATE AND MICROCLIMATE

Temperature

Plants generally have a specific range of temperatures in which they thrive. This information is usually listed in terms of hardiness or hardiness zones, although maximum daily temperature, minimum daily temperature, difference between day and night temperatures, average daytime temperature, and average nighttime temperature all have an effect.

Hardiness and Hardiness Zones

Hardiness refers to a plant's tolerance to low temperatures. Factors that influence hardiness include minimum temperature, recent temperature patterns, water supply, wind and sun exposure, snow cover, genetic make-up, and carbohydrate reserves (Figure 35-1).

Figure 35-1 ▍ *Hardy perennials, like tulips, are tolerant of the snow.*

Because of these complex interactions, gardeners may want to experiment with hardiness or take the zones with a grain of salt. Depending on the microclimate and the year, western gardeners often find that they can grow plants that are supposedly not hardy here. At other times, a plant that "should be" hardy will not be.

---

*Authors: Irene Shonle, PhD, Colorado State University Extension Gilpin County, with Linda McMulkin, Laurel Potts, Darrin Parmenter, and David Whiting, Colorado State University Extension. Artwork by David Whiting.

Hardiness zone maps indicate the average annual minimum temperature expected for geographic areas. While this is a factor in plant selection, it is only one of many factors influencing plant hardiness.

In 2012, the U.S. Department of Agriculture releases a new USDA Hardiness Zone Map at http://planthardiness. ars.gov/PHZMWeb/. The revised map has a large database correcting inherent problems with the 2003 version. It documents a climate zone creep (i.e., zone moving northwards in recent years). Zones are based on a 10°F difference in average annual minimum temperature.

Average Annual Minimum Temperature

Zone 4	−20°F to −30°F
Zone 5	−10°F to −20°F
Zone 6	0°F to −10°F

The Sunset Climate Zones claim to take into account the total climate, including length of growing season, timing, amount of rainfall, winter lows, summer highs, and humidity. This is a good concept, but they do not have enough zones for Colorado—showing Vail and Denver in the same climate zone.

Heat Tolerance

This is the opposite extreme: how much heat a plant can tolerate during the growing season. For example, Colorado summers can often be very hot and dry. In planting near stone, a south-facing wall, a driveway, or some other heat sink, the gardener might want to look for plants that "tolerate" or "thrive" in heat and drought. Keep in mind that this is not often listed in descriptions. If you live in an area with a cooler summer (such as higher elevations), heat-loving plants are not necessarily a good choice. Phrases such as "not a good choice for desert southwest" suggests that the plant does poorly in dry heat (Figure 35-2).

Microclimate

A microclimate is a variation of the climate within a localized area, usually influenced by hills, hollows, structures, or proximity to bodies of water. A microclimate differs significantly from the general climate of a region. These can be exploited to grow plants that would otherwise not be hardy (i.e., in garden beds against a facing south stone wall). Similarly, plants that prefer cooler seasons might benefit from being placed in areas that get dappled shade or only morning sun.

Figure 35-2 ▮ *Begonias are generally considered a shade plant. More correctly stated, they are intolerant of heat and can be found in full sun in cooler climates.*

Mountains and valleys create some rather complex microclimate. The bottom of valley is cooler than hillsides due to cool air draining to low spots. Valley floors may be over 10°F cooler than surrounding gardens on hillsides. Air drainage and aspect (direction the slope faces) may change growing season by one or two zones and blooming by two to six weeks.

A gardener can expand what is possible to grow by learning to create and exploit microclimates. For example, a south-facing slope may be one or more hardiness zones warmer. In hot areas of the region, avoid plants that prefer cool temperatures. In cool areas of the region, grow tender plants or ones that need more heat to bloom on the south and west.

Gardeners can also note and take advantage of the microclimates on different sides of their houses. Sunny south and west sides will be warmer. The east side of a house is typically cooler than south or west, and it may be more protected from wind. Because of this, it is perhaps the most temperate side in which to garden. The north side of houses is the shadiest, coolest, and generally moist. Grow plants that are not heat or drought tolerant here.

Many places in the West are very windy, with gusts up to 100 miles per hour common. Wind desiccates plants, increasing mortality. It can also blow away mulch. Gardeners in windy places can either grow plants that are tolerant to wind, or create or take advantage of existing windbreaks. The ideal windbreak will be semiporous, with a density of forty to sixty percent. This will provide the greatest downwind area of protection. Snow also will build up on the lee side of windbreaks, so this can be a good spot to plant more tender plants (Figure 35-3).

PLANT EVALUATION

Gardeners have a wide range of plant material available to them. Garden centers, plant catalogs, and now the Internet provide exciting new choices. However, not all plants will perform equally well in a given area or in a specific garden bed. To evaluate a specific plant, gardeners must ask questions to determine whether it is a good choice for a site. This includes interpreting catalog, garden tag, and seed packet descriptions.

Figure 35-3 ■ *This alpine garden features plants from the harsh microclimate of the high alpine meadows. Plants are small and quick to bloom, being tolerant of wind, cool temperatures, and short growing seasons.*

Developing this skill is critical to making the best choices, because few garden catalogs are written for western climates, and many gardeners did not learn to garden in the local climate where they currently reside. The ability to evaluate plants helps gardeners plant the "right plant in the right place."

Plant Descriptions

There are many pieces of information in a complete plant description that help gardeners make good decisions. These include scientific name, life cycle, preferred sun exposure, hardiness, mature size, soil preference, moisture preference, and bloom period.

Catalogs, plant tags, and seed packets generally include at least sun exposure and hardiness, but these are often not enough. Even if the description is more complete, interpreting what exactly is meant by these descriptions is often fairly tricky. This chapter helps the gardener to "read between the lines" on plant descriptions.

Scientific Name

Although the scientific name of a plant can be intimidating, it can be an important piece of information. Plants often have many different common names, and there is no way of ensuring you have a specific plant unless the scientific name is given. The name is also important if the plant description is not complete, and the gardener needs to do more research.

Life Cycles

One of the most fundamental pieces of information about a plant is its life cycle. Because of this, nurseries and plant catalogs often divide plants into categories based on life cycle or life form. Categories often used include bulbs (including rhizomes and corms), annuals, perennials, shrubs, and trees.

Annuals complete their life cycle (from seedling to setting seed) within a single year. In other words, they will not come back next year, although some may self-seed. Annuals are useful in flower beds where gardeners prefer yearly change as well as in containers and as cut flowers. Annuals can also be planted in perennial beds to fill gaps in the succession of bloom. Summer-blooming annuals typically bloom all summer long.

Biennials complete their life cycle within two growing seasons, germinating and growing vegetatively the first season and flowering the second season. The individual plant will not come back after flowering the second year (although it may self-seed). Biennials can provide quicker color than perennials and are often more architectural than annuals.

Perennials live through multiple growing seasons. Most have a short blooming period of two to six weeks. Perennials readily add structure to the garden and can provide more of a "sense of place." While individual plants may be more expensive, the one-time investment may last for years.

Bulbs, corms and tubers—Many herbaceous ornamentals fall into the category of bulbs, corms, and tubers. These plants are perennial in their native climate, but in regions with cool winter soils, some require fall digging and winter storage indoors.

Notes on Annuals, Biennials, and Perennials

Many of our annuals are actually perennials in warmer climates. Some of our more hardy annuals may live as short-lived perennials in protected areas.

Some plants are described as either being biennials *or* short-lived perennials. In a good spot, such a plant might last for three or more years—on the other hand, if it blooms extravagantly and produces many seeds, it may "bloom itself to death" in only two seasons. A factor to consider in choosing one of these plants for the garden is if the plant does self-seed. If so, is this a desirable trait? Self-seeding plants can be invasive.

Exposure

The amount of sun a plant needs to thrive is a critical factor in choosing a plant to fit a particular garden situation. The following are catalog terms used to describe the plant's preference for sun exposure.

Full sun—Due to the strong sunlight in sunny, high elevations like Colorado, a garden that receives at least 6 hours of sun each day is generally considered to be full sun. Frequently, eastern catalogs (with more cloud cover) will describe full sun as being eight to twelve hours per day.

Part sun—In Colorado, a garden site that receives 6 hours of dappled shade from trees or approximately 4 hours of direct sun with shade either in the morning or afternoon is considered part sun. Frequently, eastern catalogs may say six to eight hours.

Part shade is used interchangeably with the term "part sun."

Light shade is the shade produced from a one-story building or tree, and is characterized by bright, indirect light (Figure 35-4).

Medium shade is the shade under deciduous trees, unless the tree is large and dense. If the tree is very large, the shade may be considered deep shade. Thinning tree branches will not adequately improve sun levels for sun-loving plants.

Dark shade is very dense and dark, and is found under evergreens and very large deciduous trees. The plant palette for these areas is limited.

Figure 35-4 ▪ *Hosta and ferns make a great textural combination for a north-side shade garden.*

Irrigation Requirements

Hydrozones—Plants should be grouped into areas requiring the same irrigation amounts. For example:

- **Routine irrigation**—Watered every two to four days
- **Reduced irrigation**—Watered every five to fourteen days
- **Limited irrigation**—Watered during dry spells
- **Non-irrigated**—On sites where landscape irrigation is not desirable or possible, focus on natural growth.

Based on differences in annual precipitation, gardens with limited to no irrigation will thrive some years and decline other years.

In a semi-arid state such as Colorado, the amount of water a plant needs is a very important factor, although it is not always listed in catalogs. If this information is given, it is often through the use of symbols. Because the meaning of this varies, refer to the catalog or plant tag key for interpretation. If there is no mention of moisture requirements, and the plant or catalog is not from the West, assume that the plant in question cannot tolerate extremely dry soils.

Drought Tolerance

This is a relative term. Consider where the information is coming from. It will mean very different things if coming from New Mexico or Maine. This distinction is illustrated by the following catalog description: "Thick roots drive down deeply, making it drought tolerant; struggles in the desert southwest" (Figure 35-5).

What is a "Xeric Plant"?

"Xeric" is a relative term. Some sources consider a plant that needs no supplemental irrigation as xeric; others consider plants needing up to one inch of water per week as xeric. Xeric plants tolerate conditions of low water, bright light, and warm temperatures. Adaptations include thick, waxy, fleshy, hairy, or light-colored leaves, small narrow leaves, and taproots (Figure 35-6).

Figure 35-5 ▮ *The Colorado Springs Xeric Demonstration Garden features a variety of drought-tolerant plants. It often amazes visitors that drought-tolerant plants are not just cacti and desert-looking plants.*

For additional information on xeric plants, refer to the following Colorado State University Extension fact sheets:

- *Xeriscaping: Perennial and Annual Flowers*, #7.231
- *Xeriscaping: Ground Cover Plant*, #7.230
- *Xeriscaping: Creative Landscaping*, #7.228
- *Xeriscaping: Retrofit Your Yard*, #7.234

Soil Requirements

Eastern catalogs will often describe soil needs of plants as being **woodsy** or **woodland soils**. Western soils seldom match that description. Woodland soils usually refer to moist, acidic soils that are high in humus. Plants needing a woody soil often do poorly in Western soils even if they are hardy.

Figure 35-6 ▮ *A cacti and succulent garden can be a fun specialty garden.*

Similarly, woodland plants are usually adapted to a low light condition and soils rich in organic matter. They typically have large leaves and small flowers, and are often adapted to humid air. Again, they usually do poorly in much of the arid West.

Other soil requirement "red flags" to watch for are needs "ordinary soil" or "good soil." What is "ordinary"? Catalog writers are probably not referring to the typical western soils. In general, Western soils are either clayey, sandy, or gravelly, and are almost always low in organic matter and high in pH (alkaline).

If a catalog says the plant grows best in sweet soils, there should not be a problem, because "sweet" means alkaline. If a catalog states a plant "needs well-drained soil," it may or may not be a good choice for gravelly soils. It depends on how well drained the soil really needs to be. For example, in an eastern catalog, a plant description reads "needs well-drained, even dry soil; struggles in desert southwest." This indicates that western "well-drained and dry" is probably more well drained and dry than in the east (Figure 35-7).

Bloom Period

Another factor often listed on plant descriptions is the bloom period. This becomes of greater import when planning a garden from catalogs in January as opposed to going to a garden center where merely seeing what is in bloom at the time of purchase can be a guide. Consider when you want your plants to bloom. Does the whole garden area flower only in June, or is there color throughout the growing season?

Usually, plants are described as blooming in spring, late spring, early summer, summer, late summer, or fall, which is fairly self-explanatory. However, for gardeners who live at higher elevations or elsewhere with a short growing season, the meaning may be misleading. Here, the seasons are more compressed and most late summer or fall blooming plants will never get a chance to flower before frost (Figure 35-8).

Length of Bloom

The number of days a plant bears flowers is generally not listed in catalogs, but this can make a big difference in the garden. Perennials bloom for a period of a short-but-showy one week to six weeks or more. These long-blooming perennials can become the "backbone" of a perennial bed, unifying plants that bloom around it. Annuals can help increase the amount of color in a garden, as they tend to bloom all summer, reaching their peak at the end of summer.

Consider whether you want a changing palette of plants, or fewer, longer-blooming plants. Keep in mind that the former will be hard to accomplish in a small garden, and a small number of plants in bloom at one time may end up looking "spotty" in the garden (Figure 35-9).

Mature Size

An important consideration in choosing plants is the overall size it will reach at maturity. Often, catalogs only give information on height, which can determine whether it is better for the front or back of the border. Width is less frequently listed, but

Figure 35-7 ▮ *Iris is an example of a flower tolerant of a variety of soil types as long as it well drained.*

Figure 35-8 ▮ *Tulips and other spring flowering bulbs are popular, easy to grow, spring bloomers.*

Figure 35-9 ▮ *Daylilies are popular as a perennial with a long bloom period.*

should be given as much consideration as height. Because the final size of the plant is hard to visualize, it is easy to plant too closely, especially when starting with smaller pots. The bed should be measured and planted to take into account the ultimate size of each plant. Annuals can be used to fill in the empty space in the first season.

Growth Form

Frequently, catalogs will describe something about the growth form of a plant. These terms include the following:

- **Clumping**—Individual plants form clumps rather than spreading evenly to fill the bed.

- **Creeping, underground runners**—These usually refer to rhizomes. Plants with this growth form can be aggressive and may need to be divided or contained (such as mints or yarrows).

- **Trailing or climbing**—These are usually vining or semi-vining plants and are usually used as a groundcover or hanging basket.

OTHER IMPORTANT CONSIDERATIONS THAT MAY OR MAY NOT BE LISTED IN A CATALOG

Fragrance

You may be interested in having fragrant plants near paths, patios, windows, or doors. Even if the species as a whole is considered to be fragrant (i.e., roses), bear in mind that not all cultivars *within* a species are fragrant. Check individual listings to see whether "fragrant" is in the description. If not, it is probably not fragrant (Figure 35-10).

Figure 35-10 ▮ *When it comes to fragrance, not all roses are created equally. Some were bred for fragrance, while color patterns were the attractive features of others.*

Wildlife-Resistant Plants

Wildlife can make gardening difficult. Everything from deer to chipmunks eat cultivated plants. While there are no guarantees on what a very hungry animal will avoid, in general, most wildlife will avoid plants that are very aromatic, have prickles and spines, tough leathery leaves, milky sap, or are toxic. Further, some catalogs will actually include a little symbol or statement if, in their experience, the plant is wildlife-resistant. These are only tendencies, however, and are not foolproof.

Wildlife-Attracting Plants

Many gardeners select plants to attract wildlife, such as butterflies and birds. A large variety of pollen- and nectar-bearing flowers attract butterflies. In butterfly gardening, give attention to plants for the adults and plants to feed the caterpillars (larval stage of the butterfly). Birds are often attracted to red flowers (Figure 35-11).

Figure 35-11 ▮ *A wide variety of pollen- and nectar-producing flowers, like this maltese cross, attract butterflies and hummingbirds.*

Insect and Disease Resistance

Certain species are prone to insects or diseases, which has led to the development of resistant cultivars. Sometimes you only will notice a problem if you read through a description of *all* of the cultivars. For example, bee balm (*Monarda*) is known to be susceptible to powdery mildew. However, in one catalog, the species description of bee balm says nothing of this susceptibility, nor do two of the cultivar descriptions. However, 'Red Shades' is listed as "very resistant to powdery mildew." You must read between the lines to discover that the genus *Monarda* is susceptible to powdery mildew.

Hail Resistance

Big- or soft-leaved plants such as hosta are very vulnerable to hail. In areas with frequent hailstorms, choose narrow and tougher-leaved plants, as they are more resilient. (Figure 35-12)

Need for Staking

Many places are very windy, which means that top-heavy and tall plants may need staking. If gardening in a windy location, consider looking for shorter or lighter cultivars. For example, "a mid-size delphinium that never needs staking . . . the choice for smaller gardens."

Need for Division

Some plants need to be divided more frequently than others. For example, ornamental grasses like Blue Fescue requires frequent division as the center dies out. Peony can go many years without the need for division. Plants with need for frequent division would be considered "high maintenance." On the other hand, plants that need division frequently are good sources of plants to share with others.

Information on plant division will rarely be found in catalogs, but may be looked up in other reference materials (Figure 35-13).

Attractive or Contrasting Foliage

Consider how the plant will look out of bloom, will the foliage still look attractive? Using a range of colors, sizes, and shapes of leaves will help add interest in the garden, even when nothing is blooming. Choosing plants that have colorful fall foliage will add an extra season of interest to the garden. Planting for foliage over blooms is a new design trend (Figure 35-14).

PLANT EVALUATION PROGRAMS

There are many different ways that new plants are tested. There are two trial gardens on the Colorado State University campus in Fort Collins (the Annual Trial Gardens and PERC Trial Gardens) (Figure 35-15).

Plant Select® (a collaboration between Colorado State University, Denver Botanic Gardens, and the Green Industry of Colorado) is a program designed to seek and distribute the very best plants for gardens of the high plains and intermountain region (see www.plantselect.org). All America Selection is a national program evaluating new cultivars (see www.all-americaselections.org).

Figure 35-12 ▮ *Hail can be rather destructive to large-leaved plants, like hosta.*

Figure 35-13 ▮ *Peony is an example of a plant that rarely needs division.*

Figure 35-14 ▮ *Caladiums used for foliage color. A trend in landscape design is to replace short-blooming flowers with plants that have attractive foliage.*

ECOLOGICAL ADAPTATION

The goal is to plant "the right plant in the right place." For example, the ideal perennial for Colorado will require low water; prefer the local clayey, sandy, or rocky soils; be hardy; be long-lived; and will self-sow before dying. However, there is a fine line between choosing plants that are well adapted and plants that are so well adapted that they become invasive. Invasive plants can become noxious weeds, escaping from gardens and taking over native vegetation (Figure 35-16).

Clues to Overly Well-Adapted Plants

Plants that are aggressive in one region may not be a problem in another. These words should give clues that a plant may become a problem in some regions:

- "Naturalizes readily"

- "Quickly spreads to give blanket of color"

- "Resist the temptation to crowd plants too closely; They will spread of their own accord soon enough"

- "Vigorous spreader, but that's no vice with looks like these"

- "Give this plant lots of room"

- "Plants are typically short-lived but they seed themselves quite freely, so you'll always have plenty around"

How Aggressive Plants Spread

Aggressive plants spread by runners or seeds. They can just be aggressive within a landscape (such as a garden), spread into neighboring gardens/natural areas, or could be a Colorado Noxious Weed.

Figure 35-15 ■ *Annual Trial Gardens at Colorado State University.*

Figure 35-16 ■ *Drumstick primrose (purple) and donkey tail spurge (yellow) make a beautiful combination. However, in Colorado's climate, donkey tail spurge becomes rather invasive. It is on the Colorado Noxious Weed List.*

It is important to note that not all plants are aggressive in all climates. What is aggressive in New England may not be aggressive in Colorado, and vice versa. For example, *Euphorbia myrsinites* (donkey tail spurge) is a plant on the Colorado Noxious Weed List A. It has many ornamental and xeric qualities and was even recently promoted in Colorado as a great rock garden plant. Its invasive qualities only became apparent after. Because it is not a problem in the east, it is still offered for sale in many catalogs.

Similarly, in Colorado's climate, blackberries have marginal hardiness and will be killed in winters with lots of temperature swings. However, on Vancouver Island in Canada, blackberries thrive and have invaded thousands of acres of roadsides and native lands.

Not all catalogs will bother to find out where a plant is illegal to sell in various states. Therefore, the responsibility is on the consumer to find out which plants are illegal to grow in their state or region.

Weed Terminology

Alien is a plant that is not native to the country or state. This term is synonymous with non-native.

Aggressive usually means that it will spread widely in a garden. These plants can take over a garden or might escape into wild areas.

Invasive is loosely used, but generally means that a plant escapes into native habitat, crowding out native plants. However, it can also mean invasive within a garden only.

Noxious weed is defined by state law. Noxious weeds are always aliens and have proven to escape into native habitats or agricultural lands. Plants with this designation must not be sold or grown in Colorado. For information on Colorado Noxious Weeds, Google the Colorado Department of Agriculture. Examples of escaped ornamentals on Colorado Noxious Weed Lists include:

- Bouncing bet
- Oxeye daisy
- Yellow toadflax and dalmation toadflax
- Chicory
- Common tansy
- Dame's rocket/sweet rocket
- Purple loosestrife
- Scentless chamomile
- Donkey tail spurge (myrtle spurge)
- Orange hawkweed
- Russian olive trees

CHAPTER REVIEW
Questions

1. What parameters are the U.S. Department of Agriculture Hardiness Zone Map based on? What is the hardiness zone of your community? How well does it describe your own garden situation? Why may it be different?

2. List six factors that can influence hardiness.

3. Define *microclimate*.

4. Describe how microclimates can be influenced by the following situations:
   a. Elevation
   b. Aspect
   c. Hills and valleys
   d. Rocks and other heat-absorbing materials
   e. Structures
   f. Bodies of water

5. Describe techniques to create and exploit microclimates.

6. What are the advantages and disadvantages of gardening at higher elevations?

7. You have four sides of your house—north, south, east, and west—describe what types of growing conditions that would work best on each side.

8. Describe how windbreaks could work to your advantage or disadvantage.

9. Describe the microclimates around your home landscape.

10. Describe what makes a well-defined (complete) plant description in a catalog and a poorly defined (incomplete) plant description.

11. What attributes define the four different life cycles?
    a. Annual
    b. Biennial
    c. Perennial
    d. Bulbs, corms, and tubers

12. What are the benefits of having annuals, biennials, and perennials in your garden? Give one example for each life cycle.

13. List the five different exposure situations, and discuss challenges associated with growing plants in each situation.

14. Describe different hydrozones associated with residential landscapes.

15. Explain common misunderstandings related to xeriscaping.

16. List adaptations that make plants more drought tolerant.

17. What defines a "woodsy or woodland soil"?

18. Define "ordinary soils."

19. Given your preference for time of year flowering, what type of plants (annuals, biennials, perennials, and bulbs, corms, and tubers) would be your primary choice of plants in your garden?

20. Horticulturally speaking, what is resistance?

21. What are the parameters that define wildlife-resistant plants?

22. Give three examples of plants that you believe have attractive or contrasting foliage.

23. What are characteristics of the "ideal" plant? Which of these characteristics are applicable in your area?

24. Define the following terms about plant populations:

    a. Aggressive

    b. Invasive

    c. Native

    d. Alien

25. Give examples of wording that may suggest a plant could be aggressive or invasive in some areas.

UNIT H

Fruit

Learning Objectives

At the end of this unit, the student will be able to:

- Plant raspberries

- Prune fall-bearing (primocane-fruiting) raspberries and summer-bearing (floricane-fruiting) raspberries

- Learn trellising systems for raspberries

- Perform general care of raspberries

- Trellis and prune trailing, erect, and semi-erect blackberries

- Plant and renew June-bearing strawberry cultivars

- Plant and renew fall-bearing and day neutral strawberry cultivars

- Perform general care of strawberries

- Trellis and prune grapes in a single curtain system (including first spring, second spring, third spring, and forth spring and beyond)

- Describe planting considerations of fruit trees in the home landscape

- Describe structural training and annual pruning of dwarf, semi-dwarf, and standard size apples

- Describe structural training and annual pruning of peaches

Chapter
36*

Growing Small Fruit

Small fruits are easy to grow in the home garden. They take limited space and are relatively easy to care for. Examples of small fruit include:

- Brambles: raspberries and blackberries

- Grapes

- Strawberries

- Currants and gooseberries

- Blueberries (need acid soils)

- Huckleberries (need acid soils)

- Chokeberries (not hardy to cold winter climates like Colorado)

- Kiwifruit (not hardy to cold winter climates like Colorado)

- Elderberries

- Highbush cranberries

- Saskatoon berries (June berries or service berries)

*Author: David Whiting and Merrill Kingsbury, Colorado State University Extension. Artwork by David Whiting.

RASPBERRIES
Types and Cultivars

Fall-bearing (primocane-fruiting) red raspberry cultivars are typically more hardy than summer crop cultivars. Suggested cultivars include Autumn Britten, Polana, Jaclyn, Caroline, and Heritage. Joan-J and Himbo-Top have not performed well in Colorado trials.

Summer-bearing (floricane-fruting) red raspberry cultivars have some winter hardiness problems in climates like Colorado, with frequent winter to spring and back to winter temperature swings. Suggested cultivars include Nova, Boyne, and Killarney.

Black raspberry or "blackcap"—Suggested cultivars include MacBlack and Jewel.

Purple raspberries are a hybrid of red and black. Suggested cultivars include Royalty.

Yellow raspberries are a mutation of red. Suggested cultivars include Anne.

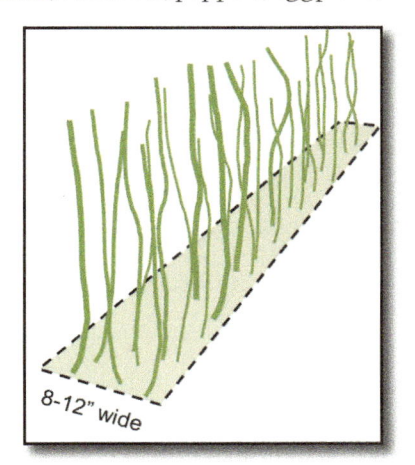

Figure 36-1 ▮ *Raspberries make a great crop for the home gardener.*

Planting Raspberries

With good growing conditions, a raspberry patch may last ten to fifteen years. Viral diseases and hardiness problems frequently shorten the life of a patch. Raspberries need full sun, but avoid reflected heat in areas with hot summer temperatures. In open windy areas, wind protection is important as dry winds can dehydrate and kill exposed canes.

Raspberries prefer a deep, well-drained, sandy loam soil. They perform poorly on compacted clayey soils and soils with poor drainage. On clayey soils, plant in a raised bed. Because raspberries are a long-term crop, extra efforts to improve the organic content of the soil to five percent gives good dividends.

Due to soil-borne diseases, do not plant raspberries where raspberries, strawberries, tomatoes, peppers, eggplant, potatoes, or vine crops (cucumbers, squash and melons) have been grown in the past four years. To reduce virus potential, do not plant raspberries next to blackberries. To help manage virus problems, purchase certified virus-free nursery stock.

In the home garden, raspberries are generally planted in a hedgerow. Place plants in a row twelve to eighteen inches between plants with four to eight feet between rows (depending on trellising system and equipment used). If planting bare-root plants, soak plants in water for a few hours before planting. Dig shallow holes large enough to spread out the root mass and set plant with the top root one to two inches below soil level. Water plants to settle the soil. Cut newly planted canes to 6 inches. Care of the new planting should be similar to vegetable transplants with frequent, light irrigation until the plants become established.

Figure 36-2 ▮ *Red raspberries in a hedgerow. For higher yield, keep width of hedgerow to only 8 to 12 inches wide for fall-bearing cultivars.*

Allow canes to fill in, making the hedgerow. By hoeing or cultivation, routinely remove any canes that come up outside of the hedgerow. For higher yields and reduced pest problems, keep the hedgerow width to only eight to twelve inches for fall cultivars and twelve to eighteen inches for summer cultivars (Figure 36-2).

Pruning

Primocane vs. Floricane—The crown and roots system of raspberries is perennial. The canes are biennial. *Primocane* refers to the first-year canes; *floricane* refers to the second-year canes.

Fall-Bearing (Primocane-Fruiting) Raspberries

In fall-bearing cultivars, the fall crop starts at the top of the *primocane* (new cane this summer), working its way down the cane with each picking. Next summer, the crop starts at the point where the fall crop ended the previous season, continuing downward.

For best yields and high fruit quality, prune to a fall crop only. In February/March, prune all canes to the ground. This eliminates the summer crop, putting all the growth into the superior fall crop. This also helps eliminate winter injury problems and many common insect pests.

For a fall and summer crop, prune the same as summer-bearing cultivars.

Summer-Bearing (Floricane-Fruiting) Raspberries

1. *Primocanes* (new canes the first year) are not pruned.

2. In spring (February/March), prune as follows:

   • Remove spindly canes, leaving stocky canes ¼ inch in diameter and larger. Thin stocky canes to about 10 canes per foot of hedgerow.

   • **For larger fruit size**, tip canes at a convenient height where they will be self-supporting, typically around 5 feet. Canes may be tied in clusters to a trellis.

   • **For larger yields**, do not top canes. Canes may be tied in clusters to a trellis.

3. Mid-summer, when the fruiting is finished, remove *all floricanes* (flowering/fruiting canes) to the ground. They will not fruit again. This makes room for the new crop of *primocanes*.

Trellising

Raspberries are considered easier to manage if trellised. Examples of trellising systems are given in Figures 36-3 to 36-5.

Irrigating

Raspberries need about 1 inch of water (rain and irrigation) per week during blooming/fruiting. Depending on soil type, this may require irrigation once to twice a week. When watering, avoid wetting the leaves and fruit, as this can cause

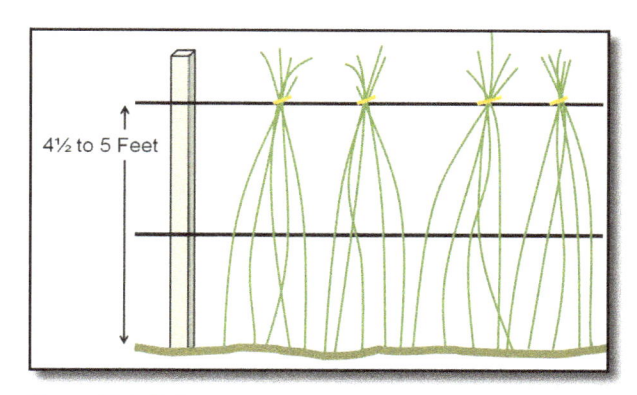

Figure 36-3 ▍ *The **one-line trellis** system has wires running at 30 inches and 4½ to 5 feet. Canes are tied to the lines in bundles.*

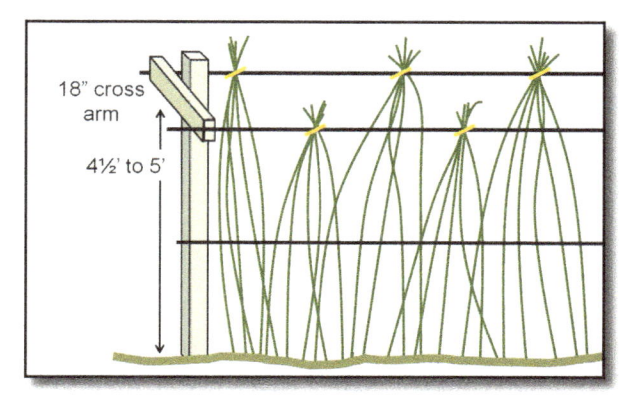

Figure 36-4 ▍ *The **two-line trellis** system added an 18-inch cross arm at 4½ to 5 feet. Wires are run at the edge of the cross arm forming a box. Canes are tied in bundles on the two lines.*

Figure 36-5 ▍ *The **T-trellis** system is popular for fall-bearing (primocane-fruiting) cultivars. At knee height, a cross arm and wire form a box. Canes are free floating inside the box.*

disease problems. Raspberries work great with drip irrigation under wood chip mulch.

Water use is significantly less during nonfruiting times. Iron chlorosis (yellowing of leaves with veins remaining green) is a common symptom of overwatering (Figure 36-6).

Fertilizing

A good guide for fertilization is to observe plant growth. Leaves should be healthy green and primocane should grow to 5 to 8 feet. Adjust actual fertilizer rate if plants grow too tall or are too short.

Figure 36-6 ▮ *Iron chlorosis (yellowing of leaves with veins remaining green) is a common symptom of overwatering. Raspberries are commonly overwatered in the spring.*

Fertilize all raspberries in the spring as growth starts and repeat in early June. For fall bearing cultivars, make a third application in August. Apply ½ to 1 cup of ammonium sulfate (21-0-0) or similar fertilizer per 10 feet of hedgerow. The fertilizer may be broadcast over the hedgerow area and watered in or placed in a band a foot to the side of the row.

If using compost or manure, make application in the late fall or early winter, but avoid early fall application which can push late fall growth. Reduce the rate of nitrogen fertilizer by one-half.

Common Raspberry Pests

Abiotic

- **Winter dehydration** is less of a problem in fall-bearing cultivars where they are pruned to the ground each spring.
- **Sunburn of fruit** (light color patches on the top side of fruit) is common in hot weather. Raspberries prefer cooler temperatures.
- **Iron chlorosis** (yellow leaves with veins remaining green) is a common symptom of springtime overwatering. Correct watering problems.

Insects and Mites

- **Grasshoppers** love raspberries!
- **Spider mite** populations explode in hot summers and following the use of the insecticide Sevin (carbaryl). Leaves are bronzed by these tiny insect relatives.
- **Cane borer, crown borer,** and **stem borer** are common borers of the canes. These are less of a problem in fall-bearing cultivars where the canes are removed to the ground each spring.
- **Plant bugs** cause misshapen fruit.
- **Raspberry sawflies** are caterpillar-like insects that feed on leaves.
- **Leaf rollers**
- **Spottedwing drosophila flies** can affect ripe raspberries, in particular fall bearing varieties.

Diseases

- **Virus complex**—Raspberries are rather prone to a variety of viruses. Simply remove the patch when the fruit becomes small and the patch is less productive. Start the new patch in another area of the garden using new, virus-free plants.

BLACKBERRIES

In blackberries, the receptacle (white core of the fruit) is the part of the fruit when picked. In raspberries the receptacle remains on the plant when picked.

Types and Cultivars

Training blackberries produce vigorous *primocanes* (first-year vegetative cane) from the crown of the plant rather than roots. Second-year *floricanes* produce long-shaped fruit with relatively small seeds and a highly aromatic, intense flavor. They are not hardy in climates like Colorado, experiencing damage at temperatures of 13°F in midwinter, and in the 20s°F range in late winter/early spring.

Erect blackberries have stiff arching canes that are somewhat self-supporting. However, they are much easier to handle when trellised and pruned. Summer prune or tip primocanes to encourage branching and increase fruit production on the second-year floricanes. Plants can become invasive to an area as it can produce new primocanes (suckers) from the roots.

Erect blackberries produce fruit with relatively large seeds. Flavor and aroma are not considered as intense as in the training blackberry cultivars. They are semi-hardy in climates like Colorado with rapid springtime temperature shifts.

Primocane-fruiting cultivars of erect blackberries produce fruit on the new canes. This makes management easier as the canes can be cut to the ground each winter. Suggested cultivars include Prime Jan and Prime Jim.

Semi-erect blackberry plants are thornless and produce vigorous, thick, erect canes from the crown. No primocanes are produced from the roots (suckering). Prune primocanes in the summer to encourage branching and increase fruit production on floricanes. A trellis is required to support the canes.

Semi-erect blackberries generally produce a higher yield than trailing or erect types. Fruit quality is similar to that of the erect blackberries. Suggested cultivars include Triple Crown and Chester Thornless.

Blackberry/red raspberry hybrids are generally natural crosses between blackberries and raspberries. Because the receptacle (white core) comes off with the fruit, they are generally considered a type of blackberry. Popular cultivars include Boysen (Boysenberry), Logan (Loganberry), and Tay (Tayberry).

Planting and Care of Blackberries

Blackberries produce best in full sun, but are tolerant of partial shade. They are more tolerant of clayey soils than raspberries. However, good drainage is essential. Because blackberries may last for ten to fifteen years, extra attention to improving the soil organic content to five percent gives big dividends.

For semi-erect cultivars, space plants five to six feet apart, space erect cultivars two to three feet apart, and space training cultivars four to six feet apart. Start with certified disease-free nursery stock. Planting would be similar to raspberries. To reduce virus problems, do not plant blackberries adjacent to raspberries.

Irrigation, fertilization, and pest management would be similar to raspberries.

Trellising and Pruning

Trellising is recommended for all blackberries.

Trailing blackberries are easy to grow on a two-wire system. Run a top wire at five to six feet with a second line 18 inches below the top wire.

After the first year, there will be fruiting floricanes along the wires. Train the new primocanes into a narrow row below the fruiting canes. Directing all canes in one direction may make it simpler.

After the fruit harvest period, the old fruiting (floricanes) are removed. However, unless there is a lot of disease, it's best to delay removing the old fruiting canes until they have died back considerably. This allows the dying canes to move nutrient back into the crown and roots. After old fruiting canes are removed, train the primocanes up on the wires. Work with one or two canes at a time in a spiral around the trellis wires. Canes from adjacent plants may overlap a little. No pruning of primocanes is necessary.

In area with low winter temperatures, leave the primocanes on the ground for the winter where they could be mulched for winter protection. In the spring, after damage of extreme cold has passed, train the old primocanes (now floricanes) up on the wires. Avoid working with the canes in cold weather, as they are more prone to breaking (Figure 36-7).

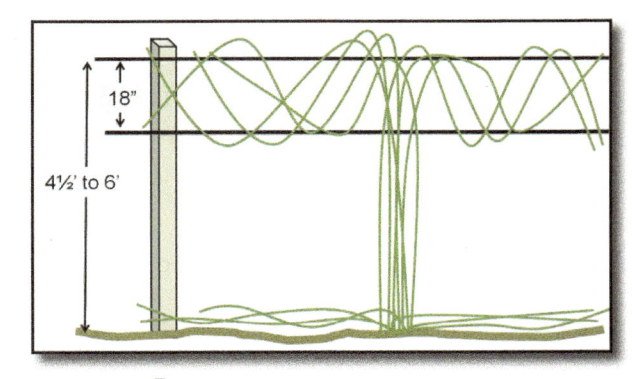

Figure 36-7 ▮ *Two-wire trellis for trailing blackberries. Spread floricanes up on a two-wire system.*

Erect blackberries produce stiff, shorter canes that come from the crown and root suckering (forming a hedgerow). A T-trellis works well to support erect blackberries.

Erect blackberries require summer pruning. Remove the top one to two inches of new primocanes when they are four feet tall. This causes the canes to branch, increasing next year's yields. This will require several pruning sessions to tip each cane as it reaches the four-foot height. Primocanes (suckers) that grow outside the hedgerow should be regularly removed.

In the winter, remove the dead floricanes (old fruiting canes) from the hedgerow. Also shorten the lateral branches to about 1½ to 2½ feet.

Primocane-fruiting erect blackberries—For best quality fruit, cut all canes off just above the ground in the late winter. In the summer, when the primocanes are three and one-half feet tall, removed the top six inches. The primocanes will branch, thereby producing larger yields in the fall.

Figure 36-8 ▮ *Pruning of erect blackberries after winter pruning.*

Semi-erect blackberries are vigorous and easier to manage on a Double T Trellis. Install four foot cross arms at the top of a six foot post. Install a three foot cross arm about two feet below the top line. String high-tensile wire down the rows, connecting to the cross arms.

Semi-erect blackberries require summer pruning. When the primocanes are five feet tall, remove the top two inches to encourage branching. This will require several pruning sessions to prune canes as they reach the height.

In the winter, remove the dead floricanes (old fruiting canes). Spread the primocanes (new floricanes) out along the trellis. Canes do not need to be shortened. However, they can be if they are difficult to train.

STRAWBERRIES
Types and Cultivars

June-bearing cultivars have one large crop in early summer (late June to early July along the Colorado Front Range) with larger fruit and higher yields. They are less hardy in climates like Colorado with rapid springtime temperature swings, and are often damaged by late spring frosts. They are popular for freezing and jams with flavorful, aromatic berries. Suggested cultivars include Honeoye, Guardian, Kent, Redchief, Delite, Jewel, Mesabi, A.C. Wendy, Cabot, Bloominden Gem, Carskill, and Geneva.

Ever-bearing cultivars have two crops: one in early summer and a second crop in the fall. They tend to be more reliable than June-bearing cultivars in cold climates like Colorado. Berries are smaller. Suggested cultivars include Quinalt, Ogallala, and Fort Laramie.

Day-neutral cultivars blossom most of the summer and fall in cycles lasting around six weeks each. Blossoming will slow or stop during hot weather. Fruit is typically small. These are popular for a light, daily harvest through most of the summer and fall. They need constant, light fertilization and regular removal of runners. Suggested cultivars include Tribute, Tristar, and Fern.

Plantings

The key to a great strawberry patch is well-drained soil high in organic matter. Strawberries need full sun (8 hours minimum), but do not like reflected heat. They need protection from wind. In clayey soils, they work better in raised beds that provide better drainage. Strawberries are shallow rooted, and thus intolerant of weed competition.

Figure 36-9 ▮ *Day-neutral cultivars provide a small, continual harvest of fresh strawberries throughout the summer and fall (except in extreme heat).*

Due to soil-borne diseases, avoid soils where strawberries, raspberries, tomatoes, peppers, eggplant, potatoes, and vine crops (squash, melons, pumpkins, and cucumbers) have been growing in the past four 4 or more years.

Blossom potential for the following year is based on plant health in the fall. The strawberry patch may need covering for spring frost protection.

Strawberry plants are fussy about planting depth. The plant crown (short segment with roots below and leaves above) needs to be at the soil line. If the plant is too deep (leaf stems buried), the plant rots. If too shallow (roots exposed), the plant dehydrates (Figure 36-10).

Figure 36-10 ▮ *Strawberries are fussy about planting depth. The short crown section needs to be at the soil surface.*

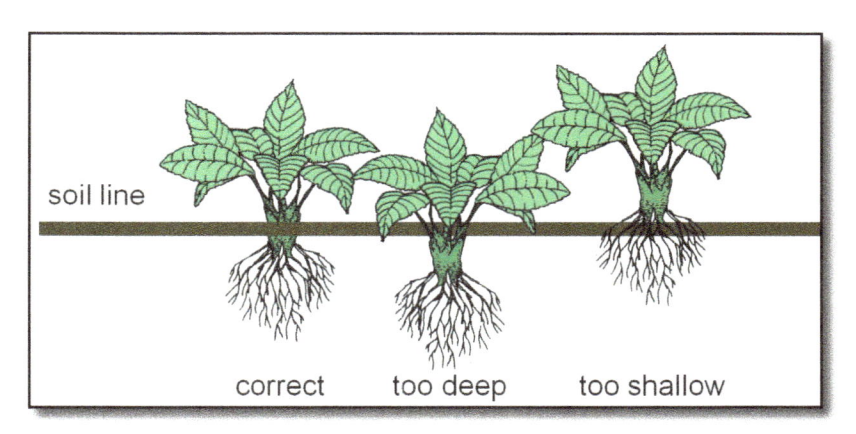

Planting and Renewal of June-Bearing Strawberries

Planting—Since June-bearing cultivars set a lot of runners, they are planted in a matted row system. Set plants eighteen to twenty-four inches apart in rows four plus feet apart. Allow runners from the "mother" plant to fill in a matted row, to a plant population of five to six plants per square foot. Remove excessive runners. Prune off runners outside the matted row and all new runners after September 1 (Figure 36-11).

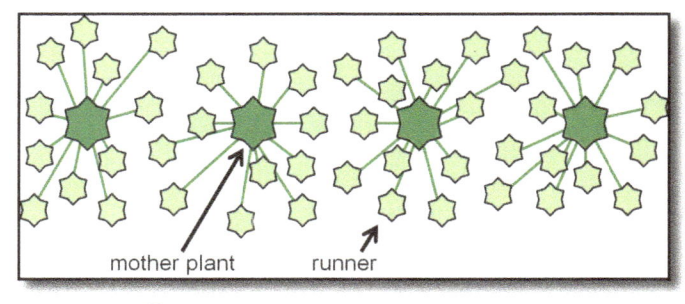

Figure 36-11 ▮ *June-bearing cultivars in matted row system. Runners from the mother plant are allowed to fill in a block 18 to 36 inches wide.*

First Season Care—Remove all flowers the first year. Flowering the first year decreases the growth and next season's yields. If growth is weak and leaves are light green, fertilize lightly in June, July, and August. Use water-soluble fertilizers (like Miracle-Gro, Peters, Rapid Gro, etc.) or one cup of 21-0-0 per 100 square feet (broadcast over bed and water in).

General Care—Fertilize after the summer crop is off with water solubles or one cup 21-0-0 per 100 square feet (broadcast over the patch and water in). Strawberries need one inch of water (rain plus irrigation) per week during blossoming/fruiting. Water needs will be significantly less when not in fruit production. Iron chlorosis (yellow leaves with veins remaining green) is a symptom of overwatering. Renovate every year or restart bed every two to four years.

Renovation of June-Bearing Growing Bed

1. After the fruiting periods, mow or cut foliage to two inches. Remove all plant debris.

2. With shallow cultivation, create alternating strips (eight to ten inches wide) of plant left and plants removed.

3. Allow runners to spread into the cleaned area, up to an optimum plant density of five to six plants per square foot.

4. Remove excessive runners and all runners after September 1.

5. In future years, alternate the strips by taking out the plants the plant strips left the previous year.

Planting and Renewal of Ever-Bearing and Day-Neutral Strawberries

Planting—Because ever-bearing and day-neutral strawberries have fewer runners, the hill system is typically used. Set plants 12 inches apart in a double- or triple-wide row bed. Remove all runners as they develop (Figure 36-12).

First Season Care—Remove the first flush of flowers and allow flowers to develop after July 1.

General Care—Periodically remove all runners. Fertilize lightly throughout the growing season using water-soluble or one-quarter cups 21-0-0 per 100 square feet (broadcast and water in). Start a new patch every three to four years.

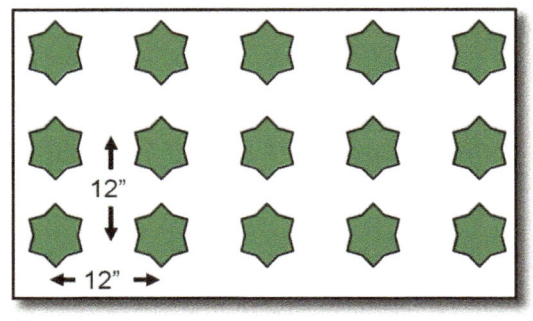

Figure 36-12 ▮ *In the hill system, plants are spaced 12 inches apart in double or triple rows 12 inches apart. All runners are removed.*

Harvesting

Pick strawberries every other day during the peak of the season. If berries are eaten or preserved immediately, harvest only red-ripe fruit and leave the caps on the plants. If the fruit will not be used for a few days, harvest the berries, caps and all, while still pink.

Winter Care

Keep soil damp until fall frost. Then, withhold water to help harden off the plants. A final November watering before soils freeze helps prevent winter-kill from drying.

In cold winter climates, like Colorado, a winter mulch of clean, seed-free straw (or similar material) is recommended. Apply it when the ground freezes (around December 1 along the Colorado Front Range). Apply two inches, but not more as it could smother the plants. In windy areas, bird netting over the mulch helps hold it in place. Mulching helps protect plants from drying winter winds and from root damage by alternative freezing and thawing of the ground.

In climates with late spring frosts (like Colorado), leave the mulch on as long as possible to restrain plant growth in the early spring. In March, start checking plants under the mulch for growth. As growth begins, remove mulch over time, allowing sunlight into the plants. Some may remain on the soil to keep strawberry fruit off the ground.

Summer Mulch

Because strawberries are shallow rooted, summer mulch helps stabilize soil moisture and also helps suppress weeds. Use grass clipping (with no application of weed killers), seed-free straw, or other mulching materials. On ever-bearing and day-neutral cultivars (where runners are not allowed to set), black plastic mulch may be used. Plants must spread and cover the plastic mulch before summer heat sets in or it will be too hot.

Common Strawberry Pests

Abiotic

- **Iron chlorosis** (yellow leaves with green veins) is a symptom of overwatering.
- **Winter injury** often kills plants.
- **Drought injury**
- **Hail** readily defoliates strawberries.
- **Wind**

Insects

- **Lygus bugs** feed on fruit—Control weeds, alfalfa, and legumes. Use insecticidal soap, avoid treating during bloom
- **Aphids**
- Slugs and millipedes—Decrease free moisture with proper watering. Reomove fruit and decaying debris. Mulch to raise fruit up off the soil.
- **Spider mites** bronze leaves. Populations explode in hot weather and following the use of the insecticide Sevin (carbaryl).
- **Spottedwing drosophila** flies can affect ripe strawberries.

Diseases

- **Strawberry leaf spots** show as red spots with tan centers on leaves.
- **Powdery mildew** shows as white mold on leaves.
- **Botrytis gray mold** is the fuzzy mold on fruit.
- **Red stele** and **black root rot complex** are common root disorders.
- **Verticillium wilt** is a common soil-borne disease.
- **Virus complex**—strawberries are prone to a variety of viruses.

Wildlife

- **Birds**
- **Rabbits**
- **Deer**
- **Slugs**

GRAPES

Types and Cultivars

Types of Grapes

- **Table grapes** are used for fresh eating. Most popular cultivars are seedless. Popular cultivars include Himrod, Interlaken, Canadice, St. Theresa, and Reliance.

- **Juice and jelly grapes**—Popular cultivars include Concord, Valiant, Niagra, and St. Croix.

- **Wine grapes**

- **Raisin grapes**

Types of Cultivars

- **American cultivars**, *Vitis labaarusca*, have a strong "foxy" (musty) flavor and aroma. They are use for juice, fresh eating, and some wines.

- **European cultivars**, *Vitis vinifera,* with tight clusters, thin skins, and a wine-like flavor are used for wines. They require more heat units for maturity and have limited potential in Colorado.

- **French-American hybrids** are popular for wine. Characteristics depend on parentage.

Figure 36-13 ▮ *Grapes on a trellis make a great living fence.*

Planting Grapes

Grapes need full sun and protection from wind. Space plants six to eight feet apart, in rows six to ten feet apart (depending on trellising system). Strong trellising systems are required to support the heavy vines and fruit. Use treated posts and twelve-gauge or heavier wire.

Trellising and Pruning

Grapes fruit on one-year-old wood (canes that grew the previous summer). Thus, pruning is a balance between growing fruit and renewing the one-year-old wood. Correct pruning is essential for production. Unpruned or under-pruned grapes give many, small clusters of tiny grapes. Correctly pruned, grapes give high yields of large clusters of large grapes. Over-pruning simply cuts the yield.

There are many methods to trellis grapes. A simple method for the home gardener is the single curtain system.

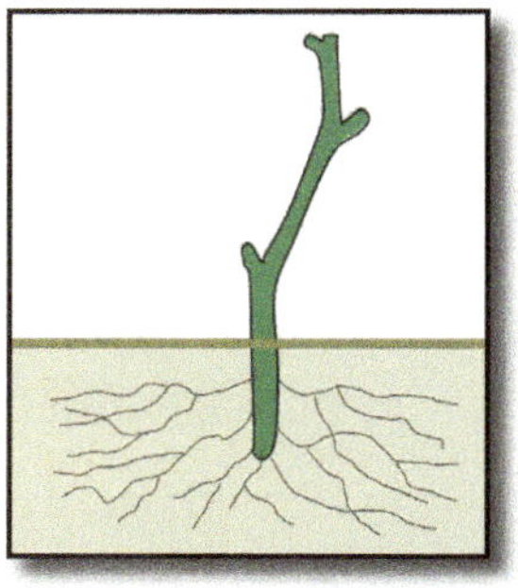

Single Curtain System

Pruning at Planting

At planting, prune back to two to three buds. Allow the summer growth to develop what will become the primary trunk.

Pruning the Second Spring

In the spring, select one of the last summer's canes to become the trunk. Remove the others, leaving one or two renewal spurs (buds close to the trunk). Renewal spurs allow for replacement growth of potential trunk wood if something damages the trunk. If growth was poor (not generating the desired trunk), start over by pruning back to two to three buds (Figure 36-15).

Figure 36-14 ▮ *At planting, prune the grape back to just two to three. This heavy pruning pushes growth of lone canes. One of the canes will become the trunk.*

Spring Pruning the Third Spring

1. Select two one-year-old canes (one to the left and one to the right) to become the *fruiting canes* and *cordon arms* along the trellis. The ideal cane is about pencil diameter with moderate spacing between buds (Figure 36-16).

2. Select two canes (one to the left and one to the right) to become *renewal spurs* by pruning them back to two buds each. The purpose of renewal spurs is to give more options near the trunk in selection fruiting canes in future years.

3. Remove all other canes!

4. Prune the two *fruiting canes* back to 40 to 60 buds per plant (more buds for smaller fruit clusters, or less buds for larger fruit clusters).

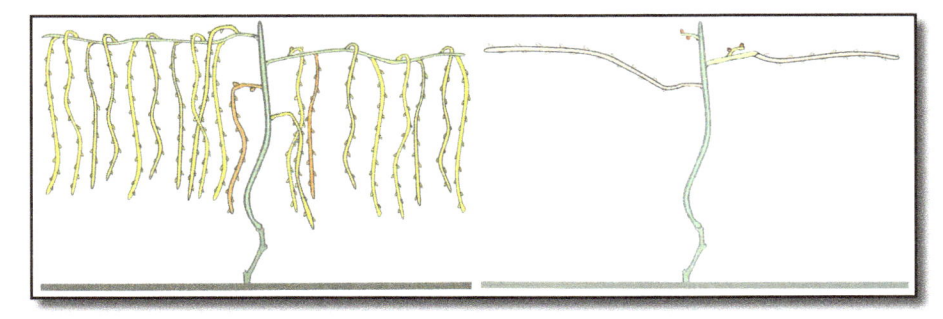

Figure 36-15 ■ *Second spring pruning: Left: Before pruning with three canes. Right: After pruning with one cane selected to become the trunk and other canes pruned back to a renewal spur (shown in red).*

Spring Pruning the Fourth Spring and Beyond

1. Select two, one-year-old canes (one to the left and one to the right) to become the new *fruiting canes* and spread them out along the trellis as *cordon arms*. The ideal cane is about pencil diameter with moderate spacing between buds. To keep the fruiting wood near the trunk, these could be selected from the first couple of canes on last year's cordon arm or from the renewal spurs.

2. Select two canes (one to the left and one to the right) to become **renewal spurs** by pruning them back to two buds each. These could be selected from the renewal spurs of the first couple of canes on last year's

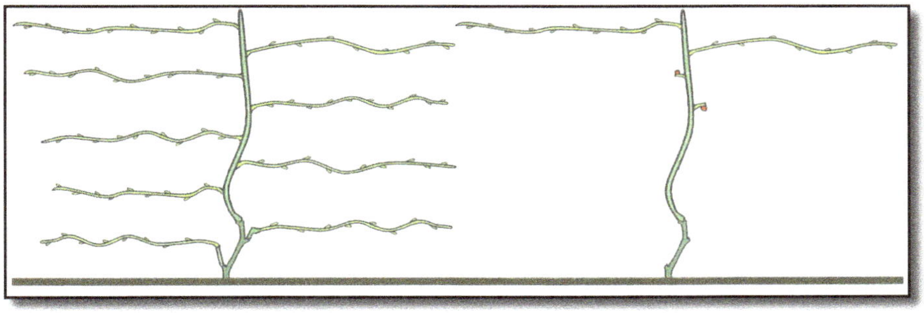

Figure 36-16 ■ *Third spring pruning: Left: Before pruning. Right: After pruning. A one-year-old fruiting cane is selected to go to the left and anther to the right. These become the cordon arms along the grape trellis. Another cane to the left and to the right (near the trunk) are pruned back to two buds as renewal spurs. All the other wood is removed. This heavy pruning balances fruit production with renewing the one-year-old wood for next year's crop.*

Figure 36-17 ■ *Forth spring and beyond pruning: Left: Before pruning: One-year-old fruiting canes shown in yellow. The one-year-old fruiting canes that have been selected to become the new cordon arm are shown in orange. Right: After pruning. A one-year-old fruiting cane is selected to go to the left and another to the right. On the left, a cane from the renewal spur as selected. On the right, a cane from last year's cordon arm was selected. These become the cordon arms along the grape trellis. Another cane to the left and to the right (near the trunk) are pruned back to two buds as renewal spurs. All the other wood is removed. This heavy pruning balances fruit production with renewing the one-year-old wood for next year's crop.*

fruiting cane. The purpose of the renewal spurs is to give options to select future fruiting canes/cordon arms close to the trunk.

3. Remove all other canes! This heavy pruning balances fruit growth with growing new fruiting wood for next year's production.

4. Prune the two fruiting canes back to forty to sixty buds per plant (more buds for smaller fruit clusters, less buds for larger fruit clusters).

General Care of Grapes

- Grapes do best with a 4-foot wide weed-free bark/wood chip mulch strip under the grape trellis. They perform poorly with lawn competition.

- Avoid overwatering. Iron chlorosis is a symptom of springtime over-watering.

- Go light on grape fertilization. Apply one-fourth cup of 21-0-0 (or equivalent) per established plant. Broadcast it under the trellis and water in.

- For home gardeners, flavor is the best method to evaluate harvest time.

Common Grape Pests

Fruit

- **Birds**
- **Botrytis bunch rot**
- **Spottedwing drosophila flies** can affect ripe grapes.

Plants

- **Powdery mildew**
- **Iron chlorosis** (symptom of overwatering)
- **Poor soil drainage**
- **Inadequate control of weeds and diseases**

1. What is the difference in raspberry fruit and blackberry fruit?

2. Describe planting for red raspberries.

3. Describe pruning for summer crop raspberries.

4. Describe pruning for fall-bearing raspberries if you want both the summer and fall crops. Describe pruning for fall-bearing raspberries if you want only the higher quality fall crop.

5. Describe irrigation and fertilization needs of raspberries.

6. Describe planting and care of June-bearing strawberries. How is the patch renewed?

7. Describe planting and care of ever-bearing and day-neutral strawberries. How is the patch renewed?

8. Describe grape pruning at planting, year 1, year 2, year 3, and year 4+. Why are grapes pruned so heavily?

Chapter

37*

Growing Tree Fruit

Tree fruits are less suited to the home garden. They require more space than can be allocated in the small home yard. To be productive they require specific training and annual pruning. In most areas, they require routine sprays to manage insect and disease problems. In regions with late spring frosts, crops are often lost to frost.

PLANTING CONSIDERATIONS

Size and Suggested Spacing

Fruit trees can be large, particularly if not carefully trained and pruned. The typical size of fruit trees is given in Table 37-1.

*Author: David Whiting, Colorado State University Extension. Artwork by David Whiting.

Table 37-1. Typical Size of Fruit Trees

		Typical Spread (Pruned)	Typical Height (Pruned)	Unpruned Spread and Height with No Competition
Apple[1]	Standard	20 feet	20+ feet	40 feet by 40 feet
	Semi-dwarf	10 feet	12–15 feet	
	Dwarf[2]	6 feet	5–10 feet	
Pear	Standard	18 feet	15 feet	40 feet by 25 feet
	Dwarf[3]	12 feet	12 feet	25 feet by 15 feet
Peach and Nectarine	Standard	20 feet	15 feet	25 feet by 25 feet
	Dwarf[4]	8–10 feet	5–10 feet	8 feet by 4–6 feet
Apricot	Standard	20+ feet	15 feet	30 feet by 30 feet
	Dwarf[4]	8 feet	6–8 feet	6–8 feet by 6–12 feet
Sweet Cherry	Standard	30 feet	25 feet	30 feet by 40 feet
	Dwarf[5]	4 feet	6–8 feet	4–8 feet by 6–12 feet
Sour Cherry	Standard	18–24 feet	15 feet	30 feet by 20 feet
	Dwarf	8–10 feet	6–8 feet	8–10 feet by 20 feet
European Plums and Prunes	Standard	20 feet	15 feet	25 feet by 30 feet
Japanese Plums	Standard	18 feet	15 feet	25 feet by 30 feet

[1] Size of apples is controlled by the rootstock and pruning techniques. Depending on rootstock, size may run from standard size down to 40% of standard size trees.

[2] Dwarf apples are recommended for home gardeners. However, they require careful training to be highly productive and staking.

[3] Dwarf pears have not proven overly successful and are not recommended.

[4] Dwarf peach and apricot require careful training to be highly productive. Dwarf apricots are not recommended. Some dwarf peach trees are very small.

[5] Dwarf cherries require careful training to be highly productive.

Pollination

Pollination is a common problem for many gardeners growing tree fruits. Bees do not fly in cool, rainy weather, common in many springs. In most of the United States, the native bee population is down due to mite problems in beehives.

Apricots, sour cherries, peaches, nectarines, and European plums and prunes are generally self-pollinated. That is, pollen from most cultivars will pollinate itself.

Apples, sweet cherries, pears, and Japanese plums are generally cross-pollinated. That is, two compatible cultivars must be planted within 100 feet for good pollination.

Spring Frost

Frost damage is a common problem in climates with late spring frost, like Colorado. Commercial orchards are typically located on side hills, where cold air drains to the valley floors, giving some frost protection. Gardens located down in a valley floor typically have a shorter growing season than surrounding hillsides, and the tendency for late spring frosts makes the location unsuitable for tree fruits. Table 37-2 gives critical temperatures at various stages of bud development.

Table 37-2. Critical Springtime Temperatures

Fruit	Swollen Buds	Buds Showing Color	Full Bloom	Green Fruit
Apples	20–21°F	24–28°F	27–29°F	29°F
Apricots	23°F	25°F	28°F	31°F
Cherries	25°F	28°F	28°F	30°F
Peaches	23°F	25°F	27°F	30°F
Pears	23°F	27°F	29°F	30°F

Soils

Being prone to root rots, fruit trees are intolerant of soils with poor drainage or heavy irrigation. Commercial orchards are often located on gravelly soils with their good drainage. Fruit trees are not compatible with the frequent irrigation of a typical home lawn.

Insects and Diseases

Each region has their local list of insect and diseases associated with growing fruit. In most areas, routine sprays are typically necessary for pest-free fruit. For example, in Colorado, refer the following Colorado State University Extension fact sheets for details:

- *Apple and Pear Insects, #5.519*
- *Backyard Orchard: Apples and Pears (pest management), #2.800*
- *Backyard Orchard: Stone Fruits (pest management), #2.804*
- *Coryneum Blight, #2.914*
- *Fire Blight, #2.907*
- *Peach Tree Borer, #5.566*
- *Spider Mites, #5.507*

TRAINING AND PRUNING

For productivity and quality produce, fruit trees require specific training and annual pruning. Training refers to the general structural shape of the tree, achieved by pruning when the tree is young. Annual pruning refers to the pruning each year to grow quality fruit.

Pruning Basics

For details on pruning basics, refer to Unit F on Pruning.

Pruning of fruit trees is similar to the pruning of shade trees. Structural training is similar to shade trees. Structural training of fruit trees involves removal cuts, reduction cuts, and, in special situations, heading cuts. Annual pruning should never include heading cuts!

The objective in annual pruning of fruit trees is to balance growing of fruit and growing of new fruiting wood. The percentage of wood to be removed is different on shade trees than on fruit trees. On shade trees, the amount of live wood to remove is generally limited to ten to fifteen percent per season. On fruit trees, much higher percentages are removed to encourage the growth of new fruiting wood. To achieve this balance, fruit trees require: 1) better general vigor with special attention to watering and fertilization, and 2) heavy pruning to promote fruiting wood.

General pruning of fruit trees occurs late winter, after the high potential for extreme cold (temperatures below zero) has passed but before bud swell and flowering. Recently pruned trees are less hardy.

Apples

Structural Training of Young Apple Trees

Dwarf apples are trained to a central leader Christmas tree shape with branches in whorls. Spread lower branches to near horizontal and upper branch to 45°. With proper training, dwarf apple trees can be kept to an eight to ten foot height. Due to increased sunlight through the tree, dwarf apples produce the best quality fruit on small trees (Figure 37-1).

Semi-dwarf apples are trained to a delayed open center or modified central leader system. When trained, semi-dwarf trees may be kept to a fifteen to eighteen foot height. In selecting scaffold branches, develop openings for ladders.

Delayed Open Center Vase Training

In delayed, open center, vase-shaped pruning, three to five scaffold branches along the lower trunk are spaced at least six inches apart creating strong branch unions. This open center allows light to reach all branches for maximum fruit production. Multiple branching originating at the same location creates weak branch unions that often fail with a heavy crop load.

To develop the open center, head back the trunk in the first pruning year. This pushes growth into the side branches. In the second pruning year, select the side branches to become the "scaffold branches" (secondary trunks). For best growth, select side branches of equal diameter and evenly spaced around the tree (Figure 37-2).

Heading back the trunk—In developing the short branching pattern, the central leader is generally headed back. After heading back, the bud immediately below the cut generally emerges at too narrow of an angle and will eventually develop

Figure 37-1 ▮ *Train dwarf apples to a Christmas tree shape, spreading lower branches to near horizontal and upper branches at a 45° angle.*

Figure 37-2 ▮ *Delayed open center vase training: The first year, the trunk is headed back a little above the desired branching height. This develops branching below the cut point.*

into a new central leader. A scaffold branch with this narrow angle of attachment will be weak.

To avoid this problem, cut back one bud above the desired branch location and nick the bark just below this top bud. In doing this, nutrients will be diverted to the bud below, which will grow at a wider, stronger angle. The following season, cut the weakened top branch off (Figure 37-3).

Modified Central Leader Training

In this decurrent style pruning, a dominant central leader is maintained with three to five *scaffold branches* (vertically spaced at least six inches apart) which becomes the primary structure of secondary trunks. By definition, the diameter of a "scaffold branch" must be less than one-half the diameter of the adjacent trunk. Being structurally strong, this pruning style is preferred for larger trees. However, fruit production and quality will be low in the center canopy due to shading.

Standard size apples are generally trained to a modified central leader system. The majority of fruit on standard sized apple trees is of inferior quality due to shading of the majority of the tree's canopy. Standard size apples are rather large for home landscapes.

Annual Pruning of Fruiting Apples

Apples fruit on two- or three-year-old twigs and spurs that are no thicker than a pencil. Avoid cleaning out of the small twigs and spurs along the branches.

The primary purpose in annual pruning is to increase sunlight penetration and to remove less productive wood. Apples need light annual thinning of the canopy, opening the tree to light. Start at the top working down into the canopy using reduction cuts and thinning cuts. Avoid any heading cuts as this leads to a thicker canopy that shades out fruit production.

If left unpruned, the quantity of fruit produced may temporarily be greater, but the quality will be much lower.

Remove any water sprouts back to the parent branch/trunk.

Pruning old neglected apple trees—Over a period of years, thin the canopy, thereby opening the tree to light. Over time, remove old wood and reduce tree height with reduction cuts.

Fruit thinning—For quality fruit, thin apples to six to eight inches between fruit, by mid-June.

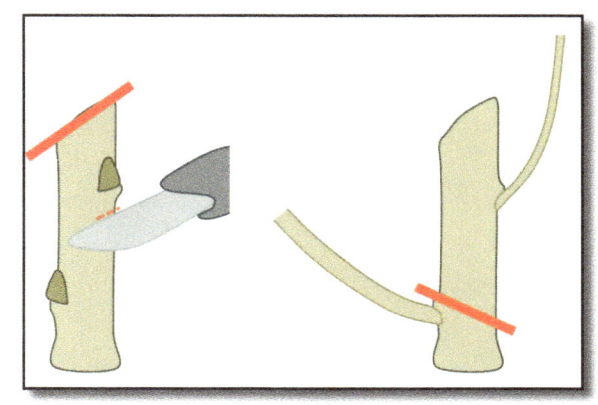

Figure 37-3 ▮ *Left: In heading back the trunk, make the cut leaving one extra bud above the desired top branch location, and nick the bark below this top bud. This will divert growth to the second bud at a wider angle of attachment. Right: The second year, remove the top bud.*

Figure 37-4 ▮ *Modified central leader training develops trees with a dominant trunk in the upper region of the trees and "scaffold branches" becoming secondary trunks. For structural strength, the scaffold branches must be spaced at least six inches apart and the diameter of the scaffold branches must be less than one-half of the adjacent trunk.*

Peaches and Nectarines

Structural Training Young Peach Trees

Peaches and nectarines (fuzz-less peaches) fruit in the top four to five feet of the tree. With careful pruning, height of a peach tree can be maintained at seven to ten feet. Untrained, it is common to find peach trees that fruit in the top four feet of a twelve- to sixteen-foot-tall tree.

Train young peach trees to a delayed open center vase shape. Space four to five scaffold branches at least six inches apart. To keep the tree height low, branching typically starts eighteen to twenty-four inches above the ground (Figure 37-6).

Select scaffold branches with wide angle of attachment and evenly spaced around the tree. It is best to develop scaffold branches all at one time and from the same diameter twigs. Otherwise, older/larger ones will dominate the tree.

In early training, allow small twiggy growth along the scaffold branches.

Do not remove all the fruiting shoots in the center of the tree. The most productive trees have fruiting wood throughout the tree canopy.

Figure 37-6 ■ *To open the tree to light, train peaches and nectarines to a delayed open vase system.*

Annual Pruning of Fruiting Peaches

The objective in annual pruning of fruiting peach trees is to balance fruit production with growth of new wood. Peaches fruit only on one-year-old wood. To promote growth of the fruiting wood, removed one-half to two-thirds of the growth each spring with a combination of thinning cuts and reduction cuts (Figure 37-7).

- Thin fruiting shoots to a spacing of four to six inches.

- Long branches produce more fruit than short ones. Generally avoid heading cuts on the primary branches.

- The ideal fruiting shoots are twelve to twenty-four inches long and three-sixteenths to one-quarter inch diameter at the base. Longer shoots may be headed back by one-forth.

- Remove three- to six-inch-long shoots that are mixed with the more desirable twelve- to eighteen-inch shoots.

- Leave small twigs that are not vigorous enough to offer competition in the tree's interior.

- Stimulate growth of one-year-old fruiting wood in the tree center by thinning out and heading back inside branches.

- Remove any water sprouts back to the parent branch with thinning cuts.

- Avoid cleaning out the small twiggy growth in the tree's interior. This eliminates the center of the tree from being fruitful.

Fruit Thinning—For quality fruit, thin peaches to six to ten inches between fruit, by the time the fruit reaches one inches in diameter.

Sweet Cherries

Structurally Training—Sweet cherries are trained to a modified central leader system. Select scaffold branches that are outward growing rather than upward growing (Figure 37-9).

Annual Pruning—Cherries are borne on long-lived spurs that produce fruit for ten to twelve years. Little annual pruning is needed on fruiting sweet cherries. Focus pruning on thinning the tree canopy, removing older wood with thinning and reduction cuts. Avoid making heading cuts in the top of the tree, as this leads to shading out of the interior.

Fruit Thinning—Cherry fruit is not generally thinned.

Sour Cherries

Structural Training—Sour or pie cherries are generally much smaller trees or shrubs. Train sour cherries to a modified central leader system or delayed open center system.

Annual Pruning—Little pruning is needed on fruiting sour cherries. With routine thinning and removal of older wood, sour cherries may be kept less than 12 feet tall.

Figure 37-7 ▌ *Peaches fruit only on one-year-old wood. Trees are heavily pruned to balance the growth between the fruit crop and production of new wood for next year's crop.*

Figure 37-8 ▌ *Sweet cherry trees are large, taking a lot of space in the home landscapes. Most cultivars require a second cultivar for cross pollination.*

CHAPTER REVIEW
Questions

1. Describe considerations in planting fruit trees in the home landscape.

2. What fruits are generally self-fruitful? What fruits generally require cross pollination by another compatible cultivar?

3. Describe the structural training of standard apples, semi-dwarf apples, and dwarf apples.

4. Describe the annual pruning of apples.

6. Describe the structural training of peaches.

7. Describe the annual pruning of peaches.

UNIT I

Vegetables

eat fruits & vegetables

5 a Day—for Better Health!

Learning Objectives

At the end of this unit, the student will be able to:

- Describe block style layout in a raised bed garden design.
- Describe garden planning and planting times.
- Describe soil preparation and fertilization for the vegetable garden.
- Describe routine garden care including mulching, irrigation, and water conservation.
- Describe routine care for tomatoes.
- List hints for growing other vegetables.
- Describe frost protection and microclimate modification.

Supplemental Reading

Web

- Assorted Colorado State University Extension publications on vegetables available online at www.cmg. colostate.edu.

Chapter

38*

Vegetable Garden Layout and Planting

WHEN TO PLANT

Cool Season Vegetables

These vegetables prefer cool growing temperatures (60°F to 80°F) and lose quality in hot weather. They are often replanted mid-summer for fall harvest.

Hardy Vegetables

Crops: broccoli, cabbage, kohlrabi, onions, lettuce, peas, radish, spinach, and turnips

Temperatures: Hardy vegetables grow with daytime temperatures as low as 40°F and may survive a frosty nip.

When to plant:

- Based on soil temperatures, refer to Table 38-1.

- Plant as soon as soil adequately dries in the spring.

- These crops may be planted as early as two to four weeks before the date of the average last spring frost.

Semi-Hardy Vegetables

Crops: beets, carrots, cauliflower, parsley, parsnips, potatoes, and Swiss chard

Temperatures: Semi-hardy vegetables grow with minimum daytime temperatures of 40°F to 50°F, but are less tolerant of a frosty night.

*Authors: David Whiting, Carol O'Meara, and Carl Wilson, Colorado State University Extension. Photographs and line drawings by David Whiting.

When to plant:

- Based on soil temperature, refer to Table 38-1.

- Plant as soon as soil adequately dries in the spring.

- These crops may be planted as early as zero to two weeks before the date of the average last spring frost.

Warm Season Vegetables

Warm season vegetables prefer summer-like weather with temperatures between 70°F and 95°F. They are intolerant of frost and may be sensitive to cool spring winds.

Tender Vegetables

Crops: beans, celery, corn, cucumbers, New Zealand spinach, and summer squash

Temperatures: Tender vegetables grow with a daytime temperature above 55°F, and are intolerant of frost.

When to plant:

- Based on soil temperature, refer to Table 38-1.

- Soil is adequately dry to work.

- These crops may be planted (from seed) around the date of the average last spring frost. Transplants of cucumbers and summer squash without frost protection should be delayed until frost potential is over.

Very Tender Vegetables

Crops: lima beans, cantaloupe, eggplant, pepper, winter squash, pumpkins, tomato, and watermelon

Temperatures: Very tender vegetables are not only intolerant of frost, but also cool spring winds. They need daytime temperatures above 60°F and prefer temperatures of 70°F to 95°F. A week of daytime temperatures below 55°F may stunt the crop.

When to plant:

- Based on soil temperature, refer to Table 38-1.

- Soil is adequately dry to work.

- These crops are typically planted two plus weeks after the average last spring frost date.

- Weather is becoming summer-like (i.e., consistently above 55°F [daytime] and breezes should have lost any cool nip).

Table 38-1. Vegetable Planting Guide

| Vegetable | Germination Temperature[1] | | | Plant Spacing[2] | Planting Depth | Days to Germination | Typical Days to Harvest | Age of Transplant (weeks) |
	Min.	Optimum	Max.					
Cool Season Crops[3]								
Beets	40°	80°	90°	4–6″	¾–1″	7–10	60	
Broccoli[4]	40°	80°	90°	18″	½″	3–10	65T[4]	5–7
Cabbage[4]	40°	80°	90°	18″	½″	3–10	85T[4]	5–7
Carrots	40°	80°	90°	2–3″	¼″	10–17	70	
Cauliflower[4]	40°	80°	90°	18″	½″	3–10	65T[4]	5–7
Kohlrabi	40°	80°	90°	7–9″	½″	3–10	50	
Leeks	40°	80°	90°	4–6″	¼″	7–12	120	
Lettuce (leaf types)	35°	70°	70°	7–9″	¼″	4–10	60	
Onion, green	35°	80°	90°	2–3″	¼″	7–12	60	
Onions, dry (seed)	35°	80°	90°	4–6″	¼″	7–12	110	
(sets)				4–6″	1–2″			
Parsnips	35°	70°	90°	5–6″	½″	15–25	70	
Peas	40°	70°	80°	4-6″ or 3″ × 8″	1″	6–15	65	
Potatoes	45°			12–15″	4–6″		125	
Radish	40°	80°	90°	2–3″	½″	3–10	30	
Spinach	40°	70°	70°	4–6″	½″	6–14	40	
Swiss Chard	40°	85°	95°	7–9″	1″	7–10	60	
Turnips	40°	80°	100°	4–6″	½″	3–10	50	
Warm Season Crops								
Beans, snap	55°	80°	90°	6″ or 4″ × 12″	1–1½″	6–14	60	
Cantaloupe[5]	60°	90°	100°	36–48″	1–1½″	3–12	85	2–3[5]
Corn	50°	80°	100°	12″ × 30″ 9″ × 36″	1–1½″	5–10	60–90	
Cucumbers	60°	90°	100°	6″ trellised 24–36″ untrellised	1″	6–10	55	2–3[5]
Eggplant	60°	80°	90°	18–24″	¼″	7–14	60T[6]	6–9
Pepper	60°	80°	90°	15–18″	¼″	10–20	70T[6]	6–8
Tomato	50°	80°	100°	Trellised: 24″ between plants	¼″	6–14	65T[6]	5–7
Squash, Summer	60°	90°	100°	36–48″	1–1½″	3–12	50	2–3[5]
Squash, Winter	60°	90°	100°	36–48″	1–1½″	6–10	100	2–3[5]
Watermelons	60°	90°	110°	36–48″	1–1½″	3–12	85	2–3[5]

[1] **Germination temperature**—Soil temperature is one of the best methods to determine spring planting time. Plant when soils reach minimum temperature measured at 8 a.m., 4 inches deep. Beans are an exception, being measured at 6 inches deep. Optimum temperatures listed in the table are useful for starting seeds indoors. Maximum temperatures are listed in regard to high soil temperatures that may interfere with seed germination in the summer.

[2] **Plant spacing**—Spacings given are equal-distance spacing for crops grown in block or close-row style beds. For example, beets, with a spacing of six inches are thinned to six inches between plants in all directions. In other words, beets are thinned to six inches between beets in the row and six inches between rows. The closer spacing listed should be used only on improved soils with four to five percent organic matter.

Close-row or block style planting works well for raised bed gardening, with blocks/beds 4 feet wide (any length desired) and 2-foot wide walkways between blocks/beds.

[3] **Cool season crops**—Cool season crops prefer a cool soil. Lawn clipping and newspapers make an excellent mulch for these crops by cooling the soil, preventing weed germination, and conserving water. Apply fresh grass clippings only in thin layers (less than one-half inch) and allow it to dry between applications. Thick layers will mat and smell. Do not use clipping from lawns treated with weed killers or other pesticides. Several layers of newspapers covered with grass clippings also work well between rows. Do not use glossy print materials.

[4] **Transplanted cole crops**—Since cole crops (cabbage, cauliflower, broccoli, and Brussels sprouts) germinate better in warmer soil, they are typically started from transplants in the spring. Days to harvest are from transplants. In the warmer areas of Colorado, these crops produce the best quality when direct seeded mid-summer (early July for the Front Range area) for harvest during cooler fall weather. Before planting out, harden off seedlings.

[5] **Transplanting vine crops**—Vine crop (cucumbers, squash, melons) roots are extremely intolerant of being disturbed, and perform best when grown by direct seeding rather than by transplants. With the use of black plastic to warm the soil, direct seeded crops germinate rapidly. If using transplants, select small, young plants, not more than two to three weeks from seeding.

[6] **Tomato family transplants**—The tomato family is traditionally planted from transplants. In warmer areas of Colorado, they can also be direct seeded with minimal delay. Days to harvest are from transplants.

Average Frost Dates

The following *CMG GardenNotes* (available online at www.cmg.colostate.edu) give average frost dates and growing season information.

- Climate Summary: Boulder and Longmont, #741
- Climate Summary: Canon City, #755
- Climate Summary: Castle Rock, Littleton and Parker, #742
- Climate Summary: Colorado Springs, #743
- Climate Summary: Dillon, #744
- Climate Summary: Eagle and Glenwood Springs Area, #745
- Climate Summary: Fort Collins, Greeley and Estes Park, #746
- Climate Summary: Gunnison and Crested Butte, #747
- Climate Summary: Northeast Colorado, #748
- Climate Summary: Northwest Colorado, #749
- Climate Summary: Norwood and Telluride, #753
- Climate Summary: Pueblo, #751
- Climate Summary: San Luis Valley, #754
- Climate Summary: Southwest Colorado, #750

BLOCK STYLE GARDEN LAYOUT

Block style garden layout (also called *close-row* or *wide-row* plantings) *increase* yields fivefold compared to the traditional row-style garden layout, and fifteen-fold for the smaller kitchen garden vegetables. The compact design reduces weeding and is ideal for raised bed gardening.

The basic technique used in close-row, block planting is to eliminate unnecessary walkways by planting vegetables in rectangular-shaped beds or blocks instead of long single rows. For example, plant a block of carrots next to a block of beets, followed with a block of lettuce and so forth down the bed area.

Plant crops with an equal distance space between neighboring plants in both directions. For example, space a carrot patch on three-inch by three-inch centers. It may be easier to visualize this plant layout as running rows spaced three inches apart across the bed, and thinning the carrots within the row to three inches. A twenty-four-foot long "traditional" row of carrots will fit into a three-foot by two-foot bed (Figure 38-1).

Design the planting beds to be three to four feet wide and any desired length. This width makes it easy to reach into the growing bed from walkways for planting, weeding, and harvesting.

Limiting foot traffic to the established walkways between planting beds reduces soil compaction. Design walkways to eighteen to twenty-four inches wide. Mulch walkways with dry grass clippings, wood chips, or other organic mulch.

Figure 38-1 ■ *Carrots planted on three-inch centers.*

As the vegetable foliage grows together, the shade cast suppresses weed germination.

After harvesting a row of radishes, beets, lettuce, or spinach, replant for continual summer production.

Due to the higher plant density, block plantings require a weed-free, fertile, well-drained soil that is rich in organic matter. Give extra attention to watering and frequent, light fertilization to nourish the dense plant population. Avoid over-crowding vegetables—the reduced air circulation can increase disease problems.

Suggested Spacing

Suggested spacing for kitchen garden vegetables: (Start with the wider spacings, reducing spacing with experience and as soil improves in fertility and tilth.)

- Beets: 4–6" by 4–6"
- Carrots: 2–3" by 2–3"
- Celery: 7–9" by 7–9"
- Garlic: 4–6" by 4–6"
- Kohlrabi: 7–9" by 7–9"
- Leeks: 4–6" by 4–6"
- Lettuce, head: 10–12" by 10–12"
- Lettuce, leaf: 7–9" by 7–9"
- Onions, bunching 2–3" by 2–3"
- Onions, dry: 4–6" by 4–6"
- Parsnips: 5–6" by 5–6"
- Radishes: 2–3" by 2–3"
- Spinach: 4–6" by 4–6"
- Swiss chard: 7–9" by 7–9"
- Turnips: 4–6" by 4–6"

Other Vegetables Suited to Block Planting

Cole crops (broccoli, cabbage, Brussels sprouts, and cauliflower)—Spaced at eighteen by eighteen inches, or three plants across a four-foot bed.

Corn—Always plant in a block to facilitate pollination. Five rows wide is recommended for the best "pollen shower" to maximize kernel set; three rows wide is minimum. Space at twelve by twenty-four inches, or four rows across two four-foot-wide beds.

Eggplant—Space at eighteen to twenty-four inches, or two or three plants across a four-foot-wide bed.

Peppers—Space at fifteen by fifteen inches, or three plants across a four-foot-wide bed.

Potatoes—Space at twelve to fifteen by twelve to fifteen inches, or three plants across a four-foot-wide bed.

Vine crops (squash, cantaloupes, pumpkins, and watermelons)—Place a single row down the center of a four-foot-wide bed. They may also be planted in larger blocks, several rows wide. Place the winter squash and pumpkins in the center of the block, and cantaloupes, watermelons, and summer squash around the edge where they can be reached for summer harvest.

Trellis tomatoes and cucumbers to save space and make harvest easier. The increased air circulation around trellised tomatoes helps suppress tomato blight.

Figure 38-2 ▮ *Kitchen garden in block style layout with (top to bottom) spinach, assorted lettuce varieties, and Swiss chard. Note that rows run across the four-foot-wide bed. As a row of lettuce is harvested, it is replanted for continual production or neighboring crops fill in the space.*

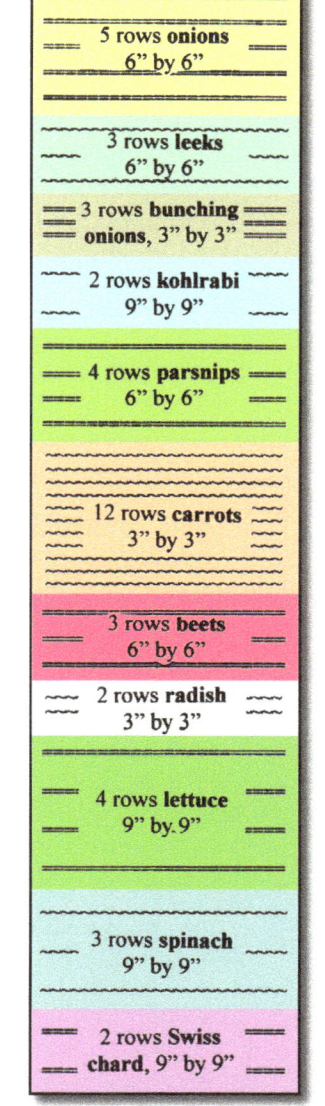

5 rows **onions**
6" by 6"

3 rows **leeks**
6" by 6"

3 rows **bunching onions**, 3" by 3"

2 rows **kohlrabi**
9" by 9"

4 rows **parsnips**
6" by 6"

12 rows **carrots**
3" by 3"

3 rows **beets**
6" by 6"

2 rows **radish**
3" by 3"

4 rows **lettuce**
9" by 9"

3 rows **spinach**
9" by 9"

2 rows **Swiss chard**, 9" by 9"

Figure 38-3 ▮ *Sample layout of kitchen garden vegetables.*

Space trellised tomatoes a minimum of twenty-four inches apart down a single row, in a block two to three feet wide. Plant cucumbers along a trellis at nine- to twelve-inch spacings.

Beans and peas may be easier to pick and are less disease-prone if planted in single or double rows, rather than block style planting. Space beans twelve inches between rows and four inches between plants. Plant a double row down a block two to three feet wide.

RAISED BED GARDENING

Raised bed gardens with block style layout have many advantages, including the following:

- **Higher yields and less area to weed**—The block style layout, eliminating unnecessary walkways increases yields by fivefold over the traditional row-path-row garden layout.

- **Reduced soil compaction**—Established walkways keep foot traffic off the growing bed, reducing soil compaction.

- **Earlier planting**—The raised bed facilitates better runoff and drainage allowing soil to warm faster in the spring. Beds can be covered with plastic during spring rains, allowing for early planting even in rainy years.

- **Frost protection**—The block style layout is easy to cover for spring and fall frost protection. It can also be shaded in the hot summer.

- **Soil improvement**—The raised bed is a clearly defined area where the gardener can concentrate on soil improvement techniques (e.g., the addition of soil organic matter). In situations where the soil is poor and limits plant growth, good planting soil may be added to the box.

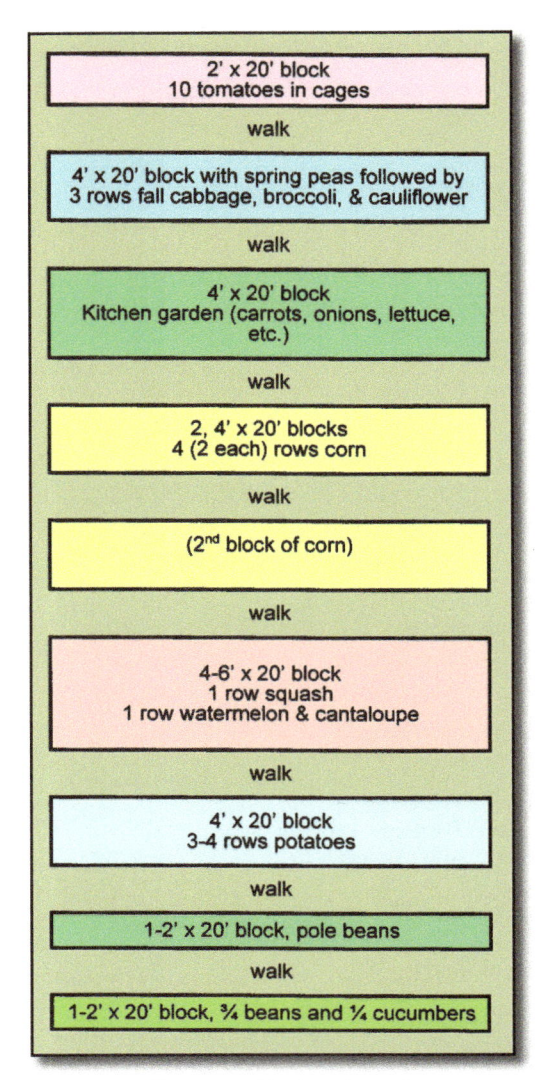

Figure 38-4 ■ *Sample block style garden.*

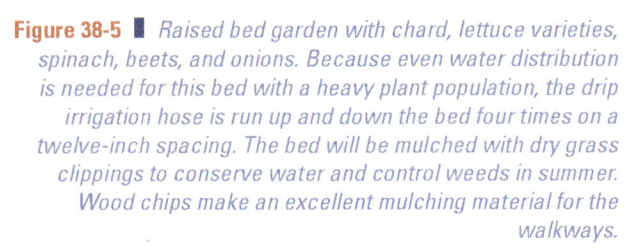

Figure 38-5 ■ *Raised bed garden with chard, lettuce varieties, spinach, beets, and onions. Because even water distribution is needed for this bed with a heavy plant population, the drip irrigation hose is run up and down the bed four times on a twelve-inch spacing. The bed will be mulched with dry grass clippings to conserve water and control weeds in summer. Wood chips make an excellent mulching material for the walkways.*

- **Architectural interest**—Raised beds become an architectural feature of the landscape design.

- **Accessible gardening**—The raised bed is ideal for enabling persons with limited mobility to garden.

Constructing a Raised Bed Garden

Size—A bed four feet wide is ideal for most vegetable crops, allowing the gardener to reach the entire bed from the side without ever stepping on the soil in the growing bed. Length can be whatever works for the space.

Tomatoes are well suited to a bed twenty-four to thirty-six inches wide, with one row of plants down the middle. Beans and peas are easier to pick in a single or double row down a bed rather than in the block style planting. Here a bed twenty-four inches wide would be ideal.

Depth / Height—The height of the beds is generally of no consequence, assuming that crops can root down into the soil below the bed. For most home garden situations, the role of a raised bed is to define and separate the growing bed from the walkway. Here a four-inch height would be adequate. Variations in heights (four, six, eight, and ten inches) among different beds may help create an appealing landscape feature.

In situations where the soil below is not suitable for crop growth, eight to twelve inches of soil is considered minimal. Deeper beds would make management easier.

To accommodate gardeners with special needs, bed height may be raised to minimize bending or to allow gardening work from a chair or wheelchair. Plan walkway space between beds wide enough to accommodate specialized equipment or mobility.

For ease of irrigation, beds should be reasonably level, both across and lengthwise.

Orientation—For frost protection, an east-west orientation has a slight advantage of collecting heat. For summer crop growth, a north-south orientation has a slight advantage of sunlight on both sides of the plant row each day. Because there is no clear advantage, orient the beds in whatever direction works best for the landscape design. Often beds are best arranged to be an appealing landscape feature of the property.

Construction materials—A simple way to construct a raised bed garden is to use construction lumber (2 by 4s, 2 by 6s, 2 by 8s, and 2 by 10s). Untreated lumber will last for several years, except in high salt areas or wet sites. Simply cut two pieces the width of the bed (typically four feet) and two others to the desired bed length. Using three and one-half to four inch decking screws, screw the corners together to make a four-sided box. Place the box-like frame on the soil and fill.

Various landscaping timbers may also be used in like fashion. Cooper-treated lumber is safe for garden boxes. However, do not use railroad ties (creosote cancer concerns) or CCA pressure-treated lumber (removed from the market several years ago due to arsenic concerns). Brick or other building materials may also be suitable.

Raised beds may also be made without sides. Here, organic matter is mixed as the garden is tilled. Walkways are dug down with the soil thrown up on the bed. Beds are four feet wide at the base and three feet wide at the top. The entire bed is covered with organic mulch such as dry grass clippings to prevent soil erosion and reduce compaction from rain and sprinkler irrigation (Figure 38-6).

Figure 38-6 ▌ *Raised bed garden without sides. Beds are four feet wide at the base and three feet wide at the top. Walks were dug down with soil placed on the beds.*

Adding soil—In the typical garden setting where crop roots will spread down into the soil below the bed, it is best to use similar soils. It may be beneficial to double-dig the beds. In **double digging**, the top six inches of soil are moved from one side of the bed to the other side of the bed. Mix organic matter into the soil below the excavated side. Return the soil to the top, mixing in organic matter. Then repeat the process for the other side of the bed.

When adding soil, avoid creating a situation where one type of soil ends and another begins. This creates a line between soil types that impedes water and air infiltration and slows, or even stops, root penetration. If the soil being added to the bed is different from the soil below, mix some of the two together before adding the remainder to avoid a distinct line of change.

In situations where the entire rooting zone will be in the raised bed, a soil on the sandy side with four to five percent organic matter would be preferred.

Figure 38-7 ▮ *A recently planted raised bed garden. Corn boxes to left, kitchen garden in center, strawberry patch on right, tomato patch in back with black plastic mulch. Growing beds are mulched with grass clippings; wood chips were used between beds.*

When purchasing soil, be aware that there is no legal definition of topsoil or planting soil. Just because it is commercially available in bulk or sold in bags, does not necessarily mean that it is good for gardening. Many bagged and bulk soils and soil amendments are prepared with compost made with manure and may be high in salts.

Gardening in a Raised Bed

Due to the high plant population, raised beds require better than average soils, and more frequent irrigation and fertilization. Concentrate on improving soils with routine applications of organic matter.

Mulching—Mulch beds to control weeds, conserve soil moisture, and regulate soil temperatures. Grass clippings make great mulch when applied in thin layers (up to one-quarter inches thick). Allow each layer to dry between applications. Do not use clippings from lawns treated with weed killers or other pesticides for at least 4 weeks after application. Wood/bark chips are great for mulching between the beds. Three to four inches of chips will minimize the compaction forces of foot traffic. However, do NOT mix wood/bark chips into the growing bed, it will interfere with seedbed preparation.

Watering a raised bed—Drip irrigation is well suited to raised bed gardening. It is rather easy and inexpensive to add a water tap at the end of each box. Alternatively, simply move a garden hose in turn to each box and connect the drip hose. Sprinkler irrigation is also suitable, but less desirable due to potential disease problems.

As a point of clarification, raised bed gardening is a water conservation technique. It does require more frequent irrigation due to the higher plant density. However, it is more efficient resulting in higher yields for the amount of water applied compared to the larger areas watered in traditional row-walkway-row culture. Raised beds become even more efficient when watered with drip irrigation or soaker hoses on timers.

Frost protection—An advantage of a raised bed, block style layout is that the bed is easy to cover for protection from spring rains and frost, allowing for early planting.

This picture illustrates a Quonset-type cold frame covering made of concrete reinforcing mesh covered with plastic. This style of frost protection adds two to six plus weeks on both ends of the growing season for cool season vegetables. Any type of covering must be opened during the day to prevent overheating.

SAMPLE PLANTING GUIDE FOR RAISED BED GARDEN

The following table is a guide for planting a family vegetable garden in a block style layout. It is based on a raised bed system with boxes four feet wide and rows typically running across the bed (four feet long).

Planting times are based on May 10 and October 10 average frost dates, typical of Colorado's Front Range. In other areas, adjust the planting dates using local average frost dates.

Estimated planting for fresh use and projected yields are estimates on what a family of four may consume in fresh use during the harvest period. Actual plantings should be adjusted to the family's likes for various vegetables and desire for canning, freezing, and storage.

Cool Season Planting Groups	Crops	Block Style Spacing	Estimated Planting for Fresh Use Projected Yield	Planting Time	Harvest Period
Cole Crops	Broccoli, cabbage, and cauliflower	3 plants across a 4' wide block (row) with 18" between rows	1–2, 4' rows each <u>per planting</u> 1 head per plant = 3 heads per 4' row	Spring planting for summer harvest: 1. Early April—Broccoli and cabbage from transplants 2. Early May—Broccoli, cabbage, and cauliflower from transplants	Spring plantings/summer harvest in June to early July (1–3 weeks per plantings, depending on temperatures) In warm weather crops come on rapidly with reduced quality (sweetness). Check every couple of days for harvestable stage, and store crops in fridge. Crops over-mature rapidly in warm temperatures.
			2–3+ 4' rows each 1 head per plant = 3 heads per 4' row	Summer planted for fall harvest: Broccoli, cabbage, and cauliflower by direct seed, mid-July for fall harvest	Summer planting/fall harvest—4–8+ weeks with excellent quality due to cool fall temperatures. Harvest crops as needed. They tolerate a mild frost into the mid to low 20s and can be stored in fridge or pit for winter use.
Leafy Vegetables & Salad Crops (Kitchen garden)	Lettuce (leaf and soft head types)	Thin to 7–9" rows, with rows 7–9" apart	1–3, 4' rows, with assorted varieties <u>per planting</u> 6 heads per 4' row 3 lbs. per 4' row	1. Early April	May–June
				2. Early May	June–July (depending on temperatures)
				3. Late July	Early September+
				4. Mid-August	Late September+
	Spinach	Thin to 4–6" rows with 6" between rows	1–3, 4' rows <u>per planting</u> 8 bunch per 4' row 2 lbs. per 4' row	1. Early April	May–June
				2. Early May	June–July (depending on temperature)
				3. Late July	Early September+
				4. Mid-August	Late September+
	Chard	Thin to 7–9" rows with 7–9" between rows	1-2, 4' rows 4 lbs. per 4' row	Late April to early May	Harvest by cutting off leaves, plants grow back, for summer long harvest
	Kohlrabi (a cole crop)	Thin to 7–9" rows with 9" between rows	1-2, 4' rows <u>per planting</u> 6 heads per 4' row	1. Early April	June
				2. Early May	Mid-June to early July (depending on temperatures)
				3. Mid to late July	September+

Cool Season Planting Groups	Crops	Block Style Spacing	Estimated Planting for Fresh Use Projected Yield	Planting Time	Harvest Period
	Dry onions	4–6" rows, 4–6" between rows	2–5, 4' rows 10 bulbs per 4' row 3 lbs. per 4' row	Early April to early May Onions are sensitive to photoperiod, the earlier the planting the larger the bulbs.	Mid-summer through fall
Onion Family (Kitchen garden)	Green onions	2–3" rows, 2–3" between rows	1–2, 4' rows 4 bunches per 4' row	Early April to early May	Early summer through fall
	Leeks (soup onion)	4–6" rows, 4–6" between rows	1–2, 4' rows 10 bulbs per 4' row	Early April to early May	Fall into winter (for winter harvest leave in garden and mulch to protect from extreme cold; dig as needed)
Peas	Peas	Thin to 3–4" rows with 8"+ between rows Note: Peas are easier to pick in a single or double row rather than in the block-style plantings	20' double row 12 lbs per 20' double row 20' double row 6 lbs. per 20' double row	1. Early April to early May, as soon as soil temperature reaches 40°—Peas are sensitive to photoperiod, early plantings give higher yields 2. Mid-July	June September Note: fall plantings are prone to powdery mildew and have lower yields, making them questionable
Potatoes	Potatoes	3–4 plants across a 4'-row, with rows 15" apart	A 16' by 4' bed of potatoes would produce around 72 lbs. of mature size potatoes	Early May	July+ Mulch with straw

Cool Season Planting Groups	Crops	Block Style Spacing	Estimated Planting for Fresh Use Projected Yield	Planting Time	Harvest Period
Root Crops	Carrots	Thin to 2–3" rows with rows 3" apart	6–18+, 4' rows 4 lbs. per 4' row	Early May	July through fall; can be left in the garden and mulched for winter harvest
	Beets	Thin to 4–6" rows with 6" between rows	1–2, 4' rows <u>per planting</u> 4 lbs. per 4' row	1. Early May	June–July—Thin for beet greens; harvest roots while young (small) for best quality
				2. Mid-July	September–October—Thin for beet greens; harvest roots while young (small) for best quality
	Parsnips	Thin to 5–6" rows with 6" between rows	2–6, 4' rows 4 lbs. per 4' row	Early May	For late fall to winter harvest, after soils cool; mulch for harvest through the winter
	Radish	Thin to 2–3" rows with 3" between rows	1–2, 4' rows <u>per planting</u> 4 bunches per 4' row	1. Early April	Early May
				2. Early May	Early June
				3. Early August	Early September
				4. Late August	Late September
	Turnips	Thin to 4–6" rows with 6" between rows	1–2, 4' rows <u>per planting</u> 4 lbs. per 4' row	1. Early May	June–July—Thin for greens; harvest roots while young (small) for best quality
				2. Mid-July	September–October—Thin for greens; harvest roots while young (small) for best quality

Warm Season Planting Groups	Crops	Block Style Spacing	Estimated Planting for Fre\sh Use Projected Yield	Planting Time	Harvest Period
Beans	Pole beans	4" in single row	10–20' row 10 lbs. per 10 foot row	Mid-May	July till frost, with adequate water
	Bush beans	4" in double row Beans are easier to pick in a single or double row rather than block style planting	10–20' row 10 lbs. per /10 foot double row	Mid-May	July till frost, with adequate water

Warm Season Planting Groups	Crops	Block Style Spacing	Estimated Planting for Fresh Use Projected Yield	Planting Time	Harvest Period
Corn	Corn	For pollination, corn must be planted in block with 4+ rows wide. In a block style garden, plant 4 rows with 2 rows each going the length of the box, in 2 boxes side by side. Space plant 9" in the row.	A block of 4, 6-foot rows will give ~60 ears	1. Mid-May 2. Mid-June	Late July to October Harvest period on any variety is only 10 to 20 days. For continual harvest of fresh corn plant varieties with 20+ days difference until harvest OR make second plants 20–30 days after the first.
Peppers and Eggplant	Eggplant	3 plants across a 4'-row, with rows 18–24" apart	1, 4' rows 12 fruit per 4' row (4 fruit per plant)	Late May, temperatures consistently above 60°	August till frost (A Wall-of-Water can be used for earlier production)
	Peppers	3 plants across a 4'-row, with rows 18" apart	1–4, 4' rows, depending on family use Yields vary with variety 18 bell peppers/4' row (6 fruit per plant)	Late May, temperatures consistently above 60°	August till frost (A Wall-of-Water can be used for earlier production)
Tomatoes	Tomatoes	Trellis in single row at 24" spacing	3–6 plants, depending on family use 26 lbs. (½ bushel) per plant	Late May, temperatures consistently above 60°	August till frost (A Wall-of-Water can be used for earlier production)
Vine Crops	Cucumbers	Trellis in single row at 6" spacing	2–4 plants, depending on family use 1 lb. per plant	Mid-May for direct seeding OR late May for transplants	Mid-July till frost For maximum yields, do not let fruit get large on the vine.
	Zucchini and other summer squash	Single row down center of 4'-wide box; two plants take 4' by 8'	2 plants	Mid-May for direct seeding or late May for transplants	Mid-July till frost (A Wall-of-Water can be used for earlier production)
	Cantaloupes, Watermelon, Pumpkins, and Winter Squash	1–3 plants per type, as desired by family 2–6 fruits per plant	Single row down center of 4" wide box with 2–3' between plants. Makes a great ground cover for garden areas. 3–4 fruits per plant	Late May, temperatures consistently above 60°	September–October

SAMPLE VEGETABLE GARDEN SEED CATALOGS

Baker Creek Heirloom Seed
2278 Baker Creek Road
Mansfield, MO 65704
417-924-8917
www.rareseeds.com

Burpee Seed
300 Park Avenue
Warminster, PA 18974
800-888-1447
www.burpees.com

Gurney Seed
110 Capital Street
Yankton, SD 57079
513-354-1492
www.gurneys.com

Harris Seed
P.O. Box 24966
Rochester, NY 14692-0966
800-514-4441
www.harrisseeds.com

**Irish-Eyes –
Garden City Seed**
P.O. Box 307
Thorp, WA 98946
509-964-7000
www.irish-eyes.com

Johnny's Seed
955 Benton Avenue
Winslow, ME04901
207-861-3900
www.johnnyseeds.com

Jung Seed
335 S High Street
Randolph, WI 53957-0001
800-297-3123
www.jungseed.com

Mountain Valley Seed
1800 W South Temple #600
Salt Lake City, UT 84115
801-486-0480
www.mvseeds.com

Park Seed
1 Parkton Avenue
Greenwood, SC 29647
800-213-0076
www.parkseed.com

Stokes Seed
Box 548
Buffalo, NY 14240-6980
800-396-9238
www.stokeseeds.com

Territorial Seed
P.O. Box 158
Cottage Grove, OR 97424-0061
541-942-9547
www.territorial-seed.com

Twilley Seed
121 Gary Road
Hodges, SC 29653
800-622-7333
www.twilleyseed.com

Tomato Growers Supply
P.O. Box 2237
Ft. Meyers, FL 33902
239-768-1119
www.tomatogrowers.com

CHAPTER REVIEW
Questions

1. Give examples of cool season and warm season vegetables.

2. What are the different temperature requirements of cool season and warm season vegetables?

3. How does a gardener know when to plant various crops? What is the best method to determine the planting time of various vegetables?

4. Describe the advantages of block style layout.

5. Describe how to design a garden in block style layout.

6. Describe the advantages of raised bed gardening.

7. Describe how to make raised bed garden boxes. How high should the beds be raised? In routine raised bed gardening, where are the crops' roots?

8. Explain "double digging."

Chapter

39*

Care of the Vegetable Garden

SOIL MANAGEMENT

In the garden, managing soils to improve *tilth* and garden *fertilization* are related but not necessarily the same process. For example, compost or manure may be added as a soil amendment to improve tilth; however, they may add a nominal amount of plant nutrients. A manufactured fertilizer may be added to supplement soil fertility levels, but it will not improve a soil's tilth. For optimum yields and quality, gardeners need to pay attention to both soil management for improving tilth and soil fertilization.

Note: *Tilth* is a term related to the suitability of a soil to support plant growth. Technically speaking, tilth is "the physical condition of soil as related to its ease of tillage, fitness of seedbed, and impedance to seeding emergence and root penetration."

Soil Amendment or Fertilizer

The term **soil amendment** refers to any material mixed into a soil. By law, soil amendments make no legal claims about nutrient content or other helpful (or harmful) properties. Compost and manure are common soil amendments used to improve soil tilth. They may also supply nominal amounts of plant nutrients. Some of the nutrient effect seen from adding soil amendments is likely due to their effect on soil microorganisms. The organic material in soil amendments is a food source that allows microorganisms to multiply. The larger numbers increase the conversion of nutrients in the soil to plant usable forms.

Mulch refers to a material placed on the soil surface.

---

*Authors: David Whiting, Carol O'Meara, and Carl Wilson, Colorado State University Extension. Photographs and line drawing by David Whiting.

By law, the term **fertilizer** refers to a material that guarantees a minimum percentage of nutrients of nitrogen, phosphate, and potash. An **organic fertilizer** is derived from natural sources and guarantees the minimum percentages of nitrogen, phosphate, and potash.

Soil Amendments

In the vegetable garden, the routine addition of organic soil amendments such as compost will optimize potential yields and quality. The goal in soil management is to increase the organic content to four to five percent over a period of years.

Common amendments include compost, manure, compost made with manure, fall leaves, straw, and peat moss. Home compost has the advantage that the gardener controls what goes into the compost, reducing problems with salts, weed seeds, and plant diseases.

In climates with long growing seasons, another method to add organic matter is to grow green manure crops in between the vegetable growing season. In some areas, this would be a winter crop, in hot areas of the south this would be a summer heat crop. In areas like Colorado, where the entire growing season is used for vegetable production, a green manure is less practical.

How Organic Amendments Improve the Soil

On clayey soil, organic matter (over a period of years) glues the tiny soil particles together into larger aggregates, increasing pore space. This increases soil oxygen levels and improves soil drainage, which in turn increases the rooting depth thereby allowing roots to reach a larger supply of water and nutrients.

On sandy soils, organic matter holds over ten times more water and nutrients than sand.

Organic matter also encourages the beneficial activity of soil organisms and helps remediate soil compaction.

Application

General application rates for compost or other organic soil amendments are based on the salt content of the materials and soil and on the depth to which it is cultivated into the soil. Ideally, cultivate the soil amendment into the top six to eight inches of the soil. On compacted/clayey soils, anything less can lead to a shallow rooting system with reduced plant growth, lower vigor, and lower stress tolerance.

Table 39-1 gives the standard application rates for compost. Compost made solely from plant residues (leaves and other yard wastes) is basically free of salt problems, and higher application rates are safe.

Table 39-1. Routine Application Rates for Compost

Site	Incorporation Depth[2]	Depth of Compost before Incorporation[1]	
		Plant-based compost and other compost known to be low in salts[3]	**Compost made with manure or biosolids** for which the salt content is unknown[4]
One-time application—such as lawn area	6–8″	2–3″	1″
	3–4″	1–1½″	½″
Annual application to vegetable and flower gardens—**first 3 years**	6–8″	2–3″	1″
	3–4″	1–1½″	½″
Annual application to vegetable and flower gardens—**fourth year and beyond**	6–8″	1–2″	1″
	3–4″	1″	½″

[1] Three cubic yards (67 bushels) covers 1,000 square feet approximately 1 inch deep.

[2] Cultivate compost into the top 6–8 inches of the soil. On compacted/clayey soils, anything less may result in a shallow rooting depth, predisposing plants to reduced growth, low vigor, and low stress tolerance. The 3–4 inch depth is shown as an illustration of how application rates need to adjust when the deep cultivate is not practiced.

[3] Plant-based composts are derived solely from plant materials (leaves, grass clippings, wood chips, and other yard wastes). Use this application rate also for other compost known, by soil test, to be low in salts.

[4] Use this application rate for any compost made with manure or biosolids unless the salt content is known, by soil test, to be low. Excessive salts are common in many commercially available products sold in Colorado. Based on soil tests of commercially available compost, this application rate may be too high for products extremely high in salts.

Compost, which includes manure or biosolids as a component, has a potential for high salt. Excessive salt levels are common in many commercially available products sold in Colorado. In compost made with manure or biosolids, the application rate is limited unless a soil test on that batch of product shows a low salt level. An amendment with up to 10 dS/m (10 mmhos/cm) total salt is acceptable if incorporated six to eight inches deep in a low-salt garden soil (less than 1 dS/m or 1 mmhos/cm). Any amendment with a salt level above 10 dS/m (10 mmhos/cm) is questionable.

Note: dS/m or mmhos/cm is the unit used to measure salt content. It measures the electrical conductivity of the soil.

Compost needs to be thoroughly mixed into the upper six to eight inches of the soil profile. Do not leave compost in chunks, as this will interfere with root growth and soil water movement.

As the soil's organic content builds in a garden, the application rate should be reduced to prevent ground water contamination issues. A soil test is suggested every four to six years to establish a baseline on soil organic matter content.

If using a green manure cover crop, till the cover crop in before it reaches four inches in height.

In the vegetable garden, do not plow in woody materials such as bark or wood chips. They may interfere with seedbed preparation and may result in soil nitrogen depletion.

Precautions When Using Compost and Manure

Manure, compost made from manure, and biosolids may be high in salts that will interfere with crop growth. Do not add more than one inch per season without conducting a soil test to evaluate potential salt buildup.

Due to a health issue (*E. coli* contamination), fresh manure additions should be made at least four months prior to the harvest of any edible crops. In other words, apply fresh manure only in the fall after crops are harvested.

Fresh manure or unfinished compost products may be high in ammonia. Avoid application of products with an ammonia smell; they could burn roots and leaves. Manure and compost may be sources of weed seeds.

Nutrient Release Rates from Compost and Manure

Gardeners need to understand that the nutrient release from compost and manure is slow, taking years. Adding compost or manure to improve soil tilth is not the same as fertilizing.

The typical nitrogen release rate from manure is only thirty to fifty percent the first year (fresh manure), fifteen to twenty-five percent the second year, seven to twelve percent the third year, three to six percent the fourth year, and so on. With compost and composted manure, the release rate is even slower, at five to twenty-five percent the first year, two to twelve percent the second year, and one to six percent the third year.

Because the nitrogen percentage of compost and manure products is typically only two to four percent, the amount of actual nitrogen release to support crop growth is very small.

For soil with four to five percent organic matter, the mineralization (release) of nitrogen from soil organic matter will likely be sufficient for crop growth.

For soils with two to three percent organic matter, the mineralization of nitrogen from soil organic matter will not likely be sufficient for heavy feeding vegetable crops. Supplement with one-tenth of a pound of nitrogen fertilizer per 100 square feet.

For the typical garden soil with one percent organic matter or less, the mineralization of nitrogen for soil organic matter will be minimal. Add two-tenths pounds of nitrogen fertilizer per 100 square feet.

FERTILIZATION

Soil fertilization is the addition of soil nutrients to support crop growth. While some soil amendments add small amounts of nutrients, amending the soil to improve soil tilth is not the same as amending the soil to provide nutrients.

Manufactured fertilizers are popular with gardeners because they are readily available, inexpensive, easy to apply, and generally provide a quick release of nutrients for plant growth. Application rates for any fertilizer depend on the content and the amount of nutrient to be applied. **In products containing multiple nutrients, the application rate is always based on the nitrogen content.**

Nitrogen Applications

Nitrogen is the nutrient needed in largest quantities by plants and the one most frequently applied as fertilizer. It is annually applied in the form of manufactured fertilizer, organic fertilizers, and/or organic soil amendments. **Application rates are critical, because too much or too little directly affects crop growth.**

The standard annual application rate for home vegetable gardens is two pounds actual nitrogen per 1,000 square feet (two-tenths of a pound actual nitrogen per 100 square feet). When organic matter is supplied, adjust the rate accordingly to account for nitrogen released by the organic matter (Table 39-2).

Table 39-2. Standard Nitrogen Fertilizer Application Rates for Gardens

	Soil Organic Content		
	Typical garden soil low in organic matter (<2% organic matter)	Moderate level of organic matter (2–3% organic matter)	High level of organic matter (4–5% organic matter)
Nitrogen needed	0.2 lb. actual N per 100 sq. ft.	0.1 lb. actual N per 100 sq. ft	0
Fertilizer examples Ammonium sulfate 21-0-0	1 lb. fertilizer per 100 sq. ft (approx. 2 cups)	0.5 lb. fertilizer per 100 sq. ft (approx. 1 cup)	0
OR Ammonium nitrate 34-0-0	0.6 lb. fertilizer per 100 sq. ft. (approx. 1⅓ cups)	0.3 lb. fertilizer per 100 sq. ft (approx. ⅔ cup)	0
OR Urea, 45-0-0	0.4 lb. fertilizer per 100 sq. ft. (approx. 1 cup)	0.2 lb. fertilizer per 100 sq. ft. (approx. ½ cup)	0

Manufactured nitrogen fertilizer can be broadcast and watered in, or broadcast and tilled into the top few inches of soil. It can be banded three to four inches to the side of the seed or plant row. Do not place the fertilizer in the seed row or root injury will occur. Some soluble types are applied in the irrigation water. "Organic" nitrogen fertilizers are typically tilled in or some can be applied in irrigation water.

Starter Fertilizers

In setting out transplants, starter solutions often promote early growth. Because transplants have been hardened-off (growth slowed to prepare the plant for movement to the exposed, windy, outdoor environment), the nitrogen in the starter solution gives the signal to resume active growth. Because phosphorus is less available in cold soils, phosphate may also be helpful in spring and before soils have thoroughly warmed.

A starter fertilizer is any water-soluble fertilizer added to the irrigation water. Common examples include MiracleGro, Peters, Schultz Plant Food, Fertilome Root Simulator, and Plant Starter Solution, etc. They generally contain ammonium nitrate since it is readily usable by the plant. Some products claim that vitamins or hormones promote plant growth. These claims are not supported by research findings.

Nitrogen "Side Dressing"

Plant need for nitrogen varies. Beans, peas, tomatoes, and vine crops (cucumbers, squash, pumpkins, and melons) are examples of vegetables with a lower need for nitrogen. High nitrogen promotes excessive growth of the plant at the expense of fruiting.

Crops such as potatoes, corn, and cole crops (broccoli, cauliflower, cabbage, and kale) use large amounts of nitrogen and need supplemental applications during the growing season (referred to as *side dressing*). For example, home garden potatoes often show nitrogen deficiency from August into fall. Symptoms start as a yellowing of lower leaves and progress into a general browning and dieback of the vine. When nitrogen stress hits, potatoes become more susceptible to diseases, including early blight and Verticillium wilt (Table 39-3).

Fertilizers commonly used in the home garden for side dressing include ammonium sulfate, ammonium nitrate, and water-soluble fertilizers such as MiracleGro, Peters, etc. Phosphate and potash fertilizers are best added in the spring or fall, when they can be cultivated into the soil.

Table 39-3. Nitrogen Side Dressing of Vegetable Crops

Vegetable	Timing	Application Rate (Based on rate of 0.1 lbs. actual N per 100 square feet)		
		Ammonium Sulfate 21-0-0	Ammonium Nitrate 34-0-0	Water-Soluble Fertilizers
Asparagus	1) Early spring 2) At end of harvest season	0.5 lbs. fertilizer per 100 sq. ft. (approximately 1 cup) Sprinkle over soil and water in, OR place in furrow to side of plant. CAUTION: an over-application will burn roots, stunting or killing plants.	0.3 lbs. fertilizer per 100 sq. ft. (approximately ⅔ cup) Sprinkle over soil and water in, OR place in furrow to side of plant. CAUTION: an over-application will burn roots, stunting or killing plants.	See label of specific product. Water soil with fertilizer added to water. Low burn potential, but significantly more expensive.
Sweet Corn	1) 12" tall 2) 1 month later			
Leafy green vegetables	3–4 weeks after emergence			
Onions	3–4 weeks after emergence			
Potatoes	Late July to early August			
Tomatoes, peppers, and eggplant	First fruits 1" diameter			
Cole crops (broccoli, cabbage, cauliflower)	1) 2–3 weeks after transplanting 2) 4–5 weeks after transplanting			See label for specific product.

Phosphorus and Potassium Applications

A soil test is the best method to determine the need for phosphate and potash. With a fertilizer containing nitrogen and phosphate and/or potash, the application rate is always based on the nitrogen percentage because nitrogen is most critical to plant growth.

Phosphate and potash fertilizers are best applied in the spring or fall, when they can be tilled into the soil.

Phosphorus

Phosphorus levels are adequate in the majority of established western soils. Deficiencies are most likely to occur in new gardens where the organic matter content is low and in soils with a high pH (7.8 to 8.3). Excessive phosphorus fertilizer can aggravate iron and zinc deficiencies and increase soil salt content.

Routine application of compost or manure will supply the phosphorus needs in most western soils.

Where phosphorus levels are believed to be low, the standard application rate without a soil test is one-quarter to one pound triple super phosphate (0-46-0) or ammonium phosphate (18-46-0) per 100 square feet.

Potassium

Potassium levels are naturally adequate to high in most western soils. Deficiencies occasionally occur in new gardens low in organic matter and in sandy soils low in organic matter. Excessive potash fertilizer can increase soil salt content.

Routine applications of compost or manure will supply the potassium needs for most western soils.

Where potash levels are believed to be low, the standard application rate without a soil test is one-quarter to one-half pound potassium chloride (0-0-60) or potassium sulfate (0-0-50) per 100 square feet.

MANAGING SOIL COMPACTION

On clayey soils, soil compaction is a common problem limiting crop growth potential. Soils are typically compacted in the construction process. Walking on wet soils, cultivating wet soils, and the impact of rain are other common forces compacting soils.

The following are suggested to help minimize soil compaction in the garden:

- Add organic matter to clayey soils.

- Avoid cultivating or working a clayey soil when wet. To evaluate, squeeze a handful of soil. Then try to crumble it. If it will crumble, it can be worked. If it will not crumble but stays in mud balls, it is too wet to be worked.

- Avoid cultivating other than to prepare a seed bed or till in organic matter and fertilizers. For weed control, use a mulch, hand removal, or shallow cultivation only.

- Use a raised bed with established walkways, and avoid walking on the growing bed.

- Mulch the soil, year round, to minimize the compaction forces of rain and sprinkler irrigation. Winter rains on bare soil are a major compaction force. This also helps manage weeds and reduces irrigation need.

MULCHES FOR THE VEGETABLE GARDEN

Benefits

The benefits of mulch depend on the material used and depth to which it is applied. In general, mulching minimizes evaporation of water from the soil surface, reducing irrigation need by around fifty percent. It helps stabilize soil moisture levels, thereby improving vegetable quality and encouraging the beneficial activity of soil organisms.

Mulching helps reduce soil compaction forces from rain and traffic. Some may later be plowed into the garden as a soil amendment, adding organic matter to the soil. Mulching may cool or warm soil temperatures. It may control weeds.

Grass Clippings

Grass clippings make excellent mulch for the vegetable garden. Apply fresh clippings in thin layers (up to one-quarter inch thick) and allow each layer to dry before adding more. The clippings quickly dry down and additional layers can be added weekly. A few layers will stop weed seed germination. Do not place fresh clippings in thick piles, as they will mat, reducing water and air infiltration, stink, and may become hydrophobic. Do not use clippings from lawns that have been treated with herbicides or other pesticides in the past month (Figure 39-1).

Around lettuce and other leafy vegetables, mulch by carefully hand placing the grass at the base of the plants. Grass sticks to wet lettuce, creating a problem in food preparation.

A couple of sheets of newspaper may be used under the clippings to help control weeds. The newspapers blow away with a light wind. They must be covered immediately with grass to hold them in place. They shut out the light preventing seed germination. Do not apply newspapers more than a couple of sheets thick or a soil carbon-to-nitrogen imbalance may occur. Do not use glossy print materials; their inks may not be soy-based like newspapers. The grass and newspaper mulch may be cultivated into the soil in the fall adding small amounts of organic matter (Figure 39-2).

Wood or Bark Chips

Do not use wood or bark chips in the growing beds since they will interfere with future seedbed preparation. It takes several years for chips to decompose in the soil.

In a raised bed garden, wood or bark chips make excellent mulch between the boxes. Apply three to four inches deep to control weeds. At this depth, chips also prevent soil compaction from foot traffic, allowing crop roots to spread out under the walkways (Figure 39-3).

When placed on the soil surface as mulch, wood/bark chips do not tie up soil nitrogen. Does not use fine sawdust for mulch because it could create carbon-to-nitrogen imbalance.

Black Plastic

Black or colored plastic mulch is extensively used in commercial tomato, pepper, and melon production in Colorado. It merits consideration for the tomato family (tomatoes, peppers, eggplant) and the vine crops (cucumbers, summer and winter squash, pumpkins, watermelons, cantaloupes and other melons). Because it warms the soil, it is undesirable for other crops.

Put the plastic on the growing bed early in the season to start the soil warming. **Crops must be planted early so plant growth shades the plastic before summer heat arrives.** Otherwise, the plastic can be too hot for crops and must be removed.

The plastic warms the soil allowing for earlier crop growth. Along the Colorado Front Range, crops average two to three weeks earlier production and produce higher yields. In cooler locations, crops could be three to over four weeks earlier in production.

Figure 39-1 ▮ *Grass clippings being applied to garden directly from lawn mower bag. Apply only in thin layers, allowing the grass layers to dry between applications.*

Figure 39-2 ▮ *Corn bed being mulched with newspapers (only a couple of sheets thick) covered with grass clippings.*

Figure 39-3 ▮ *Wood or bark chips make excellent mulch between raised bed boxes. Do NOT put wood or bark chips on the growing bed. The chips take years to break down and will interfere with seedbed preparation.*

The black plastic mulch also controls weeds and reduces the need for irrigation. Because there is no surface evaporation of water, it is easy to over-irrigate crops.

Applying Plastic Mulch

1. Prepare the soil and irrigation system. Drip irrigation with a soaker-type hose works well. Slightly mound the soil so the plastic makes direct contact with the ground.

2. Cover the growing bed with the plastic. Bury all edges two to four inches. On a raised bed box made with lumber, staple the plastic on the sides of the box.

3. Cut holes to plant or transplant into. Do not cut "X's"— the hot plastic touching tender plants can burn.

The plastic fluttering in the wind pumps air into the soil. However, covering the plastic with organic mulch like grass clippings or chips could reduce soil oxygen levels.

In the fall, do NOT plow in the plastic, rather remove and put it in the trash. Polyethylene plastic will never decompose in the soil. Because it breaks down with sunlight, it generally can be used only for a single season. Chemists are working on biodegradable plastics for horticultural uses. It will be a few years before they are available.

Some gardening magazines talk of colored plastics. For example, red plastic is reported to increase tomato yields in cloudy climates. It also makes the fruits softer in texture. With Colorado's high light intensity, color is insignificant.

Warming the soil for other crops—Plastic may also be used to warm the soil for other crops, being applied early, and **removed prior to planting**. For maximum soil warming, clear plastic is most effective. However, it will also encourage weeds to grow under the warm, greenhouse-like covering.

Straw

Weed free (seed free) straw makes excellent mulch for potatoes. When purchasing straw, look for certified weed (seed) free products. Otherwise, the potato patch may be thick with oats!

The straw protects tubers growing near the surface from sunlight, so the potato plants do not have to be mounded. When a potato tuber is exposed to sunlight, it turns green, becoming mildly poisonous (Figure 39-6).

Certified weed (seed) free straw is also a good organic source for clayey soils. After using it as a summer mulch, thoroughly cultivate it into the soil as a soil amendment in the fall.

Figure 39-4 ▮ *Tomatoes planted down a thirty-inch-wide raised bed box. Plastic mulch is stapled to side of box. Plants are spaced at twenty-four inches in the center of twenty-four-inch-wide cages.*

Figure 39-5 ▮ *Trellised tomatoes in raised bed box with black plastic mulch. With plastic mulch, crops must be planted early so plant growth shades the plastic before summer heat arrives.*

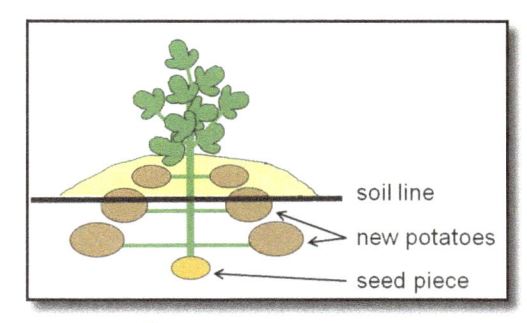

Figure 39-6 ▮ *The new crop of potatoes grows above the seed piece. To shield growing tubers from sunlight (which turns them green), soil is "hilled" (mounded) around the base of the plant. Straw mulch may be used as an alternative to hilling.*

IRRIGATION

In vegetable production, an adequate supply of water during the growing season is directly related to produce quality and yields. Many vegetables become strong-flavored or stringy with water stress.

Several gardening techniques (including soil preparation, mulching, and efficient irrigation) help conserve water in the vegetable garden.

As a rule of thumb, vegetables use around one-quarter inch of water per day during typical summer weather. If the garden is watered every four days, apply one inch of water per irrigation. Hot, windy weather will increase water demand significantly. Beans and corn will be significantly higher in water demand during blooming or tasseling/silking.

Checking Soil Moisture Content

Check soil moisture regularly. Irrigate when the top two to four inches of soil is dry to the touch. This is especially important if using mulch, where surface evaporation is reduced.

Evaluating when the soil needs irrigation is rather subjective. The "stick" method (judging moisture by the relative ease or difficulty of pushing a stick or screwdriver into the soil) is an old farmer's standard. It will be easier when wet than when dry. However, this very subjective method is specific to soil types and can be misleading to the novice. On compacted clayey soils, it may be somewhat difficult when moist and very difficult when dry. On sandy soils, it may be somewhat easy wet or dry.

To check moisture levels, a soil probe is a useful tool to pull up soil samples from the rooting zone at a six to eight inch depth. A small garden spade could be used.

Houseplant watering meters are helpful in evaluating the soil moisture content under mulch. Realize, however, that these inexpensive meters are somewhat inaccurate. If the fertility level is high, the meter will read on the wet side. If the fertility is low, the meter will read on the dry side. Learn to interpret the meter reading for a specific soil by trial and error (Figure 39-7).

Automate the System with Controllers

Sprinkler or drip systems can be easily automated with a multi-zone controller like the lawn. A small garden could be connected to the lawn's controller as a separate zone and run on a different program. However, do not have the lawn and vegetable garden on the same zone, as water needs are not the same.

Single-zone controllers connect to the garden hose. Some simple models are manually turned on and automatically turn off after the set number of minutes or gallons. More elaborate battery operated models turn the water on and off at the day and time interval set by the gardener (Figure 39-8).

Figure 39-8 ■ *Single-zone controllers connect to the hose line. Left: This style is manually turned on and automatically turns off the water flow after the set number of minutes. Right: This battery powered controller turns water on and off at the day and time intervals set by the gardener.*

Furrow Irrigation

For gardeners who have irrigation water from a ditch, furrow irrigation in the traditional row style garden layout may be most practical. As a rule of thumb, adjust water flow for the furrow so that the water reaches the end of the row one-third of the time into the irrigation period. For example, if the irrigation period is fifteen minutes, the water should reach the end of the row in five minutes. Soil erosion and runoff are major disadvantages of furrow irrigation.

Sprinkler Irrigation

Sprinkler irrigation is considered more efficient in water delivery than furrow irrigation. It is easy to measure the amount of water applied and easy to manage. Because it wets the entire soil surface, weed seed germination may be high.

Sprinkler irrigation is discouraged on vegetables prone to foliar diseases such as Early Blight (tomatoes, peppers, and potatoes). The splashing water spreads disease organisms and water on the leaves creates favorable conditions for disease development. Tall crops, such as corn and pole beans, may interfere with water delivery patterns.

As a rule of thumb, vegetables use around one-quarter inch of water per day, depending on temperature, wind, and stage of crop development. For example, if the garden is watered every four days, apply one inch of water per irrigation. The gardener can quickly learn how long to run the sprinklers by measuring the amount of water in several straight-sided cans placed around the garden.

Delivery rates depend on the type of sprinkler heads used, pressure, and the spacing of heads in the garden. For example, pop-up spray heads deliver around one and one-half inches per hour and would typically run forty minutes to apply one inch of water. Rotor type heads deliver around one-half inch per hour and would typically run for 120 minutes to apply one inch of water.

Because the water needs of the vegetable garden are different from a lawn, it should be on a different irrigation zone than the lawn. Water use will be low in the spring when crops are small and temperatures are cool and will increase as the temperatures rise and crops come into bloom.

Drip Irrigation

Drip irrigation is well suited for the block style garden layout and raised beds. Several different types of drip systems are available including:

In-line drip tubing—Emitters are found in the tubing every six, twelve, or twenty-four inches; twelve inches is most common in the home garden trade.

Soaker hose and **soaker tubing**—Emits water along the entire length of the hose.

Bubblers and **drippers**—Emitters or drippers are placed to water individual plants.

A disadvantage of a drip system is that they require relatively clean water. Systems readily plug with dirt, algae, or salts in the water. This is generally not a problem when using drinking quality municipal water supplies. Depending on water quality, drip irrigation may not practical for many nonpotable water sources. The filtering system required may be expensive and high maintenance.

Ideally, an in-line drip hose or soaker hose is placed on the soil surface under the mulch. The soaker hose may also be buried a couple of inches into the soil to protect the hose from breakdown by sunlight.

On a raised bed box, space the drip line/soaker hose at twelve-inch spacing. A four-foot-wide box would have four runs of the drip line/soaker hose up and down the box (as illustrated in Figure 39-1). For larger vegetables like corn, squash, and cole crops (three plants across a four-foot-wide bed) make three runs up and down a four-foot-wide box. On a two-foot-wide raised bed box for tomatoes or beans, the drip line/soaker hose runs down and back (Figure 39-9).

Drip systems are designed to run on low pressure. High pressure may split the hose and pop connections. The desired low pressure is easy to achieve with pressure regulators that have hose-end fitting (found with the drip system supplies). If the garden has changing elevations, a pressure regulator will be needed for every couple of feet change in elevation (Figure 39-10).

Determine the run time by examining the soil moisture content. Run time will vary with the brand of hose, water pressure, and spacing.

Soaker Hose and Soaker Tube

The soaker hose and soaker tube type of drip system allows water to seep out the entire length of the hose. It is easy to use in traditional row style or raised bed gardens (Figure 39-11).

It can be connected by manually connecting the garden hose to each line at each irrigation session or by connecting a series of dedicated garden hoses to a series of lines. On raised bed gardening, it is easy to run a water line with a tap to each box. Several small boxes may run together on the same zone (Figure 39-4).

For uniform water delivery, keep runs short, generally twenty-five feet or less. With long lengths, water delivery will be higher at the top of the hose line and less at the bottom. The ground must be reasonably level. On slopes, run several short lengths.

Several brands and styles are available in the home garden trade:

- **Half-inch soaker hose**—Some brands (like Swans Soaker Hose) are a one-half-inch hose that connects with standard hose fitting. These are found in the garden hose section. It can be cut to any length and connected with garden hose fittings.

- A small plastic disc fits inside the female hose connection as a pressure regulator (actually a flow regulator). With the reduced water flow, it may need to run for around an hour to adequately water the garden. It works better to use the pressure regulators with hose-end fittings found with the drip irrigation supplies. With this type of regulator, the drip line runs ten to twenty minutes to adequately water the garden. Without a pressure regulator of some type, the soaker hose tends to rupture, sending out steams of water at spots rather than dripping along the line (Figure 39-4).

Figure 39-9 ▮ *On this four-foot-wide box, the drip line or soaker hose makes four runs up and down the box at twelve inch spacing. Carrot rows are running across the box.*

Figure 39-10 ▮ *With an irrigation pipe, it is easy to plumb a tap at each raised bed box. Here a pressure regulator with hose-end fittings reduces pressure to 25 psi. It is connected to a ½-inch soaker hose.*

Figure 39-11 ▮ *Soaker hose seeps water out along the length of the hose.*

This half-inch hose style is more tolerant of small amounts of dirt, algae, or salts in the water than other types of drip systems, and may be successful on some nonpotable water sources. Periodically, open up the end of the hose and flush out soil deposits.

- **Quarter-inch soaker tubing**—A one-quarter-inch soaker tubing is available in the drip irirgaiton section at garden stores. Cut the soaker tubing to the desired length and connect with drip system components. An in-line pressure regulator is required; otherwise, the fitting may pop or leak (Figure 39-4).

Because the soaker tubing has a higher delivery rate, it cannot be on the same zone as other in-line drip hoses, button emitters, or bubblers.

WATER CONSERVATION

In vegetable production, an adequate supply of water during the growing season is directly related to produce quality and yields. Many vegetables become strong flavored with water stress. Unlike bluegrass and other landscape plants, vegetables cannot go dormant when the water supply is inadequate. However, there are several techniques that will significantly reduce the water requirements of the home vegetable garden.

Always follow efficient irrigation practices. The following practices will allow gardeners to have a productive vegetable garden and still reduce water consumption.

Water Conserving Techniques

Amend Garden Soil with Coarse, Decomposed Organic Matter

In the vegetable garden, the routine addition of organic soil amendments, such as compost, will optimize potential yield and produce quality. The goal in soil management is to increase the organic content to four to five percent over a period of years.

On sandy soils, organic matter holds over ten times more water and nutrients than the sand. On clayey soil, organic matter glues the tiny soil particles together into larger aggregates, increasing pore space. This process takes place over time. This increases soil oxygen levels and improves soil drainage, which in turn increases the rooting depth allowing roots to reach a larger supply of water and nutrients.

Organic matter also encourages the beneficial activity of soil organisms and helps remediate soil compaction.

Manure and compost made from manure may be high in salts that will interfere with crop growth. The standard application rate for plant-based compost (free of salts) is two to three inches per year, cultivate into the soil six to eight inches deep. After a few years, the application rate should be cut back to avoid excessive soil salts, phosphorus, and potassium.

Manure and manure-based compost may be high in soil salts. The standard application rate is one-inch maximum per year, cultivated into the soil six to eight inches deep. Do not add more unless a soil test on the specific batch indicates low soil salt levels. Soil testing on many commercially available products available in Colorado markets found extremely high salt levels in some products. For high salt products, the one-inch application rate may be too high.

Be sure that the organic matter is thoroughly cultivated into the soil. Leaving chunks of organic matter will interfere with seeding, root spread, and water movement through the soil profile.

In the vegetable garden, do not plow in woody materials such as bark or wood chips, as they may interfere with seedbed preparation and may result in soil nitrogen depletion. Wood chips take several years to decompose in the soil.

Due to a health issue (*E. coli* contamination), fresh manure additions should be made at least four months prior to the harvest of any edible crops. In other words, apply fresh manure only in the fall after crops are harvested.

Another method to add organic matter is to replant the fall garden with a green manure crop such as winter rye or Austrian peas.

Reducing Water Need with Drip Irrigation and Mulching

Use of a drip system on a mulched garden reduces water need by around fifty percent.

Other Water Saving Techniques

Plant in blocks, rather than rows. This creates shade for roots and reduces evaporation.

Control weeds that compete with vegetables for water.

Group plants with similar water needs in the same section of the garden for easy irrigation. Cucumber, zucchinis, and squash, for example, require similar water applications.

Protect plants and soil from wind with windbreaks to reduce evaporation.

Critical Water Periods for Vegetables

You can target the timing and amount of water to add. As a rule of thumb, water is most critical during seed germination, the first few weeks of development, immediately after transplanting, and during flowering and fruit production. The critical watering periods for selected vegetables follow.

Asparagus needs water most critically during spear production and fern (foliage) development. Less water is needed after ferns reach full size.

Cole crops (broccoli, cabbage, cauliflower, collards, Brussels sprouts, kale, and kohlrabi) need consistent moisture during their entire life span. The quality of cole crops is significantly reduced if the plants get dry any time during the growing season. Water use is highest and most critical during head development.

Beans have the highest water use of any common garden vegetable. During blossoming and fruit development, beans use one-quarter inch to over one-half inches of water per day (depending on temperature and wind). Blossoms drop with inadequate moisture levels and pods fail to fill. On hot, windy days, blossom drop is common. When moisture levels are adequate, the bean plant is a bright, dark, grass-green. As plants experience water stress, leaf color takes on a slight grayish cast. Water is needed at this point to prevent blossom drop.

Carrot and other root crops require consistent moisture. Cracking, knobby, and hot flavored root crops are symptoms of water stress.

Corn's water demand peaks during tasseling, silking, and ear development. Water stress delays the silking period, but not tasseling. Under mild water stress, the crop may tassel and shed pollen before silks on ears are ready for pollination. The lack of pollination may result in missing rows of kernels, reduced yields, or even eliminate ear production. Yield is directly related to quantities of water, nitrogen, and spacing.

Lettuce and other leaf vegetables need water most critically during head (leaf) development. For quality produce, these crops require a constant supply of moisture.

Onion family crops require consistent moisture and frequent irrigation due to their small, inefficient root system.

Peas need water most critically during pod filling.

Potato tubers will be knobby if they become overly dry during tuber development.

Tomato family (tomatoes, peppers, and eggplant) needs water most critically during flowering and fruiting. Blossom end rot (a black sunken area on the bottom of the fruit) is often a symptom of too much or too little water. The tomato family has a lower water requirement than many vegetables and plants are often over-watered in the typical home garden.

Vine crops: cucumbers, summer and winter squash, and assorted melons need water most critically during flowering and fruiting. Vine crops use less water than many vegetables and are often overwatered in the typical home garden.

Vegetable Gardening When Irrigation Interval Is Restricted

Restrictions that allow for thorough watering only twice a week should not have a major effect on the vegetable garden. With adequate soil organic content, a standard in vegetable production, the garden should be able to go two to seven days between irrigations. Follow recommendations listed above.

Avoid heavy water use crops such as beans and sweet corn.

Grow only what you need. Consider that one tomato plant can yield over 20 pounds of fruit.

Vegetable Gardening When No Watering Is Allowed

When water restrictions prohibit outdoor watering, do not plant a vegetable garden. Vegetables do not go dormant like a Kentucky bluegrass lawn. If water restrictions allow, consider planting containers with vegetables and consider planting non-irrigated or minimally irrigated cover crops in the vegetable garden area. Describe how adding organic matter improves sandy garden soils and clayey garden soils.

1. What are the limitations on using manure and compost made with manure in the vegetable garden? On edible crops, how long before harvest should fresh manure be applied?

2. Describe the standard application rate for compost. How does it change with incorporation depth and potential for salts in the product?

3. In the vegetable garden, what is the routine application rate for nitrogen fertilizer for soils low, moderate, and high in organic matter?

4. What is the purpose of a starter fertilizer? List examples of common fertilizers that could be used as a starter fertilizer.

5. What is nitrogen side dressing? List examples of common fertilizers that could be used for side dressing. List crops that routinely need side dressing.

6. List techniques to manage soil compaction in the vegetable garden.

7. Describe procedures and limitations on using grass clipping mulch in the vegetable garden.

8. Describe use and limitations of using wood/bark chip mulch in the vegetable garden.

9. Describe how to use black plastic mulch in the vegetable garden.

10. Describe how to set up a soaker hose drip irrigation system in a raised bed garden.

11. List gardening techniques to conserve water in the vegetable garden. What happens to vegetable quality with inadequate water supplies?

12. What is the critical watering period for various vegetables?

Chapter

40*

Vegetable Hints

Harvesting quality and quantity from a vegetable garden starts with the gardener's ability to provide nearly ideal growing conditions for individual crops. Central to all highly productive gardens is a rich soil, high in organic matter, created with annual additions of compost and/or other organic materials. The following home gardening hints summarize a variety of research projects focusing on quality in vegetable production. Crops are grouped by families that have similar cultural practices.

TOMATOES (Tomato Family: Tomatoes, Peppers, and Eggplant)

Variety Selection

There are over 2,000 cultivars of tomatoes grown worldwide. Ask neighbors, local gardeners, and garden center staff about local favorites.

Hybrid tomatoes are popular in the United States to reduce problems with Verticillium and Fusarium wilt, common soil-borne pathogens. Early hybrids were developed for their yields and disease resistance. Flavor became a driving factor in the breeding of newer hybrids. Some gardeners prefer to trade off the disease protection of hybrids for the rich tomatoey flavors of heirloom varieties.

For early production, Early Girl is a popular variety with mid-size fruits.

Celebrity, Big Boy, and Better Boy are examples of popular main season varieties. Many gardeners prefer the rich tomato flavor of heirloom Brandywine or the large beefsteak types. Pear tomatoes and yellow types are gaining popularity.

_____

*Authors: David Whiting, Carol O'Meara, and Carl Wilson, Colorado State University Extension. Photographs and line drawings by David Whiting.

Cherry and the new grape-type tomatoes are popular for salads and snacking. Many, but not all, have small size vines suitable for container gardening (Figure 40-1).

Requiring less time to cook down, paste types such as *Roma* and its descendents are preferred for making salsa, chili sauce, and other tomato products. Be aware that paste types and standard varieties are not directly interchangeable in recipes.

Where the growing season is short, select *Early Girl* and other cultivars that will mature in 50 days or less. In many mountain communities, tomatoes may only be successfully grown in a structure or adjacent to the south side of a building to provide frost protection and warmer growing temperatures.

Whatever type you prefer, VFN-resistant hybrid varieties are recommended. The abbreviation VFN indicates resistance to *Verticillium* wilt, *Fusarium* wilt, and nematodes. Verticillium and Fusarium wilts are common soil-borne fungal diseases. Nematodes are not an issue in Colorado due to cold soil temperatures. Researchers have found multiple strains of *Verticillium* and *Fusarium*, so if you are having problems with these diseases, try other VFN varieties.

Vine types—There are two types of vines: *indeterminant* and *determinant*. Most popular home garden varieties are indeterminant. The vine keeps growing through the growing season, extending fruit production until frost kills the vine. Plant size is typically large. Determinant types are common in commercial production as vine growth stops when flowering begins; plants will typically be moderate in size. Determinant types put on a large single crop. They may be suitable for container planting where trellises are not possible.

Figure 40-1 ▮ **Sweet 100** *is the most popular home garden cherry-type tomato. On a large vine, it produces hundreds of sweet, cherry-sized fruits with very tender skins.*

Figure 40-2 ▮ *Wall-of-Water protects individual plants down to the mid-teens. Notice that black plastic mulch was also used to warm the soil. Cool soil temperatures are also a growth-limiting factor with early plantings.*

Planting

Planting Time

Tomato plants need night temperature above 32°F and daytime temperatures above 60°F. They are readily killed by a light frost. A week of cool daytime temperatures (below 55°F) will stunt plants, reducing yields.

With these warm temperature requirements, planting time along the Colorado Front Range is typically late May. Do not plant tomatoes out into a cold spell and make sure soil temperatures are warm.

To get a head start on the season, gardeners use a variety of frost protection techniques. The Wall-of-Water® provides protection into the mid-teens, or lower. Cool soil temperatures also inhibit early growth. When using a Wall-of-Water, also use black plastic mulch to help warm the soil. Be cautious in filling the Wall-of-Water not to splash water around, as a wet soil will be slow to dry and warm in the spring.

Selecting the Ideal Plants

The ideal tomato transplant is dark grass-green and six to eight inches tall. Stem is about pencil size in diameter and the plant has not been pruned or cut back. Transplants are hardened off (growth rate slows so the plant is more tolerant of the move from the greenhouse environment to the bright, windy outdoors) by withholding water and/or nutrients or by exposure to cooler temperature.

Plant leggy transplants horizontally—When gardeners are shopping for transplants in the warm greenhouse conditions of May, tomato plants quickly grow from ideal size to tall and leggy. The white bumps along the leggy tomato stem are roots beginning to form.

Plant these taller leggy transplants horizontally. Dig a trench two to three inches deep. Place the plant horizontal with only the top two to three sets of leaves showing above the soil. Pinch off other lower leaves below the soil line before planting. These leggy plants readily root out along the stem in the warm soil near the surface, supporting rapid growth (Figure 40-3).

Space and Trellis Plants

To minimize Early Blight, space and trellis plants to allow for good air circulation and promote rapid drying. Trellised tomatoes are easier to pick and less preferred by tomato psyllid insects. Trellising eliminates problems with fruit rotting where they touch the ground.

The minimal spacing for trellised tomatoes is two feet apart in a hedgerow. Research has demonstrated that crowding plants will not increase yields, but will increase disease problems.

Cages—The American Society for Horticultural Science suggests a trellis two feet in diameter by four to five feet tall. It is easy to make from a six and one-half-foot length of concrete reinforcing mesh. Cut off the bottom ring of wire so the cages can be pushed into the ground. When a branch sticks out of the cage, simple tuck it back in (Figure 40-4).

For the smaller vined, determinant types, two cages may be made from a six and one-half-foot length, cutting the height in half. Cages will be two feet in diameter but only two to two and one-half feet tall.

Commercially available cages are too small for most popular tomato varieties grown on good soils.

Cages are 6 feet around, 2 feet across, and 5 feet tall. On improved soils, tomato vines will loosely fill the cage, allowing for good air circulation and easy picking.

Tender transplants are rather sensitive to cool winds. Wrapping the cages with a plastic sheet or newspapers to provide wind protection for the first week helps plants acclimate.

Single pole trellis—Some gardeners prefer to trellis tomatoes on a single pole or stake. To do this, prune plants to a single trunk by removing all side shoots. This requires constant removal of side shoots.

Fan trellis—Another method, which produces larger fruit, is to trellis to a three-trunk, fan shape, removing all other side shoots. This requires a sturdy frame to support the weight of the vine and fruit.

Figure 40-3 ▍ *Plant tall leggy tomatoes horizontal in a shallow furrow.*

Figure 40-4 ▍ *Tomatoes planted in a raised bed with black plastic mulch and cages made from concrete reinforcing mesh.*

Figure 40-5 ▍ *Wrapping the tomato cage with plastic or newspapers protects tender plants from cold winds.*

Figure 40-6 ▍ *Tomatoes trellised to a single pole.*

Mulching

As with any crop, surface mulch is recommended to conserve soil moisture and manage weeds. Mulching helps reduce the splashing of Early Blight fungal spores from the soil onto the leaves. It also helps stabilize soil moisture levels, reducing the incidence of blossom end rot.

Black plastic mulch is popular for tomatoes, warming the soil and pushing production two to three weeks earlier. When using black plastic mulch, crops must be planted early so plant growth covers and shades the plastic before summer heat sets in.

Irrigation

Avoid overhead sprinkling on tomatoes. Fungal spores are easily water-splashed from one leaf to another, and water on the leaves creates a favorable environment for disease development. Watering in the morning, allowing plants to dry before nighttime, may also be helpful.

Figure 40-7 ▮ *Tomatoes trellised into a fan shape.*

Fertilization

Tomatoes have a low nitrogen requirement. Under high nitrogen conditions, vines grow excessively large at the expense of fruit production. More correctly stated, tomatoes are a fussy nitrogen feeder. On soils low in organic matter, tomatoes typically run out of nitrogen in mid-summer, reducing yields and predisposing the plants to Early Blight.

At transplanting, apply one to three applications (depending on soil organic content) of a water-soluble, "plant starter" fertilizer. This includes any of the water-soluble products like MiracleGro, Peters, RapidGro, Schults, etc. Transplants would have been "hardened off" (growth slowed) in the greenhouse. Water-soluble fertilizers stimulate renewed growth.

If the weather turns cold late spring after tomatoes are out (that is a week with daytime temperatures below 55°F), use water-soluble fertilizers to stimulate growth when warm temperatures return. A week with daytime temperatures below 55°F stunts tomato growth, reducing yields.

Mid-summer—On low organic matter soils, tomatoes typically run out of nitrogen in mid- to late summer. Yellowing of the foliage, starting with lower leaves, is the typical symptom of nitrogen stress. Low nitrogen in the plant allows Early Blight disease to spread like wildfire. Keeping nitrogen levels up in mid- to late-summer is a primary means of Early Blight control and significantly improves yields.

Fertilize tomatoes lightly as the first fruits reach two inches in diameter. Water-soluble fertilizers (such as MiracleGro, RapidGro, and Peters) used according to label directions make a good summer fertilizer supplement. Make applications every two to four weeks, depending on soil organic content.

If using a dry granular fertilizer, apply 21-0-0 (ammonium sulfate) at the rate of one level tablespoon per plant. Sprinkle the granular fertilizer in a wide circle 12 to 20 inches out from the plant, and water in. Dry granular fertilizers can easily kill tomatoes if over-applied.

Pollination and Summer Temperatures

Tomato pollination is temperature dependent. If nighttime temperatures drop below 55°F, pollen fails to develop and flowers that open the following morning will not set fruit. Cool nights often interfere with fruit set for early tomatoes and in higher elevations. Blossom set sprays help set fruit even with cool nights.

If the daytime temperature reaches 90°F by 10 a.m., blossoms that opened that morning abort. Blossom set sprays are not effective under high temperatures.

In July and August along the Colorado Front Range, night temperatures have a 50/50 probability of staying above 55°F any given night. In unusually warm seasons, tomato fruit set may be unusually high. When poor soil conditions and/or watering problems limit plant growth potential, fruit may ripen while small. With good soil tilth and water conditions, fruit size may be unusually large.

Garden Sanitation

Control weeds—Common weeds harbor many garden insect and disease problems. Volunteer potatoes and tomatoes could be a source of Early Blight infection (Figure 40-8).

For Early Blight management, some references suggest removing lower leaves showing symptoms. Symptoms start as tiny black spots on lower leaves. Spots enlarge to light and dark target-like rings. Leaves yellow and the disease progresses from lower leaves up the plant.

If removing lower leaves, focus on leaves with the tiny black spots. Removing just the lower yellow leaves will not be adequate. Wash hands with soap and water immediately after touching diseased leaves to prevent spreading spores to other plants. Avoid working with the plants when they are wet.

Another disease, tobacco mosaic virus (TMV), can readily spread from tobacco smoke residues on the hands and clothing to tomatoes. Prevent TMV infections by washing hands after smoking or handling tobacco products.

Figure 40-8 ▮ *Early blight leaf spots (Photograph: U.S. Department of Agriculture).*

Rotation

Since the common tomato diseases (Early Blight, Verticillium and Fusarium wilt) are soil-borne, crop rotation is an effective management tool. However, this may not be practical in most home garden situations, particularly since rotation allows no tomatoes, peppers, potatoes, eggplants, vine crops (cucumbers, squash, pumpkins, and melons), strawberries, or raspberries in the same growing area for at least four years. In a garden bed, moving the tomatoes a few rows to the left or right is not an effective rotation.

Fall Cleanup

Remove all tomatoes and potato debris in the fall. Dispose of debris in municipal trash or by burial. Do not compost unless the compost heats to at least 145°F and the pile is turned occasionally. Most home compost piles do not heat adequately to kill pathogens.

Common Disorders

Refer to the following fact sheets available online at www.cmg.colostate. edu.

- *Recognizing Tomato Problems,* Colorado State University Extension fact sheet #2.949

- *Tomato Early Blight,* CMG GardenNotes #718

Ripening Fruit at the End of the Season

To speed fruit ripening in the fall, hold back slightly on watering.

Figure 40-9 ▮ *Blossom end rot on tomato is caused by water imbalance between the fruit and soil. The soil could be too wet, too dry, or root could be cut by cultivation. It could be aggravated by soil compaction and poor soil preparation.*

Ripening Fruit Indoors

With the forecast of a light frost, tomatoes may be protected by covering. If heavy frost is forecast and covering is not practical, harvest fruit before the frost event and carry indoors.

Pick ripening fruit and green tomatoes with a glossy green appearance that have reached about three-fourths of their full size. Remove stems. Wash fruit under a stream of water and allow to air dry on a clean towel. Save only blemish-free fruits for ripening indoors.

As for humidity, fruit shrivel if it is too low. If the humidity is too high, fruit mold. A gardener will have to learn by trial and error what works for their home.

Some gardeners simply hang the whole plant upside down in a dark cool barn or basement to let the fruits ripen gradually. In Colorado's dry climate, fruit tend to shrivel from the low humidity.

Other options include placing tomatoes, one or two layers deep, in a covered box for ripening. Some people find better success by individually wrapping fruit in newspaper or wax paper and placing them in a covered box. Placing a few fruit together in a vegetable storage bag has been effective for others. For higher humidity, place tomatoes up to two layers deep in a blanching pan or strainer inside of a covered pan with some water in the bottom. Make sure the fruit does not touch the water.

Ethylene gas produced by ripening tomatoes is a ripening hormone. To speed the ripening process, place a ripe tomato in the container with the fruit. To slow the ripening of green tomatoes, routinely remove ripening fruit from the container.

Green fruit will ripen in about two weeks at 65°F to 70°F, and in about three to four weeks at 55°F. Storage below 50°F will give fruit a bland, off-flavor. Ripe tomatoes may be stored in the refrigerator for a few days.

ASPARAGUS

Soil—Asparagus tolerates a wide range of soils as long as they are well drained. It prefers soil high in organic matter, and full sun (eight hours/day minimum).

Fertilizing—Asparagus is a heavy feeder. Fertilize in spring as growth starts and again in mid-summer after the harvest period.

Mulching—Asparagus competes poorly with weeds and other crops for water, nutrients, and space. Organic mulch is recommended. Mulch also provides winter cold protection for the roots.

Harvesting—The asparagus bed can be weakened or destroyed by over harvesting. The harvest period for an established bed is only four to six weeks (May into mid-June). Harvest only larger spears. Stop harvesting if spears decrease to pencil size or smaller. Leave the ferns (foliage) to grow until fall or let stand through the winter, finally cutting before new growth begins in spring.

Planting—Extra efforts in planting new beds pay off with increased production.

1. Thoroughly work in four inches of well composted and aged organic matter through the soil to a twelve inch depth.

2. Before planting, soak roots in warm water for a couple of hours.

3. Dig a trench four to five inches deep and wide enough to accommodate the spread-out roots. Space roots, typically 18 inches apart, covering with only two inches of soil.

4. Add additional soil during the growing season, as plants grow. Asparagus roots are easily smothered if initially covered too deep. (Many texts talk of planting six to eight inches deep for better protection from cold winter soil temperatures. However, this deep planting will decrease yields.)

When planting from seed, start seeds indoors 12 weeks prior to transplanting outdoors. Harden off seedlings before transplanting outdoors.

BEANS

Soil—Beans are tolerant of a wide range of soils, as long as they are well drained. Beans are rather sensitive to soil salt. A soil rich in organic matter (to hold water and nutrients for growth) is preferred.

Planting—Research clearly demonstrates that early growth sets potential yield.

Avoid planting too early in the spring. Soil temperature should be above 50°F, measured at 8 a.m., six inches deep. For example, along the Colorado Front Range, this is typically early May for well-drained sandy soils to late May for clayey soils.

Rich soil fertility should push early growth of plants. However, heavy nitrogen fertilization will lead to excessive plant growth at the expense of fruiting and increased disease problems.

Spacing affects yields—The potential for disease explodes once the plant canopy grows to cover over the patch—avoid overcrowding! Crop research suggests the following optimum spacings:

- Twenty-four inches between rows with two inches between plants

- Eighteen inches between rows with three inches between plants

- Twelve inches between rows with four inches between plants (gives twenty percent higher yield than twenty-four by two inch spacing, but may increase disease pressure)

- Six inches between rows with six inches between plants (this block style spacing will predispose the patch to foliage diseases)

High water demand—During flowering and fruit production, beans have the highest water use of any vegetable crop. If the water supply is optimum, most varieties will produce until frost. If the water supply is low, beans will respond by:

1. Dropping blossoms

2. Producing pinched, pollywog-shaped fruit

Figure 40-10 ■ *Beans have a high water use. With inadequate water, blossoms drop, reducing yields. When beans need water, plant color changes slightly from a dark grass green to a grayish green. Windy weather significantly increases the water demand.*

Depending on temperature and wind, water use during fruiting will be one-quarter inch to over one-half inch of water per day. Frequent watering in the right amount is essential for bean production.

COLE CROPS: BROCCOLI, BRUSSELS SPROUTS, CABBAGE, CAULIFLOWER, KALE, AND KOHLRABI

Quality is dependent on the weather and the grower's ability to provide conditions for rapid growth.

Soil—Being shallow rooted, cole crops require a fertile, moist, well-drained soil that is rich in organic matter and nitrogen.

Fertilizer—Cole crops are heavy feeders of nitrogen, phosphorus, and potassium. Apply a plant starter fertilizer (solution of water-soluble fertilizer like MiracleGro, Peters, and Rapid Grow) at planting, three weeks and five weeks. Starter fertilizers increase yields by twenty percent.

Mulch—Because cole crops are poor competitors, mulch to stabilize moisture and control weeds. For early spring plantings, black plastic mulch helps warm cold soils. However, plastic becomes too hot when warm weather arrives. During warm weather, a grass clipping mulch cools the soil and microenvironment.

Irrigation—Cole crops are intolerant of drying. Dry soils quickly lead to strong flavors.

Temperatures—Cole crops prefer growing temperatures between 65°F and 80°F. Hot weather reduces sweetness. Because seeds do not like cold soils, use transplants for spring planting. For a superior quality fall crop, direct seed the main planting in early July (Front Range area). Both broccoli and cauliflower tolerate some frost (down to lower 20°F) on maturing plants.

Using *Bt*—For cabbageworm and looper control, treat with *Bacillus thuringiensis* (*Bt*); a biological control product. Since *Bt* is rapidly broken down by sunlight, treat in the evening. *Bt*, a living organism, has only a two-year shelf life and cannot survive storage under extreme heat or cold.

Transplants—

- Preferred growing temperature for transplants is 60°F to 70°F. High temperatures result in too rapid growth, and tall, weak plants that are easily broken off in transplanting.

- The ideal transplant is about four inches tall and about four weeks old. Avoid transplants older than six weeks. Quick maturing varieties should be transplanted within four weeks of seeding.

Heading—Yield is based on plant size as the head (curd) starts to develop.

- **Bolting** (rapid head formation)

  —Broccoli and cauliflower are prone to bolting when exposed to cool weather before three to four pairs of true leaves develop.

  —Long days and hot weather in the summer cause broccoli to bolt and go to seed, and cause cauliflower curds to develop a red-purple discoloration.

  —Cabbage bolts if exposed to two to three weeks below 50°F. Avoid planting too early in the spring.

- **Buttoning** (development of small heads or curds [buttons] on immature plants)—Factors that restrict early plant growth (including nitrogen deficiency, cold temperatures, shock to young transplants, and drought stress) lead to buttoning. Follow practices that will result in rapid vegetative growth.

- **Blindness** (plants having lost their terminal growing points produce no head)—Damage to the terminal growing point due to low temperatures, cutworms, damage, or rough handling of transplants will result in blind plants. Handle transplants carefully, control cutworms, and avoid planting in low temperatures.

Figure 40-11 ▮ *For quality, broccoli, cabbage, and cauliflower need cool temperatures. In warm summer climates (like the Colorado Front Range) plant mid-July for harvest in the cooler temperatures of fall. They will tolerate fall frost down to the mid-20s°F.*

CORN

Variety types –

- **Normal sugary** (su)—standard varieties

- **Sugar Enhanced** (se)—Sugar Enhanced (se) genes increase the original level of sugar in the kernel and slow the conversion of sugar into starch. Isolation is helpful, but not required.

- **Super Sweet** (sh)—Super Sweet (sh) genes increase sugar content two- to threefold. Delay planting until soil temperatures reach 70°F, in June. Isolation from non-super sweet types by 300 to 500 feet or fourteen plus day differences in maturity is required.

Yield = water + nitrogen + space

- Water stress will reduce overall plant growth reducing yields. In particular, water stress will delay silking beyond the time when tassels shed pollen, thereby preventing kernel formation.

- Side dress with nitrogen fertilizer frequently (every three to four weeks) through the summer to maintain a dark grass-green color. Sprinkle one cup 21-0-0 (or equivalent) per fifty feet of row, and water in.

- Spacing affects yields. Crowding decreases sunlight to the leaves, reducing the number and size of ears. Optimum spacing is thirty-six inches between rows with nine inches between plants or thirty inches between rows with twelve inches between plants. Allow side shoots to develop, but do not plant in clumps.

Figure 40-12 ▮ *Corn needs to be planted in blocks for wind pollination. For pollination, two side-by-side four-foot-wide beds are used. Each bed has two rows going down the bed. This makes the block four rows wide. To extend the harvest season, the top of the bed could have an early planting with a later planting at the bottom.*

Plant in blocks—Corn is wind pollinated, so plant in blocks at least three rows wide, preferably four to five rows wide. Single blocks may include only a portion of the row length, with the remainder of the row being part to a block of another variety that matures at different times.

Pollination—Corn is wind pollinated, but bees collecting pollen also frequently visit it. When applying insecticides, use caution to protect pollinating insects. Do NOT spray tassels with insecticides.

LEAFY VEGETABLES AND SALAD CROPS: LETTUCE, SPINACH, SWISS CHARD, ETC.

Quality lettuce, spinach, chard, and other salad crops is the mark of a great gardener. Quality is based on the gardener's ability to match ideal conditions for rapid growth, including water, fertilizer, space, and temperature.

Soil—A rich soil, high in organic matter, is necessary for quality.

Mulch—Organic mulch (like dry grass clippings) reduces summer soil temperatures producing sweeter produce, conserves moisture, and controls weeds. Weeding by cultivation will damage surface roots.

Figure 40-13 ▮ *For quality, leafy vegetables need a constant supply of water, rich soils. For best quality, thin plants when crop is tiny. Here a variety of leaf vegetables are in a raised bed, going across the box. As one row is harvested, immediately replant for a continual harvest of young tasty produce.*

Irrigation—Keep soil moist with one to one and one-half inches of water per week (including rain). If the crop gets dry, it will become tough and stringy.

Spacing—Thin the crop to reduce competition for nutrients, moisture, light, and space.

Planting for fall harvest—Plant lettuce and spinach in mid- to late summer to produce exceptional harvest quality during cool fall weather. It can also be planted mid-fall for extra-early spring crops. Cover the small seedlings with organic mulch for winter protection.

ONION FAMILY: GARLIC, LEEKS, ONIONS, SHALLOTS, ETC.

Soils—The onion family has a poor, inefficient root system, making the crop intolerant of poor soils and competition from weeds. The plants are heavy feeders. Quality produce arises from a well-drained, fertile soil, rich in organic matter.

Mulch—The onion family thrives with organic mulch (like dry grass clippings), which cools the soil, conserves moisture, and controls weeds.

Photoperiod sensitivity—The onion family is sensitive to the length of night, which triggers bulb development. In Colorado, plant only long day varieties that start bulbing with day lengths of fourteen to sixteen hours and temperatures above 65°F. Plant size at the time conditions trigger bulb development determines the size of the bulb. Plant onions as soon as soil conditions allow in the spring.

Seed head—Keep seed heads picked. They pull plant resources away from bulb development.

Figure 40-14 ■ *Onions have a shallow inefficient root system. For quality they need an even moisture supply and rich soils.*

Seed, sets, or transplants—Onions can be planted from seed, sets, or transplants. If planted from sets, sort sets larger than a dime from smaller ones. Plant small and large sets separately. Harvest from larger sets first because they do not store as well as onions grown from small sets.

PEAS

Soils—Peas grow best in a rich soil, high in organic matter. They require a well-drained soil.

Types of peas–

- **English pea**—standard, shelled pea
- **Edible pod pea, sugar pea, or snow pea**—edible pod, pick before seeds swell
- **Snap pea**—edible pod and plump sweet pea fruit

Plant as early as possible—

- Peas are sensitive to the photoperiod (length of night), influencing yields. At Colorado's latitude, an April 1 planting will have a fifty percent higher yield than a May 1 planting.

- Plant when soil temperatures reach 40°F. Avoid planting in wet soils.

Figure 40-15 ■ *Snap peas are edible pod types eaten with plump peas filling the pod. Edible pod peas, sugar peas, or snow peas are edible pod types eaten before the pod fills with peas.*

Planting for fall harvest—Peas may be planted in mid-summer for harvest during cooler fall weather. Sweeter peas develop in cooler temperatures. However, yields of the fall crop are reduced due to photoperiodism and the vines are prone to powdery mildew in the fall.

POTATOES

Soils—Potatoes thrive in a soil rich in organic matter that provides water and nutrient holding capacity and improved drainage. However, avoid heavy applications of fresh manure or compost, as it will make the tuber surface rough and increase the occurrence of scab.

Certified seed—The use of certified seed helps reduce disease problems.

Give the plants a vigorous start–

- Plant when soil temperatures rise above 50°F, four inches deep at 8 a.m.

- Avoid using too small of a seed piece. Cutting seed pieces to one and one-half to two inches in size provides for early plant vigor. Many gardeners prefer to use seed pieces that require no cutting to reduce decay potential.

Spacing—Plant spacing determines tuber size. Learn by experience the optimum spacing for the variety in a particular garden soil. A starting point is an equal-distant spacing of twelve to fifteen inches between plants and between rows (or three plants across a four-foot-wide raised bed). Spacing that allows the plants to close in and shade the soil yields sweeter spuds. However, thick foliage and reduced airflow can also increase the occurrence of disease.

Mulch—Transplants are hardened off (growth rate slows so the plant is more tolerant of the move from the greenhouse environment to the bright, windy outdoors) by withholding water and/or nutrients or by exposure to cooler temperature (Figure 40-16).

Fertilizer—Potatoes are heavy feeders of nitrogen, phosphorus, and potassium. Running out of nitrogen by August is the most common potato problem. Symptoms are a general yellowing of leaves that starts with lower interior leaves. Nitrogen stress predisposes the crop to Early Blight.

Irrigation—If the soil is too wet or has poor drainage, tubers will rot. If the soil becomes overly dry, tubers will develop knobs.

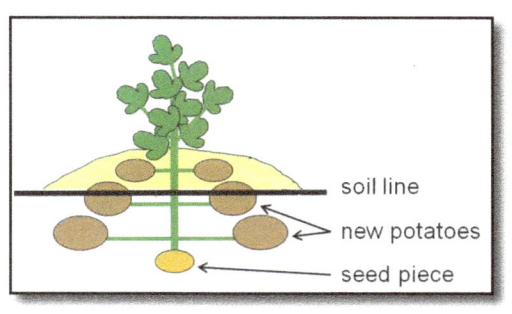

Figure 40-16 ▮ *The new crop of potatoes grows above the seed piece. To shield the growing tubers from sunlight (which turns them green) soil is "hilled" (mounded) around the base of the plant. Straw mulch may be used as an alternative to hilling.*

Figure 40-17 ▮ *Plant spacing directly affects tuber size. Learn from experience what space is ideal for any cultivar on a given soil.*

RHUBARB

Soils—Rhubarb thrives on any soil that is high in organic matter and well drained.

Yield—Yield is based on the plant's ability to store food reserves in the roots for the next year's crop.

Keep seed stalk picked off.

- Stop harvest when temperatures rise above 85°F.

- Remove oldest stalks at the base when plants grow crowded, giving room for new stalks to grow. Never remove more than one-fourth of the stalks at one time.

Mulch—Rhubarb is a poor competitor for water and nutrients. Keep mulched with organic mulch.

Sun—It prefers full sun but grows poorly with reflected heat.

Coloration—Poor coloration of stalks develops from too much shade, too much heat, overly wet soils, or an inferior variety.

Replanting—Reset when stalks become slender and the center of plant dies out, about every eight years. Rhubarb is best transplanted in the fall.

ROOT CROPS: BEETS, CARROTS, PARSNIPS, RADISH, RUTABAGAS, TURNIPS, ETC.

Soils—Root crops need a rich, well-drained soil, high in aged organic matter.

Mulch—Use an organic mulch (like dry grass clippings) to cool the soil in summer, stabilize soil moisture, and control weeds.

Moisture—Consistent soil moisture is a must!

Carrot disorders –

- Strong flavor—Many varieties have a high oil content (and the oil can turn rancid); change varieties.

- Hairy or rough root surface develops from too much fresh organic matter in the soil. Use old, well-aged compost or manure in the root crop section.

- Stubby, knobby, or cracked roots arise from uneven moisture supply, hot soil temperatures, or poor, rocky, or compacted soil conditions.

- Green shoulders result from root crowns exposed to sunlight and reduce sweetness. Mulch with dry grass clippings to shade the crown of the root.

- Failure of seedlings to emerge may arise from soil crusting, planting too deep, or high soil temperatures.

Radishes–

- Hot and/or pithy radishes arise from hot weather, hot soil, and/or plants that are past maturity.

- Thin plants as soon as they pop through the ground!

Replanting of root crops for fall harvest—For tender young root crops, replant in mid-summer (Front Range area) for fall harvest.

Winter storage of roots—Some varieties of carrots store well in the garden soil or in a root cellar for year-round use. Other carrot varieties become strong-flavored as the oil becomes rancid. Two useful options for winter storage include:

Figure 40-18 ■ *Burpee White Radish— for quality, root crops need an even moisture supply and rich soil.*

- Leave undisturbed where growing in the garden and mulch the bed with straw or other organic materials. Dig as needed.

- Place harvested carrots in straw in a garbage can storage pit.

VINE CROPS: CUCUMBERS, MELONS, PUMPKINS, AND SQUASH

Soils—Vine crops thrive in well-drained soils high in organic matter. Yearly applications of compost will likely supply needed nutrients.

Mulch—Use black plastic mulch for earlier production and higher yields. It also controls weeds and conserves water.

Planting time—Do not plant too early. Daytime temperatures should consistently be above 55°F. Protect young, tender plants from cool winds.

Seeds or transplants—Direct seeding is reported to give higher yields. If using transplants, they should be small, never more than two to four weeks old.

Blossom drop—

- Vine crops have male flowers and female flowers (small fruit behind the flower). Male flowers develop first, and generally predominate. Young fruits that are not pollinated will abort.

- When bee activity is limited, increase yields by hand pollination. Pick a male flower, remove petals, and touch the center of the female flowers with the male flower.

- Any form of stress (like too much or too little water, poor soil conditions, extreme heat, and wind) can reduce flowering and lead to abortion of fruits.

Figure 40-19 ▮ *Vine crops have female flowers (left blossom) and male flowers (right blossoms). The female blossom has a tiny fruit at the base of the petals. For production, bees or the gardener must move the pollen from the male flower to the female flower.*

CHAPTER REVIEW
Questions

1. When are tomatoes planted out?

2. Describe the ideal tomato transplant. How should tall, leggy transplants be planted?

3. What are the advantages of trellising tomatoes? How far apart should tomatoes be spaced? Give examples of trellising methods.

4. What are the advantages and limitations of using black plastic mulch on tomatoes, peppers, eggplant, and vine crops? Describe techniques for using plastic mulch.

5. Tomatoes are often referred to as being a "low nitrogen" crop. More correctly stated, they are fussy about nitrogen levels. Explain the fertilizer needs at planting and as the crop nears harvest.

6. When should beans be planted?

7. Beans have a higher water use than other vegetables. What happens when they get a little dry? What symptoms indicate that beans need watering?

8. Give examples of cole crops.

9. How does temperature affect the quality of cole crops? In warm summer areas, like Colorado's Front Range, when are cole crops planted for a fall harvest?

10. Explain the specific fertilizer needs of cole crops.

11. *Bacillus thuringiensis, Bt*, is the standard biological control approach for caterpillars (cabbage worms) in cole crops. Describe the criteria in using *Bt.*

12. Describe the need for isolation in planting corn. Define isolation.

13. What happens when corn has inadequate water during tasseling/silking?

14. Gardeners often list "poor quality" as the reason most do not grow leafy vegetables. What are the keys to great quality lettuce, spinach, chard, and other leafy vegetables?

15. What cultural practices are needed to compensate for the onion family's poor, inefficient root system?

16. What is the difference between English peas, snow or sugar peas, and snap peas?

17. Describe how to get potatoes off to a great start.

18. Give examples of "vine crops."

19. When will vine crops blossom but not set fruit?

20. Describe hand pollination of vine crops.

Chapter
41*

Extending the Growing Season
Growing Vegetables in Cold Frames and Hobby Solar Greenhouses

TYPES OF FROST

Advective frosts occur when a cold front moves into the area. Temperatures may drop significantly below critical levels thereby making crop protection questionable unless crops are being grown in a well-built solar greenhouse.

Radiation frosts occur on calm clear nights that lack cloud cover to hold in heat. Radiation frosts at the beginning and end of the growing season are typically only a few degrees below critical levels, making crop protection in the garden worthwhile.

HEAT SOURCE AT NIGHT

Soil, warmed by the sun in the daytime, is the source of heat for frost protection at night. Moist, smooth soil absorbs more heat. To trap heat from the soil around young vegetables at night, place a covering that is low to the ground and spreading. To recharge the heat source for the next night, any covering must allow sunlight to shine through to the soil or must be removed in the daytime (Figure 41-1).

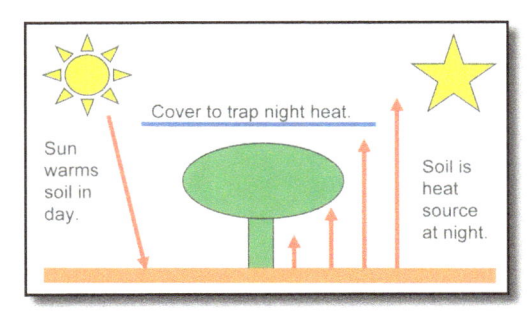

Figure 41-1 ■ *The sun warms the soil in the daytime. Heat from the soil keeps crops warm at night. A covering traps heat from the soil around the crops.*

*Author: David Whiting, Colorado State University Extension. Photographs and line drawings by David Whiting.

COVERINGS IN THE GARDEN

Blankets and Sheets

Grandma's old method of covering the garden with blankets and sheets works well as long as the fabric remains dry. If the fabric absorbs water, evaporative cooling can lead to colder temperatures adjacent to the blanket. To recharge the heat stored in the soil, the blankets and sheets must be removed in the daytime.

Floating Row Covers

Floating row covers are lightweight fabrics that lay directly over crops. Because they transmit light, they provide crop protection over an extended period of time without being removed. They provide 2°F to 4°F of frost protection, cut wind on tender plants, and screen out some insects. On insect pollinated crops, covers must be removed for pollination to occur (Figure 41-2).

Floating row covers are popular in commercial vegetable production where crops planted in large blocks are easily covered with row covers. Many brands and fabric types are commercially available.

Clear Plastic Covering on Frame

When plastic is used as a covering over a growing bed, it must be held up off the plants. Plants will freeze where the plastic touches them.

Tunnel gardening—Gardening catalogs carry wire hoops for use in "tunnel" or cloche gardening. Hoops are placed at three to five foot intervals depending on the wind exposure of the site. The wire hoops hold up a strip of plastic forming a tunnel-shape covering down the growing bed. Bury the edges of the plastic a few inches into the soil on all sides. On a raised bed box made with lumber, staple the plastic to the sides of the box. Two-inch holes cut in the sides of the plastic tunnel at two to three foot intervals are essential to reduce overheating.

Figure 41-2 ▮ *Floating row cover on broccoli and cabbage, protecting crops from cabbageworms moths.*

Figure 41-3 ▮ *Cold frame for a raised bed garden made from concrete reinforcing mesh covered with 4-mil plastic. Notice the belt-like plastic straps, which hold the covering in place. The covering is slid between the straps and mesh to open and close. Pictured open for ventilation on a warm day.*

This type of covering is popular with commercial tomato, pepper, and melon growers for an early start to the growing season. It provides 2°F to 4°F of frost protection, protects tender plants from cold spring wind, and provides warmer growing temperatures inside the tunnel. Tunnels are removed when warm weather arrives and the danger of frost is past.

Plastic-Covered Cold Frame Made with Concrete Reinforcing Mesh

An easy cold frame structure for a growing bed is made with 4-mil clear plastic (polyethylene film) draped over concrete reinforcing mesh. The structure is easily opened during warm days and closed for cold nights. It works well with a four-foot-wide, raised bed garden system (Figure 41-3).

The frame is concrete reinforcing mesh, available at hardware and lumber stores. This stiff wire mesh typically comes five feet wide, in 50- and 100-foot rolls. A six-foot length is required to make a Quonset-type frame over a four-foot-wide growing bed. In trials, the low and spreading shape was ideal for trapping heat from the soil during a frosty night.

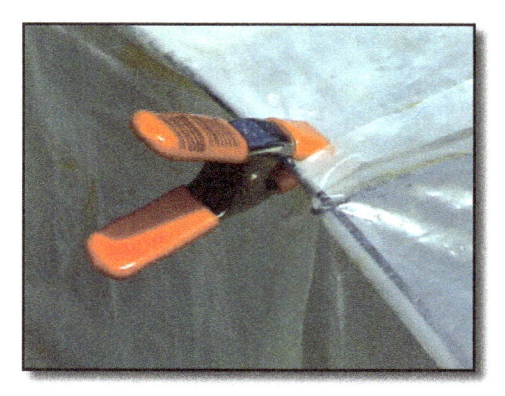

Figure 41-4 ▮ *Clip holds plastic on frame.*   **Figure 41-5** ▮ *Left: Cover must be opened at least a slit to prevent over-heating. Right: Cold frame pictured closed for a cold night.*

Cover the frame with clear, 4-mil polyethylene plastic. It typically is sold in ten-foot by twenty-five-foot rolls. For a four-foot-wide raised bed box, place a three and one-half-foot-wide section on each side, overlapping at the top. On a raised bed box, staple the plastic to the sides of the wood box. In soil bed applications, bury the plastic a few inches along the sides.

Hold the plastic onto the frame with small clips available at local hardware stores. Clothes pins do not hold in the wind. Another method is to use a series of six-inch-wide, belt-like plastic straps arching over the frame (above the plastic cover) and stapled onto the box. Open and close the cover by sliding it between the frame and the belt-like straps. Hold the plastic closed at the ends with a rock or brick (Figure 41-4).

During the day, the covering MUST be opened, at least a slit, to prevent overheating. With just an hour of sun, temperatures under a closed cover can quickly rise to over 130°F (Figure 41-5).

On cool days, open the top a crack to prevent excessive heat build-up. On a warm day, the plastic can be slid down the side, ventilating and providing crops exposure to the outdoors. On freezing nights, close the cover completely. On warm nights, the covers may be left open a crack. On stormy days with full cloud cover and no direct sun, the cover may remain closed (Figure 41-5).

Not only will the covers provide frost protection, they also increase growing temperatures for early crop growth and provide protection from cold winds.

In trials in Fort Collins, Colorado, a plastic cover on a frame typically provides 3°F to over 6°F of frost protection. It works well for cool season crops that are somewhat tolerant of frosty nights, and adds two to six weeks or more on both ends of the growing season. For warm season tomatoes and summer squash crops (being intolerant of a frosty nip), adding a small light inside the cold frame provides even better frost protection.

Adding Space Blankets

On extra cold nights, placing an aluminum space blanket over the plastic on the frame significantly adds to the frost protection. With the aluminized side placed down (toward the plants), a space blanket reflects ninety-nine percent of the heat. They are readily available where camping gear is sold (Figure 41-6).

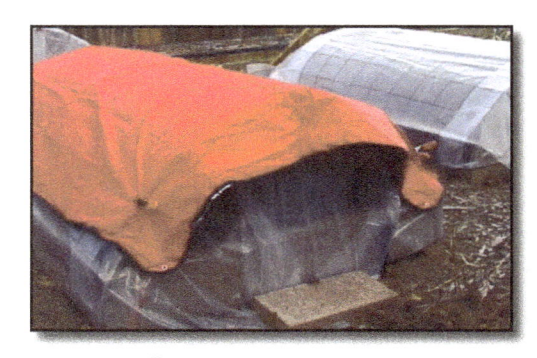

Figure 41-6 ▮ *Aluminum space blanket covering a cold frame for extra protection on cold nights.*

In trials in Fort Collins, topping a plastic-covered, concrete mesh cold frame with a space blanket prevented freezing when outside temperatures dipped to 0°F following a sunny spring day. The space blanket must be removed each day to recharge the soil's stored heat.

Lights for Additional Heat

Christmas tree lights—For additional protection, add Christmas tree lights inside the cold frame. In Fort Collins trials, one twenty-five light string of C-7 (mid-size) Christmas lights per frame unit (four feet wide by five feet long) gave 6°F to over 18°F frost protection. Lights were hung on the frame under the plastic and turned on at dusk and off at dawn. Christmas lights work better than a single, large light bulb in the center by eliminating cold corners and edges (Figure 41-7).

Space blanket with Christmas tree lights—For the gardener really wanting to extend the growing season, try Christmas lights plus a space blanket. One twenty-five light string of C-7 (mid-size) Christmas lights per frame unit (four-feet wide by five-feet long) with a space blanket on top gave 18°F to over 30°F frost protection in Fort Collins trials.

Wall of Water®

The Wall-of-Water® is a cone-shaped ring of connected plastic tubes filled with water that surrounds a single plant, like a tomato, pepper, or summer squash (Figure 41-8).

This device works on the chemistry principle of heat release in a phase change; there is a significant amount of heat released as water freezes (changes from the liquid phase to the solid or ice phase). A Wall-of-Water provides frost protection with temperatures typically down to mid-teens. It also provides wind protection for tender plants and growing temperatures may be slightly warmer inside a Wall-of-Water.

They are helpful to get a few extra weeks head start on vine ripe tomatoes. However, an extra early tomato may outgrow the protection and the tops may be nipped back by frost.

Both cold air temperatures and cold soil temperatures are limiting factors in early crop production. When using a Wall-of-Water to start early crops, warm the soil with black plastic mulch.

In filling the Wall-of-Water, be careful not to splash excessive water onto the soil. A wet soil will be both slow to warm and dry in the spring. Moderately moist soils are best.

GROWING VEGETABLES IN A HOBBY GREENHOUSE
Extending the Growing Season

Off-season vegetable production in the hobby solar greenhouse is an enjoyable way for year-round gardeners to extend the harvest season of fresh vegetables. Winter vegetable production in a greenhouse is only cost-effective with an *energy-efficient* greenhouse structure, a *well-designed solar collector*, and *optimum management*. Winter vegetables have a slow growth rate due to low light intensity. Crops should be planted to obtain a near harvestable size by mid-October. The use of artificial light for vegetable production (except for starting transplants) is generally not cost effective (Figure 41-9).

Figure 41-7 ▮ *Cold frame with Christmas tree lights for additional warmth.*

Figure 41-8 ▮ *Tomato in Wall-of-Water. Notice use of black plastic mulch to warm the soil, another limiting factor of early production. Also, note the plant has grown beyond the Wall-Of-Water and is now less protected from frost.*

Figure 41-9 ▮ *Raised bed in solar greenhouse.*

Figure 41-10 ▮ *Brick storage wall in passive solar hobby greenhouse. Thermal storage mass is a wall made with two layers of brick filled with concrete. In this well-built structure, nighttime temperatures dropped to 35°F with no supplemental heat when outside temperatures dropped to −17°F. Note young crops in raised bed style garden with drip irrigation.*

A gardener's success is dependent on the greenhouse design and construction to conserve energy and on the management care given the greenhouse crops.

Before investing in a greenhouse, carefully consider your real interests in extending the gardening season. Are you only interested in adding a few weeks to the harvest season? Are you interested in year-round gardening in a solar greenhouse OR do you need a winter break?

Passive Solar Greenhouse

For the gardener considering a passive solar hobby greenhouse, here are a few key points to consider. Refer to other greenhouse references for additional details.

For solar collectors, any area with direct sun, but not blocking solar illumination of plants, is a potential location. For a hobby greenhouse, solar collectors are typically built into an insulated north wall.

A solid brick wall on the north makes a good solar collector. Brick absorbs thirty to thirty-five percent of the solar radiation. With a brick storage wall, the greenhouse quickly heats on a sunny winter day and ventilation will be needed by mid-morning (Figure 41-10).

Water storage using plastic milk jugs makes a great storage system. Water jugs absorb ninety percent of the solar radiation, holding three times more heat than brick or rock. This increased heat storage holds night temperature higher longer into the night, resulting in slightly improved crop growth compared to brick storage (Figure 41-11).

With milk jug storage, spray the milk jugs with flat black paint, and add one tablespoon of Clorox-type bleach per jug (to prevent algae growth in the warm water). Secure the cap back on the jug with a ring of caulk. Place the milk jug on a bookcase type frame not more than two jugs high.

Disposable milk jugs develop leaks over time and require routine replacement. Heavier weight jugs (like returnable plastic milk jugs) last longer. Other

Figure 41-11 ▮ *Milk jug water storage wall in a passive solar hobby greenhouse. Disposable milk jugs on left and returnable milk jugs on right are spray painted flat black. In this well-built structure, nighttime temperatures dropped to 39°F with no supplemental heat when outside temperatures dropped to −17°F.*

types of containers may be used. Keep the size two gallons or smaller or water will stratify with hot water on the top and cooler water on the bottom, reducing efficiency.

A passive solar hobby greenhouse is only effective when built to optimum energy specifications. Because the major heat loss is through the glazing, double-glazing (which reduces heat loss by twenty-five to thirty-five percent) is required. Double glazed patio door glass is great for glazing a hobby greenhouse. Glass suppliers sometimes have recycled (used) patio door glass available at minimal prices. Night curtains may add an additional thirty to fifty percent energy conservation. On a passive solar hobby greenhouse, the north, east, and west walls are typically insulated to an R-value of R38. The foundation and floor are insulated from heat loss to the ground (Figure 41-12).

Cold air infiltration is the second major source of heat loss. For passive solar to be effective, minimize cold air infiltration with good design and construction techniques. Insulative vent covers help reduce cold air infiltration at night, but must be removed daily to allow thermostats to maintain proper temperature.

A passive solar hobby greenhouse requires an east to west orientation. In northern Colorado latitudes, an east to west orientation receives twenty-five percent more solar energy than a north to south orientation. Sometimes the hobby greenhouse may be oriented slightly to the east for faster morning warming. An orientation twenty degrees off east to west will cut four to five percent of the solar potential, whereas an orientation forty-five degrees off east to west will cut eighteen to twenty percent of the solar potential. At northern Colorado latitudes in January, a north to south orientation cuts twenty-five percent of the solar potential.

A poorly constructed greenhouse cannot be retrofitted into an efficient passive solar unit.

Figure 41-12 ■ *Hobby greenhouse being constructed with double glazed patio door glass.*

Figure 41-13 ■ *Lettuce in solar greenhouse raised bed.*

Cool Season Vegetables

Cool season vegetables do well in the greenhouse or cold frame. High temperatures are not desirable, and an occasional near freezing dip will not harm crops. High light intensity is not as critical for cool season crops as for warm season crops (Figure 41-13).

General temperatures for cool season crops

- Daytime: 50°F to 70°F
- Nighttime: 45°F to 55°F
- Short-term temperature extremes: 35°F to 90°F
- Germination: 40°F to 75°F

Vegetable	Minimum Container Size*	Minimum Equal-Distance Spacing	Remarks
Beets	8" deep	6"	Grow in fall and hold in cool greenhouse for winter use. Properly thin.
Broccoli	10" deep	18"	High yield for space used.
Cabbage	5 gallons/plant		Avoid long-term temperature extremes.
Cauliflower			Heads split with warm humid conditions.
Carrots	12" deep	3"	Extremely sweet with adequate water and cool temperatures. Use short varieties, like Short & Sweet or Scarlet Nantes. Questionable use of greenhouse space.
Chard	8" deep	9–12"	Does exceptionally well.
Kohlrabi	8" deep	9"	Does exceptionally well.
Leaf lettuce	4" deep	9"	Easy to grow in fall, winter and spring in solar greenhouse. Use softhead or leaf types. Keep temperatures under 70°F.
Green onions	6" deep	3"	Never let onions get dry.
			Sensitive to photoperiod (length of night). With short days (long nights), growth goes into leaf production. With long days (12–16 hours), energy goes into bulb production.
Peas	8" deep	6"	Use dwarf, edible-pod, or snap types for salads and stir-fry. Avoid temperature extremes. Questionable use of space. Do not transplant well, not well suited to container gardening.
Radish	5" deep	2–3"	Avoid water and heat stress. Must have 12 hours of light to root. For fall and spring crops in greenhouse.
Spinach	8" deep	6"	Needs cool greenhouse (45°F to 50°F) for best quality. Avoid temperature fluctuations.
Turnips	8" deep	6"	Good for fall and spring crops.

Many oriental vegetables are also suited for greenhouse production.

*A larger container size will make crop easier to care for, providing a larger supply of water and nutrients.

Warm Season Vegetables

Warm season vegetables require high light intensity and moderate night temperatures. They cannot be cost-effectively grown during the winter in a hobby greenhouse without solar heat collectors. Greenhouse climate control is critical for these fruiting crops to produce. Warm season crops are not compatible with cool season crops due to differing temperature needs (Figure 41-14).

General temperatures for warm season crops
- Daytime—60°F to 85°F
- Nighttime—55°F to 65°F
- Short-term temperature extremes—50°F to 95°F
- Germination—60°F to 85°F

Vegetable	Minimum Container Size*	Minimum Equal-Distance Spacing	Remarks
Beans	8" deep	6"	Not a common greenhouse crop. Good production with adequate light and spacing in spring and fall. Poor winter production. May be questionable use of greenhouse space.
Cucumbers	8" deep 3–4 gallons/ plant	18"	Requires high humidity, high light intensity, and good moisture. Needs 75°F to 80°F day temperatures and 50°F minimum nights. Avoid temperature fluctuations greater than 20°F. Poor mid-winter production. Plant gynecious greenhouse types. Needs good air circulation to minimize powdery mildew.
Eggplant	8" deep 4–5 gallons/plant	24"	Hand pollination required.
Muskmelon	8" deep 5 gallons/plant	24"	Uses lots of space for yield, try trellising. Needs 80°F day temperatures. Requires hand pollination. Needs good air circulation to minimize powdery mildew.
Peppers	8" deep 2–5 gallons/plants	15"	Minimum night temperatures of 55°F. Hand pollination required.
Summer Squash	8" deep 5 gallons/plant	24"	Hand pollination required. Needs good air circulation to minimize powdery mildew. Productive with good sunshine.
Tomatoes	12" deep 2–5 gallons/plant (depending on cultivar/ plant size)	24"	Minimum night temperature of 55°F. Hand pollination required. Productive with good sunshine.

*A larger container size will make crop easier to care for, providing a larger supply of water and nutrients.

Figure 41-14 ■ *Beans in solar greenhouse raised bed.*

- *Greenhouses for Homeowners and Gardeners*. NRAES. Cornell University Cooperative Extension. 2000. 152 Riley-Robb Hall. Ithaca, NY 14853-5701. Phone 607-255-7654. E-mail: NRAES@CORNELL.EDU. $25 plus S&H.

- *How to Build and Operate Your Greenhouse.* Charles Ellwood. HP Books. 1977.

- *Solar Greenhouses for the Home.* Cooperative Extension, Cornell University, Ithaca, NY 14853.

- *Solar Growing Frame.* Rodale Press. 1980.

- *The Solar Greenhouse Book.* James McCullagh. Rodale Press. 1978.

CHAPTER REVIEW
Questions

1. In covering plants for frost protection, what is the heat source? That is, where is the heat stored?

2. Describe use and limitations of the following row covers:

   a. Blankets

   b. Floating row covers

   c. Plastic on wire frames

3. Describe examples of heat storage systems for a hobby greenhouse.

4. Describe winter vegetable production in a hobby greenhouse.

Chapter

42*

Growing Vegetables in Containers

For basic information on container gardening, refer to Colorado State University Extension fact sheet #7.238, *Container Gardens*, available online at www.cmg.colostate.edu.

Container vegetable production is somewhat more demanding than growing flowers and other ornamentals in containers. Quality of most vegetables is based on the soil's ability to provide a constant supply of water and nutrients. Vegetables become strong flavored, stringy, and tough under dry or low fertility conditions. With the limited root spread in a container, the gardener must frequently and regularly supply water and fertilizer. In growing container flowers, minor lapses in daily care may interrupt flower production, but flowering eventually resumes with returned quality care. With container vegetables, minor lapses in daily care may significantly reduce produce quality.

COOL SEASON VEGETABLES

Cool season vegetables prefer the cool growing temperatures (60°F to 80°F) of spring and fall. Most are intolerant of summer heat. They do tolerate light frosts. Leafy and root vegetables prefer full sun, but are tolerant of partial shade. They are intolerant of reflected heat during the summer season (Table 42-1).

Spring crops are typically planted two to four weeks before the average spring frost date. Along the Colorado Front Range, spring planting times are mid-April to early May. Most are replanted in mid-July to mid-August for a fall harvest.

*Authors: David Whiting, Carol O'Meara, and Carl Wilson, Colorado State University Extension. Photographs and line drawing by David Whiting.

The quality of these vegetables is directly related to their ability to grow rapidly in a good soil mix under frequent light fertilization and a constant supply of water. Crops become strong flavored if they become dry.

Table 42-1. Cool Season Vegetables

Vegetable	Minimum Container Size*	Minimum Direct Sunlight per Day	Remarks
Beets	8" deep	8 hours	Best in cool temperatures, grow a spring and fall crop. To give space for root development, thin greens to 3". A consistent supply of water and nutrients promotes the rapid growth essential for quality produce.
Broccoli Cabbage Cauliflower	10" deep 5 gallons/plant	8 hours	Best in fall production (e.g., plant mid-July for fall harvest along the Colorado Front Range). Minimum spacing per plant is 18" by 18". A consistent supply of water and nutrients promotes rapid growth and is essential for quality produce. Heavy feeder, requiring frequent light fertilization. Crops develop a strong flavor if the soil gets dry.
Carrots	12" deep	8 hours	Best in cool temperatures, grow a spring and fall crop. Use short root varieties, like Short & Sweet or Scarlet Nantes. Roots will crack and be strong flavored if the soil gets dry. Thin early to 2–3" apart. Foliage is rather decorative.
Chard	8" deep	6 hours	Space to 6+" between plants in a row. Harvest outer leaves allowing plants to continue to grow. Makes an excellent "cut and grow again" crop. Colored varieties are very decorative. Responds to frequent light fertilization. A consistent supply of water and nutrients promotes the rapid growth essential for quality produce.
Kohlrabi	8" deep	8 hours	Best in cool temperatures, grow a spring and fall crop. A consistent supply of water and nutrients promotes the rapid growth essential for quality produce. Never allow soil to become dry. Kohlrabi is a heavy feeder, requiring frequent, light fertilization.
Lettuce (leaf)	8" deep	6 hours	Grow as a spring or fall crop; avoid hot summer temperatures. Use softhead or leaf types. As the young crop grows, thin to 9" spacing; crowding (competition for space, water and nutrients) reduces quality. A consistent supply of water and nutrients promotes the rapid growth essential for quality produce. Responds to frequent light fertilization. Lettuce becomes strong flavored if the soil become dry, during hot weather, and with crowded plants.

Table 42-1. Cool Season Vegetables (continued)

Vegetable	Minimum Container Size*	Minimum Direct Sunlight per Day	Remarks
Onions (green)	6" deep	8 hours	Onions require a consistent supply of water. Never allow soil to become dry. Thin the crop by harvesting young plants. Plant in early spring. A consistent supply of water and nutrients promotes the rapid growth essential for quality produce.
Peas	8" deep	Full sun	Not well suited to container gardening. Best in cool temperatures, grow a spring and fall crop. Use dwarf, edible pod or snap types for salads and stir-fry. May be grown in hanging baskets or trellised. Needs good air circulation to avoid powdery mildew.
Radish	8" deep	8 hours	Best in cool temperatures, grow a spring and fall crop. A consistent supply of water and nutrients to promote rapid growth is essential for quality produce.
Spinach	8" deep	6 hours	Best in cool temperatures, grow a spring and fall crop. A consistent supply of water and nutrients promotes the rapid growth essential for quality produce.
Turnips	8" deep	8 hours	Best in cool temperatures, grow a spring and fall crop. When large enough to make greens, thin to 4" allowing roots to develop. A consistent supply of water and nutrients promotes the rapid growth essential for quality produce.

* Larger container sizes will make crop easier to care for, providing a bigger supply of water and nutrients.

WARM SEASON VEGETABLES

Warm season vegetables prefer warmer summer temperatures (70°F to 95°F) and are intolerant of frost. They are typically planted after the average spring frost date as summery weather moves into the area. Along the Colorado Front Range, planting time would be mid-May to early June. Warm season crops need full sun (Table 42-2).

Table 42-2. Warm Season Vegetables

Vegetable	Minimum Container Size*	Minimum Direct Sunlight per Day	Remarks
Beans	8" deep	Full sun	In a long box 12" wide, plant bush beans or trellis pole beans. Beans have a high water requirement during blossoming. Beans drop blossoms with dry soil or excessive wind.
Cantaloupes Muskmelons	5+ gallons/plant	Full sun	May be trellised to conserve space. Compact varieties preferred for container gardening. With male and female blossoms, may need hand pollination. Needs good air circulation to minimize powdery mildew.
Cucumbers	8" deep 3+ gallons/plant	Full sun	Grow bush-types in hanging baskets or on a trellis (vines grow 18–24" long). Grow strong vining-types on trellis. Needs good air circulation to minimize powdery mildew. Young plants are very sensitive to wind burn.
Eggplant	8" deep 4–5 gallons/plant	Full sun	One plant per container. Needs night temperatures above 55°F for pollen development.
Peppers	8" deep 2–5 gallons/plant	Full sun	One plant per container or space to 14–18" in row. Needs night temperatures above 55°F for pollen development. Decorative, attractive plant with fruit.
Summer Squash (Zucchini)	36" by 36" space 8" deep 5 gallons/plant	Full sun	Compact varieties more suited to container gardening. Great in a whiskey barrel size container. One plant will produce 6 or more fruit per week. Has male and female blossoms. May need hand pollination. Needs good air circulation to minimize powdery mildew. Keep fruit picked for continued production.
Tomatoes	12" deep 2–5 gallons/plant (depending on variety (plant size)	Full sun	Varieties vary in mature plant size from determinate (bush) types to large, indeterminate vines over 6 feet tall. Patio types (small vines) are great for container gardening and may be grown as hanging baskets or trellised. Standard garden types require a larger container (like a whiskey barrel) and trellising. Needs night temperatures above 55°F for pollen development. Crowding cuts yields and increases disease potential. Blossom end rot (black sunken area on bottom of fruit) is a symptom of inconsistent watering or a soil that does not have enough water storage.

* Larger container sizes will make crop easier to care for, providing a bigger supply of water and nutrients.

1. Outline basic care of container-grown vegetables. How does it differ from growing container flowers?

UNIT J

Lawns

Learning Objectives

At the end of this unit, the student will be able to:

- Describe how lawn management practices influence turf quality and why incorrect management decisions lead to common lawn care problems.

- Describe which grass species are best adapted for lawn use, and the most important factors to consider when choosing a species for a new lawn (or when renovating an existing lawn).

- Describe how mowing height and frequency affect the aesthetic quality and stress tolerance of turfgrass; why grass clippings should be recycled back to the lawn during mowing.

- Describe why nitrogen is the most important nutrient in a lawn fertilization program, how and when to fertilize a lawn, and how to select the appropriate lawn fertilizer.

- Describe the environmental factors affecting turf water use and how to use that knowledge to most effectively irrigate a lawn (how MUCH water to apply, and how OFTEN).

- Describe thatch, understand why it forms in the lawn, what common problems its accumulation may cause, and how thatch is most effectively managed.

- Describe the negative effects of soil compaction on turf health and how to improve soil physical conditions by using common cultivation practices.

Supplemental Reading

- ***Integrated Turfgrass Management for the Northern Great Plains***. 1997. Baxendale, F.P. and Gaussoin, R.E. (eds.) University of Nebraska. Publication EC97-1557. 236 pages.

- ***Fundamentals of Turfgrass Management***. 2003. Christians, N.E. John Wiley & Sons. 368 pages. 2nd edition.

- ***Identifying Turf and Weedy Grasses of the Northern United States***. 2005. Pederson, D. and Voigt, T. University of Illinois Extension. 63 pages. Publication C1393. http://www.pubsplus.uiuc.edu

- ***Lawns: Your Guide to a Beautiful Yard.*** (2002 and 2007). Christians, N., Ritchie, A. and Mellor, D. Meredith Publishing.

- ***Weeds of the West***. 1991. The University of Wyoming. 630 pages.

Chapter
43*

Lawn Care

REASONS FOR LAWN PROBLEMS

Although there are many specific reasons to which one could attribute lawn problems, the most common general reasons include:

- Poor management decisions (soil compaction, improper mowing, irrigation, fertilization, pest management)
- Using poorly adapted species or cultivars. For additional information, refer to Chapter 44.
- Limitations in resources (water, time/labor, dollars)

MOWING THE LAWN

The two most important facets of mowing are mowing **height** and **frequency**. The **preferred height** for all species in a lawn is two and one-half to three inches. Mowing to less than two inches can result in decreased drought and heat tolerance (due to shallow rooting and reduced photosynthesis) and encouraged weed invasion. Higher height encourages insects, diseases, and weeds. Mow the lawn at the same height all year. There is no reason to mow the turf shorter in late summer or in the fall.

Mow the turf often enough so no more than one-third of the grass height is removed at any single mowing. This may mean mowing a bluegrass or fescue lawn every three to four days during the active spring growth period, but only once every seven to ten days at other times of the year when growth is slowed by heat, drought, or cold. If weather or another factor prevents mowing at the proper time, raise the height of the

---

*Authors: Tony Koski, PhD, Extension Turf Specialist, and David Whiting, Extension Consumer Horticulture Specialist; Department of Horticulture & LA; Colorado State University. Artwork by David Whiting.

mower temporarily to avoid cutting too much at one time. Cut the grass again a few days later at the normal mowing height (Figure 43-1).

Let **grass clippings** fall back onto the lawn while mowing, unless they are to be used for mulching elsewhere in the landscape. Grass clippings decompose quickly and provide a source of recycled nutrients (equivalent to one to one and one-half fertilizations per year) and organic matter for the lawn. Although a mulching or recycling mower makes this easier to do, clippings can be recycled into the lawn using any mower (as long as the 1/3 rule of mowing frequency is used). Grass clippings do not contribute to thatch accumulation.

Lawn Clippings and Surface Water Pollution

Lawn clippings and leaves mowed, swept, or blown onto the street are the major source of phosphorus pollution in urban lakes and streams. With side discharge lawnmowers, mow in a direction to prevent clippings from being blown onto the street, driveway, and other hard surfaces. Do not sweep or blow lawn clippings into the gutter and street (Figures 43-2 and 43-3).

Also, leave an unmowed grass buffer strip edging any lakes, streams, ponds, and wetlands (Figure 43-4).

In a natural setting, rain and snowmelt absorbs mostly into the soil. Air-borne pollutants and pollen washed out of the air are broken down by soil microorganism activity. The nitrogen and phosphorus released from the decay of grass, leaves, and other organic matter recycle back into the soil.

However, in the landscape setting, the water cycle is greatly changed by large areas covered by hard surfaces (streets, driveways, walks, parking lots, compacted soils, and buildings). In a typical landscape setting fifty-five percent of a rainfall moves as surface runoff, compared to only ten percent in a naturalized setting. Nutrients from grass and leaves (along with fertilizers, pesticides, and other water-soluble pollutants) readily wash off the hard surfaces into the storm sewer system. Here the pollutants end up in local streams, ponds, and lakes.

LAWN FERTILIZATION
Selecting a Lawn Fertilizer

Nitrogen (N) is the most important nutrient for promoting good turf color and growth. However, do not overstimulate the turf with excess nitrogen, especially during the spring and summer. Overfertilization can contribute to thatch buildup with some species, as well as increased mowing and irrigation requirements. Underfertilization of some species (bluegrass

Figure 43-1 ■ *Mow often enough that no more than one-third of the grass height is removed in any single mowing.*

Figure 43-2 ■ *In a Minnesota study, sixty to eighty percent of the phosphate loading of surface water in an urban setting came from lawn clippings and leaves that were mowed or blown into the streets.*

Figure 43-3 ■ *When mowing the lawn, mow in a direction to prevent clippings from being blown into the street.*

Figure 43-4 ■ *To reduce surface water pollution, leave an unmowed buffer strip around lakes, streams, and ponds.*

and ryegrass, for example) can result in poor turf color and turf thinning, which can encourage weed and disease problems. Turf species differ in both the amount of nitrogen required to keep them healthy, as well as the best time of the year to fertilize them.

Balanced or complete fertilizers contain various amounts of phosphorus, potassium, iron, and sulfur. They are a good safeguard against a potential nutrient deficiency and there is no harm in using a "complete" fertilizer. However, if you leave clippings on the lawn, these nutrients are recycled back into the lawn, so there is little likelihood of seeing these deficiencies. Besides nitrogen, the most commonly deficient nutrient in lawns is iron (Fe).

Organic fertilizers will work as effectively as synthetic types. However, it is important to understand the release characteristics of the different fertilizers so that they can be used at the correct times of the year. Organic fertilizers typically release nutrients more effectively when soils are warm and moist. Many synthetic types work well when soils are cooler, but some synthetic types work like the natural organic sources.

Better lawn fertilizers include a quick-release form of nitrogen for quick green-up, plus slow-release forms of nitrogen for sustained greening. Examples are listed in Table 43-1.

Table 43-1. Example of Quick- and Slow-Release Fertilizers

Quick-Release Nitrogen *for fast green-up*	Slow-Release Nitrogen *for sustained greening*
Ammonium sulfate Ammonium nitrate Potassium nitrate Urea	Resin-coated urea Sulfur-coated urea Isobutylidene diurea (IBDU) Methylene urea Urea formaldehyde
	Compost and manure Poultry waste Poultry feathers

When to Fertilize and How Much to Apply

The natural grass growth cycle influences proper fertilization time for lawns. Figure 43-5 illustrates typical root and shoot growth patterns of cool season turf grass species.

Figure 43-6 illustrates the influence on shoot growth when nitrogen fertilizer is applied. Heavy spring fertilization promotes shoot growth, reducing carbohydrate energy reserves and stress tolerance.

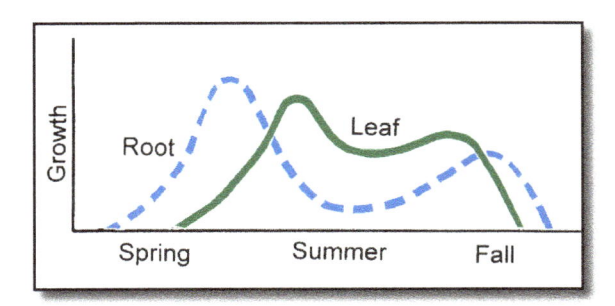

Figure 43-5 ■ *Growth cycle of roots and shoots for cool season turf.*

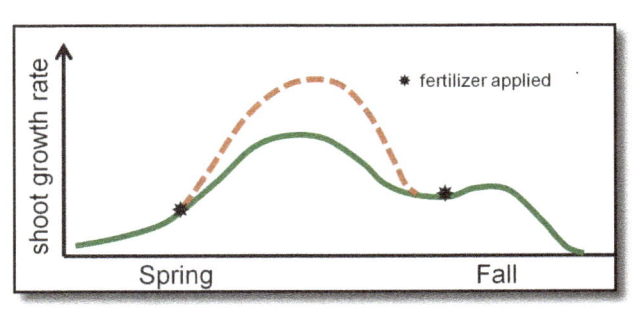

Figure 43-6 ■ *Influence on shoot growth for nitrogen fertilization.*

Benefits of Fall Fertilization on Cool Season Home Lawns

- Enhances storage of carbohydrate energy reserves
- Strengthens root system
- Increases shoot density
- Increases stress tolerance
- Better fall and winter color
- Earlier green-up in spring

Timing and Application Rate

Timing and application rates are given in Table 43-2. If lawn clippings are returned to the lawn, reduce application rate by one-quarter to one-third.

Table 43-2. Fertilizer Application Schedule for Established Colorado Lawns[1,2]

Turf Grass Species		Mid-March to April[3]	May to mid-June	July to early August	Mid-August to mid-September	Early October to early November[4]
(Nitrogen application rates are in pounds of nitrogen per 1,000 square feet of lawn area.)						
Cool Season Species	High maintenance Bluegrass and Ryegrass	½ to 1	1	Not required	1	1-(2)
	Low Maintenance Bluegrass	½	½–1	Not required	1	(1)
	Turf-Type Tall Fescue	½	½–1	Not required	1	(1)
	Turf-Type Fine Fescue	½	½–1	Not required	½–1	Not required
Warm Season Species	Buffalograss, Blue Grams, and Bermudagrass	Apply no N	½ to 1	½–1	Apply no N	Apply no N

[1] Nitrogen applications can often be reduced by 1/4 to 1/3 when grass clippings are returned to the lawn during mowing. Nitrogen and other nutrients contained in the clippings are recycled to the lawn as they decompose. **Grass clippings do not contribute to thatch accumulations in lawns.**

[2] On sandy soils, use slow-release nitrogen fertilizers (sulfur-coated ureas, IBDU, and natural organic-based fertilizers) throughout the year to reduce the potential for leaching loss. On very sandy soils, do not fertilize turf after late September. Nitrogen can leach into ground water during the winter months.

[3] The March-April nitrogen application may not be needed if fertilized in late fall (September to November) the previous years. If spring green-up and growth is satisfactory, delay fertilizing until May or June.

[4] Make the final fall nitrogen application (October–November) while the grass is still green and at least 2 to 3 weeks before the ground begins to freeze. Optional N applications shown in (). Use extra nitrogen applications where a higher quality turf is desired or on a heavily used turf.

Fertilizers and Water Pollution

Home lawn management techniques play a significant role in protecting or polluting surface water. Popular press has incorrectly labeled lawns as a major contributor to water pollution. It is not the lawn, but rather the management style of the gardener that becomes the problem.

Fertilizers and pesticides (herbicides, insecticides, and fungicides) spread onto hard surfaces (driveways, sidewalks, streets, and compacted soils) will move with surface water into neighboring lakes, streams, and ponds. (Surface water running down the street gutter is not treated before release into local lakes, streams, and ponds.)

However, phosphate fertilizer applied to a lawn or garden soil is bound to the soil and does not leach into ground water. The phosphate could move into surface water with soil erosion.

Organic fertilizers are not necessarily safer for the environment. The pollution potential is based on where the fertilizer is applied and application rates. Any fertilizer becomes a potential pollution problem when over spread into hard surfaces. Overapplication of both manufactured and organic fertilizers have been linked to ground water contamination.

Potential pollution problems arise from the careless application rather than the type of fertilizer applied. In most western soils, lawns do not need phosphate fertilizers.

LAWN IRRIGATION

Many factors influence lawn water requirements, and no two lawns will have exactly the same needs. Table 43-3 gives the typical water requirement (rain plus irrigation) per week. A healthy, high-quality bluegrass or ryegrass lawn may require up to 2 to 2¼ inches of water per week under hot, dry, windy summer conditions—but may require much less when the weather is cool or cloudy. Turf-type tall fescue may perform well with less irrigation than a bluegrass lawn, if it can grow a deep root system and the soil in which it is growing is holding usable water. In many cases, however, a tall fescue may require as much water as bluegrass to look good.

Table 43-3. Typical Water Requirement (Rain Plus Irrigation) for Colorado Lawns

October	Late April	May & June	July & August	September	Early
Inches of water per week (irrigation plus rain)	0.75"	1.0"	1.5"	1.0"	0.75"

Buffalograss and blue grama lawns can remain green for weeks without watering, even during the hottest summer weather, with rainfall.

Shady lawns (not in the rooting zone of large trees) and areas protected from the wind require less water over the growing season than more exposed turf. However, the roots of mature trees and shrubs also need water. You may have to water more in mature landscapes where the roots of many plants compete for water. Healthy turf encouraged by proper mowing, fertilizing, and cultivation uses water more efficiently.

How Much Water?

Each time you water the lawn, apply enough water to moisten as much of the root zone as possible. Use a soil probe or shovel to determine what the average rooting depth is in your lawn. If the roots grow down six inches deep, water so the soil is moistened to that depth. It is important to know not only how deep the turf roots grow, but also how deep your irrigation water penetrates. Watering too deeply, especially on sandy soils, wastes water and allows it to percolate past the root zone (Figure 43-7).

How Often Should a Lawn Be Watered?

Grass growing on a sandy soil must be watered more often than the same grass growing on clay or loam soils. Even after a thorough watering, sandy soils hold little plant-available moisture. They require more frequent irrigation with smaller amounts of water.

Conversely, turf growing on clayey soils can be irrigated less frequently, with larger quantities of water. Watering less often means more efficient water use because of less loss to evaporation. It can also reduce the number of weeds that appear in the lawn.

Figure 43-7 ▮ *Typical water requirement (rain plus irrigation) is given in Table 43-3. However, actual water use jumps around from day to day based on temperature, wind, humidity, and solar radiation (sunny or cloudy).*

With most soils, do not apply all of the water in a short period of time. If applied too quickly, water will run off of thatchy turf, from sloped areas, or from turf growing on heavy clay or compacted soils. In these cases, it is more effective to apply only a portion of the water and move the sprinkler or switch to another station to water another section of the lawn. Cycling through irrigation stations ("soak cycles") will promote infiltration and reduce runoff and puddling in low spots. This allows water to soak into the soil rather than run off.

Core cultivation (aeration) can resolve some infiltration problems by reducing thatch and compaction. Wetting agents may enhance water movement into the soil, but they should not be considered a cure-all, especially when compaction and thatch are problems.

What Are Some Signs That Turf Needs to Be Watered?

A sure sign that turf requires irrigation is a wilted appearance. One symptom is "footprinting," where footprints on the lawn that do not disappear within an hour or so following traffic. This symptom is soon followed by actual wilting, where the turf takes on a grayish or purple-to-blue cast. If only a few such spots regularly appear in the same general location, spot water them to delay watering the entire lawn for another day or so. These indicator spots help predict that the entire lawn will soon need watering.

A hardened or toughened lawn, attained through less frequent, deep irrigation, often withstands minor drought and generally has fewer disease problems. It is important, however, that the turf not be allowed to become overly drought-stressed between waterings. This weakens the turf and makes it more susceptible to insect and disease damage and to weed invasion.

During extended dry periods from late fall to spring, it may be necessary to "**winter water**" every four to six weeks if the ground is thawed and will accept water. Pay particular attention to exposed slopes, sites with shallow soil, and south- or west-facing exposures, where winter mites may infest and kill drought-stressed turf during the winter and early spring.

The most efficient **time of day** to water is late evening and early morning (between 9 p.m. and 9 a.m.). It generally is less windy, cooler, and more humid at this time, resulting in less evaporation and more efficient use of water. Water pressure is generally better, optimizing sprinkler distribution patterns. Contrary to popular belief, watering at night (after 9 p.m.) does not encourage disease development in turf.

THATCH IN LAWNS

Thatch is a tight, brown, spongy, organic layer of both living and dead grass roots and stems that accumulates above the soil surface. Factors that lead to thatch problems include the following (Figure 43-8):

- **Sod over compacted soil**—When sod is laid over compacted soils, a thatch problem will develop in a couple of years.

- **Soil compaction** is a common contributor to thatch buildup as it slows the activity of soil microorganisms.

- **Overfertilization** is a common contributor to thatch buildup as the lawn may be growing faster than the microorganism can break it down.

- **Grass species**—Thatch tends to be a problem on Kentucky bluegrass, bentgrass, and fine fescue lawns. It is rarely a problem with tall fescue or buffalograss.

- **Frequent heavy irrigation** may contribute to thatch as lower soil oxygen levels slow the activity of soil microorganisms.

- **Pesticides**—Excessive use of some pesticides may also slow soil organism activity.

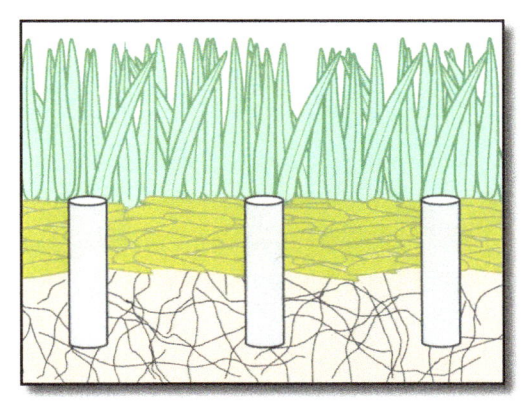

Figure 43-8 ■ *Thatch is a tight, brown, spongy, organic layer of both living and dead grass roots and stems that accumulates above the soil surface.*

Grass clippings do not contribute to thatch accumulation and should be returned to the lawn during mowing to recycle the nutrients they contain.

Measure thatch depth by removing a small piece of turf, including the underlying soil. Up to one-half to three-quaters inch of thatch is acceptable and will enhance traffic tolerance. The thatch depth can increase quickly beyond this point, making it difficult to control later. As the thatch layer thickens, it becomes the main rooting medium for the grass. This predisposes the turf to drought stress or winterkill and increases the possibility for insect, disease, and weed problems. In addition, fertilizers and pesticides applied to a thatchy lawn work less effectively.

Power Raking for Thatch Management

This method of thatch removal has been used for years. Light (shallow) power raking may be beneficial if done often. Deep power raking of a thatch lawn can be damaging, and often removes a substantial portion of the living turf. Used properly, power raking of wet, matted turf can speed spring green-up by letting air move into the root zone and warm the turf. Compost all removed thatch and organic material to kill any living grass before it is used as a mulch or soil amendment.

Core Cultivation or Aerating

This can be more beneficial than power raking. It helps improve root zone conditions by relieving soil compaction, while controlling thatch accumulation. Soil compaction, in fact, is one factor that contributes to thatch buildup. Aeration removes plugs of thatch and soil 2 to 3 inches long (the longer, the better) and deposits them on the lawn. Enough passes should be made to achieve two-inch spacing between holes.

What is done with the cores is a matter of personal choice. From a cultural perspective, there may be an advantage to allowing the cores to disintegrate and filter back down into the lawn. Mingling soil and thatch may hasten the natural decomposition of the thatch. The little fluffs of thatch and turf that remain behind can be collected and composted. Depending on soil type, core disintegration may take a few days to several weeks. Irrigation helps wash the soil from the cores. Running over dried cores with a rotary mower can be effective but will dull the blade. If the cores are removed from the lawn, compost before using as a mulch or soil amendment.

SOIL COMPACTION

Soil compaction is the most common problem in lawn quality. With reduced soil oxygen levels, rooting systems will be more shallow. With compaction, the grass roots have reduced access to water and nutrients. Irrigation and fertilization will need to be light and more frequent.

Aerating (removing plugs) once or twice a year will help reduce soil compaction in an established lawn area if enough passes are made to yield plugholes at two-inch intervals. The best time of year to aerate a lawn is late August to late September, as fewer weed seeds germinate this time of year. Aerating the lawn area around a tree is also the best method to promote tree vigor (Figure 43-9).

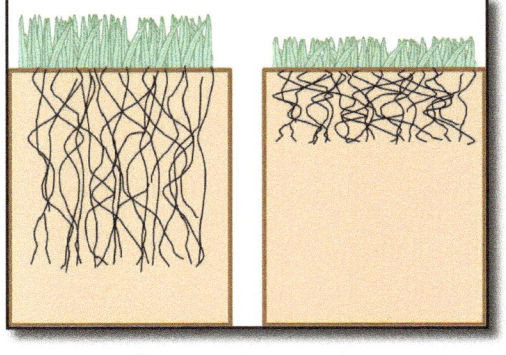

Figure 43-9 ▪ *Core aeration helps reduce soil compaction when enough passes are made over the lawn to yield plugholes at two-inch intervals.*

WEED MANAGEMENT

Lawn weed killers provide only temporary control if management factors that favor weeds are not addressed. In a thin turf with heavy traffic, weed problems may intensify following the use of weed killers. When the weeds (which help absorb the wear and tear of foot traffic) are removed with weed killers, the lawn may thin. The thin lawn opens the soil to increased weed problems.

Soil compaction is the primary cause of weed problems. Weed management factors include the following:

Figure 43-10 ▪ *Deep infrequent watering will drought out many common shallow root lawn weeds.*

- **Core aeration**—Soil compaction favors weeds and discourages lawn growth. Common lawn weeds including annual bluegrass, black medic, chickweed, clover, crabgrass, knotweed, prostrate spurge, and plantain thrive in compacted soils. Clover may be a good companion crop for lawns in compacted soils, filling in between the thin grass.

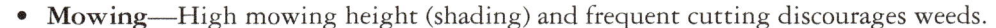

- **Mowing**—High mowing height (shading) and frequent cutting discourages weeds.

- **Watering**—Deep, infrequent watering will drought out many common shallow-rooted lawn weeds (Figure 43-10).

- **Limited fertilizer**—A thick, actively growing turf chokes out most weeds. However, fertilizer will not thicken up a turf when soil compaction is the growth-limiting factor.

For additional information on turf weed management, refer to these Colorado State University Extension publications available online at www.cmg.colostate.edu.

- *Annual Grassy Weed Control in Lawns*, Extension fact sheet #3.101

- *Broadleaf Weed Control in Lawns*, CMG GardenNotes #552

INSECT AND DISEASE MANAGEMENT

In semi-arid climates like Colorado, turf insect and disease problems are minimal, compared to other areas of the nation.

Frequent use of lawn insecticides may increase the occurrence of lawn insect problems. Some garden insecticides have a potential to kill birds feeding in the treated areas (refer to the insecticide label). Thus, avoid unwarranted treatments of lawn areas.

When controlling soil insects, the insecticide must be watered into the root zone to be effective. Some insecticides get held up in the thatch and do not water in effectively.

In semi-arid climates like Colorado, lawn diseases are minimal, compared to other areas of the nation. With Colorado's dry climate, fungicides do little to nothing for home lawn disease management. Cultural practices (fertilizer, watering, and soil compaction) are the keys to disease management (Table 43-4).

For additional information, refer to the following CSU Extension publications, available online at www.cmg.colostate.edu.

- *Ascochyta Leaf Blight of Turf*—Extension fact sheet #2.901
- *Billbugs and White Grubs*—Extension fact sheet #5.516
- *Clover and Other Mites of Turfgrass*—Extension fact sheet #5.505
- *Clover Mites*—Planttalk #1408
- *Dog Urine Damage on Lawns: Causes, Cures and Prevention*, CMG GardenNotes #553
- *Dollar Spot Disease of Turfgrass*—Extension fact sheet #2.933
- *Dollar Spot of Turfgrass*—Planttalk #1522
- *Earthworm and Nightcrawlers in the Home Lawn*, CMG GardenNotes #554
- Fairy Ring—*Mushrooms and Fairy Ring*—Planttalk #1506
- *Insects*—Planttalk #1514
- *Japanese Beetles*—Extension fact sheet #5.601
- *Leaf Blight of Turf*—Planttalk #1527
- *Leaf Spot and Melting Out*—Planttalk #1524
- *Leafhoppers on Lawns*—Extension fact sheet #5.608
- *Mites on Turfgrass*—Planttalk #1467
- *Mushrooms and Fairy Rings*—Planttalk #1506
- *Necrotic Ring Spot in Turfgrass*—Extension fact sheet #2.900
- *Necrotic Ring Spot on Kentucky Bluegrass*—Planttalk #1528
- *Patchy Lawn*—Planttalk #1509
- *Slime Mold*—Planttalk #1435

Table 43-4. Influence of Cultural Practices on Kentucky Bluegrass Diseases

	Soil Compaction	High N	Low N	Thatch	Irrigation	Mowing
Asochyta Leaf Blight	yes	yes		yes	timing	yes
Necrotic Ring Spot	yes	yes		yes	drought with heat	yes
Leafspot and Melting Out	yes	yes	yes	yes	timing (wet/dry cycle)	yes
Gray Snow Mold	yes	yes				
Dollarspot	yes		yes	yes	drought	low
Stripped Smut			yes	yes		
Fairy Ring	yes		yes	yes		

1. What is the best mowing height for lawns?

2. My neighbor mows their lawn 2 or 3 times a week. I mow only on Saturday morning. Who is right?

3. Should I mow higher or lower during the summer?

4. Will I have less turf disease if I mow my lawn shorter in the fall, just before winter?

5. Shouldn't grass clippings be collected because they create thatch in lawns?

6. How should I mow my lawn when it gets very tall?

7. Do I have to buy a mulching mower to return my grass clippings?

8. What is the impact of mowing lawn clippings and leaves into the street?

9. What is the best fertilizer for my lawn? Explain the pros and cons for spring versus fall fertilization.

10. How often should I fertilize my lawn?

11. How important is it to use a "complete" lawn fertilizer?

12. How does leaving the clippings influences the amount of fertilizer needed?

13. Explain concerns about lawn fertilizer polluting surface water. Does phosphate leach from fertilized lawns?

14. What is thatch? How does a heavy layer of thatch influence turf quality?

15. What factors lead to thatch buildup? Does leaving lawn clippings lead to thatch buildup?

16. How is thatch managed?

17. In a weedy lawn, what is the impact of removing weeds with herbicides?

18. List cultural techniques to manage lawn weed problems.

Chapter

44*

Lawn Selection

SPECIES SELECTION

There are many factors that should be considered when selecting a turfgrass species for planting in a new lawn situation:

- First, consider what will be the use of the turf. For example, is it being planted strictly for aesthetic purposes, or will it be played on heavily and/or frequently?

- What is the desired level of visual quality?

- Will the turf receive a high level of maintenance? Alternatively, will it receive only minimal amounts of water and fertilizer, and little or no pest control?

- What is the owner's interest in irrigated, summer green lawns versus a summer dormant lawn? Is there a readily available supply of inexpensive water? On the other hand, is the water supply limited or expensive? Is the owner willing to pay for the amount of water that might be required to maintain a specific turfgrass species at the desired quality level? Is the water salty?

- Is the soil sandy or clayey? Does the soil have high salt levels or poor drainage?

- Is the lawn area sunny or shady?

- What is the elevation?

- How quickly must a turf cover appear, and how hard is the owner willing to work in establishing the lawn?

- Is there a history of a certain insect, mite, or disease problems on the site?

- Is there willingness to use pesticides, or are they totally out of the question?

- Will the lawn be sodded or seeded?

*Author: Tony Koski, PhD, Extension Turf Specialist; Department of Horticulture & LA; Colorado State University.

Unfortunately, few people ask such questions before establishing a new turf. The basic assumption is that Kentucky bluegrass must be planted, and little consideration is given to alternative turfgrass species. The following descriptions of available turfgrass species, including available cultivars (a cultivar is a cultivated or man-made variety of a plant species), provide information that might allow selection of a species better adapted for a specific situation.

There are large numbers of commercially available cultivars for most turfgrass species, but all of them will never be available for sale by one seed company, much less a nursery or garden center. Local seed companies align themselves with specific national seed growers, thus limiting the number of cultivars sold by them. The selection of species and cultivars offered by even the best garden centers is generally quite limited. Local seed companies are often willing to sell smaller amounts of seed to the homeowner, and usually at a very reasonable price.

What Does "Low-Maintenance" Mean?

"Low-maintenance turf" means different things to different people. To some, it means NO maintenance (no water, no fertilizer, no/infrequent mowing, no/little pest control), such as the way in which roadside turf is managed. To most, however, it means reduced levels of irrigation, fertilization, and pest control.

The quality expectations of a low-maintenance turf should not be high, since minimal inputs can only be expected to produce a turf of minimal quality. Proper selection of species and/or cultivar is important, because some species do not persist under low maintenance or neglect.

Table 44-1. Turfgrass Persistence under Low Maintenance (1 = best persistence; 10 = worst persistence)

Common Name	Scientific Name	Persistence Ranking	
Buffalograss	*Buchloe dactyloides*	1	BEST
Blue grama	*Bouteloua gracilis*	1	
Wheatgrass	*Agropyron* spp.	1	
Smooth bromegrass	*Bromus inermis*	1–2	
Hard fescue	*Festuca longifolia*	2–3	
Sheep fescue	*Festuca ovina*	2–3	
Creeping fescues	*Festuca rubra* spp. *rubra/trichophylla*	3–5	
Chewings fescue	*Festuca rubra* spp. *commutata*	3–5	
Tall fescue	*Festuca arundinacea*	5–6	
Common Kentucky bluegrass	*Poa pratensis*	6	
Improved Kentucky bluegrass	*Poa pratensis*	8	
Perennial ryegrass	*Lolium perenne*	9–10	WORST

KENTUCKY BLUEGRASS (*Poa Pratensis*)

Kentucky bluegrass, *Poa pratensis*, has been a standard for the beautiful green lawn since the days of King Louis of France due to its dense stand, rich bluish-green color, and wear tolerance. There are hundreds of different cultivars with vast differences, characteristics, and management needs.

Advantages
+ Sod-forming (has underground rhizomes)
+ High recuperative potential and rate
+ Soft, easily mowed leaves
+ High quality (color, density)

+ Readily available in sod form
+ Excellent heat and cold tolerance
+ Good drought resistance (can go dormant and survive long periods without water)

Disadvantages
- Thatch-former
- More disease (leaf spot, necrotic ring spot, *Ascochyta* leaf blight)
- Poor to fair shade tolerance
- More frequent insect problems (billbug, grubs, mites)
- Poor to fair salt tolerance
- Higher nitrogen requirement than other grasses
- May require more frequent irrigation to maintain quality
- Will invade flower and vegetable gardens

Suggested seeding rate: three to five pounds per 1,000 square feet.

Recommended Kentucky Bluegrass Cultivars

Cultivar names in **BOLD** have exhibited better traffic tolerance

America	Full Moon	NuGlade
Arcadia	**Julius**	Odyssey
Avalanche	Kingfisher	Orfeo
Award	Langara	P-105
Awesome	Limousine	Prosperity
Bedazzled	Marquis	**Quantum Leap**
Bewitched	**Midnight**	Rampart
Bordeaux	**Midnight Star**	**Rugby II**
Brilliant	Moonbeam	SR2284
Cheetah	**Moonlight**	**Touchdown**
Diva	**Moon Shadow**	Ulysses
Everest	**NuDestiny**	

Hybrid (Kentucky X Texas) Bluegrass

In the 1990s, Dr. James Read of Texas A&M University, successfully crossed Kentucky bluegrass (*Poa pratensis*) and Texas bluegrass (*Poa arachnifera*, a bluegrass species native to the Panhandle of Texas). He named the first commercially available variety 'Reveille.' There are a number of potential advantages to using these Kentucky x Texas bluegrass hybrids for lawn and sports turf applications in Colorado. The following observations and comments are based on limited research at Colorado State University, as well as field observations and testimonials from sod producers and those who have planted these hybrids in the Western United States.

1. *Excellent heat tolerance.* This grass, in fact, seems to grow better the warmer it gets in the summer. The growth and vigor of most Kentucky bluegrass varieties will generally decline under high heat (temperatures in the upper 80s to 100s), which can reduce its traffic and wear tolerance during the hottest times of the growing season. The hybrid bluegrasses appear to maintain more active summer growth, which translates into better traffic tolerance and ability to recover from traffic injury.

2. *Deep and extensive root production.* These hybrids produce an extensive root system, which can enhance heat and drought resistance. A dense root system will also improve traffic tolerance, ability to recover from wear, and will improve footing (traction) in a sports turf application.

3. *Extensive and aggressive rhizome formation.* These grasses form large, extensive, and aggressive rhizomes (underground stems). Different from roots, rhizomes contain growing points that produce new grass plants. Grasses that produce rhizomes are better able to tolerate traffic and will recover more

quickly from traffic-induced wear—often without the need to reseed the worn areas. An aggressive rhizome system also means better traction in a sports turf situation.

4. *Low mowing height tolerance.* Its excellent heat tolerance and aggressive root and rhizome formation characteristics allow this grass, when necessary, to be mowed at lower heights than many Kentucky bluegrasses—especially during the heat of summer. This can be important for "showcase" sports turf applications.

5. *Potential to require less irrigation.* Variability exists among the hybrid bluegrasses with respect to irrigation requirement and drought resistance. Research has shown some of them to possess very good drought resistance (compared to other bluegrasses, and even to tall fescue), whereas other varieties are only moderately (or have poor) drought resistant. The ability to sustain growth and vigor with less irrigation results from deeper roots and its excellent heat tolerance.

Commercially Available Hybrid Bluegrass Cultivars
- Fahrenheit 90 (Mountain View Seeds)
- Fire and Ice (Turf Merchants)
- Longhorn (Scotts Turf-Seed)
- Bandera (Seed Research of Oregon)
- Spitfire (Seed Research of Oregon)
- Reveille (Gardner Turfgrass)
- Dura Blue (Scotts)
- Solar Green (Scotts)
- Thermal Blue (Scotts)
- Thermal Blue Blaze (Scotts)

TURF-TYPE TALL FESCUE (*Festuca arundinacea*)

Seed distributors often sell turf-type tall fescue blends that are combinations of two to five different tall fescue varieties. These blends are ideal for home lawn use and are generally less expensive than buying a single variety. The use of tall fescue named "K-31" or "Kentucky 31" is discouraged, as this type of tall fescue provides poor quality turf.

Advantages
+ Establishes quickly
+ Drought-resistant (deep-rooted)
+ Wear-tolerant
+ Few disease problems
+ Few insect problems
+ Turf types possess nice texture and deep green color
+ Excellent heat and cold tolerance
+ Slow thatch-former
+ Does well in shade
+ Good salt tolerance
+ Slow to invade flower and vegetable gardens

Disadvantages
− Seeding can produce poor results unless done very carefully.
− Sod availability more limited, compared to bluegrass.
− Leaf shredding more common when mower blade is dull.
− Some varieties must be mowed more often than bluegrass.
− Heavy use by children and/or pets can produce worn areas that may require overseeding.
− If rooting is restricted by poor soil, may require the same amount of irrigation as Kentucky bluegrass (or more!).

Suggested seeding rate: six to eight pounds per 1,000 square feet.

Recommendations for Turf-Type Fall Fescue Cultivars

3rd millennium SRP	Firecracker LS	Renovate
AST 7002	Firenza	Reunion
AST9001	Gazelle II	Rhambler SRP
AST9002	Hudson	Skyline
AST9003	Hunter	Speedway
Biltmore	Justice	Spyder LS
Bullseye	Lindbergh	SR 8650
Cezanne	Magellan	Talladega
Compete	Monet	Tulsa Time
Darlington	Mustang 4	Turbo
Einstein	Padre	Van Gogh
Escalade	Raptor II	Wolfpack II
Faith	Rembrandt	

BUFFALOGRASS (*Buchloë dactyloides*)

Buffalograss (*Buchloë dactyloides*) is a perennial, warm season grass species. It is a sod-forming grass that spreads by stolons (aboveground stems) which root at nodes, forming new plants. Buffalograss is native to the North American Great Plains, and displays a wide range of adaptability. An important range and pasture grass for both wild and domesticated animal herds, its use as an alternative lawn grass was proposed as early as the 1930s. Older range-type varieties form an open, low-density turf when mowed; the newer, turf-type buffalograss varieties can form a dense, attractive turf during its active growing season.

Because of its warm season physiology, this species becomes dormant with the onset of cold temperatures in the fall and breaks dormancy in mid- to late spring, well after bluegrass and fescue lawns become green. In Colorado's climate, Buffalograss grows most actively from late May through early September, becoming brown and dormant with the first hard frost in the fall. Its long dormant period and reputation as an expensive and difficult-to-establish lawn has made it a less attractive lawn option for many homeowners.

However, the development of attractive turf-type cultivars and greater availability of less expensive sod and plugs has generated new interest in this grass for home lawns. These new varieties are darker green, form a dense, short-growing turf, and are more resistant to weed invasion than previously used varieties. Those who choose to plant newer buffalograss varieties find that their lawn can remain green and attractive on fifty to seventy-five percent less irrigation than Kentucky bluegrass, and that buffalograss requires less frequent mowing, will thrive when fertilized only once or twice yearly, and has good resistance to weed invasion.

Advantages

+ Excellent heat and drought resistance
+ Excellent cold tolerance
+ Few disease and insect problems
+ Sod-former (aggressive stolons)
+ Low fertility requirement
+ Requires only infrequent mowing
+ Can be established from seed, sod, plugs
+ A native species

Disadvantages

− Warm season grass; becomes straw-colored with first hard fall frost and begins to green up in mid- to late May.
− Poor to fair shade tolerance. Needs at least a half day of full sun.
− Fair salt tolerance. Not adapted to soils with greater than 5–8 mmhos/cm salinity.
− Not recommended for use over 6,500 feet elevation. A protected, sunny, south- or west-facing exposure

may allow buffalograss to be used successfully at 6,500 to 7,000 feet.

— Not well adapted to very droughty, sandy soils—unless supplemental irrigation is provided.
— Will not tolerate heavy, constant traffic. Not well adapted to small, heavily used home lawns, athletic fields (soccer, football), or other situations where foot or vehicular traffic will be concentrated and constant.
— Prone to weed invasion if overfertilized or overwatered.
— Aggressive stolons may invade flower beds, neighboring lawns.

Recommended Cultivars

Turf-type seeded cultivars of buffalograss that will produce a good quality lawn include: Bison, Bowie, Cody, Plains, and Topgun. The varieties Texoka and Sharp's Improved will produce a lesser quality lawn.

Certain varieties of buffalograss are only available in vegetative form (sod or plugs). These varieties will form the best quality buffalograss lawn, but are more expensive than using the seeded types. Commercially available vegetative types include: Prairie, 609, Legacy, Prestige, and Turffalo. Prairie and 609 will suffer significant winterkill during most winters if planted along the Colorado Front Range, and are not recommended except in Pueblo and southeastern Colorado and in the Grand Junction area. Legacy, Prestige, and Turffalo have proven to be quite winter hardy throughout Colorado and will produce high quality buffalograss turf.

Buffalograss Establishment

Acceptance of buffalograss in the marketplace is critically dependent on the knowledge of proper establishment and management. Although it can be considered a low maintenance grass, proper management is necessary to realize the full benefits of the species. The amount of water required to establish a buffalograss lawn from seed, sod, or plugs will be equal to (and occasionally greater than) that amount required to establish a bluegrass or tall fescue lawn.

Seeding

Proper seedbed preparation is critical in obtaining uniform stands. Seed should be planted to one-half inch depth (drill seeding is preferred). If broadcast, seed should be covered with one-quarter to one-half inch of soil to obtain a reasonable stand. Seeding should begin in mid-late May or early June. Seeding too late in the season (beyond August 1) may result in winter seedling loss. Suggested seeding rate: two (drilled) to three (if broadcast) pounds per 1,000 square feet.

With warm soil and consistent irrigation, germination and appearance of seedlings will occur in seven to twenty-one days. Pre-emergent herbicides should not be used at the time of seeding, but may be safe after seed has germinated. Apply one pound of nitrogen (N) per 1,000 square feet two to three weeks after the seedlings appear; fertilize again about six weeks later. Irrigate to prevent excessive drying and to maintain active grass growth.

Plugging

The use of prerooted plugs can provide complete cover within eight to twelve weeks after planting. Proper soil preparation is essential for successful establishment using plugs. Plant plugs on twelve to eighteen inch centers following the last spring frost and at least six weeks prior to the first expected fall frost. Apply one pound of N per 1,000 square feet using a starter-type fertilizer at planting, and again about six to seven weeks after planting. Irrigate to maintain a moist surface for seven to ten days, and to maintain active grass growth thereafter. The pre-emergence herbicide pendimethalin (sold as Pre-M or Scotts Halts/Crabgrass Preventer) can be used to prevent weed invasion and is safe to use at the time of planting.

Transplanted plugs will often go dormant (become brown) after planting, even with adequate irrigation. This is quite normal. The grass will come out of dormancy after the plugs have formed a healthy root system. It is important that the plugs and soil be kept moist after planting, even though the plugs may appear to be dead or dormant.

Sodding

Buffalograss can be sodded like many other grass species to produce an instant lawn. Adequate soil preparation and careful post-plant care will aid in sod establishment. Transplanted buffalograss sod should be irrigated like any other transplanted sod—enough water to maintain a moist, but not saturated, root zone under the sod. It is very common for buffalograss sod to quickly turn brown following transplanting, even when irrigated. It may remain dormant for one to two weeks while new roots are being formed. New, white root growth can be seen on the bottom of the sod after a few days of watering, even though the top of the sod may be entirely brown in color. After enough rooting has occurred, the buffalograss will begin to form new leaves and green up. Proper irrigation is crucial during this root formation period.

PERENNIAL RYEGRASS *(Lolium Perenne)*

Advantages
+ Quick establishment
+ Wear-tolerant
+ Good color and density
+ Does not form thatch
+ Compatible in color and texture with bluegrass
+ May contain endophytes
+ Good heat tolerance
+ Can possess good drought resistance (if deep-rooted in well-prepared soil)
+ Moderate to good salt tolerance (6 to10 mmhos/cm)

Disadvantages
− Poor recuperative potential
− Leaf shredding common (dull mowers)
− Disease-prone (rust, leafspot)
− Poor shade tolerance
− Unavailable as pure sod
− Poor freezing tolerance if flooded or exposed to wind

Suggested seeding rate: six to eight pounds per 1,000 square feet.

Recommendations for Perennial Ryegrass Cultivars

1G squared	Defender	La Quinta
Accent II	Derby Xtreme	Line drive GLS
Allstar 3	Edge II	LS 2300
Amazing GS	Exacta II Glsr	Mach I
Apple GL	Fiesta 4	Majesty II
ASP 6004	Fiji	Monterey 3
Attribute	Firebolt	Nexus XR
Baccarat	Forever	Overdrive
Barlennium	Fusion	Palace
Brea	Galatti	Palmer IV
Brightstar SLT	Grand slam 2	Palmer V
Buena Vista	Gray star	Panther GLS
Cabo II	Harrier	Paragon GLR
Caddieshack II	Hawkeye 2	Pentium
Calypso 3	Homerun	Phenom
Cutter II	Inspire	Pizzazz
Dart	Keystone 2	Plateau
Dasher 3	Kokomo II	Pleasure Supreme

Premier II	Secretatiat II GLSR	Transformer
Primary	Silver Dollar	Uno
Prototype	Soprano	Wayfarer
Quick Silver	SR 4600	Wind dance 2
Regal 5	Stellar GL	Zoom
Repell GLS Revenge GLX	Sunshine 2	
Ringer II	Top Gun II	

FINE FESCUES (*Festuca* spp.)

The fine fescues are among the most complex groups of turfgrass species, comprising at least five different types. Hard fescue, Chewings fescue, (blue) sheep fescue, creeping red fescue, and slender creeping red fescue are the five species or subspecies. Although all are fescues, they differ both in appearance and where they are most effectively used. In general, this group of grasses performs well in the cooler, more temperate climates of the world (including cool, maritime locations). In North America, the fine fescues do well where most cool season turfgrasses are used. The relative advantages and disadvantages of using the fine fescues for turf are as follows:

Advantages
+ Quick germination (but matures slowly)
+ Fine leaf texture
+ High leaf density
+ Prefers low nitrogen fertility
+ Tolerates poor (rocky, sandy, clay) soil conditions
+ Drought-resistant (but will go dormant)
+ Moderate salt tolerance (6 to 10 mmhos/cm)
+ Very good shade tolerance
+ Very cold tolerant
+ EXCELLENT high elevation/mountain grass

Disadvantages
– Moderate wear tolerance (NOT for high traffic areas)
– Slow to recuperate from traffic injury
– Can become thatch
– May be difficult to mow (lays down; "tough" leaves)
– May go dormant during extended (1 to 2 weeks) heat (90s +)
– Susceptible to red thread, leaf spot, and dollar spot

Suggested seeding rate: five pounds per 1,000 square feet.

Types

Hard fescue (*Festuca longifolia* or *duriuscula*) is gaining wider use due to its better heat tolerance, relative to the other fine fescues. This better tolerance to warm summer conditions makes it especially well suited to use in the Front Range of Colorado. As with the other fine fescues, hard fescue performs best with minimal nitrogen fertilization and when soil is kept on the drier side (but supplemental irrigation is required to keep a good hard fescue lawn in Colorado). This is a bunch grass, so uniform seeding at establishment is essential for obtaining a good quality lawn.

Chewings fescue (*Festuca rubra* subp. commutata), named after George Chewings of New Zealand (who discovered and first sold the seed of this species in the late 1800s), is typical of the fine fescues in that it possesses excellent shade tolerance. It has a darker green color and very fine texture, resulting in a very good quality turf. This species does not creep, so uniform seeding is essential.

Creeping red fescue (*Festuca rubra* subp. rubra) is a creeping fine fescue with rhizomes that has been used in shady lawn seed mixtures for years. 'Pennlawn' was commonly used a number of years ago. A common type possessing lesser turf qualities, grown in large amounts in Canada is sold in lower quality, less expensive seed mixes (sometimes called 'Boreal' in these mixes). Improved cultivars, sometimes referred to as "strong creeping red fescue," are produced in the Pacific Northwest, with a few being imported from Europe.

Slender creeping red fescue (*Festuca rubra* subp. litoralis) produces rhizomes, but is not as vigorous a grower as (strong) creeping red fescue. These fescues are tolerant of lower mowing heights, which can allow their use in golf course fairways. However, the biggest advantage of fine fescues in this grouping lies in their generally good to excellent salinity tolerance. This makes them attractive for use where deicing salts are aggressively used. Their fine texture and compatible color allow them to be mixed with alkaligrass (*Puccinellia distans*). 'Fults' is the most commonly planted alkaligrass variety for use on salty soils.

Sheep fescue (*Festuca ovina*), sometimes called "blue sheep fescue" is generally used in lower maintenance lawns, performing especially well in infrequently or unmowed, naturalized lawn areas. They are long-lived bunch grasses that mix well with wildflowers, without dominating them. Some sheep fescues have been developed to produce a blue-green or glaucous green color (Azay Blue, SR3200), whereas others are more powder blue or "flat" blue in color (Azay, Quatro).

Recommendations for Fine Fescue Cultivars

Chewing	*Creeping*	*Hard*	*Sheep's*
Ambassador	Aberdeen	Berkshire	Quatro
Compass	Audubon	Firefly	
Intrigue 2	Cardinal	Gotham	
J-5 (Jamestown 5)	Class One	Oxford	
LaCrosse	Epic	Predator	
Longfellow II	Fortitude (TL 53)	Reliant IV	
SR 5130	Garnet	Scaldis	
Treasure II	Pathfinder	Spartan II	
Zodiac	Shoreline	SR 3000	
	Wendy Jean		

BLUE GRAMA (*Bouteloua gracilis*)

Advantages

+ Excellent cold, heat, drought tolerance
+ Low fertility requirement
+ Requires infrequent mowing
+ Few insect and disease problems
+ Rapid germination and establishment
+ Native species

Disadvantages

− Warm season grass that becomes straw-colored with first frost in fall, greening up in late spring (May)
− Not traffic-tolerant
− Not shade-tolerant
− Not a sod-forming grass
− Not adapted to high elevations (>6,500 feet)
− High seed cost
− Difficult to seed (high % inert component; "fluffy")

Suggested seeding rate: one to three pounds per 1,000 square feet.

CRESTED WHEATGRASS (*Agropyron* spp.)

Advantages
+ Excellent cold, heat, drought tolerance
+ Low fertility requirement
+ Rapid recovery from dormancy (drought)

Disadvantages
– Becomes dormant quickly under drought conditions
– Does not form a tight sod (bunch grass)
– Light green or blue-green color

Suggested seeding rate: 5 pounds per 1,000 square feet.

ZOYSIA GRASS (*Zoysia* spp.)

Zoysia grass use is not recommended for Colorado, especially when it is introduced to the lawn via the use of plugs. Solid sodding can be successful, but no zoysia grass sod is available in Colorado. Some winter dieback can be expected with this species. Since it is a warm season grass, it becomes straw-colored with the first fall frost and remains so until the following spring (May). It can be quite invasive (forms stolons and rhizomes) and nearly impossible to eradicate once established. This species requires close mowing (one to one and one-half inches), and can become quite thatchy. The cultivar 'Meyer' is the only commercially available cultivar with adequate cold tolerance.

Suggested seeding rate: usually not seeded, but some seeded types now available.

BERMUDAGRASS (*Cynodon* spp.)

There are naturalized biotypes of bermudagrass throughout Colorado, even in the northernmost portions of the state. Some people have used these bermudagrasses for home lawn purposes, often with great success. They will perform in a fashion similar to buffalograss, since bermuda is also a warm season grass. It can be quite invasive and aggressive because of prolific stolon and rhizome production. When found in most lawn situations, it is considered to be a weed. It is quite difficult to eradicate once it becomes established in a lawn. The varieties Yukon and Riviera have demonstrated excellent cold hardiness and persistence in Fort Collins, Colorado research plots since 2005.

ALKALIGRASS (*Puccinellia distans*)

This is a specialty grass, useful for high saline soil conditions. One commercially available cultivar, 'Fults,' was developed at Colorado State University. Other commercially available cultivars include 'Salty' and 'Fults II.' Alkaligrass resembles fine fescue in appearance and is a bunch grass. It requires moist soil conditions.

Suggested seeding rate: two to three pounds per 1,000 square feet.

SOURCES OF GRASS SEED, SOD, AND PLUGS

Seed

The following are Colorado seed companies that will sell seed directly to homeowners. Some may work cooperatively with select garden centers and nurseries to fill homeowner orders. They are all reputable seed companies that carry high quality, weed-free seed at fair prices.

Arkansas Valley Seed Solutions
I-25 & Highway 66
Longmont, CO 80504
970-535-4481
http://www.avseeds.com

Pawnee Buttes Seed Company
605 25th Street
Greeley, CO 80632
800-782-5947 or 970-356-7002
FAX 970-356-7263
www.pawneebuttesseed.com

Rocky Mountain Seed Company
1925 County Rd 54G
Fort Collins, CO 80524
970-493-7100
www.rockymountainseedco.com

Sharp Bros. Seed Coompany
104 East 4th Street Road
Greeley, CO 80631
970-356-4710 or 800-421-4234
Fax 970-356-1267
http://www.sharpseed.com

Southwest Seed
13260 County Road 29
Dolores, CO 81323
970-565-8722
www.southwestseed.com

Sod Producers

For information on Colorado sod producers, go to:

Rocky Mountain Sod Growers Association available online at
sod-growers.com

Buffalograss Plugs

To order buffalograss plugs (Legacy, Prestige):

- **Todd Valley Farms** (Mead, NE—near Lincoln) at www.toddvalleyfarms.com
- **High Country Gardens** at www.highcountrygardens.com

1. What factors should be considered in selecting a lawn type for any situation?

2. What is the best grass to plant in Colorado lawns?

3. What is the best grass to plant if you don't want to water a lawn?

4. What grass can grow with only a "little" irrigation?

5. Can zoysiagrass grow in Colorado? What will happen if I plant it anyway?

6. What is the best grass for a shady lawn?

7. Which grass grows best in salty soil?

8. What is the best grass to plant over my septic leach field?

9. What grass can I plant if I don't want to mow my lawn very often?

10. I would like to have a backyard putting green. What kind of grass is used?

UNIT K

Water-Wise Landscape Design

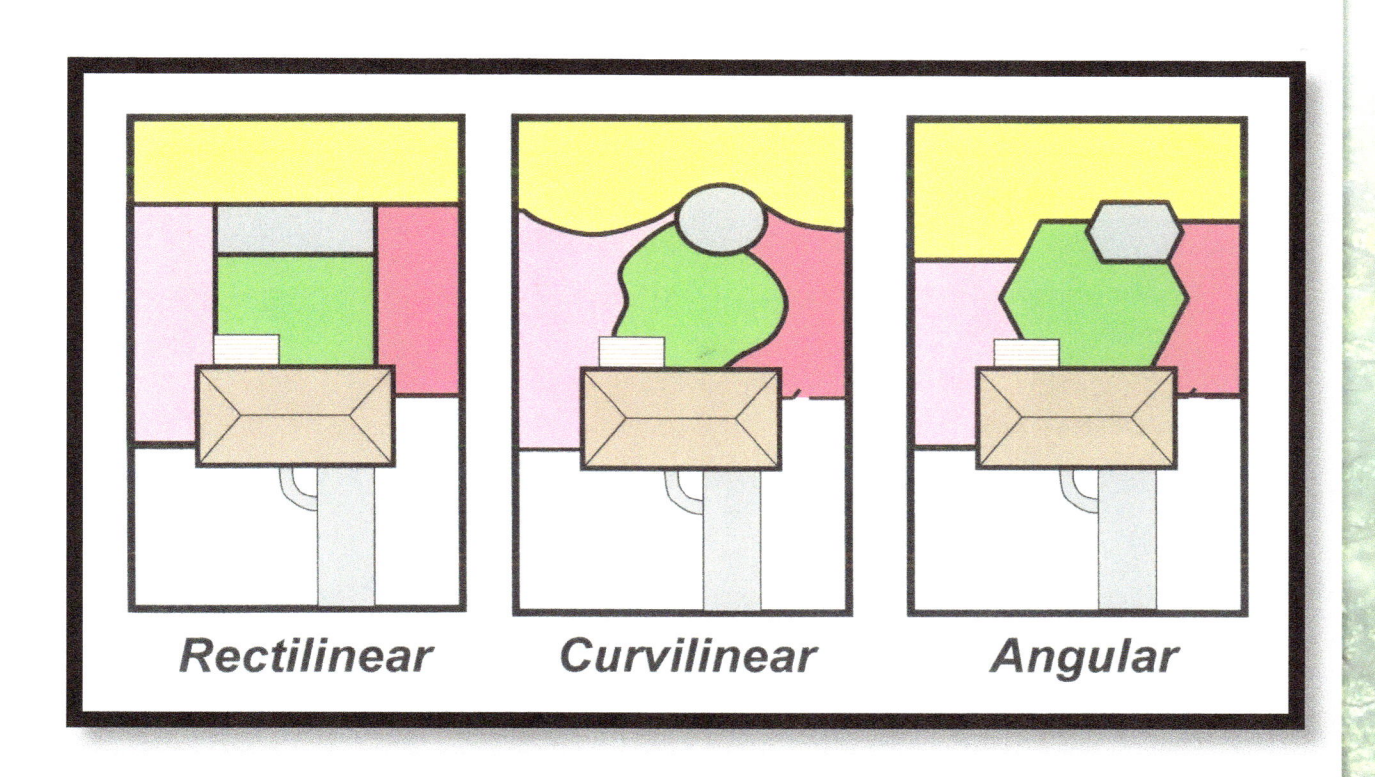

Rectilinear · Curvilinear · Angular

Learning Objectives

Working through design as a process, students will be able to design a water-wise landscape design. At the end of this unit, the student will be able to:

1. Outline the six steps in the landscape design process. Explain how the process is important to potential water savings.

2. Discuss opportunities and limitations as it relates to site analysis.

3. Explain how a story line defines the landscape around family values, needs, and wants.

4. Describe hydrozoning and its role in potential water savings and plant selection. Create hydrozone bubble drawings for a site.

5. Describe the use of rectilinear, curvilinear, and angular design styles. Convert a hydrozone bubble drawing into a basic rectilinear, curvilinear, and angular design.

6. Describe how to refine a preliminary design for efficient irrigation efficiency.

7. Describe the interplay of *line, color, texture,* and *form* with *scale, balance, simplicity, variety, emphasis,* and *sequence* to create *unity* in the design.

8. Explain hints to mix and match plants creating pizzazz.

Supplemental Reading

-   ***Basic Elements of Landscape Architecture Design.*** Norman K Booth.

-   ***Landscaping Makes Cents: Smart Investments That Increase Your Property Value.*** Frederick C Campbell and Richard L Dube.

-   ***Landscaping Your Home.*** William R. Nelson.

-   ***Residential Landscape Architecture: Design Process for the Private Residence.*** Norman K Booth and James E Hiss. ISBN: 0131140647

-   ***Xeriscape Handbook.*** Gayle Weinstein. Fulcrum Publishing. 1999.

-   ***Xeriscape Plant Guide.*** Denver Water. Fulcrum Publishing. 1996.

Chapter

45*

Water-Wise Landscape Design Process

SEVEN PRINCIPLES OF WATER-WISE LANDSCAPING

- **Planning and designing for water conservation, beauty, and utility.** The take home message is that it requires planning. Water savings does not happen by accident or by just placing a few xeric plants around the landscape.

- **Hydrozoning** is selecting plants appropriate to our climate, grouping them according to water need, and then actually irrigating according to water need. The take home message is actually watering the plants according to their need rather than watering the entire yard the same.

- **Watering efficiently with appropriate irrigation methods.** Of all the principles, watering efficiently has a greatest water savings potential for the typical landscape. The average homeowner uses twice the amount of water the lawn and gardens actually need. Efficient irrigation includes attention to design, maintenance, and management.

- **Creating practical turf and nonturf areas.** Water-wise landscaping is not anti-turf, but rather matching the turf type to the actual use of the site. This is a change from the typical landscape design where high input lawn is the common ground covering.

- **Improving the soil.** With improved soils, plants reach a larger supply of water.

- **Mulching to reduce evaporation.** Mulch with drip irrigation can reduce water use by fifty percent.

- **Maintaining with good horticultural practices.** Healthy plants are more tolerant of summer heat and wind.

---

*Authors: David Whiting, Colorado State University Extension, and Jeffry de Jong, Horticulturist, Victoria, BC, Canada. Artwork by David Whiting.

WHAT IS "LANDSCAPE DESIGN"?

Landscape design is a **process**, rather than just plunking down plants. For existing landscapes, let the process guide the evolution of the design to become more water wise.

Landscape design **creates practical and pleasing outdoor living space**. Landscape design develops a series of outdoor rooms.

Landscape design brings the **family's wants, needs, and values** into the design. These will vary from family to family and will evolve with time for any family.

Landscape design is about **how the space will be used**. It is about the connections and "feelings" created with the space. Is the space for relaxation and healing, or for action? For many, gardening is a vehicle for spiritual and emotional connection and renewal.

> *"More than anything else, a garden is a portal, a passage into another world, one of your own thoughts and your own making; it is whatever you want it to be and you are what you want to be."*
>
> —William Longgood

Paradise is from the Persian word for "walled garden."

Landscape design is about the family's investment in **time** and **dollars**.

Design is more of an art. Gardening is more of a craft. The two are not the same. Being a great gardener does not make the individual a good designer. Being knowledgeable about gardening does not necessarily give knowledge about design. Most knowledgeable gardeners are rather unfamiliar with landscape design concepts.

STEPS TO CREATING PRACTICAL AND PLEASING OUTDOOR LIVING SPACE

1. *Site analysis* identifies opportunities and limitations of the property.

2. *Family analysis* creates a story line, bringing unity into the landscape.

3. With bold *lines*, delineate softscape and hardscape areas, creating outdoor rooms.

    a. Define macro use of space with *hydrozone bubble drawings*.
       - Bubble drawings define *hydrozones for* efficient landscape irrigation.
       - Create practical turf and nonturf areas.

    b. Refine macro space (lawn areas, flowerbeds, vegetable garden, patio, etc.) with bold *lines*, in *rectilinear, curvilinear,* or *angular* design style.

    c. Refine preliminary design for efficient irrigation.

    d. Delineate micro spaces with connecting paths, plants, and hardscape features.

4. Develop plant consideration lists based on hydrozones.

5. Fit elements into the design based on the design principles of *color, texture, form, line, unity, scale, balance, simplicity, variety, emphasis,* and *sequence.*

Step 1—*Site Analysis* Identifies Opportunities and Limitations of the Property

Landscape maintenance professionals estimate that 90% of the landscape maintenance problems arise from issues that could/should have been addressed with the site analysis. For most, site analysis is an ongoing process. Keep a garden journal, recording concerns and success for future reference (Figure 45-1).

Soil Tilth—80% of Landscape Plant Problems Are Soil Related!

- Soil structure and compaction
- Sandy, clayey, or rocky
- Soil depth and profile
- Organic content
- pH and free lime
- Nutrients
- Salts

Grading and Drainage

- Slopes and land use
- Erosion potential
- Grading structures
- Drainage off the property
- Drainage onto the property
- Low spots and standing water
- Drainage down through the soil profile

Acceptable Slope

- Patio-terrace: 1 to 2%
- Entrance walks: 1 to 4%
- Ramps (with railing): up to 15%
- Steps (with railing): up to 50%
- Driveways: 1 to 15%
- Drainage swales: 2 to 10%
- Planted banks: up to 33%—Year-round plant cover to prevent erosion
- Slopes greater than 10% are hard to walk on and require year-round plant cover to prevent erosion.

Grading Structures

- For stability, retaining walls and dry walls have specific design criteria. Contact the local city building department for details on local code requirements.
- For scale, the minimum depth of the level area below the wall should be at least one and one-half times the wall height.

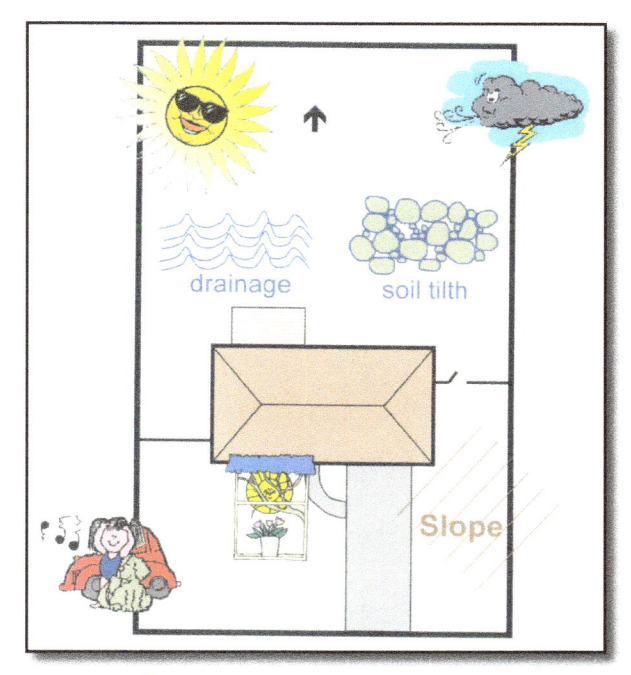

Figure 45-1 ▮ *Site analysis looks at opportunities and limitations of the property including sun/shade patterns, wind and air drainage, soil tilth, soil drainage, slopes, views, and factors outside the property line that influence use and design of the property.*

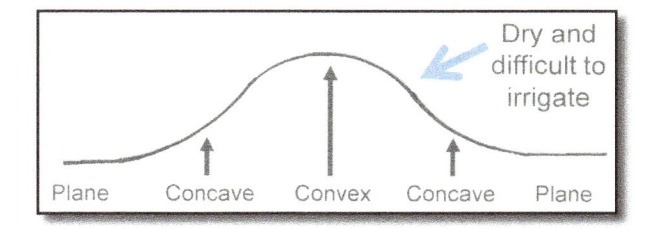

Figure 45-2 ▮ *Although berms are popular with designers, they may be high maintenance with dry slopes.*

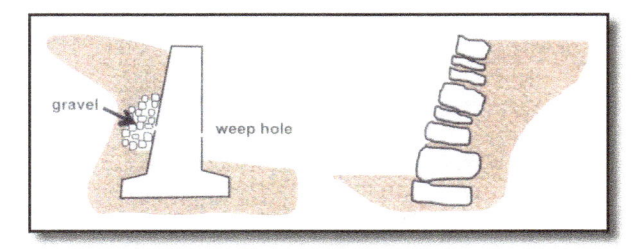

Figure 45-3 ▮ *Retaining structures have specific design criteria. Refer to local city building codes for details. Left: rRetaining wall with weep hole. Right: Dry wall.*

Microclimate

- Orientation (north and south) and shade patterns
- Prevailing winds and air drainage
- Temperature extremes (heat sinks, cold pockets)

Existing Plant Materials

- What plants are currently in the landscape?
- What is their condition?
- Which will be kept?

Extensional Landscape

- Subdivision covenants
- Views to frame or mask
- Noise
- Neighborhood landscape style
- Privacy and security

Natural Precipitation and Irrigation Potential

- In Colorado, natural precipitation varies greatly, from below seven inches per year to above 35 inches per year. What is the natural precipitation at your site?
- Colorado communities vary greatly in water resources. Due to the planning of forefathers, some have great water resources whereas other communities lack the water resources for landscape irrigation. What is the situation in your community?

Opportunity or Restraint?

Use the site analysis as an opportunity to create a unique landscape working with the limitations of the site (Figures 45-4 to 45-6).

Step 2—*Family Analysis* Creates a Story Line, Bringing Unity to the Landscape

What does the family **want and need** from the landscape? How will the family relate to the landscape? Will the space be routinely used by the family or is it simply filler space around the home?

What does the family want the landscape to **communicate**? What does the family want to "feel" from the landscape? Is it a setting of peace and relaxation, or a setting for action activities? What does the family want the landscape to communicate to others?

- *The Latin word for "sacred" gives us the word "sanctuary" denoting not only a sacred space but also a place of refuge and protection.*—Peg Streep

Figures 45-4 to 45-6 ■ *In site analysis, look at how the gardener can work with the limitations of the property to create a practical and pleasing landscape. Here at Abkhazi Garden in Victoria, BC, much of the property is covered in rock outcroppings. Working with the rock, Prince and Princess Abkhazi created an amazing garden of love and peace.*

- *Creating Sacred Space—We transform our gardens and yards into sacred space when we understand them as places of growth, not only for plants and trees but also for our inner selves.*—Peg Streep

Irrigation: What are the family's interests and values toward irrigated and nonirrigated landscape areas? How does this match with reality of the natural precipitation and irrigation potential?

Time: What are the family's interests and values toward gardening activities?

Dollars: What financial resources will be invested in the landscape?

Rather Than Filling the Landscape with Stuff, Make Some Choices!

1. Select the three most important elements in the design.

2. From these important elements, write a story line that reflects *how you want to relate to the landscape* (Figures 45-7 and 45-8).

Writing a Story Line

The story line creates a more congruent message bringing unity into the design.

The story line clarifies how the family wants to relate to and use the space. It reflects the family's personal tastes. It clarifies the "feeling" or mood the family desires from the landscape. For example, is it peaceful and relaxing space or energized for action? It clarifies what the family wants to communicate to others.

- This is the **most important design step**. Without a story line, most landscapes are not really designs, but rather collections of plant materials.

- This is the **most difficult design step** in the design process. It takes some careful evaluation about what the family really wants and needs in the design.

Figure 45-7 *Family analysis is about what the family wants and needs in the landscape. How will the family connect to the space? How will the outdoor rooms be used? The family of this Steamboat Springs garden enjoys the sitting area with fire pit.*

Figure 45-8 *Outdoor rooms in this backyard include a dining room, a fountain garden room, and vegetable garden room, creating a pleasant, relaxing space.*

Step 3—With Bold Lines, Delineate Softscape and Hardscape Areas, Creating Outdoor Rooms

Note: *Softscape features* of the landscape include all the plants (trees, shrubs, flowers, turf, vegetables, fruits, etc.). *Hardscape features* of the landscape include the nonliving elements of the design (patio, deck, fences, water features, and lighting).

Three Areas in the Landscape

Public area (front yard) is the portion of the yard openly viewed by others. Home owners' associations (HOAs) and cities often regulate what can/cannot be done in the public area (Figures 45-9 to 45-11).

- Lawn, trees, shrubs, and flowers

- Driveway and path to front door

- Community standards—Following community standards for the front yard helps create the feeling that the community is friendly and welcoming, increasing property values.

- What does the family want to communicate to the neighborhood?

Private area (back yard) is the portion of the yard not openly viewed by others. Being the family's private space, it is designed with rooms to support the family's activities and interests. (Figure 45-12).

- Cooking and eating rooms

- Sitting rooms, play room

- Fruit, vegetable, and flower garden room

- Water features

- How does the family want to relate to the space?

- How will the family use the space?

Utility areas serve specific nonlandscape functions such as the dog run and parking. They need to fit into the function of the landscape design.

- Garden shed, potting area, work area, compost bins

- Storage, dog runs, additional parking for cars, boats, RVs

- How does this fit into the landscape?

Think of Design as Creating an Assortment of Outdoor Rooms

- What makes up the floor?

- What makes up the wall?

- What makes up the ceiling?

- *Lines* connect and defines space (rooms) (Figure 45-13).

Figure 45-9 ▮ *The public area is the portion of the yard in open view by others. It may have HOA or community standards that influence the design*

Figures 45-10 and 45-11 ▮ *When the public area reflects community landscape standards it builds a welcoming and friendly feeling for the community and enhances neighborhood property values. The public area communicates about the family. What does your front yard communicate about your family?*

Figure 45-12 ■ *The private area is typically the family's primary outdoor living space.*

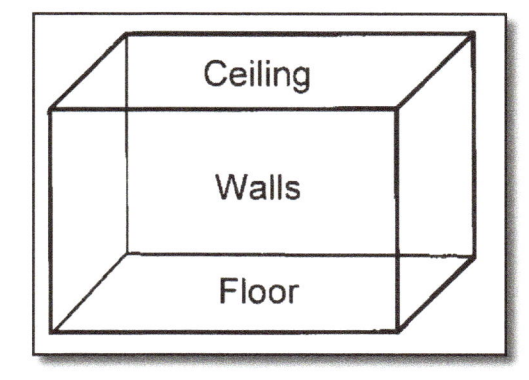

Figure 45-13 ■ *The landscape is an assortment of outdoor rooms with various activities. In design, pay attention to the floor coverings, wall features, and what makes up the ceiling.*

Step 3a—Define Macro Use of Space with *Hydrozone Bubble Drawings*

Bubble Drawings

Bubble drawings brainstorm the macro use of space. It the first and primary opportunity in the design process to be creative.

Bubble drawings are ovals that identify space allocation and use. For example, a circle represents the location and approximate size of the patio. Other circles identify the location and approximate size of lawn areas, the vegetable garden area, flower beds, etc. (Figure 45-14).

Bubble drawings do not identify actual lines, beds, path, or individual plants. These will come in future steps in the design process (Figure 45-15).

The bubble drawing step also defines hydrozones, areas with various levels of irrigation (Figure 45-16).

Landscape elements that will not change (like an existing deck or large tree) should be on the plan before starting this step.

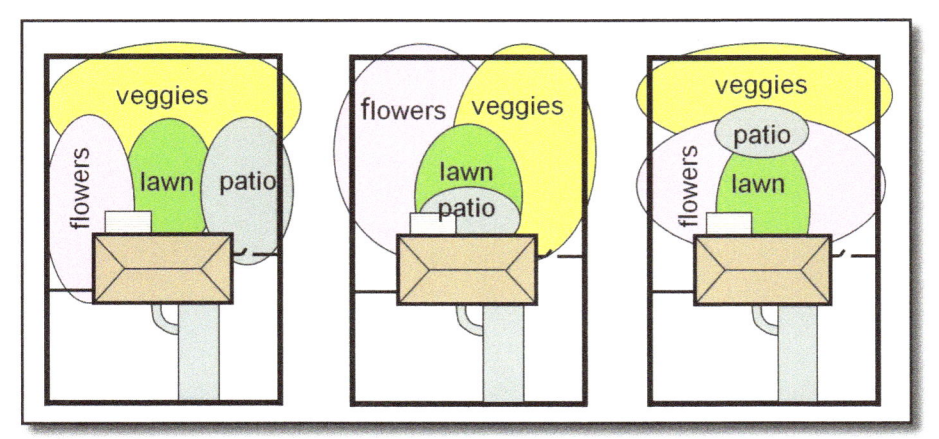

Figure 45-14 ■ *Examples of bubble drawings for a back yard with people space (patio and lawn rooms), vegetable room, and flower room.*

Figure 45-15 ▮ *Bubble drawings are ovals that depict various uses and irrigation levels of the space. Left: They need to fill the space, rather than leave large area unidentified (red in the drawing). Right: Bubble drawing does not identify the actual shape and line of the areas; this will come in the next steps.*

Do not move on too fast. Breaking out of the box, look at a variety of options. Try many options before selecting the one to use as the base for the design.

To become the design base, select a bubble drawing that best serves the design needs, best communicates "feelings," and gives the best connection with the space.

Hydrozoning—Selecting Plants Appropriate for Your Climate, Grouping Plants According to Water Needs, and Actually Watering Them According to Need

In irrigation management, individual plants are not watered plant by plant. Rather, the irrigation system waters all plants in an area (call *zone*). With sprinkler irrigation, this is easy to understand.

With drip irrigation, we apply water to individual plants, but all plants in the zone receive the same run time and frequency of irrigation. As a point of clarification, some gardener mistakenly think that using half, one, and two-gallon-per-hour drippers is an effective method to manage the differing water needs. Although this works to a small degree, the concept is basically flawed. The two-gallon-per-hour drippers will have significantly larger wetting zones than the half-gallon-per-hour dripper. However, plants with the higher water need (2 gallon/hour drippers) do not necessarily have a larger root spread. Likewise, plants with the lower water need (half-gallon-per-hour dripper) will not necessarily have a smaller root spread. (In fact, a large root spread is what makes some plants more xeric.) The factor missing here is irrigation frequency to match the water needs.

In simple terms, irrigation is done by areas not plant by plant. **Hydrozoning** groups plants with similar water needs, and then actually irrigates each group in the landscape to match the water needs of the grouping.

- In developing a bubble drawing, factor in the irrigation needs (hydrozones) (Figure 45-16).
- Areas of routine irrigation—watered every two to four days.
- Areas of reduced irrigation—watered every four to fourteen days.
- Areas of limited irrigation—watered during dry spells once plants are established.
- Nonirrigated areas

Figure 45-16 ▮ *Examples of yards with various styles of hydrozones. Left: Yard with reduced irrigated lawn in front and back, limited irrigation shrub and flower bed in front yard, routine irrigation flower bed around patio in back yard and non-irrigated side yards. Center: Larger property with a patch of lawn in the front and back yard while much of the property has limited irrigation. Right: Yard is basically non-irrigated with small limited irrigation flower beds near house in front and back.*

Hydrozones Based on Irrigation Need (Figure 45-17)

- Lawns—Routine irrigation
- Lawns—Reduced irrigation
- Lawns—Limited irrigation or non-irrigated
- Mixed flower and shrub beds—Routine irrigation
- Mixed flower and shrub beds—Reduced irrigation
- Mixed flower and shrub beds—Limited irrigation
- Vegetables—Routine irrigation
- Tree fruits—Reduced irrigation
- Small fruits—Routine irrigation
- Non-irrigated areas

Note: A common incorrect belief is that lawns are high water users and shrubs and flowers are low water users. Actually, the water demand of Kentucky bluegrass is lower middle class when placed in an ordered list of water demands for landscape plants. The typical lawn receives twice the amount of water that it actually needs.

Creating Practical Turf and Non-Turf Areas

Water wise gardening is not anti-turf, but rather about selecting the turf type to match the use of the property. This is a change from the typical Western landscape where most of the property is covered with high-input lawn.

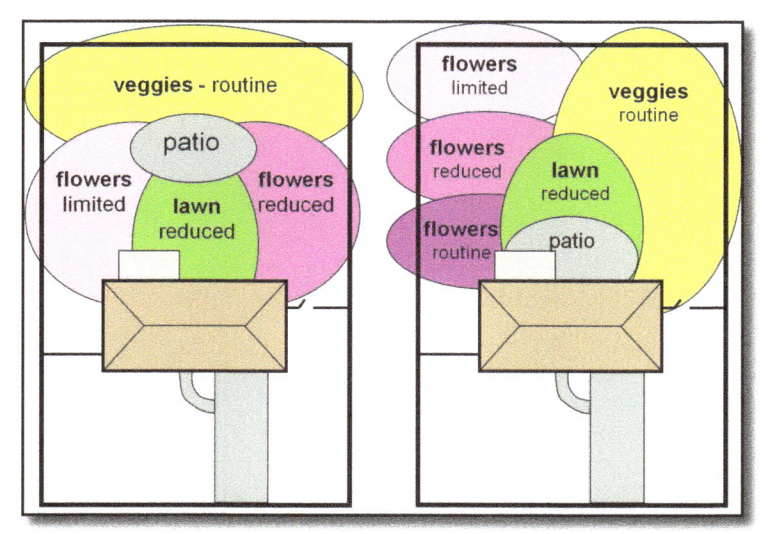

Figure 45-17 ▮ *Examples of hydrozone bubble drawings. Note the multiple hydrozone zones for flowers.*

With Colorado's population growth, water use becomes a critical issue. Water conservation helps: 1) reduce total water demand, and 2) reduce the extensive cost of expanding a community's water infrastructure.

In a typical community, water use more than doubles during the summer irrigation season. On a statewide perspective, landscape irrigation accounts for seven to ten percent of Colorado's total water use. Due to planning by ancestors, some communities have a good water supply supporting landscape irrigation. However, during drought years water may be in short supply. Other communities lack water resources for landscape irrigation. Here limited irrigation or non-irrigation may be the only practical approach. In Colorado, landscape irrigation is prohibited from newer domestic wells.

Benefits of Grass

Healthy grass is an aesthetic asset and a factor in property value. It provides a backdrop for other landscape elements and pulls the landscape design together.

The growing body of evidence points to the positive health and environmental contributions made by lawns and other grassy areas. A healthy, vigorous lawn with high plant density provides the following benefits:

- **Conversion of carbon dioxide to oxygen**—Twenty-five square feet of actively growing grass produces enough oxygen for one person per day.

  On a global basis, grasslands of the northern hemisphere are second to the tropical rain forests in the carbon dioxide to oxygen conversion. Grasslands serve a major role in reducing global warming.

- **Pollution breakdown**—Microorganisms found in the soil of actively growing turf break down organic pollutants, including air contaminates, pollen, and pesticides.

- **Wind erosion**—Grass cover prevents wind erosion of soil, trapping dust and pollen.

- **Water quality**—Turfgrass areas play a significant role in reducing surface water runoff, a key factor in *non-point-source* pollution in the landscape setting.

  —An average golf course of 150 acres can absorb twelve million gallons of water during a three-inch rainfall.

  —A thick turfgrass allows fifteen times less runoff than does a lower quality lawn.

  —A healthy, dense stand of turfgrass can reduce runoff to almost zero.

  —Compared to a garden or field planted to row crops, grassy areas reduce soil erosion by 84 to 668 times.

  —To protect surface water quality, direct surface runoff onto grassy areas allowing for natural filtering in the biologically active turf soil.

- **Soil structure**—Actively growing grass supports soil organism activity that improves soil structure.

- **People space**—Turf is basic "people space" with a cool, dirt-free activity space for children and adults.

- **Element of landscape design**—Turf brings unity to a landscape design and provides a neutral background to set off flowers and shrubs.

- **Property values**—Turf quality influences property appeal and marketability.

- **Fire defense zone**—Irrigated mowed lawns is an important aspect of fire management in communities. Dry, unmowed grass/weeds become a major fire hazard.

Turf Selection: Creating Practical Turf Areas

High input lawns are a habit in American and European landscapes. However, does the property use require the perfect green lawn with high inputs or would a moderate quality lawn with reduced inputs or a low input lawn be acceptable for the site?

Many lawn care problems arise from management differences between high, moderate, and low input lawns. For many gardeners, there is a conflict between expectations and inputs. Table 45-1 summarizes difference in high, moderate, and low input lawns.

Table 45-1. Comparison of High, Moderate, and Low Input Lawns

	High Input	Moderate Input	Low Input
Wear tolerance	best	good	limited
Appearance	best	good	limited
Water	high	moderate	limited
Exposure	sun	sun to partial shade	sun
Fertilization	spring and fall	primarily fall	fall
Species	Select KBG cultivars Perennial rye Turf-type tall fescue	Select KBG cultivars Turf-type tall fescue Buffalograss	Select KBG cultivars Blue grama Buffalograss

Grass and Water Use

Contrary to popular belief, there is no magic lawn type that delivers top quality with minimal inputs. The quality of any turf is directly dependent on the amount of summer rainfall and supplemental irrigation it receives.

A lawn's tolerance or resistance to drought is a complex situation. A "drought-tolerant" species may or may not use and/or require less water depending on many factors. Factors contributing to drought tolerance include:

- Species (including its actual water use, rooting depth, and ability to go dormant)
- Soil tilth and soil oxygen levels (rooting depth)
- Wind and sun exposure (actual water use)
- Mowing height (high mowing leads to deeper roots)
- Traffic (any lawn is intolerant of traffic when dry)
- Salt levels in soil and irrigation water
- Previous irrigation pattern (frequency and watering depth)

The bottom line is that species selection is secondary to irrigation management in water savings. A more drought-tolerant lawn species will not use less water if managed like a high input lawn!

Since Kentucky bluegrass, turf-type tall fescue, and Buffalograss make up ninety-nine percent of home lawns in Colorado, this chapter only looks at these options. Other options are available for special situations. Refer to http://csuturf.colostate.edu for additional information.

If a Turf Is Deeper Rooting

- It requires less frequent irrigation (i.e., stays greener longer between irrigations).
- However, it will also require a heavier/deeper irrigation to recharge the rooting zone, so actual water use is not necessarily reduced.
- Deeper rooting may or may not be an irrigation savings technique depending on the frequency of soaking summer rains and the irrigation pattern. If the area can depend on frequent summer soaking rains, the deeper rooting cultivars can be an advantage to keep the grass green between rain events. If the lawn is automatically watered two or three times a week, rooting depth is a moot issue (Figure 45-18).

- Many gardeners mistakenly assume that deep rooting is a water savings because irrigation is needed less often. However, the frequency of irrigation is not the primary factor to consider. The issue is total water consumption.

Figure 45-18 ▮ *Deeper rooting means less frequent irrigation, but heavier irrigation to replenish the rooting zone. It should not be interpreted as a water savings.*

Kentucky Bluegrass Makes a Great Lower Input Turf Option

- Kentucky bluegrass, KBG, is the standard for home lawns due to the rich blue-green color and its high tolerance for wear.

- Water use primarily depends on the gardener's irrigation management. On a communitywide basis, we use twice the amount of water that the KBG lawns actually need.

- Water use and growth actually slows when the soil begins to dry down. However, to capitalize on this dry down requires careful irrigation management rather than automatic irrigation on fixed days of the week.

- Irrigation demand varies significantly between cultivars. Some deeper rooting cultivars require less frequent irrigations. Some cultivars demand twenty-five percent less total water.

- KBG goes dormant with water stress. Summer dormant KBG is a standard in many parts of the Eastern United States. Just not in the arid West! Will summer dormant with green lawns in the spring and fall work for the site?

- Bottom line: It is not the KBG that demands the heavy irrigation but rather the gardener's management style.

  —High input KBG makes a great "people space" for high use areas like a ball field with lots wear and tear. Few home lawns have this high traffic situation demanding high inputs.

  —Moderate input KBG (irrigated at eighty percent ET) fits the need for most home lawns where a beautiful green lawn is desired.

  —When irrigated at sixty percent ET, KBG makes a thinner carpet. This may be well suited for lower use areas.

  —Where summer dormant is acceptable, KBG makes a great minimal input lawn. It needs to be greened up in the cooler weather of spring and fall with rainfall and supplemental irrigation (Figure 45-19).

  —The public objection to summer dormant lawns is that so many are found in unkept yards that become the neighborhood weed patch.

Note: the term "ET" stands for *evapotranspiration* which is an actual measurement of the water use of the lawn (or crop) based on crop growth, temperature, wind, humidity, and solar radiation.

Figure 45-19 ▮ *Weed-free, summer dormant KBG. Public objection to summer dormant KBG is that so many are simply no-maintenance yards, which become the neighborhood weed patch.*

Turf-Type Tall Fescue Makes a Great Lower Input Turf Option

- Turf-type tall fescue may be deeper rooted than KBG, depending on soil tilth (oxygen levels), cultivars, and irrigation pattern. This means it may go longer between irrigation, but should not be mistaken as water savings.

- Tall fescue cannot slow growth and water use as the soil dries down. Actual water use may be significantly higher than KBG.

- Tall fescue cannot go dormant. In summer dry spells, it requires irrigation.

- Based on ET, actual water use of turf-quality tall fescue is only 10% less than turf-quality KBG. Irrigation management plays a larger role in water use than species selection. Switching from a KBG to a turf-type tall fescue lawn will not save water! Water savings comes in the management of the irrigation.

- Tall fescue makes a great reduced input turfgrass for site where top quality turf is not essential for the landscape design.

Buffalograss Quality Is Dependent on the Amount of Summer Rain and Irrigation It Receives

- Being a warm season grass, Buffalograss will be dormant brown from early fall (first frost) to late spring in Colorado.

- To be green in the summer, water use for Buffalograss is about 1 inch of rain and irrigation per week. To remain green in Colorado summers, Buffalograss generally requires irrigation to supplement natural rainfall.

- Turf-quality Buffalograss requires 50% less rain and irrigation per season than KBG. This reduction is due, in part, from being dormant in the spring and fall.

Comparative Seasonal Water Requirement

The comparative seasonal water requirement (including summer rainfall and irrigation) in given in the table above. The typical lawn receives twice the amount of irrigation required for high input KBG (Figure 45-20).

Figure 45-20 ■ *Comparative seasonal water requirement (including summer rains and irrigation).*

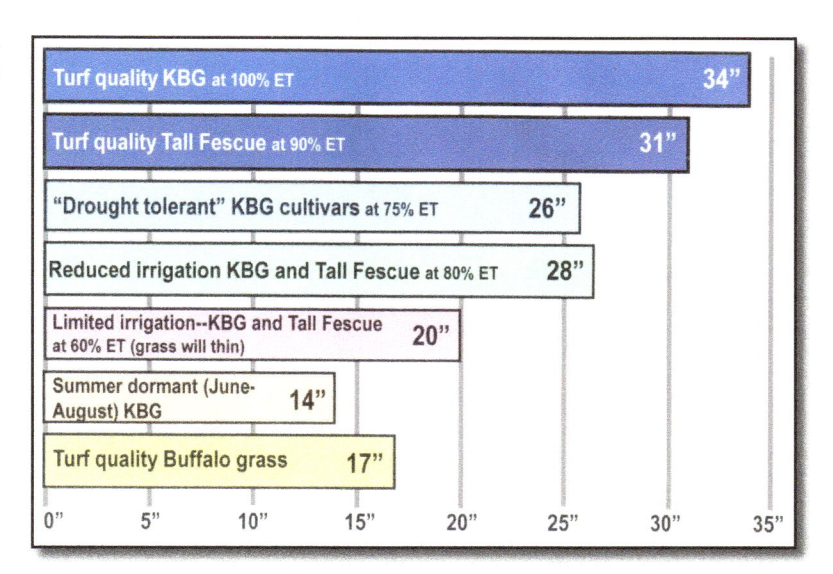

Step 3b—Refine Macro Space (lawn areas, mixed shrub and flowerbeds, vegetable gardens, patio, etc.) with Bold Lines in Rectilinear, Curvilinear, or Angular Design Style

Which Design Style Fits the Theme?

- **Rectilinear style** has straight lines and right angles in square and rectangular shapes. It is described as bold, orderly, organized, and stately; or stuffy, uncreative, and controlling (Figures 45-21 and 45-22).

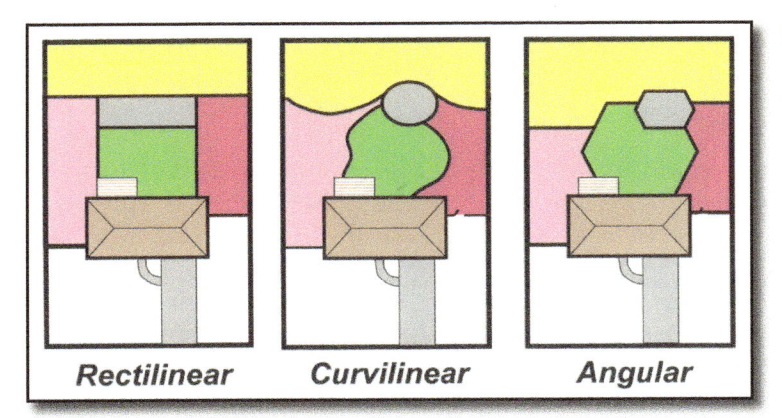

- **Curvilinear style** replaces the straight line and right angles with bold sweeping curves. (Avoid wavy lines, as this does not create the bold line for a strong design.) It is described as natural, free flowing, and friendly; or lacking form and structure (Figures 45-21 and 45-22).

- **Angular style** uses the straight lines but with a variety of angles and directions. It is described as modern, action-oriented, and bold; or hectic, chaotic, and disorganized (Figures 45-21 and 45-22).

Most people have a love/hate relationship with the three styles. Select the style that created the feeling or mood desired from the story line. A common question is "May styles be mixed?"

Figure 45-22 ▪ *Notice how lines connect and define space. The different styles bring various feelings to the site. Some are calming and relaxing whereas others stimulate action. Which design style fits the story line?*

- Basically, no, as it weakens the feelings created by the style and destroys unity.

- However, a front yard could be one style and the back yard another style. In large properties, various areas may have different styles.

- The property line and the home style do not dictate the landscape style.

- It is recognized that a rectilinear deck and raised bed garden boxes may be found in an otherwise curvilinear design.

Step 3c—Refine Preliminary Design for Efficient Irrigation

Of all the principles of water-wise landscaping, irrigation efficiency has the greatest water saving potential for most home gardeners. On a community basis, gardeners apply twice the amount of water that plants actually need. This is due to poor irrigation system design, management, and maintenance.

Efficiency in irrigation is based on uniformity of water delivery. In any irrigation zone, spots that receive more water will be overwatered to keep spots that receive less water green.

Drip irrigation systems are great for mixed flower and shrub beds, perennials, small fruits, and vegetables. Drip irrigation is not an install-and-forget-it type of system. Like any irrigation system, maintenance is required. Sprinkler irrigation is more suited for large trees and lawn areas.

Sprinkler Irrigation: Design Criteria for Uniform Water Delivery

- Uniformity of water delivery = water savings

1. Head-to-head coverage (Figure 45-23)

   - Spray from each head must reach neighboring heads.

   - A ten to twenty percent overlap may give better uniformity.

   - Less than head-to-head coverage (while popular to reduce installation costs) significantly increases water use for the life of the system.

2. Line-out along nonirrigated areas (Figure 45-24)

   - Another standard for water savings is to water from the outside in.

   - Do not water from the center out onto non-irrigation areas. The non-irrigated area will be watered or a dry edge will be found along the edge of the lawn.

   - Although lining out requires more sprinkler heads with higher installation costs, it is a primary water saving technique, reducing water use.

3. Fill in with heads in square and triangle patterns (Figures 45-25 and 45-26)

   - For uniform water distribution, fill in heads in square or triangle patterns. The overlap gives the most uniform delivery.

   - Avoid pentagons (five-sided) patterns, as this creates a dry spot.

4. Use uniform type, brand, and style of heads in each irrigation zone

   - Spray heads apply water a one to two and one-half inches per hour.

   - Rotor heads apply water at one-quarter to three-quarters inches per hour.

5. Avoid sprinkler irrigation of small irregularly shaped areas

   - To walk the talk of being water wise, avoid sprinkler irrigation on small irregularly shaped areas.

   - Minimum width of sprinklers is generally is five to fifteen feet wide.

   - In design, avoid sprinkler irrigation on smaller areas. Design these for drip irrigation, hand watering, or non-irrigation areas. Or avoid creating small irregularly shape areas all together in the design process.

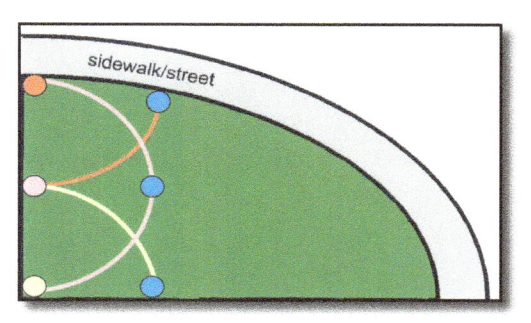

Figure 45-23 ■ *Head- to-Head Coverage is a minimum standard for water savings. Water from each head reaches the neighboring heads. A ten to twenty percent overlap may give even better uniformity.*

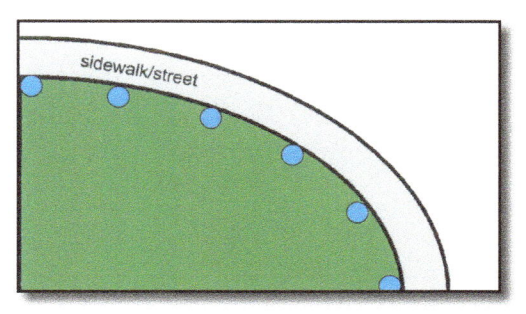

Figure 45-24 ■ *Another water saving standard is to line out the irrigated area from the non-irrigated area by watering from the outside.*

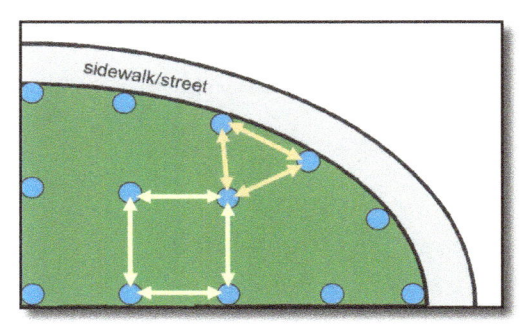

Figure 45-25 ■ *For uniform water delivery, fill in heads in square or triangle patterns.*

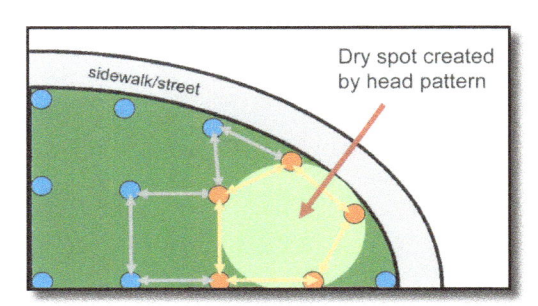

Figure 45-26 ■ *Avoid placing heads in pentagon-shaped patterns, it creates dry spots and the entire lawn will be overwatered to compensate. Pentagon-shaped patterns frequently pop up in irregularly shaped areas.*

6. Use recommended water pressure

- A mist cloud around a sprinkler head indicates excessive pressure, increasing evaporation and total water usage.

- A pressure regulator is standard on newer homes. This is typically located were the water line enters the home, just beyond the shut-off valve. It can be retrofitted into the water line in older home.

- Most sprinkler heads in the home garden trade are designed to work at 30 to 40 psi, and generally do not have internal pressure regulators.

- Heads used on commercial/industrial properties may work with much higher pressures and these more expensive heads generally have a pressure regulator built into the head.

- Many cities deliver water at thirty to forty pounds per square inch (psi). However, much higher pressures are common. With pressure above eighthly psi, automatic valves may have trouble closing.

Typical Sprinkler Patterns (Figure 45-27)

- Full circles
- Half circles (giving a straight line)
- Quarter circles (giving a right angle for square corners)
- Adjustable arc (the angle can be manually set; however, these are less uniform in delivery)
- Other patterns (like strip head) lack good uniformity in water distribution.

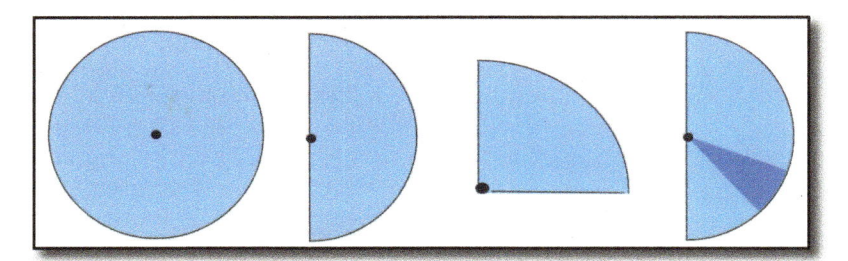

Figure 45-27 ▮ *Sprinkler heads come in full circle, half circle, quarter circles, and adjustable arc.*

Fitting Sprinkler Patterns into the Design

Pop-up spray heads are spaced at eight- to fifteen-foot intervals (depending on interchangeable nozzle installed). They have a high water delivery rate, around two inches per hour, often leading to surface runoff. They are used for small areas.

Rotor heads are spaced at fifteen- to over forty-five-foot intervals (depending on the head). They have a lower delivery rate, around one-half inch per hour, causing less surface runoff. These are use for large open areas.

For example, a thirty-foot by forty-five-foot area would have pop-up spray heads at fifteen-foot intervals, with quarter heads in the corners, half heads along the sides, and full circles in the center (Figure 45-28).

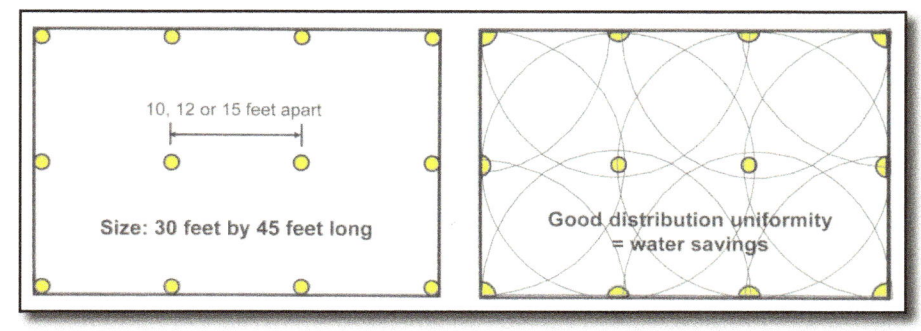

Figure 45-28 ▮ *Left: For this 30-foot-wide by 45-foot-long area, pop-up spray heads could be used at 15-foot centers. Right: Quarter heads would be placed in the corners, half heads along the sides, and full circle heads in the center. With head-to-head coverage, this would give a good efficiency for water delivery.*

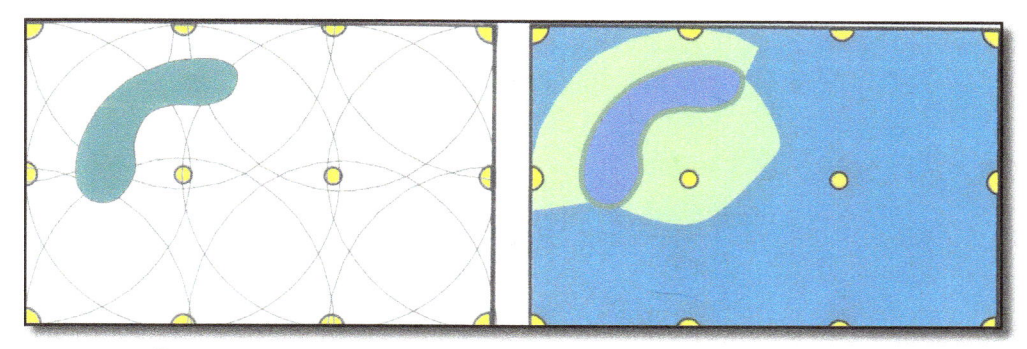

If a flowerbed was added to the area, blocked spray creates a dry area around the bed and a very wet planting bed from the intercepted water. In water wise design, AVOID blocking sprinkler delivery with flowers and shrubs (Figure 45-29).

In water-wise landscaping design, overlay the sprinkler layout onto the design. **Then adjust the lines of the design for efficient irrigation layout** (Figure 45-30).

Remember

- Head-to-head coverage with up to twenty percent overlap

- Line out non-irrigated areas

- Place heads in square and triangle patterns

- For small areas, use pop-up spray heads at eight to fifteen-foot centers. For open large areas, use rotor type heads spaced at fifteen to forty-five plus to foot centers depending on the site and heads used.

- Avoid sprinkler irrigation on spaces less than five to ten feet wide.

In a small area, sprinkler heads cannot follow the curves. Rather, they stay on the grid lines. In water-wise design, draw primary lines, and then overlay the sprinkler system looking at patterns. Adjust the head placement (staying on the grid) and redraw lines for maximum water savings (Figures 45-31 to 45-33).

Figure 45-30 ▮ *To walk the talk of being water wise, adjust the line in the preliminary design for improved irrigation efficiency. In the drawing the blue area represents a lawn that will be sprinkler-irrigated surrounded by mixed flower shrub beds with drip irrigation. The original line is indicated with the dotted line. Then the sprinkler grid pattern was overlaid. With head-to-head coverage, note that some lawn areas are outside of the water delivery zone. Sliding the heads out to compensate will significantly increase water use with the lack of head-to-head coverage. A better solution is to move the line inside the sprinkler delivery pattern. As redrawn, this minor adjustment could reduce water use by 30% to 50%!*

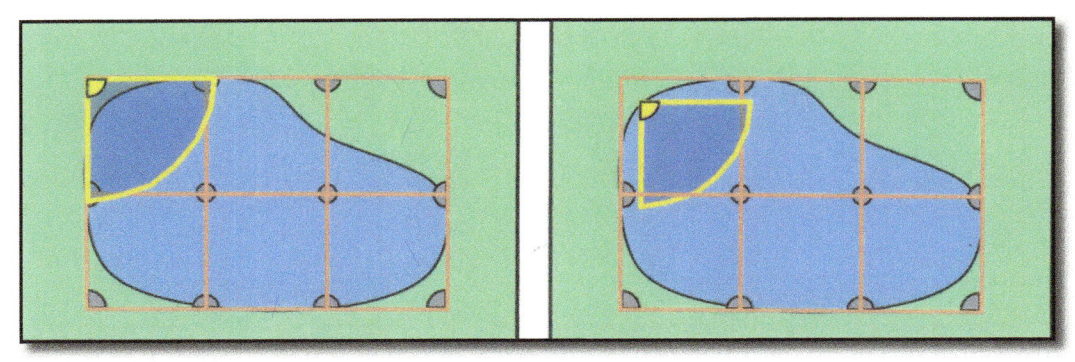

Figure 45-31 ■ *In small areas, notice how the sprinkler heads must stay on the grid lines. Plant materials along the edge of the lawn area must be kept short to allow for water delivery and must be tolerant of the water levels given the lawn. Right: If the head is moved in to the edge of the lawn (blue area), it creates coverage problems along the edge. As drawn, the final head placement is given in Figure 45-28, Left.*

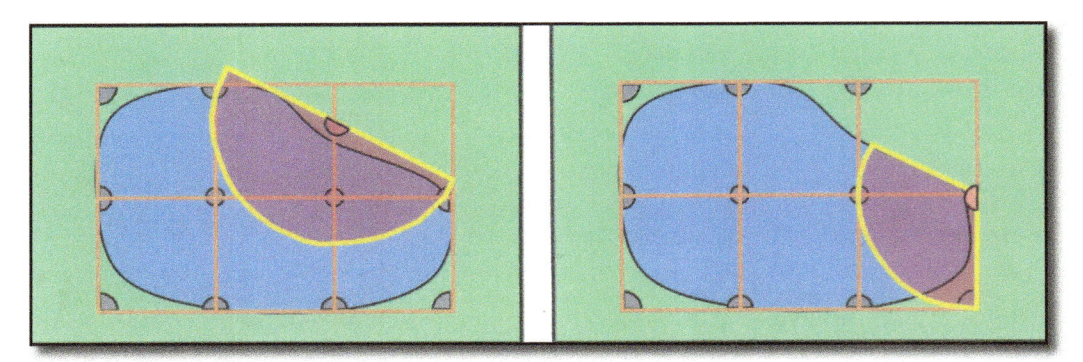

Figure 45-32 ■ *As drawn, the sprinkler head in the upper right hand corner could be eliminated. Drawings on the left and right show adjustments in placement and arc of adjacent heads. Note: For head-to-head coverage in this small area, all heads stay on the grid line. As drawn, the final head placement is given in Figure 45-23, Left.*

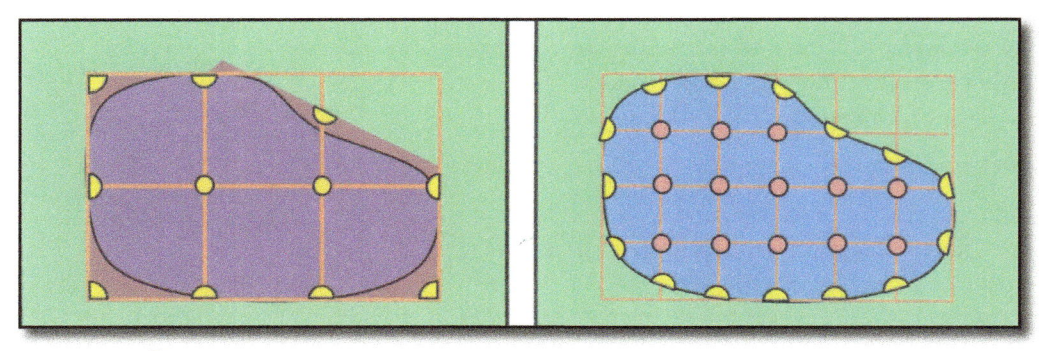

Figure 45-33 ■ *Left: Illustration of sprinkler layout for a lawn area 30 by 45 feet with pop-up spray heads at 15-foot intervals. Notice how heads stay on the grid line. The head in the upper right corner was eliminated with adjustments made in placement and arc of neighboring heads. Notice the overspray of the sprinkler system on the edges of the flower/shrub bed. Any plant materials in this area would be low ground cover types and acceptable to the watering level of the lawn. Right: Illustration of sprinkler layout for a 60- by 90-foot lawn area with pop-up spray heads at 15-foot centers. Rotor heads: In the large 60- by 90-foot lawn area, rotor heads could be used at 30-foot spacings. With rotor heads the layout would be like the illustration on the Left.*

Step 3d—Delineate Micro Spaces with Connecting Paths, Plants, and Hardscape Features

With the primary lines refined for efficient landscape irrigation, we are now ready to continue developing the design plan with secondary lines defining beds, paths, and other features.

How do folks move through the garden rooms?

- Paths direct people around a garden and are an effective way to deal with soil compaction from foot traffic.

- Paths also eliminate self-discovery of the garden.

- A threshold or peak-hole is also an invitation to enter and explore.

Step 4—Develop Plant Consideration List Based on Hydrozones

Create a Potential Plant List for Each Hydrozone

Why a potential list? Plant materials need to be identified by hydrozone so they can be grouped by water need. Flexibility in the design process at this point in time allow for exciting new plants, not previously on the list, that one finds at the nursery. Flexibility may also be needed when the desired plants are not available or are in poor quality.

Information sources on plant water needs include the following:

- CSU Extension fact sheets and *CMG GardenNotes*

- *Xeriscape Plant Guide* by Denver Water, Fulcrum Publishing

- X-rated plant lists at www.gardencentersofcolorado.org

Water-Wise Landscaping in Colorado's Semi-Arid Climate

On sites where landscape irrigation is not desirable or possible, focus on natural growth.

Xeriscaping is not a rock pile. A Phoenix style of landscaping is rather environmentally unfriendly, creating heat sinks and limiting carbon dioxide conversion into oxygen. This style of landscape feeds global warming (Figure 45-34).

Figure 45-34 ▮ *Xeriscaping does not need to be this Phoenix style rock pile. Being a heat sink and lacking plants for carbon dioxide conversion, this landscape style is rather environmentally unfriendly.*

Even xeric plants need rain and/or irrigation during establishment. Gardens with limited to no irrigation will thrive in years with heavy rainfall and decline in dry years.

Water-wise concepts support irrigation for "people space."

Step 5—Fit Elements into the Design Based on the Design Principles of Line, Color, Texture, Form, Unity, Scale, Balance, Simplicity, Variety, Emphasis, and Sequence

With the primary lines on the page, defining outdoor rooms, it is now time to decorate the rooms with various plants and hardscape features. This incorporates a variety of interrelated landscape design principles including line, color, texture, form, unity, scale, balance, simplicity, variety, emphasis, and sequence. This discussion on landscape design continues in Chapter 46, Principles of Landscape Design.

1. List the seven principles of water-wise gardening. Explain the take home message of each.

2. List the steps in the landscape design process.

3. Describe site analysis considerations in the following areas:

   a. Soil tilth

   b. Grading and drainage

   c. Microclimate

   d. Existing vegetation

   e. Extension landscape

   f. Potential for irrigation

4. Explain "opportunity or restraint" as it relates to site analysis.

5. Describe considerations in family analysis. How does potential irrigation figure into family analysis?

6. Discuss the purpose of the landscape story line (theme). What does the story line and theme bring to the design process?

7. Describe the purpose of the hydrozone bubble drawings.

8. Describe how hydrozones fit into the design process. For existing landscapes, explain why we go back to the hydrozone bubble drawings step to evolve a more water efficient landscape.

9. Describe the concept of "practical turf areas." What factors should be considered in matching a turf type for a specific site?

10. In Colorado where multi-year drought routinely occurs, how could community expectation about the lawn care change during a water shortage?

11. Discuss the following points about Kentucky bluegrass.

    a. KBG makes a great low input lawn option.

    b. KBG water use and growth slows as the soil begins to dry down.

    c. KBG irrigation demand varies significantly between cultivars.

    d. KBG goes dormant under summer water stress.

12. Discuss the following points about turf-type tall fescue lawns.

    a. Tall fescue may or may not be deeper rooted.

    b. Tall fescue cannot sow growth as soils dry down.

    c. Tall fescue cannot go dormant under water stress.

    d, Tall fescue makes a great lower input lawn option

13. Discuss the following points about turf-type Buffalograss.

    a. Summer green will be dependent on rain and irrigation.

    b. Buffalograss will be dormant fall through spring, reducing seasonal water demand.

14. Describe the "feeling" of rectilinear, curvilinear, and angular design. What determines which style would be appropriate?

15. Describe how to refine the preliminary design for efficient sprinkler irrigation. List criteria for efficient sprinkler layout.

16. In developing the plant potential lists for each hydrozone, explain the following concepts about water-wise gardening:

    a. Hydrozoning and xeriscaping is not a Phoenix-style rock landscape.

    b. Hydrozoning is not just purchasing and planting xeric plants around the landscape with other plants.

    c. Even xeric plants require routine irrigation during establishment.

    d. Hydrozoning is not against irrigated "people space" concepts.

Chapter
46*
∽
Principles of Landscape Design

The principles of landscape design include the elements of *unity, scale, balance, simplicity, variety, emphasis,* and *sequence* as they apply to *line, form, texture,* and *color.* These elements are interconnected.

UNITY IS THE QUALITY OF ONENESS.

Unity attracts and holds attention. It organizes view into orderly groups with emphasis. Unity starts with the *story line* developed in the *family analysis,* step 2, in the design process.

Figures 46-1 and 46-2 ▮ *Unity develops from the story line. Here in Jeff de Jong's garden a story line around "sacred space gardening" creates unity with the feeling of peace and tranquility.*

*Authors: David Whiting, Colorado State University Extension, and Jeffry de Jong, Horticulturist, Victoria, BC, Canada. Artwork by David Whiting.

Figure 46-3 ▪ *Notice the strong use of "line" here in the Sunken Garden at Butchart Gardens, Victoria, BC. The path (primary line) invites you into the garden. Secondary lines form the beds.*

Figure 46-4 ▪ *In this private garden, the "line" formed by the edge of the pond creates an amazing space as the plants reflect in the water. The line defines the space and pulls you into the landscape.*

LINE CONNECTS AND DEFINES THE SPACE, CREATING OUTDOOR ROOMS

Lines are a powerful design element that define rooms and connect people to the landscape. For a professional touch, use sweeping bold lines and curves rather than small zigzags and small wavy curves. Primary lines are developed in step 3 (*with lines, delineate softscape and hardscape areas, creating outdoor rooms*) in the design process.

FORM INCLUDES THE THREE-DIMENSIONAL MASS

Form is determined by the line, direction, and arrangement of branches and twigs. The resulting mass influences the scale. For unity, repeat the topography form in plant forms (Figure 46-5).

- **Horizontal and spreading** forms emphasize the lateral extent and breadth of space. They are comfortable because it corresponds with the natural direction of eye movement.

- **Rounded** forms are most common in plant materials. They allow for easy eye movement and create a pleasant undulation that leads itself to plant groupings.

- **Vase-shaped** trees define a comfortable "people space" beneath the canopy.

Figure 46-5 ▪ *Forms (left to right): columnar, oval, vase, weeping, pyramidal, and rounded.*

Figure 46-6 ▮ *Texture changes with distance. Up close, texture comes from the size and shape of leaves and twigs, plus the coloring and shading. At a distance, it comes from the mass and play of light.*

Figure 46-7 ▮ *Four-season gardening is all about texture gardening. Without the summer color, texture becomes the primary design element.*

Figure 46-8 ▮ *Texture rules here in the Japanese Garden at Butchart Gardens, Victoria, BC. Notice how the fine texture created by the moss plays with the coarse texture of the tree trunks and lantern. In Japanese gardening, the lantern is a symbol that this is sacred space, leave your cares and worries behind.*

- **Weeping forms** lead the eye back to the ground. What is below the weeping form often becomes a focal point.

- **Pyramidal** forms direct the eyes upward, so use sparingly. Grouping pyramidals will soften the upward influence. They will look more natural in the surroundings with foliage to the ground.

TEXTURE IS FINE/COARSE, HEAVY/ LIGHT, THIN/DENSE, AND LIGHT/SHADE

Texture can be defined as the relationship between the foliage and twig size, and the mass of the plants. Close up, texture comes from the size and shape of the leaves, the size of twigs, spacing of leaves and twigs, the colors and shading, the gloss or dullness of leaves. At a distance, texture comes from the entire mass effect of plants and the qualities of light and shadows (Figures 46-5 to 46-8).

COLOR GIVES GREATEST APPEAL, AND EVOKES THE GREATEST RESPONSE

How Does Color Speak to You? What Colors Work for the Landscape Story Line?

Color is powerful in creating mood and feeling. "Color therapy" is a popular topic in our rapid-paced modern world. What moods and feelings do various color create for you? What colors work for the landscape story line? What moods and feelings do you want in the garden? Is it a room for relaxation and healing or a room for action activities? Examples of common color feelings include the following (Figure 46-9):

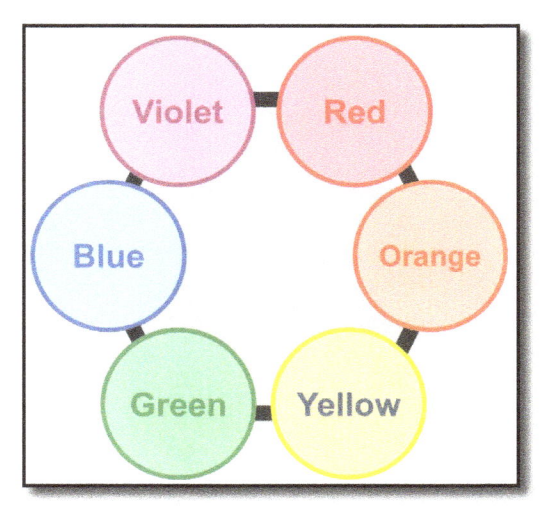

Figure 46-9 ▮ *Color is the most powerful of the design elements. Choose colors carefully to create the mood desired in the story line.*

Red	**Yellow**	**Blue**	**Green**
Passion	Joy	Imagination	Harmony
Courage	Happiness	Calm	Beginnings
Power	Communication	Serenity	Prosperity
Wealth	Inspiration	Relaxation	Nature
Motivation	Sunshine	Compassion	Growth
Fame	Optimism	Reflection	Healing

Orange	**Purple**	**White**	**Pink**
Enthusiasm	Intuition	Purity	Love
Joy	Devotion	Innocence	Sweetness
Exuberance	Respect	Faith	Uplifting
Interaction	Peace	Benevolence	Happiness
Fun	Spirituality	Honesty	Tenderness
Captivation	Awareness	Grace	Enticement
Sex	Deity		
	Royalty		

What Color Schemes Work for the Landscape Story Line?

Cool colors	*Warm colors*
Less conspicuous	Conspicuous
Restful	Cheerful
Recede	Stimulating
Suggest distance	Come forward
Low scale	High scale

SCALE EVOKES EMOTIONAL CONNECTION AND IS CLOSELY RELATED TO COLOR

- **Absolute scale** relates to the comparative value of landscape elements to a fixed structure (house) (Figure 46-10).

Figure 46-10 ▪ *In absolute scale, the small trees on the left drawing give the feeling that the house is large. On the right drawing, the large trees give the feeling that the house is small. Both houses are the same size.*

- **Relative scale** relates to comparative sizes or "values" of objects in the landscape. Relative scale is very emotionally charged and closely linked to color. It may create a feeling of relaxation and peacefulness or one of energy and action.

- **High scale** promotes action. It is used in and around large buildings and in large spaces to fill the space. Use of high scale in small spaces makes the space feel smaller (Figure 46-12).

- **Low scale** is relaxing and calming. It is used in the home landscape to give a feeling of peace and relaxation (Figure 46-13).

Figure 46-12 ▮ *Here in the fountain area at Butchart Gardens, scale is high with the brightly colored flowers. The action feeling of high scale helps move people through.*

Figure 46-11 ▮ *Relative scale compares the size or "value" of the landscape elements. Perception of tree size is based on the relative size of the person. Being emotionally charged, relative scale can create feelings of action or relaxation.*

Figure 46-13 ▮ *In this private garden in Steamboat Springs, CO, the low scale creates a relaxing, renewing atmosphere.*

BALANCE IS EQUILIBRIUM ON LEFT AND RIGHT SIDES

Formal balance repeats the same left and right, giving stability, stateliness, and dignity (Figures 46-14 and 46-16).

Informal balance differs from left to right giving curiosity, movement, and feels alive (Figures 46-15 and 46-17).

Which gives the "feeling" desired by the story line and design?

Figure 46-14 ▮ *Formal balance.*

Figure 46-15 ▮ *Informal balance.*

Figure 46-16 ▮ *The stately Italian Garden at Hatley Park, Victoria, BC, is a great example of formal balance.*

Figure 46-17 ▮ *The Herb Garden at Government House, Victoria, BC, is an excellent example of informal balance being relaxing and free flowing.*

SIMPLICITY AND VARIETY

Simplicity and variety work together to balance each other. *Simplicity* is a degree of repetition rather than constant change, creating unity. *Variety* is diversity and contrast in form, texture, and color preventing monotony (Figures 46-18 to 46-22).

- For simplicity, repeat some plant materials in sweeps and groupings.

- For variety, fill in with other plants.

- Avoid creating a horticultural zoo (one of this, two of that)!

- Zipper plantings (like red-white-red-white) lack simplicity and variety.

Figure 46-18 ▮ *In this simple drawing,* simplicity *is gained with the shrub row repeating the same plant materials.* Variety *is added with the tree.*

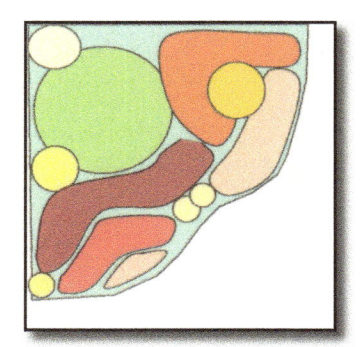

Figure 46-19 ▮ *For simplicity, repeat some plant materials in sweeps and groupings. Fill in with other plants for variety.*

Figure 46-20 ▮ *Simplicity is created by several hundred Hosta in this large bed. Variety is created by placing some in clusters of pots. Innis Gardens, Columbus, Ohio.*

Figure 46-21 ▮ *At Abkhazi Garden, Victoria, BC, simplicity is created with the row of purple heather and the lawn (the "Yangtze River"). Variety is created with an assortment of plant materials on the rocky hillside.*

Figure 46-22 ▮ *In this park, people enjoyed taking pictures of the various flowerbeds. However, they did not take pictures of this zipper planting (same elements repeated over and over again), finding it monotonous.*

EMPHASIS IS DOMINANCE AND SUBORDINATION OF ELEMENTS

The human mind looks for dominance and subordination in life. As we look at a landscape from any direction, we need to see dominance and subordination of various elements. If we do not find it, we withdraw from the landscape. Some gardens lack the dominant element. Others suffer with too many dominant elements screaming to be the focal point (Figures 46-23 to 46-25).

Emphasis can be achieved through different sizes, bold shapes, groupings, and the unusual or unexpected. What is the focal point?

Figure 46-23 ▮ *Emphasis is achieved with the tree being dominant and the shrub grouping being subordinate.*

Figure 46-24 ▮ *In this private garden, emphasis is added with the blooming Astelbe.*

Figure 46-25 ▮ *Ornamental grass often adds emphasis to a garden spot.*

SEQUENCE IS THE CHANGE OR FLOW IN FORM, COLOR, TEXTURE, AND SIZE GIVING MOVEMENT OR LIFE

Sequence with Texture

Change leaf size of adjacent different plants by at least one-half. Use proportionally larger numbers of fine-textured plants. (Figure 46-26).

In a flower/shrub bed, use coarser-texture, larger plants in the back; sequencing to finer-textured, smaller plants in the front inside curve (Figure 46-27).

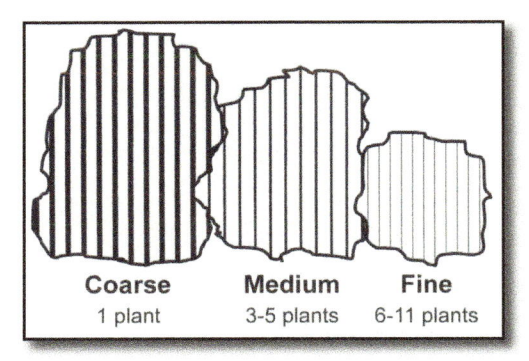

Coarse — 1 plant Medium — 3-5 plants Fine — 6-11 plants

Figure 46-26 ▮ *In a texture sequence, change leaf size of adjacent different types of plants by at least one-half. Use more of the finer-textured plant.*

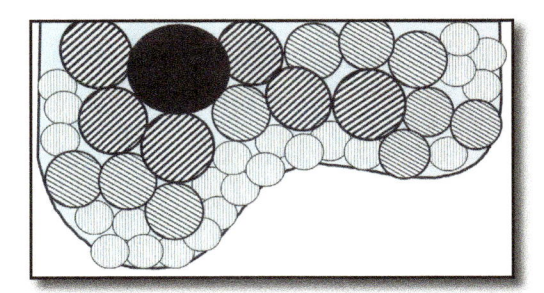

Figure 46-27 ▮ *In a texture sequence, place the fine-textured plants in the inside curve and the coarse-textured plants opposite. This is the way Mother Nature would do it. Look at the river. The sand bank is on the inside curve and the cliff opposite.*

Texture and distance—Texture becomes finer with distance. In a distant corner, place finer textures in the corner, sequencing to coarser textures on the arms (Figure 46-28).

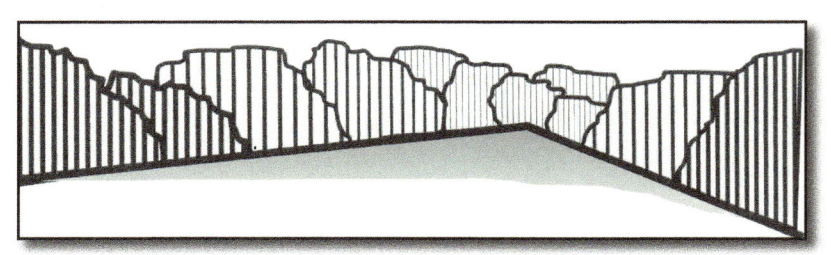

Figure 46-28 ▮ *Textures get finer with distance. Place the fine-textured plants in the distant corner with coarser-textured plants toward the viewer.*

Sequence with Color

There are few basic rules on how many warm and cool colors to use. However, watch that the scale does not become too commanding. More is NOT better. As a rule of thumb, the designs needs ninety percent green to set off the ten percent color.

Darkest shades and the purest intensity dominate and should be used at the focal point. Using cool colors in contrast is more effective than sequences. Warm colors work best in sequence.

Color Sequence

1. Decide what color(s) will be used.

2. Decide if light or dark will dominate. The darker or more intense (pure) the color, the more it will show up and dominate the scene.

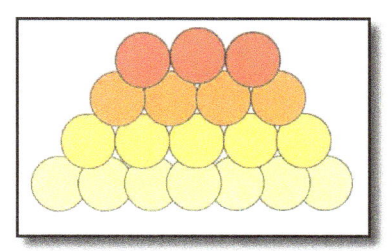

Figure 46-29 ▮ *In color sequence, increase the number of plants by one-third as the design moves from the dominant color to subordinate colors.*

Figure 46-30 ▮ *In color sequence, crescent shapes of colors give a natural flow.*

3. Calculate the number of plants of each color using this rule of thumb.

    a. Establish the largest amount of dark/dominant color that will be used.

    b. Select the next lighter shade and increase the number of plants by one-third.

    c. Select the next lighter shade and increase the number of plants by one-third.

    d. Continue the ratio to the lightest color (Figure 46-29).

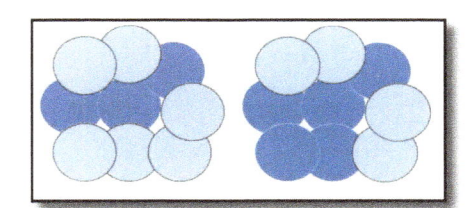

Figure 46-31 ▮ *In color contrasts, use two-thirds of one color for dominance and one-third of the other color for subordination. Not half and half.*

Grouping for best effect—Kidney or crescent-shaped groupings create a natural flowing design (Figure 46-30).

Color Contrasts

Monochrome light/dark color contrasts—Use one-third of one shade and two-thirds of the other shade (Figure 46-31).

Complementary color contrasts—Use one-third of one color and two-thirds of the complementary color.

Create Effective Plant Combinations By Pairing Opposites

To create plant combinations with pizzazz, pair opposites (Figures 46-32 to 46-35).

- Fine/Course
- Round/Upright
- Small/Large
- Short/Tall
- Thugs/Dainty
- Color contrasts

Figures 46-32 to 46-35 ▮ *Examples of great pairing.*

1. Define the following design terms:
   a. Balance
   b. Color
   c. Emphasis
   d. Form
   e. Line
   f. Scale
   g. Sequence
   h. Simplicity
   i. Texture
   j. Unity
   k. Variety

2. Describe how the following *forms* affect eye movement and feelings:
   a. Weeping
   b. Horizontal or spreading
   c. Rounded
   d. Pyramidal

3. Describe how to balance simplicity with variety. Describe how to use simplicity to bring unity to the design.

4. How does distance impact texture? In a distant corner, how should textures sequence? In a kidney-shaped planting bed how should texture sequence? In a texture sequence, how should leaf size change and the proportion of plant numbers changes?

5. Discuss how colors create moods and feelings.

6. Explain differences in warm and cool colors.

7. Describe how to sequence warm colors and cool colors.

8. In mixing colors in a bed, what is the design trick to a natural "life" to the bed?

9. Describe how to mix and match plants, creating pizzazz.

UNIT L

Irrigation Management

Learning Objectives

At the end of this unit, the student will be able to:

- Describe issues around Colorado's (western) water situation.
- Describe design criteria for efficient landscape irrigation.
- Describe maintenance criteria for efficient landscape irrigation.
- Describe management criteria for efficient landscape irrigation.
- Perform a lawn irrigation checkup.
- Set a controller for efficient landscape irrigation.

Supplemental Reading

Web

- Colorado ET: www.coloradoet.org/
- Colorado Springs Utility: http://et.csu.org/
- Denver Water: www.denverwater.org
- Northern Colorado Water Conservancy District: www.ncwcd.org

47*

Western Water Rights

WESTERN WATER RIGHTS—*DOCTRINE OF PRIOR APPROPRIATIONS*

In Colorado and other Western states, water rights are based on the **Doctrine of Prior Appropriation** or "first-in-time, first-in-right." Rights are established when water is put to beneficial use.

A water right is a property's right to use a specified quantity of the state's water for a specified purpose. As a property right, water rights can be sold, leased, or rented (like other personal properties such as a home, apartment, or car). With the *prior appropriation doctrine* used in Western states, a property owner does *not* own the water that rains, snows, or flows across or is adjacent to his/her property.

By contrast, Eastern states follow some form of "riparian" water right (i.e., water rights belong to landowners bordering the water source). Without an understanding of the *doctrine of prior appropriation*, newcomers and residents may fail to realize that the purchase of land does not necessarily include the rights to irrigation water.

Under the *prior appropriation doctrine*, water rights are established by putting the water into **beneficial use**. The person or organization putting the water to beneficial use requests the **water courts** to legally recognize the right with a **decree**.

In the establishment of water rights, the water judge decrees the location at which the water will be withdrawn, the amount to be withdrawn, the use of the water, and assigns a **priority date**. Claims with earlier priority dates have **senior rights**; claims with more recent priority dates have **junior rights**.

During times of reduced rainfall or drought, *senior rights* (water rights established in early years) take precedence over *junior rights* (water rights established in recent years). Water use will be cut off for junior rights, protecting senior rights.

_____

*Author: David Whiting, Colorado State University Extension. Artwork by David Whiting

When a water use is changed, the water courts reissue the decree amending the owner, location, amount, or use. The priority date will be based on the previous priority date. Since Colorado's water supply fluctuates continually and the typical available water in a river basin is already owned with established water rights, issues of senior and junior rights become very complex in drought scenarios.

Colorado's water future—*"As Colorado's water consumption reaches the limits of its allotment under interstate compacts and treaties, intensive water management will become even more critical. Water management decisions will involve examinations of all options. Conversation will become indispensable . . . Inevitably, as each generation must learn, the land and the waters will instruct us in the ways of community."*—Citizen's Guide to Colorado Water Law

Administration

In Colorado, the Office of the State Engineer, Colorado Division of Water Resources, administers water rights. It monitors the amount of water being taken from surface and underground sources, and oversees distribution based on the priority of water rights.

Interstate water rights are set in federal agreements based on stream flows for the Platt, Colorado, and Arkansas River basins.

WATER QUALITY TERMINOLOGY

Regulated by the Environmental Protection Agency (EPA), ***drinking water*** or ***potable water*** is water of sufficiently high quality for safe human consumption. The drinking water in many Colorado communities is of higher quality than most bottled water. Over large parts of the world, humans have inadequate access to potable water, and use sources contaminated with unsafe levels of dissolved chemicals, suspended soils, disease vectors, and pathogens.

Nonpotable water refers to water not processed to drinking water standards. ***Raw water*** refers to untreated water taken directly from rivers and lakes.

Wastewater is any water that has been adversely affected in quality by human activities. This includes domestic, municipal, or industrial liquid waste products disposed of by flushing them with water through a pipe system. *Sewage* technically refers to wastewater contaminated with feces and urine. However, in popular usage, sewage refers to wastewater. ***Gray water*** refers to water from the bath/shower and washing machine. ***Black water*** refers to water with feces and urine (from the toilet).

Reclaimed water or ***recycled water*** is former wastewater (sewage) that has been treated to remove solids and certain impurities. In most situations, it is returned to the river system, being the nonconsumptive use portion of water rights. That is, the reclaimed water returned to stream flow becomes someone's water right downstream. In Colorado, some parks, golf courses, and industrial properties are irrigated with reclaimed water. Reclaimed water may be high in salt, limiting its use for landscape irrigation.

SOURCES OF LANDSCAPE IRRIGATION WATER

In many communities, most landscape irrigation is done with potable, drinking water purchased from the city or community water provider (who owns the water right or purchases the water wholesale). The source of water may be stream flow (from snowmelt with storage in the reservoir system) or wells. During the summer irrigation season, this puts a high demand on the water treatment facilities. To deal with this, many communities aggressively market landscape water conservation.

In the West, many larger landscape sites (golf courses, parks, and industrial sites) are irrigated with nonpotable water or raw water. In some Western communities, homes have a waterline for drinking water and a second, nonpotable waterline for irrigation. This creates significant savings in water treatment costs.

Wells

For rural homes, a common water source is groundwater (wells). The Colorado Division of Water Resources also regulates the drilling and use of groundwater. In the past, the lack of strict regulations caused a significant drop in the water table in some communities, creating problems for well users. Today the use of wells is regulated, limiting the amount of water that can be withdrawn. In recent years, new domestic well permits have been very restrictive, prohibiting outdoor irrigation. Folks moving to their rural ranchette are often shocked when they learn that they may not irrigate the landscape with their well water.

On the high plains of Eastern Douglas and El Paso Counties, the community water source is nonrenewable groundwater (wells). This water supply is not refilled with annual rain and snowmelt. Conservation is extremely critical.

Rain Water and Gray Water

Landscape design can be creative in reducing the surface runoff of rain and snowmelt (reducing pollution of surface water). However, in Colorado, state law prohibits the intentional interception and diversion of rain and snowmelt (that is, the collection of the water in a retention system for later use), including rain barrels. This is an issue of water rights, as the water already belongs to someone downstream. Collection of rain and snowmelt could interfere with another's water right.

A new exception is individuals who had water rights for irrigation by groundwater (wells) may use rain barrels to catch and use water from their roof *as a substitute* for the groundwater. This requires a special permit and does not increase the water right. This exception does not extend to residents whose well permit prohibits landscape irrigation or homes with other sources of water.

In Colorado, the use of gray water is also prohibited (except under special permit) due to issues of water rights and public health. Gray water is a ***nonconsumptive*** water use, in that the water is returned to the system. After being processed, it is returned to stream flow and becomes a water right downstream. Diverting this water onto the landscape "consumes" the water rather than returning it to downstream flows, thus interfering with water rights downstream.

For additional information on using gray water and harvesting rainwater in Colorado, refer to CSU Extension fact sheet #6.702, *Graywater Reuse and Rainwater Harvesting*, available on the CSU website at www.cmg. colostate.edu.

COLORADO'S WATER USE

Eighty percent of Colorado's water supply falls on the Western Slope. With the high population along the Front Range and major agriculture in northeastern Colorado, eighty percent of the water use (that is eighty percent of the water rights) is along the Front Range and High Plains. Table 47-1 gives the breakdown of water use in a typical year.

Table 47-1. Where Does Colorado's Water Go?

Agriculture	86%
Domestic/municipal	7%
Recreation and fisheries	3%
Industrial and commercial	2%
Augmentation	1%
Recharge	1%

Source: Colorado State Engineer's Office, 2004

Production agriculture is the primary user of Colorado's water supply, using eighty-five to ninety percent for food production. To grow the typical American meal it takes 500 to 2,000 gallons of water. On an annual basis, it takes 1.6 million gallons of water to grow the food for the typical American diet of 2,000 calories per day (Source: Michigan State University Institute of Water Research).

Although the individual farmer can be rather inefficient in use, the runoff water returning to the system is used repeatedly by other farmers down the line, resulting in a ninety percent systemwide efficiency.

Landscape irrigation—Depending on the year, approximately seven to ten percent of Colorado's water supply is used for landscape irrigation, including home lawns and yards, public and commercial landscapes, parks, and golf courses. During the summer irrigation season, fifty to seventy-five percent of a community's water use may be for landscape irrigation. Because it is highly visible, landscape irrigation is often targeted for conservation.

Based on community water use, the average landscape receives twice the amount of irrigation water that plants actually need. This is due to poor irrigation system design, maintenance, and management. In research of actual yard-by-yard comparisons, most gardeners are rather efficient; however, others may be applying five to ten times the amount of water actually needed!

With the rapid growth in Colorado's population, some farmers have sold, leased, or rented water rights to communities. This creates a significant shift in water use during periods of drought and creates long-term dynamics between agriculture and urbanization.

Other demands on water flows come with power generation, recreational use, and wildlife habitats. As an important side issue, during periods of drought (decreased stream flow), hydroelectric power generation will also decrease.

A standard unit for measuring large quantities of water is the *acre-foot*. An acre-foot is the amount of water needed to cover an acre of land to a depth of one foot, or 325,851 gallons. The standard unit of measuring water flow is cubic feet per second, or cfs. One cfs equals 7.48 gallons per second or 448.83 gallons per minute.

Community Water Infrastructure

A community typically invests $30,000 to $60,000 per new household for the water and sewer treatment infrastructure. Due to landscape irrigation, Colorado communities typically experience ten to fifteen days per year when water use greatly exceeds average use. Because peak demand actually occurs only a few days a year, developing the water processing and delivery infrastructure to adequately meet water needs during these few peak days is very expensive. One Colorado community, for example, is facing a $35 million expansion to its water-processing infrastructure to meet peak demand for just five days a year!

The high cost of meeting peak water demand is why communities often adopt irrigation schedules based on address (like odd/even days or other set irrigation day programs). *Schedules are designed to spread the water demand more evenly over the week.* Just imagine the water infrastructure that would be required if most residents decided to water the lawn on a Saturday morning during a hot week!

Odd/even or set watering day water restrictions do not effectively reduce total water usage. An underlying fear with gardeners is that they cannot hold off irrigation until their next turn, so the lawn is watered just because it is their turn. Irrigation restrictions that allow for no irrigation on some days of the week more effectively conserve water.

Population Growth and Water Conservation

Colorado's rapid population growth creates growing pains for Colorado's water supply. Due to planning by forefathers, some communities have good water resources, including senior rights. Other communities seriously lack sufficient water rights to support growth. Residents who do not understand Western water rights may have strong values and opinions about where water should and should not be used during shortages. Under Western water rights, market price to purchase water rights will determine who has water. What are you willing to pay?

Water conservation, both indoors and outdoors, is essential for communities to meet the water demands for growth. Some communities with limited water resources have put restrictions on new building permits. This could be viewed as a form of discrimination aimed at keeping newcomers out of the "white" community.

Other communities, with limited water resources, have allowed for growth by purchasing "surplus" water from water rights holders (such as other communities or farmers). Some of the extreme water restrictions during the drought of 2002 are examples of what happens in years when "surplus" water is not available for purchase.

With growth, water conservation is also critical even for those communities with senior water rights. For example, Denver Water and Colorado Springs Utilities, two of the state's larger water providers, are running out of water resources to support continued growth at current usage rates. Conservation is essential.

Water for growth must come from water conservation. This will be through voluntary conservation and aggressive pricing structures to push conservation. Since Colorado's climate typically has a multi-year drought about every 20 years, water conservation is important to all residents.

1. Describe the Western water rights doctrine of "prior appropriation" or "first-in-time, first-in-right." How does it differ from the "riparian" water rights system used in Eastern states?

2. What percent of Colorado's water supply is used for landscape irrigation?

3. During the summer irrigation season, what percent of a community's water supply is typically used for landscape irrigation?

4. On a communitywide basis, what percent of the water used for landscape irrigation is wasted due to poor design, maintenance, and management of the irrigation systems?

5. Explain how landscape irrigation affects a community's water infrastructure. What is the primary purpose behind community water schedules, such as every third day or every other day?

6. What is the typical multi-year drought cycle in Colorado's climate?

7. How does population growth play into Colorado's water situation?

48*

Understanding Irrigation Management Factors

Poor watering practices lead to many common landscape problems, including iron chlorosis, low plant vigor, foliar diseases, root rots, and water pollution. On a communitywide basis, landscape irrigation typically uses twice the amount of water that the plants actually need.

Several complex factors work together in irrigation management, including the following:

- The soil's *water-holding capacity* (the quantity of water held by the soil)

- *Evapotranspiration, ET*, is a measurement of actual water use by the plant and lost from the soil by evaporation. ET is a factor of weather (temperature, wind, humidity, and solar radiation) and plant growth.

- Rooting depth

- The plant's ability to extract water from the soil

- The plant's water need

SOIL–PLANT–WATER SYSTEM

Water constantly moves in and out of landscapes. Scientists use the concept of the soil–plant–water system to explain the complex ways water moves in landscapes. The *soil–plant–water system* describes water's entry, storage, and exit in a landscape from the plant's perspective. Understanding how water moves through a landscape is important when designing or using an irrigation system.

---

*Authors: David Whiting and Carl Wilson, Colorado State University Extension; and Cathrine Moravec, Colorado Springs Utilities. Artwork by David Whiting.

Most plants constantly use water, but store little in their tissues. Therefore, plants rely on the soil water reserves being periodically replenished through entries of water into the soil–plant–water system.

Water Entries

Water enters the landscape in several ways. First, water enters through **precipitation**, such as rain or snow. Second, gardeners may add water through **irrigation**. Third, water may run over the surface of the landscape from a neighboring area (**run-on**). Fourth, water may enter as **seepage** from groundwater (Figure 48-1).

In different landscapes, some entry methods are more important than others. For example, in a wet climate most water enters through precipitation. Alternatively, in dry climates like many areas of Colorado and the West, most water enters via irrigation. If a landscape is located below a heavily irrigated property or below a melting snowfield, run-on or seepage may be the most important entry. Taking water entries into account helps gardeners determine how much water must be added through irrigation to keep plants healthy.

Water Storage

In most landscapes, soil is the major water storage site for plants. Once water has entered the landscape through precipitation, irrigation, run-on, or seepage, water penetrates the soil surface through **infiltration**.

Water infiltrates into sandy soils much more quickly than into clayey soils. For example, a sandy soil may take in four inches per hour, but a clayey soil may take in only one-half inches of water per hour—eight times more slowly. To prevent water waste via runoff, gardeners should take the soil's infiltration rate into account when scheduling landscape irrigation.

Once water infiltrates the soil surface, it **percolates** downward and sideways through the soil profile. Water moves rapidly through large soil pores, and slowly through small pores. Therefore, sandy soils with primarily large pores will accept and release water readily, holding little. On the other hand, clayey soils with primarily small pores will wet and dry slowly.

After water percolates through the soil profile, some of the water will be stored in small pores, and a water films surrounding soil particles. Plants can use some of the stored water (called plant-**available water**) by extracting it with their roots. However, some of the water is held so tightly by small pores or particle surfaces that plant roots cannot extract it. This water is **unavailable** to plants.

When plants need more water than is available in the soil, they experience **water stress**. Because water is a component of photosynthates, photosynthesis stops and growth stops. Furthermore, water stress compromises plant defense systems, making them more susceptible to abiotic stress factors as well as insect and disease problems.

Some soils store more water than others. The amount of water held in the soil and available to plant depends on the following factors:

- Clay content (the amount of small pore space) to hold water.
- Soil organic content—Organic matter holds ten times more water than sand.
- Rooting depth—Plants with deeper roots reach a larger water supply.

Water Exits

Water eventually leaves the landscape. Water may exit by running over the land surface (**runoff**). It may leave the system through **off-target application**, such as sprinklers that apply water to the sidewalk rather than the soil. Sometimes, water percolates below the plant's root zone (**leaching**) (Figure 48-1).

Water **evaporates** from the soil surface, causing soils to dry from the top downward. Mulches help ameliorate water loss by reducing evaporation from the soil surface. Mulches also improve plant growth by helping to maintain moisture in the top layer of soil, thereby stabilizing soil moisture around roots.

Some water is taken up by plant roots, transported through plant tissues, and used in photosynthesis for plant growth. Most of the water taken up by plants is **transpired** out leaf surfaces. Because evaporation and transpiration are often the two most important water exits in landscapes, scientists combine these two pathways into one term called evapotranspiration.

Evapotranspiration (abbreviated as **ET**) is a measurement of water use combining water used by plants for transpiration, photosynthesis, and growth, plus water lost from the soil surface evaporation. It is most often defined as a *rate of water loss*, such as one-quarter inch per day. In this example, an ET of one-quarter inch per day means that a one-quarter-inch depth of water was lost from the soil–plant–water system through evaporation and transpiration.

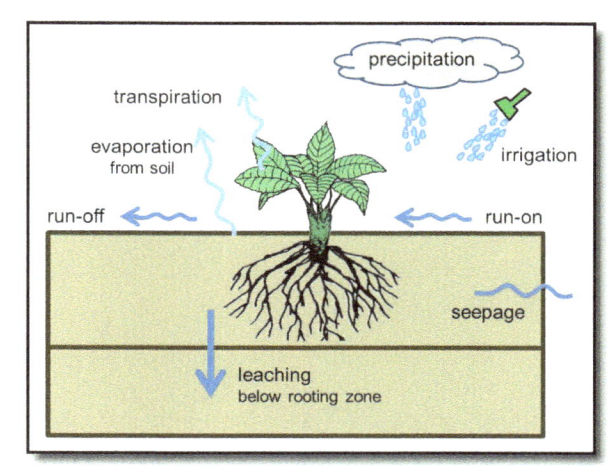

Figure 48-1 ■ *Typical water entries and exits in the soil–plant–water system.*

ET measurements help gardeners make informed decisions about how much irrigation water to add. In some Colorado communities, ET rates are available online through weather stations or water utilities.

ET rates change daily through the growing season. High ET rates occur when there is: 1) bright sunshine, 2) high wind, 3) high temperature, and/or 4) low humidity.

Summary

Water entries and exits are summarized in Figure 48-1. In order to maximize plant health in dry climates of Colorado and the West, gardeners can take two approaches. First, they can apply soil management practices to increase soil water storage. This helps ensure adequate water supplies for plants when needed. Second, gardeners can use effective irrigation management practices to ensure that irrigation water is made available to plants and not wasted.

LOCATION OF SOIL MOISTURE

Following dry winters or summer droughts, soils may be dry in the top layers with moisture only in deeper layers. Following extended drought, it is possible that soils may be dry in deep layers and wet only in the top few inches following a light rain or irrigation.

Dry soils tend to resist wetting. Alternating irrigation applications with shutoffs to allow water to soak in (cycle and soak irrigation) may be necessary to wet a dry soil profile.

Irrigation management is basically applying the correct *amount* of water at the correct *frequency* to supply water needs of the plants. Additional water would be wasted as it would leach below the rooting zone.

TYPE OF SOIL

Soil texture, structure, and organic matter content determine the water-holding capacity and water movement of a soil. Water coats the soil particles and organic matter, and is held in small pore space by cohesion (chemical forces by which water molecules stick together). Air fills the large pore space.

In large pore space, water readily moves downward by ***gravitational pull***. In small spore space, water moves slowly in all directions by ***capillary action***. Figure 48-2 illustrated water movement in a sandy soil with large pore space and clayey soil with small pore space (Figure 48-2).

Sandy soil—Large pore space dominates sandy soil, giving it rapid drainage. Thus, surface runoff of irrigation water is generally not a concern with sandy soil. Water movement is primarily in a downward direction by gravitational pull in the large pore space with limited sideward and upward movement by capillary action in the small pore space. Thus, in drip irrigation the emitters must be placed closer together than in clayey soils.

Sandy soils have a low water-holding capacity due to the lack of small pore space. Organic matter, which holds ten times more water than sand, significantly improves the water-holding capacity of sandy soils.

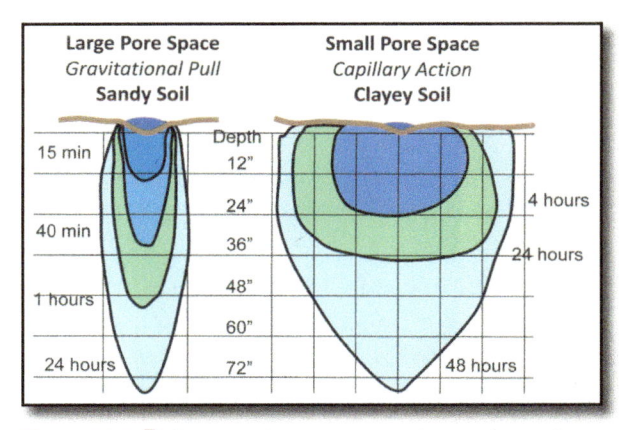

Figure 48-2 ▪ *Comparative movement of water in sandy and clayey soils.*

As a point of clarification, plants on sandy soils do not use more water than plants on clayey soils. **With the limited water-holding capacity, sandy soils simply need lighter and more frequent irrigations than clayey soils.** Water readily moves below the rooting zone when *too much* is applied at a time.

Clayey soil—Small pore space dominates clayey soil, giving it high water-holding capacity. However, the lack of large pore space greatly limits water movement. Water is slow to infiltrate into clayey soil, often leading to surface runoff problems. Cycle and soak irrigation is appropriate on clayey soils to slow application rates and reduce surface runoff.

In clayey soils, soil *structure* (creating secondary large pore space) also directly influences water movement and soil oxygen levels. Compaction (a reduction in pore space) further limits water movement and reduces soil oxygen levels, resulting in a shallow rooting depth. The total water supply available to plants is reduced by the shallower rooting.

With higher water-holding capacity but limited drainage, clayey soils need heavier, but less frequent irrigations than sandy soils. Watering *too often* can aggravate low soil oxygen levels. Because water moves slowly in all directions by capillary action, drip emitters may be placed further apart than in sandy soils.

Water-Holding Capacity

The terms *saturation, field capacity, wilting point*, and *available water* describe the amount of water held in a soil. (Figure 48-3).

Saturation refers to the situation when water fills both the large and small pore spaces. With water replacing air in the large pore spaces, root functions temporarily stop (since roots require oxygen for water and nutrient uptake).

Prolonged periods without root oxygen will cause most plants to wilt (due to a lack of water uptake), to show general symptoms of stress, to decline (due to a lack of root function), and to die (due to root dieback).

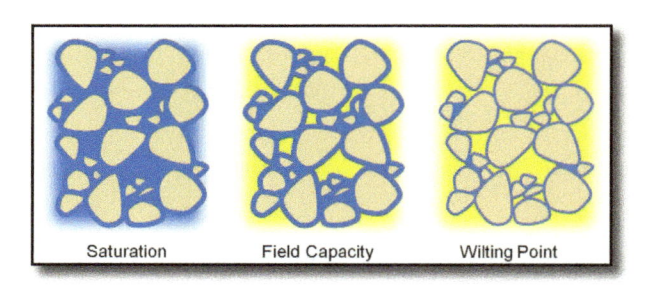

Figure 48-3 ▪ *At **saturation**, water fills the pore spaces. At **field capacity**, air occupies the large pore spaces while water fills the small pore spaces. At the **wilting point**, plants cannot extract additional water from the soil.*

During summer flooding of the Mississippi River in Iowa and Illinois it was observed that healthy trees were somewhat tolerant of a short-term flooding period, whereas trees under stress or in a state of decline were very intolerant.

Field capacity refers to the situation when excess water has drained out by gravitational pull. Air occupies the large pore space. Water coats the soil particles and organic matter and fills the small pore space. A handful of soil at or above field capacity will glisten in the sunlight. In clayey and/or compacted soils, the lack of large pore space slows or prohibits water movement down through the soil profile, keeping soils above field capacity for a longer period of time and limiting plant growth.

Permanent wilting point refers to the situation when a plant wilts beyond recovery due to a lack of water in the soil. At this point, the soil feels dry to the touch. However, it still holds about half of its water; the plant just does not have the ability to extract it. Plants vary in their ability to extract water from the soil.

Available water is the amount of the water held in a soil between *field capacity* and the *permanent wilting point*. This represents the quantity of water "available" or usable by the plant. Note from the illustration on the right that the amount of *available water* is low in a sandy soil. Loamy soils have the largest amount of

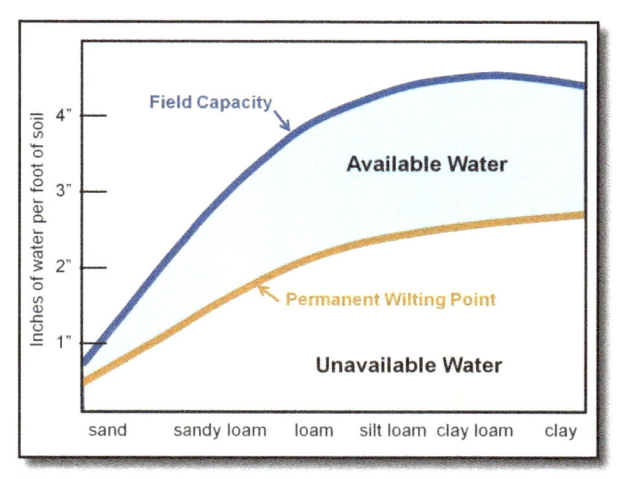

Figure 48-4 ▮ *Relationship between soil texture and available water.*

available water. In clayey soils, the amount of *available water* decreases slightly as capillary action holds the water so tightly that plants cannot extract it (Figure 48-4).

EVAPOTRANSPIRATION

Evapotranspiration (ET) is the rate at which a crop uses water for transpiration and growth plus evaporation from the soil surface. Primary influences on ET include weather factors (temperature, wind, humidity, and solar radiation) and the stage of plant growth.

On hot, dry, windy days, ET will be higher. On cool, humid days, ET will be lower. In the summer, ET changes significantly from day to day. To illustrate seasonal variations, the typical irrigation requirement for cool season turf in Colorado is given in Table 48-1.

Table 48-1. Weekly Water Requirement for Cool Season Lawns in Colorado

Inches of water (irrigation and rain) per week						
Late April	May	June	July	August	September	Early October
0.75″	1.0″	1.0″	1.5″	1.5″	1.0″	0.75″

ROOTING DEPTH

Irrigation management should take into account the rooting depth, adding water to the actual root area. Root systems may be contained or spreading. Annual plants tend to have contained root systems, whereas woody trees and shrubs have more wide-reaching roots.

A newly planted annual flower or shallow-rooted plant cannot obtain water from deeper soil depths. Deep watering of these plants is wasteful.

Roots only grow where there are adequate levels of soil oxygen. In clayey or compacted soils, where a lack of large pore space restricts oxygen levels, roots will be shallow. Plants with a shallow rooting depth simply have a smaller profile of soil water to use (Figure 48-5).

A plant with deeper roots will need less frequent but heavier irrigation than the same plant with shallow roots. This, however, should not be interpreted as necessarily using less water. For example, turf-type fall fescue may root more deeply than Kentucky bluegrass (if soil oxygen levels allow). With deeper rooting, it requires less frequent irrigations, but irrigations must be heavier to recharge the rooting zone. Actual water-use rates of Kentucky bluegrass and tall fescue are similar.

IRRIGATION: HOW MUCH? HOW OFTEN?

Table 48-2 illustrates the relationship of the soil water-holding capacity, ET, and rooting depth.

These textbook figures make a good starting point for understanding irrigation management. Most automatic sprinkler systems are set to keep the lawn green in the summer (i.e., set for the higher summer water need). Without seasonal adjustments on the irrigation controller, the lawn will be overirrigated in the spring and fall by about forty percent This springtime over-irrigation is a primary contributing factor to iron chlorosis.

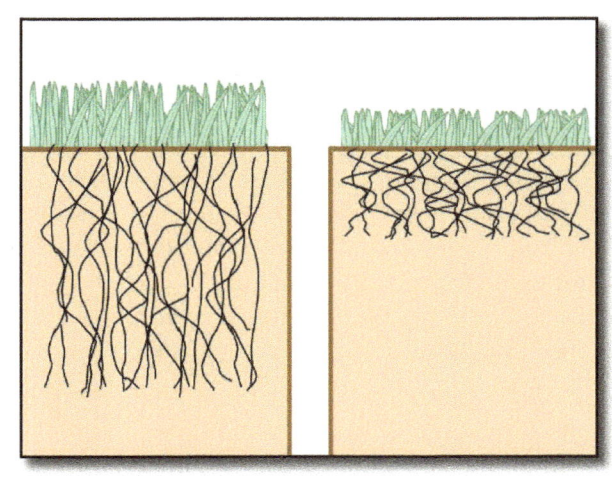

Figure 48-5 ▮ *Plants with deeper rooting systems reach a larger supply of water and can go longer between irrigations. With deeper rooting, irrigations will be less frequent but heavier to recharge the larger rooting zone. In compacted or clayey soils, low levels of soil oxygen limit rooting depth, thus reducing the supply of available water.*

Table 48-2. Irrigation Summary of a Textbook Soil

	Soil Type		
	Sandy	Sandy Loam	Loamy & Clayey
Available water per foot of soil	0.5"	0.75"	1"
6-inch rooting depths Inches of available water and **Inches of water to apply per irrigation** (Additional amounts would leach below the rooting zone)	0.25"	0.38"	0.5"
Typical days between lawn irrigation			
Spring/Fall (at 1.0 inches/week)	1.8 days	2.7 days	3.6 days
Summer (at 1.5 inches/week)	1.2 days	1.8 days	2.4 days
12-inch rooting depth Inches of available water, and **Inches of water to apply per irrigation** (Additional amounts would leach below the rooting zone)	0.5"	0.75"	1"
Typical days between lawn irrigation			
Spring/Fall (at 1.0 inches/week)	3.6 days	5.3 days	7.1 days
Summer (at 1.5 inches/week)	2.4 days	3.6 days	4.8 days
24-inch rooting depth Inches available water and **Inches of water to apply per irrigation** (Additional amounts would leach below the rooting zone)	1"	1.5"	2"
Typical days between lawn irrigation			
Spring/Fall (at 1.0 inches/week)	7.1 days	10.7 days	14.2 days
Summer (at 1. 5 inches/week)	4.8 days	7.1days	9.5days

FINE-TUNING FOR THE SITE

The textbook figures are a good starting point to understand irrigation management. When coupled with careful observations, a gardener can quickly fine-tune his/her irrigation schedule to the site-specific irrigation demands.

On a typical July day, if the lawn is using an average of 0.20 inch per day, you can estimate the water-holding capacity and rooting depth by observing irrigation needs. For example:

- **If the lawn will go five days on one inch of water**, and additional water won't extend the interval between required irrigations, the water-holding capacity (for this soil and rooting depth) is one inch. *One inch would be the maximum amount of water to apply per irrigation, as additional amounts would leach below the rooting zone.* The ideal irrigation would be 1 inch of water every 5 days.

- **If the lawn will go four days on 0.80 inch of water**, and additional water won't extend the interval between required irrigations, the water-holding capacity (for this soil and rooting depth) is 0.80 inch. *This would be the maximum amount of water to apply per irrigation, as additional amounts would leach below the rooting zone.* The ideal irrigation would be 0.8 inches of water every 4 days.

- **If the lawn will go two days on 0.40 inch of water**, and additional water won't extend the interval between required irrigations, the water-holding capacity (for this soil and rooting depth) is 0.40 inch. *This would be the maximum amount of water to apply per irrigation, as additional amounts would leach below the rooting zone.* The ideal irrigation would be 0.4 inches of water every 2 days.

These textbooks figures don't take into account exposure, wind or irrigation system efficiency. They make a good start point, **but will need adjustments to fine-tune it to the specific site.** For example:

- In full shade (not under large trees), water use could be 30% lower.

- In unusually hot weather or in open, windy sites, water use could be 20% to over 50% higher.

- In the rooting area of large trees, water use could be 30% to 50% higher (as the tree is pulling water as well as the plants in the shade under the tree).

For examples, in the author's landscape, the front lawn (open site with constant summer wind) uses 20% more water than the normal ET. While the back lawn (sheltered from the wind by the house and wood fence) uses the normal ET.

So the trick for efficient irrigation is to start with the textbook numbers then fine tune them based on observation. **Based on actual observations for each zone, adjust the run time up/down in 10% increment to fine-tune the irrigation.**

These examples are based on typical July weather. **For cooler spring and fall seasons, the amount of water to apply generally remains the same, with a longer interval between irrigations.**

OTHER FACTORS INFLUENCING IRRIGATION MANAGEMENT

Other factors also have a direct influence on the *actual* water-holding capacity and irrigation demands, for example:

- **Exposure**—The plant's exposures greatly influences water demand. Sun, heat, and wind increase water demand. Shade decreases water demand. Water use for a lawn on a windy, southwest-facing slope could be double the water use of a lawn in full sun but sheltered from wind and extreme heat.

- **Soil organic matter content**—Since organic matter holds over ten times more water than sand, a sandy soil with good organic content (around four to five percent) will hold more water than indicated in the table on page 634. Over time, clayey soils with good organic content may have an improved soil structure, supporting a deeper rooting depth.

- **Previous irrigation pattern**—Plants adjust rooting depth (to the extent that soil oxygen levels allow) to where soil water is available. Frequent irrigation eliminates the need for plants to develop a deep rooting system. A shallow rooting system makes the plant less resilient to hot, dry weather.

- **Stage of growth**—The stage of growth also influences ET. Water needs increase as a plant grows in size during the season and peaks during flowering and fruit development.

- Compared to the rooting system of a mature plant, newly planted or seeded crops do not have the root systems to explore a large volume of soil for water. Recently planted and seeded crops will require frequent, light irrigations. In our dry climate, even xeric plants generally need regular irrigation to establish.

  Confusion about plant water requirements can arise from changing needs as plants move through their life cycles. For example, newly planted trees are extremely intolerant of water stress. Established trees in good health are rather tolerant of short-term water stress. Older trees in decline are intolerant of water stress. General statements about the ability of trees to tolerate dry situations need to take into account life cycle stages.

- **Water demand of a plant**—Plants vary greatly in the demand for water to: 1) support growth, and 2) survive dry spells. (Note that the two are not necessarily related.)

- **Ability to extract water**—Plants vary in their ability to extract water from the soil. For most plants, the *available water* is about fifty percent of the soil's total water supply before reaching the *permanent wilting point*. Onions are an example of a crop that can only extract about forty percent.

- **Drought mechanism**—A similar, *but unrelated*, issue is the plant's ability to survive on dry soil. Plants have evolved with a variety of drought mechanisms, for example:

  —Small leaves, waxy leaves, hairy leaves, and light-colored leaves are characteristics of many plants with lower water requirements.

  —Some plants, like cacti, have internal water storage supplies and waxy coatings.

  —Many plants, like impatiens, readily wilt as an internal water conservation measure.

  —Trees close the stomata in the leaves, shutting down photosynthesis, during water stress.

  —Some plants, like Kentucky bluegrass, can go dormant under water stress.

  —Kentucky bluegrass slows growth as soils begin to dry down. (Does your irrigation management capitalize on this dry-down, also reducing your mowing?)

  —Tall fescue is an example of plants that survive short-term dry soil conditions by rooting more deeply (if soil conditions allow) to reach a larger water supply. However, tall fescue cannot go dormant.

TOOLS TO EVALUATE SOIL MOISTURE

Gardeners have a number of tools available to evaluate the amount of moisture in their soil.

Plant observation is a good guide to soil moisture. Look for color change and wilting. For example, Kentucky bluegrass will change from a blue-green to gray-blue with water stress. Footprints in the lawn that do not rebound within 60 minutes are another symptom to watch for. Use of an indicator plant in a perennial flowerbed is also useful. Certain perennials such as *Ligularia stenocephala* (The Rocket) and *Eupatorium rugosum* (White Snakeroot) often wilt before other perennial flowers, indicating irrigation will shortly be required.

The **hand feel method** used when digging in soil is more evidence of moisture content. Is the soil powder dry, medium moist, or even muddy?

The ease with which a **probe** can be inserted can be telling. A screwdriver will punch into the soil more easily when wet than when dry. However, this can be very misleading, as a clayey soil may be difficult when wet and impossible when dry. A sandy soil may be easy when dry and easier when wet.

Soil moisture meters are available. A simple, houseplant water meter can be used outdoors. Although the exact number reading may give little information, the overall indication of wet or dry is useful. It will read on the wet side when the soil has high nutrients or salts, and on the dry side when the soil is low in nutrients and salt. Permanently buried soil moisture sensors are available to automatically activate irrigation systems when the soil has dried.

1 List how water enters the landscape. Explain how water is stored in the landscape. List how water leaves the landscape.

2. What is ET? What factors influence ET rates?

3. Describe how these factors influence irrigation management:

   a. Location of soil moisture

   b. Type of soil

   c. Water-holding capacity

   d. ET

   e. Rooting depth

4. How does improving a sandy soil with organic matter influence irrigation management? How does improving a clayey soil with organic matter influence irrigation management?

5. Define water-holding capacity, saturation, field capacity, permanent wilting point, and available water.

6. Compare the historical ET for a lawn in spring, summer, and fall.

7. Based on a soil's typical water-holding capacity, describe the amount of water to apply and frequency of irrigation for sandy, sandy loam, and loamy/clayey soils with a 6", 12", and 24" rooting depth in the spring, summer, and fall.

8. Describe the textbook amount of water to apply if a lawn required water every 2, 3, 4, or 5 days in the typical summer.

9. Describe how these factors influence irrigation management:

   a. Exposure

   b. Previous irrigation pattern

   c. Stage of growth

10. Give examples of mechanisms that plants use to tolerate/escape drought.

Chapter
49*

Irrigation Equipment

Equipment for delivery of landscape irrigation water ranges from automated in-ground sprinkler systems and drip irrigation systems to hose-end watering. A basic outline of each with their strengths and limitations follows.

IN-GROUND SPRINKLERS

Different types of irrigation equipment are most effective to water various types of planting in the home landscape. For lawns, sprinkler irrigation with pop-up spray heads and rotor heads are generally used. Because each type of sprinkler delivers water at a different rate, do not mix sprinkler types in a zone.

All sprinkler systems must comply with local building codes, requiring building permits and inspection. In-ground sprinkler systems have the following basic components:

Point of connection—The system starts at the point of connection where the supply line connects to the water supply. This is in the basement of the typical house. The size of the pipe and water pressure determine water flow and thus influence design of the system (how many heads can run at one time) (Figure 49-1).

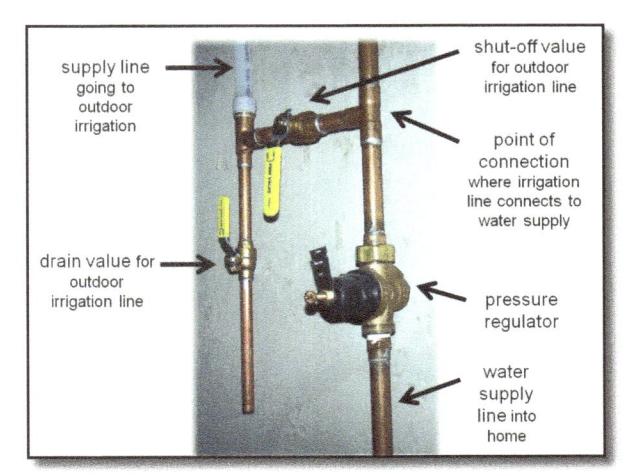

Figure 49-1 ■ *Point of connection with pressure regulator, shut-off value for the outdoor line, and drain valve that drains the outdoor line to the backflow prevention device (located just outside the house).*

*Authors: David Whiting and Carl Wilson, Colorado State University Extension. Artwork by David Whiting.

A **pressure regulator** provides uniform, lower water pressure for uniform water delivery. This is typically found just before the point of connection. It should be set at thirty to forty psi for the landscape irrigation system and household water use. Sprinkler systems have maintenance problems and valves may fail to shut off when the pressure is above eighty psi. Pressure regulators are typically not found in older homes. Due to increased uniformity of water delivery, adding a pressure regulator may result in significant water savings in landscape irrigation (Figure 49-1).

Local building codes require a **backflow prevention device** to protect the community's water supply. This is typically placed where the water line comes out of the house. Some valves have a backflow prevention device built into the valve. The type to use depends on the local building code (Figure 49-2).

The main **supply line** (water line holding water under pressure throughout the summer) splits in a **valve box** to a **valve** for each zone. To minimize maintenance headaches, use Schedule 40 PVC pipe for below ground supply lines and copper pipe for any above ground pipe. PVC fittings are connected with special glue. Copper pipefittings are soldered (Figure 49-3).

Beyond the valve, **secondary lines** (lines that have water only when the zone is running) go to sprinkler heads. Being easy to work with, these are generally made of flexible black poly pipe. Connect poly pipe fittings with pinch clamps.

The size of the pipe and the water pressure determine the number of sprinkler heads that can be used per zone. Various brands of sprinkler equipment have planning booklets with specific details for their product lines.

A **controller** (timer) runs the system from a central location (typically in the garage). In the home garden market, there are many styles of controllers with a variety of features (Figure 49-4).

In climates where the soil freezes, the lines need to be **drained** in the winter. This starts by turning off the water with the valve near the point of connection and opening the internal drain line. This drains the line to the backflow prevention valve (which is outdoors at the high point in the system).

Depending on how the system was designed, there are several methods to drain the supply line and secondary lines. Some systems are "blown out" by connecting an air compressor. Other systems have valves that are manually opened, allowing for drainage by gravity. In some systems, secondary lines have self-draining valves that automatically drain the line each time the water is turned off.

Figure 49-2 ▮ *Required by local building codes, backflow prevention devices are typically located where the line comes outside from the house.*

Figure 49-3 ▮ *Valve box with two zone valves.*

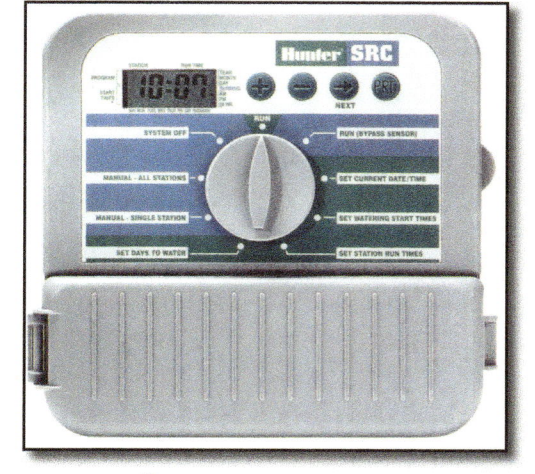

Figure 49-4 ▮ *Controller: Many brands offer a variety of features.*

Pop-Up Spray Heads

This is a generic name for sprinklers that automatically "pop up" with a fan-shaped spray pattern and do not rotate when running. The head retracts by spring action when the water is turned off (Figure 49-5).

Delivery pattern—Pop-up spray heads are best suited for small- to moderate-sized home lawn areas (larger than seven to ten feet wide up to thirty to forty-five feet wide) and irregular or curvilinear areas.

Pop-up spray nozzles are most common with fifteen-, twelve-, ten-, and eight-foot radii. The radius can usually be adjusted down about thirty percent, using the nozzle's adjustment screw. Therefore, a commonly available ten-foot nozzle can be reasonably adjusted down to seven feet. Any greater adjustment would significantly distort the pattern, resulting in poor application efficiency.

Figure 49-5 ▮ *For uniform water distribution, the spray head needs to release water above the grass height.*

The spray pattern of a pop-up spray head depends on choosing nozzles to water quarter circles, half circles, or full circles. Some manufacturers offer adjustable arch nozzles that can be set at any angle. However, do not use adjustable nozzles where a fixed nozzle would work, as the uniformity of water delivery is not as high.

Some specialty patterns to handle narrow, rectangular turf areas are available (often called "end-strip," "center-strip," or "side-strip" nozzles). However, nozzle performance is not as uniform compared to quarter-circle, half-circle, or full-circle nozzles.

Within any given brand, spray nozzles have "match precipitation rates." That is, a half-circle head uses half the amount of water per hour as a full-circle head. With match precipitation rates, full, half, and quarter circles may be used in the same zone. It is also acceptable to mix a combination of nozzle radii in a zone.

Pop-up height—For uniform water distribution, the sprinkler heads should rise above the grass height, making the 4-inch pop-up style most popular. High pop-up heads, with a twelve-inch rise, are suitable for ground-cover areas and lower flowerbeds.

Pressure—Pop-up spray heads work best with water pressure around thirty to forty psi. The water pressure at some homes may be significantly higher, and an in-line pressure regulator will be needed in these cases. A sprinkler producing a "mist cloud" around the head is a common symptom of excessive pressure. This gives a distorted distribution pattern (significantly increasing water use) and leads to increased maintenance problems.

In addition, a grade change of more than eight vertical feet on a single zone will result in significantly higher pressure at the lower end, creating distribution problems.

Small areas—Small areas less than seven to ten feet wide are difficult to sprinkle irrigate efficiently with pop-up spray heads. Consider landscape alternatives. For example, that small side yard between houses may be an excellent site for a low-maintenance, non-planted, non-irrigated mulch area. Alternatively, the small area could be a shrub/flower bed watered with drip irrigation. A narrow lawn strip may be watered efficiently with the new sub-surface drip for lawns.

Precipitation rate—Pop-up spray heads have a high water delivery rate (*precipitation rate*) of one to two and one-half inches per hour. At the typical rate of one and one-half inches per hour, the zone would apply one-half inch of water in just twenty minutes.

Rotor Head

Rotor heads mechanically rotate to distribute the spray of water. Impact and gear-driven heads are two common types in the home garden trade (Figures 49-6 and 49-7).

Figure 49-6 ▮ *Impact or impulse heads rotate as the water stream coming from the nozzle hits a spring-loaded arm. Impact heads tend to experience fewer problems with marginal (dirty) water quality.*

Figure 49-7 ▮ *Gear-driven heads use the flowing water to turn a series of gears that rotate the head. Gear-driven heads are quieter to operate than impact heads.*

Rotor heads in the home garden trade are best suited for larger lawn areas, generally an eighteen to twenty-four foot radius and greater. Some rotor-type heads in the commercial line have a radius of thirty to ninety feet.

The spray pattern depends on the head. Most can be set at any angle from 15 degrees up to a full circle. Some are adjusted at 15-degree increments. Others are designed for a quarter-circle, half-circle, or full-circle spray pattern.

In rotor head design, do not mix quarter-, half-, and full-circle patterns in the same zone. The water flow is the same for each head, but the area covered will be different. For example, a full circle (covering twice the area of a half circle) will have half the precipitation rate of a half circle. The full circle will need to run twice as long to apply the same amount of water as the half circle.

Pressure—Rotor heads typically operate at 30 to 90 psi, with 30 to 40 psi being most common for heads in the home garden trade. Better quality heads have built-in pressure regulators.

Precipitation rate—Rotors are more uniform in water distribution than pop-up spray heads and take much longer to water. As a rule of thumb, rotor heads deliver water at a rate of ¼ to ¾ inch per hour. At the typical precipitation rate of ½ inch per hour, it would take 60 minutes to apply ½ inch of water. The slower precipitation rate can be an advantage on clayey or compacted soils where water infiltration rates are slow.

MP Rotator®

The newer **MP Rotator®**, with its multitrajectory rotating streams, provides unmatched uniformity in water distribution for significant water savings. It has a lower application rate, reducing runoff on compacted, clayey soils and slopes. The streams of water are large enough to resist wind disturbance, so they reduce the amount of water blowing onto driveways, sidewalks, and roads.

Almost any type of sprinkler head can be retrofitted with an MP Rotator® sprinkler, including spray heads and traditional rotors. MP Rotators® can apply water to distances ranging from 4 feet to 30 feet. They can also be used to water narrow planting strips, which are often difficult to water effectively with traditional sprinkler heads.

Depending on the head, they perform best at 30 to 40 psi. With matched precipitation rates, quarter, half, and full heads may be mixed in a zone.

Generally used by landscape contractors, MP Rotators® are less common in the home garden trade. For the home gardener, they may be found online.

Strengths and Weaknesses of In-Ground Sprinklers

Strengths of in-ground sprinklers include the following:

- Convenience

- Time savings

- Usefulness for irrigating small areas

- Very efficient if well designed, maintained, and managed according to plant water needs (ET)

Weaknesses of in-ground sprinklers are that they can be very inefficient if poorly designed, maintained, or managed. Being "too" convenient, many gardeners give them little attention, significantly wasting water.

BUBBLERS

Small groupings of flowers and other small plants can be efficiently watered with bubblers, which flood an area and rely on the natural wicking action of the soil to spread the water.

They are ideal for level shrub and ground-cover areas. Heads are typically placed at 3- to 5-foot intervals or placed by individual plants for spot watering. Stream bubblers are directional and come in a variety of spray patterns.

Bubblers deliver water faster than drip emitters and are used to water trees and shrubs. Refer to manufacturers' literature for design and management criteria related to various models.

DRIP SYSTEMS

For flower and shrub beds, small fruits and vegetable gardens, drip emitters, drip lines, micro-sprayers, and soaker hoses are popular.

Water use rates, weed seed germination, and foliar disease problems are reduced in drip systems that do not spray water into the air and over the plants and the soil surface. As a rule of thumb, a drip system coupled with mulch can reduce water needs by 50%.

Drip emitters, micro-sprayers, and drip lines require clean water, which is relatively free of soil particles, algae, and salts. In-line filters are part of the system. Water quality is generally not a problem when using potable water sources. However, with nonpotable water sources, the filtering system required may be expensive and high maintenance, making drip impractical.

Drip systems work with lower pressures (typically around 20 psi), generally using **in-line pressure regulators**. The system snaps together with small fittings. No gluing or bands are required. It is much easier to work with if the tubing has been warmed by the sun for an hour (Figure 49-8).

The system is put together with half-inch and quarter-inch poly tubing, fittings and emitters. For the main line and branch lines, **half-inch poly tubing** is used. The **quarter-inch microtubing** serves as a feeder line to individual drippers or micro-sprinklers. Ideally, the tubing is on the soil surface under the mulch.

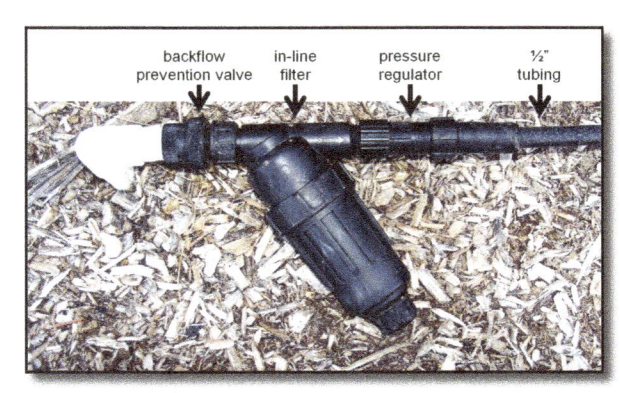

Figure 49-8 ▮ *In-line filter and pressure regulator going to drip line poly tubing.*

- **Drip emitters** deliver water at a slow, consistent rate, such as one-half gallon, one gallon, or two gallons per *hour.* Emitters can connect to the branch line or extend on micro-tubing out to individual plants or pots. Small annuals and perennials typically have one emitter per plant. Several would be used spaced around larger perennials, shrubs, and small trees (Figure 49-9).

- As a point of clarification, some gardeners mistakenly think that using half-, one-, and two-gallon-per-hour drippers is an effective method to manage differing water needs. Although this works to a small degree, the concept is basically flawed. The two-gallon-per-hour drippers will have significantly larger wetting zones than the half-gallon-per-hour dripper. However, plants with the higher water needs (two-gallon/hour drippers) do not necessarily have a larger root spread. Likewise, plants with lower water needs (half-gallon/hour dripper) will not necessarily have a smaller root spread (in fact, a large root spread is what makes some plants more xeric). The factor missing here is irrigation frequency to match the water needs.

Figure 49-9 ▊ *Drip emitter on half-inch poly tubing.*

- **In-line drip tubing** is a quarter inch micro-tubing with built-in emitters spaced at six-inch, twelve-inch, or twenty-four inch intervals. The twelve-inch spacing is readily available in the home garden trade. These are great for snaking through a bed area. For sandy soils, spacing of the tubing should be at twelve inches. For clayey soils, spacing may be at eighteen to twenty-four inches for perennial beds.

- **Micro-sprayers**, often held up on a spike, cover a radius of 2 to 13 feet. Delivery rates vary from 0.1 to 10 inches per *hour*, depending on the head selected. Because water is sprayed in the air, drift and water waste in wind resembles sprinklers more than ground-applied drip. Micro-sprayers work with a very small droplet size that readily evaporates. For this reason, their efficiency in Colorado's low humidity is questionable.

Specifications on design and management vary among manufacturers and types selected. Refer to the manufacturer's literature for details. Typical run times are 60 to 90 minutes.

Drip systems are easy to automate by connecting the zones to valves and a controller (like an in-ground system for a lawn). For ease of programming to the specific watering needs of the drip system, use a dedicated controller for multiple drip zones. In small yards, a single zone or two could be added to the controller used for the lawn, but they would run on a different program than the lawn to match the different watering needs.

When connected to the garden hose, the zone can be automated with single-zone controllers that connect with hose-end fittings at the tap. Some simple models turn the water off after a set number of minutes or gallons. More elaborate battery-operated models turn the water on and off at the day and time interval set by the gardener (Figure 49-10).

Like any irrigation system, drip systems require routine maintenance. They are not an install-and-forget type of system.

Soaker Hose and Soaker Tubing

The **soaker hose** is a different type of drip system that allows water to seep out the entire length of a porous hose. They are great for raised bed gardens and flower beds. In sandy soils, space runs at twelve inches. For flower and shrubs beds on clayey soil, space runs at eighteen to twenty-four inches. In a raised bed vegetable garden (where uniform delivery to small vegetables is important), make three to four runs up and down a four-foot-wide bed. Typical run time is ten to twenty minutes.

- **Quarter-inch soaker tubing**—Quarter-inch soaker tubing is availble in the drip irrigation section at garden stores. Cut the soaker tubing to desired length and connect with drip system components. An in-line pressure regulator (Figure 49-9) is required; otherwise, the fitting may pop or leak.

- **Half-inch soaker hose**—Some brands (like *Swans Soaker Hose*) are a half-inch hose that connect with a standard hose fitting. These are found in the garden hose section. It can be cut to any length and connected with garden hose fittings.

Figure 49-10 ▮ *Tap, pressure regulator (with hose connections) and half-inch drip hose in raised bed garden.*

A small plastic disc fits inside the female hose connection as a flow regulator. To adequately water the garden with the reduced water flow, it may need to run for around an hour. For better performance, use the pressure regulators with hose-end fittings found with the drip irrigation supplies (Figure 49-11). To adequately water the garden with this type of regulator, the drip line runs ten to twenty minutes. Without a pressure regulator of some type, the soaker hose tends to rupture, sending out steams of water at spots rather than dripping along the line.

This half-inch hose style is more tolerant of small amounts of dirt, algae, or salts in the water than other types of drip systems and may be successful on some nonpotable water sources. Periodically, open up the end of the hose and flush out soil deposits.

Because the soaker tubing has a higher delivery rate, it cannot be on the same zone as other in-line drip tubing, button emitters, or bubblers.

Strengths and Weaknesses of Drip Irrigation

Strengths of drip irrigation include the following:

- Convenience
- Water saving
- Operates with low water pressure
- Easy to change when the plantings change
- Does not require trenches for installation
- Readily automated on a multizone controller or single-zone controllers that connect to the faucet

Weaknesses of drip irrigation include the following:

- Require good quality water and filtration
- Maintenance difficulty in seeing if systems are operating and need to check water delivery to individual plants
- Cost: for large areas, the cost will be significantly higher than a sprinkler system
- Unsuitable for watering large trees

SUBSURFACE DRIP

Subsurface drip is a relatively new way to water lawns and flowerbeds. Tubes are permanently buried below ground. Water soaks upward and laterally so subsurface drip works in clay-containing soils, but not well in sands.

Generally installed by a trained and experienced professional, subsurface drip requires very exact installation depth and spacing. Without proper attention to installation, the lawn becomes striped with green and dry strips. Studies being conducted by the Northern Colorado Water Conservation District find that water use is similar to a well-designed sprinkler system.

Strengths of subsurface drip include:

- Convenience

- Operation at low pressure

- Equipment located out of sight, where it is less prone to damage

- Easy to water anytime day or night, even when the lawn is being used

- Application of water directly to the root zone

- Easy to automate with soil moisture sensors

- Potential to inject fertilizers with the irrigation water

Weaknesses of subsurface drip include:

- Requires high-quality water

- Inability to see if it is operating correctly and need to dig it up if it is not

- Prohibition of inserting stakes in the ground

- Requires professional installation

- Relatively high cost

- Evolving technology that has not stood the test of time

HOSE-END AND HAND WATERING

Hose-end watering devices include various types of spray heads, water wands and water breakers, soaker hoses, and soil needles. Such devices are commonly used for temporary situations and where permanent installations are impractical or not desired.

Hose-end watering is very inefficient in uniformity of water delivery, resulting in high water use. However, significant water savings may occur because gardeners generally do not water until the lawn/garden show signs of being dry.

A common problem with hand-held water wands is that folks tend to only water the surface, rather than deep watering of the root system. Avoid soil needles because they apply the water below the primary root system of trees, shrubs, and flowers.

Figure 49-11 ▌ *Single-zone controllers connect to the hose line. Left: This style is manually turned on and automatically turns off after a set number of minutes. Right: This battery-powered controller turns water on and off at the day and time intervals set by the gardener.*

A hand-moved sprinkler can be automated with single-zone controllers that connect with hose-end fittings at the tap. Some simple models turn the water off after a set number of minutes or gallons. More elaborate battery-operated models turn the water on and off at the day and time interval set by the gardener (Figure 49-11).

Strengths and Weaknesses of Hose-End Watering

Strengths of hose-end and hand watering include the following:

- Relative low cost of equipment
- Ability to water plants differently and usefulness for spot watering
- Allows for close observation that may result in more timely care of plants
- Being outside in the yard encourages neighborhood relationships

Weaknesses of hose-end hand watering include the following:

- Time-consuming
- Poor uniformity of water distribution with hand-placed sprinklers, leading to high water use
- Hand-held watering often leads to surface watering rather than effectively watering the root zone
- Wasting water by allowing it to run too long

SUMMARY

Any type of irrigation system (in-ground sprinklers, drip, or hand watering) can be very efficient with attention to detail. Likewise, any type of irrigation can be inefficient, wasting water. What makes a system efficient or inefficient is not the equipment, but rather the attention given by the gardener.

1. Explain basic components of an in-ground sprinkler system, including the following:

   a. Point of connection

   b. Pressure regulator

   c. Backflow prevention device

   d. Supply line

   e. Valve box

   f. Valves

   g. Secondary lines

   h. Controller

   i. Winter drainage

2. Describe the advantages and limitations of pop-up spray heads and rotor heads.

3. Describe the strengths and weaknesses of an in-ground sprinkler system.

4. Describe basic components of a drip system, including the following:

   a. In-line filter

   b. Pressure regulator

   c. half-inch tubing

   d. quarter-inch microtubing

   e. Drip emitters

   f. In-line drip tubing

   g. Micro-sprayers

5. Describe a drip system made with soaker hose or soaker tubing.

6. Describe the strengths and weaknesses of drip irrigation.

7. Describe the strengths and weaknesses of hose-end, hand watering.

Chapter

50*

Methods to Schedule Irrigation

IRRIGATION SCHEDULING

In many areas of the semi-arid West, gardeners cannot count on natural precipitation to deliver moisture at the right times or in sufficient amounts to grow most introduced landscape plants. Supplemental irrigation is necessary unless the plant pallet is limited to species tolerant of natural precipitation levels. Due to limited precipitation and periodic droughts that limit available water supplies, using efficient irrigation is of interest to all.

Scheduling landscape irrigation is a critical part of lawn and garden care. When irrigating, gardeners have two goals: 1) water enough to keep plants healthy, and 2) minimize water waste.

Irrigation management comes down to two basic questions: 1) how much, and 2) how often. Gardeners often hear recommendations such as "water deeply and infrequently" or "water to adequate depth without runoff." Such advice is usually too broad to translate into effective irrigation management practices.

Rather than using broad generalizations, this chapter looks at several management approaches with differences in the time investment and potential water savings. **The textbook figures will need to be fine-tuned to the specific site needs, taking into account soils, exposure, heat, wind, and other water use factors.**

Methods focus on cool season turf, such as Kentucky bluegrass and turf-type tall fescue. Xeric and dry land plants may need significantly less water.

*Authors: David Whiting and Carl Wilson, Colorado State University Extension. Artwork by David Whiting.

SPRINKLER-TYPE METHOD

One of the easiest ways to schedule an irrigation system is based on sprinkler type. Different types of sprinklers deliver very different amounts of water in the same amount of time. By considering sprinkler type, gardeners can begin to match their watering practices to the lawn's water needs.

Pop-up spray heads typically apply one to two and one-half inches of water per hour, whereas rotor heads only deliver one-quarter to three-quarters inches of water per hour. Therefore, zones that have pop-up spray heads can run for a short time, whereas zones with rotors will need to run longer to deliver the same amount of water.

A gardener could estimate that a zone with pop-up spray heads applies one and three-quarters inches of water per hour, and zones with rotor heads apply about one-half inch per hour on average. Table 50-1 estimates run time (based on historical water use). The typical Colorado soil requires that this be split between a couple of irrigations.

Table 50-1. Estimated Sprinkler Run Time Based on Sprinkler Type for Cool Season Lawns

	Late April	May & June	July & August	September	Early October
Inches of water per week (irrigation plus rain)	0.75"	1.0"	1.5"	1.0"	0.75"
Run Time (minutes/week)	Late April	May & June	July & August	September	Early October
Pop-up Spray Head[1]					
Irrigated 1 time per week[3]	**26**	**34**	**52**	**34**	**26**
Irrigated 2 times per week[4]	**13**	**17**	**26**	**17**	**13**
Irrigated 3 times per week	9	11	17	11	9
Irrigated every 6 days	22	29	45	29	22
Irrigated every 5 days	19	24	37	24	19
Irrigated every 4 days	15	19	30	19	15
Irrigated every 3 days	11	15	22	15	11
Irrigated every 2 days	7	10	15	10	7
Rotor Head[2]					
Irrigated 1 time per week[3]	**90**	**120**	**180**	**120**	**90**
Irrigated 2 times per week[4]	**45**	**60**	**90**	**60**	**45**
Irrigated 3 times per week	30	40	60	40	30
Irrigated every 6 days	77	103	154	103	77
Irrigated every 5 days	64	86	129	86	64
Irrigated every 4 days	51	69	103	69	51
Irrigated every 3 days	39	51	77	51	39
Irrigated every 2 days	26	34	51	34	26
Percent of July/August	**50%**	**67%**	**100%**	**67%**	**50%**

[1] Pop-up spray head estimated at 1¾" per hour.

[2] Rotor head estimated at ½" per hour.

[3] Recommended for most Colorado soils in the spring and fall.

[4] Recommended for most Colorado soils in the summer.

An easy tool for making seasonal adjustments is the **Percent Key** found on most controllers. The controller would be set for the July/August irrigation schedule. The percent key would be set at 50%, 67%, or 100%, based on the season.

The method will need fine-tuning as described below to match the actual water need for the site based on soil, exposure, heat, wind, etc.

Although this method outlines a starting point for gardeners who want an easy approach, it does not factor in the *actual* water application rates for *each zone*.

PRECIPITATION RATE METHOD

A far better approach is to do a *Precipitation Rate (Catch Can) Test* on each zone to determine the actual water delivery rate (know as *precipitation rate*). The actual precipitation rate is determined by the sprinkler type and brand, water pressure, and head spacing. It is generally slightly different in each zone.

To do the calculations you will need six identical, straight-sided, flat-bottomed cans such as soup, fruit, or vegetable cans. (Do not use short cans like tuna cans as they are too shallow, and water may splash out.) You will need a ruler, a watch, and paper/pen to record your findings. Many water providers and sod growers have calibrated plastic cups specifically designed for this test. Again, six are needed.

Precipitation Rate (Catch Can) Test

Step 1. Place 6 identical, straight-sided, flat-bottomed cans randomly around the area between sprinkler heads in the zone.

Step 2. Turn on the sprinklers for exactly 10 minutes.

Step 3. Pour all the water into one can.

Step 4. With a ruler, measure the depth of the water in the can. This is your **precipitation rate in inches per hour**. Write it down for future reference.

Step 5. Repeat steps one to four for each irrigation zone.

Step 6. Use Tables 50-2 and 50-3 to calculate the run time for each zone.

Note: If the amount of water in some containers is significantly more or less than others, the system is poorly designed or head(s) are malfunctioning.

In many lawn sections, one zone waters the area from the left while another zone waters the same area from the right. In this situation, cut run times for zones in half, so that each applies half of the needed water.

An easy way to make seasonal adjustments is with the **Percent Key** found on most controllers. The controller would be set for the July/August irrigation schedule. The percent key would be set at 50%, 67%, or 100% based on the season.

The method will need fine-tuning as described below to match the actual water need for the site based on soil, exposure, heat, wind, etc.

Table 50-2. Minutes to Run Sprinklers PER WEEK Based on Precipitation Rates For Cool Season Turf in Colorado

	Late April	May & June	July & August	September	Early October
Inches of water per week (irrigation plus rain)	0.75″	1.0″	1.5″	1.0″	0.75″
Precipitation Rate					
¼	180	240	360	240	180
⅜	120	160	240	160	120
½	90	120	180	120	90
⅝	72	96	144	96	72
¾	60	80	120	80	60
⅞	52	69	103	69	52
1	45	60	90	60	45
1⅛	40	53	80	53	40
1¼	36	48	72	48	36
1⅜	33	44	65	44	33
1½	30	40	60	40	30
1⅝	28	37	55	37	28
1¾	26	34	51	34	26
1⅞	24	32	48	32	24
2	23	30	45	30	23
2⅛	22	28	42	28	22
2¼	20	27	40	27	20
2⅜	19	25	38	35	19
2½	18	24	36	24	18
2⅝	17	23	34	23	17
2¾	16	22	33	22	16
2⅞	16	21	31	21	16
3	15	20	30	20	15
Percent of July/August	50%	67%	100%	67%	50%

Table 50-3. Conversion of Run Time PER WEEK to Run Time PER IRRIGATION

Irrigations per Week	Conversion to Run Time per Irrigation
1 time per week[1]	minutes per week
2 times per week[2]	minutes per week ÷ 2
3 times per week	minutes per week ÷ 3
Every 6 days	minutes per week × 0.86
Every 5 days	minutes per week × 0.71
Every 4 days	minutes per week × 0.57
Every 3 days	minutes per week × 0.43
Every 2 days	minutes per week × 0.29

[1] Recommended for most Colorado soils in the spring and fall.

[2] Recommended for most Colorado soils in the summer.

Determining the number of irrigations per week becomes complex as soil water-holding capacity and rooting depth are factored in. For details, refer to Chapter 48, Understanding Irrigation Management Factors.

However, many gardeners know by experience how often they need to irrigate. For the majority of Colorado soils, irrigating once per week works in the spring and fall, and twice a week works in the summer. Watering as infrequently and deeply as the soil allows gives better resilience during hot spells and helps reduce many weed species.

ADDING CYCLE AND SOAK FEATURES

On slopes or compacted, clayey soils, water is generally applied faster than it can soak into the soil, resulting in water being wasted as it runs off-site. The *cycle and soak* approach cuts the irrigation period into multiple short runs with soak-in time in between. Programming a controller for cycle and soak is simply a matter of using multiple start times.

Adding Cycle and Soak

Step 1. From the methods discussed above, calculate the total run time for the irrigation.

Step 2. Using Table 50-4, figure the number of cycles and soaks desired.

For example, if the run time is 26 minutes, three cycles are suggested.

Step 3. Divide the *run time per irrigation* by the number of cycles to get the *run time per cycle*.

For example, if the run time is 26 minutes and three cycles will be used, run time per cycle is 9 minutes (26 ÷ 3 = 8.67, rounded to 9).

Step 4. Set program with multiple start times, as needed. Generally, the controller is set to cycle again after all the zones have run. If the controller only has a few zones, start times need to be at least one hour apart.

Table 50-4. Estimated Number of Cycles to Reduce Surface Runoff

Number of Cycles	Type of Sprinklers	Run Time per Irrigation
Pop-up Spray Heads	Greater than 16 minutes	2
	Greater than 24 minutes	3
Rotor Heads	Greater than 48	2
	Greater than 72	3

OBSERVATION AND MANUAL CONTROL METHOD

A simple method to manage lawn irrigation and conserve water is to manually activate the controller as needed. With careful attention, this method can maximize plant health and water savings since the gardener continually adjusts the irrigation system to actual weather and lawn needs. The downside of this method is that it takes daily attention to the lawn's water needs.

Run times on the controller are set as previously described. The difference is that the controller is turned to the "off" position. It is manually activated when the lawn shows signs of water stress (color change from bluish-green to grayish-blue and footprints are still visible an hour or more later). After the zones run through, the controller is turned back to "off."

USING EMERGING TECHNOLOGY

Advances in irrigation technology have led to several innovations. ET controllers and soil-moisture sensors are examples. Even though they may be more expensive or require professional installation, these products can be used to further improve water delivery to a landscape. Because they automate the irrigation controller, they can potentially reduce the amount of effort needed to water effectively.

ET Controllers

The ET controller is a relatively new piece of equipment that automatically adjusts the irrigation to the daily ET. ET controllers are designed to water only enough to fulfill the lawn's water need, thereby reducing over- and underwatering.

Some models use "Historical ET," which is a multiyear average for the day. With these, dry spots will pop up with extreme heat over multiple days. They do not take into account actual rain received locally.

For a small annual fee, other models connect by cell phone, Wi-Fi, or satellite communication networks to download actual ET and rainfall from a local weather station system. On a day-by-day basis, they adjust the irrigation to match actual water need.

For additional information on ET controllers and the use of ET in irrigation management, refer to the *Northern Colorado Water Conservancy District* website at **www.ncwcd.org.**

Soil-Moisture Sensors

Soil-moisture sensors measure the water content of the soil, allowing the controller to run only when soil dries down to a threshold level. One of the advantages of a soil-moisture sensor is that it uses onsite soil conditions to control the irrigation system. Usually one sensor is buried in the home landscape in a "representative" area. Run times for reduced irrigation zones or shady zones are programmed into the controller relative to the representative zone.

Rain Shut-off Sensors

Rain shut-off devices, also known as rain sensors, interrupt the schedule of an irrigation controller when a specific amount of rain has fallen. They are wired into the irrigation controller and placed in an open area where they are exposed to rainfall. They save water by preventing an irrigation system from running during moderate and heavy rains. Many states, but not Colorado, require rain shut-off sensors on automated systems.

Fine-Tuning Any Scheduling Method

Any scheduling method will need fine-tuning to match the actual water need of the site based on soil type, exposure, wind, heat, rooting depth, etc. This is done by careful observation of the lawn.

When adjusting all zones, the **Percent Key** on most controllers provides an easy method to fine-tune for the actual site by adjusting the percentage up/down in 10% increments, as needed. It can also be adjusted by increasing/decreasing the run time for each zone in 10% increments, as needed.

When adjusting a single zone, adjust the run times for that zone up/down in 10% increments, as needed.

In typical summer weather, if the lawn starts to become dry between irrigations, increase the run time in 10% increments, as needed. By trial and error, it is easy to fine-tune each irrigation zone. On multiple days of unusually hot weather, dry spots should pop up if the controller is precisely fine-tuned. In unusually hot weather, if dry spots do not pop up, the lawn is being overwatered. Cut back the time in 10% increments, as needed, to fine-tune each zone.

Many water providers encourage homeowners to water their yards between 9 p.m. and 9 a.m. Winds are typically less at night, and evaporation loss will be lower.

Precipitation Rate (inches per hour)	Water to be Applied (inches)													
	0.2	0.3	0.4	0.5	0.6	0.7	0.8	0.9	1.0	1.1	1.2	1.3	1.4	1.5
¼	48	72	96	120	144	168	192	216	240	264	288	312	336	360
⅜	32	48	64	80	96	112	128	144	160	176	192	208	224	240
½	24	36	48	60	72	84	96	108	120	132	144	156	168	180
⅝	19	29	38	48	58	67	77	86	96	106	115	125	134	144
¾	16	24	32	40	48	56	64	72	80	88	96	104	112	120
⅞	14	21	27	34	41	48	55	62	69	75	82	89	96	103
1	12	18	24	30	36	42	48	54	60	66	72	78	84	90
1⅛	11	16	21	27	32	37	43	48	53	59	64	69	75	80
1¼	10	14	19	24	29	34	38	43	48	53	58	62	67	72
1⅜	9	13	17	22	26	31	35	39	44	48	52	57	61	65
1½	8	12	16	**20**	24	28	32	36	40	44	48	52	56	60
1⅝	7	11	15	18	22	26	30	33	37	41	44	48	52	55
1¾	7	10	14	17	21	24	27	31	34	38	41	45	48	51
1⅞	6	10	13	16	19	22	26	29	32	35	38	42	45	48
2	6	9	12	15	18	21	24	27	30	33	36	39	42	45
2⅛	6	8	11	14	17	20	23	25	28	31	34	37	40	42
2¼	5	8	11	13	16	19	21	24	27	29	32	35	37	40
2⅜	5	8	10	13	15	18	20	23	25	28	30	33	35	38
2½	5	7	10	12	14	17	19	22	24	26	29	31	34	36
2⅝	5	7	9	11	14	16	18	21	23	25	27	30	32	34
2¾	4	7	9	11	13	15	17	20	22	24	26	28	31	33
2⅞	4	6	8	10	13	15	17	19	21	23	25	27	29	31
3	4	6	8	10	12	14	16	18	20	22	24	26	28	30

Select the precipitation rate of your sprinkler zone along the left column and move right until you are in the column of the amount of water to be applied. This is the number of minutes to run your sprinkler.

Example: Your sprinkler applies water at 1½ inches per hour and you want to apply 0.5 inch, it takes 20 minutes.

Table 50-6. Sprinkler Run Time Table (in minutes)—by ¹⁄₁₀th inch

Precipitation Rate	Water to be Applied (inches)													
(inches per hour)	0.2	0.3	0.4	0.5	0.6	0.7	0.8	0.9	1.0	1.1	1.2	1.3	1.4	1.5
0.20	60	90	120	150	180	210	240	270	300	330	360	390	420	450
0.30	40	60	80	100	120	140	160	180	200	220	240	260	280	300
0.40	30	45	60	75	90	105	120	135	150	165	180	195	210	225
0.50	24	36	48	60	72	84	96	108	120	132	144	156	168	180
0.60	20	30	40	50	60	70	80	90	100	110	120	130	140	150
0.70	17	26	34	43	51	60	69	77	86	94	103	111	120	129
0.80	15	22	30	37	45	52	60	67	75	82	90	97	105	113
0.90	13	20	27	33	40	47	53	60	67	73	80	87	93	100
1.00	12	18	24	30	36	72	48	54	60	66	72	78	81	90
1.10	11	16	22	27	33	38	44	49	55	60	66	71	76	82
1.20	10	15	20	25	30	35	40	45	50	55	60	65	76	75
1.30	9	14	18	23	28	32	37	42	46	51	55	60	65	69
1.40	9	12	17	21	26	30	34	39	43	47	51	56	60	64
1.50	8	12	16	20	24	28	32	36	40	44	48	52	56	60
1.60	8	11	15	19	22	26	30	34	37	41	45	49	52	56
1.70	7	11	14	18	21	25	28	32	35	39	42	46	49	53
1.80	7	10	13	17	20	23	27	30	33	37	40	43	47	50
1.90	7	9	13	16	19	22	25	28	32	35	38	41	44	47
2.00	6	9	12	15	18	21	24	27	30	33	36	39	42	45
2.10	6	9	11	14	17	20	23	26	29	31	34	37	40	43
2.20	6	8	11	14	16	19	22	25	27	30	33	35	38	41
2.30	5	8	10	13	16	18	21	23	26	29	31	34	37	39
2.40	5	7	10	12	15	17	20	22	25	27	30	32	35	37
2.50	5	7	10	12	14	17	19	22	24	26	29	31	34	36

Select the precipitation rate of your sprinkler zone along the left column and move right until you are in the column of the amount of water to be applied. This is the number of minutes to run your sprinkler.

Example: Your sprinkler applies water at 1.5 inches per hour and you want to apply 0.5 inch, it takes 20 minutes.

1. Describe irrigation scheduling by the *type of sprinkler method*.

2. Describe irrigation scheduling by the *precipitation rate method*. Explain how to do a Precipitation Rate (Catch Can) Test.

3. What is the purpose of cycle and soak? Explain how to add cycle and soak to an irrigation scheduling method.

4. What is an ET controller? What is a soil-moisture sensor?

5. Explain how to fine-tune an irrigation schedule.

Chapter

51*

Watering Efficiently

Of the seven principles of water-wise gardening, attention to irrigation efficiency has the greatest potential for water conservation for most residents. In the typical home yard, extra attention to irrigation system *design*, *maintenance,* and *management* could reduce water use by twenty to seventy percent, with forty percent being average.

IRRIGATION ZONES REFLECT WATER NEED

Unfortunately, in the design of many home irrigation systems, little attention is given to zoning by water need.

- **Zone by irrigation demand**—The following examples have different water requirements and should be independent irrigation zones:

  —Lawns—Routine irrigation

  —Lawns—Reduced irrigation

  —Lawns—Limited irrigation or non-irrigated

  —Mixed flower and shrub beds—Routine irrigation

  —Mixed flower and shrub beds—Reduced irrigation

  —Mixed flower and shrub beds—Limited irrigation

  —Vegetables—Routine irrigation

  —Tree fruits—Reduced irrigation

  —Small fruits—Routine to reduced irrigation depending on the fruit

---

*Author: David Whiting, Colorado State University Extension. Artwork by David Whiting.

- **Zone by exposure**—Because exposure to sun, heat, and wind also plays a significant role in water requirements, irrigation zones should reflect exposure levels. For example, lawn on an open, windy, southwest-facing slope will have considerably higher water requirements than the average lawn. Design this southwest slope as an independent irrigation zone.

  Areas in full or partial shade may have lower irrigation needs than areas in full sun. As a rule of thumb, if a shady area is outside of the rooting zone of large trees, water use may be thirty to fifty percent lower. If the shady area is in the rooting zone of large trees, water use will be similar to full sun (the tree pulling water from the soil is not in the shade.) Irrigation zones should reflect site needs.

- **Drip irrigation** in flower and shrub beds, small fruit gardens, and vegetable gardens can reduce water usage by fifty percent when coupled with organic mulch.

SPRINKLER DESIGN CRITERIA FOR UNIFORM WATER DISTRIBUTION

Unfortunately, in the design of many home (and commercial) sprinkler systems, little attention is given to design criteria for water conservation.

Sprinklers do not deliver a uniform quantity of water over their distribution area. Thus to keep the dryer spots (i.e., spots that receive less water) green the rest of the area receives more water than needed. Designing sprinkler layouts to provide a more uniform water delivery can reduce water use by twenty-five to fifty percent. Most home lawn sprinkler systems have a thirty to forty percent efficiency rating, whereas a seventy to eighty percent rating is very achievable with attention to design and management.

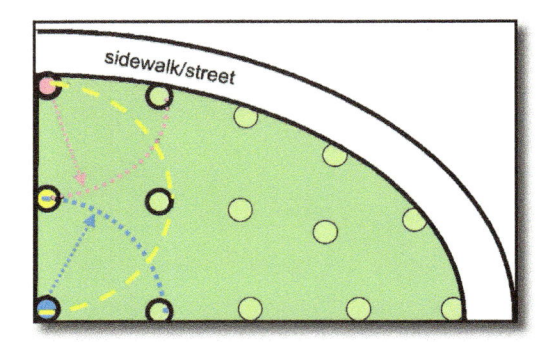

Figure 51-1 ▪ *A standard in sprinkler design is head-to-head coverage. Ten to fifteen percent overlap may give even better uniformity.*

Sprinkler design criteria for uniform water distribution include the following:

1. **Head-to-head coverage**—Designs with head-to-head coverage (i.e., the water from a sprinkler head reaches the neighboring sprinkler heads) generally give the most uniform delivery. A ten to twenty percent overlap may actually give the best uniformity. In other words, space heads at 90% of their radius of throw. For example if the radius of a pop-up spray head is 15 feet, the ideal spacing would be 13.5 feet (15' × 90%) and maximum spacing would be 15 feet. Wider spacing could increase water use by twenty-five to fifty percent (Figure 51-1).

2. *Line out* the edge—In the design process, start by *lining out* the edges (i.e., run a line of sprinkler heads down the edge of the lawn or irrigated area), spraying onto the lawn but not onto the sidewalk, street, or non-irrigated area (Figure 51-2).

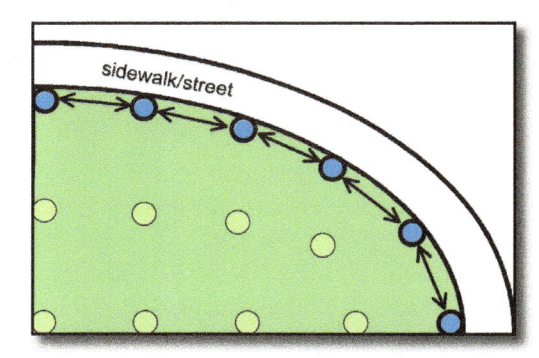

Figure 51-2 ▪ *Start the layout by lining out the edge, running a row of sprinkler heads along the edge of the irrigated/non-irrigated areas.*

In sprinkler design, avoid layouts where sprinkler heads spray from the center of the lawn area out onto the sidewalk. It either wastes twenty percent of the water as it oversprays onto the sidewalk or creates a dry lawn area along the edge (Figure 51-3).

If our society is going to deal with limited water supplies, it has to become *unacceptable* for the homeowner, private and commercial property manager, or government entity to apply irrigation water onto roads, sidewalks, and parking lots.

3. **Arrange heads in square or triangular patterns—** In the next step of the irrigation design process, fill in larger areas with sprinkler heads in square or triangular patterns. Square and triangular head patterns give the most uniform water delivery (Figure 51-4).

   In irregularly shaped areas, heads easily fall into pentagon (five-sided) patterns. Avoid these as it creates an area that receives less water than other parts of the lawn (Figure 51-5).

4. **Avoid irrigating small, irregularly shaped areas—**It is impractical to sprinkle irrigate small areas (less than eight feet wide) and irregularly shaped patches without applying water where it is not needed. In small or irregularly shaped areas, consider replacing lawns with plantings that can be watered with drip irrigation, or consider non-irrigated options. For example, in the narrow side yards around urban homes, consider a low-water-requiring ground cover or a nonirrigated mulch area.

5. **Use recommended water pressure—**Water distribution patterns change with pressure. Use the pressure recommended for the specific sprinkler head in use. Most sprinklers in the home garden trade are designed to operate at 30 to 40 psi. Commercial heads typically operate at 40 to 100 psi, and some heads have built-in pressure regulators.

New homes typically have a pressure regulator where the water line enters the home. In older homes, adding a pressure regulator may significantly reduce landscape water use.

SPRINKLER MAINTENANCE CRITERIA FOR UNIFORM WATER DISTRIBUTION

We have all noticed that blown sprinkler head down the street that goes unfixed for weeks. A problem with automatic sprinkler systems is that the gardener may not be aware of a system malfunction. Check the irrigation system's operations frequently.

As water-wise gardening concepts spread in our community, we need to adapt the practice of alerting neighbors to popped sprinkler heads and other system malfunctions. With an automated sprinkler system, many residents or landscape managers may be unaware of the mechanical failure.

Maintenance issues for uniform water distribution include the following:

- **Arc adjustment—**Sprinkler heads (particularly rotor-type heads) frequently require adjustment of delivery angle to keep water on the irrigated areas and off non-irrigated areas (Figure 51-6).

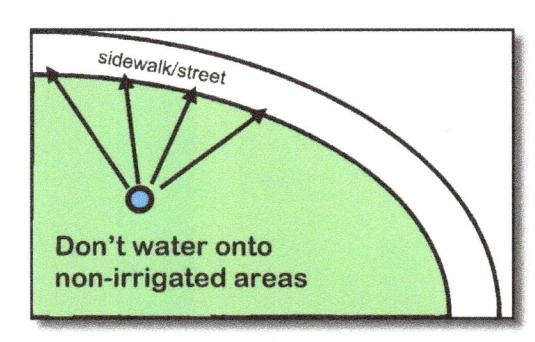

Figure 51-3 ■ *Spraying from the center out onto a sidewalk or nonirrigated area is unacceptable in water wise landscaping.*

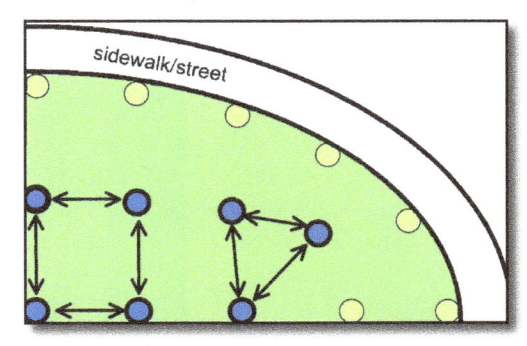

Figure 51-4 ■ *For uniform water delivery, fill in heads in square and triangular patterns.*

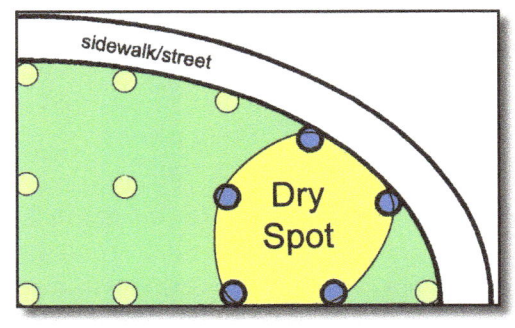

Figure 51-5 ■ *Avoid pentagon-shaped head layout. The area receives less water, creating a dry spot.*

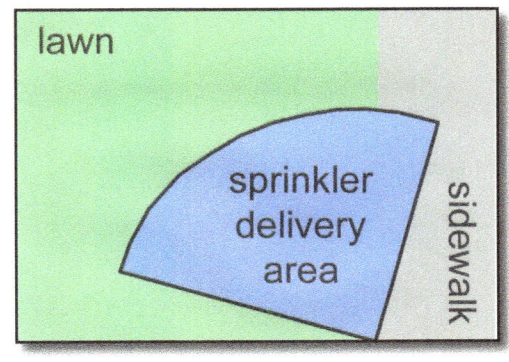

Figure 51-6 ■ *Heads frequently shift their delivery arc. Frequent adjustment is required.*

- **Adjust radius of throw**—As discussed in design, water from one sprinkler head needs to reach adjacent heads for uniform delivery. A ten to twenty percent overlap is preferred where it does not spray a non-irrigated area. Occasional adjustment on the radius of throw may be needed. This is done with a screw adjustment on the nozzle or changing out the nozzle to one with a different radius.

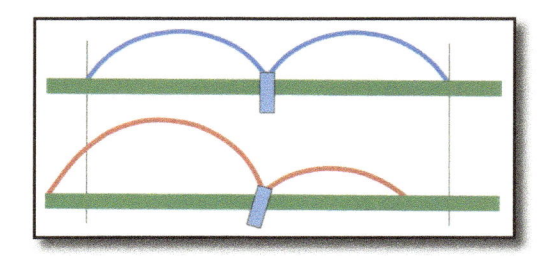

Figure 51-7 ■ *Heads require frequent adjustment back to vertical. Tilted heads change the distribution pattern.*

- **Adjust sprinkler heads to vertical**—Distribution patterns change when the head tilts off vertical alignment. To correct it, remove a donut shape of sod around the head with a shovel. Carefully loosen the soil around the head. Realign the head to vertical, and then *firmly pack* soil around the base of the head before replacing the sod (Figure 51-7).

- **Adjust head height**—When water flow does not clear the grass height, the distribution pattern can be distorted. Raise heads to release water above grass height. On the other hand, sprinkler heads set excessively high can be a trip hazard and can interfere with mowing.

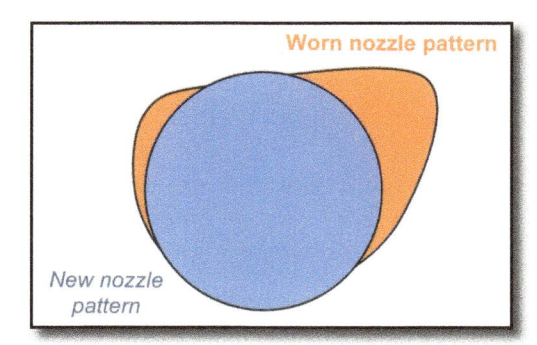

Figure 51-8 ■ *Worn nozzles distort the delivery pattern.*

To correct this, remove a donut shape of sod around the head with a shovel. Carefully loosen the soil around the head. Adjust head to the correct height, and then *firmly pack* soil around the base of the head before replacing the sod.

- **Replace worn nozzles**—As sprinkler nozzles wear, distribution patterns change, giving a less uniform water delivery. Periodically replace old, worn nozzles (Figure 51-8).

- **Adjust pressure**—A mist cloud around a sprinkler head indicates that the water pressure is too high for the head. Reduce pressure to avoid wasting water. A pressure regulator can be added to the main supply line. When adjusting pressure, slowly drop the pressure until you see water flow just start to drop, then up the pressure just a touch.

- **Replace leaky valves**—In an irrigation valve, the rubber diaphragm that actually turns water on and off ages over time. Valves that do not shut off completely need the diaphragm or entire valve replaced. Valves often fail to shut off if the pressure is above 80 psi.

SPRINKLER MANAGEMENT CRITERIA FOR WATER-WISE IRRIGATION

Sprinkler management addresses two primary questions: *how much and how often*. Irrigation scheduling is discussed in more detail in Chapter 50, Methods to Schedule Irrigation.

- **Know the *precipitation rate* for each irrigation zone, and adjust run time to match water need of each zone**—The first step in irrigation management is to calculate the precipitation rate for each zone. Once the precipitation rate is known, the controller can be set to deliver the desired amount of water. Because distribution patterns and precipitation rates generally vary from zone to zone, run times should be set for *each* irrigation zone based on precipitation rates.

Most irrigation controllers are set with all zones receiving the same run time. This results in zones that need less water being overwatered.

- **Adjust irrigation controller for the season**—As summer temperatures increase, water use goes up; as cooler fall weather moves in, water use goes down. Unfortunately, most gardeners have their controllers set for the summer, and never adjust the controllers for the season. Most lawns and gardens are overwatered by forty percent in the spring and fall. Iron chlorosis is a common symptom of springtime overwatering. Several methods can be used for irrigation scheduling.

- **Water bluegrass at 80% ET**—When water is available, Kentucky bluegrass uses significantly more water than what it actually needs to remain green. Bluegrass also slows its water use and growth rate as soil moisture decreases. Watered at eighthly percent ET, a home bluegrass lawn will remain thick and green. Watered at sixty percent ET, a home bluegrass lawn will remain green, but not as thick.

- **Summer-dormant Kentucky bluegrass**—Where appropriate for the use of the site, summer dormant Kentucky bluegrass has a very low seasonal water use. It requires only fourteen inches of rain and irrigation per year (applied in the spring and fall). For additional details, refer to Chapter 45.

- **Turn off sprinklers in rainy weather**—Manually shutting off the sprinkler system during rainy weather is another effective management tool. An inexpensive investment (around $25) to help manage the irrigation system is a rain shut-off sensor. In many parts of the country, but not Colorado at this time, local ordinances require rain shut-off sensors.

- **Soak and cycle**—On slopes and on compacted or clayey soils water can be applied much faster than it can infiltrate into the soil, leading to surface runoff. To deal with this, use multiple short-run cycles that allow the water to soak in between cycles. Most controllers readily accommodate this with multiple start times.

  On clayey soil with pop-up spray heads, apply about one-quarter inches per cycle (about eight to ten minutes) with two or three cycles to apply a total of one-half to three-quarters inch of water per irrigation. Runs are typically spaced an hour apart or, more commonly, after all the zones have run it cycles again.

- **Dry spots**—The common approach for managing dry spots is to increase the amount of water applied. Although it may green up the dry spots, it also overwaters the rest of the lawn, wasting water.

  To evaluate a dry spot, first place some identical, straight-sided, flat-bottomed cans (like soup or vegetable cans) out to measure the water applied. Compare the amount of water received in the dry spot to the amount of water received in green areas. If the dry spot receives significantly less water, it is a water delivery problem (like a malfunctioning head or design problem). If similar amounts of water are being received, the problem is soil/plant related (like compaction, thatch, and root damage).

  Note: As the gardener fine-tunes the management of his/her irrigation system, dry spots will show up in hot weather. This indicates that he/she is successfully walking the edge on ideal irrigation management.

- **Aeration** is a primary tool to increase water infiltration. Aeration may be useful spring and fall on lawns with a lot of traffic (children and dogs); compacted, clayey soils; and slopes. Refer to lawn care information for details.

- **Water deeply and infrequently** to develop a deep root system that gives the plants more resilience in hot, dry weather.

- **Water at night or early morning hours**—To reduce water loss from evaporation, water between 9:00 in the evening and 9:00 in the morning. In many areas, wind drift is less in the early morning hours. (Note: Some cities experience peak water use from 4 to 6 in the morning as automatic sprinkler systems come on. To help the community avoid spikes in water demand, remember the suggested watering window is 9 in the evening to 9 in the morning, not just 4 to 6.)

1. Of the seven principles of water-wise gardening, why does watering efficiently have the greatest potential for water conservation in the typical home landscape?

2. With attention to irrigation design, maintenance, and management, what is the potential water savings for a typical home landscape?

3. List factors to consider with irrigation zones.

4. Describe design criteria for uniform water distribution.

5. Describe maintenance techniques for water-wise irrigation management.

6. Describe management techniques for water-wise irrigation management.

Chapter

52*

∽

Worksheet

Lawn Irrigation Checkup

To complete the irrigation checkup, you will need the following items:

- Six identical straight-sided, flat-bottomed cans like soup or vegetable cans (do not use tuna or other short cans)

- Watch

- Ruler

- Colored flags (or something else) to mark sprinkler heads by zone

- Calculator

- Screwdriver and/or soil probe

WHY DO IRRIGATION CHECKUPS?

For most residents, attention to irrigation efficiency has the greatest potential for water conservation. In the typical home yard, attention to irrigation system *design*, *maintenance*, and *management* will reduce water use by 20% to 70%, or 40% on average.

The purpose of irrigation checkups is a systematic evaluation of the irrigation system design, maintenance, and management. It will identify areas where adjustments will save water and improve lawn quality. Run times for each sprinkler zone will be calculated based on the precipitation rate of the zone. Run times will be adjusted for the spring, summer, and fall seasons.

---

*Author: David Whiting, Colorado State University Extension.

The checkup is only a tool to help the gardener identify where the system is working adequately and where adjustments need to be made. Actual water savings come as findings are incorporated.

Step 1—Visually Evaluate the Lawn

a) How Does The Lawn Look?

- [ ] Green (high-input lawn)
- [ ] Green (moderate-input lawn)
- [ ] Green (low-input lawn)
- [ ] Dry spots: _____% of lawn
- [ ] Dry/Dormant

- [ ] Thick
- [ ] Thin

- [ ] Weed-free
- [ ] Few weeds
- [ ] Weedy

Other comments:

b) Soil Conditions

Stick a screwdriver in the ground to get a sense about soil compaction. The ease or difficulty with which the screwdriver can be pushed into a *moist* soil gives an estimate of soil compaction.

If possible, use a soil probe to get a sense of soil texture, compaction, soil layers, rooting depth, and thatch layer. Note: On compacted or rocky soil, it may be difficult to impossible to push a soil probe into the soil. On extremely compacted soils, it may even be impossible to push a screwdriver into the soil.

Soil compaction

- [ ] Little to no compaction (screwdriver/probe readily goes in)
- [ ] Moderate compaction (screwdriver/probe hard to push in)
- [ ] Severe compaction (screwdriver/probe extremely difficult to impossible to push in)
- [ ] Aeration needed to increase infiltration

Soil texture

- [ ] Coarse texture (sandy)
- [ ] Moderate texture (loamy)
- [ ] Fine texture (clayey)
- [ ] Rocky/gravelly

Soil profile

- [ ] Changes in soil texture evident
- [ ] Hardpan layer
- [ ] Evidence of drainage problems (such as surface pooling)

Thatch layer

- [ ] Less than ½ inch
- [ ] Greater than ½ inch
- [ ] Aeration needed to manage thatch

Slope—Does the lawn slope, allowing water to readily run off?   [ ] Yes   [ ] No

c) Run-Off Potential

☐ Low potential

☐ High potential (use *cycle and soak* application)

    ☐ Due to slope

    ☐ Due to soil conditions (compaction and/or clayey soil)

    ☐ Due to thatch

Other comments:

Step 2—Current Controller Settings

For future reference, record current settings from the controller, including watering days, start time(s), and run times. Note: Precipitation rates and inches applied could be calculated later. To calculate the water savings, the gardener could calculate the seasonal water use before and after the checkup.

Controller currently set for _____ (month)

Table 52-A. Current Controller Setting and Inches Applied					
Zone	Zone Identity	Watering day(s)	Run time	Precipitation Rate	Inches Applied
1					
2					
3					
4					
5					
6					

Step 3—Identify and Evaluate Irrigation Zones

a. Using a different color flag (or other marking implements) for each zone, flag the sprinkler heads. (Sprinklers may need to be turned on to find and identify sprinkler heads by zone.)

b. Evaluate the following hydrozone layouts.

Concept	OK—Concept incorporated	Minor—Benefits received with minor adjustments or implementation	Major—Benefits received with major adjustments or implementation	Not applicable to site
1. Lawn zones separate from flower and shrub bed zones				
2. Zone by exposure (i.e., extreme exposures, full sun, partial shade, full shade, and slopes on separate irrigation zones)				
3. Drip or bubblers used in flowerbeds, shrub beds, small fruit gardens, and vegetable gardens				
4. Design avoids sprinkler irrigation on small, irregularly shaped areas (generally areas less than 8 feet wide)				

c. If design does not meet these criteria, consider upgrading the irrigation system.

Step 4—Evaluate Sprinkler Performance

Turn on sprinklers and evaluate sprinkler performance as outlined below, repeating steps for *each* zone.

a) Design Criteria for Even Water Distribution

1. **Head-to-head coverage—Does the water from each head reach neighboring heads?**

Zone	1	2	3	4	5	6
Yes = OK						
NO = adjustments needed*						

* In some situations, adjusting heads or changing nozzles may correct the problem. In other situations, the system design may need to be upgraded for water conservation.

2. **Are sprinkler heads "lined-out" along the edge of nonirrigated areas?**

Zone	1	2	3	4	5	6
Yes = OK						
NO = upgrade needed*						

* If no, consider upgrading the sprinkler system for improved water conservation.

3. **Are sprinkler heads arranged in triangular and square patterns, avoiding pentagonal patterns?**

Zone	1	2	3	4	5	6
Yes = OK						
NO = upgrade needed*						

* If no, consider upgrading the sprinkler system for improved water conservation.

4. **Are all heads in a zone the same brand and type?**

Zone	1	2	3	4	5	6
Yes = OK						
NO = adjustments needed*						

* In some situations, replacing heads may correct the problem. In other situations, the system design may need to be upgraded for water conservation.

5. **Is there a mist cloud around sprinkler heads?**

Zone	1	2	3	4	5	6
Yes = OK						
NO = adjustments needed*						

* A mist cloud indicates excessive pressure. Lower pressure to conserve water. This may involve installation of an in-line pressure regulator.

b) Maintenance Criteria for Uniform Sprinkler Delivery

1. **For each head, does the delivery angle need adjustments (to avoid spraying the sidewalk, driveway, or other areas outside the zone)?**

Zone	1	2	3	4	5	6
No = OK						
Yes = adjustments needed						
Identify heads needing adjustments						

2. **Do heads need adjustment to vertical (straight up and down)?**

Zone	1	2	3	4	5	6
No = OK						
Yes = adjustments needed*						
Identify heads needing adjustments						

* Heads off vertical will distort the delivery pattern. Adjust to vertical to conserve water.

3. **Height—Is nozzle releasing water above grass height?**

Zone	1	2	3	4	5	6
Yes = OK						
No = adjustments needed*						
Identify heads needing adjustments						

* When water does not clear grass height distribution pattern may be distorted. Raise head.

4. **Worn heads—Look at the fan created by the water spray for each head. Is it uniform around the arc?** (Note: It is extremely hard to evaluate uniformity by looking at the spray pattern; if something is noticed, it is extreme.)

Zone	1	2	3	4	5	6
Yes = OK						
No = adjustments needed*						
Identify heads needing adjustments						

* Replace worn nozzles to improve distribution pattern.

5. **Replace leaky valves—In the irrigation valve, the rubber diaphragm that actually turns water on and off ages over time. Valves that do not shut off completely need the diaphragm or entire valve replaced.**

Zone	1	2	3	4	5	6
Valve not leaking = OK						
Valve leaking = needing replacement						

c) Evaluate Dry Spots

If the zone has dry spots, place some cans on the dry spot and on the green areas. Compare the amount of water received in each can.

Zone	1	2	3	4	5	6
No dry spots						
Dry spot(s) receiving less water than the green areas[1]						
Dry spot(s) receiving similar amounts of water as green areas[2]						

[1] When the amount of water received in dry area cans is significantly less than the green area cans, poor water distribution is a primary contributor. Evaluate irrigation design and maintenance issue.

[2] When the amount of water received in both the green area cans and dry area cans is similar, the problem is not directly related to sprinkler performance. Evaluate other growth factors, including soil compaction, thatch, runoff, insect or disease problems, etc.

Notes: All adjustments and upgrades must be completed before proceeding with the checkup process.

Step 5—Perform Precipitation Rate (Catch Can) Test

Perform a Precipitation Rate Test (Catch Can Test) for *each* zone, recording the ***precipitation rates*** in **Run Time Table 52-B.**

Precipitation Rate (Catch Can) Test

To do the calculations you will need six identical, straight-sided, flat-bottomed cans such as soup cans, fruit, or vegetable cans or coffee cans. (Do not use short cans like tuna cans as they are too shallow and water may splash out.) You will need a ruler, a watch, and paper/pen to record your findings. Many water providers and sod growers have calibrated plastic cups specifically designed for this test, six are needed.

Steps

1. Place 6 identical, straight-sided, flat-bottomed cans randomly around the area between sprinkler heads in the zone.

2. Turn on the sprinklers for exactly *10 minutes.*

3. Pour all the water into one can.

4. With a ruler, measure the depth of the water in the can. **This is your precipitation rate in *inches per hour.***

5. **Record *Precipitation Rates*** for each zone in Table 52-B, the "Precipitation Rate" column.

6. Repeat steps one to five for *each* irrigation zone.

Note: If the amount of water in some containers is significantly more or less than others, it indicates that the system is poorly designed or head(s) are malfunctioning.

Step 6—Calculate System Run Times for Each Zone

a) Run Time Per WEEK

Based on precipitation rates, use Table 52-1, to determine the **Run Time per WEEK** for *each zone* in July/August. **Record run times in Table 52-B, "Run time Per WEEK in the July/August" column.**

Table 52-1. Minutes to Run Sprinklers per WEEK Based on Precipitation Rates

Inches of water per week (irrigation plus rain)	Late April 0.75"	May and June 1.0"	July and August 1.5"	September 1.0"	Early October 0.75"
Precipitation Rate					
¼	180	240	**360**	240	180
⅜	120	160	**240**	160	120
½	90	120	**180**	120	90
⅝	72	96	**144**	96	72
¾	60	80	**120**	80	60
⅞	52	69	**103**	69	52
1	45	60	**90**	60	45
1⅛	40	53	**80**	53	40
1¼	36	48	**72**	48	36
1⅜	33	44	**65**	44	33
1½	30	40	**60**	40	30
1⅝	28	37	**55**	37	28
1¾	26	34	**51**	34	26
1⅞	24	32	**48**	32	24
2	23	30	**45**	30	23
2⅛	22	28	**42**	28	22
2¼	20	27	**40**	27	20
2⅜	19	25	**38**	35	19
2½	18	24	**36**	24	18
2⅝	17	23	**34**	23	17
2¾	16	22	**33**	22	16
2⅞	16	21	**31**	21	16
3	15	20	**30**	20	15
Percent of July/August	**50%**	**67%**	**100%**	**67%**	**50%**

b) Number of Irrigations per Week

Determine the number of irrigation per week. **Record results in Table 52-B, "Number of Irrigations per WEEK" column.**

Determining the number of irrigations per week becomes complex as soil water-holding capacity and rooting depth are factored in.

However, many gardeners know by experience how often they need to irrigate. For the majority of Colorado soils, irrigating once per week works in the spring and fall, and twice a week works in the summer. Watering as infrequently and deeply as the soil allows gives better resilience during hot weather and helps reduce many weed species. However, overwatering wastes water as it percolates below the rooting zone.

c) Run Time per Irrigation

Using Table 52-2, convert the **Run Time per WEEK** to **Run Time per IRRIGATION**. Record results in Table 52-B, "Run Time per IRRIGATION" column.

Table 52-2. Conversion of Run Time Per WEEK to Run Time per IRRIGATION

Irrigations per Week	Conversion to Run Time per Irrigation
1 time per week[1]	minutes per week
2 times per week[2]	minutes per week ÷2
3 times per week	minutes per week ÷ 3
Every 6 days	minutes per week × 0.86
Every 5 days	minutes per week × 0.71
Every 4 days	minutes per week × 0.57
Every 3 days	minutes per week × 0.43
Every 2 days	minutes per week × 0.29

[1] Recommended for most Colorado soils in the spring and fall.

[2] Recommended for most Colorado soils in the summer.

d) Adding Cycle and Soak

1. Number of Cycles

Using Table 52-3, determine the number of cycles desired. **Record this in Table 52-B, "Number of Cycles in Cycle and Soak" column.**

For example, if the run time is 26 minutes, three cycles are suggested.

Table 52-3. Estimated Number of Cycles to Reduce Surface Runoff

Type of Sprinklers	Run Time per Irrigation	Number of Cycles
Pop-up Spray Heads	Greater than 16 minutes	2
	Greater than 24 minutes	3
Rotor Heads	Greater than 48 minutes	2
	Greater than 72 minutes	3

*In extremely compacted soils or steep slope, more than three cycles may be needed.

2. Run Time per CYCLE.

Divided the *Run Time per IRRIGATION* by the number of cycles to get the *Run time per CYCLE*. Record this in Table 52-B, the "Run Time per CYCLE" column.

For example, if the run time is 26 minutes and three cycles will be used, run time per cycle is 9 minutes (26 / 3 = 8.67, rounded to 9).

Table 52-B. Run Times per Zone						
Zone	Precipitation Rate	Run Time per WEEK August (minutes)	Number of Irrigations per Week	Run Time per IRRIGATION (minutes)	Number of Cycles in *Cycle and Soaks*	Run Time per CYCLE
1						
2						
3						
4						
5						
6						

Step 7. Start Time(s)

a) Determine the First Start Time.

Most communities suggest nighttime irrigation, between 9 p.m. and 9 a.m. Winds are typically less in the early morning, and evaporation loss will be lower. However, many communities experience peak water use from 4 to 6 a.m. as many sprinklers come on, so remember that the irrigation window is 9 to 9, not just 4 in the morning. **Record your first start time in Table 52-C, Row 1, *Start Time 1*.**

b) Add Additional Start Times for Cycle and Soak (if needed).

1. Add all the *Run Times per CYCLE* together.

2. **Cycle Time**—Round this *up* to the next ¼ hour or ½ hour (depending on what start time intervals are used in your controller start options). This is the time required to run through the zones. **Add this to rows 2 and 4 in Table 52-C or add 1 hour if it is less than 60 minutes.**

3. Add this to the first start time to get the second start time. **Record your second start time in Table 52-C, Row 3, *Start Time 2*.**

4. Likewise, add this to the second start time to get the third start time. **Record your third start time in Table 52-C, Row 5, *Start Time 3*.**

Table C. Start Times	
1. **Start Time 1**	
2. Cycle time	
3. **Start Time 2** (if needed) [add line 1 to line 2]	
4. Cycle time	
5. **Start Time 3** (if needed) [add line 3 to line 4]	

Step 8. Set the Controller for July/August

1. Set Run Times as listed in **Table 52-B** "**Run Time per Cycle**" column.

2. Set Start Times as given in **Table 52-C**.

Step 9. Seasonal Adjustment

A simple way to adjust for the season is to use the ***Percent Key*** found on most controllers.

- For late April and early October, set the percent at 50%.

- For May/June and September, set the percent at 67%.

An alternative method is to repeat Steps 6 to 8 for the spring and fall season.

Step 10. Fine-Tune to Match Site-Specific Needs

These textbook figures are a good start point in irrigation management. **However, any scheduling method will need fine-tuning to match the actual water need of the site based on soil type, exposure, wind, heat, rooting depth, etc**. This is done by careful observation of the lawn.

When adjusting all zones, the **Percent Key** on most controllers makes an easy method to fine-tune for the actual site by adjusting the percentage up/down in 10% increments, as needed. It can also be adjusted by increasing/decreasing the run time for each zone in 10% increments, as needed.

When adjusting a single zone, adjust the run times for that zone up/down in 10% increments, as needed.

In typical summer weather, if the lawn starts to become dry between irrigations, increase the run time in 10% increments, as needed. By trial and error, it is easy to fine-tune each irrigation zone. In multiple days of unusually hot weather, dry spots should pop up if the controller is precisely fine-tuned. In unusually hot weather, if dry spots do not pop up, the lawn is being overwatered. Cut back the time in 10% increments, as needed, to fine-tune each zone.

SUMMARY

The checkup is only a tool to help the gardener identify where the system is working adequately and where adjustments need to be made. Actual water conservation comes as findings are incorporated.

When irrigation is done at night, it is easy to miss adjustments and system problems. On a monthly basis turn on the system to evaluate performance.

SUMMARY NOTES

Index

techniques, 487–488
    when no watering allowed, 489
Container gardening, 515–519
    cool season vegetables, 515–517
    warm season vegetables, 517–518
Container-grown nursery stock, 343–344
Contrasting foliage, 428
Control methods for weeds, 282–286
    biological methods, 284
    cultural methods, 282–283
    herbicides, 284–286
    mechanical methods, 283–284
Cool season, 16
Cool season vegetables, 459–460
Cooling in transpiration, 55
Coring devices, 364–365
Corn, 498–499
Corn gluten meal, 149–150
Corporate gardens, 10
Cortex, 31, 34
Corymb, 43
Cottonseed meal, 150
Cotyledon, 48
Cover crops, 107, 123–128
    annual species, 125–126
    benefits of, 123–124
    care, 127
    landscape uses, 125–126
    native species, 126
    perennial species, 126
    recipes, 124–125
Crabgrass, 289
Creeping perennials, 295–299
Creeping woodsorrel/oxalis, 296
Crested wheatgrass, 542
Crickets, 240
Crop competition, 282–283
Crown, 37
Crustacea, 221
Cucumbers, 502–503
Cultivar, taxonomic classification by, 23
Cultivars, types of, 444
Cultivating overly wet, dry soils, avoiding, 99–100
Cultural conditions, 287–289
Curly dock, 294
Cuticle, 38
Cuts, pruning, diameter of, 369–370
Cycle, soak features, irrigation, 613
Cyme, 43
Cynodon species. *See* Bermudagrass
Cytokinins, 66

D

Damage to plants, from insects, 256–259
Dame's rocket, 292
Damping off, 263–264
Damselflies, 239–240
Day neutral plants, 58
De-icing salts, 173
Decay
    evaluating, 363–364
    measuring, 364–366
    tree, compartmentalization of, 363–366
Deciduous, stem, leaf texture classification, 19
Declining trees, pruning, 404
Decomposed granite soils, 94
Deeply planted trees, 215
Dermaptera, 230
Design, landscape, 569–582
    balance, 573–574
    color, 571–572
        sequence with, 576–577
    color schemes, 572
    dominance, 575
    form, 570–571
    oneness, quality of, 569
    opposites, pairing, 577–578
    scale, 572–573
    sequence, 576–578
    simplicity, 574–575
    space, defining, 570
    subordination of elements, 575
    texture, 571
        sequence with, 576
    unity, 569
    variety, 574–575
Design principles
    dominance of elements, 575
    landscape design, 569–582
        balance, 573–574
        color, 571–572
        form, 570–571
        oneness, quality of, 569
        outdoor rooms, creating, 570
        scale, 572–573
        sequence, 576–578
        space, defining, 570
        subordination of elements, 575
        texture, 571
        unity, 569
        variety, 574–575
    simplicity, 574–575

Downy brome/cheat grass, 292
Dragonflies, 239–240
Drainage, 59, 549
    soil, 177–180
        drainage problems, correcting, 178–179
        French drains, 178
        pore space, 177–178
        soil tilth, 178
        subsurface drainage, 179
        surface drainage, runoff, 178–179
Dressings, wound, 374
Drill, 365
Drip irrigation, 487
Drip systems, 603–605
    soaker hose, 604–605
    soaker tubing, 604–605
Drop, 45
Drought tolerance, 425
Dry, infertile soils, 287
Dry soil, 287

E

Earthworms, 81–83
    benefits of earthworms, 82
    biology of earthworms, 81
    earthworm activity, encouraging, 82–83
    earthworm types, 81
    transplanting earthworms, 83
Earwigs, 230
Ecological adaptation
    herbaceous plants, 429–430
        aggressive plants, spread, 429
        well-adapted plants, 429
    horticultural classification by, 17–19
Edging, 130
Eggplant, 491–496
    common disorders, 495
    fall cleanup, 495
    fertilization, 494
    garden sanitation, 495
    irrigation, 494
    mulching, 494
    planting, 492–493
    pollination, 494–495
    ripening fruit, 495–496
    rotation, 495
    summer temperatures, 494–495
    variety selection, 491–492
Electrical impedance tomography, 366
Elevation, 59
    horticultural classification by, plant life zones, 17

Embryo, 48
Embryo dormancy, 49
Endodermis, 31
Endosperm, 45
Energy conservation, 322–324
Environmental quality, benefit of gardening, 3–4
Ephemeroptera, 232
Epidermis, 31, 34, 38
    plants, 29
Equipment for irrigation, 599–608
    bubblers, 603
    drip systems, 603–605
        soaker hose, 604–605
        soaker tubing, 604–605
    hand watering, 606–607
    hose-end watering, 606–607
    in-ground sprinklers, 603
    MP rotator, 602
    pop-up spray heads, 601
    rotor head, 601–602
    sprinklers, in-ground, 599–603
    subsurface drip, 605–606
Equipment for pruning, 375–376
Evapotranspiration, 593
Evergreen, stem, leaf texture classification, 19
Evergreens, pruning, 407–410
    arborvitae, 409
    evergreen trees, 407–408
    juniper, 409
    large branches, removing, 407–408
    pine, 409
    spruce, 408
Excessive cultivation, avoiding, 99
Exposure, 59
Extensional landscape, 550
External structure, insects, 222–225
    abdomen, 224–225
    head, 222–223
    thorax, 223–224

F

Fabaceae, 22
Fabrics, landscape, 282
Fall-bearing raspberries, 437
Families, taxonomic classification by, 22
Farm manure, disadvantages of, 109–110
Feather meal, 152
Fertility, 137–138
Fertilization, 45, 137–156, 478–481
    animal by-products, 150–153
        bat guano-high N, 150–151

newspaper under mulch, 133
rock mulch, 133–134
selecting mulch, 134
soil grade, 130
wood/bark chip mulch, 130–132
around trees, 132
benefits, 130–131
converting lawn to mulch area, 132
cultivating chips into soil, 132
depth, 131
general use, 131–132
landscape fabric, chips over, 132
newspapers, chips over, 132
product selection, 131
windy areas, 132
Musk thistle, 293
Mycorrhizae, 33
Myrtle spurge, 294

N

Naked bud, 35
Names, 227
common, 25–27
Latin, 24–25
scientific, pronouncing, 24
Narrowleaf, stem, leaf texture classification, 19
Native, adapted plants, horticultural classification by, 18–19
Native plants, 18
Natural precipitation, 550
Nectarines, 454–455
Needle-like leaf apex, base, 40
Neighborhood beautification projects, 8–9
Nematodes, 268–269
Net-veining, 41
Netseed lamsquarters, 290
Networks, community, building, 9
Neuroptera, 239
New seedings, 288
Nitrogen, 139–140, 478–479
Nitrogen applications, 144
Nitrogen release, compost, 115
Nitrogen "side dressing," 479–480
Node, 35
Noxious weeds, 281
legal designations for noxious weeds, 281
Nursery stock, 344–345
Nutrition, benefit of gardening, 5
Nutritional needs, 139–141
iron, 140

nitrogen, 139–140
phosphorus, 141
potassium, 141
zinc, 141

O

Observation, manual control irrigation, 613–614
Odonata, 239–240
Old lawns, 288
Oleaceae, 22
Oneness, in landscape design, quality of, 569
Onion family, 500
Onions, 500
Open shade, 57
Opposites, in landscape design, pairing, 577–578
Orange hawkweed, 297
Orders, 228–243
Organic amendments, 476
Organic fertilizers, 148–155
alfalfa meal, pellets, 149
corn gluten meal, 149–150
cottonseed meal, 150
plant by-products, 149–150
soybean meal, 150
Organic matter
adding, 98–99
soil, 79
Organic soil amendments, evaluating, 106–107
Organisms, 77
beneficial, encouraging, 83
soil, 77–78
directly beneficial, 78
indirectly beneficial, 78–79
Orthoptera, 240
Outdoor living space, creating, 548–565
Outdoors, 65
Outline style keys, 306
Ovary, 42
Over amending, 104–105
Over compacted soil, avoiding, 100
Overall leaf shape, 40
Overwatering, 164–165
Ovules, 42
Oxeye daisy, 297–298
Oxygen starvation, 271

P

Palisade layer, 39
Palmate venation, 41

topping trees, 403

    upright growing trees, 398

    utility right-of-ways, 403

    vigorously growing branches, 397

    young tree, 397

Pruning heading cuts, 373–374

Psocids, 241

Psocoptera, booklice, 241

Puccinellia distans. See Alkaligrass

Pumpkins, 502–503

Purple loosestrife, 298

Purslane, 289

Q

Quackgrass, 298

R

Raceme, 43

Radar devices, 365–366

Radicle, 48

Radish, 502

Rain shut-off sensors, irrigation, 614

Raised bed gardens, 464–467

    constructing bed, 465–466

    planting guide, 467–471

Raising, 400

Raspberries, 436–438

    fall-bearing, 437

    summer-bearing, 437

Ray cells, 362

Recently planted trees, 214–215

Receptacle, 42

Redroot pigweed, 291

Reduction, pruning, 401–402

Reduction cuts, pruning, 372–373, 390–391

Rejuvenation pruning, 415

Removal cuts, pruning, 370–372

Removal limitations, pruning, 392

Replacement pruning, 415–416

Resistograph, 365

Respiration, 54

Restoration, pruning, 402

Reticulate-veining, 41

Rhizobium, 33

Rhizome, 37

Rhubarb, 501–502

Rights to water

    administration, 584

    community water infrastructure, 586

    gray water, 585

    irrigation water, sources of, 584–585

    population growth, 586–587

    rain water, 585

    water conservation, 586–587

    water quality terminology, 584

    water use, Colorado, 585–587

    wells, 585

Rock mulch, 133–134

Rock powders, 154

    colloidal phosphate, 154

Root ball

    depth in planting hole, 338

    depth of tree in, 338–339

Root cap, 31

Root crops, 502

Root-damaged trees, pruning, 404

Root depth, spread, 210–211

Root disorders, 207–217

    compaction around trees, 213–214

    protected root zone, 210–211

    recently planted trees, 214–215

    root depth, spread, 210–211

    root function, 207–208

    root types, 208–209

    soil compaction, evaluating, 212–213

    symptoms, root/soil disorders, 207–208

    tree protection zone, 210–211

    trees planted too deep, 215

Root function, 207–208

Root hairs, 31

Root rots, 265–266

Root temperature injury, 62

Root tip meristem, 31

Root types, 208–209

Rooting depth, irrigation, 593–594

Roots, 30–33

    beneficial microorganism associations, 33

    depth, 32–33

    functions, 30

    microorganism associations, 33

    spread, 32–33

    structure, 31

    types, 31–32

    types of roots, 31–32

Rosaceae, 22

Rosette, 39

Rotor head, 601–602

Rubber mallet, 365

Rudimentary embryo dormancy, 49

Russian knapweed, 298–299

Russian olive, 299–300
Rutabagas, 502

S

Salad crops, 499
Salt problems, compost, 113–114
Salts, 273
Salty soils, 171–175
    de-icing salts, 173
    drainage, 172
    fertilizer applications, 172–173
    influence on plant growth, 171–172
    leaching salts, 173–174
    managing, 173–174
    measuring salt levels, 173
    pet urine, 173
    salt problems, factors contributing to, 172–173
    soil amendments, 172, 174
    soluble salts, 171–172
Sand, 100
Sapwood, 389
Saucer-shaped planting hole, 340
Sawflies, 225–236
Scale, in landscape design, 572–573
Scale-like leaf apex, base, 40
Scentless chamomile, 291
Scheduling irrigation, 609–617
    cycle, soak features, 613
    emerging technology, 614–616
    ET controllers, 614
    fine-tuning, 614–616
    observation, manual control method, 613–614
    precipitation rate method, 611–613
    rain shut-off sensors, 614
    soil-moisture sensors, 614
    sprinkler-type method, 610–611
Scientific names, 423
    pronouncing, 24
    taxonomic classification by, 23–25
Sclerenchyma, 29
Scorpions, 221
Seaweed, 154–155
    kelp meal, 154–155
    kelp powder, 155
    liquid kelp, 155
Seed bank, 280
Seed catalogs, 472
Seed coat, 45, 48
Seed coat dormancy, 49
Seeding, 538

Seeds, 45–49
    dicot seeds, 48
    emergence, 45–48
    function, 45
    growth, development, 48–49
    monocot seeds, 45–48
    seed growth, 48–49
        terms, 48–49
    structure, 45–48
Selection of trees
    nursery stock, 330–332
        bare-root stock, 330–331
        container-grown, 331–332
        field-grown, bailed, burlapped, 331
    size, 329–330
        establishment, 329–330
        minimum root ball size, 330
        moving trees-weight issue, 330
    species, 326–329
        climatic adaptation, 328–329
        growth rates, 327
        management concerns, 328
        mature size, 327
        soil considerations, 327
        water needs and tolerances, 327–328
Self worth, 6
Semi-evergreen, stem, leaf texture classification, 19
Semi-hardy vegetables, 459–460
Sepals, 42
Sequence, in landscape design, 576–578
Shady lawns, 288
Shallots, 500
Shearing to shape, 413–414
Shepherd's purse, 292
Shipment, 333
Shoot, 36
Short-day plants, 58
Shrimp, 221
Shrub identification, 311–318
    fruit characteristics, 315–318
    leaf characteristics, 311–312
    stem characteristics, 312–314
Shrubs, stem, leaf texture classification, 20
Silverfish, 243
Simple perennials, 294
Simplicity, in landscape design, 574–575
Sinker root, 32
Siphonaptera, 242
Slope, planting on, 342
Small fruit, 435–447
    blackberries, 439–440